Hell's Islands

TEXAS A&M UNIVERSITY

III

MILITARY HISTORY SERIES

CAPE ESPERANCE

DOMA COVE

TASSAFRONGA POINT

KOLI POINT   TAIVU POINT

POINT CRUZ   LUNGA

UMASANI   KUKUMBONA   TETERE   AOLA BAY
RIVER   BONEGI
         RIVER   HENDERSON FIELD

POHA
ER

JA

Hell's Islands

The Untold Story of Guadalcanal

Stanley Coleman Jersey
Foreword by Lt. Gen. Edward W. Snedeker, USMC (Ret.)

Texas A&M University Press
College Station

Dedicated to my grandfather,
Pvt. Miles Coleman,
12th Illinois Volunteers,
U.S. Civil War, 1861–65

and my namesake,
Cpl. Stanley Dennis, MM,
Australian Imperial Force,
World War I, 1914–18

Contents

Illustrations

Foreword

In August 1942 the U.S. Marines spearheaded an amphibious assault in the Solomon Islands. At that time, not many Americans had heard of Guadalcanal or the Solomons, but that soon would change. In the ensuing weeks and months, few days would pass when Guadalcanal was not featured in the nation's newspapers.

Hell's Islands is without a doubt one of the most comprehensive accounts of the battle for Guadalcanal. Stanley Jersey's depth of investigation into U.S. and Allied sources, as well as those of the Japanese and of the Solomon Islands, provides detail that extends well beyond the scope of the combat.

As the communications officer of the 1st Marine Division on Guadalcanal, I was in the position to be "in the know" about the famed struggle. Yet Stanley Jersey's intensive research uncovered material that had not been available to us at the time. Using "the historian as a detective" approach to the fighting and operations, he has created a prototype for future works. He has dispelled many rumors that have surrounded the battle and has cleared up many of the mysteries. He has woven a rich tapestry of supporting information that makes the book a lively account, transporting the reader to the foxhole on the front line and bringing him into the planning staffs at the headquarters level. The book is a valuable tool for anyone interested not only in the history of the nonconformist combat, but in how Guadalcanal influenced the entire course of the Pacific theater of operations during World War II.

Prior to Guadalcanal, the enemy was in an offensive role. After the battle he was on the defensive and remained so for the following two years, until the formal surrender in Tokyo Bay, 2 September 1945. It is an honor to be even a small part of this publication of *Hell's Islands*.

Edward W. Snedeker
Lt. Gen. USMC (Ret.)
August 1992
Carlsbad, California

Preface

The war in the southern Solomon Islands was in many ways the heart of the war in the Pacific. In May 1942 the Japanese seized the Australian flying-boat operations base on the tiny islands of Tanambogo and Gavutu in Tulagi Harbor, making the base, almost overnight, a focal point of both Japanese and Allied strategic planning. The Japanese quickly moved an air unit into the sector, with planes stationed on adjacent Florida and Gavutu–Tanambogo Islands. When on 1 July they traveled twenty miles across Sealark Channel to establish an airfield on Guadalcanal, the threat to the New Hebrides, New Caledonia, Fiji, and Samoa—and thus to the sea lines of communication between the United States and Australia—became acute. In response, Operation WATCHTOWER, the hastily drawn-up Allied plan to seize the lower Solomons by amphibious landings, was immediately set in motion.

The landing force for WATCHTOWER would be provided by the U.S. Marine Corps, which meant that the 1st Marine Division—in New Zealand since mid-June but not up to full strength and still undergoing further training—had to take on a combat assignment. Most of the marines were under twenty years of age and just recently out of boot camp. The U.S. Army had garrisons on New Caledonia and Hawaii for backup, but these troops were primarily "weekend warriors" from former National Guard units, with little actual training in the field. The prospect of these green troops fighting the hardened and jungle-wise Japanese logically did not augur well for victory.

The U.S. Marine landings on Guadalcanal, Tulagi, Gavutu, Tanambogo, and Florida Islands on 7 August 1942 surprised Japanese commanders, both in Tokyo and at the South Pacific stronghold in Rabaul, New Britain Island. They responded by pouring their army, navy, and air forces into the theater to dislodge the Americans. The struggle pitted the United States and Japan, two major naval powers, against each other for control of the Pacific. The battles for the islands—and in particular the torturous battle for Guadalcanal—were among the most decisive ever fought. A new history would be written by the combatants who often brutally shed blood and sacrificed their youth in these faraway places surrounded by the interminable South Pacific seas.

The pivotal battle for Guadalcanal Island was not an overnight event; it began on 7 August 1942 and continued to 9 February 1943. The center of gravity for the island was Henderson Field, named for U.S. Marine Maj. Lofton Henderson, a hero of the June 1942 battle of Midway. The Japanese would desperately want to take back the airfield once lost, as it would be a key to control of the South Pacific area.

Historians have examined extensively the significant role of the U.S. 1st Marine Division, the major player in the struggle, yet they have overlooked or touched on only briefly the many endeavors of the 2nd Marine Division. In addition, a considerable amount of latent information exists concerning the Japanese experience, even well after sixty years. This book is an effort to rectify such omissions and give a fuller understanding of the American and Japanese involvement. The manuscript evolved from a project launched in 1984 in Australia while interviewing a former coastwatcher. The undertaking was completed twenty years later, after obtaining and translating hundreds of captured Japanese World War II diaries and reading many additional hundreds of POW files and related documents. More than 225 participants in four countries were interviewed, and countless hours were spent in the Australian National Archives at Canberra as well as our own National Archives in Washington, D.C. Numerous visits were made to the U.S. Marine Corps and U.S. Navy Historical Centers in Washington, as well as trips to Tokyo to review files in the Military History Department of the National Institute for Defense Studies.

The core of the highly detailed narrative revolves around the hundreds of stories of the men who served there, experiences that are the brick and mortar holding the book together—tales of spies, coastwatchers, native scouts, missionaries, Australian commandos and aircrews, New Zealand airmen, Japanese Navy sea infantry, the Imperial Japanese Army, and Japanese construction units with Korean laborers, in addition to the American "can do" Seabees, CUBs, ACORNs, Marine Corps ground units, U.S. Army GIs, U.S. Navy sailors, and U.S. Army, Navy, and Marine air units. The story begins with a handful of Australians defending the Solomon Islands in late 1941; it continues with the evacuations of civilians from Tulagi and the outer islands, as a result of the January 1942 arrival of the Japanese at Rabaul, New Guinea, 600 miles away—the unnerving threat labeled the "Yellow Peril."

The narrative is told from both the American and the Japanese perspectives, revealing the very human, non-strategic side of the war, with particular emphasis given to those in the fierce ground combat during the critical days from August to early February. Japanese names are presented in the western style—given name first, followed by the family name.

The challenge has been to tell a many-faceted war story about these far-off islands during the early years of the 1940s, along with that of the nearby places whose roles, though some very minor, were also part of the big picture. The detailed naval or air engagements, however, although significant, are in general outside the scope of this work. The Allied air force on Guadalcanal—the Cactus Air Force—is mentioned, but its in-depth history is left to others to give the full account.

Acknowledgments

This undertaking, which began more than forty-five years after the close of World War II, required the effort of many contributors. Their generous assistance included memories sometimes obscured in the mists of time, diaries, and photographs, some of which are included in this work.

In the Far East, two individual contributors were invaluable. One was the late Akio Tani, better known to Guadalcanal veterans as the dreaded "Pistol Pete," the ingenious Japanese artillery man who was the scourge of Henderson Field during the bitter days of the 1942 campaign. Tani was a godsend, spending hundreds of hours willingly translating Japanese documents into English. A born historian, he extended himself to assist me. In the same vein, appreciation is due Yoshihiko Sagai, a former naval radio operator and student of World War II who worked with Akio Tani to help in many ways; no request was too much. During my 1990 trip to Japan, Tani and Sagai graciously assembled a number of Japanese Guadalcanal veterans for me to interview, contributions that added immeasurably to this project.

Gratitude is also due Lt. Cdr. Masao Tsunomura, Imperial Japanese Navy (IJN, Ret.), the former naval engineering officer on the Guadalcanal airstrip, who answered my many questions with clarity and furnished me a copy of his book, *Navy Engineer Facility Record.* This 770-page volume lists World War II construction units of the Imperial Japanese Navy, a rare work that provided information not available from other sources. Appreciation is also due Edward Rasmussen, a talented Japanese linguist, who translated parts of the first two volumes of *Senshi Sōsho,* the Japanese Office of War History 104-volume series on World War II, plus numerous other documents.

Kudos to Capt. Teruaki Kawado, Japanese Maritime Defense Force (JMDF, Ret.), subsequently of the Military History Department, National Institute for Defense Studies (NIFDS), who assisted in untold ways, as did Takeshi Hara, a member of his staff. Thanks are due as well to Masaichiro Miyogama and Jinsaku Sakurai, two of the four survivors of the Yokohama Air Group, who shared information on the conflict on Gavutu and Tanambogo Islands and their personal struggle to stay alive. Akira Takizawa, one of the leading authorities of the Imperial Japanese Army, also is extended appreciation.

Clear-cut details from the Japanese point of view were provided by the diaries of the late PO2c Kuichi Yamada, 81st Guard Unit, Endo Butai; SME Tomisaburo Hirai, Tanaka platoon, Kure 3rd Special Naval Landing Force (SNLF); and SM Yodoyama Mori, Tanaka platoon, Kure 3rd Special Naval Landing Force. The memoirs of PO1c Sankichi Kaneda, 81st Guard Unit, provided much information on the key land operations of naval units on Guadalcanal from July 1942 through 7 February 1943, the day he evacuated.

Ex-marine Charles A. Buser, 1st Marine Air Wing (MAW), was a friend I could always count on; his advice was wisely given and always accepted. My gratitude also is due to the late William J. Cannon, Company C, 1st Battalion, 2nd Marine Regiment, who counseled me through various parts of this work. In 1992, Bill took me to the Matanikau River on Guadalcanal and pointed out his company's November 1942 movements against Japanese-held positions. We all should have friends like these.

Col. Jon Hoffman, USMCR, the former assistant director of the History and Museums Division, U.S. Marine Corps, has always extended himself for my projects as has Richard Long, head of the Marine Corps Oral History Division. Barry Zebry, of the National Archives, worked closely with me in examining the nineteen boxes of captured enemy documents from the campaign; he noted that I was the first to ask to see them in forty years. The late Rear Adm. Ernest M. Eller, USN (Ret.), a former Director of Naval History, Naval Historical Center, provided the services of his departments, as did historian Bernard F. Cavalcante, Naval Historical Center, who has been most helpful for the past twenty-five years, always locating the out-of-the-ordinary material I was seeking.

Sister Mary Teresa, who spent most of her life in the Solomons as a missionary, also has shared a wealth of knowledge with me. She is the only person alive today who during 1942 was in contact with Terushige Ishimoto, the English-speaking interpreter attached to the Japanese Navy at Guadalcanal.

My work has benefited in great measure from two unpublished works: Dallas Bennett, "Forty-Seven Years Late," and Jim Sorensen, "Memoirs."

Their vivid descriptions helped fill information voids, first on Tulagi Island and later on Guadalcanal. In addition, Joseph G. Micek's diary provided personal insight into the detailed operations of the 132nd Infantry Regiment on Guadalcanal; and W. Marshall Chaney, as well as Lt. Col. Marvin V. Ayers (Ret.), both former veterans of the U.S. Army's 147th Infantry Regiment, contributed a day-by-day account of the January–February 1943 XIV Corps push up the island coast. Lt. Col. Felix L. Ferranto, USMC (Ret.), a talented radio-man with the 1st Signal Company, also offered assistance (his diary provided a clearer understanding of the early days of the campaign) as did Col. Sanford "Sandy" Hunt, USMC (Ret.), a second lieutenant at the time. Acknowledgment also is given to the resource of the John Miller Jr. volume *Guadalcanal: The First Offensive,* part of the history of *The War in the Pacific* in the 1949 *U.S. Army in World War II* series.

An especial debt of appreciation is due the late Lt. Gen. Edward W. Snedeker, USMC (Ret.), who during World War II was a major and Sandy Hunt's boss, and who eventually became my neighbor in Carlsbad, California. The general gave his enthusiastic support to this project from day one, and in August 1992, as the manuscript evolved, he wrote the foreword. His understanding of the scope of the endeavor was invaluable. My thanks also extend to Emmett Carter, for relating his unit's operations on Rennell Island; to Jack R. Lent, for sharing that part of his diary which covered the spot occupation of Ndeni, Santa Cruz Islands; and to J. Wendell Crain, for the details of his involvement in the Malaita raid.

In Australia, W. F. Martin Clemens—among whose many honors are the Commander of the Order of the British Empire (CBE) and the Military Cross (MC)—was a district officer and coastwatcher on Guadalcanal; he generously provided help and a copy of his handwritten diary. Jack Riddell, another Australian, whose honors include the Distinguished Flying Medal (DFM) and the Air Efficiency Award (AEA), was the historian of the Royal Australian Air Force Catalina squadrons. Jack introduced me to members of the RAAF ground crew at the Tulagi Advanced Operational Base and provided an introduction to members of the No. 1 Independent Company, Australian Imperial Forces (AIF), who had defended their installations on the diminutive islands of Gavutu and Tanambogo. Much credit as well goes to Robert K. Piper, the RAAF historian, who helped in many ways.

From the Solomons, longtime resident Jack Gaskell contributed his unique perspective on the Florida Islands and the civilian evacuation.

His assistance and openness were much appreciated. In England, I was fortunate to have the assistance of two other former Solomon Island district officers and coastwatchers: Sir Alexander N. A. "Nick" Waddell, honored with the title of Knight Commander of St. Michael and St. George (KCMG) and the Distinguished Service Cross (DSC), furnished much information on the evacuation of the western Solomons; and Dick Crofton Horton, recipient of Great Britain's Distinguished Flying Cross and the U.S. Silver Star, provided much information on conditions in the Guadalcanal area up to the spring of 1942 and on his tour with the 1st Marine Raider Battalion at Tulagi.

In the process of my research, however, I have interviewed or have contacted far too many individuals to allow me to thank them all here, and thus a complete list can be found following the bibliography. Several of those interviewed were participants in the campaign and without their selfless assistance this work would have been immeasurably poorer. I thank each of them. My regret is that a large number of those veterans have gone to serve with the Supreme Commander during the past few years. All had hoped to see this book published, and I believe it stands as a remembrance in their honor.

Special recognition is given to Joel L. Bromberg, who brought his editorial and research skills to this project and devoted the better part of two years to transforming my manuscript drafts into a publishable work. Thanks as well are extended to Lt. Col. Kenneth W. Estes, USMC (Ret.), for reading the manuscript and making corrections.

Above all, my most heartfelt appreciation is offered to my wife, Jeanne O'Reilly-Jersey, for her patience and her steadying hand over the past years. Without her help, this book would not have materialized.

Stanley Coleman Jersey

Hell's Islands

1   The Eve of World War II

The Solomon Islands in the Southwest Pacific were a primary focus of Japanese military prewar military planning. Their location in a southeast line between Japan and Australia was pivotal for future military actions. The Solomons comprise a scattered range of some nine hundred islands, atolls, and islets that stretch more than 1,000 miles from northwest to southeast between latitudes 5° and 12°30' south and longitudes 155° and 170° east, about 1,560 miles northeast of Sydney, Australia. The chain of islands covers a land area of nearly 11,000 square miles, spread over more than 500,000 square miles of sea.[1] It is not difficult to conclude that control of this area would be a significant achievement.

The Southwest Pacific Setting

The primary part of the Solomons archipelago is south of Bougainville Strait and consists of a double range of six large islands of high elevation—Choiseul, Santa Isabel, and Malaita in one group, and New Georgia, Guadalcanal, and San Cristobal in the other.[2] The two groups are separated by a body of deep water known as "The Slot" to the Allies during World War II, and to historians ever since. The archipelago extends some 249,000 nautical square miles southeastward from the strait on the west, past small Tulagi Island off Florida Island to the east. Few localities can surpass the area in sheer beauty, but unfortunately, this natural magnificence is matched in intensity by the climate. Sultry heat, frequent and heavy rain, steaming jungles, and a multiplicity of insects and disease all combined to make wartime life in the Solomons decidedly uncomfortable.

In 1568 and 1595, the Spaniard Álvaro de Mendaña de Neyra had explored the island area, but Europeans did not visit again until the eighteenth century. After 1830, British and American whalers and British warships anchored more frequently, and beginning in 1845 Roman Catholic and Anglican missionaries arrived; but the missionaries had limited initial success converting the indigenous inhabitants, and a number were

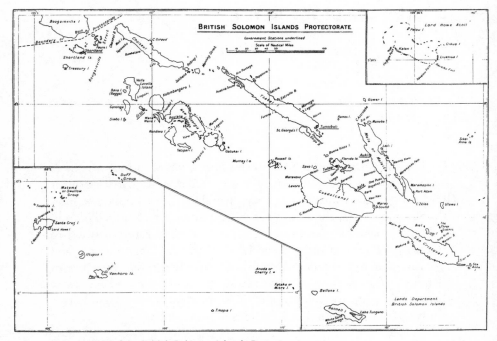

Figure 1. Map of the British Solomon Islands Protectorate, 1925.

killed by the natives. By the early 1860s, other Europeans had settled in the Solomons, and recruiting of islanders began for work on the sugar plantations of Australia and Fiji. However, predatory recruiting practices called "blackbirding"—labor recruiting by deception—resulted in retaliatory killings of white residents and ships' crews. To remedy this situation and put an end to the widespread corrupt recruiting, in June 1893 Great Britain declared a protectorate over the southern Solomon Islands.

Amateur naturalist Charles Morris Woodford is closely associated with the early history of the British Solomon Islands Protectorate. Woodford had first come to the Pacific in 1882, working for the Western Pacific High Commission (WPHC) in Suva, Fiji, and as a government agent in the Gilbert and Ellice Islands. He had made three extended trips to the Solomons between 1886 and 1889 and knew more about them than anyone, apart from the islanders themselves. In 1894, Woodford had hopes of obtaining the more permanent position of resident deputy commissioner for the Solomon Islands, but London would not authorize the funds. As acting deputy commissioner, however, he had prepared a report to be presented to High Commissioner of the Solomons Sir John B. Thurston in which he literally appointed himself. Armed with his paperwork, Woodford set out for Sydney, and Thurston gave his signature and his blessing.

During his tour as resident deputy commissioner, Charles Woodford had selected the island of Tulagi as the seat of government. Tulagi had one of the finest harbors in the South Pacific, with deep channels and spacious anchorages that would make ideal ports of entry for steamers and trading vessels—a quality the Japanese later obviously had recognized. On 29 September 1896, Chief Tambokoro and other elders met with Woodford and agreed to sell Tulagi Island to Great Britain for forty-two ounces of gold. An official Residency, government and civilian offices, and houses soon replaced native huts, and Tulagi would be the Solomon Islands' administrative and commercial center for the next forty-five years.

Between 1898 and 1900, Great Britain annexed the remainder of the Soloman Island group, offering protection for the residents and fostering further settlement and development.[3] Woodford's vision of a productive society in the Solomons depended on an efficient administration and

Figure 2. The Residency, Tulagi Island, 1940, the Resident Commissioner's house and office. On 7 August 1942 this building became the command post for the 1st Marine Raider Battalion. (Courtesy Mrs. Eugenie Murphy)

a reliable economy. The primary export was copra, the dried coconut meat that yields coconut oil, and Woodford believed that the coconut plantations and trading stations would provide sufficient revenue to support and sustain the new government. He had planned to provide registered deeds to land on Guadalcanal and other islands as distant as the Shortlands, in order to establish working estates. The concept was successful, and by 1930 more than 30,000 acres of coconut palms were under cultivation; the largest holding, more than 20,000 acres, was that of Lever's Pacific Plantations Ltd., a subsidiary of the British firm Lever Brothers.

By then, however, the Great Depression that had roots in the late twenties had begun to stall further growth. The purchase price of copra depended on European demand, but Europe also had been in an economic depression. Consumption slackened, and by 1931 copra demand had evaporated. The bottom fell out of the market and plantations could not realize sufficient profits to offset their overhead. Field hands were released once their labor contracts expired, and as a consequence many native laborers could not afford to pay the required government head tax. Resident Commissioner Francis Noel Ashley spent ten years struggling with traders, planters, tradesmen, shippers, and anyone else involved in paying taxes, and plantations facing financial difficulties were sold or in many cases simply abandoned.

Such was the situation on the eve of the Second World War. The Solomon Islands, a sleepy backwater of the British Empire, would never be the same again.

War Declarations and Early Initiatives

At 2315, the night of 3 September 1939, Prime Minister Neville Chamberlain announced on the British Broadcasting Corporation network that Great Britain was at war with Germany. Solomon Islands residents learned of the declaration on the BBC's international evening news hour, 1600 local time. At 2115, in a nationwide broadcast, Australian Prime Minister John Curtin told his country that Britain had declared war on Germany; a proclamation issued an hour later announced that Australia had joined the conflict.

What Australia's contribution to the war effort should be, however, was difficult to determine immediately. The decision was complicated by uncertainty about Japan's intent and by the fact that the strongest party in Australia's House of Representatives was opposed both to sending forces overseas and to raising home defense forces by conscription.

The Commonwealth government asked for Britain's views, and in response, the Dominions Office sent a detailed assessment by telegram on 8 September.

The British felt that if Japan were neutral it might be unwise for Australia to send an expeditionary force overseas, though she could assist by having formations ready to reinforce Singapore, New Zealand, or the British and French islands in the western Pacific. If indeed Japan were friendly, it was hoped that Australia would prepare an expeditionary force and decide whether to relieve United Kingdom units in other areas as needed, or wait until complete divisions could be deployed. Eventually, Australia would send almost four full infantry divisions to serve in the conflict under British command.[4]

Although Australia had few land forces available for duty in the South Seas, her government was alert to the threat posed by Japan. For years, the Japanese had been accumulating useful military information in the Pacific; the country's strategic planning was based on the extensive intelligence gathering by her armed services and their overseas agents before the outbreak of hostilities. Starting in the mid-1930s, skilled espionage agents often disguised as shell fishermen had swarmed into the South Pacific, charting and evaluating the military potential of every island, reef, and shoal. The *Pacific Islands Monthly* had reported the presence of Japanese "poachers" off the coasts of New Guinea, Papua, the Solomons, the New Hebrides, New Caledonia, Fiji, and the Gilbert and Ellice Islands, but nothing was done about it and the intelligence activity continued unhindered. When the Japanese went to war in December 1941, they had a fairly accurate knowledge of ground, air, and naval strength in the areas to be attacked, the locations of airfields and fortifications, and the terrain and climatic conditions in which they would have to fight.[5]

In the late 1930s, Cadet Martin Clemens of the British Solomon Islands Protectorate government service, stationed on Malaita Island, took a Japanese fisherman into custody because of the man's unusual technique: fishing without bait. The man had a long pole with a rock tied to the end and was sounding the depth of the water. Clemens took him to Tulagi for judgment, but the defendant pleaded that he was a poor man who simply caught fish for a living. He claimed he had lost his bait and was using the rock to test the water's depth in order to bait his hook properly. The resident commissioner ruled that the "poor man" be released: "He is only trying to make a living." Reluctantly, Clemens complied.

Often the islanders informed Clemens that Japanese crews were diving for pearl shells on native-controlled reefs; they took undersized shells, and thereby deprived the residents of both a present and a future livelihood. Clemens would try to catch the poachers, but by the time he had reached the locale, they usually had left the area. He later wondered if they eventually came back wearing the uniform of the Imperial Japanese Navy.[6]

Even while Clemens was investigating suspicious fishermen, a much bigger catch was at work nearby. In early 1940, Capt. Tetsuo Toyofuku, a talented 1932 graduate of the Japanese Army officer academy, received orders from Imperial General Headquarters to survey the South Pacific. From January to April 1941, Toyofuku was secretly assigned as intelligence officer to the South Seas Detachment, a unit that at the time existed in name only. He was to conduct a detailed topographical reconnaissance to determine the suitability of sites for potential landing operations in New Guinea and Papua, collect maps and related material on areas of the South Pacific, and investigate sources of war supplies in those areas. But investigating the islands was difficult, as the only maps available were British Admiralty charts dating to the turn of the century.

The captain acted alone, except where he had gained the confidence of certain local Japanese who might help him. His close-cropped hair, a sure sign of a military man, made him stand out in the tropics; he could not pass for one of the businessmen who sold Japanese wares in the islands. Toyofuku thus had to change his appearance in order to ply his dangerous trade and decided to pose as a seaman, intending to seek employment with a Japanese firm doing business in the South Seas. The largest such enterprise was Nan'yo Boeki Kaisha Ltd. (South Seas Trading Company Ltd.), a Tokyo-based concern with numerous branch offices and small trading stations in the Pacific islands. As a result of pressure from the Japanese government, the company's home office suggested to the Rabaul branch that Toyofuku be hired.[7]

Seaman Toyofuku was assigned to the Rabaul-based *Takachiho Maru*, a small motor vessel of some 350 gross tons whose master, Kiyoshi Okubo, spoke excellent English and was said to be a walking encyclopedia. As diplomatically as possible, Captain Okubo informed the crew that the new seaman was not a sailor, and that they should provide him all possible assistance. Okubo's cover story was that the government wanted Toyofuku to investigate certain locales to obtain specific information for an upcoming Japanese business venture. Toyofuku had ample funds available to accomplish his mission, and by liberal use of payoff money—the "red envelope"—he bought the cooperation of both Japanese and native crew members.

The itinerary of the *Takachiho Maru* included the Caroline Islands, New Ireland, New Britain, New Guinea, New Caledonia, Fiji, Tonga, the New Hebrides, and the Solomon Islands. Toyofuku was able to see these areas firsthand, making observations with his navy binoculars, taking photographs with his Leica camera, and writing notes in consultation with his hydrographic books and maps. However, anti-Japanese sentiment had grown considerably in the South Pacific since Japan's occupation of Indochina, and thus the islanders were suspicious of the *Takachiho Maru*. The crew's quarters were thoroughly searched by local port authorities and cameras were confiscated. But Toyofuku's Leica was never seized for he had kept it and his film well hidden, along with his Nambu 8-mm pistol. Because the vessel was in port only a short time, he generally had stayed on board and cautiously took his photographs from the doorways to avoid being seen. No doubt the sea-going spy took pictures of Tulagi and its environs, though there was then no military establishment in the area.

The resourceful Toyofuku next posed as a businessman seeking opportunities to promote Japanese products. He chartered a flight from Salamaua to Lae, on the north coast of eastern New Guinea, making mental notes of the two airfields and the coastline between them. Soon afterward, he returned to Japan with information that would be invaluable to the planners at headquarters. Among other things, his report covered the military significance of British New Guinea and the Solomon Islands.[8]

Late in 1939, Francis Ashley's long tenure as protectorate resident commissioner had come to a close and he had turned the government over to his successor, William Sydney Marchant, a veteran administrator with twenty years service in Kenya and Tanganyika. Life in the Solomons went on much as before. News of the war in Europe was heard every evening, and Europe seemed quite far away. But when German raiders disguised as Japanese transports attacked Australian shipping around the island of Nauru, just west of the Gilbert Islands, protectorate residents began to be concerned about the island's political and economic future and about their own safety. Eventually, District Officer Dick Horton at Aola, on Guadalcanal, found that the increasing war activity had made it impossible for him to leave his station.[9] In addition, all district officers were now required to send a coded weekly report to the high commissioner in Suva, Fiji Island, on unusual sightings and all movements of ships regardless of flag. This reporting continued until May 1942.

To monitor Japanese activity, the Royal Australian Navy (RAN) activated its coastwatcher network after the war began, linking local residents by teleradio—district officers, other government employees, plantation managers, traders. Among these were Martin Clemens, Donald S. Macfarlan, and F. Ashton "Snowy" Rhoades on Guadalcanal; Leif Schroeder on Savo; C. N. F. Bengough on Malaita; Michael J. Forster on San Cristobal; Donald G. Kennedy in New Georgia and the western Solomons; Geoffrey H. Kuper on Santa Isabel; Colin E. J. Wilson and Mrs. Ruby Olive Boye on Vanikoro; Paul E. Mason in south Bougainville; and W. J. "Jack" Read at Buka Passage, the narrow seaway between Buka and Bougainville.

At about this same time, the Royal Australian Air Force (RAAF) began preparing seaplane bases in the British and French territories of the South Pacific. Its first seaplane patrol squadron, No. 11, was organized in September 1939 and sent to Port Moresby, Papua New Guinea, for reconnaissance duty. The squadron was equipped with two Empire flying boats, which the government had requisitioned from Qantas Empire Airways, and two Seagull amphibians; almost half of its original personnel came from Qantas.[10]

Great Britain was supposed to supply nine Sunderland flying boats (Short four-engine) to fill out Australia's air complement, but not enough aircraft were available to meet the requirements of its own Royal Air Force (RAF). Australia therefore looked to the United States, whose aircraft industry was busy producing planes for eager buyers overseas, even though the home market was inert. In June 1940, the Australian War Cabinet ordered seven PBY-5 Catalina twin-engine navy patrol bombers from Consolidated Aircraft Corporation in San Diego; in September it ordered eleven more. The Australians numbered the planes in the A24 series. America was not prepared to go to war, and to avoid further strain on her deteriorating relations with Japan, Consolidated crews flew the Cats to Honolulu, where pilots and crews from the Australian airlines took over and ferried them on to Australia.[11]

With its deep-water Simpson Harbor, Rabaul, on the northern tip of New Britain Island, was an excellent location for both a naval base and a seaplane facility, and in 1939 the Australian Air Force established a seaplane base there. Although the Matupi volcano regularly deposited on the city a dusty, snow-like ash that fouled unhooded engines, Rabaul's geographical position made it of strategic importance. On the eve of the

Pacific War, it was garrisoned by 1,078 members of the Australian Imperial Forces (AIF), supported by a detachment of signalmen, engineers, and artillerymen in the command of Col. J. J. Scanlan. Under RAAF G/Capt. John M. Lerew, 168 airmen of No. 24 Squadron staffed the air base. The squadron's aircraft complement was just four Lockheed Hudson light bombers and six obsolete Wirraway, modified advanced trainers.[12]

On 30 April 1941, an echelon of twenty-two ground personnel arrived in Port Moresby to support the others already there; additional personnel arrived later in the year, raising the total to about 250 airmen. The seaplane facility would become the one of the primary bases for the Catalinas in the South Pacific. From there the Cats could fly search patrols covering the eastern seaboard of Australia, anchoring overnight in secluded bays and returning to Port Moresby the following day. The war spread so quickly, however, that funds allocated for completion of the seaplane complex were never fully put to use, though dirt landing strips for fighters there were improved. Nevertheless, the RAAF's current air contingent was insufficient in strength to contain the Japanese. Fighter airfields would be needed later to prevent the "sun eagles" of Japan's naval air force from destroying the RAAF contingent, along with the remnants of U.S. Army Air Corps units from the Philippines that GIs called the "Scrawny Corps." In time, with the formation of No. 20 Squadron RAAF and the arrival of new, long-range aircraft, the Catalinas were able to rotate between Port Moresby and Tulagi while flying reconnaissance missions.

Port Moresby was defended by Australian troops and, as captured documents revealed, the Japanese knew this. Based on information obtained from a Japanese national who was at Moresby in 1941, Captain Fujisaki (no doubt an intelligence officer attached to the General Staff) estimated that before 7 December there was a forty-man Australian detachment with two 6-inch guns on Paga Hill overlooking Port Moresby Harbor, as well as another group at nearby Pali Pali Point. In January 1942, Fujisaki revised his estimate of Moresby's defenses to include five thousand men housed in the vicinity of Granville East; another airdrome in the neighborhood of Rouna Road, seven miles from the town; and a seaplane anchorage north of Port Moresby. The Australians were particularly concerned about New Caledonia, the French possession lying 680 miles east of Sydney. The island was a major source of nickel and chromium, and the Japanese had more than thirteen hundred men working in the mines. After the outbreak of war in Europe, the Japanese began to purchase all the ore available. Meanwhile, at the Imperial Headquarters in Tokyo, the invasion of New Caledonia was already in the planning stage, known as the FS operation, named for the proposed sweep from Fiji through the Samoa Islands in an effort to force the Australians to surrender.[13]

The Advanced Operational Base — Tulagi

Australia was the first to have military air and ground units in the Solomon Islands. An initial survey of the area was made in November 1939 when an Empire flying boat visited Tulagi. In May 1940 a seaplane returned, bringing ACM Sir Charles Burnett for a personal inspection and discussions with Resident Commissioner Marchant. As a result of these surveys, the Australians decided to establish an advanced operational base (AOB) on the two nearly joined islands in the Tulagi area.[14]

W/Cdr. John Brogan, the Australian divisional works officer, and Group Captain Lerew, the commanding officer (CO) of No. 24 Squadron, were charged with finding a suitable site and arrived in the region in July 1940. The two officers liked the contours of Gavutu and Tanambogo Islands, which lie less than 100 feet from each other about two

Figure 3. The future RAAF advanced operational base at Tulagi Island, 17 December 1940. (RAAF photograph Courtesy Robert K. Piper)

miles east of Tulagi, all three adjacent to Florida Island. Although very small in size—Gavutu was 21 acres, Tanambogo only 13—they were sufficient and would become part of what would be called the Tulagi Advance Operating Base. Gavutu was fairly clear of undergrowth, but Tanambogo, where the air base installations were to be constructed, was covered by a thick mangrove swamp and jungle. District Officer Donald Kennedy thus hired fifty-two Malaita laborers to clear the site and assist the survey team. Meanwhile, Brogan and Lerew inspected a location for an air base at Port Vila on Efate Island in the New Hebrides, then returned to Tulagi with French surveyor Louis Page who would help expedite the project. The three men and District Officer Kennedy's labor force worked from dawn until dark, and within ten days the job was done. In addition, the surveyors visited Florida Island and mapped out a plan for a naval base there should one be needed.[15]

To provide an infrastructure for the advanced operational base, in March 1941 the Lever's Pacific Plantations initiated construction of a stone causeway eight feet wide and seventy-five feet long that would link Gavutu and Tanambogo; the company also had four galvanized huts built on Tanambogo's shore. Jack Svensen, whose family once had owned Gavutu and who was then working for Lever's, arranged a labor contract for the hiring of thirty-two Florida islanders as the permanent workforce. In all, the Tanambogo Island facility included an administrative block, stores building, kitchen, sergeants mess, airmen quarters, marine equipment store, and large T-shaped underground shelter. At the end of June, the thirteen-acre base was complete.[16]

On the northwest side of the island was a hill 125 feet by 250 yards long. On the north side of the hill a flat surface had been cut out, on which were stored 100-, 250-, and 500-pound bombs; a fuel dump in thick scrub occupied the south side. Usually the base carried 90,000 gallons of high-octane aviation gasoline, dispersed in forty-four-gallon drums; emergency reserves were hidden a few miles away in the jungle at Vura, on nearby Florida Island. The motor vessel (MV) *Wanaka* regularly delivered a thousand drums, sufficient for three weeks to two months of air operations, depending on activity.[17]

At the peak of Gavutu's hill, the Australians constructed a radio station with an antenna, enabling signalers to maintain radio contact with Townsville, Queensland, and throughout the Pacific. A water tank made of timber and galvanized iron was also situated at the crest.[18] On Tanambogo, a hidden radio transmitter was situated on the side of the hill, unobtrusively placed under a camouflaged tarp with side flaps that

Figure 4. Gavutu Island, 515 yards long and 255 yards wide, as seen from Tanambogo Island, February 1942. (Courtesy Clifford J. Searle)

could be opened to catch the sea breeze. A remote-controlled direction-finding station was set up on postage-stamp-sized Gaomi, a tiny satellite island east of Gavutu.[19]

The Tulagi Advanced Operating Base had an electric generating plant and ten refrigerators. It was kept supplied with necessities by Burns, Philp & Company's steamer from Sydney, and by Tulagi, where Lever's and W. R. Carpenter & Company had facilities, and where the Chinese stores stayed open until midnight. A small wood-frame building on Gavutu that had been a medical clinic for Lever's employees became the advanced operating base hospital.[20] The base was equipped with an 1,800-gallon refueling barge, the *Betty Jane,* a bomb barge, and a small launch with a 1.25 hp engine. A standard crash boat, used for rescuing aircraft personnel, was delivered in late March 1942.[21]

On 12 May 1941, the first Catalina from No. 11 Squadron arrived at Gavutu, assigned to monitor the seas for unusual activity and submarines. Initially, four Cats that had been drawn from No. 11 and No. 20 Squadrons at Port Moresby operated from the island. The aircraft was ideally suited for long-range patrol duty; it had a range of 2,550 miles at 115 mph and 1,500 miles with a bomb load, at slightly slower speed. If necessary, it could fly directly from Tulagi to the east coast of Australia without refueling.

An advance service unit was flown in to the Tulagi base in July, and the RAAF began shifting more Catalinas from Port Moresby to Gavutu. The balance of the personnel arrived by air at intervals through February 1942. A full complement of wireless operators was assigned to the radio unit, which was staffed around the clock.[22]

In mid-July 1941, G/Capt. F. W. F. Lukis, air officer commanding the southern area, and Commanding Officer Maj. J. Edmonds Wilson, No. 1 Independent Company, flew to Tulagi from Efate in the New Hebrides Islands where they had just arranged for Australian troops to be stationed at Port Vila. One of Wilson's commando units had moved from Australia through Rabaul on 10 July to occupy Kavieng, New Ireland. Lukis had evaluated the air installations at Vila, while Major Wilson had ironed out the details of the Australian role in the defense of the base. Among other things, the commandos would assist in training the New Hebrides Volunteer Defense Force.[23] Major Wilson made similar arrangements at Tulagi. Resident Commissioner Marchant would have operational control of the local defense force, but added to local defense plans was the shifting of one section of the 1st Independent Company from Kavieng, on New Ireland, to Tulagi.

The 271 commandos of the Australian No. 1 Independent Company were charged with defending the northeastern approaches to Australia. They were scattered in nine sections through New Guinea (Buka, New Ireland, and the Admiralties), the Solomons, and the New Hebrides. Wilson's commandos were to remain behind the lines during an enemy occupation in order to gather and disseminate intelligence and to assist and protect the coastwatchers. Their key means of transport was a lugger, the eighty-ton MV *Induna Star,* which Wilson had purchased from her civilian owners in Rabaul. She was put to work moving the detachments from Kavieng to Rabaul for further transfer to Tulagi and Vila.[24]

In 1941, the Australian Department of Air took over weather-reporting responsibilities in the area. The civilian organization was already operating in New Guinea, with a forecasting station at Port Moresby and an observing post at Salamaua; it subsequently was significantly expanded, with meteorological stations established in the Netherlands East Indies and at Vila and Nouméa. In late September, F/O J. L. Williams and Sgt. T. E. Hore set up a weather station at the Gavutu–Tanambogo locations of Tulagi AOB to supply meteorological information to the Catalinas operating from Port Moresby.

Meanwhile, Major Wilson's commandos were experiencing boredom with the prevailing monotony, a routine that consisted mostly of aircraft maintenance and guard duty. The only recreation for Wilson's commandos was visiting Tulagi or shark fishing in Sealark Channel, with an occasional excursion to Guadalcanal to shoot wild cattle on Tenaru Plantation for fresh beef. By dawn each day the Catalinas would be airborne, making reconnaissance flights between Gavutu and Port Moresby and on occasion transporting personnel being transferred to or from the base.[25] Paul Mason, the plantation manager who became a coastwatcher in south Bougainville, was able to provide Tulagi with two hours advance warning of any Japanese aircraft heading for that area, sufficient time to shift the Cats to Aola or Marau Sound on Guadalcanal for safety. Sometimes, as part of the "private" war preceding the main hostilities in the Solomons, an Aola-based Catalina would follow a Japanese flying boat back to the Maruki seaplane base at Simpson Harbor and attack as the plane was landing.[26]

Among those flying Catalina reconnaissance missions from the Tulagi advanced base were two Americans. In November 1941, U.S. Navy Lts. George H. Hutchinson and Samuel P. Weller, members of an observer team attached to the American Embassy in Canberra, were on temporary duty with the Royal Australian Air Force, Hutchinson with No. 11 Squadron and Weller with No. 20 Squadron. The two U.S. Navy Patrol Wing 10 veterans would be the only Americans to fly with the Australians in the first weeks of the Pacific War, and they have the distinction of being the first U.S. servicemen to set foot in the Solomon Islands during World War II.[27]

In May 1941, a 333-man Australian garrison force (code-named Robin Force) under Maj. D. G. Matheson had arrived at Nouméa, New Caledonia. Two months later the Australian air force established an advanced operational base at Nouméa to support its patrol squadrons. Concurrent with all this military preparation, however, uneasiness was increasing among civilians. Shortages of almost everything but whiskey were the norm, though to most people the war still seemed a long way off. Sister Mary Theresa, a Marist missionary on Guadalcanal, recalled: "During 1941, there was considerable talk about the possibility of war in the area but it all sounded like rumors and aeons away. Business went on as usual and life was lived in daily fashion. No one stopped to worry too much."[28]

At 0600 on 9 November 1941, the commando No. 1 Section departed Kavieng for Rabaul in the *Induna Star*. On the 14th, the advance party flew from Rabaul to Tulagi by a Sunderland flying boat. Late on the 18th, the sixteen-man main party sailed in the Burns Philp liner *Malaita;* they arrived at Tulagi six days later.[29] For the defense of the islands the commandos set up gun pits with three Vickers guns on antiaircraft swivel mountings. One, on the seaward (western) side of the Tanambogo hill, protected the bomb and fuel storage areas; the other two, on the southern and western sides of the Gavutu hill, covered the radio station. At the east end of the Tanambogo hill was an old cemetery; the three solitary graves, which had fallen in, were used as slit trenches.[30]

A major task assigned to the No. 1 Section was the formation and training of the Solomon Islands Defense Force on the same lines as the Papuan Infantry Battalion, with officers to be drawn from the white civilian population. Except for Martin Clemens, who was on leave, all the district officers and cadets had received appointments as second lieutenants effective 16 December 1941.[31] Three weeks later, the defense force welcomed its first commanding officer. Vivian Fox-Strangways had been the resident commissioner-designate of the Gilbert and Ellice Islands colony, but two days after war was declared Japanese forces occupied Makin Island in the northern Gilberts and he could not assume his post. He was appointed a major and flown to Tulagi.[32]

The Solomon Islands Defense Force was perhaps the smallest army in the world: it consisted of three British officers, one British noncommissioned officer (NCO), one native warrant officer (WO), a handful of Chinese, and 112 Solomon Islanders. In an appreciation of the situation prepared for the resident commissioner, Fox-Strangways lamented the force's poor state of readiness: "The European ranks . . . are in no sense fully trained. The standard of training and musketry of the native troops is low and as yet no native NCO has any real grasp of fire direction and control or of section leading. Tactical handling of troops, ammunition and ration supply, etc., has not been practiced. . . . The force is composed chiefly of native police and their officers. Guard and police duties have obviously militated against training. . . . The only hope lies in a simple basic, flexible scheme of defense."[33]

Before active recruiting could begin, however, the Japanese swept into the South Pacific, and the training scheme collapsed under the press of time. The officer ranks of the Solomon Islands Defense Force subsequently were depleted by the evacuation of a number of government officials in February 1942. Among them was Fox-Strangways, in command less than a month when he was ordered to Australia. By the beginning of March, the defense force had virtually disbanded. During the Japanese occupation, however, the force would be reconstituted around a cadre of skilled, experienced native constables, and by the end of the Guadalcanal campaign it would earn an honored place in military history.

2   The Enemy at the Doorstep

On 8 December 1941, Resident Commissioner Marchant at Tulagi learned via the BBC that Japanese troops had landed on the Malaya coast and that Pearl Harbor had come under air attack. Messages quickly were sent to residents with wireless sets. But more bad news followed: the Japanese had bombed Clark Field in the Philippines. The war had come to the Pacific.

Early Evacuation

Almost immediately in the Southwest Pacific preparations began to safeguard the women and children. The first evacuation was carried out by the *Trienza,* one of the Phosphate Commission's vessels, which served Nauru and Ocean Islands west of the Gilbert and Ellice Islands, east of the Solomons. According to the diary of Father James Wall, the Marist priest who ministered to the Australian servicemen at the Tulagi Advanced Operational Base, the evacuation of Nauru's civilian population aboard the *Trienza* took place concurrently with the boarding of the Free French destroyer *Le Triumphant.* Father Wall records that after furnishing fuel, provisions, and water to the warship at a secret location in the New Hebrides, the *Trienza* traveled north to Tulagi, where she remained for three days. Then while docked at Lever's Plantations pier at Gavutu, she boarded a number of European residents who had decided to evacuate, and subsequently she sailed back to the New Hebrides and a rendezvous with *Le Triumphant* at Port Vila.

Father Wall's account, however, clearly is incorrect. The Nauru evacuation had not occurred until 23 February 1942. It is more likely that just after the outbreak of the Pacific War the authorities diverted the *Trienza* to Tulagi for three days to evacuate civilians to Australia, particularly women and children, and that Father Wall later conflated the story and the evacuation of Nauru. Support for this explanation is found in the memoirs of Kenneth H. Dalrymple-Hay, manager of the Burns, Philp Berande Estate on Guadalcanal. Dalrymple-Hay recorded that his wife and all the other women on Tulagi apparently left without notice a few days before 16 December 1941, when he was scheduled to visit. They were evacuated on a ship that had been diverted while en route to the Gilbert and Ellice Islands, and as Ocean Island was part of that colony, the ship may have been the *Trienza.* The evacuation probably took place on 12 December; on 11 December Pvt. Reginald "Reg" Bowley (AIF), who was stationed at Tulagi AOB, had noted in his diary that "Schooners are picking up all women and children to evacuate to Australia."[1]

In December 1941 the Methodist mission's synod was held at the head station, Kokengolo, on Roviana Island, New Georgia. Attending were Rev. Clarence T. J. Luxton from the Skotolan mission station on Buka and Rev. Donald C. Alley from the mission at Teop Island, northeast Bougainville. It was decided to lay up the Buka vessel, *Saga,* for copper resheathing, and the *Bilua,* the vessel from Vella Lavella, was temporarily assigned to Buka. On the day the church council ended, the attack on Pearl Harbor became known worldwide. Both Reverend Luxton and Alley immediately sailed in the *Bilua* for Bougainville, 300 miles away. After stopping at Vella Lavella Island to pick up Alley's wife and two sons who had been visiting there, they hurried north at maximum speed, on the last night braving storms that would normally have kept the vessel in harbor. They arrived at Buka Passage on 12 December.

Preparations for a feared Japanese invasion had begun. Assistant District Officer Jack Read already had requested the use of the mission vessel if an evacuation order were issued, and shortly thereafter a native policeman brought a circular announcing that the New Guinea administration had ordered the evacuation of all European women and children from Buka and Bougainville. Nurses and missionaries could choose whether to remain, however, and that provision would create a problem for the coastwatchers, as the Roman Catholic missionaries would elect to stay. Several planters also had refused to leave.

People evacuating were to gather at the district headquarters station on Sohano Island in Buka Passage. At 0200 on 19 December the *Bilua* left Skotolan on Buka's west coast to pick up evacuees in that western area. She boarded the first at dawn, later took on four nurses from the Marist mission, and then returned to Skotolan for Mrs. Luxton and her two small children plus Sister Elizabeth Common. One more person was picked up en route to Buka Passage. At Sohano Island a launch arrived with Mrs. Alley and her children, and the missionaries spent the night aboard the *Bilua.*

At dawn on the 20th, the inter-island copra schooner *Asakaze* docked at Sohano with evacuees from Kieta, Bougainville. She boarded the Buka refugees and at 0700 they set sail for Rabaul. A short time later they ran into one of the most vicious tropical storms ever recorded in that area. The trip, which should have taken only twenty-four hours, lasted forty-two. The terrified passengers had no accommodations, only blankets spread on the deck and hatches. At last, at midnight on 21 December the *Asakaze* reached Rabaul, and twenty-nine shivering, water-soaked evacuees scrambled aboard the Burns Philp liner *Macdhui,* which was leaving for Australia.[2]

One day after the attack on Pearl Harbor, the Burns Philp liner *Malaita* had departed Sydney for the Solomons with seventy-six passengers, including seven Solomon Islanders returning home. After calling at Queensland ports, New Guinea's Port Moresby, and Samarai Island, the vessel arrived at Tulagi at 2200 on 13 December. There she lay at anchor overnight, all shore-side work having ceased at 1800 in accordance with blackout regulations. On New Year's Day 1942, the *Malaita* docked at small Makambo Island, just north of Tulagi within the Tulagi Harbor. Six people disembarked, three of which immediately booked return passage to Australia on the Burns Philp *Morinda,* then en route from Sydney. The *Malaita* departed Makambo on 2 January, making port calls through the protectorate and Bougainville and arriving at Rabaul, New Britain, on the 6th.[3]

Fifty-six people boarded at Rabaul—two returning Royal Australian Navy (RAN) personnel, seven paying passengers, and twenty-eight Japanese civilian internees locked in the hold with nineteen AIF soldiers serving as guards. From Rabaul, the *Malaita* returned through the islands, taking on single passengers at Numa Numa and Kieta, Bougainville; four at Faisi, Shortland Islands; twenty-one at Gizo; one at Fera, Santa Isabel; three in the Russell Islands at Cape Marsh; and eleven at Tulagi. The voyage was anything but uneventful. On 9 January, off Soraken in northwest Bougainville, a roving Japanese flying boat bombed the *Malaita.* She came through unscathed, however, for the pilot had either poor eyesight or inadequate training; she docked at Sydney on the 26th with ninety-eight jittery passengers.[4]

When the *Malaita* had docked at Faisi on 4 January on the way to Rabaul, William M. Klotz had disembarked; Klotz was the acting manager for Shortland Islands Plantations Ltd., which operated most of Burns Philp properties in the Shortlands. The air attacks on Rabaul had begun, and Bill Klotz found general confusion and considerable nervousness amidst the Faisi residents. When he had settled his company's

Figure 5. The SS *Morinda,* one of the ships involved in the early 1942 Solomon Islands evacuation. (Courtesy Burns, Philp & Company Ltd.)

affairs, he became involved in the plans to evacuate the European civilians from the western district of the protectorate.

The Shortlands district officer, Alexander N. A. "Nick" Waddell, had been in his post barely three months, since 25 September 1941. On his appointment, the district had been expanded to include Choiseul, as the Shortlands area was limited; however, the resident commissioner had failed to furnish the new DO a vessel with which to carry out his duties. In fact, Waddell had not been in the Shortlands long enough to acquire more than a fairly superficial knowledge of his district.[5] Nevertheless, on the outbreak of war in the Pacific, Waddell had called a meeting of the European residents and made arrangements for air raid warnings, shelters, food and oil supplies, and the disposal of shipping in the event of attack. He apprised the local native headmen of the situation and obtained their cooperation in providing lookouts and runners and instituting reporting procedures.

Nick Waddell was then a second lieutenant in the British Solomon Islands Protectorate Defense Force (BSIPDF) and had only himself and eight native constables for the security of his district. In all, they had ninety rounds of rifle ammunition. Waddell had submitted several requisitions for more, but these had not been filled. Three civilians had

Figure 6. Solomon Islands residents meet on Gizo Island in December 1941, prior to the civilian evacuation of the Solomons in February 1942. *From left to right*: Shortland Islands District Officer Sir Alexander N. A. "Nick" Waddell (later governor of Borneo), Eugenie and A. V. "Val" Murphy (Burns Philp store manager), Emily Cruickshank, Georgina and Carden W. Sexton (later a coastwatcher). *Seated, left to right*: Clara Scott, Louise Billette. Courtesy Mrs. Eugenie Murphy.

volunteered to join the defense force—Alfred Valentine "Val" Murphy, manager of the Burns Philp branch at Faisi; Ernest Mapletoft, Murphy's assistant; and Bill Klotz—but they were not accepted. Apparently Resident Commissioner Marchant wanted only district officers and other members of the civil establishment to be involved.[6]

One of District Officer Waddell's immediate concerns was the safety of the remaining European women in his district. The protectorate government indeed had advised dependents to leave, but unlike the Australians it had not compelled them to do so. Clara Scott, Emily Cruickshank, and Louise Billette, all single and all of middle age, had lived in the Shortlands for years; their plantations were both their home and their livelihood, and they were reluctant to abandon them; but Waddell managed to convince the women that relocating to Australia was preferable to having the Imperial Japanese Navy for a neighbor.[7]

Japan on the Move—Destination Rabaul

In the meantime, following up on her initial successes, Japan had moved to secure bases in the Bismarck Archipelago and New Guinea, but of key importance was Rabaul, New Britain. On 4 January 1942, aircraft of the 24th Air Flotilla under Rear Adm. Eihi Oto, from the Japanese naval base at Truk Atoll in the Caroline Islands, had bombed Rabaul's two main airdromes, Lakunai and Vunakanau. Further raids followed, and then, on the 20th, a flight of more than one hundred planes — heavy bombers, dive-bombers, and fighters — struck the Australian base. The next day forty fighters and twenty dive-bombers attacked Kavieng, New Ireland. A number of commandos were wounded; some later died. The Japanese must have thought that the town was heavily fortified to have mounted such a raid.[8]

The invasion force was already en route. On 17 January, Maj. Gen. Tomitaro Horii's South Seas Detachment, *Nankai Shitai,* having taken Guam, had boarded their transports and sailed for Rabaul. Horii's unit, which was under the control of the Fourth Fleet, was a brigade-sized force of some fifty-three hundred men; it comprised the 144th Infantry, an engineer regiment, and elements of the Maizuru 2nd Special Naval Landing Force. Based on prewar intelligence, staunch resistance was expected; but the Nankai Shitai was five times the size of Rabaul's garrison and the Japanese general had no doubt of the outcome.

Horii's brigade landed at Rabaul on the morning of the 23 January. The defenders were simply overwhelmed. Scattered pockets of resistance were quickly crushed. To avoid further slaughter, the Australian commander, Col. J. J. Scanlan, surrendered. As soon as Rabaul was in the Japanese hands, patrols were dispatched to hunt down any men who had escaped into the jungle. Many were not allowed to surrender and were just massacred. Rabaul became a large prison compound where AIF soldiers — the "Diggers" — would face starvation, ill treatment, slavery, and death.[9]

Rabaul was to be the central base for the Japanese conquest of the South Pacific, and they wasted no time in expanding their presence on New Britain. On 28 January, the 7th Construction Unit (CU) commanded by Engineering Officer Gunji Tokunaga, a civilian, began work on the reconstruction of the Lakunai airstrip. The conquerors of Rabaul planned to occupy the whole of New Britain before the end of January.[10] On 23 January, part of the South Seas Detachment had shifted to attack Kavieng, New Ireland. Their landing barges reached the western beaches at 0305, and the few remaining residents scattered for safety. The Japanese captured the town with only twelve shots fired. Kavieng was occupied by the main body of the Kure 3rd Special Naval Landing Force supported by weapons from the 5th Base Force. The 12th Construction Unit was assigned to build the base facilities and five lookout posts for the station.

The Kieta Mistake

The bombing of Rabaul had led to the belief that Kieta, on the east coast of Bougainville, was next in line for conquest. On 22 January, the Kieta district officer, J. I. Merrylees, informed his headquarters in Australia that indeed the town had been attacked and that he intended to destroy the wireless station and evacuate immediately. That day the following handbill was distributed to residents and posted in prominent locations:

> URGENT—TERRITORY OF NEW GUINEA
> In view of the broadcast that a military attack was launched on New Guinea today and that we have been unable to get in touch with Headquarters, citizens of Kieta, including public Servants, have decided to abandon their post and leave as soon as possible, probably Friday 23rd. January, by local shipping for the mainland.
> If you wish to join the party, proceed with all speed to Kieta, bringing clothing and bedding. Rations will be provided.
> /s/ J. I. Merrylees
> District Officer

The report caused a panic. Terrified that the enemy was at their doorstep, the majority of the European residents frantically made preparations to flee in any seaworthy vessel they could find. But, in fact, the "attack" was just a reconnaissance by two Japanese flying boats that had flown over Kieta. The real trouble occurred after most of the residents had departed, when islanders began looting the town. Eventually they were stopped by a small band of loyal native police, but it was too late—the damage was done. Merrylees's false report would bring chaos and disorder to every community in the Solomons and lead to the hurried exodus of island residents, many under duress.

At about 1430 on 23 January, Merrylees, along with some other nervous residents, left Kieta in the *Herald,* a ketch owned by local Chinese merchant Wong Yu. They were headed for Toimonapu Plantation down the coast. Immediately after their departure, Wong Yu sent a message to John R. Keenan, a patrol officer on Bougainville:

I just to let you know this morning have about 30 Jap ships in Rabaul, think no too good.

Today, 30 all white people have gone to Buin by my boat the Radio Station at Kieta set on fire before Mr. Doherty [H. Doherty, the Kieta wireless operator] away.

I think better you gone with Mr. Taylor [J. L. Taylor, the assistant district officer] so I am sending you three batteries so you will get some news later time all radio stations off, no on air.

Hoping to meet you all some day again. . . . [11]

En route to Toimonapu, Merrylees's party met Reverend Luxton in the *Bilua*. It is unclear whether the Reverend had returned to the Skotolan mission station after leaving on 7 or 8 December with Reverend Alley, though it would appear to be the case, inasmuch as District Officer Merrylees met him on 23 January aboard the *Bilau*. Having heard the report on the 22nd that the Japanese were at Kieta, Luxton had left the Skotolan mission and set out for Buin, at the southern tip of Bougainville. Merrylees transferred to the *Bilua,* which was much larger and in better condition than the *Herald* and could take his group well out of the area. Thus he sent the *Herald* back to Kieta with her native crew.

At Toimonapu, Merrylees found Tom Ebery, the plantation manager, and confiscated his teleradio equipment. Doherty, the wireless operator, then sent the message to Port Moresby that the Japanese had landed at Kieta. Ebery later told Paul Mason, manager of the Inus Plantation east of Bougainville, that Merrylees and his group stayed at the plantation house that night and heard the Australian radio announce the enemy occupation of Kieta. It seemed certain that the town had really been seized, but then one of the men remarked, "Don't be silly, that's only what we told them!"[12]

District Officer Nick Waddell at Faisi did not learn about the supposed invasion of Kieta until about 1730 on 25 January when he chanced to hear the news on an Australian Broadcasting Commission war news bulletin. Waddell tried to raise Kieta on his teleradio, but Merrylees was already at sea, and the Kieta line was dead.[13] The Japanese had monitored the broadcast, but apparently thought the report was a deception. Because all the war news was under strict censorship, protectorate residents lacked the information necessary to separate fact from fiction.

At the Tulagi air base, with the breakdown of the defense force training plan, the Australian role became purely one of insular defense. With three Vickers antiaircraft guns and one Bren gun—a light machine gun (LMG)—the commandos undertook the protection of the Catalina base at Tanambogo and the RAF radio station on Gavutu.[14]

The Gavatu and Tulagi Raids

Back on 9 January, when the air raids began, Reg Bowley at Gavutu had captured the excitement and frustration in his diary: "Big scare—the game's on! Japanese planes overhead. Didn't have a chance of a shot." NCO Claude Sinclair, general storekeeper in charge of the bomb dump and assistant in the marine section, recalled that one bomb that hit Gavutu left a hole forty-two feet wide and eight feet deep.[15]

That game began in earnest about 1230 on 22 January when a Japanese Mavis flying boat attacked Gavutu. All the bombs landed in Tulagi Harbor, missing the base by hundreds of feet, before the raider turned his machine guns on a Catalina (A25) that was moored off Tanambogo. As her captain, P/O Alan L. Norman, fought to get his engines started, the gunners on shore fired at the low-flying Japanese. Finally the Cat got underway and skimmed along the water, zigzagging until Norman was able to get airborne and elude his attacker by sliding into a cloud bank.[16] The islanders had a two-day respite before the next episode. On the 24th, two flying boats bombed Tulagi, then hit a small pier in Chinatown and flew off. The raid made people edgy; they realized the war was coming closer, and much sooner than they had expected.

Over the next four months the bombings would gradually increase in both size and frequency, and the Tulagi air base would become a rather dangerous place. Amazingly, no one was killed. So many attacks occurred on Tulagi that the Japanese bombardiers appeared to be completely incompetent. Their frequent attempts to knock down the wireless antenna were unsuccessful, and the town was rarely damaged. More likely, the Japanese wanted the area to be relatively intact when they took it.

On 23 January, the day before the flying boats had bombed Tulagi, Burns Philp plantations manager Bill Klotz, under instructions from Nick Waddell, went to Laumona Plantation on Purupuru Island aboard the cutter *Lofung* to pick up the owners, Katherine and Wilson Atkinson. Kitty Atkinson was eager to evacuate, but Willie refused and Klotz had to leave without him. The cutter arrived at Faisi about 0800 on the 24th with Kitty Atkinson, Clara Scott, Emily Cruickshank, and Louise Billette, who were then sent to Gizo in the *Ramada*, the schooner on loan to Waddell from the district officer at Guadalcanal.[17]

By the time Klotz returned to Laumona a day later, Willie Atkinson had heard the Australian broadcast of the Japanese landing at Kieta, and he was more than eager to leave. He realized that even his brother, Sam, who owned Ballale Island, had left earlier. Willie packed a few belongings and sailed for Faisi, arriving about 0400 on the 26th. Waddell told Klotz that the situation was dire and strongly suggested he start for Gizo immediately. After unloading some unwanted forty-four-gallon drums of diesel oil, Klotz had just enough time to visit the Lofung store, the hospital, and the office on the beach, telling the native laborers to help themselves to any remaining rations. He then picked up Eric J. "Slim" Summerland, a Burns Philp employee, and Father George M. Lepping, of the Marist mission station at Nila, Poporang Island. At about 0500 on the 26th, with Willie Atkinson, Slim Summerland, and Father Lepping, Bill Klotz set out for Gizo in the *Lofung*.[18]

In the midst of all this activity and confusion, a native canoe pulled in at Faisi. Father Richard O'Sullivan, from the Marist mission station at Patupatnai near Buin on Bougainville Island, had come to Faisi to do some shopping. On hearing of the Shortland Islands evacuation order, he immediately climbed aboard his canoe once again and headed back to Bougainville.[19]

The Confusion Lingers

At 1800 on the 26th, Waddell received an urgent telegram from the resident commissioner instructing him to burn all secret documents and destroy all stores. Waddell objected, as they had already made preparations to remain, and he was still awaiting news from his scouts on Bougainville. The only report on the fall of Kieta had come from the Australian radio broadcast, which the administration at Tulagi apparently had taken at face value. However, at 0200 on 27 January, Waddell received a message from Resident Commissioner Marchant ordering him to carry out the instructions immediately and proceed to Gizo in the *Ramada,* which was being returned to him.[20]

Nick Waddell ordered the remaining Europeans to proceed to Gizo. He and Val Murphy, the Burns Philp manager, remained behind to complete the destruction of Faisi. They arranged the repatriation of the native laborers from the various plantations to their home islands and saw that they were provided with ample food. Much of the food from the Burns Philp warehouse and all medical supplies were distributed to responsible local people in order to minimize any immediate looting depletion and shortage. The islanders were instructed to proceed to Fauro Island using all available launches, including those belonging to Burns Philp, Eric Monckton, Emily Cruickshank, and the Kamaliai Plantation.[21]

After putting the warehouse and any remaining stores to the torch, the two men sailed for Gizo in the *Ramada*. The Shortlands settlement, thirty-six years in the making, was left in ruins.[22]

The evacuation plan called for the Faisi residents to reassemble at Gizo Island, and Distraict Officer Waddell expected to remain there until receiving further instructions. But at that moment, when prompt communication was imperative, the administration—slow at the best of times—was dead on its feet. Waddell did not know that Resident Commissioner Marchant had ordered the destruction of the settlement at Gizo.

The Gizo district officer, William H. C. C. "Hugh" Miller, had been Nick Waddell's immediate predecessor in the Shortlands. Due to retire within a year, he was expecting the arrival of a cadet to replace him. He would have a long time to wait. The Australian Broadcasting Commission report of the fall of Kieta had caused turmoil and confusion at Gizo station, as it did throughout the protectorate. The central Solomons were the next step from the Shortlands, which were only fifty miles from Kieta.

The Participant Accounts

The description of the evacuation of Gizo and the central Solomons is based on several sources, the most detailed of which is an undated report, summarizing the events of 23 January to 5 February 1942 that District Officer Hugh Miller wrote for the resident commissioner. Also important is "The Cruise of the *Fauro Chief*," a mimeographed account compiled by Rev. Arthur H. Voyce from the journal of Dr. Allen G. Rutter and the diaries of Sisters Vera Cannon, Lina Jones, and Effie Harkness, all of the Methodist mission. Rutter was a medical missionary and Cannon a nurse at the mission hospital at Bilua, in southeast Vella Lavella; Jones and Harkness were teachers at Kokengolo. Reverend Voyce, a missionary at Buin, would return to the Solomons in 1943 as a chaplain with the 2nd New Zealand Expeditionary Force.[23]

According to the participant accounts, at about 0900 on 23 January, Doctor Rutter and Sister Cannon, hearing news of the Japanese advance, paddled over to Liapari Estate to confer with the manager, A. W. "Bert" Bourne, and his wife, Monica, about "the possibility of awakening a slumbering Tulagi into some active evacuation or assisting the residents of the western Solomons to leave. . . ." At midday Rutter and the Bournes went to Gizo in the mission launch *Cicely II* to inquire about the plans for evacuation should the Japanese move toward the Solomons. They found the entire population—European and native—digging trenches.

At 1400 a meeting was held in Fred Green's store, with the following people in attendance: Green; Rutter; James Kidnie, manager of Burns Philp's branch at Gizo and agent for the Shell Company; the Bournes; Ernie Mapletoft and his wife, Toni; and Hugh Miller and his wife, Margarine. Everyone seemed to be in favor of doing something, the accounts note, but there was no agreement as to what it should be. District Officer Miller suggested that the mission sisters congregate at Bilua; that the Methodist mission schooner *Fauro Chief* be held in readiness; and that if the Japanese moved toward the Solomons the residents should evacuate eastward and, if possible, join up with the Seventh Day Adventist mission staff at their large station at Batuna, Vangunu Island, New Georgia. Bourne and Rutter suggested a rendezvous at Kokengolo to prepare the *Fauro Chief* for a possible trip. Satisfied that something was being done, they returned to Vella Lavella about 2100.

Ninety minutes earlier on 23 January the Australian Broadcasting Commission had made the announcement that Kieta had fallen. The various writers indicate that Kidnie and the Mapletofts came to see Miller about the evacuation. Because Miller felt that the district schooner, *Gizo,* should remain at the station, Kidnie put the Burns Philp launch, *Marovo,* at their disposal. It was agreed that the Mapletofts and Mrs. Miller would leave for Kokengolo, via Kolombangara, as soon as possible, thereby having less chance of being seen by any Japanese entering Gizo at dawn. After advising the Kokengolo mission staff what had occurred, they would proceed to Batuna to persuade the Seventh Day Adventists to hold their schooner, *Melanesia,* as the *Fauro Chief* could not take all who were leaving. Miller immediately sent the *Gizo* to Bilua with a message for Rev. A. W. E. Silvester, telling him to come in without delay. After packing, the group met at 2300 at the Burns Philp store where Kidnie had nearly finished loading food supplies on the *Marovo.*

At that time, the accounts note, Rutter heard the news about Kieta. He dashed over in pajamas and slippers to tell Silvester and Sister Cannon. On the track he met a native messenger from Gizo with a note from Hugh Miller, asking that all the Europeans from Bilua and its surroundings be at Gizo by 0200 on the 24th. This seemed too indefinite, so Rutter and Bert Bourne returned to Gizo aboard the *Gizo,* arriving at 0300. There they learned that the *Marovo* would be leaving for

Kokengolo three hours later. No reply had been received from Tulagi, thus no help was anticipated. They would have to rely on their own local efforts.

The writings show that Bourne and Rutter had returned in the Burns Philp launch *Loai* to collect the people at Bilua. Reverend Silvester dispatched a runner to the Mundi Mundi Plantation for John Campbell and his family, then sent the *Cicely II* to Sasamunga, Choiseul, for Rev. John R. Metcalfe and Sister Merle S. Farland, instructing them to head directly to Roviana. Charles P. Beck and Mrs. Jean McEachran were brought over from Ozama, a tiny island just off Bilua.[24]

The *Marovo* left Gizo at daylight on 24 January with the Mapletofts, Mrs. Miller, and Mr. J. Gosling, a Seventh Day Adventist employee. The vessel was accompanied by the small Burns Philp launch, *Vonunu,* which was to return and let Miller know whether the Seventh Day Adventist people at Batuna would wait. About 0700 the two boats were seen passing down the coast of Kolombangara. An hour later the *Loai* left Bilua for Kokengolo, with Rutter, Beck, Mrs. McEachran, the Bournes, Sister Cannon, and Sister Grace McDonald. Reverend Silvester stayed behind.

That morning of the 24th Gizo District Officer Hugh Miller sent a radiogram to Tulagi: "Residents of the district evacuating east. Kidnie, Green and I await instructions." Resident Commissioner Marchant's terse reply came back: "Suggest evacuees concentrate Batuna." With only the *Gizo* left for their escape, Miller had no means of forwarding this message to those who already had gone.

The participant reports state that the *Marovo* arrived first in Kokengolo. The news from Gizo took the residents by surprise, but by the time the *Loai* arrived, preparations for departure had begun. The writers indicate that those at Kokengolo had made preparations previously to "go bush," as they had not thought evacuation possible. But now, it seemed wiser to depart, for Tulagi was being bombed and if that town were evacuated then it would mean no more provisions, medicines, or other supplies. They realized they would have to live in the bush in the event of a Japanese occupation to avoid internment, or worse, and they knew they would be a burden to the native people, who could protect themselves. The writings show that in addition, Grace McDonald and Lina Jones both were ill and in need of care. It was thus with "heavy and sad hearts," the reports stated, that the mission residents made their preparations, thinking about their life's work and arranging as much as possible for it to be carried on by the islanders.

The *Marovo* and her passengers meanwhile quickly moved out again for Batuna, to prevent the *Melanesia* from leaving before everyone had gathered there. Provisions from the *Loai* were transferred to the *Fauro Chief;* plenty of crude oil fuel was put on board, and the vessel was prepared as well as possible for the long voyage to Australia. Early that evening of the 24th, the *Salikana,* the auxiliary cutter from the Solomon Islands Development Company's Manning Strait Plantation, arrived at Gizo with copra from Burns Philp. Under the circumstances, Kidnie, the company's manager, had no use for it, and thus District Officer Miller sent the vessel back, along with an urgent letter to the manager of the estate, Herbert S. Brearley, telling him that Kieta had been occupied and that he should leave for Tulagi immediately.

That day, Miller had sent the resident commissioner another radiogram: "Everybody gone, do we remain?" Marchant replied: "Collaborate with agent [Mr. Kidnie] and take steps to demolish RAAF petrol in case of attack."

The participant accounts indicated that the *Ramada,* with Clara Scott, Katherine Atkinson, Emily Cruickshank, and Louise Billette, had arrived at Gizo about 1600 on 24 January. The women recounted the day and night reconnaissance by Japanese planes over the Shortland Islands. They quickly were transferred to the *Loai,* which had just returned from Kokengolo, and were told to head for Batuna with all speed, to relay to the Seventh Day Adventist staff the resident commissioner's instructions to concentrate there. The *Ramada* returned immediately to the Shortlands.

The various writers note that at 0625 on 26 January, District Officer Waddell at Faisi failed to keep a radiotelegraph session. This, and the routing of his own communications to Auki, the chief port on Malaita, led District Officer Miller to suspect that the Shortlands had been occupied and Tulagi evacuated. Then, at 0930, the Campbell family from Mundi Munda and William J. Binskin from Bagger Island, off southwest Vella Lavella, arrived at Gizo in Binskin's ketch, *Alice,* with two Japanese internees, Senanga and Pisita. It is noted that on his own initiative John Campbell had carried out a scorched-earth policy, destroying his rubber trees and stores. The writers added that because the *Gizo* would be overcrowded, District Officer Miller kept the internees on board the *Alice,* under escort, and instructed Campbell to head for Batuna and hold there for the *Fauro Chief* and the *Melanesia.*[25]

Miller and Kidnie already had begun demolition preparations. At 2200 on 26 January Waddell still had not arrived at Gizo and Miller concluded that the Shortlands indeed had been occupied and Waddell had failed to escape. Believing that Gizo would be attacked by dawn, Miller, Kidnie, and Green agreed to demolish the petrol and evacuate. The stock of petrol consisted of 250 forty-four-gallon drums, kept in a bond store on the Burns Philp wharf, less than one hundred feet from the Burns Philp store and copra shed. Miller and Kidnie opened the drums, some completely, some just enough to allow the fumes to seep out. A coconut leaf trail had been laid and saturated with paraffin; it was saturated a second time then at 2330, as the moon was failing, Miller set it afire.

Participant writings show that the three men left Gizo immediately. Due to the darkness, however, they had to anchor at Nusatupi, a small island off the entrance to Gizo Harbor. There they met the *Vonunu,* returning from Batuna. In a letter from his wife, Miller learned that the *Fauro Chief* and the *Melanesia* were heading for Australia, though the latter vessel would first stop at Gill Island, off the north coast of Santa Isabel, to pick up Pastor J. Howse. District Officer Miller also received a request from Pastor J. C. H. Perry, superintendent of the Seventh Day Adventist mission, to broadcast a message to Howse: "Meet me according to arrangements."

At 0500 on 27 January, what appeared to be the copra shed burst into flames. The glow could be seen for miles. Fearing that it would draw the Japanese, the *Gizo* and the *Vonunu* set out immediately for the coast of Kolombangara. An hour later they met up with the *Salikana,* coming from the direction of Gizo. Leaving word with the *Vonunu* to have the *Salikana* meet them at Lady Lever Plantation on Kolombangara, Miller and his party preceded there. By that time, dense black smoke could be seen rising from Gizo.

Meanwhile, after anchoring in Viru Harbor for the night, the participants state that the *Fauro Chief* had left early on the 26th for the Segi Plantation in the southern part of New Georgia island, home of long-time resident Harold A. Markham. Markham gave the evacuees his sextant and some navigation books, but was not very hopeful of their success. As they were about to leave Segi, the *Loai* caught up with them, with the four women from the Shortlands aboard; she then continued on to Batuna. The *Fauro Chief* went to Patutiva, the largest of the Methodist mission villages in the Marovo Lagoon, where the Europeans obtained potatoes and pineapples for the long trip. They reached Batuna at 1500 and found the Seventh Day Adventist mission staff preparing to leave in the *Melanesia*. The Mapletofts, Mrs. Miller, and Mr. Gosling arrived just in time to join the other evacuees.

A crew of eight Solomon Islanders, all skilled mariners, usually handled the *Fauro Chief*, but they could not leave the protectorate, so on this voyage she would not have a qualified sailor. Because the *Melanesia* was larger and the *Fauro Chief* lacked able-bodied men, the two exchanged some passengers. According to the reports, the Mapletofts joined those on the *Fauro Chief*, and Mrs. Miller, Mrs. McEachran, and the four women from the Shortlands went aboard the *Melanesia* with the Adventist men. The *Fauro Chief* passengers were glad to have Ernie Mapletoft aboard, as only Bert Bourne had some ocean sailing experience and he and Charles Beck would have been overworked. That night, they had hurriedly finished packing when the news broadcast from Australia announced, "All citizens have been evacuated from Tulagi."[26]

The *Melanesia* left first, at 0115 on the 27th. While preparations were being completed on the *Fauro Chief*, a launch arrived with the Campbell family, also going to Tulagi. Campbell told them of the scorched-earth policy that Miller had carried out at Gizo, that Sister Farland was not coming, and that Reverend Luxton had gone to Kieta to help evacuate people and most probably had been caught by the Japanese. Campbell said he could not have made the trip to Batuna, about eighty miles from his estate, without the help of the two Japanese internees, who had piloted him through the reefs and dangerous passages. He relayed Miller's request that they wait at Batuna until 1400, and then go up to Auki; however, Doctor Rutter would not alter his arrangements. The reports show that final preparations were made, and the *Fauro Chief* left Batuna at 0800. Aboard her were Rutter; Beck; Rev. E. C. Leadley from Kokengolo; Sisters Cannon, Harkness, Jones, and McDonald; Ernie and Toni Mapletoft; and Bert and Monica Bourne. Rutter asked Campbell not to radio the resident commissioner that they had sailed.

Writing again of 27 January, the participants note that Bill Klotz and his party, in the *Lofung*, reached Gizo that day, shortly before Nick Waddell and his group in the *Ramada*. They found the town abandoned and in smoking ashes—Waddell had seen the fire and smoke en route from Faisi. Perplexed because they had not received further orders from the government by radio, Klotz's party set off for Batuna to await evacuation instructions.

District Officer Miller reached Lady Lever Plantation about 0800 that morning and found the plantation unoccupied. Soon afterward, however, writings show the arrival of Edward Shields, overseer of Lever's Vila estate. Harold Mulvey, manager of the firm's estates on Kolombangara, had not heard Gizo on the air that morning and had sent Shields to investigate. Mulvey and his remaining assistant, James A. Buchanan, were at Port Vila, ready to evacuate.

Herbert Brearley, in the *Salikana*, came in to the Lady Lever plantation soon after, reporting two other vessels following. The first turned out to be the *Lofung*, with Klotz, Atkinson, Summerland, and Father Lepping; the second was the *Ramada* with Waddell and Murphy. Waddell had on board a number of Solomon Islanders who were to be put off at the Roviana Lagoon, and thus it was decided that the *Lofung* would proceed to Port Vila, collect Mulvey and Buchanan, and then head for Batuna via the eastern coast of New Georgia.

The *Gizo, Ramada,* and *Salikana* proceeded to Batuna via Roviana. The *Salikana* was sent to Tetipari on New Georgia Island to pick up a planter, Francis Thresher. District Officer Miller then transferred to the *Ramada* to try to get a wireless message through to Tulagi and sent the *Gizo* on to Batuna; however, he was unable to rig the wireless aerial. Records indicate they therefore proceeded to Markham's plantation at Segi, arriving at 0130 on the 28th. At Segi they found the vessels congregated, as it was too dark to go on to Batuna. There they learned that the *Melanesia* and the *Fauro Chief* had departed—the former to Santa Isabel, the latter to Australia. Miller then sailed at 0500 for Gill Island via Batuna, where he found the *Salikana*. Leaving word that Waddell would get there later, Miller carried on to Gill Island, arriving at 2100. The *Melanesia* and the *Loai* were anchored there, and on the *Melanesia*, in addition to Pastor Perry and Mr. Gosling, were Pastors A. R. Barrett and J. Cormack, Nurse Evelyn Totenhofer, C. Tucker, Norman A. Ferris, Mrs. Atkinson, Mrs. Cruickshank, Miss Billette, Mrs. Scott, and Mrs. Miller. Pastor Perry told District Officer Miller that they intended to make for Australia, but they had come to Gill Island first to meet Pastor Howse. On the *Loai* were John and Florence Campbell and their three children, on their way to Auki.[27]

Early the next morning, 29 January, participant writings show that Pastor Howse arrived at Gill Island. Pastor Perry decided to return to Batuna in Howse's vessel, the *Dadavata*. The *Melanesia* would carry on up the Choiseul coast in the hope of meeting Pastor C. Pascoe, who they thought would try to escape from Bougainville via the islands in the Bougainville Straits.

Privately, District Officer Miller had urged the Shortlands women and Mrs. McEachran not to undertake a dangerous ocean voyage in such a small vessel. He convinced them to come with his party to Tulagi and take passage on the *Morinda,* which was being sent directly to the Solomons on an evacuation run, and thus they and Mrs. Miller were distributed among the *Gizo, Loai,* and *Dadavata.* The three vessels left Gill Island at 1045 on the 29th and reached Batuna the next morning, the 30th. Miller radioed Resident Commissioner Marchant that he had intercepted the *Melanesia* and returned with the women and that the *Fauro Chief* had departed for Australia.

Before leaving for Gill Island, however, Miller had asked a native teacher at Batuna to proceed to Gizo on an errand. Returning on 30 January, the teacher reported that when he had arrived at Gizo Island at midnight on the 28th, he saw no one on Gizo but a fire was burning fiercely at Burns Philp's and the bond store that had contained the petrol was gone. Then, at midday on the 29th, while at the Adventist mission hospital at Kukudu, on Kolombangara, he saw a plane flying low over the island and then heard four loud explosions.

District Officer Waddell reported that the male Europeans had become restive about their evacuation, and he feared a serious disturbance if they received no immediate or definite instructions. He and Miller radioed the resident commissioner about their concern, and on 1 February they received instructions to send the evacuees to Tulagi in the *Melanesia.* However, because the *Melanesia* was not at Batuna, they made ready the *Gizo* and six other cutters and launches, and the evacuees left for the Solomons capital at 1400. Later that afternoon, Miller was instructed to send the internees, Senanga and Pisita, to Tulagi, whereupon they and their escorts left in a Seventh Day Adventist mission vessel at 1900.[28]

On returning from Isabel that evening, Pastor Perry volunteered to take to Tulagi the Malaita laborers on the Marovo Lagoon plantations. Corporal Surita of the Solomon Defense Force was dispatched in one of the vessels to collect them. Though he had promised to wait for them at the top end of the lagoon until midnight, Perry left Batuna at 2200. Surita did not return until the next day with all twenty-eight of the laborers, as he had to search for them, causing them to miss Pastor Perry.

Participants write that the *Ramada* returned from Choiseul the evening of 2 February with Reverends Silvester and Metcalfe, Sister Farland, and Father Albert Binois of the Marist mission. On the next afternoon the three Methodist missionaries decided not to evacuate and thus returned to Kokengolo in Rev. Belshazzar Gina's boat. The Malaita laborers were sent into Tulagi in an Adventist mission vessel. Reverend Silvester and Sister Farland returned to Vella Lavella, while Metcalfe remained at Kokengolo. Father Binois returned to Choiseul in the *Lofung.*[29]

On the afternoon of 4 February, District Officer Miller received a message from the resident commissioner: "Do you wish to remain in your district for intelligence?" District Officer Waddell, who was nearby, assumed that the message also pertained to him. Both men declined; their stations lay in ashes, and nothing could be accomplished by remaining. In response, Resident Commissioner Marchant instructed them to proceed in to Tulagi, and thus they left Batuna for the Solomons capital on the *Ramada* at 2315. For the most part, the Chinese residents of Miller's district had evacuated with all their stores and provisions between 8 and 12 January, moving from place to place in their vessels.[30]

On 26 January, when the Australian Broadcasting Commission had announced that Tulagi had been evacuated, and because the *Morinda* was not due for almost two weeks, the Lever's Plantation staff had quickly put into effect its own evacuation plan. The company ketch *Kombito* had collected people who wished to leave and had transferred them to a large labor-recruiting vessel, the three hundred-ton *Kurimarau,* for the trip to Australia. Fortunately, those who missed being picked up because they had not heard of the plan or were late in reaching their departure site were granted a reprieve when Charles V. Widdy, Lever's general manager at Gavutu Island, arranged for the *Kombito* to make additional stops and take them to meet the evacuation vessel in the Russell Islands.[31] On 27 January the *Kurimarau* left the Solomons for Sydney with seventy-three passengers. A few smaller vessels fled south with her.[32]

The *Fauro Chief* evacuees arrived safely in Mackay, Queensland, on 11 February 1942, after a voyage of sixteen days, though Charles Beck, elderly and very ill, was taken to a hospital immediately and died a few days later. The trip also had avoided some near disasters, for three days into the voyage Monica Bourne, who could not swim, somehow had fallen overboard. Bert, her husband, also not a swimmer, jumped in after her; apparently both were rescued. Later, the vessel experienced further distress when it became trapped for a period inside a reef.

After her arrival in Australia the *Fauro Chief* was taken up by the Australian navy and used as an examination ship, inspecting vessels entering port and checking for contraband and belligerent status. On 16 May 1945, at Milne Bay, New Guinea, she sank as the result of the collapse of the jetty alongside which she had been moored.

3   Flying Before the Storm

The small fleet of refugees from New Georgia reached Tulagi safely and waited for the *Morinda* to arrive from Sydney. District Officers Nick Waddell and Hugh Miller joined the evacuees on 5 February.[1] Meanwhile Kata Rangoso, an ordained native pastor, was in charge of the Seventh Day Adventist mission vessels and at the request District Officer Donald Kennedy had turned over the *Marara* to Hugh Wheatley, a native medical practitioner on Kennedy's staff. Wheatley used her for two weeks in repatriating plantation workers from the central Solomons to their home islands; then Kennedy took charge of the vessel. A man of forceful personality and strong character, Kennedy often operated almost independently. Having surmised that the Japanese would occupy key points in the Solomons, he had begun to collect supplies and hoard essential items.[2]

Shepherding the Evacuations

The *Morinda* finally departed Sydney at 2225 on 31 January 1942, refueled and reprovisioned, but four hours late. She had been short a third cook and could not sail until a replacement had been found. The ship had been chartered by the Australian government in response to a special request to the prime minister from the high commissioner for the western Pacific. On instructions from the government, the naval board had sanctioned her use on this special voyage to evacuate those waiting at Tulagi. The *Morinda*'s usual route was via Lord Howe Island, Norfolk Island, Port Vila (Efate), Espiritu Santo, and Tulagi, where she would dock at the Burns Philp pier on adjacent Makambo Island. On this voyage, however, she had sailed directly to Tulagi Island.[3] On board was Cadet Martin Clemens, who had been on leave in Australia when war broke out in the Pacific. He had made plans to join the Royal Australian Navy while in Melbourne, but found that avenue closed, so he had to return to Tulagi when his leave ended. Had it not been for Vic Shearwin and Jack Blaikie, who were also returning from leave, Clemens would have been the only passenger.[4]

Though the sea was calm, the crew was restless, and *Morinda*'s master, Capt. S. Rothery, was forever talking, indicative of his nervousness. Yet for all his prattle, Rothery had refused to provide any information to his three passengers, despite their constant prodding: What was the situation at Tulagi? Was it still intact? Their frustration with the captain notwithstanding, Clemens, Shearwin, and Blaikie were well served in the *Morinda*'s lounge by the young purser, Harry Lukin, and the stewardess. Lukin had the unenviable job of defending the ship with the Vickers gun mounted atop her bridge.[5]

On 5 February, European residents from all parts of the protectorate began arriving at Tulagi. Most of their cutters and schooners were scattered alongside the wharf at Makambo. Suitcases, trunks, government file boxes, cases of rifles, machine guns, ammunition, and even a load of copra were sitting on the dock awaiting the *Morinda*. The next day, Resident Commissioner Marchant appointed William V. Jardine Blake, the government accountant, as the evacuation officer. Blake was informed that the *Morinda* would arrive on the 7th, though the date was subject to change depending on clearance from Sydney; she would dock at her normal station at Makambo. In the event of an imminent air attack, or should conditions favor such action, she would proceed to a sheltered area of Port Purvis, Florida Island, and when the danger had passed she would move to Makambo to load. Blake began preparing the evacuation list and the boarding and loading plans.

In the morning sun of Sunday, 8 February, the *Morinda* steamed up between Guadalcanal and Florida Islands at about 1020. It was not good scheduling. Burns Philp had been warned to have her arrive at Tulagi either early in the morning or late in the afternoon, as the raiding Japanese flying boats usually came over about midday. It was not unexpected then that as the ship appeared off the port, an air-raid warning was received on shore. Paul Mason, the coastwatcher on Bougainville, had radioed that a Japanese Kawanishi flying boat was heading south.

A crash boat met the *Morinda* in Tulagi Harbor. On board were several armed airmen and Pay Lt. Donald S. Macfarlan, RAN, assigned to the role of port director. A recently recruited protégé of Eric Feldt, organizer of the coastwatchers, Macfarlan was decked out in his starched white navy uniform and had a tin hat on his head. Father James Wall, the missionary at Tulagi Advanced Operational Base also came out, in the Lever's Plantations ketch, the *Kombito*. All had a stern, worried look.

Although Macfarlan was untrained in maritime responsibilities—until recently he had been a department store supervisor—he issued orders to the *Morinda*'s captain to head for the Mboli Passage on Florida Island where the overhanging jungle growth would hide the ship from the prying eyes of any Japanese aircraft. The *Morinda* proceeded at a crawl. At about 1100, when she was some ten minutes away from Mboli Passage, the expected flying boat appeared out of the clouds and headed in the direction of Tulagi. Rothery stopped the engines and the old vessel became silent. Coming from the north, the Kawanishi sighted the target and descended on her bombing run. *Morinda* was a sitting duck. She resumed her movement, and slowly began to swing away just as the bombs were released. Fortunately, the channel was wide enough for her to maneuver.

Martin Clemens described the next few minutes as "hell." The flying boat dropped two bombs from her left wing, then a few seconds later two more from the right wing. Clemens thought at least one might have his name on it, but all fell off the starboard bow. Circling again the Kawanishi dropped four more bombs in a straight line 200 yards off, but astern. She circled once more, then flew off to the north. The pilot did not use his machine guns on the milling boats, which all were loaded with evacuees. Relief was evident amongst the packed small vessels, as well as on the *Morinda,* for in her hold she was carrying seventy tons of explosives and aviation fuel for the Australians. If one bomb had hit, she would have been an inferno.

The ship was now free to berth, and Macfarlan ordered the captain to take her to Gavutu for loading. In so doing, however, he greatly exceeded his authority, as responsibility for the evacuation had been entrusted to Blake, a senior civil official. Macfarlan was the naval liaison officer (NLO); his responsibilities were primarily intermediation and information. Meanwhile, the evacuees were either on the Makambo wharf or on their craft in the harbor. The European passengers were concentrated in the general area of Makambo; the Chinese evacuees remained in Chinatown on Tulagi. When they saw the *Morinda* heading for the Lever's Plantations wharf, they began loading their belongings back onto their boats and headed for Gavutu. Dozens of vessels—schooners, cutters, ketches—filled in the harbor, all trying not to bump into one another and fighting for dock space.

Blake, still on Tulagi, then went to the Makambo docks where all the government records remained, as well as the sacks of mail and boxes of rifles and ammunition. He hailed the resident commissioner's vessel,

Tulagi, and with help from others loaded the cache on her then headed for Gavutu. On docking, Blake was given a message to attend a meeting at the air mess on Tanambogo. There he found Macfarlan, Shearwin, Clemens, and Christopher S. B. Attlee discussing evacuation plans.[6] But because Blake already had devised a strategy, it seemed appropriate to them to get the evacuees aboard accordingly.

At 1430 Macfarlan handed Attlee a letter from Resident Commissioner Marchant stating that the *Morinda* would be leaving as soon as possible. Forty minutes later Blake phoned the commissioner and was informed that the ship was indeed stopping at Makambo. About 1615, however, Blake was told that she would not be coming to the Burns Philp dock. Macfarlan had interfered again.

Captain Rothery was also making Blake's difficult job worse. When Blake arrived at Gavutu at 1750, he found widespread confusion. The first of the evacuees' vessels had reached Gavutu around 1600, but Rothery had refused to permit anyone to come aboard. Somewhat earlier, F. E. "Pop" Johnson, the protectorate treasurer and collector of customs, had arrived along with other evacuating officials; he too had been denied boarding rights by the obstinate captain, who had said that "no person in the government had been over to see him about anything." Blake, as evacuation officer, had been trying to settle where the *Morinda* should be berthed and decide what action to take to protect the government records, and he had brought the evacuation list with him. But in the meantime Rothery had decided to permit the boarding of some evacuees who had arrived unexpectedly that morning from New Guinea—six Australian commandos attached to the detachment in the Namatanai Sub-District, New Ireland, which had evacuated the Namatanai area. The six commandos had been in mountainous country inside Japanese lines with District Officer Bill Kyle. Unable to raise anyone at Port Moresby or headquarters through their teleradio, they had nowhere to go and no instructions to follow. They were tired and suffering from fatigue, malaria, dysentery, and skin infections. They had obtained the use of the diesel-powered MV *Gnair* to make their way from New Guinea to Tulagi.[7]

Among those leaving aboard the *Morinda* were Fred Green and Douglas Trotter, who had departed desolate Kieta on 26 January and made their way to Tulagi by island-hopping in a small boat. They had carried with them the Kieta government records, which District Officer Merrylees supposedly had destroyed, as well as the last mail from Bougainville. Later they would learn that their cargo had been left on the dock at Gavutu.[8] Another passenger was Geoff Gaskell, whose brother Jack already had sailed for Australia in the *Kurimarau*. Geoff, who worked for Burns Philp at Makambo, was a member of the protectorate defense force and thus he was put in charge of the Vickers gun on *Morinda's* forecastle deck. His father, Dick, was also on the passenger list.[9]

Some remaining cargo on the Makambo docks was transported to Gavutu. It was normal for the prisoners from the Tulagi stockade to offload incoming ships and then load outboard cargo. But these were not normal times; all prisoners were on parole and not available for a work detail, except a few who were still held in the jail because of the severity of their crimes. Some island workers from Lever's, along with members of the South Sea Evangelical mission and the commandos, thus joined to unload the *Morinda's* cargo. Many boxes had to be put aboard as well, including guns and ammunition; however, the ship's derricks were rigged over the port side, the side farther from the wharf, and the captain and the mate refused to switch them to the wharf position. The mate agreed to accept only what would be hand carried aboard, but none of the ship's sixty-one crew members would assist. With darkness falling and the 2200 blackout in force, it was impossible to distinguish one carton from another, and the government files could not be sorted systematically and stacked. In addition, the copra was left on the wharf, a loss to some unfortunate planter.

The captain was also obstinate about how many passengers he would carry. He checked the list and refused to take anyone in excess of the number allowed by the Navigation Acts. Thereupon, it was explained to him that a Union Company ship, certified to carry fifty passengers, had taken three-hundred fifty from Tonga to Fiji, and a ship capable of carrying a few dozen had left Singapore with twenty-five hundred. But nothing moved the stubborn ship master. He stood at the top of the gangway counting noses, boarding only women and children and men accompanied by their wives. When the resident commissioner arrived from Tulagi, Rothery told him that he would not take the people remaining unless a lifeboat was supplied. Since no such boat was available, twenty-eight civilians (including nine Chinese and eleven Europeans) and four officials remained behind. It was about then, at 2100, that Lt. A. Wilson, who was standing at the head of the gangway, pointed out to Lieutenant Macfarlan, the newly appointed port director, that some government records were still on the dock. In fact, one case had just fallen off. Macfarlan simply replied, "The ship must sail." Ten minutes later the *Morinda* pulled away from the Lever's dock and headed for the open sea. The case that had fallen into the water was actually a mailbag full of thousands of British Solomon Islands stamps, part of the shipment of post office property being sent to Australia for safekeeping. Sometime after the Morinda left, the mailbag washed ashore on Tanambogo, where it was found by RAAF Cpl. John Brett.[10]

It was obvious that Lieutenant Macfarlan's stint as port director was a fiasco. His actions, and those of Captain Rothery, eventually led to much correspondence between the high commissioner and the Australian prime minister. Macfarlan subsequently would more than make up for it, however, by his later service as a coastwatcher on Guadalcanal.

The day after the *Morinda* departed Gavutu, four civilians who had been denied passage were discovered on board. The *Morinda* thus docked at Sydney with 124 passengers, including three Japanese internees and the six soldiers who guarded them. Two of the Japanese were the men from Gizo, Senanga and Pisita, who had turned themselves over peacefully, leaving behind their native wives and children. The third, Koyama, had worked for Lever's for many years.

After the Tulagi area was evacuated, the commando detachment took over the Lever's #5 bungalow on Gavutu, which provided quarters far better than those of the air unit on Tanambogo, where they had located from Tulagi when the Pacific war began.[11] With the old "bucket of bolts"—as Burns Philp's manager Val Murphy called the *Morinda*—on her way to Australia, the biggest problem left for the administration was to pay off and repatriate the native plantation workers. More than 1,500 were returned to their home islands in the vessels abandoned by the evacuees. Government officials and civilian residents who remained then had to prevent those boats from falling into enemy hands. Most were sailed into Marau Sound, at the southeastern edge of Guadalcanal. After a path was cut through the mangrove swamps, vines were strung on the vessels' masts. Within a month the boats were not noticeable, and they remained out of sight until well after February 1943. The Japanese never knew they were there.

The day after the *Morinda* sailed, the commandos blew up the W. R. Carpenter and Burns Philp marine stores, though they were later sorry they had acted so soon, for some of the items, including area maps, would have been useful later when they finally made their escape. One of the first things the government did was to take down the Tulagi wireless and move it to Auki on Malaita, some sixty miles east. A dummy structure was left, and it was this and the abandoned Tulagi antenna that the Japanese pilots always attempted to knock down, yet always missed.

At Auki, the radio station was about five miles from the district office and became the government's link with the outside world via Port Vila and Fiji, as well as Nouméa where the Australian navy maintained a station. The district office, headed by C. N. F. Bengough, was situated near the oceanfront, while Marchant and his staff were headquartered farther inland. The officials finally evacuated the capital on 13 February. Dick Horton reported that all the government records and mail sacks that had been left on the Makambo docks when the *Morinda* sailed would have gotten wet and destroyed had it not been for Father Wall who dragged them to shelter. Subsequently, they were gathered up and sent for safekeeping first to Auki, then to the New Hebrides, 500 miles away. Resident Commissioner Marchant had authorized District Officer Henry E. Josselyn to take the records, provided he could secure a boat; Josselyn managed to commandeer the Lever's ketch *Kombito.*[12]

Josselyn set out for Vila on 5 March under less than perfect conditions and sailed most of the way with gaff and then stay sails after the engine broke down. The government records were eventually put on board the *Manoora,* headed for Sydney. Josselyn remained on Efate Island, the capital of the New Hebrides Islands, until July. He would return to the Solomons 7 August as a guide for the U.S. 1st Marine Raider Battalion in the invasion of Tulagi.

Upheaval and Repercussions

The Santa Cruz Islands, some 250 miles southeast of the Solomons, played an important role in the first year of the Pacific War. In early August 1942, a patrol from the U.S. 2nd Marines scouted the islands with a view to establishing a support base for Guadalcanal, and the U.S. Navy assigned seaplane tenders there to service PBY patrol squadrons.

The false Australian radio report of 23 January 1942 claiming the Japanese had occupied Kieta had reverberations even in isolated Vanikoro, the second largest of the small Santa Cruz Islands. Vanikoro had a prewar population of a few dozen whites, who worked either at the government station at Peu or for the Kauri Timber Company, a Melbourne concern that had been logging the island's 117 square miles of forest since 1923. The diminutive town of Peu consisted of the district officer's headquarters, accommodations for the timber company employees, some native huts, and Frederick J. Jones's trading station. All communication with the outside world was by radio, and mail was delivered and dispatched when a ship arrived to pick up a cargo of the tall kauri timber. With the Kieta scare, the handful of non-native timber workers made plans to leave on the company's vessels at the earliest opportunity.[13]

District Officer Martin Clemens meanwhile also had organized an eastern Solomons evacuation party that left Aola, Guadalcanal, on 17 February for Port Vila, Efate Island, with some of the remaining civilians aboard the eighty-foot schooner the *Ruana*. The group included two men named Williamson and Roberts from Gold Ridge, as well as others identified as Bob Symes, Johnstone, and Olsen, plus five Chinese and three individuals not named. They reached Port Vila on the 26th.

Two months later, in April, a party of eleven would leave Peu, Vanikoro, Santa Cruz Islands on board Fred Jones's forty-five-foot cutter, *Quand-Meme,* a grueling trip that took sixteen days. When the ship finally pulled into the waters of Vila Harbor the passengers were so seasick that none could go ashore until several hours later. On 27 May they boarded the *Manoora* for Australia, joining the detachment of commandos and the air personnel from the base, plus the soldiers and airmen from Vila and some evacuees from Bougainville.[14]

When Martin Clemens had arrived on Tulagi in February, Resident Commissioner Marchant had asked if he would consider reopening the Gizo district. Clemens could not think of a practical reason for doing so. The Japanese were 440 miles from Gizo Island. Marchant then suggested that Clemens join Dick Horton and Henry Josselyn, the assistant district officer, at the Aola station on Guadalcanal. That still sounded unwise, but Clemens felt he had no choice. Clemens had been on Guadalcanal only once before, so he was glad to have Horton to show him the ropes. However, Horton had his mind set on joining the Australian Navy, for he knew somebody would have to show the Japanese invasion force the way back should they advance that far east.

When Clemens reached Aola on 12 February, Horton was already planning to leave the island at the first opportunity (which apparently did not present itself until early March, when he and Josselyn finally departed). Clemens had been hurried off Tulagi Island to Aola with nothing other than what he was wearing. No baggage had been unloaded from the *Morinda,* and even his toothbrush went back to Australia. Fortunately, the deserted Burns Philp store at Makambo Island had not yet been plundered of all its useful items. In a letter from Aola in March 1942 Clemens wrote of the situation there: "It appears also that Macfarlan and Pilot Officer Clive M. Hamer, in charge of the air base, had quite divergent ideas as to what was to be done and there was a complete lack of cooperation. The R.C. [resident commissioner] has stuck his head in the sand and said that the Japs would never come here. In fact he still believes it. We are getting a weekly raid over Tulagi. . . ."

If Resident Commissioner Marchant believed the Japanese would not come as far as Tulagi, he had not looked at a map of the South Pacific. With its excellent harbor, Tulagi was an ideal location for an advance base. It lay only 600 miles from Rabaul, which was being turned into the foremost Japanese base in the South Pacific. In addition, the major Japanese naval base lay within flying distance of Tulagi at Truk Atoll in the Carolines.

Clemens would remain at Aola and carry on coastwatching operations and administrative functions in the Guadalcanal district until May 1942, when the landing of the Japanese naval forces on Tulagi and their invasion in June on Guadalcanal forced him to move into the rugged hinterland. At that same time, some of the Chinese residents had created problems for him. They had lived and socialized by themselves for so long that once out of their own community they were totally lost. Those who wanted to evacuate mostly were eager for help, but they did little to assist. To make matters worse, a native had axed an old prospector to death, and Clemens had to pursue the killer. A court of justice was held off and on regarding the case, and tribal differences had to be settled. In addition, civilians who had chosen not to leave during the general evacuation now expected the district officer to accomplish miracles in relocating them. Further adding to his complications, Clemens had to play host to a German doctor and his wife, Dr. and Mrs. B. F. K. Kroening, internees from Bougainville, as well as to other Bougainville refugees, who he had to keep under surveillance.

Compounding the frustrations was a crusty World War I veteran, F. Ashton "Snowy" Rhoades. He had been the manager of the Burns Philp plantation at Lavoro, on the northwest coast of Guadalcanal, and had decided to remain on the island. He had volunteered to join the defense force, but the commissioner had offered him only an enlisted appointment, which Rhoades refused. (He was later commissioned in the Australian Navy as a coastwatcher and an aide to Macfarlan.) Rhoades was the source of many unfounded rumors, including one that the Japanese were bringing in dogs to Tulagi to hunt down the whites. Along with all this, Clemens also worried about the missionaries, whom he could not convince to leave.[15]

Two other district officers had drawn plum assignments, though they were unaware of it at the time. Michael Forster was sent to San Cristobal in the eastern Solomons where Colin Wilson was headquartered at Vanikoro, in the Santa Cruz group. The Vanikoro office did not close until 1944, and even then the post office remained open, dispatching mail when vessels were in port or when they sailed to the New Hebrides. Neither district was ever bothered by the Japanese.

But back on Efate on 26 February, the *Ruana* had not remained long. It was loaned to the Australian government to carry materiel to the Australian commando detachment at Buka. Loaded with relief supplies, she left on the 27th with Jack Webster, a resident of Port Vila, as her skipper. On board were three commandos from the No. 2 Section and Len Stevens of the New Hebrides Volunteer Defense Corps. They had arranged to meet the schooner *Malaguna* off Faisi in the Shortland Islands.[16] The *Ruana* traveled by night and hid by day to avoid the Japanese. She was frequently under sail, as her engine kept breaking down, and when she ran aground on a reef one night the crew had to jettison some heavy gear to allow her to float free.

"Sandy" McNab was among those waiting at Buin, Bougainville, for the relief expedition, but in the interim he had other concerns:

> [On] 13 March 1942, . . . Lt. Jack Mackie [CO, No. 3 Section, No. 1 Independent Company] received a message that a Cat would arrive from Tulagi at Faisi that evening to evacuate our medical technician, [Sgt. Arthur Leyden,] who had diagnosed himself as having an acute appendicitis. . . . It was pitch dark, and we could not proceed. . . . We departed Buin, Bougainville at 0300 in the schooner *Malaguna* with Father [Richard] O'Sullivan as pilot [and] two German internees on board. Mackie had me arrest Doctor and Mrs. B. F. K. Kroening. "The German Doctor" [had been a well-known] figure at Kieta since the First World War, [but] due to his empathy with the Nazis' movement he presented a threat to the Bougainville commandos. Kroening did manage to assist in preventing further looting of Kieta by the natives when the District Officer abruptly departed, yet this was not sufficient allegiance to deter his arrest. We acquired two well-known Bougainville planters, [A.] Drummond Thompson of Numa Numa and Wallace Washington Brown [of Bonis,] for evacuation. In the *Malaguna* were Sapper Douglas Otton, Private B[ernard] Swanson and myself. We arrived at Faisi at 0630 and found the Cat waiting. . . . Mackie went across with our medical technician . . . in a canoe to meet the plane—he found Lt. Don Russell aboard. [The two] section commanders [met] for about 30 minutes. A little after 0700 the Cat took off . . . and returned to Tulagi.[17]

The *Ruana* finally arrived in the Shortlands, close by Bougainville, at 1500 on 16 March and the troopers began transferring stores and ammunition to the *Malaguna*. The Kroenings were handed over to *Ruana's* crew. At 0330 on the 17th the schooner headed back to Bougainville. Instead of returning to Efate, the *Ruana* set off for Aola on Guadalcanal. Jack Webster, the skipper, now also had with him Thompson, Brown, and the two Germans. Making her way from the Shortlands through enemy-controlled waters, the *Ruana* arrived at Clemens's Aola district station at 1700 on the 18 March. The next day she left for Auki on Malaita.

At this time of upheaval, for some miners in the interior of Guadalcanal the allure of gold may have been more compelling than their safety. They had ignored the possibility of a Japanese invasion until it was too late, then had retreated to the 2,500-foot-high Gold Ridge and the upper reaches of the Sorvohio and Tsarivonga Rivers. Fred M. Campbell and his sons, Jack and Pat, along with Bert Freshwater and Ken Hay, were living in relative luxury compliments of the Burns Philp provisions from Makambo; however, with the enemy now nearing Tulagi, the Gold Ridge occupants were getting a bit restless. They could hear the coastwatcher reports over their radio and the Cats' warning messages sent back to Gavutu. Kelemendi Nabunosuno, who worked for the Guadalcanal Sluicing and Dredging Company, and Don Macfarlan picked up a coastwatcher message on Macfarlan's teleradio: the district officer on Santa Isabel, Donald Kennedy, reported that a Japanese convoy had entered Thousand Ships Bay there two hours earlier and departed after a short period, apparently satisfied that it was not occupied by Allied troops.

Enemy Advances

The bombing of the Australian military installations by the Japanese flying boats had become an all-too-regular occurrence. The Tulagi AOB did not suffer a great deal of damage, but one bomb did demolish the mess hall and with it the eating utensils and furniture. Fortunately, the Australians could borrow many household items in Tulagi town; they located the needed china and cooking utensils among the abandoned buildings. Back on 5 January Clifford Searle had arrived at Tulagi AOB by air from Port Moresby. While at the base, he was promoted to leading aircraftman. Cliff's diary describes a bombing attack:

> [The *Wanaka,* the AIF/RAAF supply vessel,] arrived after the
> morning bombing raid and [her captain] was insistent on leaving

early the same night to avoid the raid expected the following morning. Hastily Father Wall and I contacted the islanders on Florida Island, and they turned out in force to help unload the petrol and reload the ship with hundreds of empty drums. Work went on without ceasing until after dark and when it was done we were completely exhausted. Pilot Officer . . . Hamer and Lieutenant Russell had arranged for the vessel to take some of the soldiers who were unfit back with [her], and also a group of civilians who had escaped from Bougainville[. They had] traveled 500 miles to Tulagi, mostly at night, in a small and unreliable motorboat, in constant danger of capture by the Japanese."[18]

Searle spent all night in the rain, supervising native laborers as they rolled drums of petrol to the storage site. The *Wanaka* also brought a new, larger crash boat, as well as parcels, newspapers, and letters.

One of the Bougainville evacuees was Rolf Cambridge, who had often taken care of the Catalina crews at Soraken Plantation. At the request of headquarters, Cambridge was taken off MV *Wanaka's* manifest and ordered aboard a flying boat as a special passenger. He was flown to Port Moresby and later to Rathmines Air Station.[19] The *Wanaka's* arrival at Tulagi had offered an ideal opportunity for Dick Horton, the former district officer on Guadalcanal, to "bug out" and join the military service when he reached Sydney, but he almost did not get off Tulagi that day. The *Wanaka* had just pulled away from the wharf and started moving down the channel when a Japanese flying boat spotted her and began a bombing run. As usual, and luckily, the Japanese crew missed and the *Wanaka* continued on. Horton would return to Tulagi four months later as a guide for the 1st Marine Raider Battalion.

Near the end of February 1942, Father George Lepping, who had come to Tulagi with the refugee fleet, had returned to the Shortland Islands with some supplies, intent on resuming his work at Nila, on Poporang Island. There he found Father Maurice Boch, who had come down from Kieta in Father Lepping's absence; Boch had heard that the mission was unoccupied and meant to keep it going. The Right Rev. Thomas J. Wade, the American who headed the Vicariate Apostolic of the Northern Solomon Islands, arrived at the beginning of March; he decided that both missionaries should stay at Tulagi.

On 30 March, the Japanese occupied the Shortland Islands. They interrogated the priests and confined them to the mission station. Seven days later, a small vessel, the *Lauru,* arrived at Faisi Harbor. Aboard were her owner John Klaucke, Hugh Wheatley, and J. Alengi. Wheatley and Alengi were native dressers—persons trained in basic medical care—from Wana Wana, New Georgia. They had been sent by District Officer Kennedy, ostensibly to deal with an influenza epidemic but also to bring fuel for use on boats for coastwatching missions on Shortland and Fauro Islands. According to Father Lepping, when Kennedy had stopped at Nila on the 29th, he had stated explicitly that the fuel was to be distributed from the mission station. Presumably Kennedy had requisitioned the *Lauru* for the task, as Klaucke told Lepping that he had orders to go directly to Nila. Several accounts also mention that Wheatley brought a teleradio.

On their arrival at Nila, however, the men were captured by the Japanese, who ordered them to stay at the mission. A correspondence began between Wheatley and the Japanese commander Captain Asada, but it ended in August when the priests, Klaucke, and Wheatley were arrested and taken away. Hugh Wheatley and John Klaucke were never seen again. Wheatley was sent to Rabaul, but the day before he left he gave a bottle to Alengi, telling him to hide it until someone from the government came to the Shortlands. The bottle remained hidden for three years, until September 1945, when Alengi retrieved it gave it to the assistant Solomon district commissioner, Lt. S. Bolton, who was on an administrative trip to the Shortlands. The bottle contained a small roll covered with sticking plaster; written on the outside were "Diary H. Wheatley N.M.P. [Native Medical Practitioner]" and the date. Alengi identified the diarist as Hugh Wheatley.[20]

Another intrepid evacuation holdout in the islands was Emily Sprott, who had been in sole charge of the Melanesian mission station on Maranatabu, off Santa Isabel, since her husband's death from malaria in 1924. In April 1942 Mrs. Sprott went bush rather than evacuate. Although her food ran out in June and the medical supplies even earlier, nevertheless she was able to hide out for ten months, thanks to loyal islanders who had cached provisions in several different places.[21]

RAAF Response

In the strike of 30 April 1942, the Japanese dropped twenty-six bombs on Tulagi, damaging two Catalinas. Coastwatcher Leif Schroeder on Savo Island, twenty miles away, had sent an urgent message that enemy aircraft were on the hunt, and thus Eric Townsend and Terry Ekins hurried to get their Cats airborne. Townsend was in the advanced stages of lifting off and Ekins was about to follow, when both got hit. The instrument panel on Ekins's A24–19 was totally battered but, nevertheless, on the following day Townsend was able to get the plane airborne at 0300 and fly it to Rathmines, New South Wales, for repairs. He landed at 1730, having gone the distance entirely without instruments—an exceptional feat. Catalina A24–23 had mainframe damage and was unable to take off, and thus the remaining crash boat pulled it to Aola to save the plane from certain destruction. It was hoped the Cat could be repaired there with a mainframe obtained from Port Moresby.

Commando Howard J. Roberts was one of those involved in the preparations for demolition of the military installations on Gavutu and Tanambogo. His Tulagi Advanced Operational Base Activities Report notes: "[No. 1] Section's training was concentrated on methods of demolition so that everything could be destroyed if we were ordered to move out. It was found that the best method of demolishing the normal timber houses and buildings was to use a 5 gallon drum of petrol with 2 sticks of gelignite strapped to it. When the gelignite exploded the house or building was instantly ablaze. This method was applied to all the houses, offices and stores on Gavutu and Tanambogo. . . . [As of] 29 April detonators had not yet been placed in the explosive devices but Cordtex instantaneous fuse [had been] used to . . . centralize each section. The Cordtex was connected to a normal safety fuse and each [section] was to be connected to a one hour time 'pencil.'"[22]

Early in the morning on 1 May the Tulagi AOB on Gavutu and Tanambogo Islands was attacked by Japanese flying boats. It was attacked again at 0930 by two floatplane fighters—the Nakajima A6M2-N, code-named the Rufe by the Allies—and was hammered intermittently throughout the day. In the late afternoon, three RAAF Catalinas arrived. Meanwhile Sgt. C. W. "Bill" Miller, piloting Cat A24–17, sighted a five-ship Japanese task force just south of the New Georgia Islands heading for the southern Solomons. His report at 1300 to Gavutu gave the camp time to scramble and make last-minute arrangements to destroy the installations and set evacuation plans. Cliff Searle topped off the Catalinas with petrol and bombs, and he and the crews wished each other good luck.[23]

One Cat, flown by a pilot named Hirst, was airborne at 1827 that evening, heading for the expected sighting zone of the Japanese task force. At 0422 on 2 May he sighted and attacked two merchant vessels but failed to make a hit, and the Japanese continued to head south toward Tulagi. Hirst landed at Port Moresby at 1200, having flown forty-two hours in less than two days.

Flying Officer Norman took off at 0450 to conduct searches between

Tulagi and Port Moresby; Sergeant Miller followed at 0600. Just after becoming airborne, Miller saw the first wave of enemy planes start their bombing run on the base. His was the last aircraft out of the Tulagi area.

The Australians had two plans for evacuation in the event of a Japanese invasion. One was to move from Gavutu and Tanambogo to Florida Island, and then follow the government trails to the east end of the island in the hope that they could be plucked from there. The other plan was to slip out in the eighty-ton motor vessel the *Balus,* which had been hidden in the Florida mangroves for just such a move, her mast covered daily with fresh palm branches.

At 1100 on 2 May the Tulagi air base received a message from Port Moresby stating that sufficient fuel should be saved in the event that it was needed later. Then came orders to demolish the base and withdraw to Florida Island. The alarm bell clanged harshly, and the Australians put their escape plans into effect. As darkness fell, a heavy thunderstorm burst upon the islands. The Australians activated the charges and moved out of Gavutu. In his diary Cliff Searle recorded the evacuation of the airmen.

> We decided to leave the base, as the Japanese were only sixty miles away. Took *"Betty-Jane"* (Petrol Barge), Bomb Scow and all the chaps to Halavo. Just reached the shore at 0630 when over came the Jap bombers. We ran for the jungle. They dropped bombs, repeat attack, then float-fighter planes sank our crash boat with cannon fire. Leading Aircraftsman [sic] (LAC) Keith Robinson and Peter swam ashore. I went back to the base on the scow to get the C.O. [Flying Officer Peagum, who had arrived on 20 April] and the four remaining wireless operators. More fighters came over bombing our island. We got to Halavo in the scow with secret gear, also the Wireless. Another fighter overhead at 1745. We prepared for Scorched Earth System. 2030 fires going everywhere. I stayed behind with an army chap and blew up a bomb dump. 2230 We remaining chaps travel[ed] three miles in the scow and Petrol barge to track which would lead us to the *"Balus."* Blew-up petrol barge and 1700 gallons petrol, scuttled Bomb Scow and left at 0200 hours for Aola.[24]

Howard Roberts tells of the evacuation of the commandos:

> We had traveled less than a half-mile when our engine cut out in very rough weather conditions and resisted all efforts to restart.

It was found out that when the fuel tank had been filled, the cover for the fuel inlet had not been replaced and, consequently, we had water in our fuel. While we were working out the problem . . . the Tanambogo boat appeared out of the gloom. We abandoned our boat and continued toward Boli Passage. . . . Considering that it was pitch black, a rough sea and blinding rain, in an area of four square miles of sea, the odds of two small boats almost colliding were incalculable. Shortly afterwards the demolition charges started, and even though the storm still raged, the explosions and fires were awe inspiring viewed from a distance of approximately one and a half miles with an amazing reflection from the low storm clouds.[25]

From Florida Island the Australians traveled to Marau Sound, at the southeastern end of Guadalcanal. There they picked up the nineteen commandos who had gone out the "back door" of the base almost as the Japanese were coming in the front. With everyone on board the *Balus* except the crew who had taken the damaged Catalina to Aola, the boat headed for San Cristobal, arriving at Maura Bay on 5 May and Star Harbor the next day. There they waited for the *Loai,* carrying some civilians and the crew from the A24–23 (except Lieutenant Ekins), to join them. The surviving crash boat, piloted by LAC Keith Robinson, towed the A24–23 across Sealark Channel to Aola on the north coast of Guadalcanal. Four hundred Solomon islanders pulled the bulky plane as far inland as they could. The radio was removed and used by the evacuation party to communicate with their base in Vila. By that time the Kure 3rd Special Naval Landing Force was occupying what had been the Tulagi Advanced Operational Base, Gavutu and Tanambogo.

Airman Kevin Landers recorded his impressions in his diary:

The trip of the *Balus* from Guadalcanal to San Cristobal had some tense moments. The worst was when she was spotted by a Japanese flying boat. We were well briefed on intelligence reports, that there was little chance of survival if captured. . . . The . . . Japanese Kawanishi . . . circled us at 200–300 feet and at about 1000 yards, adjusting its armament as it circled, and the crews were very visible. . . . They did not know they had the total Tulagi garrison of 53 and . . . six native crewmembers [*sic*] at their mercy. We had native crew up in the rigging waving frantically and I recall a large bunch of bananas swinging from the rigging and the majority of us huddled under the main sail on the fore deck. The situation lasted 20 minutes (it seemed like hours) and it appeared they were in touch with command and they had identified us as a local native boat. They wanted to keep the natives on their side, and had let us off. Fortunately, everyone exercised great discipline, as I'm sure the main urge would have been to go over the side and take a chance of reaching the shore of Guadalcanal some three miles away. There was a feeling of great relief when the aircraft turned away.... [26]

The Kawanishi had been searching for the U.S. Navy task force that on the previous day had bombed the Japanese on Tulagi, but a navy fighter from the carrier *Yorktown* (CV 5) knocked down the Kawanishi before she could report the group's position. The *Balus* meanwhile chugged along at eight knots, with Charles Bird, a government boatswain, at the helm assisted by LAC Keith Robinson. Navigation duties fell to P/O Bob Burne, the navigator of Catalina A24–23. The *Balus* reached Maura Bay, San Cristobal, on 6 May and departed at dusk for the New Hebrides. On the 9th the party landed at Espiritu Santo; after resting, they pushed south, aiming to reach Vila on the 14th.[27]

Yet their trials were not over. Nearing Efate, the little ship was eyed by two OS2U Kingfisher aircraft from U.S. Navy scouting squadron VS-55, possibly off the heavy cruiser *Chicago* (CA 29) or the *Chester* (CA 27). According to Howard Roberts: "As we approached Efate we were challenged by two American floatplanes that were very aggressive and fired a warning burst as they approached. It all looked a little grim until the Australian flag was unfurled. They obviously reported us by radio and we were given clearance, because they gave us no more trouble. The Kingfishers waggled their wings and our vessel went on its merry way."[28]

There was another danger, however. The authorities at Espiritu Santo had neglected to inform the evacuees that Vila Harbor was mined! Fortunately, according to Keith Robinson, the *Balus* had a wooden hull and thus passed undetected directly over the mines. Had she been of steel construction, he notes, the tale would have ended differently.[29]

About the time the Australian commandos and airmen made their abrupt departure from their base on 3 May, Charles Bignell, who owned Fulakora Plantation on Santa Isabel and managed a small concession in trading goods, decided that it was time to leave. He chose to sail for the New Hebrides in his schooner, *Valere*, in company with Harold Beck from Gizo, Roy Gorringe from Santa Isabel, and twenty-two Chinese. On reaching Espiritu Santo, Bignell headed for the more civilized town of Port Vila, where the United States had recently established an advance base. He offloaded his passengers, sold his vessel to a French planter, and eventually obtained a commission in the U.S. Navy. The first vessel under Lieutenant Bignell's command was the *Resolution,* a 150-ton former Burns Philp inter-island schooner. Bignell's chief mission was the transport of military cargo and supplies to the scattered islands of the New Hebrides and as far north as Vanikoro, in the Santa Cruz group.[30]

Back on Guadalcanal, Martin Clemens allowed two days for the evacuation party to be well out of the area; then he ignited the six sticks of dynamite that LAC Duncan Ridley had placed around the damaged Catalina. The explosive was old and damp, and the entire charge did not detonate. The plane was only partially destroyed, but the locals went about hacking the remainder to pieces with machetes and threw many chunks into the ocean.[31]

Meanwhile, three civilians—A. Chant, Bill Binskin, and Lew Moon Tak—had escaped just ahead of the Japanese, in the *Hygeia,* the government health officer's vessel. At Aola, Clemens arranged for the *Hygeia* to take to Malaita some civilians and the seven airmen who had helped tow the A24–23. At Auki they would meet with the *Morinda,* which was supposed to arrive shortly to pick up the remaining evacuees.[32] In actuality, however, the *Morinda* never left Sydney. The Solomon Island government had failed to inform Clemens and other concerned parties that she was not coming again to the protectorate. A message to that effect finally was received from Auki.

At 0300, on 8 May, eight vessels left Su'u for Maramasike Passage, arriving there at noon. They traveled south to Port Vila under cover of darkness most of the way. Other than spotting a Japanese flying boat on the 10th and suffering engine trouble three times on the morning of the 14th, the trip was completed without incident. At Vanikoro on the 15th they delivered and picked up mail, purchased needed stores, and took on two more passengers, former employees of the timber company. At 1700 on the 19th, not far from Vila, two American planes flew overhead. The vessels could not make port before dark, so they signaled for a pilot boat and were met by American destroyers. After questioning, the small boats were directed toward lights in the harbor. A pinnace off one destroyer came alongside with a boarding party, and after inspection the *Hygeia* was directed to an anchorage for the night.

Much of the next day was spent on shore, then everyone except the Chinese was placed on board the *Manoora,* which sailed for Sydney at 1630. She arrived there at 1000 on 25 May 1942. The *Hygeia* was left in the charge of the resident commissioner at Port Vila, and the Chinese returned to Malaita, where they set up a settlement in the hinterland and remained there during most of the war.[33]

It is interesting that four U.S. Navy men were the first Americans to set foot on Guadalcanal during the war and not the U.S. Marines. Lt. Leonard H. Ewoldt, Lt. (jg) T. Scott McCuskey, and Ens. John P. Adams were part of the air task force that struck Tulagi on 4 May. All had run out of fuel. Brother James Thrift, from the Roman Catholic mission at Marau Sound, brought Lieutenant Ewoldt and his radio-man, Ray Machalinski, to Aola on the 13th in the *Ramada*. They had washed up off Anu, an island off Guadalcanal, after rowing in a raft for three days. They told Martin Clemens that five Japanese ships at Tulagi had been sunk, among them a supply vessel that Ewoldt had attacked and had seen go down near Savo. Ewoldt's first words to Clemens were, "Would you please get us back to Pearl Harbor?"

At about this time, Eroni Leauli, Clemens's Fijian medical assistant, had been on a trip to another part of Guadalcanal. He reported: "Two U.S. scout planes ashore at Cape Henslow abandoned. . . . [Found] parachutes, navigation boards and rubber dinghy." These were McCuskey and Adams's F4F Wildcat fighters; they were intact but slightly damaged. The two officers had been rescued by a recovery boat from the U.S. Navy destroyer *Hammann* (DD 412).[34] To their continued good fortune and true to his word, Martin Clemens commandeered the *Hing Lee*, formerly owned by a Chinese merchant at Tulagi. He shipped the airmen aboard the rickety craft to Auki on Malaita where a few other passengers joined them, including Mr. A. J. Waite, a missionary from the South Sea Evangelical mission on Malaita. The party reached Port Vila before the end of May. The two airmen returned to their carrier via the PBYs of U.S. Navy patrol squadron VP-23, attached to the seaplane tender *Curtiss* (AV 4). The *Hing Lee* remained at Vila and later was appropriated by the U.S. Army to run supplies to isolated garrisons in the New Hebrides.[35]

Clemens's newly arrived and unwelcome Japanese neighbors who now occupied Tulagi, some thirty miles from his post, soon began constructing their own advance base. They gave Clemens a great deal to worry about. He wrote in his diary: "The Nips could send a boat and be here in two hours." Fortunately, that never happened.[36]

4   The Japanese in the Southern Solomons, May–August 1942

Unlike its American and British counterparts, the Imperial Japanese Navy had its own generic infantry: the *rikusentai.* The standard unit was the Special Naval Landing Force (SNLF), a flexible organization named after the naval base where the men were recruited—Kure, Maizuru, Sasebo, or Yokosuka.[1]

Early Organization

The Kure 3rd SNLF (*Kaigun Kure Daisan Tokubetsu Rikusentai*) was formed on 2 February 1942 at the Naval Training Center, Kure Barracks. Ninety-five percent of its personnel were reservists; the balance consisted of recent inductees and apprentice seamen. The unit was led by Cdr. Minoru Yano of Sasebo, a career officer; at thirty-nine, he was younger than most of the men in his charge.[2] When Executive Officer Lieutenant Nagata read the muster roll that first day, 1,122 enlisted men and forty-four officers answered. Their average age was forty-three. Some had not been on active duty since the 1920s, most likely as deepwater sailors on combatant ships where they were trained as deck hands or engineers. Since then, as reservists, they had attended regular drills and had participated in two weeks of active-duty training each year; but that was just to keep them proficient in the shipboard billets they had held.

During the two weeks following 2 February the Kure 3rd went through a brief refresher course at Kure Barracks, but it was cut short when the unit was ordered to the field. The men did not have adequate time to work together, and the course was deficient in many ways. Yet as the U.S. Marines would discover, the rikusentai would prove to be skilled and tenacious adversaries.

On 17 February the men of the Kure 3rd boarded the MV *Azuma-san Maru,* a chartered transport that departed the Kure docks at 1700, headed for Truk in the Caroline Islands, headquarters of the Japanese Fourth Fleet. En route she was attacked by a U.S. submarine that fired a spread of five "fish"; however, either as a result of her evasive maneu-

Figure 7. The Headquarters command staff, 3rd Kure Special Naval Landing Force. *First row, sixth from right,* Cdr. Minoru Yano, commander of the Kure 3rd SNLF; *second from right,* Sp. Lt. (jg) Kakichi Yoshimoto, commander of the 3rd Company, Kure 3rd SNLF. (Author's collection)

vers or because the torpedo warheads were defective, the vessel was unharmed. She arrived at Truk on the 20th. A week later the entire 3rd SNLF complement began landing exercises.

The Imperial Navy's amphibious warfare doctrine clearly needed modernization, especially the obsolete landing tactics. Sailors had practiced going down a single knotted rope called a Jacob's ladder, hand over hand, with knots spaced a foot apart. This primitive method of disembarking had gone out with the sailing ship, but it was still the Japanese way. Training continued until orders were received transferring the Kure 3rd SNLF to Rabaul, New Britain (8th Base Force). The unit departed Truk aboard the *Azumasan Maru* on 16 March and reached Rabaul three days later. On arrival, Commander Yano's men quickly settled into their barracks adjacent to spacious Simpson Harbor.

After the fall of Rabaul on 23 January, Maj. Gen. Tomitaro Horii of the Imperial Japanese Army, commander of the South Seas Detachment (*Nankai Shitai*), had anticipated the quick occupation of Lae (code-named RXM) and Salamaua (code-named RXL) as well as the capture of Port Moresby. However, RAAF air raids on Rabaul had hampered the accomplishment of these goals. The Japanese did not move on eastern New Guinea until 8 March, when Lae was invaded by the main body of the RXM Landing Force, composed of part of the Rabaul-based 82nd Guard Unit (GU) with two platoons from the Sasebo 5th SNLF in support. The 14th Construction Unit then was transferred from Rabaul to build an advanced base at Lae. Salamaua also was taken by the RXL Landing Force, which consisted of elements of the 82nd Guard Unit, supported by two 80-mm antiaircraft weapons from the 8th Base Force.

In late March the forty-seven-man 5th Platoon, 1st Company, Kure 3rd SNLF, under WO Shigemasa Yamada, was divided into two units: the RXC Landing Force was sent to occupy Buka; the RWH Landing Force went to Shortland Bay, Faisi, Shortland Islands.[3] Knowing that the Territory of New Guinea was defended by only small numbers of Australian troops, the Japanese dispatched forces to handle them. On 6 April seventy men from two platoons of the 1st Company, Kure 3rd SNLF, led by Sp. Lt. (jg) Sakazo Takamura, were sent to occupy part of the Admiralty Islands. Other sections of the Kure 3rd and the Sasebo 5th SNLF went out on survey and patrol missions.

The presence of only small naval ground forces at Rabaul and Truk implies that, contrary to Allied intelligence estimates, the Japanese did not then have significant numbers of men in the Pacific islands. The largest army contingent was the South Seas Detachment, the force that took Rabaul. To support the Southeast Detachment—the official designation for the army forces at Rabaul—the navy had to draw personnel from the Japanese mandated islands and from Japan. These came in dribs and drabs, and by April 1942 they still numbered only a few thousand; but with each passing week Rabaul increased in strength.

In the meantime, specialized units, primarily naval, began moving into Rabaul. Airfield construction units (*hikojo setsueitai*) began to rebuild some of the old Australian fields and assist the 7th Construction Unit in establishing new airdromes surrounding the town. One large construction unit was assigned to develop miles of fortified caves in the nearby mountains; another began building the major military complex that Rabaul was soon to become.

USAAF Response–Japanese Reassessment

On the morning of 18 April 1942 Rabaul came under heavy air attack by B-17s of the U.S. Army Air Forces's 19th Bombardment Group (Heavy) out of Townsville, Australia. The Flying Fortresses plastered the harbor and sank a transport, the MV *Komaki Maru*. When a warehouse bordering the dock was hit and set ablaze, Kure 3rd sailors stationed nearby were called out to help extinguish the fire. Some of the unit's supplies and equipment were stored in the dock area, and fearing this materiel would be destroyed, Commander Yano ordered it moved some distance away for safety. Bombs also had struck the barracks of Lt. (jg) Katsutaro Makimura's 4th Company, leaving three men killed and eleven wounded. The Kure 3rd SNLF had experienced a sudden and bloody introduction to the war.

On 23 April, action appeared imminent when Commander Yano received South Seas Fleet Operation Order No. 13, spelling out the plans for the invasion of Port Moresby—the MO operation—under the Commander, Fourth Fleet. The Japanese Navy's surface forces under the command of Rear Adm. Aritomo Goto would provide direct support for the army's South Seas Detachment, which was to invade Port Moresby on 10 May at 0600 with the heavy cruisers *Aoba, Furutaka, Kako,* and *Kinugasa;* the light carrier *Shoho;* and the destroyer *Sazanami.* General Horii's brigade was to be reinforced by core elements of the Kure 3rd SNLF—the 2nd and 3rd Companies, the Dobashi transport unit, and the Chadani medical unit. To protect the eastern flank of this thrust, the navy would occupy Tulagi and the Deboyne Islands, Louisiade Archipelago, where it would establish seaplane bases and consolidate its position for potential air operations against Australia.[4] On 28 April, the troops thus embarked on the *Azumasan Maru.* The next day, on Emperor Hirohito's birthday, out of respect the contingent faced Japan, bowed, and prayed for the Emperor's health.

The stubborn resistance from Allied aircraft defending Port Moresby at this time, however, was forcing the Japanese to a strategic reassessment. Without control of the air, their naval forces would be at risk, and thus the 8th Base Force put a new plan in place: the Kure 3rd SNLF would now constitute the RXB Landing Force assigned to assault and occupy Tulagi Island. But the Japanese did not know that the Americans were intercepting and deciphering a significant percentage of their naval message traffic, including communications relating to the crucial MO operation. On May 1 the U.S. Navy Combat Intelligence Center at Pearl Harbor—code-named HYPO—broadcast a warning: "MO campaign now underway; involves south-east New Guinea and Louisiade Archipelago; suggest Moresby for MO. Forces engaged will consist of CarDiv 5; CruDiv 5 less *Nachi;* CruDiv 18, and DesRon 6 ; Gunboat Div 8 (now called 19th Division); and New Britain Air, which is known as No. 5 Attack Force consisting of Tainan Air Group, 4th Naval Flying Corps, and Yokohama Air Group."[5]

At 1930 on 30 April, elements of the Kure 3rd SNLF that had been slated to invade Port Moresby were officially reassigned as the RXB Landing Force: objective Tulagi Island. The Tulagi invasion task force was under Rear Adm. Kiyohide Shima's 19th Division. It included Admiral Shima's flagship, the large minelayer *Okinoshima;* transports *Azumasan Maru* and *Tosan Maru;* destroyers *Kikuzuki* and *Yuzuki* from DesRon 6; converted minesweepers *Hagoromo Maru, Noshiro Maru No. 2,* and *Tama Maru* from Minesweeper Division 14; subchasers *Tama Maru No. 8* and *Toshi Maru No. 3* from Antisubmarine Boat Group 56; minelayer *Koei Maru;* and auxiliary minesweepers *Wa 1* and *Wa 2.*

The fifty-four-man Mitsuwa antiaircraft unit (Mitsuwa *Butai*) under Sp. Lt. (jg) Toshichi Mitsuwa, in company with the 132-man civilian Hashimoto Construction Force (Hashimoto Butai), under Shin'ya Hashimoto, had come to Rabaul from Palau. Both units boarded the *Azumasan Maru* for transport to the Solomons in support of the Tulagi landing. The RXB Landing Force sailed initially southwest, curved to the east, continued down through The Slot, then went directly to Tulagi.[6] Intelligence reports were scanned for information. The General Staff Office directive noted: "The harbor on the north side of Tulagi is the best . . . in these islands and there are installations such as piers." At Makambo, "there are . . . warehouses and a pier. It is possible to dock a medium-sized ship." The directive added that Gavutu has "a workshop for minor repairs, an oil reservoir, a warehouse, and a pier 67 meters long"; however, the report noted, "as a result of our bombing attacks, they have been damaged considerably."[7]

On receipt of the Tulagi invasion plans the Kure 3rd SNLF elements involved were alerted for the landing. Sp. Lt. (jg) Junta Maruyama, commanding the 2nd Company, was placed in charge. The landing force consisted of Maruyama's 2nd Company and the 3rd Company, under Sp. Lt. (jg) Kakichi Yoshimoto, reinforced by elements of the 1st Company, under Sp. Lt. (jg) Sakazo Takamura, and supported by a detachment of the 7th Construction Unit and the Mitsuwa antiaircraft unit (previously on Truk). The three platoons of the 3rd Company would make up the garrison force.[8] Lieutenant Maruyama wasted no time in issuing his first order to the RXB Landing Force. Besides identifying the resistance expected, it laid out the objectives and movements of men and equipment not just for one landing site but for an alternative as well.[9]

Taking Tulagi

In the early evening hours of Saturday, 2 May, searchlights of the Japanese naval escort vessels in the vicinity of Savo Island nervously scanned the

Figure 8. Sp. Lt. (jg) Kakichi
Yoshimoto, 1941. (Author's
collection)

water and the skies for Allied ships and aircraft. They had been warned
that motor torpedo boats might be lurking in the area. Late that evening,
the RXB force reached the outer fringes of Tulagi Island; after a general
probe of the area by the minesweeping group, the force anchored in the
harbor. Combat gear and personal baggage were quickly transferred to
waiting landing craft, and at about midnight the landing force moved
in. According to WO Takeo Iwata, commander of the 1st Platoon, 2nd
Company, "In practice the transports stood offshore about three miles,
but in the RXB operation they came right into the harbor. Four large
landing boats [*Kokosukas*] were carried on the [MV] *Tosan Maru*. Each
... [could hold] 100 to 150 men, but [they were] crowded with 150."[10]

Through the haze, the men of the Kure 3rd could see the fires burning
on Gavutu and Tanambogo. They were determined to defeat the British
and the Australians — "Churchill's men" — at every turn. SME Tameichi
Shimamoto of the 4th Squad, 2nd Platoon, 1st Company, recorded his
feelings before the landing: "We are going to carry out an opposed landing on Tulagi at 0100. It is before a fight, and there is not a tremble in

our hearts. I believe the most beautiful part of a Japanese is this present mental state, transcending life and death."[11]

At 0010 on 3 May the operation began. The landing force consisted of 188 men from the 2nd Company and 210 from the 3rd Company. The 2nd Company debarked from the *Tosan Maru* in three Kosokuka landing craft. In the landing force commander's boat were Headquarters Platoon, 1st Platoon, one section of 3rd Platoon, and company signalers. The other two boats held the 2nd Platoon, the remainder of 3rd Platoon, doctors (including Lt. Tatsumi Okawa), and stretcher-bearers. The 2nd Company's landing party was split between two craft, with ninety-five men in one boat and ninety-three in the other. The landing was made on the north side of Tulagi; however, because the high-speed Kosokukas had difficulty reaching the coast, most of Lieutenant Yoshimoto's men debarked in deep water and had to wade to shore. The Japanese had expected opposition, but their arrival was uncontested.[12]

SME Yodoyama Mori of the Tanaka platoon described the events:

> We loaded our AT [antitank] guns on a large landing barge so they would be available when we faced the enemy. We packed blankets, belongings, etc., and put our name on each one and [were] ready to unload at Gavutu and Tulagi. At 1500 [on 2 May], a [minelayer, *Okinoshima*] sailed in front of our vessel, [and] reported it sighted an enemy seaplane. We recognized a four-mast warship ahead, but it was a friendly ship. At 2400 hours, we sighted island [Gavutu]. Our SNLF gathered on the stern [of the *Azumasan Maru*] and we saw something burning on the island. . . . [O]ur guard destroyers [*Kikuzuki* and *Yuzuki*] had stopped. *Okinoshima* and *Azumasan Maru* advanced. Our 120–130 men started to head for the coast in large landing craft. We placed bullets in our "I" type rifles. Approaching the coast, 500 meters, 400 meters, 300 meters, 200 meters, and 100 meters and then 50 meters and carefully landed on pier. No resistance. It seems the enemy has escaped and burned their barracks.[13]

The Australians at Tulagi air base had withdrawn only two hours earlier. Seaman Engineer Mori described the first morning on Gavutu and Tulagi:

> [W]e completely occupied Gavutu and Tulagi by 0415. The 7th Construction Unit, RXB Detachment, began unloading their equipment immediately, and missed the ceremonies of being

Figure 9. An island landing by Imperial Japanese Navy troops. (Courtesy Stephen Hasegawa)

one of the first Japanese units to land in the British Solomon Islands. . . . Before dawn they were all ashore. The required equipment would arrive later once the garrison was settled. The two platoons raised the flag on Gavutu and prayed for the celestial Emperor. We then went to the islet closest to Gavutu [Tanambogo] and waited until dawn. Sunrise was at 0605, and after the sun rose we inspected [the] enemy's barracks and arranged their weapons. There were many cans of food and goods discovered in the former enemy barracks, and we moved food to our own quarters after breakfast. The enemy left their rice and we will have it for lunch.[14]

The following day's midday meal, however, would be delayed.

The Allies Counter

On 14 April, U.S. Navy Task Force (TF) 17 operating out of Nouméa, New Caledonia, under Rear Adm. Frank J. Fletcher, had been ordered to Tongatabu in the Tonga group for replenishment and upkeep. Six days later Fletcher's force—including the carrier *Yorktown* (CV 5); heavy cruisers *Astoria* (CA 34), *Chester* (CA 27), and *Portland* (CA 33); and destroyers *Anderson* (DD 411), *Hammann* (DD 412), *Morris* (DD 417), and *Russell* (DD 414)—joined destroyer tender *Dobbin* (AD 3), hospital ship *Solace* (AH 5), and the store ship *Bridge* (AF 1) in the spacious harbor of Tonga's capital, Nuku'alofa.

Task Force 11, under Rear Adm. Aubrey W. Fitch—with the carrier *Lexington* (CV 2); heavy cruisers *Minneapolis* (CA 36) and *New Orleans* (CA 32); and destroyers *Alwyn* (DD 355), *Dewey* (DD 349), *Farragut* (DD 348), *Monaghan* (DD 354), and *Phelps* (DD 360)—had sailed from Pearl Harbor on 15 April. Fletcher sailed from Tongatabu on the 27th for a rendezvous with Fitch on 1 May, about 250 miles west of Espiritu Santo. From Australian Task Force 44, Rear Adm. J. G. Crace, of the Royal Navy—along with the heavy cruiser *Chicago* (CA 29), destroyer *Perkins* (DD 377), and oiler *Tippecanoe* (AO 21)—would depart Nouméa in time to meet Fletcher at the rendezvous point. The oiler *Neosho* (AO 23), shepherded by the destroyer *Sims* (DD 409), handled fueling chores for Fletcher's TF 17; the *Tippecanoe*, escorted by the destroyer *Worden* (DD 352), supported Fitch's TF 11. Admiral Crace, with the heavy cruiser HMAS *Australia,* light cruiser HMAS *Hobart,* and U.S. Navy destroyer *Whipple* (DD 217), left Sydney on 1 May to rendezvous with Admiral Fletcher in the Coral Sea on the morning of the 4th.

It was at 1300 on 1 May that RAAF Catalina A24–17 piloted by Sgt. C. W. Miller had sighted five Japanese vessels heading for Tulagi. Admiral Fletcher ordered an attack on Tulagi Harbor; however, the sergeant was not given permission to bomb the invasion force, even though his plane drew antiaircraft fire.[15] Two hours after sunrise on the 4th, having just landed some eight hours earlier, Rear Adm. Kiyohide Shima's flagship, *Okinoshima,* was riding at anchor close to shore while unloading. The *Yorktown*'s SBD Dauntless dive-bombers started their descent from 19,000 feet; twelve TBD Devastators followed on a torpedo run. They plastered the Japanese force with every weapon they possessed. In a second attack, between 1030 and 1120, the *Yorktown* launched all thirty-eight planes to pound Tulagi and the offshore roadstead. At that time the *Okinoshima* was anchored next to the *Yuzuki,* with the *Kikuzuki* moored about 200 yards to the east. Under attack, the vessels headed out of the harbor, led by the *Okinoshima.* Left behind were the *Kikuzuki,* the Division 14 minesweepers *Tama Maru, Hagoromo Maru,* and *Noshiro Maru No. 2,* and the sub-chasers *Toshi Maru No. 3* and *Tama Maru No. 8.*[16]

Mavis flying boats from the Yokohama Air Group had arrived recently and were riding at anchor off Gavutu. They, as well as most of their crews, were lost in the air attack. Keeping the American bandits

Figure 10. Two Japanese Kawanishi H6K4 flying boats (Allied code name "Mavis") off Gavutu Island, July 1942. (Courtesy Robert K. Piper)

somewhat at bay were the *Azumasan Maru*'s gun crews, firing their two 75-mm antiaircraft weapons and four machine guns. Sailors of Yoshimoto's 3rd Company had been unloading cargo from the transport at the time of the attack; seven were wounded and three killed. No member of the Kure 3rd on land died, but twenty-nine were wounded. The gun crew from the Mitsuwa Butai (antiaircraft unit) on Gavutu was untouched. On Tulagi, the AA unit fired its 8-cm guns from Hill 281, called *Tori-dai* (Bird Hill) by the Japanese, but none of the attacking aircraft were hit.[17]

When the assault was over, the Yoshimoto company sent barges from Tulagi to rescue survivors, collecting those who were swimming. Floating bodies were picked up and returned to Tulagi, and after being prepared, the dead were consumed in a funeral pyre while members of the unit chanted and said prayers for their departed countrymen. The Japanese suffered additional losses at sea that day as well. From the *Tama Maru No. 8* one man was killed and four wounded. Minesweeper *Tama Maru*, which was sunk, had four killed and seven wounded; the *Ichigo*, also sunk, reported twenty killed and six wounded. On the *Nigo* twenty-three were killed and fourteen wounded; on sister destroyer *Yuzuki* ten sailors were killed and thirty-two wounded. The *Azumasan Maru* suffered four men killed and five wounded; on the *Takashima* ten were wounded.

Admiral Shima's flagship, *Okinoshima*, did not get away unscathed. Limping along, she dispatched a message to Rabaul that she was in trouble. Rabaul responded by sending the *Shoei Maru* and the *Kinryu Maru*. On 11 May, while being towed by the *Kinryu Maru* just west of Buka at the northern tip of Bougainville, the minelayer was finished off. The U.S. submarine *S-42*, in the charge of Lt. O. G. Kirk, sighted the wounded warship and sank her with three well-placed Mark IV torpedoes. Three ships—the light cruiser *Tenryu* , heavy cruiser *Kako*, and ARS *Oshima*—rescued most of the Japanese crew, as well as Admiral Shima. The following day, however, the *Shoei Maru*, on returning to Rabaul, was sunk by an old World War I sugar boat, SS *44*, under Lt. J. R. Moore.

The American pilots were excited by the opportunity to strike at the Japanese Navy, though they exaggerated the results, claiming to have sunk more vessels than existed in the Japanese force. A sailor on the cruiser *Astoria* during the 4 May raid recorded the airmens' assertions: "They came back an hour and a half later saying they had probably sunk three cruisers, two transports and left one transport sinking. The second raid took place at 11 o'clock. In it they sank two cruisers, one cruiser capsized [the destroyer *Kikuzuki*], left one cruiser sinking and on fire, sunk two destroyers, strafed three patrol planes, and shot down one large vessel operating as a minelayer."[18] The airmen also showed their unfamiliarity with enemy vessels, regularly mistaking one type for another. U.S. Navy observers and historians later argued that the results did not justify the tremendous amount of ammunition that was expended. Still, the strike provided valuable experience for the U.S. aircrews, and a review of the actual losses is informative.

The Enemy Reevaluates and Steps Up

Apparently it was decided that the task of guarding the Tulagi area was too extensive for Lieutenant Yoshimoto's 3rd Company, and thus two platoons of the 1st Company—the 1st Platoon, under WO Yoshiharu Muranaka, and the 2nd Platoon, under WO Katsuzo Fukimoto—were added to the garrison force. The balance of the 1st Company and the 2nd Company (less the Tanaka platoon) returned to Rabaul.

It was soon after the 4 May air raid that the Kure 3rd SNLF took over the buildings vacated by the Tulagi evacuees. The Australians had partially burned the four former RAAF barracks on Tanambogo, but the Japanese scavenged enough building materials in Tulagi's Chinatown to repair them, even finding food and a working refrigerator stocked with cold Australian beer. On 5 May, after reporting a successful landing, the 8th Base Force redesignated the RXB force as the Yano Butai, Yoshimoto

Detachment.[19] The *Azumasan Maru,* which had transported the Kure 3rd SNLF from Rabaul to Tulagi on 3 May and survived the air attack of the 4th, returned to Tulagi on the 11th and docked at the seventy-four-foot government pier. She was immediately unloaded, amid bursts of rain. While the transport was dockside, another vessel arrived and began to discharge supplies onto eleven barges that shuttled between ship and shore, manned by the sailors of the Yoshimoto Detachment. The Japanese were wasting no time exploiting their conquest of the island.

The diary of Seaman Engineer Mori describes what was happening at Tulagi in the weeks after the Japanese takeover. On 25 May, three staff officers from Rabaul arrived by seaplane for a conference with Lieutenant Yoshimoto; they remained until the 27th. Mori writes: "Lieutenant Yoshimoto called the garrison together from the steps of his home [formerly the residence of Mr. and Mrs. J. B. Hicks, next to what had been the resident commissioner's quarters]. He informed the troops that in the sea battle of 7–8 May [Battle of the Coral Sea] there was some damage to the Japanese side, but we will make a new attempt to take New Guinea and attack both Port Moresby and Fiji soon. Yoshimoto reported, 'Our Navy sank two carriers: *Saratoga* [CV 3] and one other; two battleships, one American and one British; one heavy cruiser; four destroyers; [and] two transports; and shot down 61 enemy planes.' He reminded his troops, 'Today is Navy Day, a day when the Imperial Navy conquered the Russians in 1904.' In honor, apples were issued and beer [provided] by the supervising section at dinner. A real treat."[20]

In the following days, rumors were heard of a coming Allied attempt to reoccupy the island. On 29 May, Mori recorded that "one sea infantryman, while on pier duty at Tulagi, said that a boat came from Gavutu and warned him that an American Task Force was approaching the Solomons and may land at Tulagi and Gavutu on 30 May. At 2000, we laid sandbags at our antitank position."[21] Nothing happened.

On to Guadalcanal

On 8 June, the forty-six-man 3rd Platoon, 3rd Company, under WO Noboru Takeuchi, was shifted from Tulagi to Guadalcanal and designated as the RXI [Guadalcanal airfield] Support Force. It was to establish an encampment area on the grassy plains of Lunga for an inspection team from Rabaul. The *Kainan Maru* landed additional tents, food, and supplies for the team. The Yoshimoto company's few previous trips to Guadalcanal had been primarily to shoot cattle during food shortages. Now, there were rumors of a thousand well-armed native soldiers hid-

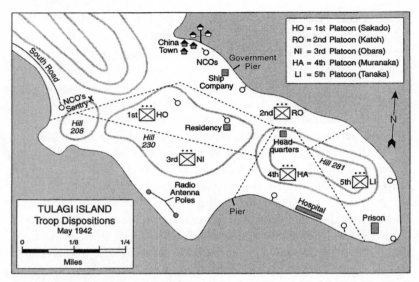

Figure 11. Map of troop dispositions of the 3rd Company, Kure 3rd Special Naval Landing Force, on Tulagi Island, May 1942, based on original in captured Japanese records. (National Archives; map courtesy Mary Craddock Hoffman)

den in the impenetrable island jungle. The Kure sailors wanted no part of that. In addition, Warrant Officer Takeuchi also heard that the islanders of the Solomons were cannibalistic.

The stinging debacle at Midway a few days earlier, on 3–4 June, where the Japanese were so unquestionably defeated, had forced a new course for Imperial Navy planners. Having lost their initiative to control the Central Pacific, they began to look for new ways to solidify their gains in the South Pacific. One possibility was to construct an airfield on Guadalcanal to defend the eastern flank of Bougainville and Truk in the Caroline Islands, and to act as an outpost for the Gilbert Islands, thus protecting Rabaul.

On 19 June, four officers—including Lt. Cdr. Tokunaga Okamura from the 8th Base Force and Rear Adm. Sadayoshi Yamada, commander of the 25th Air Flotilla—left Rabaul in a Kawanishi flying boat and arrived at Gavutu at noon. At Tanambogo, they joined Capt. Shigetoshi Miyazaki, commander of the Yokohama Air Group. The inspection team was to investigate a site and establish a plan for an airstrip in the open space on Guadalcanal's Lunga plains, in accordance with Miyazaki's suggestion. Okamura was commanding officer of the 13th Construction Unit (CU) which would begin the groundwork for the airstrip. Though not an engineer, he had been a skilled pilot and had been recalled to active duty from retirement specifically for this post.[22]

The inspection party stayed at the Residency on Tulagi, reserved for visiting dignitaries, and enjoyed the hospitality of Lieutenant Yoshimoto. At Tulagi they boarded *Kaiyo Maru No. 2* for the twenty-mile trip across Sealark Channel to Guadalcanal. There they spent two days as the guests of the Takeuchi platoon, which had set up a comfortable campsite for them. Captain Miyazaki led the team to the prairie area, as he had been to Lunga on several occasions to shoot wild cattle for fresh meat and sport. After completing their survey, the team members traveled back to Gavutu aboard the *Kaiyo Maru No. 2*. There they boarded a flying boat for the 600-mile return trip to Rabaul. Commander Okamura would return to Guadalcanal on 6 July with the advanced echelon of the 13th CU.

On 21 June, Tomisaburo Hirai recorded the sinking by torpedo of the *Keijo Maru,* which was bringing supplies and rations to Tulagi from Rabaul. Seaplanes searched for survivors; at 0700 the next morning minesweeper *No. 20* returned, having rescued sixty-two members of the crew on the 21st and twenty to thirty more on the 22nd. It was presumed that some crew members swam to nearby islands. Hirai's diary entry for 23 June reveals the shortage of food on Tulagi and Gavutu: "It seems we must find our own food by our own effort. We made fishnets and began fishing net style."[23] More bad news arrived a few days later: the *Yomoto Maru,* which had left Rabaul for Tulagi on the 24th, was sunk on the 26th.[24]

On 1 July the *Kinryu Maru* and the *Mogamukawa Maru* from Rabaul reached Guadalcanal at Kukum, west of Lunga, principally to contribute a defense framework for the expected construction units. The *Kinryu Maru* carried the advance echelon of the 81st Guard Unit—Lt. Yukio Endo's detachment, eight special duty members attached to the 8th Base Force, twenty-one men from the 85th Communication Unit under WO Seiichi Sato, and seven members of the 4th Meteorological Unit under WO Takezo Miyagama. Assigned to Lieutenant Endo's detachment as temporary reinforcements were two platoons of the Kure 3rd SNLF from Rabaul totaling 103 men. Included were two civilian English-speaking interpreters attached to the Imperial Navy, Terushigo Ishimoto and Matutaro Itoh. The strength on Guadalcanal thus increased to 257 men; their camp was set up west of the Lunga River. The howitzer gun platoon under WO Tetsuzo Nakamura was assigned to Lunga Point. The 8-cm antiaircraft guns had been the first weapons ashore, but none of Endo's men were trained as AA gunners and thus help was required to operate them. The platoon also brought a 25-mm antitank (AT) gun, three 13-mm light machine guns, and two 6-cm (Type 41) howitzers, as well as ammunition. The men established a sky-watcher observation post at the Central Control Station under PO3c Daisaku Miyakoshi. However, when U.S. planes began the bombing missions against the Japanese on Guadalcanal, they were not bothered by AA fire.[25]

On 2 July Lieutenant Endo issued his second Guadalcanal guard unit order, to establish east and west watching posts. The next day the *Nitira Maru No. 3* arrived at Lunga, bringing additional supplies, followed by the *Hokuriku Maru* with the advance echelon of the 13th Construction Unit. The islanders from the Tasimboko clan had helped the Japanese bring their supplies ashore, and now they again assisted the Japanese, though perhaps mostly out of curiosity. The locals had never seen so many men and so much materiel. They were kept busy as carriers moving oddly-shaped reed containers. PO2c Sankichi Kaneda of Toyama City, reports: "3 July, in the central [part of] Guadalcanal . . . where a grassy field in the area of [the] Lunga River right bank was to be turned into and airfield . . . the building units began by construction, first, a wharf, communication sending and receiving facilities, an electric generator building, field kitchen and barracks."[26]

From his coastwatching station on Guadalcanal, Martin Clemens observed the whole scene with anger and frustration, and he and his assistants became uneasy as the Japanese drew closer to their hideout. In his diary entry of 4 July, Clemens wrote: "Rhoades says three schooners [*Daiho Maru No. 1, Daiwa Maru No. 2,* and *Nichiro Maru No. 3*] now arriving in Visale area and searching for our traces. 1200 Corporal Andrew [Langebaea] arrived to say all is well at Aola and no visitors. 1400 Kambatimbua arrives to say all is not well. Eyes popping out of his head. One schooner passed Talaura at 1000. . . . 2100 [Scout] Dovu reports Japs ashore at Taivu."[27] On 6 July, the main contingent of the Japanese construction groups began arriving.

The story of the Guadalcanal airfield construction force begins with two organizations: Capt. Kanae Monzen's 11th Construction Unit, under the Combined Fleet, Yokosuka Naval Construction Department; and Lt. Cdr. Tokunaga Okamura's 13th Construction Unit, under the Eighth Fleet, Sasebo Naval Construction Department. Originally the two units had very different assignments. The 13th CU was to be the base construction force under the plan for the occupation of Midway Island, while the 11th CU had been tentatively assigned similar responsibilities under the FS plan, for the assault on Fiji, New Caledonia, and Samoa.

The commanders at Rabaul were seeking to protect the area they already occupied and to prevent the Allies from striking back. The simple way was to expand the conquered territories, strike mineral-rich New Caledonia, and thus contain both Fiji and Samoa. Fiji was to be invaded by a force built around the 124th Infantry Regiment, and a battalion of twelve hundred men, an element of the Seventeenth Army, would strike Samoa. The Seventeenth Army's Horii Butai, led by the veteran 144th Infantry, 55th Division, was tentatively assigned the responsibility of capturing New Caledonia.[28]

From its inception, the FS plan was a flawed concept, requiring amphibious units, which the Seventeenth Army did not have; and possibly two divisions would be required to invade the Samoa area, where ten thousand U.S. Marines were stationed. A large task force and transport unit would be required for each invasion, plus fleet commitments to deal with the threat from the American submarines and air units, the forces that had mauled the Japanese at Midway in early June. The Imperial General Staff seemed to ignore the logistics of the already extensive military commitments. The Imperial Navy had 132 Pacific island bastions assigned to the Yokosuka South Seas District, 27 stations assigned to the Kure district, and 23 to the Sasebo district. This did not include the army occupation forces in China, Manchuria, Malaya, Indo-China, Burma, the Philippines, Borneo, and the former Dutch possessions. They all had to be supplied by water transport, but the Japanese merchant marine simply did not have the necessary tonnage to support the Tokyo–Rabaul–Truk master plan.

With the Midway operation a failure, the New Caledonia–Samoa (FS) invasion plan thus was put on hold. The 11th and 13th Construction Units received a new assignment, to construct the airfield on Guadalcanal Island. It would be supported by a string of island air bases between Guadalcanal and Rabaul, New Britain Island. From there the Japanese could monitor and interdict the United States–Australia lifeline.

On 29 June at 1000, a thirteen-ship convoy carrying the 11th CU and 13th CU had departed Truk and headed for the Solomons. It was shepherded by the 6th Combat Unit, which included the light cruiser *Yūari* and destroyers *Uzuki* and *Oite,* and was supported by the 21st Submarine Chaser Squadron. U.S. submarines attacked the convoy en route, and one destroyer and one gunboat were sunk. The transport *Azumasan Maru,* which had already survived the U.S. Navy's air strike on Tulagi, was now called the "lucky ship"; five torpedoes poised to hit her either had missed or failed to explode.[29]

The Japanese landing at Guadalcanal had been set for 4 July, but word of the sighting of a U.S. Navy task force necessitated a change in course. The Japanese convoy headed in the direction of the New Georgia Islands and the waters off the Shortlands. At 1200 on 5 July it headed back to the southern Solomons, and the landing was rescheduled for the next day. The losses suffered at Midway had led the commander to take extra precautions.[30] At 1500 on 6 July, the convoy finally reached the southern Solomons. The *Kotoku Maru* had approximately four hundred construction personnel and security troops on board; each of the construction units had its own security section, made up of noncombat troops, which was to maintain discipline within the labor force. The *Kanyoh Maru* held five hundred laborers and the *Azumasan Maru* had four hundred. The *Azusa Maru* carried part of the 13th CU, plus a security detail. Transports *Meiyo Maru* and *Matumoto Maru* carried members of both the 11th and the 13th CU. The last transport, the *Nojima Maru,* transported five hundred construction workers.

The equipment aboard included thirteen trucks, one road roller, a quantity of sheet steel panels, thirteen landing craft, two five-ton derricks, two one-ton derricks, and three 6,000-watt generators, along with hundreds of reed baskets that would be used for moving gravel to the airfield. The fast-working crew of the *Azumasan Maru* unloaded first, and by 11 July all the vessels had been offloaded and had left for Rabaul.[31] But also on 6 July, the bimonthly visitors—minesweeper *No. 20,* destroyer *Uzuki,* Submarine Division 23, and the *Kinryu Maru*—arrived at the Tulagi government pier. Supplies were unloaded, including hundreds of sacks of rice and an extensive amount of wireless equipment. A detachment of 129 laborers came ashore from the 14th Construction Unit at Rabaul under Lt. Cdr. Kiyoshi Iida. Radar specialist Lt. Cdr. Dairoku Yokio also arrived to supervise the installations of communications and radar equipment on Tulagi, Gavutu, and Guadalcanal; and a small safekeeping unit under Lt. Cdr. Zeizo Nishimura disembarked the *Kotoku Maru,* with three men from the Rabaul paymaster section under Lt. Isoa Nomura.[32]

The following Japanese intelligence report could have told the arriving construction troops what to expect in terms of resources and terrain:

> Dense jungle and grassy plains, except for the strip along the beach, cover all the regions of Guadalcanal untrodden by men. There are no roads and transportation would be difficult. Generally, stored rainwater should be used for cooking. Fruit and fish are abundant; however, . . . some [fish] are poisonous.

Between Point Esperance and Kamimbo Bay, automobile passage is possible if some construction is carried out. Between [the] Aruliho [Tho] River and Point Esperance, although the area is temporarily suitable for the landing of heavier items, it will be necessary to improve facilities at river crossings in order to transport [them] inland. In the vicinity of Savaplu, the road passes at a distance from the beach to the dense jungle. East of Tassafaronga, if five or six places are repaired, automobile passage is possible. It is also suitable for landing heavy items.

The area at the foot of Mount Austen, extending in a northerly direction from the Matanikau River to the Lunga River, is composed of rolling hills. . . . [33]

The Japanese set about altering the terrain almost immediately. On 8 July, from his watch post, Martin Clemens reported that there was "enemy activity all along the coast. The grass plains are now being fired and much smoke interferes with the view." The eighth day of each month was a national holiday, commemorating the beginning of the East–West War. It was celebrated on Tulagi just as it was in Japan, with Asahi beer; the Tulagi garrison faced Japan and worshiped the Emperor from afar. Clemens reported more burning the next day.[34]

On the 9th, the *Kotoku Maru* arrived at Guadalcanal with two hundred and fifty members of the Hara Construction Force; the next day fifty were dropped off at Gavutu. On the 10th, the *Kiyomizu Maru (No. 906)* arrived off Florida Island, and the *Azumasan Maru* returned to Tulagi with twenty-two replacements from the 1st Company, Kure 3rd SNLF. She also delivered a load of three hundred shells for the Mitsuwa Butai on Gavutu, but apparently they had the wrong fuses. A message was sent from the RXB radio station at Tulagi to the base at Rabaul (code-identified as RR) complaining that the fuses were limited to 4,000 meters and that the Allied bombers flew higher than that. More trouble with fuses is recorded in a 12 July message from the Guadalcanal commander to Rabaul: "RXI Secret Cable No. 52. On 11 July we received 600 shells of 8 cm from the Gavutu unit. But those shells had no fuses."[35]

On 15 July, Lt. (jg) Toshichi Mitsuwa left Gavutu for a conference at Rabaul. The flying boat on which he departed had just brought the commander of the newly formed 84th Guard Unit, Masaaki Suzuki, who was replacing fifty-three-year-old Lieutenant Yoshimoto. The 84th GU had been formed 1 July from the elements of the Kure 3rd SNLF on

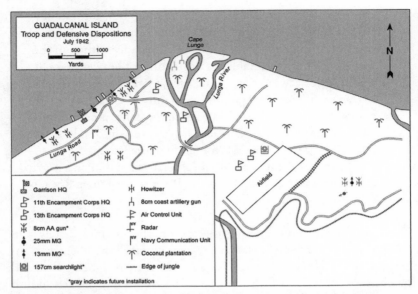

Figure 12. Map of Japanese troop and defensive dispositions on Guadalcanal Island, July 1942. (Author's collection; map courtesy Mary Craddock Hoffman)

Guadalcanal (1st Company) and Tulagi. Yoshimoto was in command of the 2nd Company, 84th Guard Unit, on Tulagi only until the 15th. Also on the plane with Commander Suzuki was a medical officer, brought to perform physical examinations of men who were to be promoted, and a chief paymaster, who was working on the money allotment plan to send funds to the sailors' families in Japan.[36]

On 16 July, Lieutenant Endo issued RXI Guard Unit (81st GU) Secret Order No. 5: "1. The 11th Construction Unit will start work on the airfield on 16 July. 2. Our RXI unit has not finished the necessary mop-up operation on RXI, but we suppose there is no enemy around here. Our unit will start to guard the airfield."[37] That same day, Endo submitted to Commander Suzuki a report for his unit, identifying personnel, progress in building several gun sites, future objectives, and conditions of food supply. Specifically, Endo noted that he had no men who were experts in firing the two 75-mm antiaircraft guns he currently had, and no one qualified to operate the stereo range finder. He reported that they kept a two-month supply of food and were resorting to cultivating farm produce for fresh food. They were investigating how to catch and store the many cattle on the island, and had a plan for using the special watcher boat to catch fish.

After Suzuki replied and asked Endo about the watcher stations, Endo sent another message, requesting assistance in mopping up Malaita and repeating his need for expert gunners and equipment specialists:

> I have not yet begun mopping up Malaita Island. The natives on this island are not gentle. I have also heard that the white men who were on Tulagi escaped to Malaita. It will be necessary to obtain help from our destroyers or our air force to mop up Malaita before establishing watching post.
>
> About the strength of our Guard Unit. I have 247 men. That is not enough! . . . I require operators for 6 AA guns, 1 of 25mm MG, 4 of 13mm MG, 2 men to operate the range finder, and 2 men to handle the searchlight. We also need sentry for five look-out posts. For the above-mentioned positions I do not have sufficient manpower. Furthermore, we expect to receive two more surface-firing cannons, 80mm. Further, it is said the 13th Construction Unit will receive two 1500mm searchlights. We must have the men able to operate the searchlights.[38]

On 23 July, the commander of the 4th Meteorological Unit at Rabaul asked the commander of the 11th CU working on the Guadalcanal airstrip for "estimates of results and charts of air currents above the runway." At about the same time, Warrant Officer Tanaka's 5th Platoon, 3rd Company, Kure 3rd SNLF, had disbanded its Gavutu camp with orders to go via Lunga to Marau Sound, in southeastern Guadalcanal, to establish a lookout station. Tanaka's men arrived at Lunga on 30 July, set up a tent camp, and began digging bomb shelters. It would not be long before the protection would be needed.

SME Tomisaburo Hirai of the Tanaka platoon wrote in his diary on 31 July:

> We started to dig shelters early in the morning, but at 0920 when I was away at headquarters an air raid began; it was too far for me to return to our area and I hid in a steel tub. Moments later I heard the sound of a bomb falling. No great problem. When I returned to my tent [2050] there was another air raid. I hid in our shelter [when] they dropped four or five bombs at 100 meters west of here. They damaged the coconut grove. God saved our life. Thanks God. But the enemy returned again and dropped additional bombs and left by 2305, a three-hour raid.
>
> 1 August: Got up at 0430. We saw a trace of last night's bomb-

ing. What a horrible sight it was. At 0630, we were told to assemble and meet the new RXI Company commander [Lt. Akira
Tanabe;] he made a patriotic speech for us. He is about 28 years
old, very young.[39]

That morning of 1 August, at 0920, the commander in chief of the
Fourth Fleet radioed the South Pacific Fleet: "According to information received enemy's condition is as follows: enemy is gathering power
along the east coast of Australia. . . . You should keep close watch. . . ."
In a communication also dated 1 August from Tokyo to paymaster Ens.
Shinzo Nagano, the sender informed the 11th CU that letters from the
families of departed Korean construction workers, thanking the navy
for forwarding the personal effects of the deceased, should be sent to a
new address.[40]

Emending the Plan

Two important changes would reshape the available combat units at
Guadalcanal. First, the 8th Base Force ordered the 81st Guard Unit,
RXI Dispatched Force, back to Rabaul to rejoin the parent unit. Appar-
ently the services of Lieutenant Endo and part of his detachment were
required in Rabaul; the feisty Endo, former adjutant of the Maizuru 2nd
SNLF, was well known there. Terushige Ishimoto and Matutaro Itoh,
the civilian interpreters attached to the navy and members of the 81st
GU, remained on Guadalcanal.[41]

It was anticipated that the newly reformed 84th Guard Unit would
assume security for Guadalcanal and the airfield. Endo left behind Warrant Officer Nakamura's howitzer gun platoon to bolster the 84th GU,
as well as some men from his unit who were manning lookout stations
on the island. Endo's force, including the 1st Platoon under WO Takezo
Hasegawa and the Command Platoon under WO Kimihide Seki, departed Lunga for New Britain Island on 2 August in the *Kinryu Maru*.
The six-hundred-mile journey normally took only twenty-eight to thirty
hours, but on this voyage the *Kinryu Maru* proceeded at a reduced speed
to allow the sailors to take and record depth soundings from the New
Georgia and Buin, Bougainville, areas all the way back to Rabaul, and
thus she did not arrive until 7 August.

The other significant change at Guadalcanal was the departure of
the Tanaka platoon of thirty-eight from Lunga for Marau Sound, along
with two radio operators and a boat crew of twelve with interpreter Ishimoto. They traveled in the *Kaiyo Maru No. 1* and *Kaiyo Maru No. 2*.

After establishing a watch post at Marau Sound, Tanaka was to move over to Malaita Island and set up another lookout post, called "Zero," at Nialaha'U Point, Cape Zélée. Tanaka's group reached the Marau Sound area on 4 August, but *Kaiyo Maru No. 1* hit a partially submerged sandbar, and there she remained.

On 5 August, three officers from the Yokohama Air Group Flying-Boat Unit at Tanambogo—Capt. Shigetoshi Miyazaki; Lt. Cdr. Saburo Katsuda; and Lt. Cdr. Takayuki Kurozaki—visited the officers of the 11th CU at the Guadalcanal airstrip. They told them that the 25th Air Flotilla would arrive at Guadalcanal from Rabaul not later than 8 August. After staying part of the day, the three men were satisfied that work on the airfield was on schedule, and they returned by launch to Tanambogo.[42]

The two major construction units labored in two shifts, night and day, on the Guadalcanal airstrip. They worked at opposite ends, moving toward the middle, with mostly shovels and pickaxes, and bicycle carts to transport the dirt and rock they dug. At the same time, workers were building the base, including a truck pool, power and refrigeration facilities, and three wooden warehouses west of the Lunga River. The beach at Kukum was fitted with cranes, a small marine railway, and a pier for unloading lighters, the flat-bottomed barges used to transport materiel relatively short distances. A bridge was thrown across the Lunga River, and a dirt road for trucks was completed from Kukum across the bridge to the airfield. The island headquarters was erected of prefabricated lumber in the Lever's Plantations coconut grove just north of the field. Meanwhile, quarters for the protection forces were put up east and west of Lunga Lagoon.

Laborer Masato Shinoda would write in his diary: "August 1—I worked hard all day with three other fellows. There was an air raid during lunch. I grabbed my food and ran away. August 2—We carried sheet iron [roofing] in the car [truck] all day. It was really hard work and very exhausting. There were two air raids. I had to flee with my lunch. [Some] 50 bombs fell on the airfield. No damage."[43]

On the night of 6 August, construction of the Guadalcanal air base was almost on schedule. PO2c Sankichi Kaneda, Nakamura platoon, 81st Guard Unit, wrote the following in his memoirs: "4 August. The first stage of construction on the runway is completed. 60m wide and 800m long. It is ready for fighter plane take-offs and landing. 5 August. Guadalcanal Guard Unit sent an urgent request to the 8th Base Force to send airplanes, but the opinion at the highest levels of command at that time was that the enemy would not mount a serious counterattack until 1943, so the request was denied."[44]

At 1940 on the 6th, the 8th Communication Unit dispatched a message from the commander of the 8th Base Force to the commander of the 84th Guard Unit, classified *Gunji–Gokuhi*—Top Secret. The 8th commander wanted the balance of the 81st *Keibitai* (81st Guard Unit) withdrawn soon, though because the "conditions" were increasing the "probability of danger," he acknowledged that the withdrawal should be postponed. He requested that the 84th GU commander confirm whether or not the Mitsuwa antiaircraft unit at Gavutu was included in the 25 July list of men in the 84th GU. By the time the message was received, however, Endo's force almost had reached Rabaul. Apparently, Rabaul headquarters sensed that something was going to happen in the Guadalcanal area, though what or when was not known.

The Americans Strike Back

When Lieutenant Endo's force arrived at the Rabaul dock at 0810 on 7 August, the dock master shouted to the seamen on deck: "Guadalcanal was attacked by the Americans and Tulagi was invaded!" Endo was furious and ran to the naval headquarters a short distance away to organize an immediate strike force to counter the Americans. His former outfit, the Maizuru 2nd SNLF, had taken Wake Island from the U.S. Marines that past December, and Endo thought that he could do it again on Guadalcanal.[45]

A hastily assembled force of 519 *rikusentais* drawn from the Sasebo 5th SNLF, the 81st GU, and the Kure 3rd SNLF boarded the transports *Meiyo Maru* and *Kankoku* for the Solomons. They were escorted by coastal minelayer *Tsugaru No. 21* and *Submarine Chaser No. 26*. The *Meiyo Maru* never made it; on the night of the 8th she was sunk by a torpedo from the U.S. submarine *S-38,* under Lt. Cdr. Henry G. Munson. The escorts picked up 177 survivors. Lieutenant Endo was not among them.[46]

Anyone who believes that the U.S. Marine invasion caught the Japanese completely by surprise is mistaken. The 8th Base Force had been alerted that something was afoot, but it had neglected to adequately brief the Tulagi and Guadalcanal garrisons of its suspicions. The Japanese had been diligently sending their flying boats off each morning about 0700 on reconnaissance surveys over assigned tracks of the Pacific Ocean. Their normal schedule called for a three-plane unit to fly a pattern 400 miles in a southeasterly direction. On 6 August, however, the

Kawanishi flying boats remained tied to their moorings in Gavutu Harbor because of atmospheric conditions and the misty cloud cover that blanketed the area. Had the weather been clear, the U.S. invasion fleet would have been spotted and its nineteen transports and their precious cargo put in jeopardy. The struggle for Guadalcanal would have had a different beginning, perhaps even a different ending. But fate chose to favor the Allies that day.

That evening an immense Emily flying boat landed at Gavutu Harbor, bringing some sorely needed oil for the Kawanishi. Aboard was Lt. Cdr. Noboru Sato on an inspection trip to the advance base. A party was held in his honor at the Kasen unit club on Gavutu—a former RAAF building—with beer, *sake,* and much storytelling and entertainment.[47] About 2100, before the reception was over, the radio watch clerks reported receiving numerous unusual radio signals from the enemy. Excitement in the camp ran high. All air group personnel were put on immediate alert. Captain Shigetoshi Miyazaki decided to extend the normal search pattern to 600 miles. MCPO Masaichiro Miyagawa was placed on watch duty from 0200 to 0600.

Meanwhile, the maintenance crews performed last-minute checks of the Kawanishi that were riding at anchor 80 to 150 yards off Gavutu, with fuel tanks that had been topped off the day before. The pilots were awake at 0300, and within forty-five minutes they reached the ramp area and were ferried to their planes. They warmed up their engines by taxiing about in Gavutu Harbor, their blue and white guidance lights flickering.[48] PO Kyosho Mutou was at the controls of his flying boat, waiting patiently for the signal to take off. Lt. Cdr. Soichi Tashiro, third in command of the air unit, was making his final instrument adjustments. When the green takeoff signal flare was fired, the Kawanishi jockeyed into position.

Then at Tanambogo headquarters, the telephone rang. It was Tulagi. The caller yelled, *"Ku-shu-keihoh!"*—*"Air raid!"* Master Chief Petty Officer Miyagawa at his lookout perch could not hear any engines, but glancing in the direction of Guadalcanal he could see numerous black dots approaching Gavutu, like swarming bees.

A mass of attackers from the U.S. Navy aircraft carriers *Wasp* (CV 7) and *Enterprise* (CV 6)—sixteen fighters, twenty-four dive-bombers, and one torpedo bomber—struck the three-island complex, overwhelming the flying boats before they could get airborne. The fully fueled planes became flaming pyres, spurting burning gasoline that saturated the area. Fuel drenched the gray rubber boats used to ferry crews to the Kawanishis; when hit, they too burst into flames, the occupants burning as they dove or were hurled into the water. Few escaped the inferno. "It was a horrifying sight," Miyagawa recalled. Ens. Raymond F. Conklin, a pilot from U.S. Navy fighting squadron VF-71 aboard the *Wasp* who attacked flying boats off Makambo, commented that one of his victims flamed so fast that it was like "flying through a prairie fire."[49]

Having devastated the flying boats, the F4F Wildcats of VF-71 went on to deal with the fighter component of the Yokohama Air Group, the seven war-painted Zero floatplanes (Rufes) based at Halavo on Florida Island. Coming in at only fifty feet off the water, two fighter divisions took the Rufes under fire. They sank immediately. Another division clobbered Haleta village, where the U.S. Marines would go ashore two hours later.[50]

The attack was over within minutes. Nothing was left of the Yokohama Air Group. Lieutenant Commander Katsuda was overheard saying, "All prizes and honors of our air group have been lost."[51] Lieutenant Commander Sato, who had arrived for an inspection the day before, was found dead on Gavutu, apparently by concussion, for there was not a scratch on him.[52]

Reveille on Tulagi was at 0400 each day. Morning worship began at 0415 and ended at 0440. Breakfast was ready twenty minutes later. Work normally began at 0630. This had been the routine on 7 August, except that Commander Suzuki and Lieutenant Yoshimoto were sleeping later. At 0610 the explosion of shells on nearby Florida Island abruptly wakened them. Partially dressed, they headed for the limestone caves located not far from their command post at a hill near the former government station. Lieutenant Yoshimoto, who was very much afraid of air attacks, in anticipation had the rikusentai excavate dugouts and caverns throughout the lower end of the island.[53] That early August morning, others running for the shelters included medical officer Lt. Ryoichi Chadani and supply officer Lt. Ko Nomura.

Almost instantly the bombardment shifted to Tulagi, tearing up the moss-green ground cover and blasting the beautiful bougainvilleas that adorned the Residency grounds. The caves that had provided safe haven many times during air raids in the last three months now did so again. But this time the salvos from the enemy warships made everyone jittery, wondering if they would be invaded.

PO3c Osamu Yamaoka of the Tulagi radio communication section had been on duty when at 0600 a runner alerted him that a group of

Figure 13. The Yokohama Air Group Floatplane Fighter Unit (Hama Air Unit) at Halavo, Florida Island, July 1942. (Author's collection, via Maru)

strange ships had been seen near Savo Island. As others crowded into the radio shack, a hurried message was sent off to Rabaul:

From: Commander, Tulagi Communications Base

To: Commander, 8th Base Force

20 vessels, enemy surface force attacking RXB by air raid; preparing to land.

Further messages of increasing urgency followed. At 0630 Tulagi reported, "All seaplanes on fire." At 0635, "Enemy mobile force sighted." At 0715, "Enemies commenced landing on Tulagi." At 0725, "Enemies commenced landing on RXB." Two minutes later the 8th Base Force radioed: "When required, set fire to equipment." At 0729 Tulagi replied: "Situation requires setting fire to equipment immediately."

The invasion and supporting bombardment were overwhelming. At 0730, Tulagi reported, "Receiving naval gunfire." At 0749, "Enemies both shelling and beginning disembarkation." At 0800, "1 battleship, 3 cruisers, 15 destroyers plus transports." At 0810 on 7 August the Tulagi communications base radioed the 8th Base Force for the last time:

"Enemy strength great. Defending to the last; may the fortunes of war be with you."[54]

Commander Suzuki, who had been on Tulagi only three weeks, had studied the defense plan drawn up by Lieutenant Yoshimoto. However, the strategy, drafted in May, was by August out of date and Suzuki had to improvise. Suzuki ordered one part of the 4th Platoon under WO Fukimoto to take up positions in the government wharf area. The headquarters unit under WO Takeo Ikeda and the Command Platoon under WO Tsurusaburo Shigeta covered the sector between the Residency and Sasapi. Half of the 1st Platoon under WO Yoshiharu Muranaka, stationed in the hospital area, butted up against PO3 Harubumi Ishida's 2nd Squad, 2nd Platoon (under WO Sadayuki Kato), which was guarding Chinatown. The lines were stretched thin. Suzuki had a total of about 175 effectives from his four platoons. Most of his 2nd Platoon was on lookout duty on Florida Island, and the other half of his 1st Platoon was garrisoning Malaita. On Guadalcanal, thirty-eight men from the 5th Platoon under WO Kikuo Tanaka were on detached service at Marau Sound, and WO Noboru Takeuchi's 3rd Platoon of forty-six was attached to the newly formed 1st Company, 84th Guard Unit, at Lunga. Takeuchi had ten men on observation duty off Banika in the Russell Islands.

The strength of the Japanese defense on Tulagi lay in the 1st and 4th Platoons, which were reinforced by the headquarters unit and thirty-six men from the Command Platoon who functioned as a floater unit, moving around the island as needed. Part of this force was the original machine-gun company of the Kure 3rd SNLF, now the 2nd Company, 84th Guard Unit, which provided Suzuki with great firepower. Normally he had a squad stationed at the commanding Hill 281 (Bird Hill), with sentries on duty around the clock, in six shifts of four hours apiece. Other guards, likewise in six shifts, were stationed at the government pier. Another group was at the wireless station, while a squad covered the east end of the prison.

In the way of ordnance, Commander Suzuki had five automatic rifles, two at the foot of Bird Hill behind the hospital, two near the harbor close to the former post office building, and one on top of Bird Hill; two light machine guns, one in Chinatown and one near the hospital; two 8-mm antiaircraft guns on top of the southeast promontory of Bird Hill; two 13-mm machine guns and three antitank rapid-firing guns in various parts of the defense zone; and twelve grenade launchers. The key

Figure 14. WO Tsurusaburo Shigeta platoon (information platoon, 3rd Company), 17 February 1942, Kure 3rd Special Naval Landing Force, Kure Barracks, Kure, Japan. *First row, left to right*: PO3c Tokio Ishihara (or Isjiwara), PO3c Kazuo Kano, PO3c Yoshiaki Murakami, PO1c Katsuo Takano, WO Tsurusaburo Shigeta, Sp. Lt. (jg) Kakichi Yoshimoto (commander, 3rd Company, Kure 3rd SNLF), WO Takeo Ikeda, PO3c Toyosaku Saito, PO3c Shigeo Kanbara, PO3c Goro Hayashi, PO3c Masajiro Yoshimura. (Author's collection)

defensive position was in and adjacent to Bird Hill, which had the most concentrated firepower of the 84th Guard Unit.[55]

Standing orders to Lieutenant Mitsuwa, whose men on Gavutu had 13-mm and 25-mm machine guns, were to fire when he thought it would be an effective deterrent against any landing forces. Supplementing the defenders were 185 personnel from the construction detachments, under the command of Lt. Cdr. Kiyoshi Iida—50 noncombatants from the 7th Construction Unit, 129 men from the 14th Construction Unit, and 6 men from the 13th Construction Unit. The 14th EU, to be transferred to Lae, New Guinea, was awaiting replacement by the 15th Construction Unit, a new force of three hundred men. Also still at his post was the ill-starred fifty-three-year-old Lieutenant Yoshimoto, who was being replaced by Commander Suzuki and was to be released from service into retirement. Yoshimoto was scheduled to leave Tulagi on 8 August aboard the *Nichiran Maru*.

When their dull routine was shattered on 7 August by American shells, the sentries on Tulagi were unaware that a great Allied armada was at their very doorstep. They had known something was amiss, because the flying boats had been churning the water since early that morning. But no one from the air group had informed the garrison commander of their suspicions. The Kure men and the construction workers remained in the caves and air-raid shelters until about noon.[56] Near 1207 that midday, the rikusentai shifted to form a line across Tulagi's eastern slopes and ravines. There Suzuki's "non-seagoing sailors" would wait for the U.S. Marines to show them their fighting abilities.

5 Preparing for Battle

A Joint Chiefs of Staff (JCS) directive approved by President Roosevelt on 30 March 1942 divided the Pacific theater into three parts: Pacific Ocean Area (POA), Southwest Pacific Area (SWPA), and Southeast Pacific Area (SEPA). The Pacific Ocean Area was divided into the North Pacific Area (NPA), Central Pacific Area (CPA), and South Pacific Area (SPA). The South Pacific Area included every Pacific Ocean Area land-mass south of the equator except the Phoenix Islands. The Southwest Pacific Area included the Bismarck Archipelago, New Guinea, and the Solomon Islands.

The Starting Point

Gen. Douglas MacArthur was appointed Supreme Commander, Allied Forces, Southwest Pacific Area (CINCSWPA), and Adm. Chester W. Nimitz, Commander in Chief, Pacific Ocean Area (CINCPOA). Nimitz was given command of the North Pacific Area and Central Pacific Area but was directed by Adm. Ernest J. King, Commander in Chief, U.S. Fleet (COMINCH), to appoint Vice Adm. Robert L. Ghormley as commander for the South Pacific Area. On 18 April, Admiral King ordered Ghormley to establish his headquarters in Auckland, New Zealand, with an advance base in Tongatabu (Tonga). Ghormley arrived at his headquarters in Auckland on 22 May. On 2 July 1942 the JCS issued the Directive for Offensive Operations in the Southwest Pacific Area, the order that leads to the invasion of the British Solomon Islands by the 1st Marine Division, reinforced by elements of the 2nd Marine Division.

In January 1942 the 2nd Marine Brigade had deployed to the Samoan Islands as reinforcements, and the U.S. Army and Navy occupied Bora Bora in the Society Islands. There the navy constructed a fuel tank farm to support fleet operations. Other task forces meanwhile occupied the Phoenix and Fiji Islands.

On 12 March, Army Task Force (ATF) 6814 landed at Nouméa, New

Caledonia (code-named WHITE POPPY) and in May ATF 051 garrisoned Tonga (code-named BLEACHER). The next jump was 400 miles from New Caledonia to Efate Island, New Hebrides, when ATF 6814 Detachment A landed at Port Vila. Two months later the small task force moved 100 miles west to Espiritu Santo Island, also in the New Hebrides group. The Japanese had not been motionless. They had occupied Rabaul on New Britain Island on 23 January, and by March were in Lae, New Guinea, and the Shortland Islands in the northern Solomons. While the Americans moved west, the Japanese moved east. In May, the Japanese special landing party had captured Tulagi Island, the capital of the British Solomon Islands while seaplane units moved into Florida, Gavutu, and Tanambogo Islands.

To prevent the Japanese from expanding farther east, the U.S. Navy planned to establish stepping-stone bases on key islands in the South Seas. The immediate objective would be the occupation of Ndeni (code-named APRICOT), the main island in the Santa Cruz group (code-named CYANIDE), located 335 nautical miles east-southeast of Guadalcanal. The reinforced 2nd Marines on the U.S. West Coast were the most readily available unit for the task.

The Joint Chiefs of Staff planned to assign the 1st Marine Division reinforced to the Ndeni–Tulagi operation. The 2nd Marines were to assault Ndeni, 335 miles from general target area. Guadalcanal (code-named CACTUS) was not part of the original 2 July directive; it was later added when an enemy airstrip was reported being constructed. The SPA did not have sufficient combat aircraft or support units to conduct both operations simultaneously. Moreover, it lacked the required stocks of war materiel and support facilities for a protracted minor war, much less a major one. The U.S. Navy had secured small advance bases in the South Seas since January 1942, but all were rudimentary. Rear Adm. John S. McCain's chief of staff had noted: "Everything they eat, everything they wear, every place they live has to be brought from the US. . . . There are no dock facilities, no cranes and . . . very poor beaches for landing craft. Heavy engineering equipment . . . must be brought ashore so that you can build [needed] facilities. . . . Everything has to be manhandled. . . ."[1]

The ultimate objective of the United States, code-named PESTILENCE, was the seizure and occupation of the New Britain–New Ireland–New Guinea area in order to deny it to Japan. The operation plan divided PESTILENCE into three phases or tasks: Task One, the seizure and occupation of the Santa Cruz Islands, Tulagi, and adjacent positions; Task Two, the seizure and occupation of the rest of the Solomon Islands, Lae, and Salamaua, and the northeast coast of New Guinea; and Task Three, the seizure and occupation of Rabaul and adjacent positions in the New Guinea–New Ireland area.

Task One (Operation WATCHTOWER) was tentatively scheduled for 1 August 1942 but later changed to 7 August. The boundary between the SPA and the SWPA was moved westward by one degree of longitude, a change that placed the entire Task One target area—Santa Cruz Islands, Tulagi, Gavutu, Tanambogo, Florida, Guadalcanal, Malaita, San Cristobal, and the Russell Islands (in the British Solomon Islands)—in the SPA under Vice Admiral Ghormley. In brief, the target area was reassigned from the SWPA, General MacArthur's command, to Vice Admiral Ghormley's command.

WATCHTOWER was the brainchild of Admiral King, who had conceived the operation in early 1942. King saw that Tulagi would serve as "an additional bastion to the America–Australia lifeline, . . . the starting point for a drive up the line of the Solomon Islands into Rabaul, and . . . a deterrent to any further expansion by the Japanese."[2] On 25 June, Admiral King issued an alert notice to his Pacific commanders to prepare for offensive operations against the Santa Cruz Islands and Tulagi. Subsequently a movement warning order was sent to the 2nd Marine Division, as it had already been determined that the reinforced 2nd Marine Regiment would be earmarked for the invasion of Santa Cruz. On the 30th, the regiment was detached from the 2nd Marine Division and assigned to the Amphibious Force, South Pacific, commanded by Rear Adm. Richmond Kelly Turner. This force would be augmented by green troops from the training base at Camp Elliott, outside San Diego, California. Some recently graduated "boots" were transferred from the newly formed 22nd Marines to bolster the component's 2nd and 10th Regiments.[3]

On 10 March, the artillerymen of the 10th Marines with their 75-mm pack howitzers and 155-mm guns had moved to Camp Dunlap, at the tiny town of Niland in southern California. It was an ideal site for practicing cannonades under the hot sun, with the Chocolate Mountains as a backdrop. The locals didn't seem to mind the all-day firing, though pictures often fell off the walls of their modest wooden houses, and occasionally a distant rumbling could be heard at night when the big guns went into a barrage of firing. By April, however, most of the regiment had returned to San Diego, and in just two months, on Wednesday, 1 July, they were aboard their transports, heading for the South Seas. The vessels that carried them later were called the "Unholy Four." The *President Adams* (APA 19) held the 3rd Battalion, 2nd Marines (3/2); the *President Hayes* (APA 20) held the 2nd Battalion, 2nd Marines (2/2); the *President Jackson* (APA 18) held the 1st Battalion, 2nd Marines (1/2) and Company G, 3rd Battalion, 10th Marines (G/3/10); and the *Crescent City* (APA 21) held the Headquarters Company, 2nd Marines (HQ/2). The transports sailed in company with the cargo ship *Alhena* (AKA 9), carrying HQ/3/10.

All the vessels were overloaded with combat gear and armament. In addition to the infantry, each transport carried one battery of 75-mm pack howitzers. On the *Jackson,* the 37-mm antitank guns and baby howitzers were lashed on the aft deck. Slung from pulleys, cables, and large cranes (davits) were the landing craft, Higgins boats, barges, and deck-mounted tank lighters, the flat-bottomed boats used to take their cargo to shore. PFC William J. Gilomen (G/3/10) remembered: "There must have been close to fifty or sixty [landing craft] aboard and all [were] capable of holding thirty or more men. The hatches were boarded over at each deck and then we loaded everything we possessed: amphibious tractors, trucks, jeeps, tanks, recon cars, guns and anything else that could be . . . piled on. We had a tremendous supply of ammunition down in the hole, most of the reserve ammunition for the whole regiment. The *Jackson* was crowded, jammed, odoriferous and dirty."[4]

That first day of July 1942 was 68 degrees at 0800, hazy with a slight ocean breeze, as the green utility-clad marines crowded the rails of the troop ships to take a last look at the beautiful port city of San Diego. Many hoped they would have the opportunity to see it again, thinking they might even relocate there once the war was over. Most had never seen the Pacific Ocean before, much less been a passenger on a transport, but they soon settled down as they watched their convoy, accompanied by the carrier *Wasp* and a destroyer screen. When the ships finally were at sea, the sealed orders were read to the men: "This [is] Task Force Number 18, headed south by southwest in the Pacific Ocean for aggressive action against the Japanese."

"That hit us like a bolt," Gilomen recalled. It was less than a month since the Battle of Midway, and "most of the troops believed we were going to reinforce the Midway Island garrison."[5]

Holed up in the bowels of the hot and sticky transports, the marines broke up the dull days by playing poker, many for the first and last time as the big-city boys began to rake in money, mostly from the inexperienced and gullible. Yet, what would they need money for where they were going, wherever that might be? The men were accustomed to Marine Corps cuisine, but now it was U.S. Navy chow aboard the crowded rocking vessels, and most did not like what they were offered. On Saturday, 4 July, however, Ens. L. P. May, USNR, the ship's commissary officer, had a surprise for the troops on the *President Hayes*. Chief Commissary Steward H. W. Watson had prepared an Independence Day feast: tomato juice cocktail, sweet pickles, olives, celery hearts, waldorf salad, roast tom turkey, oyster dressing, buttered peas, giblet gravy, mashed potatoes, asparagus tips, candied sweet potatoes, cranberry sauce, hot finger rolls with butter, apple pie, ice cream, coffee, and cigars and cigarettes.

Preparations at Nouméa

On 10 July, the 1st Marine Raider Battalion arrived at Nouméa, the pleasant capital of the French oceanic colony of New Caledonia, from its recently conducted commando-style training in Samoa as a component of the 3rd Marine Brigade. The cigar-shaped island of New Caledonia lies about 900 miles from Sydney and Auckland and 700 miles from Suva, Fiji. It is known as *la grande Terre* (the great land) and has been described as the most interesting place in the Pacific, laced by a thousand-mile coral reef with an enormous lagoon at its doorstep. Although New Caledonia has a subtropical climate, there is little tropical growth beyond occasional clumps of bamboo and coconut palm. The dominating features are shingle streams flowing through greenish valleys and scattered farms flanked by steep, rugged hills.

Sanitary conditions for the U.S. troops on the island were poor, but it was free of malaria, dengue fever, and amoebic dysentery, including filariasis, which was prevalent in Samoa. Regardless, the sailors, soldiers, and marines loved it. Nouméa was unlike any town they had ever seen. Only a few locals spoke English, but the American dollar did a lot of talking by itself. In the "Paris of the Pacific," you could pick up fresh baguettes at any local bakery as well as Australian beer. According to Robert C. Muehrcke of the 132nd Infantry, "If you had any rank at all, [you] could once in a while wrangle a date with some French dolly. That is, if you beat the New Zealanders and the Australian officers to the action. But they were there first and had all the choice goods already staked out."[6]

The 1st Marine Raider Battalion, one of the four new, elite, special commando-type battalions, was under crusty "old Corps" Col. Merritt Austin "Red Mike" Edson, who had received his baptism in jungle fighting in Nicaragua. That experience, and the familiarity with the Japanese that Edson had gained with the 4th Marines in China, would be greatly to the marines' advantage during the forthcoming operations on Tulagi and Guadalcanal. As soon as the Raiders had reached New Caledonia, Edson put his men on a grueling training program, running and climbing through the rough terrain of the island's back country where they set up a tent camp in the bush. The Raiders loved the role and added "bush craft" to their commando skills.

The Navy Department had assigned a special code word, BELMONT, to the 1st Raiders—the only marine organization to have its own code name. The unit continued its arduous training in New Caledonia until late July; it was in an ideal geographic locale for the pending Solomon Islands operation. In the interim, a few Raiders who obtained liberty sought out entertainment in Nouméa, some simply staying around the water fountain at Place Curbed, perhaps to admire the few French ladies. The three movie houses in the town were not often places of choice, as they were small and hot and stuffy, and all the films were in French. The men had to go prepared to stand through the two verses of our National Anthem and the "Stars and Stripes," as well as the French "Marseilles," as an overture to the program. A few religious servicemen may have attended services at the Catholic cathedral or the Protestant church on Sunday.

One particular building in Nouméa, a large pink house on a small hill, seemed to beckon to the marines. It was the town's principal bordello, properly named *La Maison Rose*—the Pink House. The officers had their own entrance; but for the others, the lines were so long they were patrolled by the military police, and the U.S. Army opened up a prophylactic station not far away. The bordello remained open for business through most of the war, though sometimes a well-meaning chaplain would cause its temporary closure. Generally, La Maison Rose operated with the tacit blessing of the Force Surgeon and the Navy Medical Department. The Force Medical Inspector later described it as "maintaining a zero venereal fall-out."[7]

On 22 July 1942, three former British Solomon Islands Protectorate district officers with detailed information about the islands joined the 1st Marine Raiders. Nick Waddell and Dick Horton had been ordered to Port Vila from Sydney, and with Henry Josselyn had been cooling their heels at Vila, held there at the request of Solomon Island Resident Commissioner Marchant. For some reason Marchant thought they would be able to return to their former posts in the Solomons. Waddell had been released from the Australian military service, and Horton had been denied permission to enlist in the Royal Navy. Josselyn had been in Vila ever since carrying the protectorate government records there from Auki, Malaita, in March in the ketch *Kombito*.

Marine Colonel Edson jumped at the opportunity to obtain the services of the three men, who had detailed knowledge of Tulagi, the Raiders' initial objective. Rather than sit idle at Vila, they could be very useful as his guides, as they knew the 3½-mile Tulagi Island from top to bottom. The office of Rear Adm. John S. "Slew" McCain, Commander, Air, South Pacific (COMAIRSOPAC), interceded on Edson's behalf by arranging with the High Commissioner for the Western Pacific, Sir Philip E. Mitchell, to release the three for temporary service with the U.S. Marines. McCain also arranged a priority flight on a PBY from Vila to Nouméa.[8]

Converging the Task Forces

"Edson's Raiders," as his men liked to call themselves, would leave the Paris of the Pacific on 27 July without fanfare. They were split among the four fast transports (APDs) of Transport Division 12—*Colhoun, Gregory* (APD 3), *Little* (APD 4), and *McKean* (APD 5)—which had been converted from World War I-vintage destroyers (four-stackers). The APDs reached the Koro Islands, Fiji, on the 28th to meet the WATCHTOWER task force coming from New Zealand, San Diego, Hawaii, and Australia, for pre-invasion landing exercises. While the Raiders were still at New Caledonia, the 2nd Marines convoy was headed for Tonga. Bill Cannon, with Company C, 1st Battalion, 2nd Marine Regiment described the voyage from San Diego: "The trip over was almost unbearable with so little air to breathe; the intense heat almost pushed us to a breaking point. . . . Everything was wet from perspiration and water was rationed!"[9]

Cpl. James Sorensen (A/1/2) was aboard the *President Jackson*.

> Our quarters [were] on B deck, above the water line and
> right under the main deck. . . . It could be awfully hot in these
> steel walled quarters. . . . We had about 200 men in the compart-
> ment, sleeping in tiers of bunks, four high. All you could do in
> a bunk was roll over. If you lifted your head more than a few
> inches, you would scrape a layer of skin off your nose. The bunks
> were built up around four sides of a big hatch, which extended
> down to the hold of the ship. It didn't leave much room for

movement in the compartment. . . . We were up in the forward part of the ship with the head right next to the compartment. At that we were lucky because there weren't very many heads and washrooms for all the men aboard. We washed our clothes in the big sinks, the same ones we used to wash ourselves when there was water to wash. . . . The head was a long metal trough with a pair of smooth shaven boards laid over it. . . . At intervals of a few minutes, salt water was supposed to flush out the entire trough. Sometimes it did and sometimes it did not. The odor of sweating men became part of the ship. You could not get away from it. . . . [The] ventilation system . . . followed the example of everything else that wouldn't work aboard our scow. Chow became worse as the days went by.[10]

The 2nd Marines endured weeks on board the stinking transports, some of the men with just fifteen weeks of boot training in the States. They were physically exhausted from the long ocean journey, as were all the marines in the task force, particularly those unlucky enough to be assigned to the bowels of the troop ships. All the officers shared deck cabins and as a result were in better physical shape than the enlisted men. They could roam the transports at will, and most had better food and better eating conditions than the men below deck; they would be much better prepared for the strains and fatigue of combat.

The discomfort of the poorly ventilated and crowded transports finally came to an end when the 2nd Marine Regiment arrived at Tonga, known as "where time begins," or "a place where time stood still." Her Majesty Queen Salote Tubou, a Methodist monarch who had ascended the throne in 1918, knew a few days beforehand that the U.S. Marines were coming, but not how many. They would soon take over the quaint town and country. The missionaries of the London Missionary Society, the Seventh Day Adventists, and Latter Day Saints, plus a handful of others who operated mission stations throughout Tonga, could hardly believe their eyes when they saw so many young marines walking around and sightseeing. They had warned the females to beware of men in uniform.

The enlisted men who had departed San Diego seventeen days before were apprehensive at their new environment yet overjoyed to set foot on solid ground. All the officers and most of the enlisted personnel were allowed shore privileges. At the rural community of Tongatabu (Sacred Tonga), the thirsty battlewagons refueled and the marines caught a glimpse of island life in the South Seas. Businesslike natives sold them their first taste of green coconut milk, much to the marines' regret. The tiny capital, Nuku'alofa (City of Love), now had hundreds of American soldiers and some four thousand U.S. Marines milling around. The soldiers were from the U.S. Army, 147th Infantry Regiment, with a few airmen from the USAAF's 67th Fighter Squadron. The marines later would meet the GIs from the 147th Regiment and the airmen from the 67th Squadron on Guadalcanal. But in the meantime, the marines soon would be gone, leaving only the U.S. Army and a small group of the sailors, plus a handful of New Zealanders from the 34th Battalion.

On 24 July, Tonga's marines boarded their transports once again, their shore leave over, and the next day the flotilla moved out to sea. Two days later the convoy rendezvoused with invasion Task Forces 11, 16, 18, and 62 roughly 370 miles south of the Fiji Islands. The next stop was the rugged Koro Islands of Fiji, which had characteristics similar to those of the target area, though fortunately the target area would not have a dangerous coral reef as did Koro.

Charles O. Hall of Company D, 2nd Medical Battalion, back on board the *Jackson,* described the events: "We were then told that we were to make a landing on Guadalcanal, Tulagi and Florida Island. . . . A few days before the landing, we made a practice landing on Fiji. I later read this was the most fouled up landing, ever, and I believe it. . . . [W]e never did anything correct, as nobody knew where anybody was and just small sections were together. There were no Beach-masters and the place where we landed was coral and full of holes. Many marines drowned, or almost drowned, during the mediocre landing. Our battalion ate fresh bananas, mangos and native chicken while on the beach. We returned to the *Jackson* and I guess everybody else got aboard the correct ship. Then we sailed towards Guadalcanal."[11]

On 30 July the convoy was at the Koro transport area. A staff conference held aboard the *Crescent City* revealed future commitments of the 2nd Marines in the WATCHTOWER operation. The APRICOT plan, to deny Ndeni in the Santa Cruz Islands to the Japanese, was still in effect. Regimental Secret Operational Order 2–42 specifically outlined that the 2nd Marines, reinforced (less the 1st Battalion), as the division reserve, was to be prepared to take over the mission assigned to either the 1st Marines or the 5th Marines in the event that either or both units were unable to perform their assignments. The "Gyrenes" in the average outfit could not be described as amphibious troops; and even though they were considered to be sea soldiers of the U.S. Navy, they simply did not have sufficient long-term training as a professional seaborne force. Nevertheless, the U.S. Marines were the best available for the task that lay ahead.

On 31 July, Combat Teams B and C (less attached units aboard the *President Hayes*) of the 2nd Marines rehearsed in the Koro Islands by landing on make-believe enemy-held shores. The troops had participated in very limited practice in Higgins-boat landings. On the 30th the 3rd Battalion, 2nd Marines, from the *President Adams* was to disembark and "hit BEACH GREEN" on the last day of the exercise. Then a change in orders arrived from the *Crescent City* to land the 3/2 at rocky Nola Point on the 29th. But before this could transpire, once again new orders were received for the landing exercise that was to acquaint untested marines in a ship-to-shore movement; the original landing date of the 30th was back in place. The 3/2 boarded the Higgins boats and headed for the shore as directed. However, when the boats were a few thousand yards out, the whitecaps breaking just ahead signaled nothing but trouble, and the 3/2 landing force turned around and returned to the *Adams*.[12]

Former Lt. Richard E. Bennink, USNR, landing boat commander on the transport *Heywood* (AP 12), recalled: "As we approached the Koro Islands, with the Marines [paratroops] in the boats, I saw that its shore was ringed with a coral reef, black and sharp, like sharks teeth, that would have chewed our boats [plywood LCPs] to pieces. I returned to the ship without attempting to land. Fortunately, the other landing force officers did the same or we would have [had] no boats for Guadalcanal."[13]

The practice landing in the Koro Islands proved to be a bust. The first U.S. Marine war-related landing exercise of moving men en masse from transports at sea to land indicated the marines were not ready to storm the shores of an enemy-held area. Maj. Gen. Alexander A. Vandegrift, commander of the 1st Marine Division, appraised the exercise: "These rehearsals did not work out well, mainly because hidden coral prevented the boats from reaching the beaches. Although I later described the rehearsal as a 'complete bust,' . . . [a]t the very least it got the boats off the transports, and the men down the nets and away. It uncovered deficiencies such as defective boat engines in time to have them repaired and gave both Turner and me a chance to take important corrective measures in other spheres."[14]

Meanwhile, CUB-13, a small U.S. Navy specialized air and base facility unit was activated in 1942 on the West Coast specifically for the Ndeni operation; personnel and supplies would be taken from the recently formed LION-1 facility, also on the West Coast. This large unit was formed in the United States as a complete naval base for Espiritu Santo Island, New Hebrides (code-named BUTTON). However, by drawing men and materiel from LION-1, CUB-13 delayed the progress of Base BUTTON. Supplies were requisitioned, but only limited quantities reached the advanced bases. Espiritu Santo, which was the closest location to the target area, was to be the major backup base for operations in the southern Solomons, yet it lacked everything.

Nouméa, the advance headquarters for the South Pacific command, was in no better shape. On a visit in late September 1942, Gen. Henry H. "Hap" Arnold, head of the U.S. Army Air Forces, found that "[Admiral Ghormley, the commander of the South Pacific area] had eighty ships in the harbor which he could not unload. . . . Ghormley's people . . . didn't know what was on the ships; consequently . . . the transports had to be sent down to New Zealand to be completely unloaded and new manifests made out. This, when there was a distinct shortage of shipping in all other theaters of the world!" Arnold felt that "the Navy had taken one hell of a beating and . . . did not have a logistic setup efficient enough to insure success."[15]

But CUB-13 drew the required materiel from the West Coast depots and was hurriedly shipped off to New Caledonia, reaching Nouméa on 1 September. The unit was to occupy Ndeni and construct a backup base for Guadalcanal, but by the time it had reached Nouméa circumstances had change. It was too late for the proposed base. Nevertheless, the operation remained on hold pending the outcome of Guadalcanal. Several plans were considered, including one, which was later canceled, involving the Tonga-based 147th Infantry Regiment. CUB-13 eventually was dissolved and became part of the New Caledonia naval base.

Operation WATCHTOWER Proceeds

At 1750 on 31 July, the WATCHTOWER invasion forces of eighty-two warships of Task Force 61 had departed the Koro Islands. On the following day, plans were made for the select landing party for Ndeni—actually nearby Trevanion Island—Santa Cruz Islands, headed by Capt. George F. Doyle, an engineering officer with the 2nd Pioneers. Included in the group were six marines from the intelligence section, 2nd Marines under Sgt. Jack T. Lent, Cpl. Mahlon R. Kruse, and Sergeant Hawkins as the photographer. They were to land in the Santa Cruz Islands and make a reconnaissance to see if the area had the potential as a backup base for the Guadalcanal–Tulagi operation. On board the transport, the men drew maps of their destination, Trevanion Island.

On 2 August, Captain Doyle's recon party left the transports by destroyer for Port Vila, on Efate Island, New Hebrides. There they boarded the *McFarland* (DD 237), where they were temporarily housed. On the 6th the men were taken to Trevanion Island on one of the *McFarland's* motor launches, and the next three days were spent surveying and photographing potential sites and making maps. On the morning of the 11th, the *McFarland* sent a boat to pick up the party, with orders that they were to evacuate the island at once. Two days later, she reached Segond Channel, Espiritu Santo Island, New Hebrides.

Captain Doyle reported to Colonel Arthur, CO 2nd Marines, that "[t]he only good transport areas are at the head of Graciosa Bay and that only three or four transports can anchor there but require air protection. . . . The estimated time to prepare and occupy this island upon arrival is about three weeks. . . . It is my opinion the Trevanion Island is too small to tactically accommodate a reinforced regiment and supplies." The occupation of Trevanion, however, would prevent the enemy from using the "back door" approach to recapture Guadalcanal. While Doyle's recon patrol was already in the Santa Cruz area, a mailgram from the commander of Task Force 62, dated 5 August, altered the involvement of the 2nd Marines in the Santa Cruz Islands. It read in part: "On August seventh 1st Marine Division reinforced with the 2nd Marines will recapture Tulagi and Guadalcanal Islands. . . . In this first forward step toward clearing the Japanese out of a conquered territory we have strong support from the Pacific Fleet and from the air, surface and submarine forces in the South Pacific and Australia. . . . R K Turner Rear Admiral US Navy Commanding."[16]

Jim Sorensen, aboard the *Jackson,* was a scout-sniper with Company A, 2nd Marines. Company A noncoms had been summoned to a briefing session where their destination was made known to them. Sorensen recalled: "I never heard of Guadalcanal or Tulagi. . . . Our unit was given very little information of Guadalcanal, since our initial assigned role was to take part in the assault on Tulagi. At this briefing, we were given a reasonable description of the Tulagi terrain and told that our role would be to land somewhere in the area of the harbor following which we would have to scale precipitous cliffs or a steep ridgeline and gain the heights above the harbor. Later, we learned that our mission had been changed and we were now to make a landing on Florida Island."[17]

The first order of business for the 2nd Marines was to secure positions around the initial target area, the islands adjacent to Tulagi, Florida, Gavutu, and Tanambogo. This accomplished, the lead team of 2nd Marines was to head for Florida Island, code-named RUNABOUT. D-day opened with an overcast sky of low cumulus clouds and a slight mist—a gift to the Allies, for it kept the enemy's Mavis flying boats moored at Gavutu, preventing them from carrying out their daily reconnaissance missions. Had the Japanese ever sighted the expedition, especially at the start or finish of the operation, the outcome might have been entirely different. At midnight that day the carriers *Saratoga, Enterprise,* and *Wasp* would arrive just south of Guadalcanal Island.

Task Force 62, the amphibious force was commanded by Rear Adm. Richard K. Turner; it included the Fleet Marine Force formations of six heavy cruisers, two light cruisers, fifteen destroyers, thirteen attack transports, six attack cargo ships, four destroyer transports, and five minesweepers.[18] Turner divided his forces into eight groups: Transport Group X (X-Ray), Transport Group Y (Yoke), the Guadalcanal Fire Support Group, the Tulagi Fire Support Group, the Minesweeper Group, the Screening Group, the Air Support Group, and the Landing Force Group, which consisted of the 1st Marine Division reinforced. Transport Group X, assigned to the Guadalcanal landing, consisted of four transport divisions. Two of the divisions were each composed of three transports and one cargo ship; the third, of two transports and one cargo ship; and the fourth, of one transport and three cargo ships. Transport Group Y, assigned to the landings in the Tulagi area, consisted of two transport divisions—one made up of four transports and the other made up of four destroyers previously converted to troop transports (APAs). Four more ships, the *Zellin* and the *Betelgeuse* (AK 28) and their escorting destroyers, transported the 3rd Defense Battalion from Pearl Harbor.[19]

The Guadalcanal Fire Support Group consisted of three fire sections composed of one heavy cruiser, and two sections of two destroyers each. The Tulagi Fire Support Group consisted of one light antiaircraft cruiser and two destroyers, plus five minesweepers in the Minesweeper Group. The Screening Group consisted of three Australian cruisers, one U.S. heavy cruiser, nine destroyers, two fighter squadrons based on aircraft carriers but detached to the Screening Group on D-day, and eight observation seaplanes on the cruisers. The Air Support Group was made up of one fighter and one dive-bomber squadron, plus one additional fighter and one additional dive-bomber squadron for the initial mission, all drawn from the carriers.

The men of the 2nd Marine Regiment would have the honor of being the first members of their brotherhood to land on Solomons soil. The 1st Battalion, 2nd Marines (1/2) inaugurated Plan U by assigning three companies to land on one island at two different points where they would be in a position to protect their comrades engaging the enemy on Tulagi and Gavutu. The battalion was to be split for the Florida Island landing, with Company B making the landing at Haleta and Companies A and C going ashore on the Halavo peninsula. The battalion was briefed that it was to remain on Florida no longer than thirty-six hours; if all went according to plan, the 2nd Marine Regiment would be reembark for the APRICOT operation at Ndeni (the recon party was still on Trevanion Island). At this stage, the 1st Battalion, 2nd Marines would be either a reserve for the operations in the Tulagi area or the primary invasion force at Ndeni.

While the initial assignment of the 1st Battalion, 2nd Marines, on Florida was to protect the Tulagi–Gavutu flanks, the 3rd Battalion, 2nd Marines, remained in reserve at sea. The 1st Raider Battalion was to assault Tulagi Island with the 2nd Battalion, 5th Marines, and an artillery detachment from the 11th Marines. Four hours after the Raiders were ashore, the 1st Parachute Battalion would hit the beach on Gavutu, some two miles away.

At dawn on 7 August, the reinforced 2nd Marine Regiment was poised to wrest the first Solomon Islands foothold back from Japan. On D-day, at 0613, the morning was clear and the usual rainfall missing. The project was feasible only in the absence of effective opposition from the Imperial Navy. The former San Diego marines were now on their way to destiny, an apprehensive group of young untried "mud marines" mixed with a few "old China hands," plus a couple of marines who had been in "the war to end all wars" over a quarter of a century earlier. Some were so green as to be called "molded" marines—they were told simply to obey orders; and some in the landing crafts were mustangs, who at one time were elbow to elbow with the enlisted men. There were second lieutenant "shavetails" and other reserve officers called up for active duty, plus a few aged regulars who had been around from the old 1st or 2nd Brigades.

But few on that day in 1942 knew jungle warfare in any form, nor about war in the tropics. They held only vague notions of the enemy and the composition of their target, and until final details were provided as to the locations of the landings, the target name was given merely as HOCOMPOCUMBOLIO, something dreamed up by one of the briefing officers.20 Before the day was over, the U.S. Marines, much to their surprise, would be running about seeking an unseen enemy. One marine with the intelligence section reported that they had been told they were going to attack Florida. His reaction: "What's Florida?"

6 The Early Air War

From May through early August of 1942 the air war in the Solomon Islands centered on a bombing campaign by RAAF Catalinas and USAAF Flying Fortresses against Japanese positions on Tulagi and Guadalcanal. It was an exercise in waste. The crews had to fly hundreds of miles to reach their targets and were frequently hampered by unpredictable weather. In all, they dropped only a few hundred bombs; from a high altitude, most missed their targets. The Allies paid a significant price, for there is no doubt that more Allied airmen lost their lives in this endeavor than did the Japanese.

Bombing and Reconnaissance

The military significance of the southern Solomons was not appreciated until after the Kure 3rd SNLF invaded Tulagi on 3 May. Flight Engineer Jack Riddell recalled: "Even through the haze we could see our old RAAF base the Japs had occupied and wished that we bothered them as much as they troubled us in the 60 raids they made on our AOB."[1] On 17 May, a B-17 from the Port Moresby-based USAAF 19th Bombardment Group flew a daylight mission to photograph Japanese-held Tulagi, and on the 29th the peaceful nights of the sea infantrymen changed. The RAAF Catalinas had added Tulagi, Gavutu, Tanambogo, and diminutive Makambo to their target list. That day they were able to dispatch five Cats for operations in the Solomons loaded with either sixteen 250-pound bombs or eight 500-pounders—aircraft from Havannah Harbor on Efate Island in the New Hebrides, from Nouméa on New Caledonia, and from Bowen Air Base at Queensland, Australia.

Unless they were being bombed by a B-17 flying at 14,000 feet, the Japanese generally could identify which aircraft was overhead by the sound of its engines. The Flying Fortress, with its four Wright Cyclone engines, had a roar like no other airplane; the Catalina, which was equipped with two Pratt and Whitney fourteen-cylinder power plants, had a different sound. Just after noon on 13 June, Guadalcanal coastwatcher Martin

Clemens heard a large plane pass over his station: "The sound of its engines was new to us; we began to hope that it was a B-17.... We heard bombs being dropped in Tulagi, and then the plane, in the distance, returning to the south."[2] Three days later, another aircraft created a flurry among Clemens and his crew:

> At 1100 a Flying Fortress, returning from Tulagi, flew directly over the station.... She really impressed the locals.... Forty minutes later she was still majestically cruising about ... when the hum of a Kawanisi [*sic*] was heard. Excitement grew at the prospect of an aerial battle ... The Kawanisi suddenly banked to port, turned ..., and shot upward into the clouds.... "Our" plane appeared to see it; she came roaring in from the seaward and ... sailed over.... The Fortress appeared tremendous, and as she swung back out to sea the air was filled with leaves sucked off the top of the trees. Then she flew round several times in a wide circle; while she was over Nggela we could hear the Kawanisi ... "treading air" in the cloud. Just after 1200 the B-17 gave up the game and flew off.... About five minutes later the Kawanisi sneaked out of the cloud and, after a cautious look around, chuffed off sheepishly toward Tulagi; he must have been quite scared.... The Fortress was cheered to the echo every time she went over the station.[3]

In his diary, SME Tomisaburo Hirai, of the 5th Platoon, 3rd Company, Kure 3rd SNLF, kept a more accountant-like record of the bombings of Tulagi and Gavutu and of the damage they inflicted. On 28 May, Hirai recorded a bombing "at 1935—four men slightly wounded." On 29 June: "2130 dropped three bombs on Tulagi, and hit the coast; 10 feet from shelter yet most hit the sea." On 6 July: "At 1445 suddenly someone shouted *'Ku-shu keihoh'* [air-raid]. They dropped five bombs on the *Azumasan Maru* about 150 meters distance—no damage and flew off."[4]

Sometimes the Japanese counterattacked these raids, sometimes not. On 7 July, Hirai had recorded: "0400 raid on Guadalcanal, no Zero counterattacked." On 10 July, however, he noted: "1120 a B-17 was hit and downed by a Zero." Hirai's reports of the results of the engagements are hauntingly terse: "1200 two Zeroes took off; at 1300 only one returned"; "1030 two B-17s, four Zeroes took off, three Zeroes [Type A6M-2, Zero floatplanes—Rufes] returned."[5] After a bombing raid on 29 July, Capt. Kanae Monzen, the Guadalcanal base commander and CO of the 11th CU, reported that one sailor-fireman, Kenkichi Shishikura, was injured at 0430 on Tulagi and later died. The cause of death was listed as *Tobu-bakudan-hahen-so* [appears to be bomb fragment to the head].[6] The Japanese reported few casualties.

Another danger to Allied bombers in addition to the Zeroes was friendly fire, as RAAF Capt. Mike Seymour and copilot Sgt. Jack Brammel of No. 11 Squadron discovered on 27 June while returning from a bombing mission in Catalina A24–17: "The morning of June 25 we flew to *Nouméa,* where we refueled, armed and departed that afternoon for Tulagi—a seventeen hour round trip involving a midnight attack—and returned to Havannah Harbor about 0800 hours the following morning. The raid was successful. Fires were seen burning as we left. The return . . . was without incident until, with the harbor in sight and on descent about ten miles out, we were attacked by an American Wildcat aircraft [from VMF-212] from a nearby fighter base [Bauer Field]. This aircraft . . . was flying a standard patrol north of Havannah Harbor. . . . It had not been informed of our presence and [had] sighted from above a large camouflaged aircraft approaching the flying boat base with red roundels on its wings. . . . We were subjected to three diving attacks from vertically overhead. . . . Most of the 50 caliber rounds passed us, but there were some hits on each pass. Both fuel tanks were holed, the port aileron was shot away, the hull was holed in seven or eight places and the wings in about twenty. . . ."[7]

The attack finally was broken off when Captain Seymour did not return fire—though his crew certainly wanted to! He lowered the floats, rocked his wings, and gave the recognition signal on an aldis lamp. His Cat was subsequently patched up and flown to *Nouméa,* where final repairs were made by the seaplane tender *Curtiss.* Seymour flew A24–17 back to Havannah Harbor on 3 July, rearmed, and again struck Tulagi en route to the home base at Bowen. How a U.S. fighter pilot could confuse an RAAF Catalina (whose configuration was identical to that of a U.S. Navy PBY) with a Japanese Kawanishi H6K seaplane is difficult to comprehend. Happily, Seymour and his men lived to tell the tale.[8]

The Allied planes were not just bombing, however; they were also carrying out reconnaissance photography, including flights on 29 May and 23 July. In fact, this reconnaissance work would be perhaps the greatest contribution of the B-17s that later joined the bombing missions.[9]

At about this time, the U.S. Navy entered into the bombing of the southern Solomon Islands when three PBYs from Patrol Squadron 71 (71-P-10, 71-P-11, and 71-P-12) departed *Nouméa* Harbor at 2320 on 29 May 1942. Approaching Gavutu at about 12,000 feet, the PBYs made a normal bombing run, dropping twelve 500-pound "eggs" on the target area. After releasing their load, they climbed to 20,000 feet and headed back to Nouméa. They ran into a storm there, however, and trouble began. As the dark clouds descended, the PBYs continued as a trio for a short period; the trio became a pair, then finally each plane was on its own. Somehow they could not raise anyone on the radio, and thus they flew until they were almost out of fuel. PBYs 71-P-10 and 71-P-11 landed at sea amid seven- to eight-foot waves, but "Lady Luck" was on board, for they at last were able to transmit their approximate location with their Mayday distress signal before heading to the waves below. At dawn, sister aircraft 71-P-1 arrived and maintained a vigil over the downed PBYs. She was later relieved by 71-P-7, which flew cover during the night. The crews were rescued thirty hours later by the destroyer *Meredith* (DD 726). PBY 71-P-11 could not be salvaged, and the *Meredith* had to sink her; however, 71-P-12 reached Mare Island in the Loyalty Islands, part of the New Caledonia colony.

The PBYs claimed to have inflicted significant damage. VP-71's squadron intelligence report noted: "Gavutu damaged. Results: Large fires in vicinity of docks and buildings (estimated). Many oil tanks and buildings destroyed, and if any ships present, they were at least damaged."[10] Seaman Hirai, however, reported less damage: "Warehouse burned where we stored the 'Churchill' clothes, plus furniture, I stayed 45 minutes, burned till the next day."[11] The "Churchill clothes" belonged to the former residents of Tulagi Island. The Kure 3rd sailors had cleaned out all the houses for use as their barracks and had placed clothing and furniture in a vacant local building. When the PBYs hit the storage area, the accumulated pile was set afire, and belched black smoke as it burned.

The Unrelenting Allies

If ever there was a "tried, tired, and taxed" air group in the U.S. Army Air Forces, it was the SWPA-based 19th Bombardment Group (14th, 28th, 30th, 93rd, and 435th Bombardment Squadrons). As part of the Far East Air Force (FEAF), this group had fought its way all through the Philippines with wearied B-17s and spent weeks on Java at a forward airfield trying to forestall the Japanese Imperial Army. It continued to bomb the Japanese on dozens of islands. On 5 February 1942, the FEAF was renamed the Fifth Air Force, and its aircraft, though not in great condition, continued to hammer the enemy whenever a mission was ordered.

In May, B-17s from the 435th Bombardment Squadron initiated attacks against Tulagi and the other small islands in Tulagi Harbor. On 15 July, the 19th Bomb Group (BG) was designated as the Mobile Air Task Force for the Southwest Pacific, which included the British Solomon Islands. At the same time, the Hawaii-based 7th Air Force was named as the Air Task Force for the Central Pacific area. The B-17s of the 19th BG, along with the PBYs of VP-71 and the RAAF Cats, formed the backbone of the Allied air strike forces in the southern Solomons until late July, when the USAAF 11th BG assumed the responsibility for the bombing of Guadalcanal and the satellite islands.

The air strikes against the southern Solomons were being carried out principally by the command from Australia — the U.S. SWPA group, including the RAAF. Occasionally U.S. Navy PBYs from the patrol squadron base at Ile Nou, New Caledonia, were involved. To remove jurisdictional uncertainties between the Southwest (SWPA) and South Pacific (SOPAC) areas, the boundary lines were moved westward to the 159th meridian as of 1 August. This placed all of the southern Solomons under the direct control of the South Pacific commander (COMSOPAC) at *Nouméa*.

To support the bombing effort and prepare for Operation WATCH-TOWER, the 11th Bombardment Group moved from its home base in Hawaii to the South Pacific, with the air echelons staging down in their planes and the rear echelons following by ship. The 431st Bombardment Squadron went to Nandi, Fiji. Other elements went to the New Hebrides: part of 11th BG Headquarters and the 98th Bombardment Squadron to Espiritu Santo, the remainder of 11th BG Headquarters and the 26th Bombardment Squadron to Efate. On 22 July, the 42nd and 69th Bombardment Squadrons reached Plaines des Gaiacs, New Caledonia. The 11th Bomb Group's ground echelon reached Suva, Fiji, on 2 August and arrived at Efate Island three days later.[12]

The airfield nearest to Guadalcanal, 558 miles to the southeast, was a primitive landing strip at Espiritu Santo, New Hebrides. The island lies on a north–south axis and is about seventy-five miles long and seventy-five miles wide, with its main portion and two peninsulas extending northward, one on each side. A new 4,500-foot airstrip was to be hacked out of raw jungle and felled coconut groves, with a completion deadline of 29 July 1942. Through back-breaking manpower under the most primitive conditions, the enlarged makeshift airfield was finished on time; downed coconut trees and stumps lined the edge of the 200-foot-wide strip. The overriding problem, however, was servicing the aircraft with the several thousand gallons of avgas required to fill the tanks of one B-17.

The 11th BG had brought with them to the South Pacific a few essential crew chiefs and a couple mechanics, but the B-17s were plagued by engine failures. The Espiritu Santo base involved inescapable drudgery, and flying to a target area was worse. Between Espiritu Santo and Guadalcanal Island the 11th BG was forced to fly above 17,000 feet to get over the muddy cloud cover. Some flew at lower altitudes below the clouds, risking a downdraft that could toss a B-17 into the sea. The magnificent group of airmen survived endless hardships and faced countless challenges, yet they received little credit for their effort. Some of the history of the 11th BG was recounted by the group's commander, Col. LaVerne G. "Blondie" Saunders:

> I got the 11th, in January of 1942. . . . I had no information on any of the islands down there or what their background was. . . . We had to just go with our airplanes and a few administration people and a few mechanics. Our ground echelon didn't get down. . . . I got hold of Admiral McCain [at *Nouméa*] and asked him, "What am I going to do with bases?" [He said,]
> "Well, you go up to Vila Field on Efate, see what they can do there." . . . I looked at the map and I got in [a B-17] and flew it up there. . . . The airstrip was . . . a single strip. He said there was a Marine Fighter Squadron; this major came out and I told him who I was and that Admiral McCain had sent me. . . . "I want to see if I can get a squadron up here . . . nine B-17s, but we have no ground equipment, . . . just air crews." [He responded,] . . . "Well, let's take a look." He . . . had tentage but he said, "We couldn't feed everybody at once. . . ." [I told him,] . . . "Well we can stagger them . . ." [and] I went back . . . and told Admiral McCain; I said, "How about the rest of them? He said, "Well, Espiritu Santo [is] about 150 miles north of Efate, why don't you go up there and see what's happening? There's a naval detachment, a construction detachment and a little company of army engineers; see what they have." . . . I took a B-17 with two bomb bay tanks in it and went up and I circled the field. They had a strip down there. . . . They'd knocked the coconut trees down; it was all coral of course. I landed and taxied up in a little place they had chewed out there and I told them what my problem was and they said,

"Well we have nothing up here. There's no gasoline, no bombs, no service, no nothing."[13]

Saunders had flown from Efate to Espiritu Santo in a B-17F piloted by Maj. Allan J. Sewart, CO of the 26th Bomb Squadron. The field where Sewart set his plane down was just a plain expanse on that sweltering day, 30 July. No Army Air Forces veteran who served on Santo in late 1942 would have called this incomplete, primitive, unfinished landing area an airstrip. It was surrounded by dense green jungle, populated by coal-black people who as recently as the turn of the century had enjoyed eating "long pig."[14]

The Espiritu Santo Airstrip

The story of Espiritu Santo (BUTTON) began on 27 April 1942 when a Grumman JF2–5 (Duck) piloted by Marine Sergeant Wolley from Efate landed in Segond Channel, Espiritu Santo Island, with Brig. Gen. William R. Rose, USA. Rose commanded the Efate Detachment (Detachment A) of Army Task Force (ATF) 6814. He had been on New Caledonia, but Maj. Gen. Alexander M. Patch Jr, commander of ATF 6814, did not want another buck general around, so he shipped Rose off to the New Hebrides.[15] His assignment was to canvas the Lugainville area of Santo as a possible site for an airstrip.

Espiritu Santo is the largest island in the New Hebrides, and the remaining European settlers were concentrated in the south and east, adjacent to Segond Channel. Lugainville was a simple government outpost, with a Catholic mission station and hospital and a handful of European and Chinese stores. At the suggestion of Burns Philp's branch manager on Efate, General Rose met with Tom Harris, the manager of the BP store on Espiritu Santo. Apparently they discussed the possibility of arranging a site for a future airstrip. The company had been doing business in the New Hebrides before 1900, and the BP people knew all the locales.

General Rose returned on 12 May and Harris introduced the general to Pascal Michel, a plantation operator at the time. Michel, Harris, and Rose visited some sites, one of which was the Bencoula Plantation at Pallikulo, then operated by Michel under lease from its owners, Société des Iles du Pacificque, whose headquarters were at *Nouméa*. Two days later, three officers visited the Bencoula site: Lt. Kenneth Tonking, of the Royal Australian Navy, and two Americans, one of whom was Army Capt. Ritchie Garrison, assistant intelligence officer (G-2) at Efate (III

Island Command). As they looked over the Bencoula location, the first naval station essentially was established on Espiritu Santo when two Kingfishers (OS2U-3) piloted by Ens. Roger S. C. Walcott, USNR, and Ens. Raymond N. Traynor, USNR, of VS-5-D14 flew from Efate and anchored in Segond Channel near Alhena Landing. The pilots' barracks were to be in Tom Harris's house.[16]

An interesting reminiscence was provided by Dr. Arthur G. King, who was with the medical section of Army Task Force 6814 that flew from Nouméa to Espiritu Santo: "My first visit to Santo was in June 1942 . . . with several other staff officers to inspect the situation. . . . A battered PBY-4 flew us in, and I was seated in the starboard machine [-]gun blister, getting sicker by the minute. We landed in a pouring rain and my first view of the island was a shack near the water to which we ran for shelter. To the right of it was a heap of old whiskey bottles (at least 150 I would estimate). A grizzled, unkempt but actually pleasant man who introduced himself as Tom Harris . . . greeted us. All that was missing was Sadie Thompson to complete the perfect tableau of the South Pacific."[17]

On 28 June, General Rose's Detachment A (ATF 6814), along with nine VS-5-D14 air maintenance men, had arrived at Segond Channel on board the New Zealand warship *Leander,* escorted by three destroyers. U.S. Army Detachment A consisted of members of Companies L and M, 182nd Infantry Regiment; part of Headquarters Company, 3rd Battalion, 182nd Infantry; Company B, 57th Engineer Combat Battalion (Lt. H. V. Eliott); and a small medical unit from the 182nd Infantry.[18]

On 1 July, a lease was initiated and signed by representatives of the U.S. Army, the owners of Bencoula Plantation, and Pascal Michel, the leaseholder. The property involved 1,700 hectares (approximately 4,200 acres), including 85 hectares (210 acres) of coconut trees and 67 hectares (166 acres) of cocoa trees; the balance was raw jungle. The United States secured three leases for a monthly rental of $1,400.[19]

Five days later, on 6 July, three officers — Lt. H. V. Eliott, USA, 57th Combat Engineers; Maj. Harold W. Bauer, USMC, CO, VMF-212; Lt. Samuel Mathis, 3rd Detachment, 1st Naval Construction Battalion (NCB) — informed Michel that they soon would begin cutting nine lines of coconut, thirty feet between each. Lieutenant Mathis, with construction experience, had been appointed foreman for the Santo airstrip. On 7 July, marking of boundary lines started and surveying continued until the next day when the Santo islanders saw their first bulldozers being unloaded at Pallikulo Bay.

On 10 July, the workforce included Detachment A (ATF 6814); fifty men from the 3rd Detachment, 1st NCB; thirty-seven men from the 57th Engineer Combat Battalion (USA); and five officers and 145 engineers from the Efate-based 4th Marine Defense Battalion. In addition, about four hundred islanders were recruited from Malekula. The airstrip was to have an overall length of 4,500 feet. While the bulldozer was knocking down coconut trees, one little native boy could not contain his excitement. He danced around trying to explain to everybody: "Big fella moto killem coconut. Coconut done finish." Former Pvt. Joseph B. Chin, 182nd Infantry, recalled: "The landing field above Wrights Ranch [Pallikulo] was first started by L and M Companies along with the engineers. We cut down the coconut trees by hand and with native labor moved them aside. Then later the CBs [Construction Battalion] came in with their heavy equipment to finish the landing strip."[20]

Through stamina and determination the composite force completed the arduous task by 28 July, a day ahead of schedule. But the airstrip construction project was not without problems. If it was not the adverse weather, it was the problematic native workforce. And everything was primitive. One airman reported that the runways were soft and often flooded. For night or early morning liftoffs to bomb Guadalcanal, the end of the airstrip was indicated by truck headlights; and both sides of the strip were marked off with cans and bottles stuffed with gasoline-soaked rags set ablaze. On the day the work was completed, an AT-6 Texan aircraft from Efate, piloted by Major Bauer with General Rose on board, was the first plane to land on the strip. (Later, Bauer would be awarded a posthumous Medal of Honor for air action on Guadalcanal.)

The days immediately following the 28th were hectic; bombs and gasoline had to be obtained in order to continue the assignment. But the initial planning and construction work had been a success; the 11th BG now had a landing space that was the closest base to the target area. The group had six B-17s stationed on Espiritu Santo, and though there were no accommodations for the airmen, they slept under the aircraft, along with the island's voracious mosquitoes. Coordinating the B-17s from four different airfields hundreds of miles apart in order to launch an attack on Guadalcanal would be a demanding task. The islanders— much like those earlier on Guadalcanal, as reported by Martin Clemens—were astonished when they saw their first Flying Fortress. For a long time they just stood around gaping and staring, then they edged a little closer, finally touching the enormous bird. But after a few weeks they lost interest and would hardly look up when one landed.[21]

On 4 August the government-contracted transport *Nora Luckenback* arrived at Santo, carrying 3,000 barrels of avgas and 160 drums of aviation lubrication oil. The ship did not unload; instead, she headed for Efate Island on 7 August, arriving on the 8th. Limited quantities of avgas were stored in the Burns Philp warehouse at Port Vila on Efate, brought there in brilliant red fifty-five-gallon drums aboard small inter-island vessels owned by the native inhabitants. About fifty yards offshore the drums would be heaved over the side of the vessels; the islanders would push them ahead as they swam them to shore, then roll them up to the beach.

The B-17's gas tanks had to be filled by hand. One crew, anxious to get into combat, filled the big reservoirs by "bucket brigade" swinging five-gallon fills from ground to wing. Later, a few hand-held Billy pumps were borrowed from the Navy, but it still was a difficult job. Each Fort took no fewer than thirty to thirty-five drums of fuel. It could take a day to top off by hand one of these "gas eaters."[22]

The B-17s Strike

From late May to late July, RAAF Cats flying from Australia via Port Moresby had carried out air strikes on the Tulagi–Gavutu area, though the attacks, from altitudes of about 10,000 feet and with small bomb loads, caused only minor damage. At the end of July, the 11th Bombardment Group—called the "Blondie Bombers" after their commander, Colonel "Blondie" Saunders—became the principal heavy bomber component for the South Pacific. On 31 July, nine B-17s of the 26th Bombardment Squadron from Bauer Field, Efate Island, augmented by the Santo-based B-17s, struck destination target Guadalcanal (code-named ORANGE airfield by Allied planners). The flight, led by Colonel Saunders, was under the cover of inclement weather. The B-17s spray-bombed the shadowy island with 100- and 500-pound bombs from an altitude of 14,000 feet. "Resistance was slight, the AA ineffective, and the Zeros (Rufes) at Gavutu, probably without functioning radar, failed to leave the water in time for interception. The bombers came through Mission One against Guadalcanal undamaged."[23]

On the ground at Guadalcanal, CPO Yasuo Yamamiya, who was assigned to the headquarters of the 11th Construction Unit and was a close associate of the commanding officer, Captain Monzen, recorded the results of the bombing in his diary: "Heard whirl, an air raid, felt the vaguely uncanny sound of dropping bombs, just for a moment, very clear. . . . Lay flat on the ground, exploded with a pillar of fire, hit the storehouse, the former headquarters building, two laborers were killed and two or three men were seriously wounded; regretfully, grind my teeth with annoyance. Yesterday we had just completed a telephone line between Headquarters, the garage and community kitchen, now some lines were torn up. . . . KIA were a civilian attached to the Navy, Mr. Kenkichi Shishikura, and another; we buried them in an area surrounded by coconut trees [Lever's Plantations]. Platoon Leader WO Sashihata who said 'Present Arms' led a burial service; let us pray for their souls We would meet everybody in the home of Kudan."[24]

On 1 August another raid occurred. Ten B-17s of the 11th BG struck Japanese bases near Tulagi, destroying one patrol plane and damaging another. The bombing ignited fires in the Tulagi Golf Club building, and four 500-pounders were dropped on the Lunga airstrip. Two Zero floatplane fighters attempting to intercept were shot down. Yamamiya noted: "0900 enemy planes attack while flying over our head, then they drop about 30 bombs, hit the former headquarters and the coast outpost; two men wounded. Afternoon, again another air raid but heard some firing from Tulagi, but results remain unknown. In the night it was quiet, maybe enemy enjoy a dance on Saturday night."[25] Similar attacks were made through 5 August; there was no raid on the 6th.

Judging by the small number of bombs dropped, it appears that most of the B-17s did not find their mark, possibly because Tulagi–Guadalcanal was such a small target area. There could not have been heavy antiaircraft fire, because Lieutenant Endo's 81st Guard Unit on Guadalcanal did not have experienced gunners and not all their guns were operational.[26] In a letter dated 1 August, PO Tada Kuni of the 81st GU had turned aside from what he could not talk about for security reasons—the war itself—to tell a correspondent back in Tokyo about the coconuts, cannibals, and crocodiles. However, SM Shizuko Takahashi, Security Force, 11th CU, vividly described his feelings of helplessness in the face of the bombings:

> This time I think it is truly hopeless when I watch them over
> our head. Our forces are shooting more and more at the enemy.
> However, not one bullet seems to hit anything. The enemy circles
> around calmly over our heads and drops the bombs. If our planes
> appear the enemy will immediately flee. Thus, I hope the com-
> bat planes arrive here as soon as possible. It is very regrettable
> because we do not have any weapons for fighting against the air.
> Thus, the only thing we can do is hide. The time they usually ap-

pear is around 0910 to 0930. I wonder if there is a good method of preventing it? Four [enemy] planes assaulted us at 0900. No casualties. Five enemy planes dropped approximately 20 bombs at 1100. Around 1200 there was an air assault for the 3rd time. However, there were no losses. . . . Approximately 20 bombs were dropped in the vicinity of our tent, but fortunately there was no damage. I do not feel as though I'm alive for hiding out. Our combat planes cannot get close to the enemy Flying Fortresses. It is very regrettable; however, the only option is for us to flee from being killed.[27]

SM Norio Ogihara, Command Platoon, 3rd Company, Kure 3rd SNLF, reported: "American reconnaissance planes appeared over Tulagi two or three times a week. Bombings most commonly took place during the day between 11 and 12 in the morning. From July 31 through August 5 Tulagi was bombed every day. My platoon took shelter, but one man of their number who was on observation watch was killed. The bombs damaged the motor park north of the underpass, hit the cook shack, and struck an ammunition dump near the parade grounds. . . ."[28]

Back at Pallikulo Field on Espiritu Santo, Colonel Saunders was unhappy with the bombing results of the 11th Group on Guadalcanal. He thought the famed secret Norden bombsights were off-kilter and wanted them adjusted. He asked the engineering officer, Lieutenant Eliott, to have his men construct a perfectly flat five- by seven-foot concrete slab next to the airstrip so that the ordnance specialists could adjust the bombsight. Whenever one was out of its fittings, armed guards were posted. The adjustments, however, did not help. Although subsequent bombing caused some damage to the Guadalcanal airfield, the results were far less than expected. Yasuo Yamamiya's diary notes: "Even though three enemy planes assaulted at 0900, the bombs only dropped at the working place and barely missed the runway and hangar. However, there was no damage. Even the accurate enemy fortunately did not drop bombs in the vicinity of our tents, thus everybody was overjoyed at being safe."[29]

That day, 4 August, was ill-fated for B-17 41–9218 from the 26th Bomb Squadron and for 1st Lt. Rush E. McDonald and his crew. They were on the third raid, which took place between 1030 and 1200. The three B-17s were flying fast from the northwest over Tulagi and Gavutu at between 16,000 and 19,000 feet. All their bombs had found nothing but the ocean. Seven Type 2 Zero-Sen float fighters from Florida Island, led by Lt. Cdr. Riichiro Sato, attacked the three B-17s with 20-mm cannon and 7.7-mm gunfire, apparently with little effect. Then one floatplane, flown by nineteen-year-old NAP1c Shigeto Kobayashi, singled out Lieutenant McDonald's Flying Fortress; he attacked from the rear to the upper right side and rammed it. The disabled Fort began pouring out white smoke, then black. The Japanese on the ground knew the Fortress was in trouble, and their own pilot surely lost. The remaining two B-17s flew off and six remaining Zero-Sen returned to Halavo.[30] The security boat from Tulagi took off and raced to the spot where the Zero was last seen, but they found mere bits of the plane. The only things recovered from McDonald's B-17 were a helmet, a chest jacket, and a piece of clothing.

Participating in that raid was 2nd Lt. Jack Lee, USAAF.

> Spent the night at Espiritu Santo then took off at daylight to bomb Tulagi. McDonald and Heard [John A. Heard Jr.] had damaged #4 prop the night before on a barrel near the runway. Our three ships took off. Mc and Heard were to turn back if the engine vibrated. Over Tulagi there were seven float type Zeros waiting for us. They worked around for a frontal attack and made their first try before we started our bomb run. Two of the first group of the three . . . dived and cut loose with their guns in turn. The third was killed in his dive by the top turret gunner. He came between us in the lead ship and McDonald on our right wing. He was in a vertical bank and his top or right wing hit [McDonald's] ship between the two left hand engines. The Zero exploded and blew the wing off the B-17. I turned in my seat to watch the Zero as it went by and saw the crash. There was a terrific flame from the burning gasoline. The 17 turned on its side with the stub up then nosed down and fell out of sight. The gunner said that four Zeros were shot down. They continued to make passes as we dropped our bombs and turned down to the coast of Guadalcanal toward home. A very tough day.[31]

An interesting turn of events was discovered to have occurred on 5 August 1942. Captured Japanese documents show that the Gavutu Detachment of the Japanese 14th Construction Unit had noted they had captured two fliers that day—crewmen. However, nothing further is known. These documents had long been misfiled at the National Archives, placed erroneously in the translated Japanese records regarding Attu and Kiska in the Aleutian Islands.[32]

On 5 August, SM Shizuko Takahashi with the 11th CU recorded: "Three enemy planes assaulted at 0930; three enemy planes assaulted at 1040. Few losses were received at petroleum depot, working place, etc. [the airfield]. Black smoke was rising from the petroleum of the guard unit that was hit by enemy bombs. This is a fearful sight. We were bombed constantly from 0930 to 1400." On 6 August, he reported, "No attacks." It would be the lull before the storm. SM Norio Ogihara, in his POW interrogation report, stated: "That evening, though nothing was said about it among the men, [I] felt for the first time that the Americans were coming."[33]

In support of Operation WATCHTOWER on D-day, 7 August, the B-17s of the 11th Bombardment Group had a number of their aircraft carrying out reconnaissance flights to scan the area for any signs of Japanese forces. Early that morning, the B-17s of the 431st Bombardment Squadron flew from Nandi, Fiji, to Efate, where they refueled, then were airborne for Guadalcanal. Maj. Marion N. Pharr, USAAF, commanding officer of the 431st, piloted one plane. His crew included Lieutenant Pate, copilot; Lieutenant Warren, navigator; Lieutenant Lehr, bombardier; Staff Sergeant McKee, engineer; Sergeant Rogers, gunner; Technician Sergeant Hendrix, radio operator; Staff Sergeant Winey, radar; Technician Sergeant Nelbach, aircraft chief; and Private 1st Class Decker, tail gunner. Pharr's Fortress, a B-17E, is believed to have been shot down by friendly fire, possibly having been mistaken for a four-engine Japanese flying boat. A tail gunner on another B-17 reported hearing, "We're hit! We're going in!" That was the last message from Pharr's craft; it was never found. Pharr and his crew were the first members of the U.S. Army to lose their lives in the Guadalcanal campaign.[34]

Between 31 July and 6 August 1942 the 11th BG flew fifty-six bombing missions and twenty-three reconnaissance sorties over the Tulagi–Guadalcanal area, losing one Flying Fortress. Pharr's plane was lost on D-day, 7 August, as were two others, due to mechanical problems or accidents.[35] By 8 August, Colonel Saunders, who had begun the Solomons air war with twenty-six B-17s, had lost fifteen percent of his strike force, a stiff price to pay for the 11th BG's participation in the early air campaign. In those earliest days of their missions in the Southwest Pacific, it seemed that the B-17s had better success in reconnaissance than in bombing. On bombing surface targets they had almost a zero record. Nevertheless, Colonel Saunders believed that "the ease of the landings at Guadalcanal and Tulagi was attributable to the destruction his planes had inflicted on the two areas and, conversely, that the heavy opposition encountered on Gavutu was due to the absence of preparatory air attacks." This evaluation, however, appears exaggerated. The 11th BG flew missions and bombed from 14,000 feet, causing minimal damage. "[General] Vandegrift's engineers found the runway on Guadalcanal in a damaged condition but not badly hurt and his troops captured an amazing supply of undamaged equipment useful for completing the field."[36]

When on 8 August the U.S. Marines had reached the Guadalcanal airstrip, they realized that all the bombing efforts by the Allied air force had made little difference. The base was almost intact.[37] One historian gave the following assessment of the bombing: "Far less satisfactory was the offensive work of the B-17s, which scored hits with less than 1 percent of their bombs. The reasons for this slender contribution acknowledged by the Army Air Forces historians included the limited number of planes overall, diversions for reconnaissance duties, small bombing formations, aircrew and maintenance crew shortages, adverse weather, inaccurate intelligence, and inadequate facilities. The inability of the Flying Fortress to hit or sink ships represented a profound doctrinal embarrassment to the Army Air Forces; but the B-17 squadrons made a signal contribution through their reconnaissance work."[38]

The extraordinary bombing efforts of the RAAF and the air units of the U.S. Navy and Army Air Forces under arduous conditions were not rewarded by the results. Japanese bases in the southern Solomons were not put out of commission; in fact, they were barely scratched, though the bombing did slow down Japanese construction of the Guadalcanal airstrip. The enemy should have been more alarmed by the increased bombing tempo of the Allies, a telltale sign that an invasion was imminent, but apparently the Japanese commanders on Guadalcanal did not heed the warning signs that X-day was beginning to unfold.

7   Day One, Guadalcanal

On Friday, 7 August 1942, the calculated risk of Operation WATCH-TOWER began. The weather that morning was overcast—low-hanging cumulus clouds mixed with a shallow mist. At dawn, a Curtiss SOC Seagull catapulted from the cruiser *Astoria,* then dropped a flare to signal the start of the attack. At 0614 a cascade of fire was expelled from the guns of the invasion fleet, led by the heavy cruisers HMAS *Australia* and *Quincy* (CA 39), bombarding the shoreline of BEACH RED, the area chosen for the Guadalcanal landings. The first step on the long road to Tokyo had been taken

The Beginnings of Hell

The 13th Construction Unit, whose workforce was Korean, was billeted around Kukum, not far from Lunga Point, on the north-central coast of Guadalcanal; the 11th Construction Unit was in the general area of the Lever's and Tenaru Plantations. The first Allied shell demolished the community kitchen building at Lunga. At about the same time, the Grumman F4F Wildcats of the *Saratoga* (U.S. Navy Squadron VF-5) and the *Enterprise* (U.S. Navy Squadron VF-6) strafed the beach, including the landing site. The stunned workers scrambled. Some ran for the nearest slit trenches; the rest, terrified, fled in all directions.[1]

PO2c Sankichi Kaneda of the 81st Guard Unit recalls:

> [On] 7 August was the beginning of Hell. In the darkness before dawn, the Landing Forces men and [the] construction units men who the night before had celebrated with *sake* the successful completion of the airfield, drinking and singing until midnight, were sunk in slumber. About 0330 [0630], I was awakened by the communication man on duty telling me that the Guadalcanal Defense Unit HQ had telephoned, "Tulagi is being bombed. Take warning!" I got right up and naked except for a loin cloth, went down to the beach to relieve myself, while urinating, look-

Figure 15. Principal geographic locations on the north coast of Guadalcanal Island (Courtesy Tom McLeod).

ing over toward Tulagi and saw a red-tinged cloud mixed with flames billowing up, gleaming off the water.

Then came a loud boom from the direction of the Defense Unit HQ and, shocked and horrified, I became aware of incoming naval shell fire, and I found myself instinctively running barefoot through clouds of sand and gunpowder smoke, jumping head-first into an air raid shelter. Quicker than [I] thought, the trench was full of men. . . . Everyone was saying, it's an enemy strike force and what if we get a direct hit? Like a turtle, I eased my head out of the trench to look around; smoke was rising from the roof of our hutment. It was beginning to burn. Our uniforms and equipment were in there. "What the hell, I'll be left naked!" I thought, and then I shouted, "Our weapons! Hurry or they'll burn." We rushed into the burning hutment and grabbed up armfuls of clothing, rugged shoes, helmets, swords and sidearms, canteens mess kits and first aid supplies, and dashed back to the air raid shelter. Shells bursts blasted fronds off coconut palms and others blew holes in the ground. I skirted the holes and reached headquarters. I found the building on fire. Behind the headquarters building was an uncompleted air raid shelter, nothing but a hole with no cover. In the hole was decoder Seaman Second Class (SM2c) Okumura and SM2c Takami.

In the faint light of dawn, the construction units had melted away as each man for himself grabbed up all the provisions he could carry and then each on his own scattered. . . . Some took

off before the enemy landed and fled to the east of the airfield.
Since they were heading toward the enemy, many were captured. . . . The fortunate ones were those who fled to the west
where they found coconut groves and adequate water and so
were able to survive.[2]

The deadly Allied barrage started at Lunga Point and to the west of
Kukum. Palm trees were slashed and debris flung in all directions. The
gasoline dump was set on fire, and the tent camp west of the Lunga River,
south of Kukum, had shrapnel holes the size of boulders. Salvos from
the *Australia*'s main battery struck between Lunga Point and the Tenaru
River, while the transport *George F. Elliot* (AP 13) fired her deck guns at
a supposed Japanese encampment. The heavy cruiser *Astoria* plastered
the area east of the Lunga River with her 8-inch guns; those of her sister
ship, the *Vincennes* (CA 44), blasted the coast east of BEACH RED
from Lengo village (Makile) to Tetere. The destroyers *Dewey*, *Hull* (DD
350), and *Ellet* (DD 398) peppered the eastern third of the beach with
their 5-inch "pea shooters," while the *Wilson* concentrated on the center.
The burning Japanese fuel dump sent up a cloud of black smoke so concentrated that the spotter planes could not see the targets. Fortunately
the special prize, the 2,600-foot airstrip, remained almost intact, though
a 196-foot stretch was still to be completed. Three aircraft hangars were
nearly untouched, and the fourth was only partially damaged. The pre-
landing barrage was lifted at 0907; it had smashed foliage, but killed
only a few of the Japanese.[3]

The big island, occupied by an unknown number of enemy troops,
was to be invaded by 11,349 men of the 1st Marine Division. The "ground
pounders" that boarded the waiting LCPs for the Guadalcanal landing
were hardly fresh troops—they had been holed up in cramped quarters
for days, some for weeks—but their adrenaline was flowing.[4]

Navy crewman Ray Whitaker was aboard the transport *Barnett*
(AP 11):

Just before dawn. We had a Roman Catholic lay person lead
everyone who desired to participate in Mass. He . . . apologized,
saying that it should have been done by a priest but [that] under
the circumstances, he was sure no one objected. After regular
chow the night before, we would have nothing to eat but sandwiches and coffee until the operation was over. There wasn't
much sleep that night. Lights went out. . . . I saw [Lt. Cdr. Joseph
G.] Pomeroy throw his four-cell flashlight at a Marine who was

lighting up a cigarette in the mess hall. Portholes were not covered. The only lights during a "darkened ship" are dim red lights [that illuminate] just enough area for one to see his own way.

The approach to the landing area was from the western side of the Solomon Islands, up to the northern tip of Guadalcanal. Then a swing was made east, southeast and finally south, passing between the northern tip of Guadalcanal on our right and Savo Island on the left. . . . General Quarters was sounded a couple of hours before dawn. Everything was proceeding smoothly and quietly. Dawn was breaking in the east. The silence was broken with gunfire forward of the *Barnett* [crew members called the *Barnett* the "Barney Maru"]. One of the line warships had fired on a small boat or ship of some sort, setting it on fire and sinking it. One group of ships with the screening force had broken off and moved to the Tulagi side. About 0600 a line of cruisers and destroyers commenced bombarding the shoreline at "Lunga Point" . . . , as well as nearby shorelines on both sides. This went on for probably an hour. In the meantime, the landing boats were lowered, heavy rope netting was dropped over both sides . . . to the landing craft, and finally the Marines climbed down. They left behind a huge pile of heavy shoes on the ship's fantail. I suppose they figured one pair would be all they would need.[5]

BEACH RED had a surprise for the landing force: there was no enemy resistance. Captain Patterson's Company K, 3/5, landed at Alligator Creek to the east of BEACH RED, and the young marines first ashore immediately had fallen prone onto the sandy shore, pointing their 1903-vintage Springfield rifles at the expected enemy. They met none. The only unfriendly obstacle facing the invaders was an abandoned Type 88 antiaircraft gun pointed seaward. The Americans then began their pass through the undergrowth and dense jungle where the only noises they heard were their landing craft pulling away and the occasional screeching of an unfamiliar bird.[6] They quickly recognized that this was not a tropical paradise, but a hot, humid hell-hole.

The marines were somewhat stunned that the Japanese did not greet them with blistering fire. Cpl. Ore J. Marion (L/3/5) was in the first wave ashore. He wrote: "My Sergeant [Henry Klemicki] said, 'Go.' He went over the gunwale and I followed."[7] Marion manned one of the two old Lewis machine guns, which he began firing about 600 yards out from BEACH RED; he halted his fire within 100 yards of land, just as the

boat started scraping the gravel. The man with the dubious honor of being the first marine to set foot on "Hot Acres" was PFC James A. Snodgrass, Company K, 3/5. Later, Snodgrass was accidentally shot through
the heart by another marine, who was manning a sniper outpost.[8]

Companies K and L were on shore within minutes of each other.
Close on their heels was Company A, 1st Medical Battalion (Company
B was attached to the 11th Marines). In the third wave were a marine
officer, Capt. R. O. Hawkins, and two U.S. Navy radio-men, RM2c
M. Mulkey and RM3c R. V. Brown. The three-man shore observation
party was to establish and maintain communication with the *Vincennes.*
Communications were initially a problem, however; the equipment did
not work well in the jungle and it was inadequate for the task. Captain
Hawkins's party had established contact with the *Vincennes,* but they
were using portable 25-watt transmitter-receivers and 100-watt transmitters driven by 400-cycle gasoline generators for both voice and code
messages. Nevertheless, once set up, the communication crew was able
to report that the landing party had not encountered any Japanese and
that the landing was going according to plan—except that the beaches
were being swamped with cargo.

Headquarters, 1st Marines, Combat Group B, was busy executing
Plan Q, the landing on BEACH RED. It was followed by the 1st Battalion, 1st Marines, Combat Team 1, which initiated Plan S by landing
on BEACH RED and then moving inland through the 5th Marines,
Combat Group A, under Col. Leroy P. Hunt. The artillerymen of the
11th Marines came ashore with their 75-mm pack howitzers, followed by
the regiment's second echelon, the 105-mm tube artillery.

Accompanying Colonel Hunt as guides were two seasoned former
Solomon Islands residents: J. A. Johnstone, known as "Butcher," because
he had run the butcher shop on prewar Tulagi, and C. H. V. "Viv" Hod-
gess, who had managed the Paruru plantation on Guadalcanal. The fifty-
year-old Colonel Hunt was well familiar with warfare, having fought at
Chateau–Thierry in France during the Great War as a member of the
"old" 5th Marine Regiment. He was never without his leather quirt, carried in hand or stuffed into his trouser pocket.

At 0935 on 7 August the 3rd Battalion, 1st Marines, came ashore on
the left half of the 800-yard landing zone. Following the 1st Battalion,
5th Marines, and the 3rd Battalion, 1st Marines, elements of the 3rd Defense Battalion under Maj. J. S. O'Halloran disembarked at 1100. The
plan was for the defense battalion to secure a thousand-yard strip along
the beach, but when they met no opposition, they moved forward, and

their beachhead was lengthened. The battalion, however, which was to be the principal air defense unit on the island, was understrength in both men and weapons; its commanding officer, Col. Robert H. Pepper, and one detachment were at the time temporarily on Tulagi with one-third of the antiaircraft weapons. The remainder of the battalion's elements on Guadalcanal had landed with only three .50-caliber machine guns.

Division headquarters moved ashore the afternoon of Day One and set up near the invasion beach not too distant from the 5th Marines. The command post was established next to the beach near Block Four, a processing shed on the Lever's plantation. The division message center was set up nearby in a tent under a palm tree just south of BEACH RED, with the Lunga River to the west. To that point, the operation was progressing well, with no evidence of hostile forces other than a stray sniper. It was not until the following day that the 3rd Defense Battalion received its important air defense weapons, when one 90-mm antiaircraft gun was brought ashore by a special barge from the cargo ship *Betelgeuse,* along with dual 20-mm machine guns and a .50-caliber antiaircraft machine gun on mounts. The 90s and 50s could exact a heavy toll on enemy aircraft.[9]

On the afternoon of the 7th, the division command post (CP) was established against a hillside not too far from the airstrip, and the message center moved to a tent nearby. The marines were finding their captured island to be miserably hot; the burning sun that morning was the cause of some heat prostration. Progress was slow and tough. The men were fatigued, and the possibility that unseen enemies were lurking in the jungle made them jittery; they often responded to any unrecognized movement by releasing a blast of gunfire. Colonel Hunt's marines were less than aggressive in reaching their objective; some of them acted out their tension by shooting at coconuts or a make-believe enemy, much to the displeasure of the 1st Marine Division commander, General Vandegrift. Complicating things further, their advance was hampered by crude, hand-drawn maps of the north coast of Guadalcanal, which placed almost everything in the wrong perspective.

Meanwhile, the engineers had put a temporary bridge upstream on the Tenaru River, using amphibian tractors as pontoons. The 1st Marines crossed the river and turned southwest toward the area called Mount Austen. On the beach, the 1st Battalion, 5th Marines, crossed the mouth of the Tenaru at 1330 and marched west toward the Ilu River. Neither regiment met any Japanese. The 1st Marines progressed slowly as they advanced inland with battalions echeloned to the left and rear. The only map the regiment had to guide it was vague; the angle of declination between grid and true north was not shown. Had commanders been able to study aerial photographs before the landing, they might have picked easy, natural routes instead of a straight and difficult compass course through the jungle.[10]

General Vandegrift could see lofty the crest of Mount Austen in the distance, about six miles from the landing site; it was actually a sort of sloped plateau with heavily wooded ridges—hills that were numbered by both the Japanese and the Americans. Early in his career, General Vandegrift had learned that you seek and take the high ground early; but the Americans would not take Mount Austen until 1943. Meanwhile, Lt. (jg) Ichizo Hoshino of the Yokohama Air Group was inducted into the air battle of 7 August strictly by accident. According to a POW report some five months later, Hoshino was flying his four-engine Kawanishi flying boat, probably at about 1130, with a crew of four enroute to pick up five navy men. Although the POW report states he was going from Rabaul to Tulagi, more likely it was to Gavutu or Tanambogo. He was also delivering two petty officers who had been in training in Japan and were returning.

Lieutenant Hoshino's luck ran out that day. Because his radio was not working, he did not receive the message that the Americans had landed on Guadalcanal. His seaplane was attacked by a Grumman fighter near Savo Island; the engines were knocked out and it crashed at sea. Hoshino and his navigator, Fujita, along with the two passengers, Petty Officerss Kimata and Takahashi, managed to escape and swam to nearby Savo Island. They remained there until 1 September when the four left in a native sailboat for Kolombangara Island in the New Georgia group.[11]

By sundown of the 7th, the 1st Marines were far short of their objective and were ordered to dig in. The regimental commander, Col. Clifton B. Cates, appears in Guadalcanal campaign photographs as clean-shaven, well dressed, with clean pressed pants and polished riding boots. But Cates was no armchair warrior; he was a splendid strategist and a much-decorated combat leader who had fought with the 6th Regiment during World War I. Between the wars he had bounced around Shanghai with the 4th Marines and had observed the Japanese first-hand. Cates's guide that day on Guadalcanal was F/O C. V. Widdy, RAAF, who was attached to the 1st Marines for Operation WATCHTOWER. Widdy had been Lever's general manager in the Solomons and was very familiar with the terrain where Cates landed, as it was right in the middle of his former employer's holdings; in fact, he once had an office on the property. With Widdy as guide, Cates's men reached the banks of the Tenaru River just south of the 5th Marine encampment. The 2nd and 3rd Battalions, 1st Marines, had moved landward, and by evening they had reached the outskirts of the airstrip, just east of the Lunga River. The 1st Battalion, 1st Marines, held up briefly by snipers, joined them later, and the three battalions then camped adjacent to the airfield.

The U.S. Navy had promised a radio station as part of the invasion unit, but somewhere along the way this important detail was over-looked—nor were any cryptographic aids brought ashore. For security reasons, notably fear of capture by the enemy, the division's crypto-graphic material was left with the rear echelon in a secure area.[12]

The Japanese Strike Back

The quiet the marines were experiencing on landing would soon be disrupted. On receiving news of the Allied attack on Tulagi and Gua-dalcanal, IJNAF Rear Adm. Sadayoshi Yamada, commander of the Rabaul-based 25th Air Flotilla, ordered his naval "sea eagles" to meet the newcomers. At 1155, just before noon on 7 August, thirty-two Mit-subishi G4M Type 1 (Allied code name Betty) high-level bombers from Rabaul flew in between Savo Island and Guadalcanal in three perfect, flat-V formations, headed straight for the transports. At the same time, twenty-four Mitsubishi A6M Type O (Zero or Zeke) fighters flew cover overhead. All the vessels were underway before the planes appeared, thanks to advance warning by coastwatcher Jack Read, who was behind the Japanese lines in northern Bougainville in the hills overlooking Buka Passage. Read had sighted the bombers heading south, and knowing that the Allies had landed in the Solomons, he passed on the word that the attacking Japanese aircraft were heading in the direction of Guadalcanal. The message was sent to Port Moresby (call letters VIG), decoded, and transmitted to the RAAF base at Townsville, Australia, which in turn informed Task Force 62 of the impending raid. This invaluable informa-tion no doubt saved many lives. All shipboard antiaircraft weapons went into action, including machine guns manned by marines.[13]

The *Crescent City* was credited with dropping five attackers in her vicinity, one of them attributed to Cpl. Edward S. Stelloh, a marine gun-ner on the transport. A single aircraft flying erratically and in flames had headed directly for the ship, apparently on a death plunge. According to his Silver Star citation, "Corporal Stelloh, with great coolness and ac-curacy, opened fire, and shortly thereafter the pilot was seen to slump in his seat; the plane went out of control and crashed into the sea about 50 yards from the ship. By his display of coolness, Stelloh probably saved the *Crescent City* and her personnel from disaster." The only casualties on the transports were two marines slightly wounded by flying fragments.[14]

Charles Hatfield, a member of the weapons company, 2nd Marine Regiment, was on the transport *President Hayes:*

> On August 7 we were preparing to land on Tulagi when we came under an air attack from the Japanese. Our platoon furnished anti-aircraft support for . . . the *President Hayes.* Our .50 Cal air-cooled machine gun was mounted in a landing boat mid-ship on the upper deck. . . . [W]e were under attack from Zeroes straf-ing our ship and things were very hectic with the aircraft flying close enough to read the markings on the Zeroes as they zoomed past our ship. Our crew, firing 50s, was about ready to run out of ammunition, so I jumped to the deck to assist in handing up another case. A case of belted shells weighed over 100 pounds and we had to lift the case to about seven feet above our heads. A Company cook pitched in and helped. Just at that moment, a Zero dived on us; bullets ricocheted on our position. The cook didn't wait for me to help him lift the case, but with his eyes open wide and bulging so that all you could see were the whites, he lifted the case by himself and threw it to the loader above, then dived under the landing craft. He could never have lifted it up to his chest at any other time.[15]

The leathernecks on deck had a front row seat when U.S. Navy F4F Wildcats trounced the attacking Japanese; by contrast, those marines in the ships' horribly hot holds were restless, wondering what was going on. Bill Becker of the 1st Military Police Company, on the cargo ship *Bella-trix* (AK 20), came up from below just before the attack: "On D-day my platoon [was] part of the unloading detail; I was down in the hold . . . off-loading ammunition, and it was hotter than hell[;] we were shirtless. In time, I'm sweating so bad I am sick. I was brought up on deck to be revived and was given salt tablets by the medic. Just about that time, it happened so fast, the Japanese air unit . . . attacked and they were com-ing in only a few feet above the water. All guns were firing at them from our ship, and the other transports were firing too. It is a wonder they didn't hit the other vessels."[16] The sky contest lasted just eleven minutes. The Americans claimed eleven Bettys and five Zeros; the Japanese de-clared only two aircraft lost and claimed to have shot down forty-three U.S. planes.[17]

The destroyer *Jarvis* (DD 393) had been hit in the action and the transport *George F. Elliot* had suffered minor damage. The *Elliot's* crew continued to unload cargo far into the night and stopped only when the beach assembly area became congested; the ship's assigned lighters remained unattended and beached on Guadalcanal. The 703 marines of the 1st Pioneer Battalion, assigned to handle the cargo, were too few for the Herculean task of clearing the beach. Had the Japanese known this and bombed the supplies, the campaign could have been over in a few weeks.

Two hours after the Japanese midday air attack and before the anti-aircraft guns of Task Force 61 had cooled off, nine Aichi D3A Type 99 dive-bombers (code-named Val) from the 2nd Air Group hit the invasion area. Admiral Yamada had expected the second flight to finish off any crippled Allied warships that the Bettys had failed to send to the bottom. He did not know that the pilots of the *Saratoga* and *Enterprise* had taken a big chunk out of his first flight. The second attack fared little better, but in all, nine Vals, nine Bettys, and two Zeros failed to return.[18] The Americans lost nine pilots and aircraft.

Father Joseph Lamarre, the Marist missionary on Buka, described the signs that Yamada's air assault had faltered: " . . . On the afternoon of the 7th of August, there was a lot of activity in the air; Japanese planes were returning from the Solomons. A large bomber made a forced landing near Lemanmanu; half a wing had been cut away by machine-gunning. Other planes passed over Hanahan, in a hurry, out of formation, and seemed to have the devil on their tails. Five Zero Fighters have been forced down at Buka Passage. The natives related to us how these were riddled with American bullets. Friends on Bougainville sent us the news of the landing of the American Marines on Guadalcanal. An Allied victory! Our hopes soared sky-high!"[19]

8 Day One: Tulagi, Gavutu, and Tanambogo

On the night of 6 August, over the *President Jackson* loudspeaker the 2nd Marines communication officer announced that the regiment would disembark on enemy-held Florida Island the next day. The men of the 2nd Marines would be the first Allied troops to strike a counter-blow to the Japanese on 7 August. The 1st Battalion, 2nd Marines, would be the first to go ashore, led by Company B, commanded by Capt. Edgar J. Crane, and supported by four seven-man squads of the 4th Platoon, Company D, the 1st Battalion's weapons company. The formation would be guided by twenty-seven-year-old Plat. Sgt. John H. Bowler Sr., called "Grandpa" by the younger marines.

The Landings

At 0640 the morning of 7 August, Captain Crane's men climbed down the nets to the rocking wooden-hulled LCPs. They were scheduled to hit the Florida Island beach at 0800, a few hundred yards from Tulagi Island. Twenty-minutes later, Companies A and C backed by the balance of Company D, departed the assembly area in fourteen landing craft. Their mission: knock out the seaplane base at Halavo on Florida Island. It turned out to be an uneventful milestone, a landing of the RINGBOLT operation—the invasion of Tulagi—that ran like a textbook exercise. But this would be the only mission in that area to fit that description. The rest—Guadalcanal, Gavutu and Tanambogo—would be bloody and grim.

At 0740 (H minus twenty minutes) twenty-year-old Clarence Frederick Miller of Duncan, Oklahoma, was in the lead landing craft. He was a scout-sniper, a post he had been assigned to by Gunnery Sgt. Emery Noble of Orofino, Idaho. Miller's position was in the bow so that he could dash off into the jungle as soon as the craft hit the shore. When he and another scout jumped onto land that day he became the first American to step ashore on an enemy-held island during World War II. Close behind them reaching the shoreline was the 1st Platoon under 2nd Lt John J. Smith.

Once on land the marines fanned out and headed for their target, the native village of Haleta, not far from the landing zone and a suspected enemy post. But Haleta was deserted. Company B combed the area for the Japanese, and finding none, they regrouped and waited for further orders.

Everything was new to them; unfortunately, know-how would come with deadly "on-the-job training," and all the marines of the 2nd Division thus became known as "second to none." What they did not know, however, was that the islands they hit essentially were like pre-heated ovens—ready for action. Both landings that day were made to protect the left flank of the Tulagi landing force. The total casualties for D-day on Florida Island were no enemy dead, two leathernecks wounded, and one killed.

As dawn broke that day, the fire support for the landings on Tulagi and Gavutu was beginning to maneuver on various courses to bombard the predetermined targets. At 0610, the first Douglas SBD Dauntless dive-bombers hit Tulagi Island. When the bombing started, the rikusentai scattered and headed for the caves and air-raid shelters. At 0700, the landing craft transporting the 1st Marine Raider Battalion bound for Tulagi were sighted east toward the line of departure; the *Hovey* (DMS 11), *Hopkins* (DMS 13), and *Trever* (DMS 16) executed a simultaneous turn to close with their targets. As they did so, the Mitsuwa antiaircraft unit under Sp. Lt. (jg) Toshichi Mitsuwa, on Gavutu Hill, opened fire at about 4,000 yards—the maximum range of the island guns. The *Hopkins* immediately returned the fire.[1] The guns of the Mitsuwa unit found the range of the *Hopkins* and fired several times without scoring any hits. There were close calls, but the Japanese shells were of a small caliber and their light charges inflicted no damage. However, the *Hopkins,* firing at the beach line on Gavutu, managed to put several rounds on top of Gavutu Hill (Hill 148), where the Mitsuwa antiaircraft unit held the commanding position.

At 0730, the *San Juan* (CL 54) began a bombardment and sent one hundred rounds in the vicinity of Tulagi's southwest coast. In the meantime, two guardians, the *Monessen* (DD 436) and *Buchanan* (DD 484), moved into position to provide additional Tulagi pounding with five minutes of shelling while the Raider Battalion's landing craft were within 2,500 yards of the island's BEACH BLUE. The two destroyers also fired an additional two hundred rounds each at the landing site on

Figure 16. The Australian Imperial Forces machine-gun pit on Hill 148, Gavutu, March 1942, before it was taken over by the Japanese invaders. U.S. Marines would attack this position on 7 August 1942. (Courtesy Clifford J. Searle)

the south side of Tulagi. Some were wild shots; the shell holes can still be seen on the side of the island where the U.S. Navy peppered the solid rock. The *San Juan* poured 560 5-inch rounds from mounts 1, 2, 3, 4, 6, and 7 at Tulagi's Hill 208 starting at 0743 and completed by 0759. But the bombardment was a washout. The Japanese sea-infantry on Tulagi were safe; not one was killed.

At 0804, a spotter on the *San Juan* informed Lt. Cdr. Matt Radom that a submarine periscope had been sighted at a distance of 1,500 yards. Alarm bells rang as Radom bumped the speed up to twenty-five knots and went after the sub at 0809, dropping six depth charges. No other sighting was reported.[2] Meanwhile, at 0830, the *Trever* scored one hit near the Gavutu gun emplacement, momentarily disrupting the action; but the Mitsuwa's gunners were soon back at work. To help reduce Gavutu's strongpoint, the command center on the carriers dispatched SBDs, which dropped loads near the battery, but only damaged a nearby building. Like Tulagi Island, Gavutu was full of the limestone caves that were safe havens during the bombing.

At H-hour, 0800, the 1st Marine Raider Battalion put Plan T into effect, the operational concept for the invasion of Tulagi, code-named

Figure 17. Aerial photograph showing the 1st Raider Battalion's advance westward on Tulagi Island during the morning of 7 August 1942. (USMC photo)

RINGBOLT. The mission was led by Col. Merritt A. Edson and reinforced by the 2nd Battalion, 5th Marines (2/5), and E Battery, 11th Marines (E/11).[3] Edson's staff had expected it to be a "cookie party": "It will be the type of quick operation for which we had trained; we would hit hard, capture the island, and be back on the ships in a day or so. . . ." The Japanese on Tulagi—they called it *Tsuragi*—had other plans.[4]

Edson's Raiders had been divided: 104 aboard the *Neville* (AP 6), 110 on the *Heywood,* and the balance, 604 men, on the four ships of Transport Division 12, the *Colhoun, Gregory, Little,* and *McKean.* As soon as the Raiders were settled in the swaying landing craft—LCPs, more popularly called Higgins boats—they headed for Tulagi's BEACH BLUE on the southwest coast of Tulagi. The *Little* acted as the control ship, with the *McKean, Gregory,* and *Colhoun* providing fire support. But not one landing craft of the first wave was able to set its occupants on the shore; they had to wade in. They were led by Baker (B) Company then followed by Dog (D) Company.

The Raiders had some difficulty reaching BEACH BLUE, the designated landing area. Maj. Justice "Jumping Joe" Chambers, who commanded Company D, reported: "It was the last place that the Japs thought we would land. It was completely surrounded by coral reefs and this made it necessary to halt the boats on the edge of the reef. Then everybody had to plunge into the water and wade to shore. (Tom Pollard, a mortar man remembers jumping over the side 100 yards from shore and sinking into a pothole; someone pulled him up.) This was no fun, as we had found out during our training at Samoa, because coral reefs are dotted with holes and at any moment you are likely to step into water that is over your head. The best beach on Tulagi was at the other end of the island, and the Japanese had clearly expected any hostile landing would be made there. So they had very lightly fortified the beach where we landed."[5]

Despite their difficulties, the Raiders landed exactly on the button at 0800 (H hour). They were forced to wade, some neck deep, in the foaming surf while the two landing craft were hung up on the coral outcrops that partially surround the island. (The Japanese had had the same problem three months before.) Not knowing the depth of the water certainly had presented a problem. Only when the first Raider landed with his head above water and stumbled forward to the sharp-edged beach did the others swarm over the gunwales. Able (A) Company was next, then Charlie (C) Company followed in the second wave. They were fortunate, as the Kure 3rd had not set up barbed wire or installed Type 98 hemispherical anti-boat mines. It was also their good fortune that the marine height qualification was a minimum of five feet six inches, or else many would have drowned pushing against the turbulent waters with more than seventy pounds of gear.[6] Some nevertheless did.

Company D, the weapons company with 60-mm mortars, led by Capt. George W. Herring, was responsible for the beachhead security. Meanwhile A and C Companies were stuck on the coral outcrops, though the lead element by 0830 had reached the crest of a very steep hill and ended up in the Tulagi cemetery. The target—Tulagi—was a steep island measuring 5.7 miles in circumference. Its largest ridge on the rugged interior rose 347 feet near the northwest sector, sloping down to 300 feet. The uneven island levels off near the government Residency, with a few houses nearby. The island is shaped somewhat like an hourglass, with hills and ravines and jungles, but it also had a former developed govern-

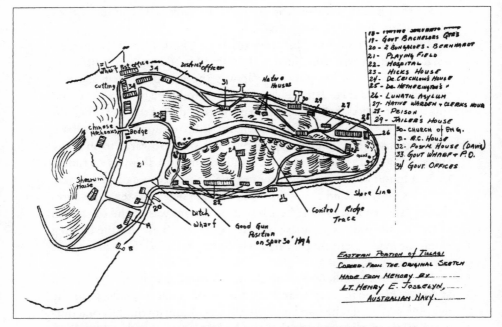

Figure 18. Map of Tulagi town made by Lt. Henry E. Josselyn, RANVR, illustrating the eastern portion of Tulagi Island. (From Rosenquist, Sexton, and Buerlein, *Our Kind of War*, 39.)

ment area at the southeastern end, complete with a cricket field, tennis court, and golf links. While at Nouméa, Lt. Henry E. Josselyn, RANV, the former assistant district officer on Guadalcanal, had constructed a plaster cast of Tulagi complete with molded terrain landscape. Josselyn also had been a district officer on Tulagi and knew it well. The detail of his casting was so fine that, after having observed it before their invasion, some of the marines would later say, "It was like I had been there before D-day." The present occupants of Tulagi were not friendly, however; nor were the former government grounds a pretty sight, now smashed and full of shell holes, compliments of the U.S. Navy.

At 0834 the morning of 7 August, the *San Juan* was back in the business of lobbing shells at Tulagi. This time it was at the prison far from the advancing Raiders; she shot 280 rounds. Subsequently twenty-minutes later, she began firing at Tanambogo Island and within a span of six minutes she fired 410 rounds. At 1004 she flew 280 rounds at Gavutu, but on board she ran into trouble; a power charge had exploded, killing seven and wounded eleven.

Raider Pvt. August R. Montgomery was a member of the first wave that landed on Tulagi and according to orders immediately pushed inland to the depths of the jungle. The Raiders pressed on through thick vegetation to the narrow midsection—the crown—of the island, briefly harassed by snipers. Meanwhile, Company B pushed forward to the opposite coast where it occupied the small boat-building village of Sasapi.

"BEACH BLUE sector was not the ideal place to land," Lt. Dick Horton, RANV, noted. He had been on Tulagi four months before the landing and was at the time tutoring Colonel Edson and his "not so jolly" Raiders about the little-known island. Tulagi was passable, but it promised to be troublesome; and it was hot as hell. Horton had come ashore this time with the third landing wave, which had brought the command unit. He recalls wading toward BEACH BLUE next to Colonel Edson and suddenly stumbling into one of the many coral potholes, loosing his balance, while the ice-eyed Edson plowed on ahead.[7] Once ashore, Horton joined Lt. John "Tiger" Erskine, the Japanese-language officer.

The Raiders were relieved to have arrived unnoticed on hostile shores, and thus they regrouped and climbed the steep slope reaching the local cemetery, easily occupying the western sector. Colonel Edson was cautious but not wearing "clay boots," following an old military adage to "go slow, then move out." At 1120, he reported to Brig. Gen. William H. Rupertus, the assistant division commander still on the *Neville* in Tulagi Harbor, that he held line "A," which extended from the high ground northwest of Hill 281 (Bird Hill) to Carpenter's wharf, belonging to W. R. Carpenter & Company Ltd., a South Sea island trading company. Edson would attack from that position with a green rocket signal at 1130.

Earlier, at 0916, the 2nd Battalion, 5th Marines, the backup support force for the Raiders, had landed on BEACH BLUE. Raider reinforcements consisted of Combat Team 2, Combat Group A (2/5), plus E Battery, 11th Marines, the first of the "cannon cockers" to land in the Solomons. They comprised 1,085 marine officers and men from *Neville* (APA 9) plus the rear echelon of Edson's Raiders who had joined the 2nd Battalion, 5th Marines, on 29 July at the close of the rehearsal landings at Koro Island, Fiji Islands. At 0932, 2/5's command post was set up just west of the cemetery. There were no enemy defenders to greet them, and thus Company F moved into the northwest portion of the island. Company E headed for the high ground overlooking Sasapi. At 1109, 2/5 reported that the northwest end of Tulagi had been cleared of enemy forces.

The Enemy Reality

Robert Caufield, at the time a Private 1st Class with Company F, 2nd Battalion, 5th Marines, recalls the Tulagi experience:

> Truthfully speaking, I didn't realize that we were in a real fight until we started to land. Cpl. Theodore F. Himmelsbach and I reached the beach about the same time; we saw marines floating in the water [that had drowned while landing—potholes]. Then I knew we were in for a real fight. You are not scared until you actually see it. . . . When things quieted down a bit . . . we started to take a break. . . . We were sitting around, not too far from a house with a tin roof. Some guys were smoking and all of a sudden a shot rang [out] from the roof. No one was hit, but we saw the Jap jump off the roof and everybody fired at him. As machine gunners, our side arms were not .45s but '03s. But we smashed the S.O.B. I don't know who hit him; I suppose it was everyone. He must have had a dozen slugs in him, maybe more. Second Lieutenant Carroll, our Platoon leader, stressed that our mission was to reinforce the Raiders and to provide security to prevent any enemy landings, and as a result our gun teams were spread along the coastline. Every once in a while someone would try and land either by swimming or by barge (whatever they call [those] things), and we would plaster them with .50s until there was nothing left.[8]

A motion picture photographer, PFC Richard K. Hance of the division intelligence section (D-2), landed with the 5th Marines but other duties took precedence over his camera work. As a result, no film record was made of the events on Tulagi. It was a significant loss for historians.

At 1000 Company E 2/5 arrived at the high ground overlooking Sasapi. There it rendezvoused with Raider Company B, moving along the north shore trail. Company E reported that the Japanese had evacuated Sasapi; the evidence suggested a quick departure. By 1100, the 1st Platoon, Company H 2/5 (weapons company), moved in the direction of Hill 203 and phase line "A." This provoked enemy fire and the platoon retaliated at the defenders. The 2/5 had its own secret one-man army, or rather a one-man force—Sgt. Lou Diamond, from Bedford, Ohio. The bearded, legendary fifty-two-year-old Diamond was rough and it was said his voice was so strong that if he yelled (he was nicknamed "the Honker"), the Japanese would run—almost. His ability with mortars was so accurate and his senses so keen that it was said if an enemy soldier hiccuped, Lou could drop a mortar shell right down his throat.

At 1135, Company D of the Raiders reached phase line "A," in the island's center; then, relaying orders, they fired a cluster of green shells to notify the ships to bombard the eastern and more populous end of the island. The Raiders now found the going extremely difficult at Tulagi's eastern end. Company C lost two men in the early minutes of combat when Pvts. Leonard A. Butts and Lewis A. Lovin were hit. They were on the reverse slope of the ridge adjacent to line "A" and were a part of the skirmish line. They moved to the crest of the ridge, and then faced a slope that was void of bush or vegetation. They hurried down the slope, and on reaching the base were sprayed by machine-gun fire. Butts died on the spot; Lovin was evacuated but later died aboard the *Neville*.

At 1600 both Able and Charley Companies—Able under Capt. Lewis "Silent Lew" Walt, Charlie under Maj. Ken Bailey, called "Ken Dill"—had reached their initial objectives. At 1625, Charlie Company encountered stiff resistance in the area of Hill 281, yet the advance continued until dark. Handfuls of the Kure 3rd sea infantry were well dug in, protecting the hill, and were determined to stop the invaders at any cost. The air and ship bombardment had killed only a small number of the island laborers and none of the Kure 3rd men, who had quickly sought shelter after the first shell had landed. Diarist SM Tomisaburo Hirai would write: "During the air raids our commander [Sp. Lt. (jg) Kikichi Yoshimoto] would be the first one in the shelter. He would often tell us to always be brave. But he is the one who is not brave."[9]

The Kure 3rd had dozens of long-tunneled caves dug deep into the island's limestone cliffs and the U.S. Navy was using the wrong type of ammunition against the rock formations. When the marines entered the area, the Japanese emerged unharmed from the caves and octopus holes to fight furiously from machine-gun and sniper positions.[10] They demonstrated their philosophy of sacrifice, behaving in a way that baffled the attackers, who could not fathom such self-destruction. The Americans had shouted in English to the hole-bound "termites" to surrender, and a few who had picked up a smattering of Japanese yelled, *"Buki wo wawase, Koosan Se!"* ("Surrender, self and troops!"), assuming that some could understand the Americanization of their language. However, not one of the enlisted sailors of the Kure 3rd SNLF could comprehend a word of English, though some of the officers could.

Cornered and forced back into the caves, some of the Japanese escaped through other openings. Those refusing to surrender were killed by grenades or Molotov cocktails, or were shot when they ventured out. Most were laborers; some had the ill-conceived notion they were descendants of ancient warriors. Although the marines were able to move forward at a reasonable pace, they repeatedly found it necessary to retrace their steps to hunt down the snipers.

At 1246 that midday of 7 August, the *San Juan* was called back for bombardment service on Tulagi's Hill 281. By 1250 she had tossed 280 rounds of 5-inch shells at the problem knoll.[11] At about 1300, 1st Lt. Rex Crockett's platoon of B Company ran into a group of frightened islanders near Carpenter's wharf. The platoon shepherded the islanders to the rear, but what Lieutenant Crockett did not know was that the group was George Bogese and his family. George was a native medical practitioner who had been living amidst the Japanese on Tulagi by permission—the only family to do so—because he was the garrison's contact with the natives on Florida and Savo Islands. Bogese had first met the Japanese on Tulagi when he had gone there to demand payment for his services as native doctor to some wounded Japanese seamen that had washed on the shore of Savo Island after their vessel had been sunk. George was considered a turncoat and his word was not trusted.

Maj. Justice Chambers of Company D recalled those first days on Tulagi: "Every building that we met had its quota of Japs and we had to drive them out or kill them with hand grenades. We had thought that coconut trees would not have enough branches to conceal snipers. But we found that the Japs were small enough to hide in them easily and so we had to examine every tree before we went by. If they had been good shots, few of us would have survived, but, happily, there was no comparison in marksmanship between the Marines and Japs."[12] Chambers was wounded when he was too near a mortar firing position as a round hit a tree and splattered. Capt. William E. Sperling, then took command of Chambers's Company D.

Pvt. Edward G. Sexton, the still photographer assigned to the Raiders, was shot at several times: "The Japs had been only about seventy-five yards from me. They couldn't hit a bull in the ass with a board if it were sitting on its back." One Raider had an opposite view: "These guys were as tough as nails. Their snipers were very good." 1st Lt. Eugene "Tex" Key, commander of the 1st Platoon, Company B, was in a forward position when one of his men was hit by a sniper. No sooner had the marine hit the ground when Key also was shot. Lt. (jg) Samuel Miles, one of the doctors, saw Key fall and rushed to his side. The Sun Devil sniper took their lives.[13]

WO Tsuneto Sakado's platoon had several snipers: from his 2nd Squad was SR Haruo Okamoto; from his 3rd Squad, SA Takeo Sumi; from his 4th Squad, SR Katsuyoshi Ikeda; and from his 5th Squad, SM Syuichi Fuchikawa. Snipers from WO Sadayuki Kato's platoon included PO3c Roysuke Kuwabara, SA Yoshimi Hamaoka., SA Tadao Hironaka, and SR Yoshihiro Taniguchi. Half of WO Yoshiharu Muranaka's platoon was on Malaita Island on garrison duty; he had no sharpshooters. WO Noburo Obara had four shooters in his platoon: PO3c Torao Morishige, SA Tomehachi Itoh, SA Shigeo Kawamura, and SR Mitsuo Nakajima. Most of the Kure men were reservists with an average age of forty and included a small number who had served in the Great War. A few recruits were added in February of 1942 to fill out the rikusentai's full complement. Most of the Japanese snipers, however, had not fired much since basic training and were afraid to waste the ammunition. On board ship they had conducted "dry firing." Nevertheless, they made a dent in the marines' advance; they used smokeless powder and could fire from the bush, remaining almost undetected.[14] What the marines did not know was that the 3rd Company of the Kure 3rd SNLF was the machine-gun unit of the force.

Meanwhile, at Hill 208, the Company C Raiders were held up for an hour by enemy machine guns, which were finally reduced with small arms fire and grenades. The Japanese were far from being a spent force, however, and Companies A and C moved on to the hill west of the cricket grounds. Maj. Kenneth D. Bailey, the CO of Raider Company C and a gifted leader, was wounded; Capt. Robert H. Thomas then took command. So vigorous was the enemy's resistance that only one platoon of Company C could continue, but it managed to edge along the southern shore to the eastern tip of the island. Colonel Edson's biographer describes some of the Tulagi struggle:

> As usual, communications broke down just when they were most needed. Edson could not get a report from Walt's A Company, so he decided to go there himself and get a firsthand look at the situation. He called for Lt. John B. Sweeney [code-named "John Wolf"] who was in charge of CP [command post, Hill 301] security, and the two set out for the right flank. They moved along Company B's lines for a short time, and got challenged every few steps by alert, nervous marines. No one knew where [Capt. Lewis] Walt's CP was located. [Walt's CP was twenty yards behind A Company lines but the captain was somewhere in the

boondocks with the first sergeant and did not show up until the next morning. However, his executive officer (XO) 1st Lt. John W. Antonelli was there, as was 2nd Lt. Thomas P. Mullahey.] It became clear to Sweeney that the odds of reaching their objective were not good. After a brief halt and a reassessment, 'Red Mike' decided to head back to his headquarters. . . .[15]

The snipers of WO Sadayuki Kato's 2nd Platoon harassed the marines as they tried to converge on the main position between the cricket grounds and Hill 281. PO1c Nakasuke Miyagi and his squad of nine—with sharpshooter PO3c Ryosuke Kuwabara, supported by PO3c Harubumi Ishida and his seven men with sniper SM Yoshimi Hamaota—were able to block the marine advance.[16] Supporting the rikusentai were members of the 14th CU Detachment led by PO1c Hiroshi Furuichi, but they were not combat trained. They were electricians and engineers and had been busy on construction projects on Tulagi, Gavutu, and Tanambogo, and thus the Kure 3rd had to assist in repelling the invaders. The 14th CU had completed work on wireless stations and was awaiting transportation back to Rabaul when the marines landed.[17]

The Fight Intensifies

As the events proceeded, Company G, 2nd Battalion, 5th Marines, was moving toward the southeast part of the island along the well-worn ridge trail. Company E was having trouble in Chinatown, with snipers picking off marines as they ventured away from protected areas. A concealed machine-gun nest opened fire on Company G and five marines fell. The mortar platoon (2/5), "the Honker's own [Sergeant Diamond]," moved forward by 1345 and established a firing position. At 1400, the battalion command post was moved forward to the former Solomon Islands constabulary barracks and then later moved to the Residency, by then almost in ruins. It had been the home and office of forty-nine-year-old Masaaki Suzuki who became island commander on 15 July, and once was the most beautiful residence in the Solomons when it had been surrounded by green moss and beautiful bougainvillea.

As the battle wore on, Colonel Edson was growing concerned at the chaotic conditions, and for a time considered calling for reinforcements, except that communications were then nonexistent. Although they had expected the Japanese counterattack, the ferocity and determination of the assaults had surprised Red Mike and his XO. At one point the enemy fought to within fifty yards of the Residency; Edson later called this threat to his command post one of his "few exciting moments" in the Guadalcanal campaign.[18] The outnumbered handful of diehard Kure 3rd warriors gave a solid account of themselves and taught the marines a few new tricks. Raider Capt. Robert P. Neuffer of Company D heard an unusual command in an American manner near his position: "C'mon, get your stuff together; we're pulling out of here." A marine sergeant had started to obey what sounded like an order, but almost as he got to his feet, someone else recognized that it was not a marine at all who had spoken, but an enemy. The English-speaking Japanese officer, one of the nine, and six others hovering nearby were shot. "That trick indicated just how tough Tojo is," Neuffer said. "It took guts."[19]

At 1800, the early evening of that first day of the invasion, Company B of the Raiders established itself for the night adjacent to the government wharf to the north and placed guards, while Companies A and C protected the right flank to the south. Edson's weapons company was in support along the ridge to the west. According to Pvt. Pete G. Sparacino:

A little behind line "A" Company A (in the front of Company C) was Cpl. Frank J. Guidone's squad that set-up a defense position facing up the slope to the crest of the ridge (there were ridges and hills all over Tulagi). He was actually on the reverse slope and expected the enemy to sneak over the ridgeline to attack. Guidone told his men not to move ahead or back unless he ordered to do so. Somehow a fire was started in a building on a ridge in front of Guidone's position and this provided a clear picture. Anyone moving over the ridge would be silhouetted. The CP was about 20 yards to the rear and Guidone, taking advantage of the moment, needed more grenades; he went back to the CP and obtained a case. Not too long after that . . . full darkness set in. There was a movement to the front. . . . You could hear them jabbering. Then, the enemy found a gap and began running through the opening. The gap was [sealed] when another squad closed the gate. Some Japanese had crawled within twenty yards of Guidone's squad. Frank began throwing grenades from a prone position. His grenades were going off 15 yards from our position [and] we had to duck as they exploded. The enemy was all around. It was brutal and deadly. We had to be careful not to kill our comrades. We were tired but had to stay awake or be dead. Early in the morning Frank went back to the CP to obtain more grenades as the squad had used them all. . . . I have fought on Tulagi, Guadalcanal and Iwo Jima, and I had not encountered a battle such as this one.[20]

The next morning Corporal Guidone would be Sergeant Guidone.

Two companies of the 2nd Battalion, 5th Marines, had been busy cleaning out the snipers in the western end of Tulagi: Capt. Harry J. Connor's Company E and Capt. Charles R. Baker's Company F. Capt. Harold T. A. Richmond's Company G followed the Raiders to the government house area in the eastern end, where they reported to Colonel Edson. Meanwhile, the 3rd Platoon, Company H (2/5), was ordered to relieve Company E; E had been ordered to move across to Gavutu to support the 1st Marine Parachute Battalion, which had been badly shot up. The securing of that island was then still in doubt. Before Company E could leave for Gavutu, however, the order was countermanded.

PFC Howard Schnauber of Company E, 2nd Battalion, 11th Marines, was assigned to a 75-mm pack howitzer unit attached to 2nd Battalion, 5th Marines, for the invasion of Tulagi.

It seems wherever 2/5 moved, so did 2/11. I went ashore in one of the older Eureka landing craft, the kind [where] you roll over the side instead of going out the bow. On the way in we lost some men because of a light machine gun hidden in a small cave not too far from the landing site and to the left. . . . A 75-mm pack howitzer was a difficult piece of weaponry that was manhandled ashore piece by piece, then put together and pulled by a jeep. We got ashore and lugged the ammo. To get to the other side of the island where we were assigned, we had to move through the "Tulagi Pass," the short-cut through the steep hill separating one side of the island from the other. The slot was level, but it had two caves [air-raid shelters] dug into the limestone, large caves that housed quite a number of Japs. The only way past them was for the foot marines to shoot into the entrance as the jeep pulled the howitzer past. This system worked well and we managed to get the gun to the opposite side.

On the northwest side of Tulagi, it is leveled out, and the ground slanted toward the beach. After we got all the equipment to our assigned area it was decided to dismantle one howitzer and lug it up the steep slope of a large hill. The advantage was a perfect spot for a view covering the water between the Canal and Tulagi, a perfect field of fire. [The 75-mm shell traversed a lofty, curving trajectory with a range of about six miles.] We all expected the Japs to retaliate at anytime, so our positions were all set up as a defense perimeter. My section had a machine gun with light and heavy [air-] cooled .30 caliber guns and some air-cooled .50 caliber along with rifles and BARs (Browning automatic rifle).

By evening, everyone was alert and in place. Fox holes dug, but on edge, not knowing what to expect. Some enemy started to move around in the dark. We knew it was the Japs because our orders were implicit to stay put and stay awake. Sometime during the night I heard a Marine call out "Hollywood," the answer came back "Rollypop."[Then . . .] "Rollypop hell," and the next thing we heard was the sound of a .30 caliber machine gun filling the night air. . . .[21]

Another artilleryman, Cyrus J. "Jim" Moore (E/2/11), was pressed into service as a stevedore in the rush to get supplies ashore on D-day.

We were in the process of off-loading equipment and supplies for our assault on Tulagi. We received word that the Japanese Navy was on the way and would arrive at our position soon. We began fanatically loading everything we could into Higgins boats and when they were filled to capacity, began throwing food (which was stored in wooden containers) over the side in hopes they would float ashore and could be retrieved later. During this rumpus, someone suggested that . . . the possibility of having to use a gas mask on a small island was very unlikely. . . . We proceeded to dump our gas mask paraphernalia and fill the bag with such things as we thought we'd need a lot more of . . . such as cigarettes, candy, and anything we could think of. . . .

We proceeded to our designated area and set up our artillery pieces (75-mm pack howitzers) for support of the Marines still engaged. We received word that we would pack up and move the weapons overlooking Tulagi Harbor. We were in the process of manually moving the guns along the beach, when suddenly a Japanese submarine appeared about a half-mile off shore and began to shell Marine positions on the island with their deck gun. Our CO ordered our forward observers to immediately go up a hill near the beach . . . to return fire on the sub. We set up our guns in record time and began firing at will. We saw some of our shells hit the sub and it was reported that we got five direct[s] and it was sent to the bottom. Whether the claim for the sinking is true

Figure 19. The "Tulagi Pass" short-cut path through the steep hills dividing Tulagi Island, ca. 1930. (Courtesy Mrs. Eugenie Murphy)

or not, I couldn't say for certain, but I know we hit it a few times. [The Japanese did not report the loss of any submarines that day.]

We continued relocating and had just settled ourselves for a much needed rest, after manually pulling the guns all the way from one end of the island to the other and getting them set up again. Suddenly someone shouted "Gas!" . . . You can imagine how we felt after dumping our masks for other unnecessary items. There we sat just waiting for the end to come. . . . As it turned out the enemy had fired a couple of rounds filled with something that smelled like chlorine. Maybe they did and maybe they didn't. Who knows? From that time on, when we were called up for invasions, we always had our gas masks . . . even if it meant no cigarettes or candy.[22]

Japanese Cdr. Masaaki Suzuki had concentrated his sea infantrymen on the steep slopes of Hill 281, around which his command post was deeply entrenched, protected by sandbags and supported by machine-gun pits in the shovel-shaped ravine west of the hill and slightly north of King

George Field. Several light machine guns covered the valley between the southeastern slope of Residency Hill and Hill 281. A heavy machine gun was emplaced to cover both BEACH WHITE and the southeastern slope of 281. While alone on the east end of King George Field, Pvt. E. L. Speicher was hit by a sniper's bullet. He was buried where he died.[23]

That evening zealous banzai charges carried the Kure 3rd men straight into the muzzles of the American machine guns. Although they showed fanatical courage, each successive attack resulted in the further loss of what essentially was cannon fodder, making the next assault less potent. Other charges took place that evening of 7–8 August and the morning of the 8th. A belly full of *sake* possibly had influenced these suicidal attacks, a technique that had previously proved effective when fighting the poorly armed Chinese. The cold steel charges, now called "bamboo spear tactics," were a method the men from Nippon had perfected over the years. Experts who analyzed the Japanese forces during the war in the Pacific theorized that they were an army of humans, supported by machines of war; in contrast, for the United States, machines of war were supported by men.

On that first day of the invasion, the corpsmen attached to the Raiders became heroes in their own right. Not only did they risk their lives time and again to attend to the wounded, but in addition they even dispatched some of the enemy. One especially brave and courageous "pill-pusher" was Harold P. McCann, who had killed four Japanese with his .45 sidearm on D-day. Apparently the enemy had sighted McCann, who was wearing his Red Cross armband, and began shooting at him while he was administering aid to wounded Raiders.[24]

Day One had seen a tough afternoon. The night, Major Chambers recalled, was even worse. "The Japs tried every trick on us that we had been told they would, yet that we really never imagined they would. They shouted, whistled, and sniped at us all night. In fact, you might say that they slept with us. At first there was considerable promiscuous night firing, the Japs trying to locate our units by [shooting] at us at random. But our men learned to hold their fire and not give away their position unless attacked in hand-to-hand assault."[25] During the night, the Kure 3rd sea infantrymen conducted piercing attacks and counterattacks, succeeding in driving a sharp wedge between Raiders Companies A and C and isolating Company C along the beach. Then they turned on Company A in a vain attempt to attack up the ridge toward the British Residency—Edson's command post. In this mad assault the rikusentai failed; the marines of Company A lost some good men in the skirmish, but they killed twenty-six Japanese within yards of the defense line, and the attack was thwarted.

The Kure men made five determined attacks between 0300 and 0530 in the early morning hours of 8 August. Through constant pushing by small groups or individual probing attempts they were able to infiltrate almost to Edson's command post. Dick Horton reported that the Japanese reached the CP at the Residency and a half dozen or so were killed under the building. He recalls: "My particular post was to be nearby Red Mike—Colonel Edson. . . . The battle heated up from the afternoon of the landing until the Japs had been driven down and off the island. . . . The really noisy and exciting time was early the next morning when the Japs tried to counterattack. . . . Henry Josselyn had been with [Raiders] Company C and they were cut off during the night and had to form a defensive circle in and around a crater into which the Japs lobbed or tried to lob grenades—however the Marines held fast and in the morning they saw they had killed a number of the enemy and I think it was at light cost to themselves."[26]

The Japanese citizen—and therefore the Japanese soldier or sailor—was schooled in devotion to his country and respect for his superiors to a degree that aroused wonder among Americans. Japanese drama and literature made war glorious; American films and literature often balanced war was as futile and tragic. The American was impatient and volatile; the Japanese was patient and obedient. Deep in the Japanese character was the image of the Samurai bowman, who was obliged to take his own life if he missed the target.[27] Japanese strengths and weaknesses were summed up by an analyst in the 1930s: "Rapidity of attack is a marked feature of all [their] training on land and sea as well as in the air. . . . Where rapid thinking is required in order to improve against the unexpected, the Japanese probably leave something to be desired; provided nothing intervenes to upset their carefully thought-out plans . . . they have few equals and no superiors."[28]

According to SME Giichi Nohara (Kato platoon), the Kure 3rd SNLF had practiced night ambush operations and trench warfare at the base of the antiaircraft station. The attacks against the marine lines on Tulagi occurred between 0200 and 0500 on 8 August, but the rikusentai did not have sufficient manpower or reinforcements to break through the American positions. Even if they had, there was no place to go.[29] At 0300 that morning, Raider PFC Edward H. Ahrens of Company A was on the right flank of his battalion as part of the security detail when a Japanese officer, with two companions, attempted to infiltrate

the American lines. Though shot and knifed several times in the melee, Ahrens helped repel the assault. After dawn had broken, Captain
Walt found him wounded and barely alive. Author Joseph H. Alexander
would write: "Ahrens managed to kill the Japanese lieutenant and the
other a sergeant and several others. . . ."[30] However, the only lieutenants
on Tulagi were Sp. Lt (jg) Kikichi Yoshimoto, the fifty-four-year-old
former detachment commander, Lt. Royoichi Chadani, the doctor, and
Lt. Ko Numura, the supply officer. Ahrens could not have killed a sergeant because there is no such rank in the Imperial Navy; they all were
sailors. Historian Samuel Eliot Morison, in his *History of United States
Naval Operations in World War* II, would describe them as "non-sea-
going-sailors."

The Enemy Battles On

On 8 August, the marines secured a building and discovered a quantity
of Japanese medical supplies—medicines, linens, pans, and fine surgical
instruments.

> [According to] PhM2c Huey M. "Whitey" Love . . . : 2nd Lt.
> "Tiger" Erskine, the Raiders' Japanese interpreter, would trans-
> late the Japanese medicine and then write the English name on
> each bottle. This was our basic medical supply; came in handy,
> just in the nick of time. We used all the Japanese medicine that
> we could. I have no recollection of receiving any medical supplies
> from our sources. When things quieted down, supply ships and
> destroyers would come into Tulagi bay and unload supplies for
> transfer to Guadalcanal by patrol vessels (YP), ex-California tuna
> boats (YPs). Our medical officers would go aboard any vessel
> and try to persuade the medical officers and/or corpsman [to]
> provide whatever medical supplies . . . they could spare.
>   . . . [A] cache of Japanese quinine powder . . . with a very bit-
> ter taste [was located] and soon put to use. We had no (natural)
> gelatin capsules to put it in; therefore, we would mix it with
> water and give it to any patients who had malaria. We had to
> watch them like a hawk to be sure that they swallowed it.[31]

On the morning of the 8th, Companies E and F, 5th Marines, were hitting the island's big trouble spot, Hill 281. The aggressive Company C
Raiders finally captured and controlled it, though their task remained
to flush out the isolated Japanese hidden in every corner. From their key
position, the marine mortar and machine-gun teams could apply aggres-

sive firepower to any area of resistance. Later on that D + 1, Colonel Edson declared Tulagi secure; but he subsequently changed his mind when he kept encountering resistance from unexpected locales.

On the evening of D + 1, Cpl. Robert B. Pape of the 1st Raider Battalion, Headquarters, Company B, found himself under a house during a fight, when to his surprise fifteen Japanese, some wounded, crawled in not far from him to escape the cascade of machine-gun fire. He knew he had company, but they were unaware of his presence. At dawn, Pape was slowly inching his way out when he was suddenly recognized. The enemy opened fire, and he was hit in the leg, though he managed to pull himself away and call for help. A nearby machine-gun post recognized his situation and zeroed in on his attackers, killing them all.[32]

During Day Two, the 1st Raider Battalion was directed to clean up any armed stragglers from the western part of Tulagi, while the 2nd Battalion, 5th Marines, was ordered to clean up bypassed pockets from the beach area of the eastern side. Companies E and F, which had tangled with the Japanese survivors on the western part of Tulagi, were the lead units. From a line northeast of Hill 281—Tulagi's much-blasted principal elevation—with F Company on the right and E on the left, they moved cautiously over the prominence to the southwest side of the island. Hill 281 was honeycombed with unexposed chambers in which the enemy could hide. Some of the Japanese emplacements were shattered, but the outnumbered defenders fought on.[33]

At 1300, Company G, 5th Marines, and the Raiders advanced on the last Japanese stronghold on Tulagi. E and F Companies, nudging cautiously along the north coast, trapped a number of Japan's iron men between two prongs—the Raiders on one side and the 5th Marines on the other. The 81-mm mortars of the 5th Marines weapons company pounded the enemy into submission, and the remaining few Japanese were almost annihilated. Nonetheless, the contest for Tulagi was far from over.

In the senseless screaming banzai charges, many Kure men died in savage-hand-to-hand fighting. Marines also paid the price for bravery: Chuck Barcomb, Wood Barr, Ken Bowers, Marion E. Bradley, Lou Carpellotti, Jerry Diovisalvo, Ben Fairbanks, Lt. Miles Fox, Joe Giffels, John Gilligan, Ed Gyatt, Art Hampton, Julian Hansen, Frank Huber, Lt. Eugene M. "Tex" Key, Milton Lewis, Lewis "Art" Lovin, Alexander Luke, Claude Miller, Francis Nee, Tom Nickel, Robert Paine, Bill Renye, Bill Strandvold, Bill Trowbridge, and others died in the battle for Tulagi,

some of them well after General Rupertus had declared the island secure. Lt. (jg) Samuel S. Miles, USNR, was killed while attending the
injured on 7 August, and corpsman Ted Parker was almost killed a number of times during his heroic efforts attending the wounded. PFC Clifford C. "Red" Hills of Company A won the praise and respect of Capt.
Lew Walt for his outstanding devotion to duty during the night attacks
of 7–8 August, and Hills received the Navy Cross.[34] On the day Lieutenant Key was killed, headquarters in Washington had promoted him to
captain.

The 2nd Battalion, 5th Marines, had twenty-four casualties with
eight killed in action (KIA) and sixteen wounded; the 1st Raider Battalion suffered ninety-nine casualties, including thirty-nine KIA, but
on D + 3, three badly wounded Raiders got a real break: Gunnery Sgt.
Angus Goss and Privates Pike and John W. Hambrock were flown out
of Tulagi Harbor on a PBY from VP-23, bound for hospitalization in
the New Hebrides Islands. "Gunny" Goss, a demolition expert, was at
least ten to twelve years older than his brother Raiders and was their
Senior NCO. His story is typical. Although wounded by a sniper from
a cave, he charged the dugout, which was occupied by a handful of sailors, killing all of them. The Raiders were awarded eight Navy Crosses
and their share of Silver Stars and Purple Hearts; the 2nd Battalion, 5th
Marines, received a bucketful of Purple Heart medals. The only Bronze
Star awarded for the Tulagi campaign was presented to Navy corpsman
PhM2c John A. Gallagher of 1HqA; Lt. (jg) Samuel S. Miles M.D. received a Silver Star posthumously.

B. P. Wenver with *The New Nation Magazine* wrote: "Daylight the
next morning found us steaming [along] and a short while after[,] we
anchored in Tulagi Harbor, only a few hundred yards from the land.
And what a land it looked to us! The beauty of that early morning scene
beggars description and one had a feeling that God had especially en-
dowed this earthly paradise with all beauty and glory."[35]

Toward the end of that second day, at 2130 the night of the 8 August,
while the light cruiser *San Juan* was navigating the waters adjacent to
Tulagi Island a deck spotter saw an SOS signal from a small light. The
CL 54 maneuvered toward the glow to investigate and saw a Higgins
boat. She moved alongside for a closer inspection and found that the
craft contained wounded Raiders. Some kind saint had brought the injured from Tulagi out to the harbor looking for medical assistance. The
men were taken on board the warship and cared for.[36]

The 1st Parachute Battalion — Gavutu

At 1056 on D-day, 7 August, the paramarines — another special unit of the Marine Corps, men skilled in parachute-drop invasion — headed for Japanese-held Gavutu (code name ACIDITY), the twenty-one-acre island a mere 250 by 500 yards in size. The 1st Parachute Battalion was comprised of 338 enlisted men, 23 officers, and 30 naval personnel, along with four doctors and a U.S. Navy chaplain. Also attached was an enlisted marine, Pvt. Robert M. Howard, the photographer from Headquarters Company, 1st Marine Division. His job was to take photos, not to kill the enemy. The omens for the paramarines, however, were disconcerting, for on the *Heywood,* one of the transports carrying them to Gavutu, a sergeant and a corporal were practicing knife fighting and the corporal somehow sliced the sergeant's abdomen from hipbone to hipbone. The landing force would be short one non-commissioned officer.[37]

These marines were assault troops, sent to hit the small tightly held island enclave, similar to the landing at the Australia-New Zealand Army (ANZA) Cove at Gallipoli in 1915, but on a miniature scale. Whereas the Turks had held a controlling ridge at Gallipoli, the Japanese at Gavutu had a compact defensive position backed by the island's commanding hill, much to the paramarines' disadvantage. A major handicap as well was the lack of up-to-date details of Gavutu's terrain. When Lt. Col. Frank B. Goettge, the 1st Marine Division intelligence officer (D-2), had traveled to Australia seeking data on the Solomons for the operation, he had overlooked interviewing the fifty-odd Australian commandos and aircrews who had served on Gavutu and Tanambogo for eight months during 1941–42. They knew every nook and cranny of the islands and could have furnished information not available elsewhere. These men were then serving in Australia or New Guinea and could have been brought in for a briefing; but none were contacted. Goettge and his staff should have combed Australia and New Guinea for information in general, but especially regarding Gavutu. However, Goettge had to work through General Macarthur's staff, a handicap to begin with, and he was not a trained intelligence officer.

The paramarines were an elite group within an all-volunteer service that had received extensive parachute training but had never jumped in combat. They had excellent tactical instruction and like the Raiders were considered to be ideally suited for their task. Dubbed the "Chutes," the men of the 1st Parachute Battalion were under the command of Maj. Robert H. Williams, a daring bulldog of a leader. Gavutu was to be the

Figure 20. U.S. Marine Corps paratroops (paramarines) photographed at Tent City, New River, North Carolina, June 1942. *Left to right*: PFC John P. Hurn (KIA, Bloody Ridge), PFC Leonard Kiesel, PFC Gerald F. Donahue (WIA, Gavutu). (Courtesy Leonard Kiesel)

most difficult to crack of the three-island complex, and before Day One was over, the marine landing there would set new mortality rates.[38]

Someone from the *Heywood*—the twenty-year-old former *City of Baltimore* (CA 68), which the marines now called the "Haywire"—had scattered rose petals on the pathway to Gavutu, implying that this would be an easy show: hit, run, leave the Jap bodies where they fell, get out with your skin. The 1st Parachute Battalion, overconfident, was destined to wade into a hornet's nest. Its entire mission as a component of Operation WATCHTOWER had been jinxed since the men had left San Francisco on 22 June. The government had charted a commercial ship, the *John Ericsson,* to move them from the West Coast to Wellington, New Zealand, to join the 1st Marine Division for the upcoming operation. The voyage was a disaster from beginning to end. The beat-up vessel's refrigeration broke down after seven days at sea, and all the fresh food spoiled and had to be thrown overboard. The marines aboard survived on meager hardtack and sardines.[39] By the time they had reached New Zealand, they were starving and exhausted—most had lost twenty pounds.

Shortly after the *Ericsson* docked at Wellington's Pipitea wharf, the unpatriotic New Zealand longshoremen, always strike prone, were again engaged in a work stoppage, and the wearied paramarines, with no dock-side assistance, were forced to unload their misery ship and then combat-load the *Heywood* in drizzling rain. They finally shoved off for the Koro Islands, Fiji Islands, to participate in the pre-invasion practice landing, another unanticipated failure.[40]

The paratroops were slated to invade Gavutu as infantry, with the landing scheduled for H + 4 hours, or 1200. When exiting the *Heywood*, the Chutes had disembarked into thirteen blunt-nose LCPs painted gray to give the appearance of steel, with a few shallow-draft Higgins Eureka boats mixed in. Major Williams would comment, "This battalion was unique in that in reality it was 'The Old Breed'"—all sergeants and many corporals who were on their second four-year enlistment. Some of the staff NCOs had eight or ten years of service, and thus an attitude of professionalism had characterized the battalion.[41]

The Gavutu hill—Miwa Hill (Hill 148), an abbreviated name after the commander of the unit on the hill, Sp. Lt. (jg) Toshichi Mitsuwa—as well as nearby Tanambogo were honeycombed with dugout strongholds that had sheltered most of the Japanese during the bombardments. Since the dawn attack on the twin islands' air complex, the now-grounded Japanese airmen on Tanambogo had limited number of weapons readily available, other than a handful of Nambu 8-mm pistols and thirty-two old 1905 .38-caliber rifles. But the maintenance shop contained several 20-mm and 13-mm machine guns and 7.7-mm (light Nambu) weapons in various stages of repair. The ordnance men thus worked feverishly to put the guns in working condition, cannibalizing other weapons to make them operable should the enemy Allies venture onto Tanambogo.[42] In any event, they fully expected that the Japanese Navy would to come to their rescue before the day was out. Surrender was absolutely unacceptable.

The Gavutu–Tanambogo invasion plan, set forth in Operations Order No. 5 (revised) of 4 August 1942, was clear and simple. Under Plan R, the 1st Parachute Battalion was to attack Gavutu, seize the island, then attack and grab Tanambogo. It was to defend those islands until relieved. Under Plan T, elements of the 2nd Battalion, 5th Marines, after seizing Makambo, were to be prepared to send one reinforced company to relieve the forces on Gavutu and Tanambogo; that, however, was never executed as the Japanese kept them busy on Tulagi.

The paramarines at Gavutu were equipped with a few JLMGs

(Johnson light machine gun) called the "Johnny gun" and, if in sufficient supply, the Reising folding-stock submachine gun. The JLMG was
the weapon of choice, but there were not enough for all the troops. The
Reising, called a "grease gun," was a disappointment; chronic jamming
problems were caused by rust residue from the salt water and the island
climate. The gun was plagued by constant malfunctions. In the initial
jungle fighting, it was effective at only 150 yards, which left the Chutes
at a disadvantage, even before the first shot was fired.

The paramarines had received stateside parachute training in securing an enemy-dominated position by jumping from an air transport; but
their jump training was of no value on their initial combat operation, as
they headed for one of "hell's islands" in boats. The leadership had been
lax in its assessment of the deployment and had led the paramarines to
believe the operation would be effortless. This misguided assessment of
Gavutu injected a nonchalant attitude, which led the Chutes directly
into a hotbed of lethal firepower. The primary error, however, lay not
with the paramarines' combat management but with the U.S. Navy that
should have assigned a few cruiser "big guns" to pound Gavutu and
Tanambogo. Although the big gun warship attack on Guadalcanal did
little harm, it played a role. Had this attention been applied to Gavutu
and Tanambogo, it may not have produced a "walk in the sun" for the
paramarines, but at least it wouldn't have been a "ride into hell."

The seven-mile journey from the *Heywood* began late morning on
7 August. The Chutes were delayed in taking off because they had to
wait until Edson's Raiders, who had landed on BEACH BLUE Tulagi, released the landing craft for the paramarines' use. The first wave,
Company A, shoved off at 1056; it was followed five minutes later by
Companies B and C. The passage had an ominous beginning. The sea
was anything but calm, and the Chutes were jolted around in the rocky
landing craft like so many corks in stormy waters; the bouncing Higgins
boats and the constant spray of seawater drenched them. Their carefully
cleaned weapons packs and assorted assault gear were soaked, their eyes
stung, and most were seasick.

While the parachutists were inbound, the *San Juan* pumped more
than 800 rounds of armor-piercing into Gavutu within thirty minutes.
One marine watching that day said later, "I didn't see how the Japs could
live through all that shelling." But *San Juan's* pounding did little damage to the defenders, who were holed up in the caves and beach dugouts;
the armor-piercing shells were worthless in a staged bombardment.[43]
Maj. Robert H. Williams, the CO, was in the lead craft and stood next

to Lt. Richard E. Bennink, USNR, the landing-craft commander. Williams was anxious to get underway and had urged Bennink ahead. Under pressure, the lieutenant reluctantly gave an early "go" signal, and the *San Juan*'s last salvo landed in the water just ahead. Furious, Lieutenant Bennink cursed the major: "God damn it! I am in command until we hit the beach, and don't ever do that again!"[44]

Unfortunately, the naval gunfire was lifted too soon, and the Japanese were quickly able to reorganize and marshal their forces to greet the invaders. Their reception for the Chutes was machine-gun fire. The defenders of Gavutu had been expecting the American troops for hours, watching the landing craft every step of the way. Gavutu was essentially just over a handful of acres, and the Japanese could shift men and automatic weapons to any threatened sector in a matter of minutes. Once they knew where the marines would land, they brought concentrated firepower to bear on that location.

Because sharp coral clusters border most of the island, the initial landing was made on the northeastern side, not too distant from the causeway connecting the island with Tanambogo. As a result, the landing craft had to pass along the eastern part of the island, between it and Cape Haroro on Florida Island, then make a sharp left toward the proposed landing area. The *Monssen* and the destroyer *Buchanan* by then had been firing at Gavutu, and they lifted fire only a few minutes before the Chutes landed.[45] But from the wreckage of a downed Emily flying boat in Gavutu's harbor came scattered machine-gun fire as the landing boats passed — a menace that was not corrected until the following day by a platoon under Sgt. Warren Fitch (L/3/2). Compounding the landing problems, some coxswains were so frightened that they dropped their passengers far from the beach, and paramarines had to wade through a barrage of bullets.[46]

The preceding shelling had caused additional problems. "These boats intended to land at the concrete seaplane ramps," said General Vandegrift, "but because the heavy naval gunfire and bombing preparation had tumbled huge blocks of cement in the path of the leading waves, several of the boats were forced to land along the concrete dock to the right."[47] Had the Chutes landed on the ramp, it would have provided a running start for them, and the outcome might have been different. One coxswain, lanky Larry Michaels, who stood six feet four inches, brought his landing craft right up to Gavutu's gateway for the dubious honor of having his craft be the first to arrive at hell's doorstep. Being so tall, Michaels made an ideal target for Japanese snipers, but somehow they missed him.

Figure 21. Part of the causeway linking Tanambogo and Gavutu Islands, March 1942.
RAAF airmen Cyril Minchenberg (*left*) and Laurie Cummings (*right*) are on the Tanambogo
side. In August, the U.S. 1st Parachute Battalion and the 2nd Marine Regiment would
fight their way across this deadly stretch to retake the islands from the Japanese.
(Courtesy Clifford J. Searle)

However, they did hit his boat's machine gunner in the shin. Twenty-
year-old seaman John P. Lanigan recalled: "In going in, I was lying down
on the side of the gunwale next to my Lewis gun and I could hear Larry
singing a hymn and a marine sergeant was telling me where he wanted
me to direct my fire. When we hit the beach all hell broke loose. . . . This
marine radio operator fell just as he got up and over the ramp and I went
to assist him to his feet; and I think that's when I caught it. I thought I
bumped my shin on the gunnel but Larry said I was bleeding. After pulling away from the slaughter, Larry took me to the hospital ship."[48]

The Chutes went into Gavutu promptly at 1200 on Day One, right
on schedule. The first wave, with Company A, beached at three selected
landing points, about twenty-five yards apart. The Japanese defenders
let them land with ease, and some stumbled ashore almost too seasick
to care what would happen next. Capt. Kermit Mason caught a Japanese
bullet even before he landed. Lieutenant Bennink had noted that he lost
one boat to a hand grenade and two men, and overall, one man of every
ten that landed was a casualty. The first man ashore was 1st Lt. Norman
R. Nickerson, commander of the 2nd Platoon, Company A; Major Wil-

liams, the gallant leader of the 1st Parachute Battalion, was up and over, and as soon as he had debarked he was out of sight. He slowed down when stopped by a bullet. Nickerson recalled: "I saw Williams fall and rushed to his aid with my platoon, where we formed a protective shield around the major until a corpsman arrived."[49]

Four boats transporting paramarine Company C had landed to the right of Lever's wharf. On board each landing craft were two Lewis guns, left over from World War I and of questionable value—good for only ninety-seven to one hundred rounds. After that the guns were usually "dead." The Chutes carried the Reising submachine guns and 60-mm mortars, plus a few Johnson rifles and .45-caliber Colts for the officers, as well as a few stray pistols bearing the markings of the U.S. Army Smith and Wessons. The first wave had three Bangalore torpedoes, one on each Higgins boat, yet only one was carried to the beach.[50]

Japanese Lieutenant Mitsuwa, the crafty Gavutu gun commander, had honeycombed the commanding hill with automatic weapons. His fifty-four gunners had the main responsibility of holding back the paramarines. They were supported by the civilian laborers of the Hashimoto Construction Force (Shin'ya Hashimoto, 132 men) and the Hara Construction Force (Inoure Hara, fifty men); eleven airmen from the avgas unit of the Yokohama Air Group Floatplane Fighter Unit based at Halavo, Florida Island; and one casual air officer. A total of 248 Japanese were present on D-day. They had let the first wave land, and when the Americans were within range, the order came: *"Hassha o hajime!"*— "Commence firing!"

This took a quick toll on the leathernecks as they beached or were out in deep murky water. The Mitsuwa Butai spent more than its share of time on Nambu machine guns and used them very effectively. Although the marines thought the marksmanship of the defenders was poor, the Japanese inflicted a sizable toll.[51] Mitsuwa's gunners kept up a steady stream of fire as the paramarines cautiously crept forward on the left flank. Fortunately for the Chutes, the antiaircraft gun on Miwa Hill could not be lowered or there would have been even more hell to pay. Since the dawn attack on the twin islands' air complex, the Japanese aircraft crews and service personnel had managed to obtain some of the machine guns from the repair shop on Tanambogo that had been urgently made operative. Defending their base, the airmen joined the fray, pouring fire on the advancing marines. MCPO Masaichiro Miyagawa of the Yokohama Air Group Flying-Boat Unit, reported: "Unfortunately, there was no strong resistance set up at the landing sector [and] some

Marines managed to get to shore." Yet the 1st Parachute Battalion still had no major beachhead.[52]

The second wave of paramarines landed a minute and a half later, facing heavy gunfire. Three were hit before they left the boat, and others were hit as they splashed toward shore. While the Higgins boats were pulling away, one was hit and sunk by a well-placed hand grenade thrown from shore and two sailors were killed.

On Tanambogo, twenty-one-year-old SA Jinsaku Sakurai, also of the Yokohama Air Group, was sleeping on a cot beneath the quarters of the medical officer, Lt. Cdr. Mankichi Hoshino. Hoshino's quarters were in a building on stilts, near the water's edge, a typical spacious and breezy native construction that allowed one to walk underneath. This was Sakurai's home away from home. On the morning of 7 August, he was awakened with a start by an unfamiliar shrill sound. He wondered what it was he had heard, and upon jumping up he saw an aircraft with American markings flying so low that he could distinguish the goggles on the pilots. As Sakurai ran for cover, he picked up a *Chinkesy* (tin case) and started banging on it and yelling, *"Teki no kyûshû!"*—"Enemy raid!"

The planes were coming in to the west from over Florida Island, flying low through the morning mist. Sakurai joined six officers (Lieutenant Commander Tashio; Lt. Tadao Shima, the accountant; and four ensigns) who were quickly heading for the officers' shelter. Ten minutes later, a flight of Grumman fighters appeared, bombing and strafing in successive waves. Sakurai could see that the waters around Tulagi were full of warships moving about while shelling Tanambogo. The attack continued for two hours. He could not remain in the officers' shelter, and thus during the break in the barrage he ran out. When a shell hit and exploded, he lay flat, then before the next salvo, he ran again. This continued until he was able to reach the large shelter on the opposite side of the small island where he was momentarily safe.[53]

The assignment for the Chutes from Capt. William McKennan's Company A, 1st Parachute Battalion, was to secure the landing area and offer a protected haven; this was accomplished under intensely difficult conditions. The Gavutu defenders had the Arisaka Model 38 weapon, whose high-velocity bullet made of nickel iron packed a terrific wallop at distances under 300 yards. This weapon, in skilled hands, took an exceptionally heavy toll on the landing units.[54] The second wave, Company B, which had landed to the left of A Company in a rock-pile area, had been under brutal fire while still on board the Higgins boats; the third wave, Company C, also encountered fire from Gavutu's Hill 148 and from Hill 121 on Tanambogo, but they landed in the beach sector behind Company A. They were even subjected to machine-gun fire from the microscopic offshore islet, Gaomi, called "Dead Man's Island." Capt. Richard J. Huerth of Company C was killed while going over the gunwale, and others nearby were also struck. Shortly after, Huerth's young friend, 2nd Lt. Walter W. Kiser, took a hit that ended a promising career.[55] One landing craft was lost and several crewmen were killed. Cpl. Crescenzo P. Demattis was on Gavutu soil less than ten minutes when a sniper's bullet killed him.

While the Chutes were engaged in the lethal fields of Gavutu, the U.S. Navy had its hands full handling the Imperial Japanese Naval Air Force (IJNAF) on the waters surrounding Guadalcanal. The Chutes on shore could hear the aerial contest, but could not actually see it. They had trouble of their own — staying alive. One of the battle pests on Gavutu was an antitank gun built into a concrete bunker, a weapon that would cause considerable problems before the day was over. The bunker had been constructed by members of the Tanaka Butai during their brief stay on Gavutu, and the builders had left their antitank weapon there when they were transferred to Guadalcanal.[56] A much smaller pest on the island was the red ants, swarming on Gavutu soil in the millions. The crawling Chutes had them on their hands and fingers, on their faces, in their ears, and down their backs — all the while confronting the constant deadly Japanese cannonade. Typical of their commitment was PFC Warren L. Givens, a Lewis gun operator on his Higgins boat, who had poured fire at the enemy. He never ducked to safety and continued to shoot in face of intense opposition. When his gun jammed, Givens grabbed the closest rifle and kept firing until he was hit. He later died of the wound.[57]

When the third wave of 140 men landed at 1206, some of the craft were forced to pull back 1,000 yards because of the murderous weapons fire. Those who landed faced brutal firepower, and several Chutes were hit while still aboard their craft. Ens. Galen Craig Brown, USNR, the third wave landing commander, managed to beach at about 1300; he found a platoon of paramarines held up by heavy fire behind the protection of the smashed concrete debris along the Lever's dock.[58] When the 1st Parachute Battalion finally gained a foothold, it was confined to a small area on the tiny island, and the defenders concentrated their firepower on that sector. The paramarines had fire coming from all directions and could solve only one problem at a time. The first one was Gavutu's hill. Lawrence Moran of Company B recalled:

We left the *Heywood* around 1000 and circled her for about
two hours. . . . I got seasick from all the bouncing around. We,
the second wave, landed about mid-day, not on the beach but
[on] a concrete ramp at about a 45-degree angle. I had a hell of
a time getting out . . . the Japs were not zeroing in on our boat
or I would have been a goner. My entire magazine went into the
"drink." . . . Our company was supposed to go through Company
A and take the hill, but it didn't quite happen that way. I stopped
off and was left behind, by the others who headed for that pesky
hill, to see where the other Japs were located. What I saw was
a sandbag fortification at the other end of the causeway with a
machine gun, and this weapon was shooting at our guys trying
to take the hill. Some paramarines from Company A managed
to toss a grenade at a cave entrance and killed two of the three
enemy, but I imagine some were still alive. This was adjacent to
the risky hill and a fortified position. The entrance was slightly
plugged by sandbags. I could not see too much because of that
small entrance just seeping light and dust. I told the guys with
machine-guns, who set up . . . weapons about 20 yards from
the entrance, that I saw some enemy, still alive. Arriving on the
scene about this time . . . was this 2nd Loolie with a Reising-gun
who set his gun on full automatic, and perhaps playing the Hollywood part, started blasting at the sandbag emplacement. From
the emplacement came a single shot[;] it seemed loud to me
because I was so close. . . . Then I heard that a Lieutenant [Wal-
ter X.] Young was shot through the neck. That was real and not
Hollywood style, because in Hollywood the victims don't bleed
real blood.

About this time I realized I had to get going to catch up
with my platoon now charging up the hill [148]. As I started up
the incline two dive-bombers started to drop bombs and they
exploded near the top of the hill, yet the Nippon flag was still
flying. That cured me from moving to the top, so I just went
halfway up the hill to protect myself from the wild carrier
pilots.

When I came down, the sandbag emplacement was on fire
and the bags were peppered with holes so the sand was pouring
out. I guess the two Japs were in there. We finally took the hill at
a terrific cost of lives. We buried our dead and were relieved by
the 2nd Marines.[59]

Company A attempted to neutralize the deadly hill from a different angle. Plat. Sgt. Thomas P. Driscoll was killed at 1430 while attempting to dislodge the defenders. Shortly afterward, Plat. Sgt. Ronald F. Kachinsky, also from Company A, was killed while leading his 3rd Platoon. The parachutists were encountering heavy concentrated fire from Tanambogo, where the Japanese airmen from the flying-boat detachment were supporting Hill 148 from their side of the causeway. Another adversary, this one unintended, was a U.S. Navy dive-bomber. While flying over Gavutu its gunner opened fire at the paramarines below. They madly waved at him, but he kept on shooting. On his second trip around, the leathernecks fired back and the Dauntless finally flew off. Reportedly the gunner killed at least two Americans.[60]

Pvt. Leo M. Gagnon (2nd Platoon, Company A) grappled with some Japanese in a hand-to-hand struggle, and though outnumbered he managed to kill one of them. When another man threw a grenade at him, Gagnon quickly retrieved it and tossed it back, silencing the thrower; but the gallant marine then was killed by one of the defenders. PFC Theodore J. Houle also in the 2nd Platoon had a different experience with the Japanese. After hours of fighting he finally reached the heavily defended Hill 148 when someone set off the ammo dump nearby and sent Houle flying. The next thing he remembers was that he was on board the *Neville*. Pvt. William J. Taylor Jr. (HQ/1) earned the title "Wild Bill," as he was all over the island. According to one ex-paramarine, Taylor never remained still. In contrast, one officer [Miller] was dubbed "Fox Hole" because he found an empty pit and directed his platoon from his stationary headquarters with orders to "Get 'em, boys."

The parachutists were trained to fight as individuals, and PFC Robert G. Fuller of Company C, from Newburyport, Massachusetts, did just that. Fuller was a one-man hurricane. He attacked a fortified machine-gun emplacement against withering blasts from the enemy and in perilous hand-to-hand combat killed eight of Mitsuwa's men. Another standout was Cpl. Ralph W. Fordyce of Company A, one of the first to beach and one of the first in action. While inland, Fordyce overpowered an enemy navy man and, taking his gun, shot and killed his opponent and another enemy soldier. Then he daringly attacked a machine-gun emplacement, killing all five defenders.[61] Cpl. Carmen C. Delia single-handedly attacked another fortified position, fighting until he neutralized the enemy post. In that action Delia took a Japanese slug in the shoulder; he was taken to the Gavutu makeshift hospital (the former Lever's store) and later evacuated to New Zealand. In yet another daring assault, Sgt. Wilfred V. Michaud killed eight of the enemy, eliminating a hazardous obstacle and thus helping clear the way for the marines' advance.[62] The U.S. Navy doctors, Lt. Harold Schwartz and Lt. Harry Eisenberg, had their hands full patching up these casualties as best they could and sending them off to the better-organized shipboard medical facilities in the harbor. The *Neville* was declared the hospital vessel for the casualties, but some wounded paramarines ended up on the "Unholy Four," the name given the other transports.[63]

With Major Williams down, Maj. Charles A. Miller, CO of Company B, succeeded to command of the battalion. Williams's runner was unable to contact Miller for thirty minutes, however, and this complicated the leadership problem, as Miller's command post had not yet been established. The battle raged on Gavutu without leadership; Miller was in a vacuum. Capt. George R. Stallings, the commander of the weapons unit, played an important role in securing the island by reducing the Japanese strong points with the proper placement of his 60-mm mortars. Meanwhile, Lt. William C. Ellis, USNR, the third-wave commander, was instructed to transfer the wounded to the *Neville* in one of the damaged boats, but while his Higgins boat was withdrawing, two of the crew were wounded. During this period Japanese small-arms fire from both Tanambogo and Gavutu had become so intense that each of the sailors who were boating the wounded back to safety wondered if any one of those flying slugs had his name on it.

By 1400 of 7 August the Chutes on the left flank had made suitable progress and were able to apply constant mortar fire on the right flank. Lieutenant Gregory's platoon was tied down as they attempted to reach Miller's command post to provide protection. The command post was also the short-term hospital, temporarily set up in Lever's store. It was a two-story structure, one of the largest buildings on the island, but was subject to intense sniper fire. Eventually, however, the exhausted paramarines established some minor control over Gavutu. Company A of the 1st Parachute Battalion had a number of exceptional men, among them PFC George F. Grady. Grady was having difficulty with his Reising gun but, nevertheless, he rushed three of the enemy who were firing on his squad and engaged them in hand-to-hand combat. He killed two before he was mortally wounded; he died five hours after landing.[64]

Some remnants of Company B, under Capt. Richard S. Johnson, finally managed to subdue the Gavutu hill, but they suffered losses for their bravery. Marine gunner Robert L. Manning of Company B, 1st Parachute Battalion, heroically charged the hill and bolted through the key entrance, then engaged several of the enemy in a hand-to-hand struggle that resulted in the death of Lieutenant Mitsuwa. Finally, the Stars and Stripes were raised over Gavutu, possibly to inform the U.S. Navy fliers that the island was now United States territory. But at that moment, the Rising Sun still flew over Tanambogo.[65]

Day One at Gavutu, morning to night, is relived in two more individual accounts. Leonard Kiesel of Company C, 1st Parachute Battalion, was part of the third wave:

> Breakfast 7 August, one apple! What a way to go to battle. That morning we were all lined up on the railing of the *Heywood* watching the Navy planes strafe the two target islands, Gavutu and Tanambogo. I remember seeing a Japanese gas and oil storage unit go up in smoke, the result of shooting and bombing by our Navy. We were all anxious and excited, but had to wait our turn to board the Higgins boats, as they were committed to the 1st Raiders for the Tulagi landing. We were called upon to make the Gavutu landing at 1200.
>
> When we finally climbed down the rope net into the barges, the water had turned a bit rough. The barges were bouncing up and down and when I attempted to drop off the net into a waiting Higgins, my knees were almost driven up to my shoulder blades. Brief distress but nothing like I would feel later on. The U.S. Navy started shelling and blasting the shoreline; their shells were streaking over our heads. We were on our way in — finally.
>
> As we came closer to Gavutu one of our coxswains was hit and instantly killed; his assistant took over and hunched down in the bottom of the barge, steering by reaching his hand up to the wheel. About 50 yards off shore he uttered, "This is as far as I go boys." We had to bail over the sides, no landing ramps on these old plywood babies. Over we went — chest deep in water, bullets singing by, some hitting the water. It was so concentrated at one time, I considered ducking under the water and going in that way. Two of our mortar men, with mortars strapped on their backs, stepped into deep holes in the coral and never did come up. Another Chute [Pvt. Lawton R. Crumpler Jr.] (C/1) just in front of me stumbled and went down, I thought he had slipped; after catching him by the shoulders, I dropped him instantly, half his face was gone! All this happened in a few seconds.

Finally, getting to move along a little, now up to my belt line, then knee deep and beginning to move better, when "wham" I am knocked off my feet. Getting up, I tried to run, but my right leg buckled under me. It was then I knew I was hit. I managed to crawl up to the beach and headed to my left and got behind a piece of concrete [from the blasted seaplane ramp] to shelter me from the gun that hit me. I called "Corpsman," but none came. I applied a tourniquet to my leg to stop the bleeding.

Every time I moved to change my tourniquet, the Japs would pepper my area. I finally made up my mind that this was my area to defend and set things up accordingly. A knife stuck in the ground near my head, two grenades nearby and my piece by my side. Looking over the top of the concrete slab, I noticed three enemies about 70 yards away, along the beach in a downed Jap seaplane or what was left of one. They were busy manning the one gun that was operating. I quickly took aim and fired three shots, I know I killed one of them and wounded the other. Now I waited. No more firing from that pesthole. "Thank God."

Next I heard a dragging . . . or crawling sound coming in my direction; I reached for my rifle but he was quickly upon me, swinging a knife; instead I got him. I felt exhausted . . . for some reason it was quiet. . . . I began to get a little scared. I heard muffled sounds and put my ear to the ground and could hear Japanese voices around me; the sounds seemed to be coming from the ground itself. I guess there were tunnels everywhere. My leg still hurt badly and I was almost immobile. . . . After three hours, I decided to give a corpsman another call. To my surprise, two corpsmen appeared almost at once. . . . I was taken up to a makeshift hospital, a partially damaged galvanized building high on a hill on Gavutu. Sulfa powder was applied to my leg and [it was] stretched out and bound.

Later that night two Higgins boats were called in to evacuate the wounded, including myself. We were put in metal-mesh stretchers and loaded on board for a trip to [the *Neville*], which acted as a hospital vessel. Then they were hoisting the stretcher to the deck—I was in the lower basket being raised up with one stretcher above me. The Marine in the stretcher above me had been hit in the lung area and was bleeding badly; his basket was full of blood. As it reached near the deck area, his stretcher

158   Hell's Islands

partially tipped, causing his blood to splash on me. Then when I reached the deck, I heard a medic call out "Get this guy over to the operating room right away." I said, "This is not my blood, I was hit in the leg—that guy (pointing my finger) he is the guy you want."[66]

Likewise, the events of that day remained etched in the mind of ex-paratrooper Robert Walter Moore of the 3rd Platoon, Company B, fifty years after the battle:

On August 7, my platoon was together on the deck of the Higgins boat heading into Gavutu. We were told there [were] about 600 Japanese and . . . that there were laborers. We asked how could we tell who was who and were told, "You can't, just kill them all." As we approached the cement dock [Lever's pier] Marine Gunner Robert Manning (MG) looked over the bow of the landing craft and said, "There couldn't possibly be anyone alive there[.]" It had been blasted and shelled from one end to the other and the island was absolutely bare except for a few coconut trees that seemed to have survived.

As we were approaching the sea wall and dock [about 75 yards out] we hit a coral reef and the bow of the boat swung to the left and the bow was lowered, we all plowed into the water, not realizing the water was up to our necks. We started heading for the sea wall . . . bullets were whizzing around us and heavy fire hitting the water and you could hear the sound of shells flying by. After a vexing time, we reached the sea wall . . . there [were] cement blocks about 3' × 3'. My platoon assembled about at the base of the sea wall and we commenced firing. That is, every one except me. My piece would not fire. . . . I tried everything I knew how to get it to operate. No luck. I was weaponless with the enemy firing at the Marines, including yours truly. . . .

Manning also tried to fix my weapon. Still no luck. Finally he said "Throw the damn thing away" and handed me his .45 pistol, a Colt A1 "Sauce" weapon. He still had a workable Reising submachine gun and said "Follow me and stay close." Believe me, I did.[67]

Finally we were able to crawl up the sea wall and land. It was slow going [as we] headed east to the base of the hill [Hill 148], . . . facing a murderous fire coming from [there]. We attempted to make ourselves the smallest target you could imagine, struggling all the way, and finally managed to reach the base of the hill. . . . There was some sort of a small wash running from [its] base . . . to the water. It was there that I saw my first dead Marine, Cpl. Harold E. Johns, who was a rigger in Headquarters Company. I have never forgotten it.

. . . We got to the end of the island and started up the east side of the hill under extreme fire. It was very slow going with casualties all along the route. The hill was approximately 140 foot high and there were caves and dugouts all the way up. The first Japs I saw in one of the dugouts were big men in gray uniforms [from the Mitsuwa AA gun unit]; . . . [William K.] Vesey (B/1) was in the Jap dugout swearing and stabbing any enemy within bayonet distance, over and over with his bayonet. . . . I saw Platoon Sgt. Howard D. Pumroy (B/1) and 2nd Lt. Walter W. Kiser had been killed. The two were close friends, perhaps from the same town.

. . . There was constant machine[-]gun fire coming from a tin roof building [Lever's store]. . . . We were pinned down for some time, I don't recall just how long, and we had not reached our goal. One of two planes [an SBD] dropped a bomb at the top of the hill, killing some of our own people and inflicting injuries on others. Somehow we finally got to the top and wiped out the machine[-]gun nest.

That night we dug in as best we could on the side of the damn hill. It rained buckets and we lay in our foxhole, alert but soaked and shivering. About 2200 there was a rumbling and an upper part of a battle scarred coconut tree came crashing down in our area. It killed [Cpl. Joseph G.] Bresing (B/1). Joe had gone through the day without a scratch only to be killed by a falling tree. The next morning, I received Joe's Reising gun and gave Manning back his .45.[68]

Reworking the Plan

Col. W. J. McKennan would later write: "As commander of 'A' Company I was convinced by nightfall of D-day that the combined small unit tactics of both 'A' and 'B' Companies had overcome all organized resistance on Hill 148 and Gavutu was, indeed, secure."[69]

But the battle had not ended, only subsided. The paramarines' mission was to seize Gavutu and then attack and secure Tanambogo. The plan was to commit Company C to overrun the opposition airmen (though they didn't know they were airmen at the time) and seize Tanambogo, utilizing the remainder of the shot-up Chute battalion to grab the island via the causeway.

A systematic destruction of enemy trouble spots began on D + 1 using TNT, gasoline, and dynamite. Capt. Harry L. Torgerson (HQ/1), a demolition expert, became well known for his part in blowing up the caves on Gavutu—blasting the Japanese "to kingdom-come" or sealing the caves shut. Torgerson held to the "cockroach theory": uncover one and there are likely to be more. However, the majority of Japanese cave holdouts were terrified laborers from the construction units.[70]

While the exhausted Chutes commanders began working out a plan to invade the twin island, the Yokohama airmen planted drums of gasoline across the portal to block the passageway between Gavutu to Tanambogo, hoping against hope that the Imperial Navy would rescue them before the marines broke through the barriers. Lt. Cdr. Saburo Katsuda, the air group's executive officer, planned the operation involving the gasoline drums. He was certain the Americans would not make a landing before nightfall. A coral reef extended through the waters adjoining the officers' dugout, and since the invaders' landing craft would hit the bottom and be stranded, they probably would not approach there. Katsuda believed the landing would be either at the wharf or by the causeway. When the air attacks subsided, he organized a large group of airmen to move a quantity of 200-liter gasoline drums from the wharf and place them everywhere along the water's edge and across the portal to block the passageway between Gavutu and Tanambogo. Some drums were placed near the radio shack. That evening between 2200 and 2300, just as Katsuda had predicted, enemy assault craft cut their engines and began attempting to land. But his plan had defects, and eventually it would cause more harm to his Tanambogo defenders, because smoke and flames from the burning gasoline would block the machine gunners' view, allowing the marines to rush in.

The constant fire coming from Tanambogo prevented the marines from crossing the causeway and was taxing the push-pull energies of the tired Chutes. One of the aggravating spots was the island's water tower, where snipers took shots at the invaders until the nest was cleaned up. The Japanese airmen on Tanambogo had whittled away at the Chutes, killing some, wounding others. The paramarines' commander had planned to employ the depleted Company C in an attempt to secure the dangerous passage across the causeway, but only about seventy worn-out paramarines were available for the thrust. A strong supporting force was

Figure 22. The water tower on Gavutu Island, March 1942. In August, Japanese sharpshooters were located here, preventing the U.S. Marines from quickly crossing the causeway during the battle for the islands. (Courtesy Clifford J. Searle)

required to impel the drive across the stone walkway, and a message was sent out seeking reinforcements.

In another location, earlier having completed its mission on Florida Island, Company B, 1st Battalion, 2nd Marines, was ordered to return to the *President Jackson* for reassignment. The ship's captain sent six boats to retrieve Captain Edward Crane's troopers at 1500, but while en route they were intercepted by Maj. William K. Enright, the executive officer of the 2nd Battalion, 5th Marines, who issued verbal orders to Crane to land on Gavutu and transfer control of his company to the commanding officer, 1st Parachute Battalion. That CO was Maj. Charles A. Miller, who had replaced the wounded Major Williams. However, Miller was often off somewhere, and Capt. George R. Stallings became the part-time CO. Company B was now to shift to Gavutu in a supporting role. The difficulty was that Captain Crane was informed that only a small pocket of snipers held the island; actually there were about 240 Japanese air-unit personnel.[71]

Three of Captain Crane's Higgins boats were ordered to proceed to the northeastern portion of Tanambogo to attack the defenders from the rear. The others headed in another course; one boat containing the

2nd Platoon hung up on a coral reef and took no part in the assault. In the meantime, the destroyers began shelling the wharves and the jetty on Tanambogo's eastern shore. Crane had anticipated a landing at about 1845 under the wrap of darkness, but this cover literally was blown when one of the last shells fired, a wild one, hit Gavutu's fuel dump. The marines were silhouetted in the glare of the burning oil, a shooting gallery for the enemy shore guns. Bedlam prevailed, with Company B's LCPs going in all directions, some out of control and some headed for the shore. A couple of leathernecks were killed while manning the Lewis guns on one bow; a coxswain in another craft also was killed. A few landing craft crashed the beach area near the docks, and as they tried to approach, the heavy fire drove the marines back to their boats. Two boats were wrecked and the wounded ended up in the water—some swam back to Florida Island. The Japanese managed to perforate one of the boats, causing six casualties.

The bonfire on shore clearly outlined Captain Crane's marines before they all had an opportunity to fully disembark. Many became casualties. A machine-gun unit (4th Platoon, Company D) managed to reach shore and set up two of its weapons on Lever's dock, but it came under heavy gunfire and was forced to withdraw. The Japanese had a "duck shoot" and took advantage of it. Coxswain John S. Evans, USNR, who had taken Crane's troops to Florida early that morning was now involved in boating some Company B marines to Gavutu. At high risk he managed to disembark passengers from his LCP, including Cpl. George F. Goodspeed Jr., Cpl. William S. Parks, and PFC Everett J. Rodgers, who somehow obtained a foothold on that rock.

Evans and his crew remained at Gavutu until 0400 on D + 1, the LCP serving as an aid station. They were under constant fire as casualties were loaded, but Evans successfully withdrew and delivered the wounded to the *Neville*. Then he took his landing craft back into the maelstrom, transporting more 2nd Marines from the *Jackson* to Gavutu in support of the beleaguered 1st Parachute Battalion.

According to Chief Pharmacist's Mate William F. Graham:

> After we had been shot out of the Higgins boats, it was Captain Crane who gathered us together and led us back to Gavutu, wading chin deep in water along the causeway. . . . In the darkness, both Japs and the Marines on Gavutu were firing at us. The coolness displayed by Captain Crane held us together. Some men from Company B who did manage to land were to scratch

small cuts of Gavutu real estate as shelter from anything that would offer protection. Even Gavutu's scrub brush would find a Marine behind it, hugging the rock soil. Crane's determination and the stalwart remnants of Company B who managed to get to shore established a toehold. His problem was not so much the Japanese, but the paramarines who were trigger happy; they were unaware that a number of unannounced 2nd Marines were in their midst. Crane noticed some men, who were not too far from him, and not knowing the password he shouted, "I'm Captain Edgar Crane, Company B, 2nd Marines!"

A word comes from the crowd "No he is not." A Chute yelled "He is a Jap. I can tell by his accent, shoot the Jap son-of-a-bitch!" [Crane came from Galveston, Texas, and had the well-known southwestern drawl.] Torgerson yelled "Hold your fire, I know this guy."[72]

Captain Crane's Gavutu landing cost the 2nd Marines eight dead, fourteen wounded, and twenty-six missing. Among the survivors, Elmer R. Wetsel of Company D, 2nd Battalion, 2nd Marines, and his companions who had supported the landing, would spend a miserable night in the chilly water hugging the pilings of Lever's pier to avoid the withering enemy fire. He was cold, hungry, and tired, but Wetsel hung on for dear life—the water was twenty fathoms deep.

Early the following morning the remnants of Companies B and D were able to leave their cover and fight their way inland to join the battle. Miyagawa reported losses on Tanambogo for 7 August of only ten air service personnel KIA, with approximately two hundred fifty still alive.

The uncertain struggle would continue.

9 Day Two: Tulagi, Gavutu, and Tanambogo

At 0230 on 8 August 1942 the captains of the *President Adams, President Hayes, Alhena,* and *Crescent City* received orders to shift from the reserve force section off Guadalcanal to anchorage off Tulagi. By 0600 the four ships were moored in transport area YOKE (Transport Group Y). At 0300 the alarm bells rang for reinforcements to support the 1st Raiders and 2nd Battalion, 5th Marines, on Tulagi. In the predawn hours, the 3rd Battalion, 2nd Marines, plus elements of Batteries H and I of the 3rd Battalion, 10th Marines, aboard the *Alhena,* were ordered to land with their 75-mm pack howitzers. At 0705 the orders were rescinded and a new directive issued. The invasion forces were doing well, but the marines there could use some help in a final mopping up.

There was no reason why the RINGBOLT operation should have been in trouble, as more than 1,500 marines were on Tulagi. The situations on Gavutu and Tanambogo, on the other hand, were still very much in doubt. There the few battle-weary paramarines who were still able to stand were lucky; the others were either on stretchers or awaiting burial. The tactical reserve of the 2nd Marines and its supporting units thus were alerted at 0800, and ordered to proceed to Tulagi and Gavutu.

The Bitter Fight

At 0945, Combat Team A—the 1st Battalion, 2nd Marines, less Companies B and C—landed at BEACH BLUE on Tulagi with orders to mop up and sweep to the center and the rock area of snipers. The Japanese forces had dwindled, yet an occasional sea infantryman took potshots at stray marines, until they were whittled down one by one. James Sorensen (A/1/2) described his company's part in clearing out Tulagi:

> At dawn on the . . . 8th [we were] re-boated from [Florida] and told we were to make a landing on Tulagi to back up the Raider Battalion, which had found itself in a rather stiff fight.[1] We

were picked up on Halavo Beach by Higgins craft and shifted to Tulagi. Due to the coral at the landing zone, we disembarked at a point about 50 yards from the shoreline and waded in. . . . The landing zone was directly opposite the Chinese cemetery and we moved across this area quickly to the base of the ridge running down from the center of Tulagi . . . .We came under automatic weapons and sniper fire from the ridge, but it did not last for more than a few minutes. . . . [WO Katsuzo Fukimoto had pulled most of his squad (snipers) out of the sector to join the main force adjacent to the middle of the island, leaving a few men behind to harass the marines.]

The Raiders were engaged in a major fight at this time towards the eastern end of Tulagi. Our Company A, under Capt. Paul W. Fuhrop, was ordered to move over the ridge above the cemetery and to the east of Sasapi to the north of the ridge. We turned west, then on the northern slope, and . . . proceeded to sweep this side of the ridge. We came under intermittent automatic and persistent sniper fire as we cleaned out this side. . . . The movement lasted no more than a couple of hours and in the process a handful of enemy snipers were eliminated. At this point we had apparently reached the extreme west end of the ridgeline. We reversed our move, then traversed back to Sesapi, then crossed the ridge by a deep cut through the ridge in the vicinity of Sesapi, and then crossed the ridge and back to the cemetery.[2]

Although no longer facing an expected hail of bullets, the marines could not take safety for granted, as Bill Cannon of Company C, 1st Battalion, 2nd Marines, witnessed when part of his battalion deployed from Florida Island to Tulagi: "[On] D + 1 dawn saw us re-embarking in our Higgins boats for a quick trip to Tulagi. We landed on Tulagi at [the] Chinese Cemetery and had to suffer through another combat landing at the hands of the nervous gunners on the landing craft. This barrage lasted about 20 minutes, doing nothing . . . just shredded vegetation. We were assigned to patrol the mid-island and clean out the enemy. At one point we were feeling safe, then one shot rang out. A sniper sent a bullet through Pvt. Joseph H. Jenks's neck; he was the company's first casualty. Jenks was evacuated on the *Neville*. I never heard any further from him."[3]

One of the responsibilities of Headquarters Company, 2nd Battalion, 2nd Marines, was guarding the assistant commander, Brig. Gen. William H. Rupertus, who was placed in charge of the Tulagi Northern Landing Force (NLF), and operations of the satellite islands of Gavutu, Tanambogo, and Makambo. He landed with his staff—all in well-pressed, starched uniforms—on Tulagi's western BEACH BLUE from his command post aboard the *Neville* at 1234 on Saturday, 8 August. Dallas Bennett (HQ/2/2) remembers:

> BEACH BLUE was at a place where the Japanese had established a cemetery and was heavily forested. On arrival, we did not get a small greeting card from the Jap troops in the form of machine gun fire. I thought that maybe Japs don't shoot at generals? I was mistaken. We took off our packs and were just about to plot our position when . . . [a] sniper took a pot shot at someone, and we all hit the ground[;] then, all our machine guns, and rifles opened up and the blasting lasted about five minutes. No more discriminating shots were fired our way. Then quiet. A "cease firing" order was issued.
>
> At the time Headquarters Company 2/2 landed [on the] beaches of Tulagi, they had been outside the zone of fire riding in the waves of Tulagi harbor attempting to land, and it was noontime before they could reach their disembarking point. . . . Tulagi was in shambles. We safely delivered the General to the 1st Raider Battalion command post at a house called the "Residency" situated on one of the highest elevations and about midway on this less than 100 acre island. He took no part in the active field command until he turned up at 1300 on the 8th.
>
> Snipers took advantage of the cover afforded by underbrush and trees, caves, bomb shelters, and rocks, as well as buildings. Many of Tulagi's buildings were built two to three feet above ground level with metal roofs and water tanks to catch the rain water since there was no fresh water on the island. The enemy utilized these buildings, their attics, and water tanks for sniper cover. Each had to be destroyed or given a spray of machine gun fire and grenades. One such building, clearly marked as a hospital, contained snipers.[4] [This would have been the position of Lt. Ryoichi Chadani of the medical corps, with the snipers being any of the six stretcher-bearers in his unit; even the hospitalized patients participated in the fight.]
>
> Eliminating snipers and machine-gun nests sometimes took ingenuity. Gunnery Sgt. Jessie R. Glover, an old "China Hand" from Company H, used his team and grenades to greet these

holdouts. He had once climbed up on the shoulders of squad members to reach the attic of a Japanese occupied building used as a sniper post. He threw two grenades through the window and yelled "Good morning you poges!" Glover then climbed down and calmly walked inside to check his handiwork. All six occupants were dead. One of the last caves to be neutralized was one dug midway through the ground-level passageway cut from the Government wharf to King George field on the opposite side of the island. This was cut only about ten feet wide and nearly 30–40 feet deep. This had been a shortcut to the other side. Caves dug into the limestone sidewalls by the Japanese made it almost impossible to approach the openings without being exposed to those [inside]. Directly in front of the caves the Nippon warriors set up a sandbag fort and had men facing either way and firing. Marines of Company D poured fire of every caliber gun or weapon on hand at the barricade from both ends of the hill cutout. Actually, it is a wonder Marines did not hit their buddies who were on the other end, as both were firing at the Japanese barricade in the middle. The fire kept up for some time with the Kure men firing in both directions, occasionally running into the cave for more ammunition. Someone in Dog Company conceived the brilliant idea of burning them out. They got hold of a 55 gallon drum of gasoline and managed to get it to the top of the hill and poured it down on the Japanese below, setting it on fire. That obstacle was removed.[5]

About 0950 on 8 August, the first wave of the 2nd Marines, Combat Team C, reached the fringe of Gavutu and landed between the two cement piers. By 1000 they were treading on death's doorstep; in the second wave, Company K found numerous dead paramarines in its path. Company M landed under sporadic fire, for the Japanese they were still full of fight. Attached to the 2nd Marines in support of the assault on Gavutu was the 3rd Platoon, Company A, 2nd Pioneer Battalion, under 2nd Lt. Harold A. Hayes. Hayes's demolition experts—the "go-to-hell" men—were just what was needed to blast out the island's resolute defenders and seal the caves. They came ashore on Gavutu right next to the landing craft of Lt. Col. Robert G. Hunt. Among Lieutenant Hayes's Pioneers were Illinois-born Russell L. Jarrett; "Henry" Duke, a quiet Texan; and Barney Boos. Emory B. Ashurst, a demolition squad leader, recalled: "We took up our position at the intersection of the causeway

Figure 23. The 3rd Platoon, Company A, 2nd Pioneer Battalion, 2nd Marine Division, photographed at Tulagi Island, September 1942. *Front row, left to right*: Harley R. Simmons, Axel Friedstrom, William Hill, Joe McEntree, Robert Wilson, Abe Simon, Ed Susans, Leo Pakula, Robert Jackman, M. D. Woods. *Second row*: L. Brown, Joe Sobol, Paul Baran, Frank Brookner, William Glasner, Tom Thomson, Everett Baker, Frank Smith, Emory B. Ashurst, Jimmie Read. *Third row*: Richard F. "Pappy" Dortch, Roy Hulse, Robler (?), Sam Herman, Gene Young, William Pressley, Donald Lazzari, David McGary, Russell L. Jarrett, U.S. Navy Corpsman Gene Getchel. *Back row*: 2nd Lt. Harold A. Hayes (platoon commander), Charles Snelling, Gene Seng, Perry Johnson, Charles Kinder, Donald Perry, Jimmie May, Daniel Vollmer, Charles Mull, Henry Duke, August Gustafson, U.S. Navy Corpsman Roy M. Ford. Present but not identified: Jack Noonan, John Bass, Plat. Sgt. Gerald Christiano. (Courtesy Joe Sobol and William Bethard)

and Gavutu and manned a 13-mm antiaircraft machine gun. We proceeded to dispose of bomb duds and blow caves after the Japanese refused to come out. . . . At one cave, as I was placing a charge, a shot went off and I wasn't sure if someone was shooting at me or killing himself. It turned out an officer [had] shot himself with a rifle, using his toe to pull the trigger."[6]

The 2nd Platoon, 2nd Pioneers, under 2nd Lt. Arthur K. Simonson, with Sgt. George Gable, Corpsmen Harold B. Rice and Roy M. Ford, and machine-gun specialist Michael A. Masters, were among the mere thirty men who made the Tulagi landing about noon on the 8th. They passed beat-up Chinatown and went ashore at the Sasapi jetty, the former boat-building area of Tulagi. Meanwhile, 2nd Lt. John S. "Skip" Henderson Jr. and his 1st Platoon landed on Gavutu and shuttled men between there and Tanambogo. Only ninety-eight Pioneers were on the three islands.

Elements of the 10th Marines were fed into the Tulagi–Gavutu–Tanambogo meat grinder at a later stage of the struggle. The "cannon-cockers" of Company I, 3rd Battalion, 10th Marines, in company with elements of the 2nd Marines, landed at Levers' dock on Gavutu, while Company H (3/10) was shifted to Tulagi and landed at the government pier. Battery H moved inland between the Sasapi jetty and Chinatown and faced Gavutu and Tanambogo. Warren Fitch of Company L, 3rd Battalion, 2nd Marines, from the *President Adams,* recalled his company's arrival on Gavutu:

> The paratroops had met stiff resistance; at the end of the 7th they called for help. Company L was alerted at 4:00 A.M. on the 8th to get ready to go ashore and to take what we needed for 72 hours. At daybreak we loaded into landing boats. The [1st] Platoon led the way; this was my Platoon, I had the second squad. When the boat hit the beach I was first out. There were several Marines lying [there] and I landed in the middle of them, thinking to get news from them as to what the situation was. I looked to the right where there were four-dead; I looked to the left, there were also four dead. Advancing about twenty-five feet I was told to keep my squad down. There was a log and sand[-]bagged bunker just ahead. They were having trouble getting the bunker cleared out. We had one more trick to try. About five sticks of dynamite were tied to the end of a 12-foot board. This was lit and shoved into the bunker. When it exploded the whole top seemed to raise about two feet and then settle to ground level. The bunker was then quiet.[7]

Company L, having landed on the north end of Gavutu, then made a sweeping line toward the south. It eliminated a couple machine-gun nests along the way and then came upon a disabled Japanese plane half above water. When the marine who waded out to check on it was fired on from the plane, Fitch's company shot back and killed whatever enemy was there. Fitch relates that Company L was motivated by the memory of the reported Japanese atrocities after the enemy had taken Wake Island on 23 December 1941:

> Several times [there on Gavutu], two or three Japs tried to surrender, but we cut them down. We had a battle cry, "Remember

Wake Island." As far as we knew all Marines were killed on Wake [and we] were not going to take any prisoners. If the Japs [had] announced they had taken prisoners on Wake, it would have saved some of their men. As we advanced along the south shore of the south end of the island, we came to the ridge that ran [its] length . . . . We encountered some caves in a rock edge of the shoreline. A couple of nude Japs ran out of them onto the shallow coral reef, but with about 25 Marines firing at them, they didn't make it far. Now we started receiving fire from the caves, some at ground level and some at a height of fifteen feet. In order to return the fire directly into the caves we had to get out on the coral reefs in about ten inches of water. To the Japs we must have looked like ducks in a shooting gallery. Our Platoon Sergeant Hill took a bad groin hit; and a corpsman was killed going to his aid. A Marine behind me told me to step to one side as I was in his line of fire. The split second I moved over he was hit in the left shoulder. As he was about three inches shorter than I was, it would have been a heart hit [for me]. Several more were wounded around me. The firing from the caves let up and we retraced our route on the island.

That evening at sunset "Taps" [was] played. We had about an hour of resting before taking beach defenses for the night. During this lull, the words "war is hell" kept going over and over in our minds. I had a pretty good idea of its meaning.[8]

While the leathernecks were clearing out the stragglers as best they could, the nooks and crannies hid some enemy airmen. PO Marakazu Yasuta from Osaka, Japan, found a spot in which to hide near the Gavutu wharf; it was a locale he knew well, as the flying boats were usually fueled there. The area was crawling with marines, some within feet of his hiding place, but somehow Yasuta managed to conceal himself. That night he emerged slowly, managed to get to the beach unseen, and swam to Florida Island. Yasuta's war was almost over.

1st Lt. Frederick W. Riggs landed on Gavutu with Company K, 3rd Battalion, 2nd Marines, he recalls:

It wasn't long after the 0200 alert on 8 August, on board our transport, *President Adams,* that the [2nd] Platoon of K Company was in Higgins boats and headed for Gavutu, presumably to relieve the paratroopers, who had met considerable opposition there. On approaching the island it was evident that the Marines from the previous landing group had not pushed up to shore, but we were still taking cover in the deep water surrounding the [island's] banks . . . . Pushing ahead and climbing on shore we were immediately subjected to intermittent fire from Tanambogo, off our right flank.

Cpl. Jonnie Blackburn of Tyler, Texas, on attempting to take cover under a fallen coconut palm found the space already occupied by the enemy; Blackburn was able to shoot before the terrified Japanese could react.[9]

Then the Platoon moved up the steep slope of the dominating hill and from that vantage point the surrounding islands, including Savo, were in clear view. We watched Tanambogo undergoing attack by our own SBDs, which flew from the south, dropped their bombs and continued northwards towards Tulagi. Unfortunately, one of the pilots approaching Tanambogo spotted us on Gavutu and, evidently thinking we were Japanese, banked his plane to the west and dropped his bomb, with fatal results on Mike (M) Company's machine gun squad, which was temporarily attached to the 2nd Platoon.

That afternoon and evening, a heavy rain fell, soaking us, and we were near incapacitation from the cold. In the dark we were able to locate and move into a big water[-]filled depression where in we sat, somewhat warm and relaxed. We watched the fireworks and heard the gunfire of a tremendous naval battle off Savo and waited for the rain to stop. . . . When dawn arrived, by the faint light, we discovered that we were sitting in a shell hole warm and red with the blood and body parts of our comrades; the victims of the previous day's bombing.[10]

A temporary aid station was set up on Gavutu at the Lever's bullet-peppered store; it was manned by three Naval Reserve doctors—Lt. Gilbert C. Campbell, Lt. John N. Roberts, and Lt. Erwin T. MacCamy—all assigned to the medical team of the 2nd Marines. Their skilled hands meant some relief for the Chutes's doctors, who were now nearing exhaustion. The corpsmen all went in harm's way. Two of these unarmed medics, though wearing the Red Cross red and white armbands, were killed as they went after a wounded marine; a third then attempted to rescue the downed marine, but he was also shot to death. Apparently the

Japanese did not respect the Geneva Convention guidelines regarding the safety of medical personnel. One corpsman, PhM1c Eugene Edward Baxter of Company D, 2nd Medical Battalion, was recommended for the Navy Cross for this action.[11]

Richard N. Vorwaller of Company M, 3rd Battalion, 2nd Marines, tells the story of his company on Gavutu:

> In the early morning of August 8 just after daylight, the 3rd Platoon, Company M, 3rd Battalion, 2nd Marines moved down the cargo nets of the *President Adams* into the waiting Higgins boats. Our heavy .30 caliber machine guns along with spare parts and boxes of ammunition were lowered into the waiting boats. Our packs held three days' "C" rations, a poncho, an extra pair of socks, and a belt of machine[-]gun ammunition. We also carried 100 rounds of .30 caliber ammo for our 30.06 bolt action Springfield rifles. We had one canteen of water, a bayonet, a fighting knife, and a gas mask.
>
> All boats formed up and started for the shore of Gavutu. . . . Because none of us really knew what war was like . . . we were not afraid, a little apprehensive maybe, but not really scared. It was very quiet going in, then an older man in our Platoon by the name of Bill Windham opened the bolt in his rifle and fed a clip of shells into it. Private Acherman said, "Are you loading your rifle?" to which Windham answered, "Hell yes man! This is war!" At his reply everyone in our boat loaded his weapon.
>
> Lt. Robert O'Brian, our Platoon leader, said, "We have done everything according to rank and we're going out of this boat according to rank." O'Brian was the first out. As we left the landing craft and headed up the beach there was fire coming at us, but every man in the Platoon made it ashore without being hit.
>
> We moved to the Lever Brothers store and up to the foot of the hill and there we set up our guns to cover the island of Tanambogo. From there we could see the end of Gavutu, the causeway between the two islands and the whole side of Tanambogo that faced us. After our guns were set up, we began an applied wrapper fire of the whole island of Tanambogo. We covered it from top to bottom.
>
> One incident I recall . . . happened to me during this heavy firing, as I was shooting from a natural depression about a foot and a half deep, . . . I saw a dual heavy machine gun firing from a posi-

tion on top of the hill of Tanambogo back at us. They were using tracers and everything seemed to be moving in a very slow motion. It looked to me as if the tracers were just floating in the air but they were coming directly at me, so I rolled to my left as fast as I could and the bullets impacted in the ground right where I had been [lying].[12]

Robert C. Libby, also of Company M, describes 8 August from landing to nightfall:

For information on events we were very much left in the dark. However, later in the day we were informed we would be put ashore on the following morning. Saturday, August 8 dawned bright and clear. Once in our landing craft, we pulled away from our ship and headed across open waters towards the island of Gavutu–Tanambogo. The 1st Paramarines had landed [there] on D-day. We were told that due to this outfit having been mauled somewhat by defending forces, we were being sent to relieve them. . . .

Drawing in to . . . the waterfront, we bailed out of our boats and moved along the pier, towards the island itself. My team . . . [had] 81-mm mortars, [and] I got the job of hauling the shells! With each shell, in that heat they got heavier and heavier and I wished I had another assignment. Right after landing, on that pint[-]sized island, with sporadic gunfire going on, it was then that I saw my first dead Japanese defender lying face down, with a rather large hole in the back of his head. Naturally, momentarily stunned, I stared and then moved on . . . past an old corrugated iron building, which was used as a sick bay, not too far from the dock. I was soon inland taking a survey of my surroundings.

Directly before me rose a steep hill of some 100 feet or so, by my estimation [actually 148 feet]. To my right and left was flat terrain and facing the hillside and looking to my right, I could see the causeway linking Tanambogo. It appeared to have a flat area stretching away from a hill similar to that on Gavutu, but not as high. From the top of the hill rose a tall mast with the Japanese national flag fluttering in the breeze. . . . We set up our 81-mm mortar and prepared to fire on this outstanding target. Under direction of a special non-com range finder, we attempted to topple the flag. A short spurt of firing failed . . . [though] I . . . believe a supporting destroyer lying hove to the island successfully carried out the task. With no ground action . . . taking place in our sector at the moment, we were ordered to dig our shelter.

Information was given out stating we could expect the Imperial Navy to pay us a visit around midnight. As the afternoon wore on plans were set in motion for the night's defense of our position ashore. Patrols were organized—the password was given as darkness settled over the place. . . . [We were told] the Japanese were unable to say words containing double "L"—so the word Yellow was the password for that night.

Somewhere between 2200 and midnight heavy rain set in. The night became even blacker . . . [until we were] unable to see anything moving about. This, of course, brought a sense of panic among the troops. It got so that while on patrol, one had to incessantly repeat the password or else die right there. Having done my stint on one such patrol, I returned to my water[-]logged shelter. Barely settled down in the water, [I got] a call from the shoreline . . . that Japs were swimming from close by Florida Island towards our island. All hell broke loose! Rifle fire screamed across the flat area before me in all directions. Sizing up the situation, I came to the decision to remain where I was—even though an order had been passed for everyone to move to the beach. Obviously, more casualties ensued as a result of our own trigger-happy troops than [were] caused by enemy action.[13]

Louis Carr of M Company, 3rd Battalion, 2nd Marines, witnessed one of the most horrifying incidents of the day:

Our first few hours of enemy contact on Gavutu seasoned us for what lay ahead and we soon found out that this game . . . was a deadly one. We were fighting a merciless, cruel foe. In just a few short hours we built up such animosity and anger you would not believe it. What really set us off was that our unarmed corpsmen [were] nothing but a target, despite the Red Cross band on their arm. I saw two Corpsmen killed trying to care for one of our wounded. While we were halfway up the hill one of our men was wounded. A Corpsman [HA1c Robert Wilson] came to his aid. They shot Wilson, pulled him inside a cave and started cutting him up one piece at a time. First a hand, then an arm. We could hear him screaming above all the other noise of rifle, machine gun and explosives. There was no other alternative but [to] blast the caves with TNT, killing all.[14]

Another marine from Company I, 3rd Battalion, describes D + 1:

> I/3/2 was in the reserve force and because the landing on Gua-
> dalcanal went so well we were not committed to any action on
> D-day. The Marines not committed to the battle had no knowl-
> edge [of] just how it was progressing. Our Sergeant had drilled
> into our minds over and over on the ship: "When you hit the
> beach, stay low. Don't make a target." Amazingly, he lit out [on]
> a streak and ran straight in and was killed immediately. After
> landing, I found myself next to a Navy corpsman who had a soft-
> ball[-]size hole in his shoulder. Under his direction, I packed his
> wound with sulfa and bandaged it. He said he was O.K., so
> I started to crawl forward. About this time, my Lieutenant
> [J. Wendell] Crain, motioned for me to join him. As I dropped
> next to him my rifle accidentally went off and the bullet went
> right past his head, almost blew it off. He just looked at me,
> shrugged his shoulders and pointed out our two tanks. They
> were in trouble. The Japanese were pouring out of caves and
> had surrounded [them]. They were beating on them with sticks,
> throwing rocks and they set one on fire. . . . We concentrated our
> fire on them and afterwards counted over 40 bodies around the
> two tanks. But, not in vain as it was the turning point in control-
> ling the battle.
>
> By that time it was getting late so they positioned some of
> us along the top of the ridge for the night. Our orders were to
> control the ridge and not let anyone go through. Soon darkness
> came and then heavy rain and it poured all night. I remember
> sucking the water of my helmet chin-strap. After a short time we
> began to hear noises down below and we began firing. I noticed
> a discharge flame from my rifle due to the dampness and began
> to hear a "FFT," "FFT' in the mud around me. I suddenly real-
> ized they were firing at the flame my rifle produced and I told
> the guys around me to hold their fire and why. The buddy on
> the right quit firing, but the one on the left kept on. . . . In the
> morning we found him dead. It was so cold [lying] there my only
> relief was wetting my pants once and a while, for a few seconds
> of warmth. Morning finally came; we were surprised to see how
> bad we all looked. The earth of Gavutu is red and our dungarees
> had changed from green to red. We stayed that way for a few days
> until we could climb in the ocean and wash off.[15]

When Louis Carr of Company M (3/2) had reached the hilltop on Gavutu, he could see the adjoining island of Tanambogo: "I saw a Japanese
flag on top of the high ground, another area with natural caves and dug[-
]in tunnels. You could see the Japanese running around from place to
place. Company K set up machine guns, firing across the body of water
between Gavutu and Tanambogo. Our 81-mm and 60-mm, also [the
3rd Battalion, 10th Marines'] pack howitzers, were shelling Tanambogo,
knocking down the Japanese flag, but somehow they kept putting it back
up. Meanwhile, the command structure called for aircraft and additional
bombardment to soften up Tanambogo, our next attack."[16]

At about 1500 on D + 1, Richard N. Vorwaller wrote:

> [The] Navy destroyer [Buchanan] moved in on Tanambogo and
> began shelling the island at point[-]blank range. It was so close
> to the island that some of the shells did not have sufficient arch
> on them to hit so that they would explode; they would glance
> off the ground and back out to sea with the sound of a locomo-
> tive. After the destroyer pulled back[,] Company I, led by Capt.
> William G. Tinsley, landed on the right of the island. At the
> same time a platoon led by 2nd Lt. [John] J. Donahue started
> across the causeway and most of them made it. Our platoon was
> the machine[-]gun support for Company I and we were attached
> to them in combat. For as long as it was possible our guns kept
> up a steady fire, but finally had to halt for fear of hitting our
> own men.[17]

The reinforcements arriving at Tanambogo included Company I and
sections of Company K, 3rd Battalion, 2nd Marines. When Lt. Col.
Robert G. Hunt (3/2) was making plans for an attack on Tanambogo,
Louis Carr (M/3/2) and Joseph A. Michuda of Company M found
themselves "volunteered" to assist Company K with their Browning automatic rifles. Carr wrote:

> We regrouped around Lever Brothers buildings where we could
> see the causeway. While we were regrouping there was no let-up
> from our mortars, pack howitzers, planes and naval gunfire. Ma-
> chine guns (.30's & .50's) were getting in position to provide us
> fire support while going across the causeway. Finally the shelling
> and bombing diminished; the moment had come. You got a deep
> hollow sunken feeling in your stomach as we proceeded down
> the causeway. A Japanese machine gun swung back and forth like

a windshield wiper. First one man would fall, then another but we kept right on going across. Finally the machine gun was put out of commission by one of our mortars or machine guns from Gavutu.

As we reached the end of the causeway we were greeted by screaming Japanese sailors who came out of holes. Hand to hand fighting, man against man, Japs with bayonets, knives and pitch-forks. I had a small bayonet on my BAR. At times one could not shoot because of the chance of hitting one of your fellow Marines.[18]

Along with Company I and sections of Company K were two tanks from the 3rd Platoon, Company C, 2nd Tank Battalion, led by 2nd Lt. Robert J. Sweeney. The "iron monsters" had as their principal weapon a 37-mm turret gun. They embarked for Tanambogo in two LCMs, called "Mikes," and while the tanks were enroute, the destroyer *Buchanan* poured fire from her 5-inch guns onto Hill 121 on Tanambogo. Then she moved near the very small Gaomi Island and commenced firing from another direction at the southeast side of Tanambogo. As the two tank lighters approached their starting point, they signaled the *Buchanan* to lift her barrage. At the same time, the 3rd Platoon, led by 2nd Lt. John J. Donahue (K/3/2), started across the causeway, as Richard Vorwaller had described. Pvt. James McCoy recalls:

We were brought off the hill on Gavutu and assembled on the small flat around the end of the causeway where Lieutenant Donahue told us what was expected of us. We were to charge over the causeway and attack Tanambogo while I Company and two tanks were to hit the north. Donahue commanded, "fix bayonets" and to follow [him]. He led us at a pretty good clip[;] after a brief period I hear a steady crack of rounds going over our head. I was burdened by my Browning so I began to lag to the rear when Willie was hit and that speeded up my pace. Why the Japanese fired so high I don't know, but three feet lower, they would have slaughtered us. I remember the charge over the causeway very clearly because I was so dammed convinced that I could not have survived. As I recall [among] Platoon Sgt. Ferguson, Pfc. Cable, Corporals Miller and Tropea, Privates "Curley" Graham, Leonard E. Skinner and "Willie" Smith[,] Willie was the only one to get hit[. He] got hit in the neck, and went over backwards. He was later evacuated.[19]

Pvt. Leonard E. Skinner remembered: "It did not take us long to cross the causeway as it was a smooth surface; about six feet wide. We ran the entire [way]. We were probably exposed for only 3 or 4 minutes."[20] During the crossing, the marines were also subject to harassing fire from Gaomi.

The crewmen on the LCMs, which had the tanks headed for Tanambogo on board, began firing their automatic weapons at shore positions on Gavutu, then added their 37-mm punch in an attempt to blast open a stretch of the beach, their anticipated landing zone. At 1700, lighter #1 was to clear a path with its main weapon. On board were several leathernecks seeking protection behind the tank. The naval petty officer in charge of the lighter, BM2c G. L. D. Sporhase, had made a landing on Gavutu earlier and had thoughtfully scrounged several sandbags for additional protection for the marines. At this time the *Buchanan* began pounding Tanambogo for several minutes; when the cease-fire order was given, the destroyer and lighter #1 moved to the eastern shore of Tanambogo and prepared for a landing. On reaching the shore, the lighter lowered its ramp, and as the tank drove off, it and the marines disembarking faced a hail of fire; one marine was killed instantly.

With its tank on shore, lighter #1, which was having trouble raising its ramp, finally was able to pull away and go back to Gavutu to pick up additional troops. On its return to Tanambogo, the lighter again experienced problems with the retractable ramp, and the marines had to climb over the gunwale. When the last man was off, the lighter pulled away. Lighter #2, with its troops and Lieutenant Sweeney's tank on board, was less successful. It had hit Tanambogo's coral outcrops and remained stuck. The boatswain, BM2c B. W. Hensen, signaled the tank commander to ram through the ramp door, which Sweeney did. Fourteen marines followed in fast pursuit.

When Lieutenant Sweeney's tank reached the shore at 1615, it took an aggressive lead, quickly outdistancing the marines of Companies I and K (3/2) attempting to follow it. That was Sweeney's first mistake. His second was boldly sticking his head and shoulders out of the tank and popping away with his Tommy gun as the tank sped around, which caused him to fire haphazardly. The sound of a single rifle bark was heard and a bullet tore into his skull, killing him. Seeing that the tank was in difficulty, about fifty of the Japanese air crewmen scampered out of their caves and surrounded it. The frenzied horde dumped cans of gasoline on it and used hand-made bombs as grenades. According to Louis Carr's published account, all the crew were killed except two, who miraculously managed to escape.[21] MCPO Masaichiro Miyagawa of the Yokohama Air Group wrote: "I recall seeing my officer Lt. Cdr. Saburo Katsuta on top of the tank [possibly he was the one who used the hand-made killing tools to destroy the tank and its crew]. This was the last time I saw him."[22]

Similarly, once ashore companion tank #14, commanded by Cpl. Leon "Bud" Richardt, also had outpaced its supporting marines. The single objective in the driver's mind had been to reach a pest-hole pillbox that was causing casualties. Some leathernecks caught up and gathered behind Richardt's tank for protection, but the vehicle got stuck in between two palm trees. The Japanese airmen ran out from a cave by twos and threes and struck it with hand tools and bottles filled with gasoline, much as had been done to Lieutenant Sweeney's tank. Bud Richardt was killed and Danley, the driver, was shot and killed as he exited. The infantrymen fired at the attackers, but the damage was done. The Japanese airmen had ignited the gasoline-soaked tank, and Pvt. Eugene O. Moore, the radio operator, and PFC Ben Pugsley, the gunner, fled the smoke-filled vehicle, willing to take their chances outside. The credit for their survival to goes Pvt. Kenneth Koon (I/3/2).[23] He was one of the infantrymen busy shooting at the Japanese to keep them away from Richardt's tank. Koon is credited with killing thirty-one of the attackers.

Meanwhile, Private Moore, outside the tank, was being beaten to a pulp by frenetic Japanese. There is no report on what happened to Pugsley after he exited. Private Koon recalled:

> Well the Japs banged Moore something terrible. He was bleeding something terrible. He was bleeding and I could not get a shot at them. Then they quit. They moved away. I guess they figured he was cooked. So did I. I never saw anyone [lie] there so dead. . . .
> I decided it was time for papa to get going too. That tank was out and I was there alone. There was firing behind me now. The Japs obliged by streaking for the pillbox [cave]. When they were inside, I decided to get going. So I crawled [away] easy like and there was no one in sight. . . . I got up and made a break for it—heading for a Jap bomb shelter. I hadn't gone two steps . . . when bang—I got hit. In the leg. Must have been a sniper. They were all over the place . . . raising holy hell. Funny they got me and the Japs around the tank didn't. Finally I made the bomb shelter. [Nobody] was in it. I lay there six hours until some Marine pals found me.[24]

The next thing Koon remembered was that when he regained consciousness, a corpsman bandaging him up and he was on transport. Later,
Koon and Moore were bed partners in a rear area hospital.[25]

By then, the pillbox was out of commission, but many marines had
fallen. Meanwhile, roughly half of Company I slowly crawled up the
southern slope of Hill 121, while the remainder drove to the east and
north slopes and covered the coastline. At the end of D + 1, Louis Carr
and his companions spent a frightening night on Tanambogo:

> It wasn't too long before darkness had overtaken us and we dug
> in for the night. It was one of many sleepless nights, with miser-
> able, hair-raising experiences. It started to rain, like pouring water
> out of a bucket; your foxhole filled up and to top things off we
> learned the Japanese *could* pronounce "L" as well as we could!
> We learned this after one or two Marines had been bayoneted
> because of our password. We lay down in our foxholes face up
> with a poncho covering our weapons. One didn't dare sit up.
> The darned sand crabs were crawling all over you, sometimes
> pinching. There were hogs running around feasting on the dead
> and wounded. The Japanese soldiers tied buckets of junk around
> a couple of hogs and ran them through our lines. One didn't
> dare move or stand up as you would either be shot by your own
> men or knifed or bayoneted by the Japanese. It was so dark you
> couldn't see your hand three inches from your nose. We were not
> only wet and miserable, we hadn't had anything to eat since 0630,
> when we had a simple Navy breakfast of baked beans, bread and
> black coffee so strong it would grow hair on a billiard ball.[26]

Company I spent the next day rooting out the last of the Japanese. Most
would not surrender, so their caves were blown up and the entrances
sealed. The next night the marines were put on full alert and struggled
to stay awake. The day after, the men sat down for their first food in
two days, then immediately turned to bury the dead.[27] Occasionally, in
the days that followed, a Japanese was captured. One such prisoner, on
Gavutu, was put to work digging a burial site, and obviously thought he
was being made to dig his own grave:

> Having completed the task, he carefully laid away the shovel he
> had been using and turned his face to us, even as he stood in the
> hole he had dug. He was offered a cigarette and with much bow-
> ing he gratefully accepted what he surely must have thought to

be a kind gesture by the enemy before dispatching him to the land of his ancestors. He sat on the edge of the hole and calmly smoked in silence. Once completed he shredded the remains and stood up in the hole looking at us—undoubtedly expecting his execution. It was then pointed out to him the fact of a dead Jap lying beneath a heap of rubbish. He was directed to bury the body in the hole he had dug. With a sudden smile crossing his face, he bent to with a will and soon had his chore completed. From that moment on he conveyed to us a cheerful manner in carrying out his task.[28]

MCPO Masaichiro Miyagawa and a companion, SA Jinsaku Sakurai, spent fifty days hiding in one of Gavutu's caves; they periodically ventured out only at night to replenish their water. The shelters and caves had ample storage of food for air raids and kegs for water. When the marines began to close the remaining caves with explosives, Miyagawa and Sakurai began scheming to escape to Florida. They stole out late one night to the coast and thought they might swim to the island; but because Sakurai could not swim, Miyagawa found a barrel lying on the beach area and, using it as a float, Sakurai was able to paddle, with some difficulty. The two lived on Florida for about a month eating sweet potatoes and coconuts and living in abandoned native huts. They were caught by islanders in mid-October and turned over to the marines on Tulagi. Sakurai later wrote that he believed Lt. Cdr. Takayuki Kurozaki and Capt. Shigetoshi Miyazaki had killed themselves or were sealed in Gavutu's caves.[29]

The taking of Tulagi, Gavutu, and Tanambogo by the U.S. Marines ended a terrible cycle of death and destruction. Of the Yokohama Air Group Flying-Boat Unit on Tanambogo, only four survived; from the Floatplane Fighter Unit (Hama Air Unit) at Halavo on Florida Island, only two. From the Iida Butai, the 14th Construction Unit on Tulagi, and other construction elements, sixteen are known to have survived. Of the Kure 3rd SNLF on Tulagi, seven men were left alive: SME Kyoichi Takahashi, SM Masakane Iwata, SME Yoici Hayami, POIc Shikie Yamamoto, SA Yuko Takamoto, SR Haruji Matsumoto, and Saburo Watanabe.[30] The ten officers did not survive.[31] Of Lieutenant Mitsuwa's antiaircraft unit on Gavutu, four gunners surrendered; fifty perished. Of the Hashimoto construction unit, also on Gavutu, almost all of the 132 were killed; Shin'ya Hashimoto and one other survived.[32] The eight radio operators from the 85th Communication Unit also lost their lives. As for

Figure 24. The U.S. Marine and Navy cemetery at WHITE BEACH, Gavutu Island. (Courtesy William Bethard)

the paramarines, out of 361 men, they suffered 250 casualties, with 23 being consigned to the cemetery at WHITE BEACH on Gavutu. Plat. Sgt. Ronald F. Kachinsky, Company A, 1st Parachute Battalion—buried in plot 52, with the Pacific Ocean on his left—was one of them.

Holding Ground

In the Battle of Savo Island on the night of 8–9 August, one Australian cruiser and three American vessels—the *Astoria, Quincy,* and *Vincennes*—went to their watery graves taking with them 1,077 sailors and marines. Combined with the withdrawal of the carriers by Admiral Fletcher the previous day, this forced Admiral Turner to order the departure of the transports and cargo ships from the Guadalcanal waters, taking the supplies much needed by the marines ashore. It took a few days for leathernecks to get over the shock of the U.S. Navy's disappearance from the Solomon waters; yet they knew the war effort must continue on. The "best of the marines," the 2nd Regiment, made Tulagi their fort to hold. Mike Masters wrote:

> The largest caliber weapons in the company [Company A, 1st Pioneer Battalion] or on the island were our .30-caliber machine

guns. . . . [They were] of little value against the formations of Jap bombers that came over Tulagi every day around noon—flying at about five to six thousand feet, making their final turn, then heading for the airfield on the Canal. . . .

It bugged me not to be able to take any action against the bombers or the snooper planes that buzzed us. . . . I located a disabled landing craft . . . with an operable air-cooled 50-caliber machine gun, [and] set up a gun position on a hill overlooking the North Channel, with a clear field for any enemy landings or planes. Having the only gun on the island firing at the Japs stirred the Marines who were down on the beach. They cheered as if they were at a ball game. . . . [33]

The 1st Marine Raider Battalion was to remain temporarily on Tulagi, and the much shot-up 1st Parachute Battalion was to shift there from Gavutu. On 10 August, the first of the Chutes to arrive on Tulagi was Company A, assigned to defend the Sasapi area; Companies B and C followed. The next day, the Chutes were ordered to move to the ridge in the vicinity of the J. B. Hicks house, where Assistant Division Commander (ADC) Brig. Gen. William H. Rupertus had set up his command post.[34] On their arrival, the paramarines were designated as force reserve.

On D + 2 the defense of Tulagi was divided into three major sections. Major Miller of the 1st Parachute Battalion, Combat Team A, took over the southwest sector, west of line A and south of the ridge; Major Pressley of Combat Team B took over the northwest sector, west of line A and north of the ridge. The island sector of Gavutu, Tanambogo, and Makambo was assigned to Lt. Colonel Hill, Combat Team C.

On 10 August, elements from Companies E, F, and G of the 2nd Marines seized Mbangi and Kakomtanbu Islands without any opposition. The following day, the 3rd Marine Defense Battalion (MDB) Detachment, which had landed on Tulagi at Sasapi on the 9th, took over as the defense unit for the Chinatown sector. The balance of the 1st Parachute Battalion arrived on Tulagi on the 11th. Temporary control of the Tulagi Chutes was transferred to E Sector, commanded by Lt. Col. Harold E. Rosecrans, CO of the 2nd Battalion, 5th Marines. The 1st Raiders were assigned as force reserve, with Colonel Edson given the additional duty as assistant chief of staff, assistant division commander.

The plan included the 1st and 2nd Battalions, 2nd Marines, occupying Tulagi; Companies K and M of the 3rd Battalion would remain on Gavutu. Company L, plus the 5th Platoon, Company M, with 223 men, and Battery I, 3rd Battalion, 10th Marines, were assigned to defend Makambo Island. Regarding the Makambo operation, Cpl. Claude R. Blanchard (HQ/3/2) wrote:

> After 36 hours of no sleep I was told to go with Company L; I was the only wireman. I was to take two EE8 field telephones and a reel of telephone wire weighing about 80 pounds. Staff Sgt. John Revel assigned me to Company L under Lt. Michael Ryan. My very words were "Why me?"
>
> The landing came off beautifully and not a shot was fired. We lived on captured Japanese rice and green coconuts. We had little food, because the ships had left after the Japanese Navy hit the area. The only clothes we had were on our backs and we landed with only our rifles, radio and telephone equipment. Life on Makambo was great for a week or so. My only assignment, after laying the telephone line and hooking up two telephones, was to crank the generator mounted on a wooden stool for the radio operators to send coded messages at night. However, most of the time we were saddled with dead batteries.
>
> [On Makambo, Blanchard found a pair of buildings belonging to a trading company, presumably Burns Philp.] . . . In the larger of the two was a walk-in steel safe with the door blown [open.] We selected the smaller one as our communications shack . . . the "message center." Some Jap warships took [shots] at us[,] intending to hit the Message Center building; they came close. After that, we moved our communications unit to one of Makambo's small hills, and would use the larger [building] with the walk-in safe in the event of an air raid or in case the Jap Navy improved their shooting. We lived in the open area with no shelter, only a poncho. It was good duty with no flies or the stink of dead bodies as encountered on Tulagi. Truly, a beautiful island.[35]

Meanwhile, back on Tulagi, all was not quiet even after the island was declared secure. An occasional sniper would appear from nowhere and take pot shots at the marines while the noisy 2nd Pioneers were busy blasting caves with demolition satchels and stubby fuses attached to long poles. The demolitionists continued their handiwork off and on during the month.

The marines always expected that the Japanese would attempt to recapture Tulagi, but would first take control of Florida Island, then jump to Tulagi, and then move over to Guadalcanal. As a result, the command powers at Tulagi considered the island susceptible to attack at any time. S2c John M. Braloski, USNR, was called on to help defend it during one of the condition "Red" alert days:

> ... One Marine sergeant had our group of eleven sailors to assist in defending the island from Jap invaders. He took us out to one of the beach areas and spread us out so many feet apart and gave us instructions on what to do if the Japs tried to come ashore. We took our .30 caliber machine guns off our Higgins boats and secured them along the bank. He also gave us a handful of grenades and a quick explanation of how to use them. None of us had any grenade throwing training and I understand it's almost an art. He told us: "All you have to do is pull the pin, wait a few seconds" (he never explained just how many seconds), "just a few seconds, and get rid of the grenade." Talk about a fast course in grenade training—we got it. When morning came we were secured from condition "Red" as it was now condition "Green" and we went back to our shacks.[36]

Coast Guardsman John P. Lanigan from the *Heywood* recalled: "In the days we manned the Higgins boats and at night we were added to the forces that guarded Tulagi. We were assigned a machine-gun position in the native cemetery and our defense post was manned by myself, and fellow seamen Ed Seturman, and Harry Wilde, and we had a Corporal Davis and CWO Dave Sauls, USMC. Right after the Savo battle, we had to go out and look for survivors."[37]

The marines on Tulagi received a pleasant surprise package when five amtracs (LVT) of 3rd Platoon, Company A, 2nd Amphibian Tractor Battalion, delivered ammunition, food, and water from the *President Adams* and evacuated wounded on the return run. The Tulagi leathernecks were forever grateful.

10 Guadalcanal: Hanging On

On 8 August, D + 1 at Guadalcanal, the men of the 5th Marines uncovered the Japanese communication control center—a radio transmitter station complete with antenna and electrical substation. Thinking the small green and red lights flashing inside the structure were the enemy, the young marines sprayed the building with automatic fire, which caused some damage, but this was later repaired. The power substation was a special prize; it was just what the 1st Signal Company required.

The Framework of a Base

The radio station was in a prefabricated wood building containing two 1,000-watt continuous-wave (CW) radios, with its own power supply generated by a stationary diesel engine. From the station, a high-voltage cable was run underground to supply energy to the transmitter station and to the Pagoda, a Korean-style building the Japanese had planned to be an officers club. The one-story Pagoda was now to become the nerve center for the Cactus Air Force, the aviation units of the U.S. Army, Navy, and Marine Corps assigned to Guadalcanal Island, code-named CACTUS.

Maj. Edward W. Snedeker, General Vandegrift's signal officer, put 2nd Lt. Sanford B. "Sandy" Hunt in charge of getting the radio operational.[1] As a buck sergeant, Hunt had been responsible for the 1st Marine Division's cipher and code room when the division was headquartered in Wellington, New Zealand. Before the division sailed for Guadalcanal he was commissioned and became the new communication officer. On Hunt's team was TSgt. Felix L. Ferranto, a crackerjack radio-man, who repaired the captured equipment and made it usable. Ferranto, who had accompanied Admiral Byrd on one of his trips to Antarctica, deciphered the Japanese radio markings and by the evening of D + 2 the 1st Signal Company was able to transmit. Incoming messages, via the fleet broadcast from Pearl Harbor, presented no problem; outgoing messages were the challenge. Tuning the receivers to where they thought

Figure 25. The Japanese radio transmitter station captured on Guadalcanal and put in service by TSgt. Felix L. Ferranto on 9 August 1942. (Courtesy Lt. Col. Felix L. Ferranto, USMC, Ret.)

the South Pacific Navy might be located, the men found a radio circuit and made a call to an unknown station. It turned out to be the U.S. Naval Station at Auckland, New Zealand. With that command's assistance they managed to contact CINCPAC at Pearl Harbor, which cleared the circuit and set up a permanent, round-the-clock operator network for CACTUS traffic, with the call sign NGK. With "Radio Guadalcanal" activated, the marines no longer had to depend on vessels at anchor to clear their messages.

Station NGK, using a hand-operated paper-strip cipher system and key lists, took over the radio guard for all message traffic, and the division began copying all incoming traffic in cipher. NGK was used not only for official business but also for sending the war correspondents' stories back to Nouméa or Hawaii.[2] General Vandegrift saw no harm in sending the correspondents' messages without encryption, but before Lieutenant Hunt could transmit them they would have to be cleared through 2nd Lt. Herbert C. Merillat, the division historical officer and correspondent liaison. Part of Merillat's job was to approve the press releases and get the permission to transmit from Col. W. Capers James, the division chief of staff. James disliked reviewing the reporters' work,

Figure 26. Maj. Edward W. Snedeker on Guadalcanal, D + 2. (Courtesy Lt. Gen. Edward W. Snedeker, USMC, Ret.)

which he considered "a lot of crap," but by late September he had been replaced by the more amiable Lt. Col. Gerald C. "Jerry" Thomas, who had received a spot promotion to colonel. Sandy Hunt, then under Thomas's wing, received the title of Signal Assistant to the Chief of Staff. His job entailed handling routine encoded messages for General Vandegrift and Colonel Thomas, as well as what Hunt called "paraphrased ULTRA information"—high-level coded messages already deciphered and re-encrypted, to be directed only to those who needed to know, which meant General Vandegrift and Colonel Thomas. Long after the war, Colonel Hunt wrote:

> After the Navy took over Naval communications from me[, ULTRA] information was transmitted to their station in paraphrased form and I delivered it to Col. Thomas—no one else. So far as I know no one ever saw an ULTRA message on the [i]sland except Gen. V[andegrift] and Jerry Thomas. . . .
>
> There was no ULTRA operation on the [i]sland. We were just recipients of the information resulting from [the] Navy's

deciphering operations in Pearl Harbor and Washington. The only history of Naval communications ciphering and deciphering operations is that of my Naval Radio Station NGK. All the traffic we handled was normal everyday variety[,] which included some paraphrased ULTRA information. The source of this information was never stated. Most of it turned out to be quite solid because it was from deciphered Japanese messages. The major reason we received by radio and messenger ULTRA information rather than ULTRA messages was because for security reasons we did not have "high class" cryptographic aids (materials). ULTRA messages were enciphered on electrically operated machines using very minimum distributed keylists held only by higher commands in secure areas.[3]

Once read, that material was returned to Lieutenant Hunt and burned. In the meantime, while the cipher system was being organized, the division radio-men took over the former Japanese Kukum telephone exchange, and the photographic reproduction unit that had been aboard the transport *Hunter Liggett* (AP 27) was moved to that building's adjoining darkroom.

At 1159 on 8 August the transport *George F. Elliot* again became a prime target, as it had on the 7th; forty Bettys attacked, flying low over Florida Island to avoid detection. One flaming enemy aircraft, in a death lunge, suddenly swerved and crashed into the *Elliot* amidships. Burning debris was flung about the hold, spreading flames and rupturing the water mains. Flames gutted the ship, and thus the destroyer *Hull* was compelled to sink her with four torpedoes. However, with the *Elliot* went most of the supplies.

The Confrontations Begin

The men of the 1st Pioneer Battalion also were a target. On the evening of D + 1, two members of the Pioneers, Privates Benson and Peterson, had volunteered to be part of an LCP crew, equipped with a TBX radio, that was to patrol the sea off Lunga Point, Guadalcanal, on the alert for any enemy activity. They never made a report and never returned.

That same day, 8 August, the Japanese 11th and 13th Construction Units had moved to the west bank of the Lunga River. They had two problems: one was food, the other was radio communication. Capt. Kanae Monzen, the commanding officer of the 11th CU, took charge, with Lt. Cdr. Tokunaga Okamura as his deputy. Captain Monzen apparently had a short-wave radio and was able to contact submarine *I-121* offshore; in turn, the submarine forwarded his reports to the Japanese Eighth Fleet and received messages for him in a similar manner.

Monzen had planned a suicide attack, but he abandoned the idea as he had only a small force around him. The next day, 9 August, the 11th CU moved a short distance west, to the Point Cruz area, and set up a defense line with about two hundred combatants from the security force under Lt. (jg) Soichi Shindo. In addition, the 11th established a second camp at the mouth of the Matanikau River (the *Ma*), some 2½ miles west of Lunga. The river formed a natural barrier, and the men from Japan took advantage of its strategic value. The 11th CU's main body now numbered a few hundred, including officers. Most of the laborers had scattered, but they did not take much food with them when they had bolted out of their camp, and what little they carried was gone by the third day. The construction unit, also out of a food supply, was thus divided into three groups to check out native gardens.

PO2c Sankichi Kaneda remembered:

> The Kure 3rd [84th Guard Unit] and the 81st Guard [Unit, Nakamura platoon] 2nd Howitzer Battery set up a Line of Resistance . . . digging foxholes at strategic locations under the command of WO [Tetuzo] Nakamura. The 2nd Battery squads of PO[3c Isamu] Matsuda and PO3c Tan were positioned in the crossing area north of the river. On 10 August, Petty Officer Matsuda led a recon party to reconnoiter the situation of the enemy on the opposite bank. They encountered what were perhaps enemy scouts, and a skirmish followed. [They ran into a patrol from the 5th Marines and] SM2c Nagayoshi Takayanagi . . . was wounded. On 11 August, they ran into about 30 infantrymen . . . [then] came back across the river and called out "Enemy attack. And there is a tank!" . . . but the enemy remained on their [own] side of the river. . . . [On 13 August we were a] . . . Howitzer Battery without howitzers[;] we were armed only with handguns, and found it hard to muster up [a] fighting spirit. We had with us [a] short[-]wave radio we had captured from the enemy on Wake Island, and could tune in on broadcasts from Sydney, and keep informed on the general war situation.[4]

Food was also a severe problem for the Americans. Of the sixty-day allotment of supplies and ten units of ammunition that the 1st Marine Division had loaded at Wellington, only a few days worth had been unloaded. About four units of fire—the number of rounds expected to be fired on a given day—were available on Guadalcanal and Tulagi; Guadalcanal had six million rounds of .30-caliber ammunition and eight hundred 90-mm shells. When an inventory was completed about 15 August, it was found that the troops had sufficient food on hand for only thirty days: adequate B rations for seventeen days, C rations for three days, and captured Japanese rations for ten days. The marines were reduced to two skimpy meals daily—if they were lucky.

Pvt. Gaetano Gerace of Company C, 1st Battalion, 5th Marines, recalled finding the Japanese food:

> On the second day we crossed the river and found the Japanese camp abandoned. I don't recall how many tents there were; all I remember is that [the camp] looked like they were ready to eat breakfast. One large tent had a safe with an abundance of Japanese funds, occupation money and stationery. There were two warehouses stacked with food, rice, dried fish, canned grasshoppers; you name it, it was there. The other was loaded with Jap beer and Saki [sic]. This food became very important to our survival on Guadalcanal, yet we did not know it at that minute. Somehow the beer and Saki disappeared. A few leathernecks were seen wobbling around after sampling the Jap beverages, but in the island's sweltering heat, and the lack of food in their bellies[,] many became unwell and ended up on sick call. One interesting detail[:] the engineers made the Japanese power plant operational, and this outfitted the ice plant, and we had ice that made life a bit easier.[5]

Establishing a Defense

By Sunday, 9 August , the 1st Battalion, 5th Marines, had established a beach defense from the east branch of Lunga River to about 1,000 yards west of Kukum Creek. The Japanese indeed had deserted the area, as Private Gerace had noted. The marines found a 3-inch naval AA gun, a 25-mm and a 13-mm machine gun, and a Type 41 6-cm howitzer. But at 1000, another forward patrol from Company A, 5th Marines, operating behind enemy lines in the Matanikau sector, was surprised and driven off by a Japanese force under PO1c Goro Sakurai of the Guadalcanal RXI Security Force. Both sides lost warriors. The marines backed off for the time being, assured that they would meet the enemy again.

The next day, 10 August, twenty Bettys and fourteen Zeroes flew over from west to east, but no bombs were dropped. Four fighters made a low sweep along the beach line, dropping two parachutes in the area of the Japanese Navy forces west of Lunga Plains. Apparently, they were looking for Admiral Turner's transports, which by this time were halfway between Guadalcanal and Espiritu Santo. The aircraft dropped their bombs and flew back to their nest. The Japanese 5th Air Attack Force reported: "Observed along the coast about 50 enemy-type small landing craft. Received intense machinegun fire while in the air above the mouth of the Lunga River. There is a pile of crates beside the Lunga River."

On 11 August, six Bettys flew over from east to west; again they dropped no bombs, but this time they apparently took photographs. The next day, Lt. Cdr. Keisuke Matsue, senior staff officer at the Headquarters, 8th Base Force, reported on reconnaissance by Japanese land-based attack planes: "Some enemy troops were observed near the Guadalcanal airfield, but their feeble movements appear unhealthy[;] also abandoned boats were observed along the coast. . . . It is now possible to believe recapture will be easy. Following the shock from the sea battle on the 8th [at Savo Island, where the Imperial Navy sank four Allied cruisers,] . . . enemy units went to such trouble to land [and] are now in confusion, and . . . anxiously trying to withdraw them. We should be able to mop up the remnants quickly."[6]

With the U.S. 1st Marine Division were seven men from the Samoa-based 8th Marines, part of the "other breed," the 2nd Marine Division, which had been temporarily detached and ordered to join the 1st Division in the Koro Islands for the trip to Guadalcanal. Sgt. Elmer R. Widman of Company L, 3rd Battalion, 8th Marines, and the six others in his party were cartographic specialists. They were ordered to report to Headquarters, 1st Marine Division, where they were directed to measure and study the characteristics of Guadalacanal's rivers and report their findings. Widman and his companions essentially on their own, and had to seek food from various outfits since they belonged to no particular organization.

Ray Whitaker from the *Barnett* recalled: "After the boat crews discharged the Marines, they returned . . . to take off supplies and ammo. Things got bogged down on the beach. Lieutenant Eubanks, who was in charge of the *Barnett*'s landing craft and the boat crews, reported that supplies were piling up and the Marines were doing little, if anything, about moving them. Some supplies were lost in the ocean when the tide came in." Karl Thayer Soule (D-2), a second lieutenant, remembers: "Crates and boxes were piled high for almost a mile. Many, too near the water, were partially submerged at high tide."[7] The mess was not cleaned up until D + 10, when the 2nd Pioneers appeared.

Lt. Harold A. Hayes commanded the 3rd Platoon, Company A, 2nd Pioneer Battalion, which was attached to the 3rd Battalion, 2nd Marines, on board the *Adams:*

> During the morning of 7 August, a message was received aboard ship requesting that shore party personnel be sent to the beach from the 2nd Pioneers to man at least one unloading point. I took about half my platoon and we landed sometime before noon on D day. I reported to Major Bob Ballance, [1st Pioneer Battalion,] whom I knew, as instructed and was informed to move down the beach and help move supplies off the beach and into the dumps. We landed without equipment other than ourselves, so the work effort was all manual. We did all sorts of things[:] helped direct traffic and move vehicles off the beach. This continued until late afternoon when we received a message from the CO of the 3rd Battalion to return to [the] *Adams.* As soon as possible, we were to move out in the evening for another destination. I reported to Major Ballance and found an LCP from the *Adams,* then embarked and returned to the ship, arriving about dusk.[8]

Moving Forward Amidst Disarray

The staff officers who had planned the WATCHTOWER operation were novices and pressed for time. No one had done a thorough analysis of Plan Q, the strategy for moving the supplies to shore and then moving them inland; it had not been entirely worked out at staff meetings. Consequently, by D + 2 the beach was piled high with an assortment of materiel. At one juncture, the beach held one hundred lighters, and fifty Higgins boats were lying offshore. Had the Japanese struck the beach, it would have spelled doom for the expedition; but the marines' luck held. A few combat troops were relieved from defense duty and ordered to move the cache inland; however, the "ground pounders" paid for the command negligence, as they had only a small number of trucks, and most were broken-down Japanese vehicles. Some of the troops, instead of moving the supplies, simply walked away from the area. They felt that they had come to fight, not to become stevedores.[9]

While the marines were holding on to a small portion of Guadalcanal real estate, the Southwest Pacific U.S. Army Headquarters issued a press release headlined, "The Army Lands in the Solomon Islands Spearheaded by the U.S. Marines." General MacArthur was claiming recognition for a minor role in what others had indeed "spearheaded" and accomplished. This attempt to seize the limelight vexed Admirals King and Nimitz and resulted in a flurry of messages between Hawaii and Washington. The U.S. Navy had to ignore the situation, much to its disgust.[10]

The U.S. Army Air Forces in Australia was to assist in the WATCH-TOWER operation by using the 5th Air Force to neutralize the Japanese airfields on Rabaul, tying down their aircraft so that they could not interfere with the island landings. Sgt. Edmund L. Troccia of the 93rd Bomb Squadron, 19th Bombardment Group, flew in B-17E (412461) in the D day attack against Vunakanau Airfield and Rabaul-East: "Thirteen B-17s took off at dawn on [7 August] enroute to the target, reaching the area at about 1115. We spent five minutes bombing, only to be jumped by about 30 Zeroes. In the fray, we lost one fortress, commanded by Capt. Harl Pease Jr., AAF, and his crew."[11] At the time the B-17s hit Vunakanau, a squadron of North American B-25 Mitchell bombers also attacked the Japanese airstrip at Lae but did negligible damage. Consequently, the Imperial Japanese Naval Air Force was able to send off four flights of bombers and accompanying Zeroes to attack the WATCH-TOWER invasion fleet on D day.

Capturing the Guadalcanal airfield was uppermost in General Vandegrift's mind. The objective was to grab the airstrip and use it against the enemy. By midmorning on D + 1, the 1st Battalion, 5th Marines, and 1st Platoon of Company A, 1st Tank Battalion, crossed the Ilu River and moved cautiously along the coast. The uneasy marines returned imaginary gunfire. By nightfall Col. Leroy P. Hunt, commander of the 5th Marines, had his 1st Battalion in possession of the airfield, a property of great value as it made Guadalcanal a "land-locked carrier." The only thing lacking was a complement of aircraft.

Col. George R. Rowan. commanding officer of the 1st Pioneer Battalion, directed his executive officer, Maj. Robert G. Ballance, to assist the marine engineers—the airstrip builders—in every way possible. The 490 men of the Pioneers had been parceled out to various units, and they were fortunate to have landed one regimental supply (R-4) bulldozer, which became the airfield's workhorse. The engineers and the men of the 1st Pioneer Battalion worked on the strip from morning until just before dark and rebuilt it foot by foot. The Japanese had left eight small but useful tandem rollers and several Kato tractors; they also had installed huge lights, most of which were high and untouched by the bombardment, but the marines would not dare use them with the Imperial Navy controlling the sea and each night prowling for targets. The 1st Special Weapons Battalion did set up its weapons on D day—.50 caliber machine guns; 37-mm antitank guns; and 20-, 40-, and 90-mm antiaircraft guns. These, plus the weapons of Maj. J. S. O'Halloran's 3rd Defense Battalion, helped keep the Japanese aircraft far above the airstrip, limiting their effectiveness.

The goal was to complete the airstrip south of Lunga Point as soon as possible, so that it could be used against the enemy. But the engineer in charge, Maj. James G. Frazer, commanding officer of the 1st Marine Engineer Battalion, had problems. The 11th and 13th CU had been working from opposite ends and were to meet in the middle. However, a hole existed in the airstrip, caused by a 500-pound bomb dropped by the 11th Bomb Group during the early August raids. The islanders from the Tasimboko and Matanikau clans that the Japanese had used as slave labor had carried reed baskets of crushed coral to the strip to fill the unfinished section; it was slow, backbreaking work, and when the American bombing started, the frightened islanders disappeared.

Now, with the U.S. Marines in command, Major Frazer's understrength battalion had to finish the task. The engineers had to use captured, worn-out tools, which no doubt already had suffered from tropical weathering. They had inherited a score of well-used shovels, some TNT, and thirty beat-up three-ton stake-body trucks, ex-Nippon (Model 1 1941 4 × 2 Toyota), as well as the eight road rollers. One hundred low-bed trucks had been in the Japanese truck pool, but most were not serviceable. It had been hoped that the marine engineers could have the airfield operational by D + 3, but this was no longer possible, for their essential equipment was still on board the transports *Hunter Liggett* and *McCawley* (APA 4) and the attack cargo ship *Libra* (AKA 12), and some critical items were lost when the *Elliot* was sunk. Among the items needed were 2½-ton trucks, which were not landed because the U.S. Navy had decided they would not be necessary.[12]

On D + 1 the engineers surveyed the airfield and determined that 2,600 feet of the runway about 160 feet wide was acceptable, but that the remaining large cavity needed to be filled and graded. Under exhausting conditions the marine engineers had moved thousands of cubic feet of crushed coral and had a crude strip completed by D + 4. All that was then required was for their work to be tested. On 12 August, a PBY-5A from VP-24, flying from Ile Nou, New Caledonia, landed and bumped along on Guadalcanal's rudimentary airfield. The pilot was

Lt. William S. Sampson, naval aide to COMAIRSOPAC, Rear Adm. John S. "Stew" McCain. Sampson was accompanied by Lt. Cdr. W. K. Goodney, a member of McCain's staff. A small mishap occurred when the plane rolled into a bomb crater and twenty marines were needed to haul it out. Nevertheless, Lieutenant Sampson observed that if the pot-holes were fixed up, they certainly would have a landing field. The PBY was refueled from five-gallon Jerry cans, and Sampson returned to his base with two wounded marines.[13]

The hard-working 1st Engineers faced considerable problems with the airfield, as it had been laid out by the Japanese in a basin. Because of the constant rains, it often was like a river of mud, and thus a ditch had to be excavated to carry off the rainwater. Oil drums were substituted for drainage pipes, though later the engineers installed pre-cast concrete ducts. The work started simultaneously with sub-grading, using the cap-tured Japanese equipment. The machinery was in poor shape for lack of proper maintenance, but it enabled the men to complete their tasks.

Ferreting Out the Enemy

While the land engineering work was proceeding, patrols from regimen-tal headquarters and the 1st Battalion, 5th Marines, moved along the beach south and southwest of Kukum. Combined patrols of regimental headquarters and Company A engaged an enemy party about five miles southwest of Kukum, killing two Japanese and wounding several. On 11 August, a patrol from the 3rd Battalion, 5th Marines, moving west of the Lunga River spotted two Japanese. One jumped into the river trying to escape and was shot; the other surrendered. The captive, WO Tsuneto Sakado, a rikusentai, was taken to division headquarters, where Capt. Sherwood F. Moran, the Japanese-language officer, questioned him. The man looked "tattered and hungry," and he indicated there were others who also were sorely in need of food and might wish to surrender.[14]

Lt. Col. Frank B. Goettge, head of the 1st Marine Division's intelli-gence section, had limited information on the Japanese, and this seemed an ideal opportunity to expand on it. He approached Lieutenant Colonel Thomas, the operations officer, with a plan to seek out the enemy, hope-fully locating some of those willing to come forward. Thomas did not wish to expand offensive operations at that time, but Colonel Goettge was adamant—his job was intelligence, and he had inadequate infor-mation. There was little that Thomas could do, other than suggest, as Goettge outranked him; and although General Vandegrift heard about the proposed mission, he offered only tepid encouragement. Because the division was not interested in his initiative, Colonel Goettge decided to carry it out on his own. He planned to land his men near Point Cruz, investigate, and then hike back.

On 12 August Colonel Goettge formed a patrol to search out enemy positions where captured rikusentai Sakado had indicated some of his compatriots might be found. However, the executive officer of the 5th Marines, Col. William J. Whaling, who had led previous patrols to the area, warned Goettge to avoid the Matanikau basin and the land west of Point Cruz, as he suspected a heavy concentration of Japanese in that sector.[15] Whaling was right: the sea infantrymen of the 1st Company, 84th Guard Unit, under Lt. Akira Tanabe, had joined the Matanikau defense line that morning. Worse, Lt. (jg) Soichi Shindo's 11th CU Security Force, 222 strong, also had moved into the basin, and the 119-man 13th CU Security Force under Sp. Lt. (jg) Inado Yasuda was in the district. A deadly hornets nest of enemy combatants had massed just where Colonel Goettge intended to land.

Capt. Wilfred H. Ringer Jr., the intelligence officer (R-2) of the 5th Marines, had been in favor of moving at an earlier hour; as it was getting late, he was growing more hesitant. Ringer had asked Capt. Lyman D. Spurlock, the CO of Company L, 3rd Battalion, 5th Marines, if his men could come to the aid of Goettge's group if they got in trouble. Spurlock's reply was not encouraging: "It would be difficult at night." Thirty-nine-year-old 1st Sgt. Stephen Armstrong Custer, a former World War I soldier and distant relative to General George Armstrong Custer of Civil War and Little Big Horn renown, wanted a large, heavily armed patrol to investigate the area. Colonel Goettge, however, wanted to travel light, and despite the wishes of the others he opted for a small party.

The patrol comprised twenty-five men, the majority from the 5th Marines, R-2 Section (intelligence), under Captain Ringer, and the rest from the division intelligence, D-2. The party included forty-three-year-old 1st Lt. Ralph Cory, the Japanese-language officer of the 5th Marines and an expert cryptanalyst, and fifty-two-year-old Lt. Cdr. Malcolm L. Pratt, the 5th Marines surgeon.[16] The enlisted ranks included 1st Sgt. Stephen A. Custer; Plat. Sgts. Denzil Caltrider and Frank L. Few; Sgts. Charles C. Arndt, Robert Stanfill, and David Stanffer; Cpls. William Bainbridge, Ralph V. Benson, Aaron Gelzer, Joseph F. Kashuba, Henry L. Kowal, Robert R. Lyons, Theodore E. Rhat Jr., Stephen Serdula, and Joseph A. Spaulding; and PFCs John L. Delano, Blaine G Walter, Daniel L. Gauntt, Jack B. Kelly, and Robert W. Lovelace.[17] Lieutenant Soule, the division photographer, was to go with the patrol, but at the last minute it was decided that taking photographs at night would not be practical. Twenty-one-year-old Cpl. Vernon C. Stimpel, also from D-2, asked to go along but was advised by Colonel Goettge to remain with the others and "keep an eye on things." He assured Stimpel that they would "be back shortly."[18] The patrol then left the Kukum docks by LCP at 1800 on 12 August. As Goettge pointed out the landing site, POW Sakado pleaded: "*Iie, Iie*"—"No, No!" The colonel insisted. The conversation was loud enough to be heard over quite a distance.[19] But the Coast Guard coxswain had difficulty taking them in to land, as the Higgins boat had run aground. They finally went ashore at 2030 on the left bank of the Matanikau River—directly in the midst of the Japanese.

The marines went over the side and rocked the Higgins boat free. It then returned to its base. From that moment, Colonel Goettge's party was on its own. His plan indeed proved to be quite ill-conceived: he had taken no radio; the men had no automatic weapons; they had departed late in the day; and they had sailed into an enemy-dominated area. The Japanese had been watching the craft and when the men went ashore just west of the river, the 2nd Platoon, 11th CU Security Force, led by Lt. (jg) Soichi Shindo, was waiting for them. Two shots rang out, and Custer and Goettge went down. The colonel was dead, the sergeant wounded. Lieutenant Cory was hit in the abdomen; each time he cried out in pain, shots would be fired in his direction.

The night was pitch black until enemy flares illuminated the Americans' position; then machine guns began barking. Captain Ringer helped move Custer to the beach before the group ran for cover and fought; but they were outnumbered and outgunned.[20] Back at Lunga, members of the 5th Marines heard the distant muffled shots. Captain Spurlock, knowing of Ringer's concern about the mission, had phoned headquarters with his information; he was told to monitor the situation. Nothing was done to assist Goettge's patrol until the next day, when a reinforced patrol was assembled. The colonel's poorly thought out operation had cost the lives of twenty-one marines and a U.S. Navy doctor. Somehow three of Goettge's men managed to escape when they moved out under orders to seek help. Sgt. Charles C. "Monk" Arndt arrived back at 0530 on the 13th by swimming along the beach. Plat. Sgt. Frank L. Few arrived back at 0800; he had suffered a chest bayonet wound in the struggle. Cpl. Joseph A. Spaulding also returned by walking through enemy lines. The Japanese reported seven men lost, including the platoon leader, PO1c Goro Sakurai.[21]

After a brief interview with Sergeant Arndt, a rescue party from the 5th Marines was put together at 0615. However, Arndt could not pinpoint the landing zone. Company A, 5th Marines, led by Capt. William B. Kaempfer, boarded a Higgins boats at 0650 and headed for the Point Cruz area. At 1010, Kaempfer radioed that his company had landed about ten miles from the base and had sighted an enemy unit. A support force headed by Colonel William J. Whaling, who organized two platoons from Company L plus a machine-gun section, set out to join Company A. Both detachments were in radio contact. At 1645, Whaling radioed the regimental command post that he was unable to find where the patrol had met its fate and that he was moving to the mouth of the Matanikau River to work his way back. Late that afternoon both units returned to the dock at Kukum.[22]

When word of the disaster reached the perimeter, the marines were predictably angered. The incident would set the stage for a "take no prisoners" response. To add to the uneasiness, a small earthquake woke up the camp at 0235 on the 14th.[23] The next day, the 15th, Pvt. William J. Carroll of Company C, 1st Pioneer Battalion, was on guard duty with an eleven-man squad on the outer flanks of the Ilu River near the deserted village of Volonavua. Suddenly a single file of native constables appeared, their rifles properly shouldered. In the middle of this strange entourage was a tall, bearded white man. Puzzled by the stranger's rough appearance, Private Carroll and his mates held their weapons ready. In a crisp British accent, the man introduced himself as Captain Clemens of the British Solomon Islands Protectorate Defense Force and asked to be taken to the marines' headquarters. Bill Carroll turned to his companions in amazement: "Now I have seen everything."[24]

With the landing of the Americans, Martin Clemens had decided to come in from his coastwatching post deep in the Guadalcanal mountains with his sixty native scouts to join the liberators. Private Carroll brought the party into the marines' lines and a jeep soon appeared with Capt. Halstead Ellison, commanding officer of Company C, 1st Pioneer Battalion. Clemens was whisked off to Col. Clifton B. Cates's 1st Marine Regiment Headquarters, but before he left, Clemens asked Carroll to take his scouts forward, and the private obliged. The odd procession received curious glances from the marines on the sidelines.

Buildup on the "Canal"

On 16 August the first Japanese reinforcements arrived on Guadalcanal when a 197-man detachment landed, the remnants of the Sasebo

5th SNLF. The main body of the unit had been lost on 8 August while headed for the island, when the *Meiyo Maru,* the ship transporting the troops, was sunk by U.S. submarine *S-38* with a lucky shot from one of her usually unreliable Mark XIV torpedoes. The 17th became a significant day when the Americans renamed Guadalcanal's ORANGE airstrip Henderson Field, after Maj. Lofton R. Henderson, a marine dive-bombing squadron commander who was lost in the victorious 4–7 June Battle of Midway. It was a fitting memorial for a gallant airman. General Vandegrift's prize was now ready to receive support aircraft. The mile and a half area surrounding the airstrip immediately became some of the most valuable property in the world, for Henderson Field was the key to the Allies's ability to defend Guadalcanal and turn the tables on the enemy. Unfortunately, when the cow-pasture strip was almost ready for aircraft, the Japanese staged a bombing raid that left seventeen new holes in the runway, and the weary engineers worked two days to repair the damage.

With Henderson Field now operational, albeit barely, avgas and spe-

Figure 27. ORANGE airstrip on Guadalcanal, renamed Henderson Field on 17 August 1942. The one-story Pagoda in the background was the nerve center for the Cactus Air Force. (USMC photo)

Figure 28. Capt. Hank Adams (*left*) and Lt. Fred Kidde (*right*) hold the Japanese "sun disk" flag that flew over Guadalcanal's ORANGE airstrip. (Courtesy Lt. Gen. Edward W. Snedeker, USMC, Ret.)

cialized personnel to service and arm the aircraft were urgently needed. Fortunately, the U.S. Navy had 939 trained men from CUB-1, the airfield operating unit that had arrived 11 August at Espiritu Santo in the New Hebrides along with the 6th Naval Construction Battalion—the Seabees—aboard the transports *President Polk* (AP 103) and *Wharton* (AP 7). The CUBs originally had been assigned to Auckland, New Zealand, which would have been heaven compared to Espiritu Santo; but even Santo was heaven compared to Guadalcanal.[25]

En route to Espiritu Santo the *Polk* and the *Wharton* had stopped for twenty-four hours at Samoa and boarded 858 members of the 7th Naval Construction Battalion; the Seabees could do more to advance the war effort on Santo than at Pago Pago, Samoa. Meanwhile, while still at sea, the 6th NCB was assigned to the WATCHTOWER operation, but no one on board was aware of the assignment or what the future would hold. The Bees learned of the marine landing in the Solomons on the day they reached the New Hebrides. The "fighting builders" of the 6th knew something was in the winds when they were confined to their transports while their comrades in the 7th were immediately transferred to shore. The 7th NCB subsequently became the backbone of the construction force on primitive Espiritu Santo Island. Pending the stabilization of the

Guadalcanal beachhead, it was decided that the 6th NCB would be the initial construction unit to move there. The bulk of CUB-1 would become the aviation component for Espiritu Santo Island, with sections transferred to Guadalcanal in increments as required.

During the second week of August, Col. Akinosuka Oka's 124th Infantry Regiment had received orders to move from Palau to Guadalcanal.[26] On the 17th, at Tasivarongo [Tassafaronga], Guadalcanal, the destroyer *Oikaze* landed 113 men of the 2nd Naval Force from the Yokosuka 5th SNLF. The group was designated as the 1st Camp Relief Unit, under Lt. Tatsunosuke Takahashi, IJN. The unit's primary task was to transport vital radio transmitting equipment to the 11th CU, Japanese Navy Headquarters, near the Oki River (*Oki Gawa,* Rove Creek) not far from Point Cruz; the 11th CU had left its heavy communications gear at Kukum when it evacuated that area.[27]

The 1st Camp Relief Unit, which had started out from Truk with 1,069 men in a convoy of eight warships, had encountered numerous problems. The principal vessel in the convoy, *Kinryu Maru,* was attacked by B-17s and eventually sunk. The destroyer *Mutsuki* had picked up the water-weary survivors; however, she too came under attack and was sunk. Two patrol boats plucked from the water the remaining survivors that could be rescued and ferried them to Faisi in the Shortland Islands. At the Faisi base, the men received orders to deliver the much-needed radio equipment to Guadalcanal. Until then, radio communication with other units had been by runner, and communication with Rabaul had been via submarine, the boats acting as forwarding agents.

As all these events were transpiring, however, Colonel Goettge and his men were not forgotten. On 17 August, Companies I and L of the 5th Marines, in nine Higgins boats, made a landing at Kokumbona to the west of Point Cruz, seeking information on the Goettge patrol. A passing Japanese destroyer spotted the landing party and fired a few shots, but caused no casualties. Capt. William Hawkins's Company B, 5th Marines, was to advance overland and join the others on his side of the Matanikau River.[28] Company L, 3rd Battalion, 5th Marines, led by its executive officer, Lt. George Mead Jr., was assigned the task of crossing the river upstream and attacking the enemy at the river's mouth. During the afternoon of the 18th, they had reached the crossing point, which was adjacent a small stream running into the Matanikau. The following morning, the 19th, Company L, engaged the Japanese while intercepting them trying to outflank the marines. Lieutenant Mead and his platoon commander, Plat. Sgt. John Branic, were killed. Branic was buried where he fell. Some forty-nine years later a body was found while excavating for the U.S. Guadalcanal war memorial. It was not identified at the time and the spot marked "Unknown soldier," but later DNA testing identified the remains as that of Sergeant Branic.

The marines continued searching out the enemy by checking the villages of Matanikau and Kokumbona. In what became known as the First Battle of the Matanikau, 17–20 August, the leathernecks met stiff resistance when they confronted a mixed structure of naval units under Japanese Capt. Kanae Monzen. The force consisted of about 140 men (including seven officers) from the 84th Guard Unit under Lt. Akira Tanabe, 328 men from the 11th CU and 13th CU security units under PO1c Morikiyo Sashohta, and the recently arrived 1st Camp Relief Unit, which was bivouacked nearby. WO Tetuzo Nakamura of the 81st Guard Unit had twenty sailors from his howitzer platoon.[29]

Almost immediately, Capt. Bert Hardy Jr. and Company I ran into a fusillade of gunfire from the brush. Meanwhile, Capt. Lyman Spurlock and Company L, with Colonel Whaling leading, was engaged in fierce fighting around Hill 73, including hand-to-hand combat. The Japanese launched three separate assaults. At first the marines buckled under the attack and took cover; then they counterattacked and regained the lost ground. On the 18th, the two villages were pounded by the 11th Marines. PO2c Kaneda records: "The enemy installed what we took to be field artillery on [the] high ground on the opposite bank, and at a regular time twice a day we would receive shell fire. It caused almost no damage, but the shells hit terrifying close."[30] As Company I entered Kokumbona, the Japanese withdrew to the brush. The marines recorded sixty-five enemy killed during the clash; Company L had four men killed and eleven wounded, and Company I lost one.

Licking their wounds, the Japanese retreated to the hills with all their weapons. They would have more use for them when they made their next stand, at the bank of the Mboneghe River. They had a considerable number of wounded, as Sankichi Kaneda records: "When it was dark, the unarmed construction workers, commanded by commissioned officer [Lt. Cdr.] Masao Tsunomura [engineering officer at Koku Kichi RXI, the air base on Guadalcanal] at their head, moved out in the moonlight into the grass and trees. After them came the ambulatory sick and wounded, leaning on a cane or another shoulder. Next were the heavy-laden litter bearers [carrying fifty patients] and the landing force men set out from [the] 3rd Camp Area [Sigilow Camp], carrying weapons ready for an enemy pursuit.[31]

Marine Headquarters ordered the companies back to the perimeter; Companies I and L returned by boat, while Company B marched to Kukum via the beach route. Radio-man Kuichi Yamada of the 8th Communication Unit reported that the 11th CU then had a strength of 428 and the 13th CU had 850. The Japanese felt a special urgency to have a "lightning attack unit" drive the Americans from Guadalcanal. The force selected for the task was Col. Kiyonao Ichiki's crack 28th Infantry Regiment—the Ichiki Detachment—which was then at Truk. Its original task had been to assault Midway Island, but because the Imperial Navy had made a misstep there in June at the Battle of Midway and suffered losses, the detachment was at Truk pending transfer to Japan.

The day after arriving at Truk, Colonel Ichiki received an order from the Seventeenth Army: "Ichiki Detachment, with cooperation from the Navy, will recapture RXI (Guadalcanal Airfield). They are to seize without delay a position on RXN (Guadalcanal) where they will await the [arrival] of their backup unit. As a vanguard they will board six destroyers and leave for RXN immediately."[32]

At 2300 on 18 August, the advance echelon of 916 men were delivered by six ships of Destroyer Division 14: the *Arashi* (1st Lt. Hideo Goto, engineers and headquarters), the *Hagikace* (1st Lt. Magoz Maurama, 3rd Company), the *Hamakaze* (1st Lt. Shigenao Komatsu, 2nd Battalion, 28th Infantry Regiment Machine-Gun Company), the *Tanikaze* (Maj. Nobuo Kuramoto, 4th Company), the *Kagero* (1st Lt. Yusaku Higuchi, 1st Company), and the *Urakaze* (Capt. Tetsuro Sawada, 2nd Company). The U.S. military had named these destroyer-transports the "Tokyo Express," though subsequently the Cactus airmen would call them "the Rat Patrol," as they transported Japanese forces to Guadalcanal under the cover of night, essentially unopposed. The Japanese troops, most ex-China veterans comprising the 1st Battalion, 28th Infantry Regiment, were under Major Kuramoto. The formation landed at the 81st Guard Unit naval lookout post at Tiabo Misaki (Taivu Point) under PO3c Tan. Earlier, also at Taivu, an echelon of the Express dropped off 160 men from the 3rd Company, 1st Independent Shipping Engineer Regiment, under Capt. Masaharu Mushitan. These soldiers operated the *shōthatsu* (small landing craft) and *daihatsu* (large landing barge) and would ferry the detachment to shore.

Col. Kiyonao Ichiki was an impatient officer, and within hours after his force had landed a reconnaissance patrol was organized to scout the attack route. He believed the report that only two thousand Americans were on the island, and his strategy was to be a surprise night attack; he had boasted that the Americans would be "dog meat" for his "die-hard soldiers."[33] Ichiki met with Major Kuramoto and planned the assault, based on the forthcoming results of an intelligence- gathering party. A thirty-eight-man party was put together consisting of five teams. It was led by Capt.Yoshimi Shibuya, the communication officer, and included four other officers—1st Lt. Shoji Tate, 2nd Lt. Masanobu Hagyuda, 2nd Lt. Kenji Matsumoto, and an engineer, Provisional Officer Shigemi Wada. Two enlisted sailors from the 81st Guard Unit were to act as guides.

The patrol set out at 0830 on 19 August, taking the sandy coastal route to familiarize the men with the terrain and the point of attack. At 1200, the men stopped for a rest and lunch at *Kori Mura* (Koli village), a little off the route; at 1307 they were on the move again. The two guides were in the lead; Captain Shibuya's team, with Lieutenant Tate on his left, was about 100 feet behind them. In the middle were Lieutenant Hagyuda's men, followed by Lieutenant Matsumoto and his group; Provisional Officer Wada and his fifth team brought up the rear. At the bend in the road at *Kori Saki* (Koli Point) they ran into an ambush laid by a patrol from Company A, 1st Battalion, 1st Marines, under Capt. Charles H. Brush Jr. His sixty-man force was equipped with automatic weapons, and guiding the patrol were four of Martin Clemens's scouts—Daniel Pule, Beato, Gumu, and Vura. Daniel and Vura were with Captain Bush; Beato and Guma were with 2nd Lt. John J. Jackym.

Shibuya, Tate, and the guides were killed instantly. Others took cover, but they faced a hail of gunfire. Meanwhile, Lieutenant Jackym steered his platoon around the right flank in an enveloping movement to cut off the enemy's rear. Jackym recalls: "We came across the Japanese quite suddenly: they were all cleverly camouflaged and hard to see until they seemed to pop out of the bush only yards away. It was horribly frightening, uncertain and confused: they seemed to be all around. I just fired furiously whenever one came into view."[34] In the fifty-one-minute skirmish, thirty-two Japanese were killed, including all five of the officers. Most died immediately, except Engineer Wada, who though severely wounded managed to escape into a thicket; he died there afterward. Another wounded man, Cpl. Kiyonobu Akasaka of the 1st Squad, Tate platoon, also crawled into the underbrush. Sergeant Sudo, despite his severe wounds, was able to return to Taivu Point to give a report, then collapsed and died. Superior Privates Hirano and Isamu Mashiko, both slightly wounded, were slowly making their way back to Taivu. Leading Pvt. Masamitsu Okamo and PFC Katajiro Tomano, also wounded, returned to their base and reported the disaster.

On hearing the news, Colonel Ichiki was stunned. How could this happen? A relief party from the 1st Company, led by 1st Lt. Yusaku Higuchi, was immediately assembled and rushed to the scene; the group included a medical team under 1st Lt. Giji Nakai. Lieutenant Higuchi and his platoon took the lead. Some 325 feet behind, the 2nd Platoon, under 2nd Lt. Yuzo Kudo, kept a close watch for the Americans; the 3rd Platoon, under 2nd Lt. Tadayoshi Uchizawa, protected the rear. Accompanying Higuchi's men was the 1st Platoon, 4th Company, under 2nd Lt. Kiyoshi Sato. The patrol arrived at 2000 to find that the Americans were gone and that bodies and blood were spread all across the area. In the faint evening light they found five dead marines wrapped in tarps and apparently ready for interment. One by one, the men of the patrol located their comrades in the jungle; all had been killed except Corporal Akasaka, who was breathing but unconscious. Members of Lieutenant Sato's platoon buried their dead.

Before the Japanese had arrived however, 2nd Lt. John J. Jackym's platoon had searched the bodies of the Japanese for information. Emptying the pockets of the dead, they found notes, photographs, and in some cases badges. One key discovery was a dispatch case, which revealed evidence of a recently arrived strong army force, including an aerial photograph showing the layout of the marines' camp. These men were not sailors; they were first-class Japanese Army troops—the first of their breed on the island. The 1st Marines would soon meet the rest of the newcomers at the Ilu River basin.

The Fight Continues

Back on Espiritu Santo, meanwhile, the message was received to send an air service support unit to Guadalcanal—the airplane specialists. The only men available were the "Bluejackets" of CUB-1, and thus it was that 120 sailors were hauled out of their beds at midnight and given a handful of M1903 .30-caliber Springfield rifles. The echelon was commanded by Ens. George Washington "Wash" Polk, USNR, assisted by WO Robert Fickles, USN. They were accompanied by an older flying officer, Maj. Charles H. "Fog" Hayes, USMC, executive officer of VMO-251.Vice Adm. John S. McCain, Commander, Air, South Pacific (COMAIRSOPAC), had ordered Major Hayes to go to Guadalcanal to get the airstrip prepared to receive aircraft. Hayes would play a key role in the completion and operation of the field and would be the first operations officer.[35]

The men of CUB-1 were herded aboard the same converted four-stackers of Transport Division 12 that had taken the 1st Raiders to Tulagi on 7 August—the *Colhoun, Gregory, Little,* and *McKean.* Nestled on the decks of the refitted "tin cans" were 400 fifty-five-gallon drums of avgas, drums of aviation oil, 282 bombs (100 to 500 pounders), several hand pumps, various boxed belts of ammunition, and a few aircraft tools. The green CUB-1 sailors reached Guadalcanal at sunset on 15 August. There they were unceremoniously dumped onto the unlit, squashy beach and introduced to the basic facts of their new life of foxholes and mud in a hot mucky hell-hole of disease, bombing, and assured misery. The CUB-1 specialists included ordnance men, gas crews, mechanics, a parachute rigger, medics, and a postal clerk. Metalsmith PO3c Luie Fuller said, "We had four master tool boxes. Period! That is all we had to work with. . . ." Fortunately, among the 120 enlisted men was a radio technician, RT1c Virgil R. Rambow, who carried a Collins transceiver radio (TSC). He would shortly put the set to good use.[36]

On 20 August the leathernecks saw thirty-one aircraft land on lumpy Henderson Field—a gift from the gods and the highlight of the day. It was the first echelon of Marine Air Group 23, (MAG-23) comprising one squadron (VMF-223) of nineteen F4F-4 Wildcat fighters and another squadron (VMSB-232) of twelve SBD-3 Dauntless dive-bombers. The following day, the seaplane tender *McFarland* pulled into Kukum Harbor and unloaded 102 ground crew and six pilots from VMF-212. Another 170 members of VMF-223 were shipped on the transport *William Ward Burrows* (AP 6), which departed Pearl Harbor on 3 August and reached Tulagi on the 29th; the next day they boarded LCPs for a wet ride across Sealark Channel to Guadalcanal to rejoin their squadron. The air group—including a headquarters, with its own post office—was now complete. Two days later the Wildcats of VMF-224 and the SBDs of VMSB-231 would arrive to augment the mixed air units of the Cactus Air Force.[37]

On the night of 20 August, when the first aircraft had touched down on Henderson Field, Pvt. Wilbur F. Bewley and PFC Leo Campbell of Company G, 2nd Battalion, 1st Marines, were on outpost duty near the 1st Marines' beach defenses. A few minutes after midnight the two heard bursts of machine-gun fire from the direction of the river—the opening shots of what would be called the Battle of the Tenaru. Suddenly, out of nowhere, a large, bedraggled Solomon Islander came staggering toward

Bewley's post. Bewley had been told that anyone in front of him would be the enemy, and to act accordingly. Bewley states he had shouted to the man: "You better stop or you're a dead son-of-a-bitch!" The man raised his hands above his head, pleading that Bewley not shoot him, as he was "no Japanese."[38]

Jacob Vouza, the man Bewley was detaining, had been a retired sergeant major in the Solomon Islands Protectorate constabulary and now was one of Clemens's scouts. He had been captured by Colonel Ichiki's soldiers while on a local patrol; they had interrogated and tortured him, bayoneted him repeatedly, and left him for dead. But Vouza had chewed through his ropes and escaped. Bewley had indeed noticed the man's blood-stained *lava lava,* the rectangular cloth that native islanders wore around their waist. He called out to the corporal of the guard, Elias D. Holtz, who took charge and delivered Vouza to Lt. Luther Jordan; Jordan took the man to the command post of Lt. Col. Edwin A. Pollock, 2nd Battalion, 1st Marines. There, Vouza—who believed he was dying—poured out his heart to Martin Clemens in a long message for his family. But before he passed out from loss of blood, the indomitable scout also gave Clemens detailed information on Colonel Ichiki's force, including numbers of men and weapons; Clemens immediately telephoned the information to Lt. Col. Jerry Thomas at the command post, which the occupants called the "impact center."

Earlier the Marine Corps leadership had considered that the ideal location for the enemy to land would be on the beaches, and consequently that was to be the main line of resistance (MLR). The marines built a 9,600-yard defense—nearly 5½ miles—from the west side of the mouth of the Ilu River, just west of Tenaru, continuing on around Lunga Point to the abandoned village of Kukum. The Ilu flank was set 600 yards inland on the first high ground of the coastal hills. Two battalions of the 5th Marines garrisoned the line from Kukum village to the west bank of the Lunga River, just east of Lunga Point, and the balance was held by the 1st Marine Regiment along the tidal lagoon called Alligator Creek, which was set apart from the ocean waters by a 100-foot-long sandbar, 25 to 50 feet wide. South of the Henderson airstrip a 9,000-yard stretch was guarded by the 1st Pioneer Battalion, the guns of the 11th Marines, the 1st Amphibian Tractor Battalion, and the 1st Engineer Battalion.

On 21 August at 0240, the vanguard of the 2nd Company of the Ichiki Detachment (1st Battalion, 28th Infantry Regiment), after a twenty-mile night march from Taivu Point, struck from the jungle at the flimsy but determined defenses of the marines who held positions on the western side of the airfield at the Alligator Creek lagoon. The sand pit there represented the open door to the airfield defenses, but there was a deadly obstacle: behind it were 930 leathernecks from the 2nd Battalion, 1st Marines, with a similar number from the 3rd Battalion on their left and the 1st Battalion in reserve.

The night was pitch black, and it was raining. Ichiki's soldiers shed their knapsacks and all non-essential equipment so as not to impede their attack. At about 2200, a flare went off and lit the jungle east of the Lunga River. Nothing happened; all was quiet. To check it out, part of Company A, 1st Marines, led by Captain Brush and 2nd Lt. Victor Valenti had been aggressively patrolling the outskirts of the 1st Marine defensive sector to determine the enemy's strength beyond the coconut groves; finding nothing, they had returned to the bivouac area.

Just in front of Company G, 2nd Battalion, 1st Marines, was the sand-bar formed by the Tenaru River and the ocean tides—the place where Ichiki's men would attack.[39] The sandbar formed near the mouth of the Tenaru because the stream flowed only at high tide; at low tide there is a sizable area of exposed beach. Within minutes the major assault was underway. To see where they were heading, the attackers set off another flare; momentarily, it was like daylight. The time was 0310. The battle began with a mass of preparatory fire from the attackers' Model 99 Arisaka that sent sheets of 7.7-mm shells toward the leatherneck lines.

The marines, however, had a primitive secret weapon that was effective only at dark—a band of rusty barbed wire strung across the fifty-foot sandbar between the lagoon and the beach. The wire had been stripped off a plantation fence used to control cattle and had been installed on the east bank of the sandbar. The lead wave of about two hundred from the 2nd Company, under Capt. Tetsuro Sawada, made a dash across the Ilu River—the *Nakagawa*—only to be met with a hail of deadly fire from Capt. James F. Sherman's Company G. Pvt. Masahiro Hayashi of 2nd Lt. Goro Ohashi's platoon was the 2nd Company's only survivor. He had been wounded in the left hip and had remained in the water until almost daybreak, then slowly made his way back the way he had come.

On the opposite side of the river was Pvt. P. C. Becker who could see nothing. He said the battle came on suddenly and the firing was intense; he thought the Japs were "crazy." Pvt. Gilbert Delloff of Company E, 2nd Battalion, 1st Marines, also remembers: "It was [a] dark, moonless night and difficult to see very far. Bill Wallace had a position to my left and on my right there was a machine gun post and a 37-mm gun beyond that. Suddenly all hell broke loose as Wallace started firing towards the surf. Directly in front of me was a dead tree. . . . Wallace shouted to me that the Japs were hiding behind it so I began firing at each end of it." Meanwhile Japanese artillery fire from 2nd Lt. Taisuaruh Hamani's #1 field gun (Type 92, 77-mm) continued, and Delloff recalls:

> The artillery fire seemed to be wounding quite a lot of our guys and the machine gun near me got knocked out. The only survivor brought me some ammunition. It was a godsend because I was getting low. . . . Most of the firing was coming from the river with artillery, mortars [from the Capt. Tetsuro Sawada company's mortar squad], and machine guns [from 1st Lt. Shigenao Komatsu's heavy machine guns (eight squads)] and rifles. We kept firing until Jap artillery began to land among us. One hit [Pvt. William] Wallace's [D/1/1] position and he got hurt bad. Then, [Pvt] Ray Roberts [E/2/1] got killed nearby [and] another hit on the emplacement and killed Ray [Pvt. James P.] Edlin [E/2/1] and two others, all guys I'd been through training with.[40]

In the darkness, at least two companies of the attackers became partly enmeshed in the barbed wire—1st Lt. Yusaku Higuchi's company and 1st Lt. Hirozo Maruyama's 3rd Company. The marines were under tremendous pressure. The Japanese were met by lethal fire from machine guns and two 37-mm antitank guns, manned by two platoons of Battery B, 1st Special Weapons Battalion, under 2nd Lt. James F. McClanahan. The antitank guns, which had been placed in an ideal position on the point opposite the sandpit (later called "Hell's Point"), were loaded with canister shot, large shells filled with shrapnel; during the battle they were fired every five to six seconds. For a short while Ichiki's men were in disarray, then they plowed on, only to be killed in the onslaught.

One group of Lieutenant Maruyama's attackers, under 2nd Lt. Matsuo Yoshimoto, took possession of an abandoned amtrac that was standing in the river. (About a week before the attack, the marines had sunk two LVT1 Alligators in a stream that was the headwaters of the Tenaru and built a bridge over them.) Matsuo's men set up their own machine gun on the amtrac and fired at the marines. Meanwhile, back at Tenaru Point the enemy had struck the marine line using mortars and grenades to knock out the troops of B Battery who were manning and protecting the 37-mm antitank weapon. The attackers—1st Lt. Hideo Goto's engineers—broke through on the right flank and one of the antitank gun crews was wiped out; but the marines regrouped and in hand-to-hand combat killed the enemy. Pvts. Harry R. Horsman and E. Carter, Cpl. Larry DiPietroantonio, and Sgt. James W. Hancock took over and kept the gun firing. For his extraordinary performance during this action, Sergeant Hancock, one of the many heroes, received the Silver Star. 2nd Lt. William Whorf, CO of Company H, had his four machine guns in place close to those of Company G's .30- and .50-caliber weapons. Three of his crew—Al Schmid, LeRoy Diamond, and Johnny Rivers—were awarded the Navy Cross for this action, the second-highest award given by the Marine Corps; Rivers's award was posthumous.

Company G's 60-mm mortars took a terrible toll of the Japanese across the river in the coconut grove; bodies and body parts flew in all directions. Pvts. Harry "Trigger" Briggs and George Hoffman, two of the Browning automatic rifle men, were situated at Tenaru Point; they reported that their weapons were so hot from firing that they were afraid the BARs would lock up. Pvt. Henry Brunkhurst, a former baseball pitcher, was able to throw hand grenades smack in the middle of the on-rushing Japanese. The battalion commanding officer, Lt. Col. Edwin A. Pollock, was seen bending low while moving along the line of riflemen, telling everyone in his calm and competent way, to "stay low, sight your target, and squeeze 'em off." Pollack proved to be an inspiring combat leader. All of his company commanders—Lieutenants Jordan, Matthews, and Codrea—similarly demonstrated superb leadership. Both Colonel Pollock and Lt. George Codrea would receive the Navy Cross for heroics in the battle. Lieutenant McClanahan would receive the Silver Star but was recommended for the Navy Cross.

At 0400, 1st Lt. Toshiro Chiba's company plunged forward under 2nd Platoon leader 2nd Lt. Akiro Imano. At about this time, 1st Lt. Shigenao Komatsu, the commander of the 2nd Battalion, 28th Infantry Machine-Gun Company, had his eight Type 92 heavy machine guns in place on the left flank and began firing in unison. When the gunfire briefly abated, Komatsu urged his men to continue. The marines, momentarily stunned, had been directing their fire on stopping Ichiki's soldiers, who had fallen by the hundreds; then they concentrated on silencing Komatsu's gunners.

At 0410, the 1st Battalion, 5th Marines, received orders from the division to support the 1st Marines by combing the area for stray enemy. Marine guts and tenacity would play a key role in blunting the enemy assault.[41] Heroism was everywhere. The Japanese phalanx fell apart. At sunrise, 0445, the remnants of Colonel Ichiki's men withdrew to the jungle to renew the attack, only to be hammered by three 75-mm guns and one 105-mm gun of the 11th Marines, whose weapons had zeroed in on their assembly area and about 1,000 yards of the beach. The Japanese would not surrender, though only a handful survived. They crawled away to their rear area, no doubt telling their comrades of the unceasing ferocity of the U.S. Marines. After the battle, one of Colonel Ichiki's infantrymen would comment: "The American volume of fire was wild beyond imagination." Another, Ldg. Pvt. Yoshimasa Niide of 2nd Lt. Masao Ingaki's platoon, a gunner who had service in China, said: "Our heavy machine guns were firing coordinated probing fire, so Mr. Enemy returned fire like a madman."[42]

At 0800 that morning of the 21st, Lt. Col. Leonard B. Cresswell, commanding officer of the 1st Battalion, 1st Marines, ordered Captain Bush's Company A and 1st Lt. Nikolai S. Stevenson's Company C to advance west in a flanking nutcracker movement to squeeze and annihilate any enemy in the groves. Cresswell placed his B Company under 1st Lt. Marshall T. Armstrong as a rear guard at the mouth of the Ilu River.[43] At 0830, the division ordered Lt. Col. Frederick C. Biebush's 3rd Battalion, 5th Marines, to move overland to the east bank of the Matanikau River to prevent any Japanese from filtering past. During that morning, the newly arrived F4F-4s of MAG-23, flying along the coast, also attacked and sank a few small enemy supply boats that were heading toward the battle zone.

The light tanks of A Company, 1st Tank Battalion, were ordered to seek out any enemy, and Sgt. Earl J. Mowery, one of the commanders of an M2A4 tank (later called the Stuart tank), remembered: "A platoon of four Stuarts, led by 1st Lt. Leo B. Case advanced to support the riflemen. We drove down a trail through the coconut palm, to a spit of sand across the mouth of the Ilu River. The tanks lumbered across the sandbar and engaged the enemy, crashing into the palm trees to knock them over and eject the hidden Japanese hidden there. One tank was knocked out by enemy fire, but the crew was rescued and the tanks continued the advance firing canister as they moved. They ran over many bodies during the battle[,] crushing them under the tracks."[44] Most of the marine casualties occurred as the leathernecks followed the tanks. The wounded enemy pretended to be dead until an American passed, then from behind the Japanese would shoot, or stick him with a bayonet, or throw a grenade.

All the while the engagement had been raging, RT1c Virgil Rambow, the CUB-1 radio operator, had set up his Collins transceiver on a nearby hill to report the various stages of the battle to the division. The melee lasted sixteen hours, with the division on edge until it was over.[45]

Touring the area late on the 21st, the marines could not believe the grisly scene before them—terribly mangled bodies now covered with maggots and flies. Most of the men gagged and vomited. About 777 of Colonel Ichiki's infantrymen would not return to Asahigawa City, Hokkaido. They either were buried at Koli Point, in a sandlot or in the coconut grove, or were washed out to sea. Excerpts from the diary of Lt. Jack Fuller, USNR, of the Lunga boat pool describe the horror: ". . . [Regarding what we called] the Tenaru battlefield[,] I have never seen in my life such a sight. The bodies did not only have gunshot wounds, but [were] horribly mangled. The heads of most of them were blown off. The bodies were all ripped open and the entrails spilled on the ground. Arms and legs were [lying] all over the area."[46]

Fifteen wounded Japanese, heavily blood-stained, were captured and taken within the marine lines. Thirty survivors, in mixed physical and emotional condition, including two officers—2nd Lieutenant Toshio, the assistant adjutant, and 1st Lt. Yoshiaki Sakakibara, the assistant communication officer—somehow managed to crawl away and get back to Taivu Point. One of the thirty, Sup. Pvt. Isamu Mashiko, had staggered in after four days of wandering around.[47] Others that made it back included Corporal Tanaka, PFC Takeshichi Makabe, Cpl. Shoji Setoda (Goto engineering company), Sgt. Sadanobu Okada, Sgt. Masatoshi Mae, Pvt. Tadshi Suzuki, PFC Kuragand, and PFC Kiyoshi Ono (2/28 Machine-Gun Company). Ten that had returned joined the rear echelon of forty men from 2nd Lt. Daizo Umeda's transport unit. Another forty soldiers from the Sato platoon were fortunate, as they had missed the battle because they stayed behind to bury those killed at Koli Point.[48]

Thirty-four marines were lost forever and seventy-five wounded. The 2nd Battalion, 1st Marines, lost the most men, with twenty-five killed and forty-four wounded. The 1st Battalion lost seven KIA and thirteen WIA, while the Special Weapons Battalion, a division unit, lost two KIA and fourteen WIA. One man was wounded from the 1st Marines Regimental Weapons Company and three from the Headquarters and Service Company. One doctor, Lt. L. G. Saphier, USNR, was killed as he went forward to give immediate first aid. After the battle, the most severely wounded were evacuated in the high-speed transport *Colhoun* to Efate Island in the New Hebrides for treatment at the U.S. Naval Base Hospital #2 at Port Vila.[49]

On 21 August, Captain Kanae Monzen sent the following message to the Eighth Fleet at Rabaul, from the Imperial Japanese Navy Headquarters located near Point Cruz: "From [about] 0200 [0400] we heard sounds of a furious battle near the airfield area. Five small planes took off at 0400 [0600] and circled above. The five that took off landed between 0500 and 0530. They did not take off again. We continued to hear the sounds of gunfire. We saw no takeoffs or flights. . . . We guessed that our advance troops' attack on the airfield [was] proceeding favorably for our side. Please convey to the Ichiki Detachment that many construction units workers are retreating through the tropical forest around the airfield."[50] Late that evening, however, IJN Headquarters at Rabaul received another wire: "The Ichiki advanced troops were almost completely annihilated this morning at a site near the airfield, without reaching the field."[51] This communication was received from the East Point lookout station (Point Taivu) via the *Boston Maru*. The message came from 1st Lt. Yoshiaki Sakakibara, Colonel Ichiki's assistant signal officer.

Maj. Gen. Akisaburo Futami, the former chief of staff, Seventeenth Army, later recalled the reaction to the news about the Ichiki Detachment:

> We at the Oki Army [Seventeenth Army] Headquarters had acknowledged a communication from the Navy earlier that the Ichiki Detachment made a bloodless landing. . . . But, later there was no more contact with the Ichiki Unit. When I was resting in my quarters on August 22 and at about 2325 [Tokyo time], Lt. Col. Hiroshi Matsumoto, the senior staff officer, came to me and [said]: "They tell me the Navy received a wire saying the Ichiki Detachment was annihilated." Matsumoto smiled and added: "I think it's a false report." Wireless communication from Guadalcanal could not reach us without Navy transmission. We had no recourse but to rely on the Navy. On the 23rd, the Navy analyzed in detail all wires we received. As a result, we reached a conclusion that the battle situation of the Ichiki Detachment was not necessarily to be viewed with optimism. Also, if they had succeeded in taking the airfield they would have reported it immediately. Four days had passed since they landed. It might have been an overstatement to say "annihilated." However, we could not help but reach the conclusion that they were forced into a desperate battle. At this point, we canceled the planned summons of a detachment of one battalion from the Kawaguchi Shitai [Maj. Gen. Kiyotake Kawaguchi's detachment] to Rabaul as a reserve unit and decided to throw all three battalions of the Kawaguchi Detachment into Guadalcanal.[52]

Figure 29. Maj. Gen. Kiyotake Kawaguchi and staff, 35th Brigade, Koror, Palau Islands, 13 August 1942. *First row, left to right*: Unknown, Maj. Kanehisa Yamamoto, Maj. Gen. Kiyotake Kawaguchi, Lt. Col. Yoshihiko Osone, Capt. Kiyoshi Kurashige. *Center row*: 1st Lt. Koichi Ihara, 1st Lt. Masao Takenaka, 1st Lt. Tadatsugu Kato, 1st Lt. Kazuo Yamaguchi. *Top row*: 2nd Lieutenant Ozawa, 1st Lieutenant Iwaizumi, 2nd Lieutenant Yamada. (Officers' names furnished by Akiko Kawaguchi, the general's daughter.) (National Archives)

At 2200, on 21 August, the one thousand men of the 2nd Battalion, 5th Marines, from Tulagi joined the 1st and 3rd Battalions on Guadalcanal and were assigned as the division reserve, positioned near Henderson Field, between the Lunga and Tenaru Rivers. The only action they had seen on Tulagi in the past ten days was the burying of dead Japanese. However, on the 21st, the marines also saw the U.S. Navy for the first time in almost two weeks when the supply ships *Alhena* and *Fomalhaut* (AKA 5), escorted by the destroyers *Blue* (DD 387), *Helm* (DD 388), and *Henley* (DD 391), arrived at Lunga Roads, the offshore anchorage.[53] The next day, 22 August, the first USAAF aircraft landed on dusty Henderson Field. Five P-400s—the export version of the Bell P-39 Airacobra that the RAF had rejected—were flown from Tontouta, New Caledonia, via Efate and Espiritu Santo; two B-17s from the 11th Bombardment Group shepherded the fighters from Santo to Guadalcanal.[54] The superb mechanics of the 67th Fighter Squadron had assembled the P-39s at Tontouta from crated models and without blueprints—a Herculean task. But the aircraft were inadequate surplus models from

Lend-Lease, without oxygen equipment. They were called "Pete" and "Repeat" by the marines, yet they ultimately would do yeoman service in the hodgepodge assemblage of aircraft and pilots of U.S. Marine, Navy, and Army air units of the Cactus Air Force, which would carve itself an honored place in military history.

The day after the pilots and aircraft arrived, the *Fomalhaut* carried to Guadalcanal an advance ground crew of thirty from the 67th Fighter Squadron: "The Marine pilots showed the airmen of the 67th a palm grove with some scattered tents—'Our camp,' they said. To bed down, they provided them with straw mats, courtesy of the departed Japanese. When asked where the Japs were, the Marines replied, 'See that river over there?' Pointing to a stream about 200 yards away. 'They are on the other side.'"[55]

On the 24th more help arrived when twenty-nine SBD-3 Dauntless dive-bombers and six Grumman TBF Avenger torpedo bombers from the carrier *Saratoga* landed on the airstrip and spent the night. They took off the following morning, leaving behind twenty-seven 1,000-pound bombs, which were pulled to the side and stacked. However, Rear Adm. Sadayoshi Yamada's Imperial Japanese Navy "eagles" spotted the cache and planted a bomb nearby; it missed the 13½ tons of explosives, but the blast flung the 1,000-pounders around the area like bowling pins. The CUBs subsequently gathered the bombs and moved them to safety.

While the marines were rejoicing in the new air power on the field, the Japanese at Truk had their own plans for Guadalcanal, as outlined in the following order:

> The enemy surface force task force including 1 or 2 aircraft carriers has appeared Southeast of the Solomon Is. The enemy seems to be reinforcing his strength in the Tulagi area, and about the 20th, 25 enemy planes landed on the Guadalcanal Airfield.
>
> Our fleet is proceeding rapidly to San Cristobal Island area in order to destroy it.
>
> The 1st Echelon of the Ichiki Detachment is advancing toward the airfield mainly by night movements, and by the morning of the 20th its front line has reached Tetere. It is now making preparations to capture the airfield by night attack.
>
> The 2nd Echelon of the Ichiki Detachment should land on the night of the 24th.
>
> The Guadalcanal Navy Garrison Unit, besieged by the enemy, is engaging in desperate fighting and will defend its positions until the last.

The Kawaguchi Detachment, cooperating with Navy Forces, will first quickly destroy the enemy on Tulagi and firmly secure it.

2. The Regiment (less one company and two platoons) will exert every effort to conclude quickly the debarkation of the Kawaguchi Detachment.[56]

Meanwhile, the Cactus Air Force was continuing to add all the aircraft the rear bases could muster. On 24 August additional air reinforcements were received when eleven SBDs from the carrier *Enterprise*—Flight 300—flew in to Henderson Field. The SBDs dropped their 500-pound bombs in Sealark Channel before landing in order to prevent accidents. The following day a Consolidated PBY-5A flying boat from Espiritu Santo landed at Henderson. On board was Lt. Cdr. Joseph P. "Paul" Blundon, USNR, commanding officer of the 6th Naval Construction Battalion. Blundon had been ordered to Guadalcanal for two reasons: first, to inspect the airfield and note what was required; second, to pave the way for the transfer of the 6th NCB from Espiritu Santo to Guadalcanal. He dallied at Henderson, however, and lost his ride back to Espiritu Santo when the PBY took off without him, leaving him the lone Seabee on the "Canal." This, however, gave him the honor of being the first Seabee under fire in World War II in the Pacific. While Blundon was working on plans for base improvements, his staff on Espiritu Santo was making plans to transfer the first echelon to Guadalcanal.

On 27 August, nine P-39s, dubbed the "Klunkers from the 67th Fighter Squadron from New Caledonia—the "Game Cock Squadron"—landed on the Henderson airstrip, guided to the field by B-17s of the 11th Bomb Group. On the same day, one of Col. Leroy Hunt's battalions—the 1st Battalion, 5th Marines, under Lt. Col. William E. Maxwell—moved out from Lunga Plains on a patrol to the Matanikau area via Kokumbona, directly amidst a Japanese naval concentration and supply point. They ran into some remnants of Lt. Akira Tanabe's 84th Guard Unit there, as well as the security units of the 11th and 13th CU. Colonel Maxwell, playing it safe, radioed back and asked for help, requesting landing craft to transport his unit back to the perimeter. No one knew what the Japanese had in the way of troop strength, as most of the 5th Marines intelligence staff had been killed on the Goettge patrol. But Colonel Hunt did not like Maxwell's plan, and therefore sacked him. He took direct command of the 1st Battalion and continued to recon the area. The enemy force under Lt. Akira Tanabe, seeing the size of Hunt's force, decided to break contact, and thus the 1/5 made its way back to the perimeter via the coastal route.

The vanguard of the 6th Naval Construction Battalion, consisting of 387 enlisted men and five officers under Lt. (jg) Thomas L. Stamp, boarded the *Betelgeuse* at Espiritu Santo on 30 August and arrived at Lunga Roads two days later. By the time the Seabees reached Guadalcanal, the airfield's coral off-ramps were filled with aircraft, though not all were in flying condition. Some had already reached the boneyard, the result of unsuccessful takeoffs and landings due to potholes or enemy activity. The day before, 29 August, had brought bad news for the marines when five Imperial Japanese Navy destroyers landed 750 troops at Taivu Point—300 from the 2nd echelon of the Ichiki Detachment and 450 from Maj. Yukichi Kokusho's 1st Battalion, 124th Infantry, 35th Brigade. On the 30th, another five destroyers delivered seven hundred men from the 2nd echelon of the Ichiki Detachment to Taivu Point. The 31st brought to Taivu some eleven to twelve hundred men on eight destroyers from General Kawaguchi's 35th Brigade.[57]

That same day, 31 August, aircraft from the *Saratoga*'s squadrons (VS-3, VF-5, and VT-8) landed at Henderson to augment the Cactus Air Force. Two weeks later, unexpected help arrived when eleven aircraft of VS-71 from the carrier *Wasp* flew in. The *Wasp* later was sunk, on 15 September, in "Torpedo Junction," the area between San Cristobal and Espiritu Santo. Cdr. Takaichi Kinashi's *I-19* submarine torpedoed her with an array of three out of six fired, while she was en route to Santo. The balance of the *Wasp*'s aircraft were flown to Luganville Airdrome, Espiritu Santo, New Hebrides; the maintenance crews were sent to Efate Island.[58]

By the end of August the recently arrived Lt. Hugh Mackenzie of the Royal Australian Navy, the deputy supervising officer from Port Vila, Efate Island, had set up a radio station in a former Japanese dugout at the northwest side of Henderson Field. Major Snedeker, the division communication officer, gave Mackenzie five marine radio operators from the 1st Signal Company to monitor the coastwatcher network, and they were able receive advance word of any incoming air raids. Added to that, a recently received radar set was put in operation, picking up incoming enemy aircraft 125 miles away. Both enhanced the air defense of the island, as the Japanese unfinished radar station the marines had discovered was so incomplete that it was impossible to put in service.

11 Bloody September

On 1 September 1942 Companies A and D of the 6th Naval Construction Battalion came ashore at Lunga Point from the *Betelgeuse*. Lt. Cdr. Mark H. Jordan, executive officer of the 6th NCB, fondly referred to these CBs as the "Confused Bastards." Their campsite, located on the Lever's plantation and called "mosquito gulch," was centered between two clearings—Henderson Field and the soon to be built Fighter Strip No. 1. Upon their arrival, a lone Betty bomber had initiated the 6th CBs to the air war over Guadalcanal. It was an ineffective attack, but bombs hit the strip at a few spots and the Bees came to call Henderson Field "Pothole Hen."

The Henderson Locus

On their second day on Guadalcanal Company D immediately took over construction and maintenance of the airstrip from the leatherneck engineers, led by Lt. (jg) Alma P. Pratt with CMM Floyd L. Johnson as crew chief. The marine engineers had made the runway 3,800 feet long and 150 feet wide, with a 150-foot clearance zone adjacent to the runway. The Seabees used an odd assortment of machinery, including two HD7 bulldozers, six International 1½-yard dump trucks, twenty-four Japanese low-bed rolling stock vehicles, one Adams patrol grader, and one "traxcavator." Later, five-yard Garwood carryall scrapers and two smaller scrapers were borrowed from the 1st Engineer Battalion.

The pilots loved the Seabees. They knew they would be able to land when they returned from a "hunt" because the 6th NCB had developed a fill-in system to take care of the potholes. Flying squads—dump trucks loaded with crushed coral—were stationed adjacent to the field, with just the right amount of the gravelly fill to cover a hole made by a 500-pound bomb. At the end of a bombing, the trucks would dash out and unload the crushed coral, then Chief Johnson's crew would quickly fill the craters.

The airstrip was the 6th's primary construction assignment. Although

Figure 30. The 6th Naval Construction Battalion, Henderson Field, Guadalcanal Island. (National Archives)

the marine engineers had completed sufficient work to make the field usable for fighters, the flat cross section gave no slope for drainage and little was done to provide a wearable surface. With pelting rains, the heavy flight traffic constantly dug up and rutted the surface. The Seabees had the dual task of keeping the strip continuously in usable condition and later of extending it to 5,000 feet or more for the use of B 17s and B 24s. For the problem of water accumulation on the soil-bed base, the CBs created a cross slope that would shed rain and provide a wearable surface. While one group tackled the first field project, the other crews began felling coconut trees to clear the way for the airstrip's extension. As soon as a power shovel was obtained, it was put to use in the bed of the Lunga River, excavating gravel for the crowning surfacing job.

On 4 September, an R4D transport from VMJ-253 flew the 880 miles from New Caledonia to Henderson Field. On board were Brig. Gen. Roy S. Geiger, commanding general, 1st Marine Air Wing; Col. Louis Woods; and Lt. Col. John C. Munn, the wing's D 2, under whom the staff of MAG-23 became an intricate part of the 1st Air Wing operations. The inter-service Cactus Air Force made its headquarters in the

Pagoda, the former Japanese officers lounge. The R4D—the U.S. Navy's version of the ubiquitous Douglas DC-3—served as either a cargo carrier (the Skytrain) or a passenger plane (the Skytrooper). The Skytrains of New Caledonia-based MAG-25 (comprising VMJ-152 and VMJ-253) would become the backbone of a unique airlift service that supported the ground and air forces on Guadalcanal. They flew everything imaginable, from food to wire, torpedoes, aviation gasoline, medical supplies, personnel, and the U.S. mail. On 24 November, they became part of the South Pacific Combat Air Transport Command (SCAT), which was sometimes referred to as the Southern Cross Air Line. Eventually, thirty-eight MAG-25 R4Ds were engaged in transporting critical supplies to the island and returning with sick and wounded for hospitals in the rear area.[1] Later, the C-47s of the USAAAF's 13th Troop Carrier Squadron were merged into SCAT to augment the Skytrains. The C-47s were the workhorses of the 13th Air Force and became the backbone of the Army Air Forces's air delivery service. These "Flying Boxcars" were a godsend to the men on Guadalcanal; two were lost during the campaign.[2]

The Japanese Push

When Martin Clemens's scouts reported the landing of a large number of enemy troops in the vicinity of Tasimboko, about eighteen miles east of the Lunga delta, Clemens had informed the marine command. General Vandegrift promptly dispatched the 1st Raider and 1st Parachute Battalions under Col. Merritt A. Edson to confront the Japanese. The tenacity of the Raiders and paramarines seems to have impressed Vandegrift so much that he gave them unusual and demanding assignments, such as the one to Tasimboko. The Raiders would spearhead the attack, with the Chutes as the supporting echelon. On the evening of 7 September, the Raiders embarked on the destroyer-transports *Manley* (APD 1) and *McKean*. The plan was to have Company B land on the right of the beach, with Company A on the left and Company C as the battalion reserve.

Although the Raiders landed a short distance from the Japanese lookout post at Taivu Point where the majority of Maj. Gen. Kiyotake Kawaguchi's 35th Brigade was bivouacked, they did not bother to attack, but headed instead for Tasimboko village.[3] Clemens's scouts had reported about three hundred Japanese in the area; however, that estimate, although accurate when it was made, had radically changed. During the evening of 7 September Clemens's men brought word that the enemy force at Tasimboko had grown to several thousand—the actual count was 6,722.[4] Similarly, Major General Kawaguchi had arrived on

Guadalcanal with inadequate intelligence information. Like Colonel Ichiki he believed there were no more that two thousand marines on the island and that they could be quickly dispatched.[5] This was based on information he had received at Truk on 20 August. He was later to regret that he was not better prepared.

That night of 7 September, 1st Lieutenant Hagiwara landed at Tasimboko from the minelayer *Tsugaru,* commanding fifty-three men in a battery of 75-mm field guns from the 1st Company, 1st Battalion, 2nd Field Artillery Regiment (2nd Infantry Division). Hagiwara had left his four 75-mm guns at Tasimboko under the protection of the 124th Infantry before leaving for Taivu Point with his artillerymen to report to the 35th Brigade. The bulk of General Kawaguchi's troops had encamped near Tetere, some ten miles to the east of Tasimboko. Bivouacked in the Tasimboko sector was just the guard unit—two companies of the 124th Infantry under Lieutenants Eisei and Uyenura. At about 0630 that following morning they sighted the two smoking old destroyers, the *Manley* and *McKean,* and several other warships behind them; thinking that a major landing was about to take place, they faded into the jungle. In fact, what they saw steaming behind the two destroyers was a convoy of two transports and five warships headed for Lunga Roads. Adding to the Japanese woes, at 0647 their position was attacked by two Douglas SPD Dauntless dive-bombers of MAG-23 and four P-400 (P-39) Airacobras from the 67th Fighter Squadron.

The Tasimboko landing force consisted of 501 men of the 1st Raiders.[6] Capt. Robert P. Neuffer took a flanking column around through the jungle as the main body of the Raiders approached Tasimboko village from the south. Instead of three hundred Japanese, they found Kawaguchi's supply point, complete with hundreds of neatly stacked knapsacks, including bedrolls and packets of condensed food. Later they discovered Lieutenant Hagiwara's four field guns and one 37-mm antitank gun of the 124th Infantry. All were destroyed. The *Manley* and the *McKean* returned to Kukum late in the morning and embarked 208 members of the 1st Parachute Battalion; these were joined by 103 men from Company E, 1st Raider Battalion, who boarded two district patrol vessels, *YP-298* and *YP-346*—100-foot-long wooden tuna fishing boats from California. At 1210, this rear echelon arrived at Tasimboko, allowing the combined forces to push on. A subsequent firefight ensued in which twenty-seven Japanese were killed; two Raiders were killed and six wounded.[7] The marines ransacked the Japanese supplies, destroying a great quantity of stores and equipment, much food, and all types of am-

munition. Several large radios were smashed—a major loss. A good haul
of *sake* was salvaged, however, and General Kawaguchi would miss his
white duck trousers, which ended up in the possession of coastwatcher
Martin Clemens.[8]

The Japanese were on the island with a primary purpose in mind: to
push the Americans off and recapture the airstrip. The 1st Marine Division was aware the enemy would strike, but where that would be was the
concern. Colonels Edson and Thomas, both gifted officers, surmised that
Kawaguchi would attack at the west entrance to the airstrip from over
a protruding, grass-covered knoll south of the strip, which they called
Lunga Ridge. Maj. James C. Murray, the division adjutant, informed a
group of officers that the Japanese were coming with five thousand men.
Red Mike Edson, who had made his mark as the conqueror of Tulagi
and captain of the Tasimboko raid, was given the task of defending this
position. He was one of General Vandegrift's most resolute commanders. The Raiders and the paramarines would be the brick wall the sun soldiers would have to breach to reach their objective, and the able Edson
would prove a stalwart gatekeeper.

Meanwhile at the Japanese naval camp, PO2c Sankichi Kaneda had
been summoned to the headquarters of the Guadalcanal Defense Unit
located in the jungle about a half mile southwest of Point Cruz. There
he was told that because he had escaped the enemy and returned to his
unit by way of the area south and west of the Lunga airfield (Henderson
Field), he was to immediately guide Colonel Oka's 124th Infantry Regiment there. Kaneda was dismayed, telling his superior, "The sun is about
to set. When I escaped it was in daylight and I just had to watch . . . the
sky for enemy planes. I couldn't travel at night." But, he was told, "No
one else knows the area. Go!"

Kaneda continues:

> "[I] was permitted to ask for a subordinate, so [I] chose SM1c
> Yoshio Takada. The [124h Infantry] unit promptly moved out
> with the two of us in the advanced guard . . . [and] marched
> along the left bank of the Matanikau River. . . . It was pitch
> black. . . . We moved at a crawl. . . . At 1200 we reached a log
> bridge over the river. . . . It was difficult crossing at dark. . . . I
> followed my compass east[,] pushing and cutting a path. By the
> 11th, we were through the upper reaches of one of the branches
> of the Lunga River. Colonel Oka was able identify the target . . .
> [and] he gave orders for a long rest. Being so close to the enemy,

the men could not smoke. . . . [We ate] . . . hardtack. . . . [We were tired and] we slept like dead. We were awakened [and] the march was resumed. It was a daylight movement[;] . . . our long file stretched out like a giant snake. . . . At noon [we] reached *Shishi* [Lion] Hill . . . where through field glasses we could see the airfield. . . . . That evening we enjoyed white rice. [The plan was for the Oka Butai to attack when they heard the *Kuma* Battalion—the 7th Infantry Division—on the east begin their shelling.] After that Colonel Oka gave the order to attack[;] it seems almost an hour had passed before they had assembled while a long line file of men straggled out of the bush and formed squads and then platoons. Finally the attack began.[9]

The Battle of the Ridge

At the airfield, one of the first tasks of division ordnance was to send a ton of grenades to the ridge where the marines were digging zigzag trenches and foxholes along a thousand-foot line. It was there, on 12–14 September, that General Kawaguchi and his 35th Brigade would suffer an historic defeat. The Battle of the Ridge marked a turning point in the Pacific War, for it was the only time during the land campaign when the Americans could really have been so soundly defeated that the Japanese could have retaken Henderson Field.[10] After the battle, Lunga Ridge became known as Edson's Ridge; later, war correspondents coined the name Bloody Ridge.

General Kawaguchi's 35th Brigade was split into three assault forces: the central body, and the left and right wings. The central body consisted of twenty-one hundred men under General Kawaguchi with the brigade headquarters and a unit from the guard company. The force included the 1st Battalion, 124th Infantry, under Maj. Yukichi Kokusho; two guns of the 124th Regimental Gun Company under 1st Lieutenant Chifiwa; two 37-mm guns of the 124th Regimental Antitank Company under 1st Lt. Kaoru Hisatomi; the 3rd Battalion, 124th Infantry, under Lt. Col. Kusukichi Watanabe; one platoon each of the 7th and 15th Independent Engineer Regiments under Second Lieutenant Mortoto; thirty-seven men of the 24th Water Purification Unit; the Kudo medical unit from the 67th Line of Communication Hospital; and the 6th Radio Unit.[11]

The left wing, led by Col. Akinosuka Oka, included the 124th Infantry Regimental Headquarters under adjutant Capt. Masato Yamazaki, the 124th Signal Company under 1st Lt. Yukio Moriguchi, the 28th Regimental Machine-Gun Company under 1st Lt. Shigenao Kokatsu, and

Figure 31. PO2c Sankichi
Kaneda (81st Guard Unit) was
selected to lead the soldiers
of the 124th Infantry Regiment
to the perimeter for the
September 1942 attack because
he knew the area. (Courtesy
Sachimiko Kaneda)

a small engineering unit and a radio unit. Colonel Oka was dependent
on his two infantry battalions, supported by his gun contingents. They
included one 75-mm gun of the 124th Regimental Gun Company under
1st Lt. Yoshibei Nagao; two 37-mm antitank guns of the 124th Regimental Antitank Company; the 2nd Battalion, 124th Infantry (II/124i), under Maj. Etsuo Takamatsu; and the 3rd Battalion, 4th Infantry, under
Capt. Morie Sasaki, led by the 5th Company, 4th Infantry. Due to tar-
diness, however, the 3rd Battalion, 4th Infantry, missed the battle. The
bulk of the 4th Infantry, with Col. Naomasa Nakaguma commanding,
was still aboard the *Sado Maru* in Kamimbo Bay when the 35th Brigade
was attacking the airfield. .[12]

The right wing was composed of the rear echelon of the Ichiki Detachment, identified as the Kuma Battalion, which was commanded by
Maj. Eiji Mizuno. The 7th Company, 124th Infantry, was commanded by
1st Lt. Shingo Shimokawa. It was supported by fourteen guns: four 75-
mm of the 28th Regimental Gun Company under 1st Lt. Kakuro Wada,
four 37-mm of the 8th Independent Antitank Company, four 37-mm of
the 28th Regimental Antitank Company under 1st Lt. Yoshio Okubo,

plus two 75-mm of the 124th Regimental Gun Company. This assemblage of weapons was identified as the Nakaoka artillery unit—Capt. Isoa Nakaoka originally had commanded the 8th Independent Antitank Company. The Nakaoka artillery unit's six 75-mm guns would be set back into the hills to support the drive.[13]

The central body, spearheaded by the 124th Infantry, planned to approach the ridge from three directions, exiting from the jungle. General Kawaguchi had his overworked 6th Independent Shipping Engineer Regiment cut, with machetes and swords, a sodden jungle trail that ran from Kawaguchi's rear assembly point to the outskirts of the ridge, a path well concealed by the thick tropical growth. The muddy, narrow course permitted the men to move only single file, and the march through dense jungle in 110-degree inland heat and no breeze taxed the already exhausted troops. But it was not just the devilish jungle that distressed the general. First it was the maps. Kawaguchi had an old piloting chart of the island with its unknown interior; thus he shifted around by compass. Then, it was his headquarters, challenging his patience as it moved around, keeping him out of contact. In addition, the force was moving north, but was unable to reach the assigned position by noon, and with the next shift to the south, the command had become scattered. Nevertheless, moving through the jungle from the east, west, and south, the group (composed of elements of the 4th and 124th Infantry Regiments, reinforced) infiltrated the base of Lunga Ridge, known to them as *Mukade Gata* (Centipede Hill).

A thin line of 1st Raiders and remnants of the 1st Parachute Battalion manned the hill, with the 105-mm artillery of the 5th Battalion, 11th Marines, supporting. The 5/11's communication line was connected to the Raider's line, with a direct connection to the 11th Marines forward observer. At this time the 3rd Battalion, 1st Marines, held the area west of the Tenaru River, while K Company (3/1) was on outpost duty adjacent to the Overland Trail. The 2nd Battalion, 1st Marines, was dug in at the coast, with minute patrols extending out to 3/1. Gaps existed here and there, though in time the engineers would plug one breach with elements of the 5th Marines as backup. Because General Vandegrift had recently moved his command post and occupied an area not too far from the ridge, to protect him the .30-caliber machine guns were temporarily removed from one of the six tanks of Company B, 1st Tank Battalion, and repositioned in the event of an enemy breakthrough.

The evening of 12 September was pitch black, reducing visibility for both the attackers and defenders. The assault forces were not 100 percent sure where they were heading as they trampled noisily through the darkness, thus losing any tactical surprise. The parachutists were positioned on the left, with the Raiders (less Company A) dug in the central portion of the ridge. One company of the 1st Engineers held a line through the jungle to the Lunga River, with Raider Companies A and C on the right. The right flank of the Company A Raiders abutted the Lunga. The 2nd Battalion, 5th Marines, under Capt. Joseph J. Dudkoski, formed a reserve line northeast and southwest across Hill 2, and Company C of the parachute battalion was on the left flank in the draw between Hills 1 and 2, in the vicinity of the ridge, about fifty yards east of the trail. Sections of the 1st Pioneer Battalion were established on both banks of the Lunga River.

The 3rd Battalion, 1st Marines, under Lt. Col. William N. McKelvy Jr., defended the eastern perimeter, spanning 3,400 yards north to south from a place 1,500 yards south of the slow-winding Ilu River and ending due east of the crest. Company L, 3rd Battalion, 5th Marines, covered the left flank, with Company K (3/5) on the right and Company I of the 5th Marines concentrated in the middle. To provide more firepower, three machine-gun platoons were added to each company. The weapons platoon sited its 60-mm mortars to blanket the grassy plain with fire; the 81-mm weapons of Company K, fixed farther back, were also set to zero in on the plain, where the enemy was expected.

Late that evening, at about 2130, four enemy cruisers launched an intense bombardment on the perimeter, but none of their shells reached the positions on the ridge, splattering instead within the jungle. The three-day attack actually began at about 2200 on 12 September, when the Japanese spilled out from their cover. The 1st Battalion, 124th Infantry, with about nine hundred ninety soldiers, backed by the 124th's 3rd Battalion (III/124i), then jabbed the far right edge of the marines' position, clashing with the Company C Raiders. Nearly all of Company C was holding the jungle line in between the Lunga River through to the lagoon at the base of the ridge. At the same time, the cannoneers of the 11th Marines fired. Silence followed for a few minutes while the attackers moved ahead to a position about 200 yards in front of the 11th's forward observer. Alerted to the proximity of the enemy, Colonel Edson gave the command to fire at the exact moment the Japanese troops bolted out of the underbrush heading for the ridge and Edson's command post northwest of Hill 2. Earlier, at 2000, a dozen sun soldiers had managed to infiltrate between Hills 1 and 2, which had caused Edson to move his command post twenty yards behind the forward line (the paramarines' command post was twenty yards behind Edson's). During the battle that night, Plat. Sgt. Lawrence H. "Pappy" Holdren, a machine-gun commander, bravely stood his ground while surrounded by the enemy after the other units had pulled back; his continued fighting gained time for the Raiders to form a new line. He would be awarded the Navy Cross for his deed.

A second battery of marine 105-mm howitzers was shifted from the west to the south and a third battery was then moved into position to support the defenders. The 105s of the 5th Battalion, 11th Marines, under Lt. Col. Eugene Hayden Price, were elevated high, firing by map reference or simply guided by the uproar of the advancing Japanese. If the marines heard cries from beyond the ridge, they knew their direction had been correct. At 2200, another heavy bolt of fire was dumped on the approaching enemy. That evening the 5/11, the Raiders, and the Chutes fought unrestrained, with both sides severely bloodied. In the hands of the skilled marines, the hand grenade dominated the battle. That late night and early morning hours of the 13th, they fought off five attacks involving hours of hand-to-hand combat.[14]

With General Kawaguchi's troops at the doorstep, MG Robert Manning of Company B, 1st Parachute Battalion—recipient of the Navy Cross for Gavutu—commanded a 60-mm mortar squad between Hills 1 and 2. The enemy infantry was stabbing at the middle and left flank in an intense rush, aided by green overhead flares. Gunner Manning organized his men to fire the 60-mm tubes at remarkable speed, which helped break the back of the assault. The marines were forced to pull back to Hill 2, with paramarine Sgt. Keith Perkins of Company A, 11th Marines, positioning his machine gun to cover the withdrawal, while he was protected by a handful of Raiders. Later his body was found with dozens of enemy dead nearby. Another machine gunner reported firing twenty-five thousand rounds that first night.

By this time, the enemy was hitting the front sector and both flanks. Colonel Edson had been attempting a regrouping, but when he could not locate paramarine Maj. Charles A. Miller, he grabbed Capt. Harry L. Torgerson, another parachutist and the expert "cave sealer" on Gavutu. Edson ordered Torgerson to prepare a counter-punch against the threatened left flank. Torg gathered enough paramarines and raiders to form two composite companies and personally led them to firm up the endangered area. The Chutes were able to defend the position and, amidst the confusion, repel the infiltrators in close-quarter fighting, some of the fiercest of the night. Many on both sides were struck down.[15]

While the Americans were falling back to an imaginary second line, they were rallied and took up new positions. The line waved and was bent; the Special Weapons Battery, 11th Marines, was overrun, but it regrouped and re-established positions between the division command post and that of the artillery and prepared to hold. The Japanese charged up the ridge, throwing grenades and using 50-mm mortars effectively. The paramarines suffered casualties, as did the Raiders and a few members of the 2nd Battalion, 5th Marines, that were fed into the line. Those positions were overrun several times, yet the ridge held, and the 3rd Battalion, 1st Marines, was shifted to a position far to the left.

The attack of the Japanese right wing, the Kuma Battalion, under Maj. Eiji Mizuno (the Ichiki rear echelon), began on the evening of 13 September. It was led by the headquarters unit, followed by 177 men of the 1st Company under 2nd Lt. Kiyoshi Sato and 169 men of the 2nd Company under 2nd Lt. Toshio Hanehara of the 28th Infantry. Also from the 28th Infantry was the machine-gun platoon, commanded by WOI Kosaku Nakeo. The reserve unit, the 28th Regimental Antitank Company under 1st Lt. Yoshio Okubo, would be located adjacent to the west bank of the Higashikawa River (the Tenaru). They hit a position well secured with barbed wire at the south bank of Alligator Creek manned by Company K, 1st Marines. As they attempted to breach the wire, every weapon in the Company K, 1st Marines, arsenal fired at the attackers. Most were killed within minutes. 1st Lt. Shotaro Maruo, commanding officer of 1st Company, 124th Infantry, described the attack on the ridge:

> By the 12th, we had marched five kilometers during the morning and were four kilometers from the enemy lines. We were much encouraged when 26 planes of our air force attacked the airfield. At 0400, we advanced and at 1100 we took out an enemy lookout post. Within the next hour two of our planes were shot down by enemy anti-aircraft fire. In the meantime, one of our planes dropped a bomb in the midst of the 1st Company, 124i (1st Lt. Shotaro Komatsu), killing one and wounding four. [It] was meant for the Americans. At 1430, we reached a point near the position where preparations for the attack were being made. Major Kokusho assembled all the company commanders with our attack orders.
>
> Second Lieutenant Kobayashi and four men left on a scouting patrol of the enemy lines. As soon as dusk fell, we began

our march along the Higashikawa River (Tenaru) with the 2nd
Company now in the lead, followed by the 4th and the 3rd, and
moved across the river. We approached to about two kilometers
from the enemy's front lines and received heavy gunfire. . . . The
3rd Company was the battalion reserve and it moved to the
rear. 0100 and 0200 had passed and we still had not obtained
our goal, and we had no knowledge of the terrain or the enemy
position. The 2nd Company opened the attack, but was stalled.
In early morning, the battalion commander [Maj. Yukichi
Kokusho] withdrew all the companies and planned to regroup
and attack again. As dawn drew near, the enemy planes attacked
and provided an intense bombing and strafing.

Major Kokusho gave a spirited talk stating that "this was a
difficult operation and we must sacrifice our lives to serve our
Emperor and our country." The second attack started at 1400
with the 4th Company in the lead and hit the enemy's barbed
wire and captured a position there. The battalion concentrated at
this point but received intense enemy artillery fire [from the 11th
Marines]. The companies scattered and casualties mounted.[16]

According to PFC Haste Sakamoto—an ammo carrier with the 3rd
Battalion Machine-Gun Company, 124th Infantry, under Capt. Kichita Hatanaka—his unit cut through the jungle to a point southwest of
the airfield and attacked from there while the 2nd and 3rd Battalions
came from the south and the Kuma Battalion from the west. Just before
1900 on the 13th, Colonel Oka's west wing, then numbering just under
1,000 men, was in place to make its move.[17] Sup. Pvt. Kiyoshi Sonoda's
antitank company, 124th Infantry, a segment of the central body of the
force, recorded that his unit "had 150 men plus two platoons with two
37-mm antitank guns; the guns were seldom used for fear of attacks by
the Marine artillery fire. In fact, in the attack, the weapons were actually
hidden as everyone expected a quick victory and that there would be no
need for fire support. Later, the guns were used for harassing effect."[18]

Second Lieutenant Kashii, the intelligence officer of the 124th Infantry, recorded in his diary:

2030 arrived at an outpost on the eastern side of HYO [mean-
ing "Leopard," code name for the hill not too distant from
the airfield]. At 2100 Headquarters, II/124i, 5th, 6th, and 8th
Companies[,] plus the 2nd Battalion Machine-Gun Company

(First Lieutenant Kiya) advanced northeast to attack the enemy positions. During the movement active artillery fire was heard to the east. Involved in the advance [were] the 124th Infantry Machine-Gun Unit[,] 124th . . . Infantry Signal Unit, 2nd Battalion Light Mortar Unit, and elements of the Naval Landing Party [the 81st and 84th Guard Units]. The 1st Battalion occupied Hill 15, and then withdrew. One battalion commander and several men became casualties and so they were incapable of engaging the enemy. The situation of the 3rd Battalion and [the] Aoba Detachment [II/4i] is not known, but the Nakaguma unit withdrew along the *Okawa* (Lunga) River. There was mortar fire all night. It seems the 2nd Battalion is gradually withdrawing from its advance positions.[19]

When 2nd Lt. Kenji Matsumoto contacted battalion headquarters for instructions about the next move, his 1st Company received orders to advance. However, the assault was disorganized, and the companies lost contact with each other. In the interim, Matsumoto, with the ten-man command section, captured a position and secured it with the help of Lieutenant Furubayashi's machine-gun platoon, a part of the machine-gun company of the 3rd Battalion under Capt. Kichita Hatanaka. "Meanwhile," wrote Matsumoto, "I was searching for enemy positions. I met the Aoba Commander [Col. Naomasa Nakaguma, CO, 4th Infantry], who clued me in on the battle [the night before]. During the brief lull, Lieutenant Yukitake and 24 others, all wounded, joined me. At 1500, each unit was ordered to withdraw, and we were not ashamed of the way we fought; the only disheartening point was that the enemy employed his firepower so well."[20]

PFC Hiroshi Iwamoto, a rifleman with the 3rd Battalion, 124th Infantry, reported that about two-thirds of his battalion was destroyed in the attack, with the remaining men attached to the other two battalions. Matsumoto reported other losses: "The battalion commander Kokusho was killed, [along with] five other officers; 180 men were KIA and 100 more wounded and were litter cases. There were many men who were hit, yet still able to walk. The return trip was exhausting—it took us three days to a point 10 kilometers up the Okawa River." In his account of the retreat, Private First Class Sakamoto noted in his diary that the 3rd Battalion took ten days to reach the Bonegi River basin.[21]

An unknown diarist from the Guard Company, 35th Brigade, would write:

12 September—Finally, tonight at 2000 there was a general attack. The soldiers were tense and winding through the jungle advanced toward their objective.

By marching day and night, crossing many steep mountains, we neared the enemy positions. Enroute communications were cut and at this point dawn broke. With the loud cannons roar and tracer bullets, the time for the engagement arrived. The 1st and 3rd Aoba Battalions of the front line force attacked at night, but because of preparations were lacking it ended regrettably in failure.

13 September—This morning the Butai [guard company] first retreated and then made preparations to attack. Since morning, enemy planes droned overhead all day in formations of seven. A shell burst near me but I was not scratched. About 1030 our planes came over and aerial combat took place for about 30 minutes.

14 September—Last night's attack ended in failure. And tonight, we are waiting in the jungle to prepare for another attack. At 1300, each front line Butai settled in position for the attack. Detachment Headquarters started action at 1600 [2200 Guadalcanal time]. [I c]limbed a grass-covered hill; I observed the situation of the front line Butai. Tonight's general attack was a severe one. The concentration fire from the enemy's heavy artillery lasted from evening to the following morning and continuously showered us with several hundred shells. During that time our machine guns and the shouts of our men attacking could be heard. However, our forces bravely rushed into the enemy's front line and inflicted many casualties[. I]t ended up in failure. The necessity of retreating was regrettable. The Butai retreated west along the Lunga River. Therefore the Guard Company, and the 15th Independent Engineer Regiment, in order to open a path by cutting the jungle trees, departed at 0930, advanced two kilometers[,] and bivouacked.[22]

Private Yamame Yutaku of 1st Lt. Kakuro Wada's 28th Regimental Gun Company also reported: "Only 70 men of the Ichiki Detachment survived this attack. Most of the 1st Battalion of the Oka unit was also destroyed. Following their defeat they started out through the mountains heading for the coast west of the airport. They only had three days rations when they went into the attack and soon ran out. Four days they pulled their cannons over the trails but had to give up and bury [them—Type 41 75-mm mountain guns]. It took around two weeks to make the trip and over one-half the men became sick and died on the way. Only a few men of the Ichiki unit reached the coast. These were attached to the 2nd Division as a labor unit for unloading ships."[23]

On the American side, all of the marines on that ridge were heroes. Col. Merritt A. Edson was first in that group, verifying one of his axioms of command: lead by example. The same could be said for Maj. Kenneth D. Bailey; Maj. John B. Sweeney, who commanded Company D, 1st Raiders; Maj. Houston "Tex" Stiff, who played a major role in the Raiders' mortar and weapons platoon; TSgt. Francis E. Pettus, of the Raiders' intelligence section; Capt. Harry Torgerson, who rallied the parachutists; and Capt. Richard S. Johnson, who commanded one of the paramarine companies on the knoll. On 13 and 14 September, when communication lines were cut, Cpl. Walter J. Burak, Colonel Edson's runner, was busy quickly carrying messages, dodging bullets, and jumping in gun pits to deliver orders. Others from the rear—cooks, mailmen, radio-men, paper-pushers—all rushed to help. Calls continually were heard for "more grenades! . . . more ammo!" Grenades were used by the hundreds.[24]

At daybreak on the 14th the assault was partially broken off. Bodies lay scattered around the ridge. The attackers were heavily bloodied. In the area alone covered by the 3rd Battalion, 1st Marines, two hundred enemy were killed. In all, an estimated one thousand Japanese were killed in action, and an untold number died during the retreat.[25] Following a report that the enemy was in front of the 1st Marines' sector, six M3 Stuarts from Company B, 1st Tank Battalion, were summoned to investigate. As they approached the site, the four 37-mm antitank guns of 1st Lt. Yoshio Okubo's 28th Regimental Antitank Company were in place to deliver fire from a distance of approximately 1,600 feet. This surprise smashed tank #1; tank #4 was soon hit and toppled down a steep embankment into the Tenaru River; the headquarters tank was also disabled. In the action, a total of eight members of Company B were killed.[26]

As events transpired, the marines' lines were infiltrated. Eighteen-year-old Cpl. Carlo Fulgenzi of the Headquarters, 1st Engineers Battalion, was positioned across a jeep track near the division command post, overseeing wounded comrades. He had left the sector to check the ridge line when suddenly he heard a disturbance. He encountered five Japanese within minutes of each other; he shot all five as he successively came upon them.[27] The Japanese, however, had captured two marines and were torturing them; their horrific screams penetrated the ridge for hours.[28] At this same time, Pvt. Harry Dunn, a member of Company B, 1st Marines, was involved in a fight in which twenty-four of his comrades were killed. Dunn was reported as missing in action; however, he showed up a week later, totally exhausted from having carried a wounded comrade to safety.[29]

According to Sgt. Shohei Haga, the 2nd Battalion, 4th Infantry, became the second wave of Japanese. The 2nd's orders were to follow 1st Lt. Tetsuji Ishibashi's 7th Company and 1st Lt. Yoshimi Onodera's 5th Company and, after passing through those units, to penetrate the enemy's position. At dawn the 2nd Battalion reached Henderson Field, but it had no time to regroup as the marines counterattacked from the southern edge of the ridge. Ordered to advance and conduct a frontal attack, the Japanese made a hurried dash in the black of the night. The effort failed, and the Japanese soldiers had no choice but to leave their dead and return to the jungle's edge. The 3rd Battalion, 4th Infantry, under Capt. Morie Sasaki, also was to participate in the attack by being barged to the Matanikau River from Kamimbo Bay. But the Cactus Air Force had destroyed so many barges that Sasaki could not get his disorganized battalion in place to help in the offensive, and he remained inactive.[30] Late on 14 September, what was left of the attackers' shredded units began to forge their way back west through the jungle to the Matanikau River and temporary sanctuary. It was a diminished force. The 1st Marine Division sent low-flying P-400s of the Cactus Air Force to strafe them, in the area where the attack from the previous night had originated.[31]

The two Raider doctors, Lt. Cdr. Edward P. McLarney and his assistant Lt. Robert Skinner, were busy men. Before they could establish a proper aid station they were inundated with casualties. In an emergency clearing site set up behind the ridge they skillfully treated more than two hundred wounded marines. Many paramarines and Raiders owe their lives to the medical handiwork of the doctors and the U.S. Navy corpsmen.[32]

Martin Clemens estimated that the Americans had crossed the Matanikau seventy-six times during the battle. The paramarines already had been worn out and thinned in ranks by the time the battalion had moved from Tulagi to Guadalcanal at the end of August. When the battle was over, thirty-seven Raiders had been killed and 103 wounded. Only eighty-five paramarines were able to stand; their heretofore decimated battalion had sustained a further thirty-two killed. Among their 101 wounded were Capts. John E. Gorman, Victor S. Malinowsky, and

Norman R. Nickerson. The 5th Marines lost five killed and fifty-five wounded; losses in the 1st Marine Regiment totaled thirty-one killed or wounded. Colonel Edson and Raider Maj. Kenneth D. Bailey, who had rallied the leathernecks on what now was called Bloody Ridge, were awarded the Medal of Honor, though Ken Bailey would not live to receive it. [33]

The dead were buried in Guadalcanal's military cemetery, enlisted men and officers side by side. Raider Maj. Robert S. Brown was interred near Raider PFCs Herman F. Arnold and Jimmy W. Corzine and Sgt. Daniel W. Hudspeth. All would be awarded the U.S. Navy's second-highest decoration, the Navy Cross. History would note well the service of Colonel Edson and his defenders of the ridge, but they could have ended up as forgotten dead. if not for the cannoneers of the 11th Marines whose 105-mm howitzers had pumped 1,992 shells into the midst of the assaulting Japanese.

The Marines Push Back

On 13 September, the 3rd Battalion, 2nd Marines, had been alerted for transfer from Tulagi to Guadalcanal as reinforcements, and on the 14th it had headed for the transports. At 0730, Company I departed for Guadalcanal by YP boat, and by 0900 the second echelon—all of Company L and the balance of Company I—was aboard the *Bellatrix*. By 1600 the *Bellatrix* left the dock for the journey to Lunga Roads. The remainder of the battalion—part of Company K—was shifted to Gavutu. On reaching Guadalcanal the 3/2, acting as the division reserve, was moved into line on the friendly side of the Matanikau River. The battalion occupied the beach defense position from Lunga Lagoon to Alligator Creek—not exactly a quiet spot for the 2nd Marines. While they remained as the division reserve, they witnessed action when Japanese snipers tried to infiltrate.

On 17 September, Japanese Imperial General Headquarters ordered the 7th Heavy Field Artillery Regiment under Col. K. Shimpdo, then in Manchuria, to select one company with four 105-mm cannons and prepare it for transfer to the area north of Australia—i.e., New Guinea. The company was to move out within twelve hours, an exacting task. The 2nd Company, under the command of 1st Lt. Akio Tani, IJA, was selected; however, due to the shortage of transportation, it did not deploy for ten days. The *Tani Tai* (Tani company) finally reached Rabaul on 2 October, but there the company was reassigned to the Seventeenth Army and was not shipped to New Guinea. It was destined to play a

Figure 32. 1st Lt. Akio Tani
(Pistol Pete), Tokyo, 1941.
(Courtesy Akio Tani)

more demanding role on Guadalcanal, where Lieutenant Tani would soon come to be known as the infamous "Pistol Pete."[34]

On 18 September, the Samoa-based 7th Marines, 4,262 strong, landed on Guadalcanal amidst much rejoicing, though the celebration was not so much from seeing the reinforcements as from the food and equipment they brought. With the division strengthened, headquarters had plans for westward expansion and General Vandegrift had fresh troops to bolster his defenses and extend his protective screen. The arrival of the 7th Marines enabled Vandegrift to plan a strong defense sector by dividing the Lunga area into ten zones. Defenses of the seven inland sectors on the west, east, and south were buttressed by the addition of infantry battalions. The 3rd Defense Battalion, with the 1st Special Weapons Battalion attached, would continue to be responsible for beach and antiaircraft protection—downed Japanese airmen would attest to their accuracy. Although some sectors could not be conclusively held, there were no large exposed flanks, rather only small gaps here and there. Yet the inland area still presented problems. Key positions on open ridges were organized in depth, but on the lower ground the solid jungle prevented the creation of mutually supporting positions.

Nevertheless, outposts were maintained and manned on a twenty-four-hour basis, though not enough leathernecks were available to carry out the huge task of clearing fields of fire for 14,000 yards of jungle—nearly eight miles. Whenever possible the controlling line of resistance followed the ridges and sloping valleys. The Samoa marines had brought enough barbed wire to wire up the front behind two ensembles of double-apron fence backed by trip wires between the bands. The cannoneers of the 11th Marines's 75-mm pack howitzer battalions remained in positions spread within the perimeter to furnish fire to any threatened sector. Although this defensive design was far from ideal, it provided potent firepower and presented a nearly continuous line to prevent possible enemy penetration. The Americans held a line that stretched along the beach from a point halfway between the Matanikau and the Lunga Rivers, east to the Ilu River, a distance of some five miles. From there, its perimeter looped around inland, south and then west, then north to the beach, thus completing an oblong-shaped defensive area along the Lunga River about three miles across at its widest north-south axis. The leathernecks also held a prominent column some 2½ miles long and three-quarters of a mile wide, extending west along the beach to the Matanikau.

The 1st Marine Division was ready to take the offensive. After the engagement at Bloody Ridge, headquarters knew that a major enemy force was operating west of the Matanikau, in Kokumbona, and active in the Mount Austen sector. Miller's *Guadalcanal: The First Offensive* describes the terrain that dominated the area:

> Mount Austen, a spur of Guadalcanal's main mountain range, juts northward between the Matanikau and Lunga Rivers toward Lunga Point . . . [and] provided the enemy with an excellent observation post from which to survey activity at Lunga Point—traffic at Henderson Field and the fighter strips, unloading of ships, and troop movements. . . . From the hill they could see the American areas west of the Matanikau, and over the hills west of the mountain into Kokumbona, 9,000 yards to the northwest.
>
> Mount Austen, where the Japanese were to make their strongest defensive effort of the campaign, is not a single peak, but the apex of a confusing series of steep, rocky, jungled ridges. The main ridge forming the summit rises abruptly out of the foothills

about two miles south of the shore, and east of the Matanikau River. . . . Hill 27, a separate rocky mound, 920 feet high, lies southwest of the summit. . . . Hill 31, a grassy area about 750 yards north of Hill 27, overlooks Lunga Point.[35]

What General Vandegrift did not know, however, was that the Japanese were far stronger than his staff had anticipated. The Tokyo Express had shuttled troops from Rabaul to Buin to Guadalcanal, and the U.S. Navy had not been on hand to intercept the sea caravan. Although the Cactus Air Force pilots had managed to annoy the fast Japanese destroyers, they still moved freely down The Slot at night to Guadalcanal. On the other hand, although the Imperial Navy could unload its forces in record time, it simply could not provide them with sufficient supplies, a problem that eventually would be the undoing of the Emperor's troops.

The soldiers in the Matanikau–Kokumbona area were from Col. Naomasa Nakaguma's 4th Infantry Regiment. Conceivably the enemy could offer no immediate threat to the south and east sectors, and thus General Vandegrift planned to clear them from the west by a series of thrusts of regimental strength. Once the Japanese had been driven out, the division would be able to establish strong defensive positions to keep them beyond striking distance of Henderson Field. The plan called for operations in the west by elements of the 7th Marines and the 1st Raider Battalion. Lt. Col. Lewis B. "Chesty" Puller commanded the 1st Battalion, 7th Marines, and the Raiders were led by Lt. Col. Samuel B. Griffith II. In the meantime, an urgent call had been sent to CUB 1 on Espiritu Santo seeking radio operators to be shipped to Guadalcanal "ASAP." On 21 September, five CUB 1 radio-men—Louis Stark, James Smith, Leon Woodward, Keith Upton, and Frank Rathke—were taken off waiting destroyer-transports and rushed to Santo's Bomber 1 base for transport to Guadalcanal via Col. LaVerne G. Saunders's "Blondie Bombers" of the 11th Bomb Group. Each flew alone in one of the five B 17s during the 2½ hour flight to Henderson. These men were the team that would run 2nd Lt. Sandy Hunt's NGK radio.[36]

On 21 September Colonel Edson took command of the 5th Marines, replacing Col. Leroy P. Hunt. Edson immediately began planning a move to check the Japanese in the west. Two days later he ordered Colonel Puller's 7th Marines to proceed southwest to Mount Austen, move west along its northern slopes, and then cross the Matanikau inland to patrol the expanse between the river and Kokumbona. On the 22nd, while Puller's leathernecks were searching for the enemy, the Japanese moved into a small cave on Mount Austen that permitted a clear view of the airstrip. The marines had little intelligence beyond what their patrols had discovered in the past few weeks and thus they continued to act without the benefit of adequate information. One company ran into Japanese guarding the Naikuro Road water supply point; it attacked the patrol, commanded by Lieutenant Ojima, but was driven back. Part of Colonel Puller's force also had confronted Japanese on the right bank of the Lunga River; the 124th Infantry's outposts named HYO (Leopard), TORO (Tiger), and KUMA (Bear) were attacked, but the defenders did not weaken, and their strong counter-thrust pushed the Americans aside. On the next day, a marine patrol reached the Mount Austen area, surprising and scattering a Japanese force. Colonel Edson meanwhile had ordered Lt. Col. Walter Reaves, the new commander of the 2nd Battalion, 5th Marines, to reinforce the 1st Battalion, 7th Marines, in the west; Reaves's battalion arrived early the following morning. In this sector the Japanese would put up a stubborn resistance and concede but a few yards of ground.

The 2nd Battalion, 5th Marines, attacked across the river with Capt. Harry Connor's Company E in the lead, but it was beaten back. The marines ran into a veritable stone wall where the Japanese were protecting their primary river crossing. The 124th Infantry Headquarters was only some 550 yards to the east and was supported by elements of 1st Lt. Shingo Shimokawa's 7th Company, 124th Infantry. Connor's Company E sought protection of the jungle while Capt. Harold Thomas A. Richmond's Company G attacked. The lead platoon under 2nd Lt. Paul Moore Jr. attempted to cross about 300 yards from the mouth of the Matanikau River, but it was too deep and casualties were taken. Another attempt slightly upstream was made to ford the watercourse; as they reached the western side, one man was shot in the face but was alive. Lieutenant Moore rescued him while under constant fire and returned to the eastern side.[37] In all, Company G took twenty-five casualties.

Meanwhile, on 26 September Colonel Puller (1/7) had been ordered to abort his circuit; he did not cross the river but turned north along the east bank to the river mouth, where he intended to ford. When his troops reached the mouth, they moved across the sandbar. Heavy fire from the opposite bank greeted the formation, and they were forced back under the intense mortar barrages. Puller's battalion had encountered 1st Lieutenant Taniguchi's 6th Company, 124th Infantry, and 1st Lt. Yoshibei Nagao's 124th Regimental Gun Company, with elements of the 4th Infantry. The marines attacked at 1100 on the right bank, a short distance away from the secondary river crossing, where they were engaged by 1st Lt. Takabumi Kojima's 9th Company, 124th Infantry. The marines would later call this flowing stream the "River of Death." The Japanese could well have named it the same.[38]

The leathernecks were not without firepower. The 5th Battalion, 11th Marines, under Lt. Col. Eugene Price had supported the drive and had some moderate success with spotting by an observing infantry officer. By 27 September the 2nd Battalion, 11th Marines, also was involved. Before the push was over, the guns of the 11th Marines had deposited on the enemy positions in the riverbed area 940 75-mm pack howitzer rounds and 340 105-mm shells. In the engagement, the second in command of 1st Lt. Takabumi Kojima's 9th Company was killed and Kojima was mortally wounded.

Elements of the 124th Infantry were defending the *Nippon-bashi*, a one-log footbridge that was a key crossing point on the Matanikau; they reported killing five Americans and wounding ten in a firefight when the marines had attempted to cross. The Japanese controlled the ground and had the upper hand in the engagements. At the secondary river crossing, another well-guarded ford, the area was solidly defended by the 8th Company under 1st Lt. Masayuki Kamei and components of the 12th Company, 124th Infantry, under Capt. Gensuke Bito. Colonel Puller radioed the 11th Marines for artillery support, but the fire failed to dislodge the strongly entrenched Japanese in their well-prepared positions—they simply brought up more mortars and automatic weapons to stiffen the sites.

At about this same time the 1st Raiders under Lt. Col. Sam Griffith, along with Selea, one of Martin Clemens's scouts, were to proceed west along the coast road to establish a temporary patrol base at Kokumbona where the route crossed several inland native trails. The sector was deep in Japanese country and control of Kokumbona would not only deny good landing beach to the enemy but also prevent them from using the track to move inland. The 1st Raiders probed the primary Nippon bridge crossing where Second Lieutenant To and his 3rd Independent Trench Mortar Battalion company—plus two attached machine-gun units, Lieutenant Nakashima's 2nd Platoon, and Lieutenant Moita's 3rd Platoon—were entrenched. In the skirmish, the Raiders's executive officer, Maj. Kenneth D. Bailey, was killed and Colonel Griffith was wounded. The Raiders shifted positions, seeking safety, but were still pounded by the 3rd Independent Trench Mortar Battalion's fire.

Casualties had mounted without the marines making a dent in the enemy's position. Three of Chesty Puller's companies—A, B, and D—were assigned to escort the wounded back to the perimeter; the balance of Puller's troops edged slowly toward the Matanikau River, reaching it the following day. On the 27th the division ordered the Raiders to join forces with Puller's unit and attack west the next day. Colonel Edson was assigned to command the force, with Colonel Puller as his second. Edson ordered the 2nd Battalion, 5th Marines, to attack west across the river mouth, but they were hurled back; upstream about 2,000 yards the Raiders moved inland to cross the Matanikau. Both forces moved to attack again in the morning, but failed to gain any ground. The Raiders and 2/5 were facing 1st Lt. Makoto Hirota's 5th Company, 124th Infantry, with the company's machine-gun unit attached. But while 2/5 was having difficulty in installing itself on the west bank, the Raiders had advanced to the high ground on Hill 67 (*Saru*, Monkey) on the east bank, about 1,500 yards south of the beach; there, however, they were held up by unexpected fire. During the previous evening Japanese forces under Maj. Masuro Tamura's 2nd Battalion, 4th Infantry, and elements of the 2nd Battalion, 124th Infantry, had crossed upstream to the east bank and occupied Hill 65, about 850 yards south of Hill 67.

The Raiders quickly dispatched a message to Edson that they had a problem, but due to bad reception, the communication was distorted and misconstrued. Colonel Edson, mistakenly thought that Griffith's men had crossed the river and were encountering resistance in Matanikau village. He thus decided on a new plan, calling for a three-battalion attack using the 1st Raiders along with the 2nd Battalion, 5th Marines, and the 1st Battalion, 7th Marines. The Japanese, however, had their own blueprint to stop the Americans, and they did. Upon receipt of Edson's orders, the Raiders moved out while 2/5 approached the river. In attempting to cross, F/2/5 and G/2/5 sustained casualties totaling sixteen killed and sixty-eight wounded.[39] Because of the strong Japanese resistance, the moves had become confused and 1/7 was ordered to return to the perimeter.

Colonel Edson's new scheme involved attacking the Japanese from the sea. The operation, using Companies A, B, and D of 1/7, would be run by Colonel Puller's executive officer, Maj. Otho "Buck" Rogers, USMCR. Rogers's force would make an amphibious landing west of Point Cruz in the vicinity of Kokumbona and attack the Japanese in the Matanikau River basin from the rear. It was a good plan, but it suffered from poor intelligence. The marines could not disembark at the prescribed site because the jungle penetrated right to the water's edge.

The landing craft thus were forced to move slightly west, where the marines landed at 1100. The Coast Guard unit that had carried Rogers's men received orders that one craft should stand by to evacuate any casualties should the marines run into trouble. S1C Ray Evans was one of the Coast Guard coxswains involved in the landing:

> Commander Dexter . . . gave us the information ordering several Higgins landing craft and three Tank Lighters to embark the troops. . . . The plan was to land the Marines at the head of the cove at Point Cruz following a shore bombardment by the destroyer *Ballard* [(AVD 10)] and from the end of the cove the Marines were to drive straight inland. Unfortunately it did not work that way.
>
> After the bombardment, the first boat to land found too much coral to land at the head of the cove, so we hastily informed the Marine commander [Rogers] we would have to land on the right[-]hand side of the cove and after getting ashore they would have to make a flanking movement to the left to regain their former plan. The beach was about eight feet wide, quite steep with immediate jungle growth. In some places the bows of the boats were actually in the jungle.[40]

Unknown to the attackers, the Japanese had prepared positions on the ridge overlooking the landing site. Ready to meet the marines were members of 1st Lieutenant Yoshida's Headquarters Unit, 2nd Battalion, 124th Infantry, coupled with a machine-gun platoon and the 3rd Battalion Infantry Gun Unit and supported by 1st Lt. Shoutaru Maruo's 1st Company and one-third of the 1st Battalion Machine-Gun Unit commanded by 1st Lieutenant Futami.[41]

W. Ray Thomas of Headquarters Company, 1st Battalion, 7th Marines, who was with Major Rogers's expedition, recalled the ambush:

> When we disembarked from the Higgins and moved inland we were surprised there was no resistance. As we made our way up Hill [84], about 500 yards inland we encountered some sporadic bursts of machine[-]gun fire and I felt sure we would soon meet some heavy resistance. I recall crossing one clearing of about 40 yards where we would be vulnerable to enemy fire, but our group continued without incident. We started up a steep portion of the hill; I remember passing a horse corral, where we saw dead enemy, and we continued on until we reached the crest of the hill

and we could observe the area, yet nothing unusual. (For some reason, the main bodies of our forces were unable to complete their part of the operation. Even though I was a radio operator, we had no radio with us and were unaware of the main body's action.) Now in retrospect, it became clear why we met so little opposition as we moved up to the crest of the hill. Instead of the Marines' tightening the trap, we found ourselves completely surrounded.

Suddenly, all hell broke loose; mortar and artillery fire seemed to be coming from everywhere, and we instinctually hit the deck. [Sgt. Roy Fowler 1/D/7 of the mortar platoon had only fifty rounds of ammunition, which was soon exhausted. Major Rogers was killed by a mortar round and Capt. Zach Cox was wounded.] When Puller was made aware of his battalion's predicament, he boarded the *Ballard* and directed her to sail close to the beach.

Someone noticed a destroyer off shore flashing light signals in Morse Code. Sgt. Robert "Bob" D. Raysbrook could read the signals and he was instructed to signal back and give yardage so the DD could lay down a barrage to keep the enemy occupied so we could make our way back to the beach, which we did. [Meanwhile, 2nd Lt. Dale M. Leslie of VMSB 231 was flying in an SPD dive-bomber and spotted some T-shirts laid out to spell "Help." Leslie called Cactus radio Z604 and reported what he saw, then stayed and flew a protective cover.]

As we made our way down hill[,] two . . . or three Marines would position themselves on each side of the clearing to help cover the withdrawal . . . [lying] down . . . diagonally enabling others to cross. By changing places as each group made it across, we were able to reach the beach while still carrying our wounded.[42]

The situation was dire. With Major Rogers dead, Capt. Charles W. Kelly Jr. assumed command. But the Japanese were wreaking havoc on Kelly's men. In an heroic rear-guard action, Plat. Sgt. Anthony P. Malinowski Jr. held the enemy at bay with his Browning automatic rifle until he was overrun. Kelly's marines, still fighting, picked up their wounded and climbed aboard the LCPs that had roared back from Lunga to evacuate them. Among the courageous that day, many stood out: Sgt. Robert D. Raysbrook received the Navy Cross as did Plat. Sgt. Tony Malinowski;

but Tony's was awarded posthumously. Another hero was Coast Guard Signalman 1st Class Douglas Albert Munro. A born leader, he was among the first to volunteer for the rescue mission and was placed in charge of the detail. Knowing that the last marines to leave would be the hardest pressed because they had been covering the withdrawal, Munro placed himself and his boats so that they could act as the covering agents for the final man, and by his successful maneuver he brought back many more than had been hoped. Ray Evans, Munro's shipmate and close friend, tells the story:

> The debarkation was done under intense fire. We had a few guns on the landing craft; Munro and I carried an air[-]cooled Lewis machine gun from one boat to another as we sent boats to the restricted beach. We managed to load most of the Marines from the same beach they landed on, but I was told they had 25 wounded and about the same number of dead left behind. . . .
>
> As we passed the end of the point we saw another LCT loaded with Marines stranded on the beach and unable to back off. Munro directed the LCT with us to go in, pass a towline and get them off, which it did. . . . When both LCTs were headed out to sea we fell in after them and were at full power when I saw a line of waterspouts coming across the water where the LCT had been grounded and realized it was machine gun fire.[43]

Evans shouted a warning, but Munro, who was facing forward and did not see the line of bullets, could not hear him over the roar of the engine. A single bullet struck Munro in the neck at the base of the skull. When they were out of range, Munro momentarily regained consciousness. He asked just one question: "Did we get them off?" Assured that the marines were out of harm's way, Doug Munro smiled, then he died. He was two weeks short of his twenty-third birthday.[44]

By the time Puller's battalion was safe, the Raiders and the 2nd Battalion, 5th Marines, had withdrawn. This unfortunate action cost the marines sixty killed and one hundred wounded. The Japanese reported finding thirty-two bodies, one water-cooled machine gun, one BAR, fifteen rifles, and fifteen boxes of machine-gun ammunition. Their losses included 1st Lt. Masayuki Kamei, CO of the 8th Company, 124th Infantry, and 2nd Lieutenant Shisida, a platoon commander.[45] History would record the action as the Second Battle of the Matanikau, but several marines would name it the "Dead-Man Patrol." Some marines still loved Colonel Puller. Those who did not called Puller's patrols "meat grinders."

Between 8 September and 2 October the Tokyo Express brought more trouble for the marines, delivering the 3rd Company, 1st Independent Artillery Mortar Regiment, under Capt. K. Watanara, with its twelve Type 98 (1938) 50-mm mortars; the 1st Company, 1st Battalion, 2nd Field Artillery Regiment, under Capt. Kunie Ogiware, with its four 105-mm guns; the 2nd Company, 1st Battalion, 2nd Field Artillery Regiment, under Capt. Masanao Nagao, with its four 75-mm guns; and the 2nd Company, 21st Heavy Field Artillery Battalion, under Capt T. Tanaka, with two batteries and four 15-cm howitzers. These weapons would be the source of problems for the Americans.

While on an air search from Henderson Field in an SPD 3 Dauntless during the morning of 27 September, Lt. M. P. MacNair of Scouting Squadron 3 spotted and strafed a sailing schooner, the *Daiwa Maru No. 2,* carrying eight or ten Japanese troops—sailors—off Moe Island in the Russell Island group, presumably heading for Cape Esperance. However, the weapons of Lieutenant MacNair's gunner, ARM2c W. M. Rambur, had jammed and thus MacNair returned to the field and obtained another plane. He flew back to the vicinity of Moe Island where he strafed the enemy troops as they neared the beach. On this second attack he was accompanied by Ens. E. Fink in an SPD 3 of Bombing Squadron 6. MacNair believes that in the two attacks he killed or wounded five or six enemy.[46]

On 30 September, 2nd Lieutenant Kashii, the 124th Infantry Regiment's intelligence officer, set up his observation point one kilo—approximately a half mile—east of Kokumbona. Seventeenth Army Headquarters ordered the 4th Infantry, commanded by Col. Naomasa Nakaguma, to grab positions east of the Matanikau on 8 October for use by the artillery. The 1st Battalion, 4th Infantry Regiment, was to occupy the Point Cruz area and cross the Matanikau at its mouth, while the 3rd Battalion, 4th Infantry Regiment, crossed further inland. If the 4th Infantry pushes were successful, the Japanese would be able to deny the Matanikau Basin to the Americans.

At about this same time, the transport *Fuller* (APA 7) arrived at the offshore Lunga roadstead from Santo and discharged her passengers, among which was radio-man Ted Kemper from CUB 1. Kemper had been at the Espiritu Santo radio station operation at a distant lookout post. Upon his arrival at Lunga Roads he carried a heavy canvas U.S. mail bag filled with secret code books that included cryptographic aids and key lists for the NGK radio network. Up until then the command had been operating without any specific codes and had managed, but barely. Kemper was met at the beach by the middle-aged Lieutenant Commander Lincoln, the radio officer of CUB 1, who took the sack from him and never said a word. When Lincoln ignored his salute, Kemper concluded that the place and the men there were not too friendly; he later learned that saluting in a combat zone was dangerous because it identified officers and presented attractive targets for snipers.[47]

The 1st Marine Division was still determined to destroy the Japanese adjacent to Point Cruz and drive them beyond the Poha River, about 9,000 yards to the west. If this operation succeeded and a patrol base could be established at Kokumbona, Henderson Field would be safe from artillery fire. However, General Vandegrift's staff did not know that 1st Lt. Akio Tani—Pistol Pete, who was also called "Hillside Harry"—was bringing his four Type 92 (1932) 105-mm Osaka arsenal guns all the way from Manchuria. These arrived early in October on the *Sado Maru* via Buin, Bougainville, and were stationed in the hills near the White River (the *Isamu Gawa*) about five miles west of Point Cruz. Lieutenant Tani had added an extra charge so that the shells would reach the perimeter. He had a spotter stationed on Mount Austen, between the Matanikau River on the west and the Lunga on the east, who would relay messages to the gun site; and he usually would fire in the morning during takeoffs or landings, which forced General Vandegrift's headquarters to rethink all moves west.

The 1st Division's plan of attack called for the 5th Marines, less one battalion, to execute a holding attack at the mouth of the Matanikau; they were to cross the river on divisional order while the 7th Marines less one battalion, plus one battalion of the 5th Marines, commanded by Colonel William J. Whaling, covered Point Cruz. A noted hunter and a keen marksman, Bill Whaling had formed and trained the Whaling Group scout-sniper detachment. He had no staff position at the time, but simply acted as a floater, filling vacancies where required. The Whaling scouts were to follow the 5th Marines along the coast road, then turn southwest and advance inland to a point about 2,000 yards southwest of the Matanikau's mouth where the river was narrow. The group was to travel over a rickety bridge made of logs thrown across the stream and then turn right (north) to attack. The ridges west of the Matanikau, 200 to 300 feet high, run from north to south. The Whaling Group was to attack north along the first ridge west of the river.

Colonel Puller's 1st Battalion, 7th Marines, was to follow the Whaling Group across the river, then move forward beyond the first ridge and attack northward with all formations abreast on Whaling's left. If these attacks succeeded in reaching the beach and destroying the Japanese, the 5th Marines would pass through Whaling's position and the 7th Marines would attack west toward Kokumbona with the 3rd Battalion, 1st Marines, in reserve. Simultaneously in the plan, the Cactus Air Force was to support the thrust with dive-bombing and strafing while furnishing liaison planes for the infantry reconnaissance and spotting aircraft for the 11th Marines.

12 Black October

October marked the critical phase of the Guadalcanal campaign. To the Japanese Imperial Army, the enemy on *Ga Tō*—Guadalcanal—had become a festering sore. Japanese commanders thus had decided to marshal major land and sea forces to drive the Americans off the island and out of the southern Solomons. To accomplish that task they began sending reinforcements to Guadalcanal.

Buttressing *Ga Tō*

On 28 September, the Seventeenth Army (code-named *Oki* Army) issued orders to execute its reoccupation plan. The mission of retaking Guadalcanal was assigned to the 2nd Division—the Sendai Division, identified as the YU Division—reinforced by elements of the 38th Division. To prevent enemy landings to the west, the much-contested Matanikau River sector would be held by the Nasu Detachment—the 4th Infantry Regiment, reinforced, under Maj. Gen. Yumio Nasu—also known as the 2nd Infantry Brigade Group. In addition, the Nasu Detachment would place a heavy concentration of artillery fire on the airfield.

At the time, however, the 2nd Division was in the Dutch East Indies on occupation duty. It was alerted for immediate deployment, and to make the necessary arrangements the division's chief of staff, Col. Harukazu Tamaoki, flew to Rabaul, New Britain Island, where the Japanese had held firm since late January 1942. The commanders believed that victory on Guadalcanal would be swift; officers and men thus were to carry only essential field equipment and ten days of rations. All nonessential materiel would be left behind at Rabaul or in the Shortlands and supplies would soon follow—a task later assigned to the 230th Infantry Regiment.

The movement of elements of the 2nd Division from the East Indies to Rabaul and then to Guadalcanal began on 13 September and continued for approximately two weeks. On the 15th, Regimental Headquarters, 9th Company (under Capt. Tsuneo Sato), 3rd Battalion, 16th Infantry

Regiment (under Maj. Zenichi Morokado), with parts of the regiment artillery of the rapid-fire gun battalion, plus the communications unit— a total of 350 men—sailed from Batavia, Java, on the cruiser *Kinu*. With them were 450 men, part of the 3rd Battalion, on the *Isuzu Maru*. By 20 September this force was on New Guinea soil. Once at Rabaul, New Britain, they waited for the balance of the 16th Infantry Regiment under Col. Toshiro Hiroyasu, along with the 29th Infantry Regiment led by Col. Shojiro Komiya, plus other segments of the 2nd Division.

The remainder of the force went into bivouac in the Shortland Islands under Maj. Tadao Yoshi (CO, III/29i). Part of this formation and the rear echelon of the 4th Infantry Regiment left the Shortlands base for Guadalcanal on 24 September in four destroyers, but they were forced to return that evening when the ships were attacked by the aggressive Cactus Air Force from Henderson Field. Some damage to the vessels resulted in crew casualties, though the bulk of the troops disembarked intact in the Shortlands. After re-embarking a few days later, they reached the final debarkation point of Kamimbo Bay on the northwest end of Guadalcanal.

The principal force that transferred from Java was in two echelons. The first convoy consisted of the *Kyushu Maru*, *Sakido Maru*, and *Oikawa Maru*, with approximately 4,450 men; it arrived at Simpson Harbor, Rabaul, New Britain, on 29 September. The second echelon, consisting of approximately 4,200 troops under the command of Lt. Col. Shiro Minamoto (CO, I/16i), traveled on two transports along with five cargo vessels—the *Origami Maru*, *Havre Maru*, *Brisbane Maru*, *Aden Maru*, *Kozan Maru*, *Mume Maru*, and *Takaoya Maru*. The echelon arrived in the Rabaul area on 7 October.

Meanwhile on Guadalcanal the disorganized elements of General Kawaguchi's 35th Brigade and the Ichiki Detachment's 2nd Battalion, commanded by Maj. Eiji Mizuno—the remnants of the Bloody Ridge defeat of 13–15 September—finally reached their bivouac area several miles west of Henderson Field. However, harassed by low-flying P-39s of the Cactus Air Force, the Japanese had little rest. The constant American activity along the Matanikau River and the possibility of a marine amphibious landing somewhere along the coast were major concerns, along with the lack of rations.

Guadalcanal had many Marine Corps heroes throughout the fighting, and one 6th Battalion Seabee joined their ranks on 3 October. S2c Lawrence "Bucky" Meyers, who worked on Henderson Field, was the first decorated Seabee. In his off time he had salvaged and repaired

Figure 33. Japanese soldiers of the 35th Brigade meet for orders, October 1942. (Courtesy John Gen Nishino)

an abandoned machine gun, which on 3 October he used to shoot down a Japanese Zeke fighter making a strafing run. For this he was awarded the Silver Star; but it would be a posthumous honor, for on 16 October Meyers was killed in action when the avgas barge he was working was struck by enemy naval gunfire.

In the overall plan to retake Guadalcanal, the Seventeenth Army on 8 October established its rear echelon headquarters at Faisi, Shortland Islands. Lt. Gen. Haruyoshi Hyakutake, the commander, assigned Maj. Gen. Shuichi Miyazaki as his new chief of staff, replacing Maj. Gen. Akisaburo Futami. The Miyazaki name was well known at headquarters, for the general's younger brother, Shigesaburō, was the commander of the 31st Division in Burma. General Hyakutake had lost patience with General Futami's defeatist attitude; Futami had been critical of the Ga Tō campaign, suggesting that reinforcing Guadalcanal was pointless after the defeat of the 35th Brigade and the loss of the Ichiki Detachment. General Futami was thus put on the retired list and remained inactive.

Maj. Gen. Shuichi Miyazaki was the former chief instructor at the Japanese War College. His posting with the Seventeenth Army was the first step in a promotion, and he gathered his new staff officers and selected enlisted men to escort his party to the assigned duty station. Among them were thirty-nine-year-old Col. Masanobu Tsuji and Lt. Col. Taro Sugita who were attached to the Imperial General Staff. Colonel Tsuji had commanded a small group of select officers that had formulated the plan and tactics for Japan's seventy-day campaign for the conquest of Malaysia; in addition, he had been involved in the Kuantung Army campaigns of the 1930s. The young staff officers celebrated him as Japan's "God of Operations," for his plans had worked well in Malaya and Singapore. Guadalcanal, however, might be a different situation.

At 0400 on 9 October General Hyakutake and his officers boarded the destroyer *Oyashio* and sailed for RXN. They landed on the northwest coast at Kokumbona at 2100, where General Hyakutake established his advance headquarters in the area, identified as the *Sento Shireijo* (Battle Command Station), with a complement of ninety-eight, including thirty-seven civilians. Upon his arrival, Hyakutake assumed administrative command of the forthcoming planned assault. He made a speech to the officers about the importance of the impending battle, emphasizing that, if necessary, the men should "die for the Emperor." Three weeks later Hyakutake would return to his headquarters in the Shortlands, and before his troops would depart the Solomon Islands in another three months the general would lose some of his snow-white hair. He would be faced with four major problems: the Cactus Air Force, the shortage of food and medicine, a depleted army, and the unyielding Americans.

Japanese transports that sailed out one day from the Shortlands or from Rabaul would return the next, forced back by Allied surface and air attacks. Troop losses en route were negligible, however, and all in this phase managed to reach Guadalcanal after the first or second attempt. Troops from the transports *Kyushu Maru* and *Sakido Maru* boarded the destroyers *Shigure, Ayamai, Shirayuku,* and *Murakumo* and the cruisers *Nisshin* and *Yura* in the Shortlands; they landed at Mamara on Guadalcanal, east of Kokumbona, the night of 5 October. The convoy then departed with General Kawaguchi on board who had been ordered to Rabaul for a conference on the pending strike. He subsequently returned to *Gadarukanaru* (Guadalcanal) on the 10th, reportedly with some small treats and cigarettes for his staff. The convoy that carried the general back to the island also disembarked 824 sea-infantrymen from the Maizuru 4th SNLF; they would remain at the docking area as stevedores and guards.

With the arrival of 2nd Division Headquarters, command of the forces on Guadalcanal passed from General Kawaguchi to Lt. Gen. Masao Maruyama, commander of the 2nd Division. Maruyama immediately ordered the 4th and 124th Infantry Regiments to prepare for an attack on the airfield. They were to occupy the south side of Point

Cruz, which was between Kukumbona on the west and Lunga Point on the east, then force their way across the mouth of the Matanikau River, just east of Point Cruz, with the 124th Infantry attacking farther south down the river. On 8 October the 1st Battalion, 124th Infantry Regiment, under Maj Yukichi Kokusho, began a move across the first river-crossing point; it succeeded, but then encountered the 1st Battalion, 7th Marines, and Col. William J. Whaling's scouts. A severe battle ensued and the Japanese were driven back. Maj. Gen. Yumio Nasu noted that the 4th Infantry had lost two companies from Maj. Hichiro Usui's 1st Battalion. A Japanese report stated: "The 2nd Bn [was] almost annihilated. The 1st Battalion was driven back by the enemy."[1]

Nevertheless, elements of the Japanese 2nd Division continued to pour onto Guadalcanal, arriving on fast destroyers that made nightly landings along the west coast between Kamimbo Bay and Kokumbona. In contrast, supplies dribbled in on landing barges that staged down from the Shortlands. Transports bringing a large number of men to the island during the nights of 11 and 12 October were protected by a covering force of Cruiser Division 6, comprising the *Aoba, Furutaka,* and *Kinugasa.* Although the cruisers were mauled by the Cactus Air Force, the transports managed to get through safely.

The 230th Infantry Regiment—the Shoji Butai—under the command of Col. Toshinari Shoji was also involved in the Ga Tō reinforcement effort. Sgt. Hisakichi Hara, who spent one hundred days on Guadalcanal as a member of the Headquarters Company, 1st Battalion, related the story of the Shoji Butai. On 20 September 1942 Sergeant Hara's 230th Infantry Regiment, which was part of the 38th Division, was assigned to the Seventeenth Army for duty in the forward area. After reaching Simpson Harbor at Rabaul on 7 October, the 230th received orders to deliver ammunition and supplies for the 2nd Division, which was then engaged in fierce fighting on Guadalcanal. On the Rabaul wharf, six transports were loaded—the *Sasago Maru, Nankai Maru, Sado Maru, Sakido Maru, Kyushu Maru,* and *Azumasan Maru.* The convoy carried thirty-eight pieces of heavy artillery—from 15-cm guns to 28-cm howitzers—along with Maj. Eiji Sekiya's 1st Battalion and Maj. Yasuhei Oneda's 3rd Battalion, 230th Infantry; one battery of the mountain artillery regiment; the 38th Field Antiaircraft Battalion under Lt. Col. Yasuzo Nakamura; the 45th Field Antiaircraft Battalion; the 3rd Battery less one platoon under 1st Lt. Masanori Yamada; one company of the 47th Field Antiaircraft Battalion under Lt. Col. Masayo Fuchiyama; the 1st Company, 38th Engineer Regiment, under Capt.

Tadao Wakabayashi; and one section of the 38th Division Signal Company under Maj. Ryoichi Ito.

At 1400 on 12 October, about one hundred miles from the Shortland Islands anchorage, the Japanese transports were attacked by thirty aircraft of the Cactus Air Force; a second attack occurred at 1530. Both were ineffective however, and the ships sustained no damage. The convoy arrived off Tassafaronga Point, on the northwest coast of Guadalcanal, early in the evening of 14 October; the effort began to unload onto lighters, which plied between the transports and the shore. According to Maj. Eiji Sekiya, commander of the 1st Battalion, 230th Infantry, almost ten thousand crates and boxes had to be on shore within twenty-four hours.[2] At 0830 the following morning, 15 October, the Cactus Air Force again began bombing and strafing the transports. The *Sasago Maru, Kyushu Maru,* and *Azumasan Maru* were seen burning, but personnel, ammunition, rations, and most of the equipment had been successfully landed before the three ships were sunk or beached by air strikes the next day. Additional Japanese forces subsequently arrived on the northwest coast between Kamimbo Bay and Kokumbona, and replacements for the 124th and 4th Infantry Regiments arrived in late October.

October was also a critical month for the Americans. On the 3rd, a handful of marines had arrived on Guadalcanal from Nouméa, New Caledonia, as part of the forward echelon of the 1st Marine Air Wing—the specialists that were to help manage the day-to-day operations of the Cactus Air Force. Radio-man Cpl. Charles A. Buser was among them. Eleven skilled radio and radar men had flown to Guadalcanal aboard a South Pacific Combat Air Transport (SCAT) R4D of Marine Corps Squadron VMJ-252. Buser wrote:

> We were hardly the most valuable part of the cargo; lashed down were about a dozen 55-gallon drums of aviation gas. None of our group had experienced even one hour of combat and we only had a vague idea of where Guadalcanal was located. We were in for a shock. On arrival, the area on and around Henderson Field gave the appearance of a moonscape due to the numerous bomb and shell craters . . . in fact . . . the strip had been the target of an air raid just prior to our landing. . . . We did not have the slightest hint of where to go or what to do. . . . We spent that first night on the slope that ran from the west end of the airfield down to the Lunga River. . . . The following morning . . . Lt. Walter R. Giles, USMC, the officer in charge of communications on Pagoda Hill,

    . . . instructed us to find a couple of tents in the coconut grove
. . . and to dig at least two foxholes. We were to report to him at
1200 on 5 October at the Pagoda. . . . ³

Chuck Buser's radio work area was a tunnel near the famous Pagoda.
The tunnel system had been constructed by crews from the 6th Naval
Construction Battalion under Chief Carpenter's Mate Walter H. Joslyn and Shipfitter 1st Class Irwin J. Rose. They had worked around the
clock to dig four underground passages to protect the surface-housed
equipment from Japanese air and sea attacks and to provide a zone of
safety for key command functions. The crews worked three eight-hour
shifts on the side of Pagoda Hill, a few hundred feet from Henderson
Field. The first shaft, which was named the "Joslyn Tunnel," was 107 feet
long by seven feet wide; it housed irreplaceable equipment. The second
tunnel was sixty-eight feet long and had three rooms: an air operations
center, a switchboard area, and a radio communications area. The third
tunnel housed the division command post—the impact center. The
fourth tunnel, 125 feet in length, had two rooms, each thirty feet long,
eight feet wide, and eight feet high; it had been built for naval intelligence. These underground crawlways became the nerve center for the
direction of the Guadalcanal campaign.

    Buser notes:

    The radio room . . . was roughly timbered and large enough to
accommodate our transmitter, a receiver, some worktables and
benches. Radar was new and primitive and you could identify
the operators by their bloodshot eyes.

    At that time, Lieutenant Giles was the only man there who
understood the system. He set up the equipment and then had to
teach us how to use it. We . . . had gone through radio school at
Jacksonville, Florida, but were ill prepared for the work at hand.
We were in touch via code with our bases in New Caledonia,
Efate, and Espiritu Santo. We were in voice contact with the aircraft in the immediate vicinity of [Guadalcanal]. That included,
but was not limited to, contact with our fighters during enemy
air raids or with the scout planes during their search for enemy
vessels or aircraft. At such times, the air crackled as we tried to
pass on numbers, bearings, altitude, and whether the aircraft's
identity was Zero, Val, or Betty. Typically, our fighters would
climb upwards of 20,000 feet in time to intercept the attacking
aircraft. Some of the pilots . . . kept their throat mikes on and we

received blow by blow, picturesque accounts of the characteristic action upstairs....

As enlisted men, we radio operators were limited as to what information we could pass on to the pilots, and it was sometimes touchy. When asked for information by a pilot we had to answer: "Roger, wait."... We then had to receive information from ... General Geiger [Brig. Gen. Roy S. Geiger, commander, 1st MAW, in charge of all aviation on Guadalcanal], Lieutenant Giles, or some other nearby officer.... This delay irritated the men upstairs, who had their lives (and ours) on the line. But, somehow it worked.... Our call letters were Z604 and that number was burned into the brain of everyone who ever worked the circuit.

The Japanese-constructed Pagoda was demolished in mid-October 1942 when it was learned that the galvanized roof reflected moonlight or flares at night, providing a good sighting aid for enemy aircraft or warships. [Even] with the Pagoda gone, however, we continued to work the radio system from the depths of our "tunnel home."[4]

Renewing the Battle

On 6 October, when the advanced echelon of the Japanese 2nd Infantry Division had established its headquarters in the Kokumbona area, west of the Matanikau River, it immediately began making plans for the assault. General Hyakutake put his faith in the 29th Infantry Regiment as the muscle of the attack, and he believed that Col. Shojiro Komiya, its commander, would punch through the enemy lines and provide an opening for the others to follow. The Japanese planned to secure the entire island, but the U.S. Marine command intended to establish permanent positions on the east bank of the Matanikau, a natural dividing line, as the river ran through a valley with thick undergrowth and compressed jungle. With a strong presence there the marines believed they could hold the enemy in check. To accomplish this, they assigned a sizable bridgehead force consisting of the 3rd Battalion, 5th Marines, commanded by Maj. William H. Barba and Whaling Sniper Group, including a detachment from the Special Weapons Company, 5th Marines, commanded by Col. William J. Whaling. The force had a few odd amtracs for command-post security, and in addition, the 1st Raider Battalion was supported by the 7th Marines and the guns of the 2nd and 5th Battalions, 11th Marines. All were in position by 6 October.

The 3rd Battalion, 5th Marines, was tasked with the protection of the 7th Marines' river crossing. The 1st Raiders along with the 1st Battalion, 7th Marines, and the 2nd Battalion, 5th Marines, commanded by Maj. David S. McDougal, had been in the same area in late September and they were back, this time hoping for better luck. The Raiders' mission was to set up a blocking position to prevent the Japanese from escaping over the sandpit located at the mouth of the Matanikau while the 3rd Battalion, 5th Marines, moved across the river. Historians would name this operation "The Second Matanikau." The Raiders then would move back to the perimeter, and this would be their last operation, as they had been in almost constant combat since 7 August when they were part of the forces that had invaded Tulagi.

Initial contact with the Japanese was made when elements of Company I, 3/5, under Capt. Bert W. Hardy Jr., crossed the river just seventy-five yards inland. Company I soon met the Japanese along its entire front; Company K, 3/5, under Capt. Lawrence V. Patterson, cautiously moved across the river in an attempt to connect with Company I, which was on its right flank. The Japanese forces in play were the 1st and 2nd Battalions, 4th Infantry, commanded by Maj. Hichiro Usui and Maj. Masuro Tamura, respectively; they were supported by the 1st Machine-Gun Company under Capt. Moriji Sigibashi. The 5th Company under 1st Lt. Yoshimi Onodera and the 7th Company under 1st Lt. Tetsuji Ishibashi, 4th Infantry, were guarding the Point Cruz sector, while the elements of the 124th Infantry and the 4th Infantry, under the command of Capt. Morie Sasaki, occupied the left bank of the Matanikau at the river's mouth.

Marine Company K was ordered to attack in the bush on the left flank of Company I, but a large gap existed between the two groups. Company L, in regimental reserve, was released and ordered to attack in the jungle in a westerly direction; however, the gap could not be filled, and the Japanese plowed in.[5] Captain Sigibashi's machine guns wreaked havoc on the marines, then adding to their misery were six 75-mm howitzers of Lt. Col. Matsujiro Kaji's 20th Independent Mountain Artillery Regiment (IMAR), which showered the leathernecks with thirteen-pound (six killogram) projectiles. The commander of Kaji's 1st Company, Lt. Matsataka Kurokawa, claimed they were firing ten rounds per minute.[6] The 11th Marines returned counter-fire, but the artillerymen were stymied by limited visibility and the lack of essential sound-and-flash ranging equipment necessary for effective counter-battery fire, which had been left with their rear echelon in New Zealand.

At 0800 on the 6th, with Raider officer Maj. Lew Walt in command, Company A of the 5th Marines moved in a westerly direction through the tangled brush toward the Matanikau River with L/3/5 on its left flank. Strong resistance was holding up Company L, but Company A pressed forward to the shore and hastily installed a barbed-wire defense at the area's former positions held by I/3/5. Meanwhile, Company C, 1st Raiders, was ordered to move from its rest area at dawn and report to Colonel Edson, the new commander of the 5th Marines, as the regimental reserve. The formation was then placed under the temporary command of Major Walt now regimental operations officer (R-3) of the 5th Marines, recently promoted to major. Walt had won the Silver Star at Tulagi and was considered a rising star in the Marine Corps.

Hostile resistance stalled two unsuccessful attempts to advance up the river; then at 1500, Raider Companies B and E also were ordered to report to Major Walt. That evening, Company A Raiders held a triangular defense position of the river and the beach; Company B held the left and rear of Company A; and Company C held the left flank of Company B, with its left section connected to K/3/5, a well-protected position.[7] But yet another problem appeared: the drenching rain that turned the river banks into soupy mud.

On 8 October the Japanese attempted to break out from the dense jungle, attacking in small groups from isolated spots, in the process discharging several smoke canisters. Raiders from the 60-mm mortar section were involved in hand-to-hand combat. PFC Dennis F. Thomas refused to be dislodged from his position, as did most of the section; he fought until he was killed. PFC Michael P. Fedorak, manning a light machine gun, continued firing until it jammed, then he removed the back plate and withdrew, leaving fifteen corpses in front of his position.[8]

On 9 October, Companies B and C of the 1st Raiders took up positions between Company A and the 3rd Battalion, 5th Marines, to trap the Sun Soldiers where they stood, and the heavy fighting continued. One section of half-tracks with 37-mm weapons covered the mouth of the river to the Point Cruz peninsula with deadly effect.[9] The 11th Marines had used 105-mm white phosphorous, producing a smokescreen from a terrifying incendiary shell that ignited the grasses in several areas. But communication with the forward observer was difficult, and thus the battery fire control was faulty. The 11th Marines discharged 2,188 rounds of 75-mm, and the 105s blasted the Japanese with 1,063 shells. However, the operation was broken off when the 1st Marine Division received a message that a new threat was en route.

The 11th Marines were replaced by the 1st Battalion, 1st Marines. The
formations on the west were pulled back to a more stable area, since the
airstrip was the key to holding Guadalcanal. The marines claimed seven
hundred Japanese killed; their own casualties totaled sixty-five killed
and 125 wounded.[10] A report that recorded twelve Raiders killed and
twenty-two wounded noted: "This was truly a minor action but in reality it was the ugliest. The conditions were brutal; rain, fog and jungle.
We, in the ranks, awakened on the morning of the 8th in a nasty mood.
Wet from the rain and hungry most of us were bearded, and muddied.
Hardly ready for battle. Generally, we felt that the Division had other
units they could have added to their reserve. Despite these conditions
the leaders took us in hand and instilled in each of us the necessary will
to fight—blame the Japanese and take it out on them—we did. The
loss of ten mortar men was disturbing—had we made an attack on the
pocket in the daytime we may have saved some lives. But I am certain
that the conditions were not right for a daytime attack."[11]

According to Frank J. Guidone, now a sergeant with Company A,
1st Raiders:

> The fight was hours of hell. There was yelling, screams of the
> wounded and dying; rifle firing and machine guns with tracers
> piercing the night—[a] combination of fog, smoke, and the nat-
> ural darkness. Truly an arena of death. I remember vividly look-
> ing seaward from my foxhole and seeing the Japanese tangled up
> in our barb wire while our machine guns cut them to pieces. I
> was on a patrol the next morning and viewed the bodies of our
> slain mortar men—most of them were killed in their foxholes—
> bayoneted and knifed. They were armed with pistols, and were
> killed as they filed in to fill the gap we had in our line.
>
> A few days later the 1st Raiders embarked on APAs and
> headed for New Caledonia. We did this sadly in view of the per-
> sonal losses we suffered at the battle on the Matanikau River.[12]

The next day, 2nd Lieutenant Nakayama's Seventeenth Army Mobile
Ground Radio Squad was assigned to the 35th Brigade as the communication unit for the pending new assault on Henderson Field. Within
a few days a radio command post under Lieutenant Takeoka was established at the foot of the Mount Austen mass of hills. This important
communication junction later established phone connections between
the Seventeenth Army Headquarters at Kokumbona and the artil-

lery spotters on the Mount Austen range and its Hill 903 (called *Ko-chi*, meaning "high ground"—U.S. Hill 89). On 14 and 15 October the weapons of the 47th Field Antiaircraft Artillery Battalion began firing to assist in softening up the airfield prior to the attack, yet all they did was make a racket.[13] Col. Tomojiro Akamatsu, commanding officer of the 4th Heavy Field Artillery Regiment, also had received orders at his command post on Hill 903 to shell the airfield; he used all of his twelve Type 96 15-cm howitzers during the Cactus Air Force takeoffs and landings, successfully restricting flights.

At dusk on 14 October Colonel Akamatsu's 1st Company under 1st Lt. Takeo Fuse positioned its 15-cm howitzers about 400 yards west of the old Nippon Navy Headquarters at Point Cruz to harass the marine perimeter. At dawn the next morning, the group started shelling; fires were started in the hangar area and the oil dump, which further disrupted air activities. Using his spotting binoculars from his perch on Hill 903, Akamatsu could see six guns in the vicinity to the rear of the pier at the marines' naval operating base (NOB) and four of what appeared to be 155-mm howitzers on the northeast side of the airfield. He counted six B 17s and about thirty fighters. He relayed this information to Capt. Kouta Miyabe of 2nd Company and to 1st Lt. Naburo Hara of 3rd Company, and both put their 15-cms into play, dropping ninety-five rounds on the airstrip. The commander of the 2nd Field Artillery Regiment (2nd Division), Col. Masuo Ishizaki, also had received a copy of the directive to shell the airfield, and thus he ordered Capt. K. Onodera's 5th Company and Capt. K. Suzuki's 9th Company to begin firing their Type 38-improved 75-mm howitzers every thirty minutes on 15 and 16 October. By the 18th, they had blanketed the area four times during the day.

As this had been proceeding, 1st Lt. Akio Tani's 7th Heavy Field Artillery Regiment had arrived from Manchuria, via Rabaul, on 14 October with his 2nd Company and had established a forward observation post on Hill 903 of Mount Austen. His four 10-cm weapons were set up in the White River area at 0800 on the 16th where he ordered his gunner to fire for three hours at ten-minute intervals.

Meanwhile, COMSOPAC continued to ship reinforcements to Guadalcanal. On 13 October, 210 men from the second echelon of the 1st Marine Air Wing and a detachment from the 4th Marine Replacement Battalion arrived aboard the *Zeilin* (APA-3), one of the vessels in what the marines called the "Nouméa Express," the convoy of some nineteen warships with men and materiel from Nouméa, New Caledonia. With the airmen came 2,852 GIs of the 164th Infantry Regiment from North Dakota, the vanguard of the New Caledonia-based American Division, a new unit that had been officially formed in May 1942 from three National Guard regiments. The 164th—men generally older than most of the Guard units—was a tough regiment with a proud history and sorely needed on Guadalcanal to replace some of the men of the 1st Marine Division who were beginning to suffer from the unrelenting tropical diseases and inadequate food. They arrived at Guadalcanal in Admiral Turner's flagship, the *McCawley*—the "Wacky Mac"—and disembarked on the Kukum docks. That evening, the brave and tired men of the 1st Raider Battalion would embark on the *McCawley* and *Zeilin* to return to Nouméa.

Just as the GIs had set foot on Guadalcanal a green alert sounded, the all-clear notification; but shortly after that it was once again "Tojo Time." Twenty-four Bettys left their calling cards in the form of 500-pound bombs. When some cartons of the 164th's total 3,200 tons of foodstuffs vanished during the melee, directly under the watch of the regiment's MPs, the army GIs were quickly introduced to one of the marine credos: "Take what you can and don't get caught." Sgt. Roy A. Lindberg of the 164th Infantry wrote to his sister: ". . . Stuff [was] piled up on the beach. It was [in] this condition that our first bombing raid caught us. . . . 'Condition Red' [air raid] someone yelled—the Marines told us to find a hole. I found a shallow ditch which . . . seemed like ample cover at the time and good observation spot. . . . My curiosity soon came to and end, however, when a whistling bomb fell some hundred feet away. We saw men scurrying with stretchers."[14]

For radio-man Chuck Buser, the most terrifying time on Guadalcanal was the "black night" of 13–14 October. The 15-cm weapons of the Japanese 4th Heavy Field Artillery Regiment under Col. Tomojiro Akamatsu had hit the perimeter during daylight on the 13th; that evening, a solo spotter plane dropped a flare, then an illumination shell—a star shell. It announced trouble. The Imperial Navy had sent the "heavies" from the Eighth Fleet, the battleships *Haruna* and *Kongo,* to neutralize the marine compound. At 2336, shortly before midnight, their 14-inch guns began to pound the island with the new antipersonnel high-explosive shells (Type *San Shiki*) beginning at a point off White River. Moving at twenty-eight knots, the two ships shelled the Henderson Field area from one end to the other; at 0023, the ships began firing again on their return course. The *Kongō*'s assistant gunnery officer, Cdr. Ikichio Shima, reported that his ship had fired 331 armor-piercing and

104 incendiary shells; the *Haruna* had fired 294 armor-piercing and 189 antipersonnel high-explosive (APHE) shells. The *Kongō's* 6-inch guns deposited twenty-seven shells on the airstrip; the *Haruna's* dropped twenty-one. In eighty minutes the battleships threw twelve shells per minute at Henderson Field, setting in motion the plan to keep the airfield in disarray.

To all who were there, the assault seemed to span a lifetime. Yet the torment was not over for those on the receiving end. That night the cruisers *Chōkai* and *Kinugasa* accompanied by the destroyers *Amagiri* and *Mochizuki* flung their 5- and 8-inch shells into the airfield, setting afire the airfield's fuel dump. When the attack ended it had almost decimated the Cactus Air Force, leaving only eleven Dauntless SBDs operational. Forty-seven other aircraft were damaged, including all the Navy's TBF Avengers, which were hauled off to what the men called the "Geiger boneyard," in the clearing next to the airfield.[15] One bright spot: most of the aircraft parked on Fighter Strip No. 1, the new dirt airstrip, were saved, and Lt. George Cole, USMC, a former World War I soldier and an aviation specialist, was able with his team to rebuild part of the depleted aircraft arsenal.

At the time of the shelling, sixteen Espiritu Santo-based B 17s were resting on Henderson Field following a bombing run on Buka, Bougainville, including a new Flying Fortress from the 431st Bombardment Squadron. The Japanese assault had left Henderson with twenty-one holes in the pierced-steel planking (PSP) Marston runway mats, but only one aircraft was mangled beyond repair. However, forty-one Americans in the camp had been killed and many were wounded. Six pilots had died, four from VMSB 14—Maj. G. A. Bell, Capt. R. R. Abbott, Capt. E. F. Miller, and 2nd Lt. H. A. Chaney Jr. When the all-clear finally sounded, the undamaged fifteen B 17s took off for Espiritu Santo, maneuvering around the potholes and using only 2,500 feet of runway to get airborne, though one was caught in the matting, tearing it up, and had to be abandoned. The aircraft of the 67th Fighter Squadron also escaped serious mishap that day: the P-400/P-39s—the "Klunkers" or "Winged Trucks"—were left intact; only two of the P-39s were damaged. Nevertheless, when the dust finally settled, the camp area was filled with enormous shell holes. Lt. Harold H. Larson, detachment commander of U.S. Navy Squadron VT-8 torpedo planes, had no aircraft to fly because of the destruction and thus joined the infantrymen on the perimeter.

The 164th Infantry Regiment had lost three of its members in the shelling. Cpl. Clifford R. Kurtz (HQ/164) and most of the other soldiers of the 164th had been busy unloading the transports and had not dug the mandatory foxholes—no one had told them to do so. They were sleeping on the ground when the Japanese battlewagons started pounding the area. Kurtz complained, asking if every night was as disruptive as his first on the island. The tents were in shreds, and many good men were buried in the rubble, including PFC Bernard Seiden.[16] Shells also hit the phone cable set against the ridge, cutting the master line. When a shell hit a line going in the other direction, the phone service was temporarily dead.[17]

Michael J. O'Dea Jr. of the 6th Naval Construction Battalion wrote of that day and night: "13th: Air raid three times today. Hit the airport hard and damaged our fuel supply. Shelled from battleships from 1:00 AM until daybreak—stayed in foxhole all night—no sleep, no food, one meal today. Two shells near my foxhole—dirt struck my neck—one killed and seven wounded near my tent. Fired at from hills nearby— this has been our worst day and night. Army landed today[;] shelled for four hours tonight. 14th: Air raids all day—bombs dropping all night. Haven't slept for 48 hours—will try and get a few hours sleep tonight. 15th and 16th: These last four days can be explained as plain Hell."[18] Arvil L. Jones of CUB 1 recalled: "Oh God! What destruction! Shattered palm trees dangled at odd angles. Our tent was flat, a pile of rags. A huge piece of shrapnel rested right in the middle of it." Although PFC Larry Gerkin of Company L, 3rd Battalion, 5th Marines, came through the barrage, he almost had a 1,400-pound Japanese souvenir to take home. During the bombardment an unexploded 14-inch shell landed near his foxhole and rolled, nearly covering his deep pit.[19]

Forbidding weather that Sunday grounded the Cactus Air Force, but the Japanese planes were active and they bombed and strafed the Lunga area in seven different attacks. The day had a touch of humor when the ground crew around the airstrip hauled damaged aircraft hulks from the boneyard and parked them in a regular formation along the edge of the field; the Japanese airmen took the bait and destroyed them. With bad timing, Cpl. William W. Rogal of Company A, 1st Battalion, 2nd Marines, had just arrived in the Lunga area from Aola, on the northeastern portion of Guadalcanal, with a downed airman he had rescued at sea. Rogal recalls: "Things were perplexed when we got to Lunga. This was Pistol Pete's [1st Lt. Akio Tani] first day and everyone in the area was unused to being shelled by land. As I recall, I got a ride to sick bay. The flier was ambulatory, but not feeling real chipper. As ordered, I went on to report to General Vandegrift on the accomplishments and current position of the patrol [the 2nd Marines in the Aola sector]. I was dug in that night with some headquarters types who had a deep dugout. It was a very bad night!"[20]

No American who was there ever forgot that night. All had jangled nerves. Believing the Japanese might land, the officer in charge (OIC) of the base radio station and five other officers got panicky and without orders started to burn the code books. When the chief of staff, Col. Gerald C. Thomas, heard of the destruction he had it stopped; by the time he intervened, however, seven mailbags with confidential and secret publications had been destroyed. The OIC was sent packing to Nouméa.[21]

Fuel was always in short supply on Guadalcanal, and after the last bombing the reserve situation was critical; without fuel the Cactus Air Force would be grounded and Guadalcanal would be lost. AM1c August "Marty" Martello of CUB 1 was responsible for keeping the fuel inventory and became one of the many unsung heroes of the campaign. In the bush near the former Japanese camp, Martello had secreted 488 drums of avgas, sixty-seven drums of 1120 oil, seven drums of 1100 oil, and five barrels of 3065 oil—the major supply for the next flight action. Had he not taken the initiative and stowed the fuel away from the strip, the campaign might have had a different ending.[22] CUBs AM2c Arvil Jones, AM2c Jack Evans, and AM2c Rick Kaymier had also stored twelve drums in the bush, which they soon retrieved. Another sixty-five drums were found near the Tenaru River, and caches totaling two hundred barrels were found huddled in various areas, well camouflaged under palm-tree leaf cuttings. Jones, who was on the gas-truck detail, records that three tankers full of gas (750 gallons) were untouched by the shelling.[23]

Following the Japanese bombardment, on 20 October nineteen sick and wounded marines boarded a 13th Troop Carrier Squadron C-47 Skytrain evacuation plane—a Gooney Bird; it was airborne at 0750, bound for hospitals in New Caledonia. All went well for several hours, and then the aircraft developed engine trouble. The pilot made a safe emergency water landing on the D'Entrecasteaux reef—the Huon or French reef—northwest of Belep Island off the New Caledonia group. There the sick marines and aircrew remained for eight days until a patrolling PBY spotted the downed C-47 and reported seeing survivors. The command at Nouméa sent three PBYs the following day to conduct a rescue. On the 29th, three Catalinas landed off the reef and boarded the haggard men, but heavy seas and swells prevented the Cats from taking off. One PBY from VP-11 floated to the reef, while the others (P-5 from VP-23 and P-5 from VP-51) drifted to the open sea. On the 30th, a fourth Catboat flew to the scene and located the wayward PBYs. It flew cover and assisted in directing the destroyer *Barton* to the reef area to retrieve the downed patients and aircrews. All were saved, but the three PBYs were lost to the unyielding sea.[24]

At about the same time, communication progressed for the besieged airmen at Henderson Field when Lt. Col. Chesty Puller's 1st Battalion, 7th Marines, set up a private radio station from six radios they had salvaged from wrecked aircraft at the boneyard; they put together headsets so that the command post could listen to stateside news as well as talk with airmen in flight. Division headquarters was unhappy with Puller's pirate radio network, but did not order it disbanded.

Carrying Out the Japanese Plan

The Japanese planned attack on the perimeter was beginning to take shape with a blockbuster assault by the 2nd Division. In the division camp at Tassafaronga a directive from Lt. Gen. Masao Maruyama dated 14 October was issued as YU Order #2, stating that "control" of the troops would be the "key to success" in any jungle rushing attack. Maruyama asserted that there was "no position" that could not be breached if a charge was made simultaneously.

On 17 October, the Seventeenth Army had issued tactical orders to the 2nd Division. The coast force, under Maj. Gen. Tadashi Sumiyoshi's command, consisted of the 3rd Battalion, 4th Infantry (III/4i) with 2,100 men; the *Meada Tai* with twelve tanks, two Type 95 and ten Type 97, with eleven artillery pieces; the Tani Tai, with four 10-cm cannons and sixteen artillery pieces of the 4th and 21st Heavy Field Artillery Regiments under Capt. Masuo Ishizaki; and segments of the 124th Infantry. The tank unit staged at Kokumbona, but on 20 October lost one vehicle from the 3rd Platoon due to gunfire from a U.S. warship. Japanese assault forces were being deployed along a line nearly four miles (six kilometers) south of Henderson Field, with the attack scheduled to begin at 1700 on 21 October. The Seventeenth Army order noted that the Sumiyoshi Force (Commander Artillery Force) would fake an attack from Mount Austen while the 35th Brigade—the spearhead—would capture the enemy positions and the artillery units—the 11th Marines—at the edge of the woods on the north side of the airfield, then advance along the coastline.

The Seventeenth Army had planned a three-stage flanking movement, and thus the 4th Infantry placed its 1st Company led by 1st Lt. Kanji Inoue on the left side of the *Shiba* position (code name for Shiba

[Lion] Mountain). The 5th Company, under 1st Lt. Yoshimi Onodera, and the 6th Company, under 1st Lt. Junichiro Kurnoki, were on the right shore, north of Shiba Mountain. The advance order for the attack force of the 124th Infantry was 1st Lt. Kazuo Yamaguchi's 4th Company and machine-gun unit; then the 1st Company and machine-gun unit; and finally 1st Lt. Manuos Shoutarou's 2nd Company, with one platoon of the 7th and 15th Engineers plus a platoon from 1st Lt. Choishoo Saaki's 3rd Independent Trench Mortar Battalion (ITMB). The 3rd ITMB would head for the center. In another move setting the stage for the assault on the airfield via the middle sector, the 76th Line of Communication Hospital in conjunction with the 2nd Medical Unit had established medical receiving services in the Tassafaronga area.

While the enemy was thus preparing to push the Americans off the island, the U.S. Navy was trying to furnish enough avgas to keep the Cactus Air Force flying. Japanese aircraft and submarines often harassed the slow-moving tankers attempting to haul fuel to Guadalcanal, and although some made it through, some did not. One of the U.S. Navy's newest "silent service" vessels, the submarine *Amberjack* (SS 219), was temporally assigned to COMAIRSOPAC and ordered to report to Espiritu Santo for assignment. The mission was to deliver high-octane gasoline and supplies to Guadalcanal. At Santo, the men from the seaplane tender *Curtiss* welded two fuel tanks for the *Amberjack*. When the conversion was completed, 9,000 gallons of avgas was loaded, and the passenger list included fifteen U.S. Army Air Forces fighter pilots assigned to 347th Fighter Group. Keeping the aviators company were two 100-pound bombs stacked in each of the ship's lounges. The *Amberjack* reached the Lunga area on the morning of 25 October but was ordered to move to Tulagi for unloading, as it was a safer anchorage.

For the Japanese, the fighting in both New Guinea and the Solomons was under the command of the Seventeenth Army. Putting the New Guinea operation aside would permit the Seventeenth to extend all efforts to recapture Guadalcanal, yet combat conditions in New Guinea and in the north of Australia sector also demanded attention. To consolidate both efforts, Imperial General Headquarters (IGHQ) activated the Eighteenth Army under Lt. Gen. Hataso Adachi to the New Guinea sector with the ultimate goal to capture Port Moresby, relieving Lt. Gen. Haruyoshi Hyakutake of that responsibility. The IGHQ then activated the Eighth Area Army (under the code name GO) and assigned fifty-six-year-old Lt. Gen. Hitoshi Imamura as its commander to coordinate both the Eighth and the Eighteenth Armies. The sole task of General

Hyakutake's Seventeenth Army thus would be to send reinforcements to Guadalcanal and take back the island.

For the push east, the main body of the 2nd Division, led by Maj. Gen. Toshio Nasu, would move up the Lunga River as they crossed the south foothills of Mount Austen. The Nasu unit (the 29th Infantry and the 1st Battalion, 10th Independent Mountain Artillery Regiment) and attached contingents would advance upstream of the Lunga via the Maruyama Trail (Maruyama Road), the pathway cut through the dense jungle by Lt. Gen. Masao Maruyama's troops. In addition, Maj. Gen. Kiyotake Kawaguchi's force, supported by two battalions of the 230th Infantry, was to join the Nasu unit. On 18 October, the 29th Infantry led by Maj. Tadao Yoshi (CO, III/29i) took the lead. Its main objective was to smash through the Mukade Gata (Bloody Ridge)—the same ridge that the 35th Brigade had failed to take in September—and occupy the airstrip.

1st Lt. Kozaburo Miyazawa would write in his diary:

> Oct. 20—It was planned to carry out the general attack, but because of the inaccuracy of maps and the unknown terrain, the progress of road construction by the Engineers . . . and the advance of units, especially the heavy weapons units, was very slow. Therefore, the general attack was unavoidably postponed to the 23rd, the 24th and the 25th.
>
> Oct. 25—At 1700 it was planned to enter the enemy position together, but because of imperfect communications with the 29th Infantry Regiment, that one regiment did not move and the point of the general attack was completely lost.[25]

Combat Order #3 of the 10th Independent Mountain Artillery Regiment (code letters DAN) called for the Japanese Army to form plans for a decisive battle at 1700 on 23 October. The order had been issued by Maj. Mutsuo Ogasawara, commander of the 10th's 1st Battalion. At 1115 the Sumiyoshi wing was to advance and attack the main enemy positions; at 1200 the Fuji unit, including the 124th Regimental Gun Company under 1st Lt. Yoshibei Nagao, was to open its attack.

In support of the assault many heavy guns were assigned to rain fire on the American lines. On 18 October the 75s of the 10th and 20th Independent Mountain Artillery Regiments, plus the four guns of the two batteries of the 21st Heavy Field Artillery Regiment and the Type 41 regimental guns, had begun preparations for their move from the general bivouac area west of the *Bonegi Gawa* (Bonegi River). The troops had started to dismantle the weapons on the 18th and by noon on the 19th commenced the advance forward. Forty men in two teams were required to transport each gun over the narrow Maruyama Trail, with seven men needed just to carry the frame. In addition, as would be done elsewhere, each soldier had been ordered to shoulder one shell plus his pack and rifle. The men dragged the guns up and down the hills in the stifling heat of Guadalcanal's seemingly impenetrable jungle, but by 21 October the weapons became too heavy. The troops were exhausted and hungry. Col. Toshiro Hiroyasu's Shiba Operation Order 179 of 20 October had stated: "Cooking fires after sundown must be absolutely prevented. . . ." Commanding Officer Lt. Gen. Masao Maruyama had reinforced the directive that same day in his 2nd Division YU Operation Order A—No. 172: ". . . Again, cooking and going to the river and openings during the day, are strictly prohibited." The men were not to build fires until noon of the 21st, as the smoke would signal the enemy. It should have been no surprise then when the overtaxed force began dropping the heavy armament shells trailside.[26]

All of the regimental 75-mm guns were left beside the road. Men were falling, unable to take another step, and finally only one independent mountain artillery regiment would be dragged onward. On 22 October Capt. Kyohtaroh Oishi, commanding officer of the 3rd Company, left the group with a small party to seek a location for setting up the remaining weapons. On the 23rd rain began to dissolve the jungle floor into mud. In the meantime, however, Captain Oishu had selected a site some seven kilometers (4½ miles) south of Henderson Field, and on the 23rd the group arrived. The one gun, a 1908 Type 41 75-mm mountain weapon was set into position.

With Y-day now immediately approaching—the Japanese equivalent to the Americans' D-day—Lt. Col. Matsujiro Kaji, commander of the 20th IMAR, on the 24th was to support the 35th Brigade's drive through the Mukade Gata. Colonel Kaji, however, received a new order, to support the left wing under General Nasu, and thus he positioned the 10th IMAR's Type 41 weapon that had been moved up to pound the airstrip. The gun had a maximum range of only 7,800 yards, equivalent to the 4½-mile distance to the airfield. It barely made the target, but was efficient enough to harass the Americans. 2nd Lt. Kazumi Yokoyama, commander of the 1st Platooon, 3rd Company, 1st Battalion, 10th IMAR, claimed the weapon was only fired twenty times because of the compelling counter-fire from the 11th Marines; Yokoyama lamented that they had dragged the 75-mm weapon all that way only to fire a few rounds.[27]

Just before the battle, the 35th Brigade was bivouacking in the area adjacent to the Lunga River crossing. Orders were received attaching the brigade's guard company to the Nakaguma Butai (4th Infantry) for the pending attack; they would be just over six miles from Henderson Field.[28] However, the Seventeenth Army's steamroller movement toward the airfield defense line was hampered by the weather, terrain, and disrupted communications, as well as later by the marines and GIs—the 1st, 5th, and 7th Marines; the 3rd Battalion, 2nd Marines; the 3rd Battalion, 10th Marines; the 11th Marines; and the 164th Infantry Regiment of the U.S. Army's Americal Division.

The arrival of the 164th Infantry had been a "shot in the arm" for the men on Guadalcanal, as it permitted General Vandegrift to make additional support changes in the Lunga defense structure. The 1st Division intelligence officer, the G-2, believed the Japanese would strike from the west where their main strength was concentrated. In sector #1, a 7,000-foot stretch of beach on Lunga Point was under the 3rd Marine Defense Battalion, supported by elements of the 1st Special Weapons Battalion. The 1st Amphibian Tractor Battalion, 1st Engineer Battalion, and 1st Pioneer Battalion were ordered to hold the beach lines during the evening hours. In addition, two sea-watch stations were set up just east and west of the Lunga River; consisting of twelve men each, they were manned twenty-four hours a day. The left outpost commanded an excellent view up the entire northwest coast, including the ground that rose inland as far as Cape Esperance, the horizon from Guadalcanal to Savo Island and from Savo to Florida, and the outline of Florida itself. The right lookout station faced northward across Sealark Channel to Tulagi and Koli Point. Both stations were wired into the 1st Division Headquarters.

Part of the 1st Special Weapons Battalion and segments of the 164th Infantry Regiment were assigned to sector #2 and deployed across a 2,500-yard front. Later, the sector that the 164th defended was named "Coffin Corner." This long defense line extended along the beach from the 3rd Defense Battalion's position on the right flank to the Ilu River, inland along the Hu River about 4,000 yards, and then west through the forest to the left flank of the 7th Marines. The 7th occupied about 2,500 yards of sector #3, between the 164th Infantry's right flank (3rd Battalion) and the Lunga River, including the south slopes of Bloody Ridge (Edson's Ridge). The 1st Marines held a 3,500-yard expanse of jungle area between the Lunga River and the left flank of the 5th Marines, who held sector #5, the western corner of the perimeter. The two battalions—both the 1st and 7th Marines—held the Matanikau line called "Dead Man's

Corner," supported by segments of the 1st Special Weapons Battalion and one battalion of the 11th Marines. These were the airfield garrison's staunch defenses set up to meet the upcoming Nippon offensive.

The Japanese 2nd Infantry Division had issued its attack plan back on 10 October. In principle, the division would concentrate its components at the head of Matanikau River and under cover of artillery fire would assault the enemy position and seize Henderson Field with one blow. The main movements extended from the northern edge of the Mount Austen mass to an area adjacent to the beach. The attack had been prearranged to commence about 18 October, and the 4th Infantry Regiment (less the 3rd Battalion) was to be responsible for holding the landing point between Kamimbo Bay and the Matanikau River and for protecting the roads. On the right flank was to be the Headquarters, 35th Infantry Brigade; the 24th Infantry Regiment; the balance of the Ichiki Detachment (the Kuma Battalion under Maj. Eiji Mizuno); the 2nd Antitank Battalion (less one company); half of the 2nd Company, 2nd Engineer Regiment, under Capt. Akimasa Kishi; and a unit of medical troops. At the center were to be two companies of the 29th Infantry Regiment's light mortar unit; the 9th Independent Rapid-Fire Gun Battalion under Lt. Col. Jiukichi Yamamoto; part of the medical troops and engineers; and part of one company from the 2nd Engineer Regiment under Capt. Akimasa Kishi.

On the left flank was to be the 2nd Infantry Division Headquarters group; Capt. Morie Sasaki's 3rd Battalion, 4th Infantry Regiment; Maj. Shiro Gen's 1st Battalion, 16th Infantry Regiment; Capt. Sumuto Meada's 1st Independent Tank Company; the 1st Company's light mortar unit; the 3rd Company, 6th Independent Rapid-Fire Gun Battalion; the 1st Independent Artillery Mortar Regiment (three batteries) utilizing the deadly Type 98 32-cm spigot mortars; one company of engineers; General Sumiyoshi, the artillery group commander; the 2nd Battalion less the 6th Battery and the 3rd Battalion less the 9th Battery, 2nd Field Artillery Regiment; the 4th Heavy Field Artillery Regiment, less one battalion; the 2nd Battery, 21st Heavy Field Artillery Battalion led by Capt. Junzo Tanaka; the 1st Battery, 2nd Company, 7th Heavy Field Artillery Regiment; and the 2nd Engineer Regiment less the 2nd Company, plus the 39th Road Construction Unit, with Col. Takuzo Takahashi (2nd Engineers) as the engineer commander.

The attack reserves were to be under Col. Toshiro Hiroyasu, commander of the 16th Infantry Regiment. The reserve was to include the 16th less the 1st Battalion; an air defense unit of Lt. Col. Yasuzo Nakamura's 38th Field Antiaircraft Battalion; Maj. Inawa Tamada's 45th Field Antiaircraft Battalion; 1st Lieutenant Yokota's 3rd Company, 47th Field Antiaircraft Battalion; Capt. Koichi Ezaki's 2nd Division Signal Unit; the medical unit less one-third; part of 67th Line of Communication Field Hospital; the 76th Line of Communication Hospital; part of 24th Water Supply and Purification Unit; and a transport unit.

Each flank was to make preparations at the line—the departure starting point—oriented at 0600. On the night preceding the attack, they were to advance to a position approximately 100 meters (some 325 feet) in front of the enemy. Like the 4th Infantry Regiment, the 16th would concentrate its main force at Kokumbona to hold the landing point in the area between Kamimbo Bay and the Matanikau River and to protect the roads there. Pending an attack order, Capt. Sumito Meada, commander of the 1st Independent Tank Company, was to reconnoiter the coastal areas suitable for tank action.[29] Thus on the 19th, Meada sent two tanks from the 2nd Platoon led by 1st Lt. Tsukasa Ikeda in tank #1 along the coast route, but found the area near the Ma [Matanikau] River basin especially sandy. On the 20th another party was sent out, this time 2nd Lt. Hiroyasu Yamaji in tank #2 and Sgt. Y. Nishimoto in tank #3 from the 3rd Platoon. They traveled as far as the Ma River and were accompanied by one platoon from the 4th Infantry Regiment. The group found an outpost line strongly defended on the east bank by the 3rd Battalion, 1st Marines. When the marines saw the tanks they fired one shot from their 37-mm antitank gun from about 160 yards and hit Nishimoto, damaging the tank's gun and hatch and smashing the vehicle. Yamaji's tank escaped, but along with the troops it was soon after strafed by the Cactus Air Force, which was returning from a mission to the west. A trail of bodies was left behind.

Upon his return to Captain Meada, Yamaji reported what had been discovered about the American positions, and with that information Meada approached General Sumiyoshi to suggest that the tanks should not attempt to cross the sandbar, but only be used to break through the airfield defenses. The general's response: "The plan stands." Captain Meada's junior officers were not pleased with the prospect of operating on sandy soil, as they were trained tank operators and knew the difficulties of crossing that surface. They originally had anticipated heading directly to the airfield and blasting through the marine lines. Thus, on 21 October another set of tanks set out to explore the river basin once again, this time from the 1st Platoon, led by 1st Lt. Sanae Harada in tank #1, Sgt. Seizou Watanabe in #2, and MSgt. Minoru Tanaka in #3.[30]

The 11th Marines were warned of the presence of tanks by the men at the impact center, on the east bank, and although they hammered the Japanese with the sector 75s and 155s, the tanks escaped damage. This third encounter, however, had alerted the impact center of the strong Japanese interest in the sector and as a result the marine troop strength was boosted on the east bank. Interestingly, as meticulously as the Japanese had outlined their offensive orders, they had not taken into adequate account Guadalcanal's concentrated jungle, steep hills, debilitating weather, and their own ineffective resupply system, nor had General Maruyama adequately addressed the need for both appropriate reconnaissance and proper route preparation.

Stepping Up for the Attack

The 1st Marine Division radioed Nouméa seeking the greatest possible amount of air and surface support, and Admiral Ghormley, who was generally detached from the Guadalcanal campaign (named "timid Ghormley" or "Tiny Tim" by the troops), on this occasion was fully attentive to the urgent predicament. Capt. Miles Browning, Ghormley's chief of staff and an effective administrator, requested help from SWPAC to have the 5th Air Force and the RAAF search the western approaches for an enemy carrier force. When the B 17s of the 11th Bombardment Group were forced off Henderson Field for the lack of fuel, Rear Adm. Aubrey W. Fitch, commanding South Pacific land-based aircraft, also suggested that the 5th Air Force relieve the pressure on Guadalcanal by intensifying its strikes on Rabaul, Kahili, and Buka. The records are vague on what support General MacArthur actually gave to the Guadalcanal campaign; in any event it was paltry.

At the time, the U.S. Navy was still operating on borderline support level, with few warships in the South Pacific area. The *Enterprise, Saratoga,* and *North Carolina* (BB 55) were in Pearl Harbor undergoing repairs, but Admiral Nimitz ordered the work on the Big "E" to be rushed. The *Enterprise* was able to sail for the South Pacific on 16 October — sooner than expected — in the company of the battleship *South Dakota* and nine destroyers. Meanwhile, Admiral Fitch's air force at Espiritu Santo was increased to eighty-five patrol planes and heavy bombers.

It was about this same time on Guadalcanal that the Japanese 4th Heavy Artillery Regiment (twelve guns) and the 2nd Battery, 21st Heavy Field Independent Mountain Artillery Regiment (four guns), had established the regimental command post on Hill 903 (U.S. Hill 89). And it was on 14 October that the plan had been set in motion to neutralize

Henderson Field by shelling it with 150-mm howitzers and 10-cm cannons. The intent had been to hit everything, including the fuel dump and the Cactus Air Force planes, which indeed often were fired at, preventing takeoff. Thus it was that by the 18th the Japanese had shelled the area four times that day. The Sun Soldiers were to smash through the airfield defenses from the south flank with 5,800 men, backed by artillery, engineer, and medical support, a force divided into two wings. The right wing, under General Kawaguchi, was to attack the southeast sector of the ridge. It consisted of Maj. Etsuo Takamatsu's 2nd Battalion, 124th Infantry; two battalions of the recently arrived 230th Infantry (38th Division); parts of the 3rd Independent Trench Mortar Battalion under Lt. Col. Yoshihatsu Onizuka; the 6th Independent Rapid-Fire Gun Battalion; the 9th Independent Rapid-Fire Gun Battalion; and the 20th Independent Mountain Artillery. The left wing, under Maj. Gen. Yumio Nasu, comprised the 29th Infantry (main body) and elements of the 3rd Independent Trench Mortar Battalion, less detachments; a rapid-fire gun battalion; a mountain artillery battalion; and one company from the 38th Engineer Regiment under Lt. Col. Tsuneo Iwabuchi.

General Kawaguchi's wing included the 35th Brigade, which after moving inland from Kokumbona was to travel northward east of the Lunga River under cover of darkness to strike the airfield and destroy the Americans in the area. General Nasu's left wing was to attack northward from a point between Kawaguchi's front and the Lunga River. In reserve was the 16th Infantry under Col. Toshiro Hiroyasu and additional engineering formations. The Seventeenth Army ordered the reserves—the 16th Infantry troops—to guard the sector between the Poha and Mamara Rivers and from the Poha to the Bonegi River, and ordered the Sato engineers to repair the road. Elements of the 16th Infantry became the support unit to forward supplies to the front.[31]

Back on 15 October, Martin Clemens's scouts had reported the landing of a large enemy force, alerting the 1st Marine Division to a possible renewed attack. A captured Japanese map made by the 124th Infantry indicated a possible triple-pronged assault from the east, west, and south, but there were no indications of a recent landing of enemy forces east of the perimeter (Koli Point). Air and ground patrols had not located any organized bodies of enemy troops along the upper Lunga, only groups of stragglers. The increasing artillery fire and growing Japanese troop strength west of the Matanikau convinced the Lunga defenders that the brunt of the attack would again fall in the west.

On 16 October, Lt. Col. Robert G. Hunt's 3rd Battalion, 2nd Ma-

Figure 34. Martin Clemens's scouts and Cpl. Ralph R. Wendling, D-2 Section, 1st Marine Division, at Aola, Guadalcanal, October 1942. (USMC photo)

rines, as reinforcements moved to a bivouac area to the rear of the 5th Marines; the 3/2 had just recently arrived from Tulagi. On the 17th, a group of Betty bombers accompanied by a flight of Zeroes attacked and several bombs fell in the 3/2 sector, injuring five. 1st Lt. Frederick Riggs's platoon (Company L) was taking shelter under the large roots of a banyan tree when a bomb hit the tree and fiercely propelled steel fragments. Riggs was seriously injured, and Sergeant Richter, who had recently arrived from Espiritu Santo, received a hole in his back and spine the size of an eighty-eight-count apple.[32]

As the Japanese Seventeenth Army meanwhile slowly approached the perimeter, their activity remained mostly undiscovered. General Maruyama moved his combat formations, field guns, ammunition, and major supplies into position for the offensive, enabled by the 2nd Division Engineers who had constructed and improved byways leading from the landing beaches eastward to Kokumbona. The Imperial engineers—the "path-builders"—and the assault troops had begun work on the back-country Maruyama Trail, over which the 2nd Division could move into position south of the airstrip, hidden from the American aircraft flying overhead. This nearly iron-bound thin path ran southward from the Seventeenth Army assembly point at Kokumbona, turned east to cross the Matanikau and Lunga Rivers south of Mount Austen, then followed the Lunga north, downstream, to a point near the American lines. The Japanese movement along the thirty-five-mile narrow spiral trail extended for about fifteen miles through the bottom expanse of Guadalcanal's jungles where enormous trees, thick vines, and slippery hills with dense undergrowth made walking difficult for a soldier. Nevertheless the Japanese troops advanced amidst the inhospitable vegetation, through the overhanging forest that blotted out much of the sun and strictly limited their vision. The route they took south of Mount Austen led through tangled bush and a sequence of ridges and muddy ravines—a spongy quagmire.

Sgt. Hisakichi Hara of the 230th Infantry described the difficult march on the Maruyama Trail:

> The path that ran along the coast made a right turn at a place called Kokumbona into a valley between two hills. From here, laboring under miserable conditions our engineers had opened a way. For a painful time before nightfall, vines armed with thorns wrapped around our necks and we continued stubbing our toes on tree roots and projecting rocks. After a few days of this, our uniforms were in tatters and we had many open sores constantly irritated by being soaked with sweat. [The jungle was filled with] rotting trees and luminous insects, which we took and smeared on the backpacks of each man, so we could see the [one] in front as we marched. . . . We trudged on at the bottom of an ocean of foliage that denied us the benefit of sunshine, in extreme discomfort. The trail had taken us through the jungle, but now high and steep mountains thrust up before us. Sweat streamed from us as we marched, and a canteen full of water was a lifeline. Scrambling up and tumbling down, we kept going. Thinking to fall by the way would be the end, we shrugged off the shadow of death and I urged myself on, saying, "We have not yet engaged in battle with the enemy. Dying here would be dying in vain."
>
> Coordinating with the naval bombardment, we were told, the army would attempt to envelop and destroy the enemy in one stroke. However, our units making our miserable way over bad terrain were advancing too slowly and one or two precious days were lost; so we were unable to reach our deployment point at

the scheduled time. On the 20th, the date set for the offensive to begin, we had finally reached the Lunga River crossing, but there was no airfield and there remained 15 to 20 km [approximately ten to twelve miles] of rough trail still ahead. That evening we began to make the crossing. The provisions we brought with us had already reached bottom; being only enough for one day remaining. Then we received the word that the offensive had been postponed to the 24th. Soon we [would] feast on Yankee food! Roosevelt rations, breakfast biscuits, and coffee.[33]

The Seventeenth Army units continued on their grueling march from their assembly point at Kokumbona toward the line of departure east of the Lunga River. Because the trail was narrow, the men tramped single file in an extended irregular column; despite the vanguard group beginning the procession early each morning, the rear component usually could not move until afternoon. As rain soaked most of the trek, the 2nd Division inched along, encumbered with heavy shells and full combat equipment. Despite their heavy load, they subsisted on their limited half rations of raw rice and with ropes pulled the General Sumiyoshi artillery pieces and automatic weapons along the unyielding muddy track until eventually they were compelled to abandon some of their guns, packs, and extra ammunition shells.

With no road-building equipment, the Japanese engineers simply had chopped their way by hand using axes, saws, and machetes. Their horses had been left at Rabaul, and with no significant motor transport the 800-some tons of supplies would be carried to the jungle front from as far away as Cape Esperance. Timing was important to the plan, yet the attack management team did not take into account the uncertainties of jungle travel. As a result, when the attack actually began, most of the troops were not in place to jump off at the proper moment. The result would be a meager, though indeed determined, thrust at the onset rather than a protracted assault.

Adding to October's complications was the pervasive island malady. Except for Kawaguchi's formations, the Japanese 2nd Division attack troops were almost untouched by what was called the "Ga Tō sickness." In contrast, General Vandegrift's marines were suffering from malaria and dysentery, as well as from malnutrition and the lack of sleep and replacement clothing. Operation "Shoestring" should have been the name for the Guadalcanal mission. Everything was in short supply, even writing paper.

It is understandable that the Japanese no doubt fully expected to surprise the Americans in such a situation, especially considering that the jungle and mountainous terrain allowed them to remain hidden from the Cactus Air Force. However, the Americans were well entrenched in positions on the ridge mounds in anticipation of an attack, and cannoneers of the 11th Marines could zero in firepower for any threatened sector.

The Flawed Swift Blow

General Maruyama faced problems when his attack forces fell far behind schedule. He had rescheduled Y-day, and then because some troops were still not at their line of departure, he rescheduled it again, to the 24th. Even so, some formations, although in place, were not aware that the attack date was changed. One such unit was the coast wing. The scheme was to involve a swift "knock-out blow"; instead it became a two-night dragged-out battle.

According to Sergeant Hara: "The plan of the operation was for Sumiyoshi's Artillery in the western shore area to launch a diversionary attack while the main assault force, traveling over the trail, was deployed south of the airfield with the right wing commanded by General Kawaguchi and the left wing commanded by General Nasu in one concerted assault, [to] drive the enemy to the beach and then annihilate them." On the 24th, as the 1st and 2nd Battalions, 124th Infantry, moved out to deploy at their appointed place, an order came through that the commander of the 230th Infantry under Col. Toshinari Shoji would relieve General Kawaguchi and assume command of the right wing. Colonel Shoji would launch the attack by the first light of the 25th. Sergeant Hara added: "The right wing, in order to be able to make our approach to the enemy's left rear, turned off the mountain trail and pushed on to the headwaters of the Ilu River and then waded down the river to arrive at the appointed place."[34]

An unknown diarist from the 4th Infantry Regiment would write: "The general attack is to be made on the 24th. The 2d Battalion of our 4th Infantry Regiment [under Maj. Masuro Tamura] is to defend the coast; the 3d Battalion [under Capt. Morie Sasaki] and the Oka Regiment [124th Infantry] are to attack the airfield located on the right bank of the Matanikau River. The 29th Infantry is to attack on the rear flank of the airfield. The 230th Infantry [under Col. Toshinaro Shoji] will participate in the capture of the airfield. The 16th Infantry [under Col. Toshiro Hiroyasu] will be in the reserve for the division."[35]

Sergeant Major Taneka of the 29th Infantry surveyed the American lines and reported: "The enemy munitions assembly point and storehouses are located in the various [sites] along the shore extending from ... 1.5 K to 3 K in the river mouth on the right side of the Lunga River. There seems to be an enemy munitions assembly area in the vicinity of the Nakagawa [Ilu] River and the enemy defense equipment in the grassy plateau [Bloody Ridge]."[36]

The initial Japanese offensive action was an early mistake that occurred in the Matanikau River section named "Hell's Gate" by the marines. Due to a communication muddle, elements of the 4th Infantry and the 1st Independent Tank Company had not received word of a change in the plans and therefore began their action a day early, on the 23rd. At 1440 that day, the attack had been rescheduled to 1700 on the 24th, but the message took four hours to reach the tank unit, which already had begun its move.[37]

Capt. Sumuto Meada's tanks on the 23rd were supported by the troops of Maj. Masuro Tamura's 2nd Battalion, 4th Infantry. Meada's company included 104 men in four platoons, including the Command Platoon with one Type 95 Ha-Go light tank; the 1st Platoon with three Type 97 Chi-Ha tanks; the 2nd Platoon with three Type 97 tanks; Meada's own 3rd Platoon with three Type 97 tanks; and one maintenance vehicle. The scheme was to hit the marines with the initial wave on the right led by 1st Lt. Tetsuji Ishibashi's 7th Company, 4th Infantry, and on the left by 1st Lt. Yoshimi Onodera's 5th Company, while 1st Lt. Junichiro Kurnoki's 6th Company was held in reserve. The 2nd Machine-Gun Company under 2nd Lt. Chikanosuke Sato set up its guns on the west bank and prepared to support the assault.

At 1700, 23 October, the tanks began their run. Major Tamura's 2nd Battalion, 4th Infantry, approached the west bank of the Matanikau River; this sector was vital to the success of the attack, as it was the only point where tanks could cross and then head directly for the airfield. The problem, however, was the obstacle of the sandbar and the defenses on the other side of the river. The infantry was to engage the Americans and break through in cooperation with the 2nd Division's frontal assault on the airfield, but when the coast force had jumped off too soon, it had signaled that an attack was under way—a costly mistake. In addition, the tanks were slow in their breakout because they had to maneuver around a litter of Japanese that had been killed earlier.[38] Captain Meada had planned to attack using all his tanks in a direct assault on the marine lines, but his own was having engine trouble and had to be left on

Figure 35. Japanese tanks caught on the sandbar at the Matanikau River, Guadalcanal. (National Archives)

the coast route; he was forced to join 2nd Lt. Hiroyasu Yamaji in the #1 tank, 3rd Platoon.

At dusk on the 23rd, the marines were quickly alerted by heavy blasting of weapons as nine tanks, supported by the 6th and 7th Companies, 4th Infantry, burst out of the jungle on the west bank. What was anticipated as a battle-winning lightning strike quickly turned into a disaster. Meada's tank commanders used an action that had been successful in China. Three tanks began firing their short-barreled 57-mm guns at the other side, hoping the Americans would return the fire and expose their positions. However, the marines had become combat-wise and did not respond. When the nine noisy "iron-monsters" appeared out of the west jungles in an attempt to smash a passage across the sandbar, the tracers from the marine gunners set the brush on fire so that the tanks were fully silhouetted and became choice targets. The tanks in the lead, which were followed by Lieutenant Itabashi's 7th Company, took heavy casualties as they crossed the sandbar and were stopped cold. Bodies were floating everywhere.

Facing the Japanese was a fire base of 81-mm mortars of the 3rd Battalion, 1st Marines, and 3rd Battalion, 7th Marines, with their regimental 75-mm antitank guns mounted on half-tracks. They were backed by artillery of the 11th Marines, which had zeroed in between the Matanikau River and Point Cruz. The 75-mm half-tracks were dug in the center of the sandlot, behind the emplaced 37-mm anti-tank guns of the 1st Battery, 1st Special Weapons Battalion. The 11th Marines pounded the area; they had a combination of ten 75- and 105-mm guns set up to concentrate on Kukum on the coastal trail, just where the tanks and troops had gathered, and they immediately began firing. In a series of barrages encompassing a 600- to 800-yard-wide boxed-in area between the Matanikau River and Point Cruz, the marines on the east side of the Matanikau attacked the oncoming troops with every weapon they had.

The loose sand hampered movement and the support infantry—two companies of the 4th Infantry—took a beating as they fought to cross the sandbar. Sgt. Shohei Haga (II/4i) remembered: "Others who were in the front line, undeterred, hurtled over the dead and penetrated."[39] In the run, the first tank was that of the 2nd Platoon leader, 1st Lt. Tsukasa Ikeda; it was disabled when PFC Joseph D. R. Champagne of Company M, 1st Battalion, 1st Marines, slipped a grenade in the tracks. Its engine was still running and as the tank backed away from the barrier, the half-track of 2nd Lt. Thomas C. Mather opened fire at point-blank range. Lieutenant Ikeda's tank slid sideward twenty yards into the sea.[40] Ikeda and his gunner, Sgt. Nagayoshi Miyashoita, were killed, though two others escaped. Tank #2 (Sgt Kuniharu Yamada) and tank #3 (Sgt. C. Hara), both of the 2nd Platoon, were halted by the sand and were wrecked by gunfire. Two were killed and two saved in each tank. Meanwhile, as Japanese infantrymen attempted to take the lead, they jumped over the dead by twos and threes and continued the advance. But the marines held fast, and some of the Sun Soldiers, seeing the battle going badly, became disheartened and confused.[41]

1st Lt. Sanae Harada's tank was the fourth knocked out. Initially Harada was unable to leave the vehicle because of the heavy fire; he could hear the bullets bouncing off the armor plate. When the barrage abated he managed to escape while the tank burned.[42] The fifth *Chi-Ha*—#2 Tank, 1st Platoon—commanded by Sgt. Seizou Watanbe toppled into the river killing two, though two escaped. The sixth tank, #3 of the 1st Platoon, took a direct hit that killed the commander, MSgt. Minoru Tanaka, and three others. The next tank, #1 of the 3rd Platoon, led by 2nd Lt. Hiroyasu Yamaji with Captain Meada, was stopped by a direct shot before it entered the river; only Sgt. Y. Nishimoto escaped. The tank with Sgt. Mitsuo Koshikawa was next, and as it began to cross the river it took a direct hit; Mitsuo was killed, but the driver and gunner escaped. The last tank adjacent to the river, #2 of the Command Platoon, driven by Cpl. Atsuj Ishii, was damaged by shellfire from the 11th Marines, as was Captain Meada's tank that had been stalled on the coast route. The #3 tank, 3rd Platoon, that was damaged earlier was also crushed.

Thirty tankers were killed in the skirmish.[43] The marines had wreaked havoc on men and machines, and the remnants were forced to return up the coast route.[44] The Japanese assault had been halted so suddenly that the few surviving infantrymen withdrew. About midnight, however, the 4th Infantry made another attempt to charge across the river farther upstream, but that effort also was blunted. When the attack was over, the 1st Marines listed twenty-five killed and fourteen wounded; they estimated the Japanese losses at six hundred.

Japanese artillery continued its intermittent fire during the day on 24 October, and during the afternoon two incidents forbode a serious situation for the Americans. The 3rd Battalion, 7th Marines, which was holding the southeast line of the forward position of the Matanikau sector along Hill 67, observed an enemy unit moving eastward over the Mount Austen foothills, some 1,000 yards to the south. It was an area the 7th Marines had traveled a month earlier. Apparently the Japanese had crossed the upper Matanikau hoping to outflank that forward position. The 11th Marines' artillery immediately directed fire to the area, and the Cactus Air Force lifted off to strike. The enemy column evaporated within the jungle, however, and the bombing and strafing were ineffective.

The enemy was not to be deterred, for not long afterward in a second incident at 2200 on the 24th the fireworks started again when the Japanese attacked the southwest flank of Bloody Ridge. They were met by an effective response from the 1st and 5th Battalions, 11th Marines, who fired in support of the threatened 7th Marines, while the 3rd Battalion, 11th Marines, fired in support of the 164th Infantry Regiment.

Col. Akinosuka Oka's force of General Kawaguchi's wing was to hit the airfield from the right bank of the Lunga River and move to the southwest side of Mount Austen: the 124th Infantry less the 3rd Battalion; the 3rd Battalion, 4th Infantry; half of the 4th Infantry gun unit under Capt. Kunio Sato; one squad of a mobile radio unit also from the 4th Infantry; the 10th Independent Mountain Artillery Regiment, less one platoon, under Lt. Col. Masaji Kitayama; the 4th Company under 1st Lt. Katsuyoshi Tokuyama; the 5th Company under 1st Lt. Torasaburo Kato; and the 6th Company under Capt. Masatoshi Oka. The 1st Battalion, 124th Infantry Regiment, was the spearhead of Colonel Oka's force, with the 3rd Battalion, 124th Infantry (less the 10th Company), in the second line.

The 164th Infantry's position on Bloody Ridge was turned over to Chesty Puller's 1st Battalion, 7th Marines, which was ordered to the Matanikau to relieve the 3rd Battalion, 1st Marines. Jon Hoffman writes:

> On October 20, the 1/7 moved back into the lines, reassuming responsibility for the left half of the 7th Marines sector, while 2/7 (Lt. Col. Herman H. Hanneken) contracted into the right half. The men went to work again improving their defenses, which Puller considered only 30 percent complete. Despite his low estimate, it was a formidable position. In addition to fire lanes, barbed wire, bunkers and fighting holes, both battalions [were] generously equipped with heavy weapons. Each had a normal complement of mortars (six 60-mm and four 81-mm) and .30-caliber machine guns (24 heavy and six light). Infantry battalions also rated a pair of 50-caliber machine guns. The regiment had three anti-air, anti-tank guns and four 37-mm anti-tank guns.[45]

Following the tank attack of the 23rd and the observation of the enemy movements the next afternoon, the 2nd Battalion, 7th Marines, moved into position to cover the break between the Matanikau sector and the Lunga perimeter, with the 3rd Battalion, 7th Marines, and Edson's 5th Marines in the Lunga perimeter. The discovery of the Japanese 124th Infantry adjacent to the Matanikau sector was followed by the report of a second force, indicating that a two-pronged attack might be in progress. The leathernecks of Puller's battalion, now spread thin over an extended front, awaited the attack. The 3rd Battalion, 2nd Marines, the division reserve, bivouacked north of the airstrip.

The Drive Grinds On

By noon on the 24th elements of the 35th Brigade had crossed the Lunga River and were positioned in the dense jungle east of the river and south of Edson's Ridge. On the left center were Col. Shojiro Komiya's 29th Infantry less the 2nd Battalion and Capt. Satoru Suzuki's 7th Company, along with elements of the 124th Infantry, as well as the 3rd Company, 1st Battalion, 2nd Engineer Regiment, under 1st Lt. Goro Ichijo, and part of the 6th Independent Rapid-Fire Gun Battalion, 1st Company, under Capt. Kazuo Kitayama, equipped with 20-mm antitank weapons. Elements of the Shoji Butai prepared to attack to the east; their heaviest weapons were machine guns as most of the artillery pieces and the Type 97 81-mm and Type 98 heavy mortars had been abandoned along the trail—a lack of firepower that certainly placed the Japanese at a disadvantage.

The marine line rifle companies were supported by their heavy weapons and artillery as well as the weapons of the 164th's Company M, one heavy machine-gun section of its Company H, and its 37-mm antitank guns—an array of machine guns lined up bumper to bumper. The 164th was spread out on a 1,000-yard front with the four canister-firing 37-mm antitank guns it had borrowed from the 7th Marines. These weapons were influential in a close encounter, as they would cover heights as tall as a boxcar, and a good gun loader could pack twenty canister shells per minute. Events unfolded quickly that afternoon. Cpl. George C. MacGillivray of the 1/7 weapons company had manned gun #1 of the 37-mm antitank weapons. He recalled: ". . . In front of my position on the Ridge, a mass of infantrymen were attempting to bust through the barbed wire, just at a wired gate, when I let go a canister shot of rusty nails and spent shells, killing the lot. One enemy soldier was later identified as Sergeant Yomishito, with the 29th Infantry. The other three 37s of Weapons 1/7 also blazed away, mowing down the oncoming Japanese. That night, H/2/7 fired more than one thousand 81-mm mortar rounds, which helped paralyze the rush."[46]

Capt. Juro Katsumata, commander of the 11th Company, 29th Infantry, was part of the 2nd Division attack. His notes of the event support many of the previously documented details of the Japanese advance and assault, but add his own experience to the mix. His observations provide a narrative that begins with the night of 12 October when the destroyer *Shirayuki* had closed in toward Guadalcanal's northwest coast near Tassafaronga, landing 140 men of his 11th Company, 29th Infantry Regiment. According to Captain Katsumata, the company was immediately assigned to guard duties on Hill 96, one mile west of Point Cruz. Although the hill was only five miles from where the company had disembarked, the men traveled three days to reach it, as they were constantly machine-gunned and bombed by American planes and they could move only by night. From Hill 96, Captain Katsumata's company guarded the sea flank of the Maruyama Trail that had been cut through the thirty-five miles of jungle by General Maruyama's engineers as part of his planned attack against Henderson Field from the south.

On 16 October, Katsumata's men joined the main force of General Maruyama's 2nd Division and set off along the trail on their way to the planned airfield assault. They found the first day's march to be relatively effortless as they passed through coconut groves along the coast, then over a range of hills inland. On the second day, however, they entered dense, hilly forest land and Katsumata noted how the trail had become so narrow that they had to travel single file. They soon approached a series of steep hills slippery from the rain and covered in thick undergrowth. Katsumata wrote that progress was slow in the hot, humid jungle, and the hills were so steep that ropes, blocks, and tackles had to be used to haul the 70-mm cannon up the inclines. By the third day, he adds, the men were slowing even more, becoming exhausted, and Captain Katsumata notes that he sent his NCO along the line to lash the men with canes in a desperate attempt to drive them forward.

Katsumata details that General Maruyama realized that the column was getting behind schedule and thus sent a message to General Sumiyoshi at the Matanikau River to postpone the planned combined attack on the airfield by twenty-four hours. He put the men on half rations, as their advance was taking longer than expected and their supplies potentially inadequate. On the fourth day, Katsumata notes, the men hauling the guns simply abandoned them along with other heavy equipment. Machine guns, mortars, and boxes of ammunition began to litter the trail as the men sought to rid themselves of everything except their most essential equipment. Heavy rain slowed their progress even more as they slipped on the muddy steep hills and the sides of ravines. After five days Captain Katsumata's 11th Company had covered only twenty-six miles, and again General Maruyama was forced to postpone the planned assault.

On the afternoon of 24 October, Katsumata describes the 2nd Division finally reaching a position two miles south of Henderson Field. The 9th Company under Lt. Yukio Makita was then sent forward to probe the American defenses, and Captain Katsumata's 11th Company was ordered to follow Makita's 9th Tai and support it. The 11th and 9th Companies set off at 1500 in heavy rain through the thick jungle toward the airfield. By nightfall they had made limited progress and had seen nothing of the American forces. The darkness settled in so completely that it was difficult to see the man in front, and Captain Katsumata writes that he and his men lost contact with the 9th Company. At that point he ordered his troops to place their hands on the shoulders of the man in front, and in this manner they pushed on. At 2100 they found an American telephone line, which they cut; however, having realized this might alert the Americans, Katsumata ordered his men to search along the line and eliminate any American listening post they found.

As Katsumata's men traveled down the cable, a voice from the jungle called his name. It was Lieutenant Makita, from whom they had been separated earlier. He and ten of his men had been moving back when they heard Katsumata's troops. Makita told Katsumata that after being separated from Katsumata's company he and his men had proceeded forward until they came to a field with a line of barbed wire across it. Lieutenant Nakagome of the 2nd Platoon had wanted to lead a patrol through the field, but Makita denied the request, as it might draw the attention of the Americans and subvert the regiment's attack later.

At that point, Katsumata states, he and Lieutenant Makita took their men back to the field, and Katsumata sent a squad to the right to reconnoiter. Across the field he could see what appeared to be a line of empty trenches; as he was discussing the situation with Lieutenant Makita a sudden burst of machine-gun fire came from their right, toward the squad he had sent out. As the men hurried back, a second machine gun opened fire from the left. Katsumata writes that he hid at the edge of the jungle watching the colored tracers stream across the night. He realized that the two guns would have to be destroyed before he could move across the field, and thus he sent back a request for a squad of engineers with dynamite to come forward. To his dismay, he learned that the dynamite had been dumped on the Maruyama Trail earlier by the exhausted engineers. Katsumata then gave orders for a machine gun to be set up to counter the American guns while his men advanced across the field

As Katsumata was talking to his NCOs, Maj. Eiji Mizuno arrived, the 2nd Battalion commander of the Ichiki Detachment; he had been drawn by the firing. Major Mizuno disagreed with Captain Katsumata's plan for taking out the American machine guns and instead ordered him to send one squad to the right to destroy the gun there while Katsumata led the rest of his men across the field, then turned left to take the other weapon from behind. At this point Captain Katsumata's notes indicate that he realized his men were wet, tired, and hungry, and also probably apprehensive and frightened at the thought of their first attack against the Americans. He was concerned that some of them would panic or get lost in a night attack, and thus he would follow the major's order and lead them across the field in a short rush, keeping them together. After he sent the squad to the right, he took the rest of his men to the edge of the field and passed his instructions to the NCOs. Katsumata states that the rain had stopped by then; the clouds were beginning to break up, and the moon shone through occasionally. Across the field he could see a large tree and told his men that it would be their initial objective, after which they would swing to the left as Major Kuramoto had ordered.

The men ran forward in a rush for thirty yards, then hit the ground. The Americans were still firing intermittently, but the tracers were passing over their heads. Captain Katsumata had been lying prone and could not see the tree, but after a word to an NCO he crawled forward twenty yards until it was within his vision. Kasumata notes that as he turned to go back to his men he was horrified to see them all suddenly get up, start shouting, and charge over to the left. He quickly ran after them, calling for them to lie down and be quiet. But it was too late. The American machine guns lowered their fire and the men in one section were cut to pieces. Dozens fell with bullet wounds in their chest, waist, or legs. In addition, they had run into a minefield, and a line of explosions erupted among them, flinging men into the air. From the light of the explosions the rest of Katsumata's men could be plainly seen, and the American fire instantly shifted to them.

Within moments, Katsumata states, he caught up with his men and ordered them to lie down. From the darkness nearby, a soldier shouted that he had found some barbed wire. The captain realized that they could not stay there with fire from both flanks and barbed wire ahead, and thus he crawled forward to the wire, then worked his way along it until he came upon a part that was only two feet high. He called to his men that the wire at that point was low enough for them to jump over it.

When Katsumata stood up to go over the wire two bullets immediately hit him. One grazed his right cheekbone, tore his helmet strap, then took off his right ear lobe. The second grazed his right knee. He hardly felt either projectile as he jumped over the barbed lines, running forward some twenty yards before falling to the ground. Above the din of the continual firing and the screaming of the wounded, Katsumata states he called repeatedly to his men to join him. A short time later from out of the black of the night 1st Lt. Kanichiro Shirai of Headquarters Company and two others appeared. The firing stopped and Katsumata sent Lieutenant Shirai back to the wire to bring the rest of the men forward. Katsumata writes that after several minutes Shirai returned alone; he had found no one alive.

Not long after that Captain Katsumata stated he could hear the rustling of grass about fifty yards to his left. He thought it might be the 9th Company, which Kurimo had ordered to support him, then suddenly he heard the voice of 2nd Lieutenant Kimio Nakagome shouting *"Kogeki! Kogeki!"*—"Attack! Attack!"—and the rush of men toward the wire. Katsumata instantly called a warning to them, but at that moment the American machine-gun fire broke out again from both sides. The agonized screams of the wounded filled the night air, yet above it all Katsumata could hear Nakagome still urging his men forward.

The American attack increased in intensity and a third machine gun directly ahead of Katsumata began firing. Nakagome's men seemed to have reached the wire as again Captain Katsumata heard "*Kogeki! Kogeki!*"—and then a piercing scream of pain, after which he heard Lieutenant Nakagome no more. The firing continued for several minutes. The cries of the wounded and moans from near the barbed wire were everywhere, but eventually they faded and Katsumata was almost overwhelmed by the silence. He notes that as the moon broke through the clouds, he looked at his watch and could see the hands near midnight, only thirty minutes since he had led his men into the field.

Then the shelling started. Most of the barrage landed in the jungle on the other side of the field. Unknown to Katsumata at the time, the shelling broke up Japanese forces moving toward his position. A shell-burst nearby tore off the top of a tree, sending it crashing to the ground only ten yards from Katsumata's small group. Sensing potential shelter, the men crawled toward the huge tree and hid beneath it. A short time later a shell hit near the barbed wire and shrapnel whipped through the air, hitting the captain in the right ankle, Lt. Seiaichi Shirai in the left leg, and one of the soldiers in the hip. A few minutes later more shrapnel tore into the chest of the second soldier, who died within minutes. Throughout that night, Katsumata states, the three survivors huddled close to the ground as the shelling continued.

Captain Katsumata hoped that his comrades' successive attacks would sweep toward his position, but as the night wore on the charges became fewer and weaker and he realized that if they stayed there, they would be shot by the Americans as soon as the dawn broke. He decided to go back across the field and look for the squad he had sent toward the right. Lieutenant Shirai thought it would be impossible to get back and that they simply should commit suicide before the Americans found them. As Shirai raised his pistol, Katsumata tells that he had put his hand on Shirai's shoulder and told him they could do that at any time, but they had to try to make another attack before dawn.

Machine-gun fire was still occasionally kicking up the dirt nearby the men, but after watching for a clear run Katsumata dashed to the wire. When he reached it he found four or five of his men dead, hanging over it. He climbed across and in short dashes made his way back through the field, once stumbling and falling, then discovering he had tripped over the feet of a dead soldier. Looking around, he saw a group of almost fifty other dead nearby. Just before dawn, Katsumata notes, he reached the edge of the jungle, then turned off to the right, stopping at intervals and shouting, "This is Katsumata! Gather here . . . we will attack again!"

In about an hour Katsumata had assembled about fifteen survivors. As they stood together, he heard Japanese voices coming toward him through the dense growth. Leaving his men he moved toward the sound and saw Col. Shojiro Komiya with about twenty men, including Lt. Col. Katsutoshi Watanabe, commander of the 2nd Battalion, 29th Infantry. Colonel Komiya informed Katsumata that he was preparing for another attack, but Katsumata told the colonel what had happened the previous night and suggested he get some machine-gun support. Komiya agreed and sent back for a machine-gun detachment while Captain Katsumata went to gather his fifteen men to join in Colonel Komiya's attack. Records show that at 1700 Colonel Watanabe enlisted the help of 1st Lt. Kozaburo Miyazawa, commanding officer of the 2nd Machine-Gun Company, 2nd Battalion, 29th Infantry, and they subsequently attacked the center of Bloody Ridge.

Meanwhile, Captain Katsumata's notes show, he found that his fifteen men had scattered; only one remained at the place where he had left them. He sent this man to locate the others, and eventually most were gathered again and joined up with Komiya's group. Katsumata then discovered that most of the others already had left for the attack mission, except for Colonel Watanabe who remained with about fifty of his own men. While the captain and the colonel were discussing the situation a sudden shout announced that the Americans were coming. They all scattered to take up defensive positions, and Katsumata states he found himself with about twenty men and a light machine gun. They ran to the top of a small hill, but despite the sound of frequent shooting they saw no enemy troops.

After an hour had passed, a runner arrived with a message telling Captain Katsumata to report to brigade headquarters, some 1,000 yards to the rear. When he arrived, he was surprised to find that no one seemed to know what had happened during the night, nor did they have any knowledge of Colonel Komiya's attack that morning. He concluded that the American shelling probably had destroyed the telephone lines.[47]

A less graphic version of the fierce encounter was presented by 1st Lt. Kozaburo Miyazawa, commander of the 2nd Machine Gun Company, 29th Infantry, who wrote on 20 October: "It was planned to carry out the general attack, but because of the inaccuracy of the maps and unknown terrain, the progress of road construction by the engineers, and the advance of the units, especially the heavy weapons unit, was very slow. Therefore, the general attack was unavoidably postponed to the 22nd, 23rd, 24th, and 25th. . . ." On 25 October Miyazawa noted: ". . . At 1700 it was planned to enter the enemy's positions together, but because of imperfect communications with the 29th Infantry Regiment, that one regiment did not move to the point of the general attack [and the thrust] . . . was completely lost."[48]

The POW interrogation of Sup. Pvt. Yabuchi Ichiji, 6th Company, 2nd Battalion, 29th Infantry Regiment, also offered a brief view of the events: "Immediately after landing his unit joined the rest of the regiment and they marched through the jungle to the southeast of the airport. The regiment at that time was estimated to be about 2,000 men. They entered the battle with the 16th Regiment on their right and the 4th Regiment to the west of the airfield. In the resulting night attack Ichiji stated that they lost 800 men. Regimental Commander Colonel Komiya and the commanding officer of the 2nd Battalion, Lieutenant Colonel Watanabe, were also killed in this battle. The remainder of the unit the retired to the beach area in the vicinity of Mamara."[49]

PFC Masao Nakagawa, 2nd Platoon, 1st Company, 3rd Independent Trench Mortar Battalion, would report that the men of his company of twelve guns were capable of firing thirty rounds per minute. The 29th Regiment was advancing with the 3rd Battalion under Maj. Tadao Yoshi in the lead and the 1st Battalion under Capt. Kohei Nakajima on the right, but due to darkness they could not make contact with each other. The 2nd Battalion under Lt. Col. Katsutoshi Watanabe was to be the reserve, but it followed directly behind the 1st Battalion. Nakagawa states:

> I learned during the night of the problems of the vanguard units which intended to join the battle but the enemy had concentrated its fire on the road and by dawn only a few members were able to join the attack.
>
> The 3rd Battalion plowed ahead. Even though it was night the enemy had good fire zones. Major Yoshi with strong determination strove to break through and each company, in accordance with its orders, began the assault, but because of the heavy concentration of machine gun and mortar fire the break[-]through was impossible. The battalion was having great difficulty and made no progress but one party [got] through. By dawn the [enemy] fire became more intense and as a result the 3rd Battalion [29th Infantry] was practically annihilated.[50]

The Battered Enemy

The Americans watched the assaulting forces drift away. The Seventeenth Army was withdrawing its tattered units to regroup and prepare for another strike. At dawn on 25 October the 3rd Battalion, 2nd Marines, was fed into the lines of the 7th Marines east of Lunga covering the south slopes of Bloody Ridge. The 164th Infantry Regiment assumed command of the sector in a draw between the marines' left flank and the right flank of the 2nd Battalion, 164th Infantry. The doggies of the 3rd Battalion, 164th, were prepared to defend its area with four rifle companies: L on the left, K in the center, and I on the right. Company E of the 164th reinforced Company A, 1st Battalion, 7th Marines. The 164th's 60-mm mortars were set behind the lines in order to place precise fire in front of the barbed wire; the 81-mm mortars were set behind the 60s, to hit the edge of the jungle that was beyond the range of the short shells. The 2nd and 3rd Battalions, 164th Infantry, were covered by four 37-mm guns where the two joined at a narrow trail leading north to the Lunga road. The 164th reserves—consisting of 175 men of the service and antitank companies—and the 5th Marines, to the west in sector five, moved southwestward to join with the left border of the 2nd Battalion, 7th Marines.

In the murky night of the 25th the troops of the Seventeenth Army struck in the same fragmentary manner as on the previous night, though this time the 16th Infantry, which had been behind the 29th Infantry the evening before, was the spearhead. The 29th had lost most of its muscle the day before, yet it was willing to fight on. Both regiments attacked along the entire front, supported by machine-gun fire; clusters of two hundred to three hundred Japanese hit the perimeter. Colonel Oka's force, which had been observed crossing the foothills of Mount Austen the day before, during the night hours of the 25th–26th struck north at the diminished line of the 2nd Battalion, 7th Marines, east of Hill 67 (Saru) on the east bank of the Matanikau. The Japanese managed to breach the marine line at one position and were fighting desperately at close quarters, but before they could organize they stumbled around in the darkness and a marine counterattack forced them off the knoll.

The 2nd Battalion, 7th Marines, led by Lt. Col. Herman H. Hanneken ("Horrible Harry") meanwhile was in a bitter firefight near the coast, just east of the Matanikau River.[51] At 0230 on the 26th, his battalion was attacked by a mixed force comprised of the 1st Battalion under Maj. Eiji Sekiya and the 3rd Battalion under Maj. Yasuhei Oneda, 230th

Infantry; the 3rd Company under 1st Lieutenant Yokoi, 3rd Independent Trench Mortar Battalion under Lt. Col. Yoshihatsu Onikzuka; plus the machine guns of the 9th Independent Rapid-Fire Gun Battalion led by Lt. Col. Jiukichi Yamamoto. The 2/7 weapons company under Capt. Louis Ditta held back firing its 60-mm mortars until the enemy was thirty yards beyond Hanneken's lines. The first wave of the Japanese was stopped cold, but others plowed ahead. The marines knew that anyone in front of them was the enemy and when Colonel Shoji's infantrymen reached the top of Bloody Ridge they were in a series of life and death struggles with the men of the 2nd Battalion, 7th Marines. The enemy pressure was relentless. Marines prefer to kill at a distance — 400, 200, 100 yards at tops; man-to-man is not the preferred choice. The night of the 26th was one of terror.

Remembering the ferocity of the battle, Sgt. Harry Wiens, 3rd Battalion, I Company, 164th Infantry, wrote in admiration of the supporting marine artillery: "The thirty-seven mm canister rounds were at first most bizarre. We had never seen any weapons flare out that way, and weren't sure. . . . Then the welcome blasts. . . . Our Marine artillery was magnificent. They laid their rounds just forward of our wire, and tore the Japs to bits. . . . It was an interminably long night. . . . K and L Companies were still in the path of the major charge [and] they disseminated them. . . . Come dawn the Japs pulled back. . . . Then all too quickly the night was upon us. . . . It was long, endless, unconscionably so. . . . [A total of] 1749 enemy bodies were buried in front of our 3rd Battalion sector alone."[52]

Typical of the courageous battling on Bloody Ridge — now also dubbed "Hanneken's Ridge" — is the story of twenty-four-year-old Plat. Sgt. Mitchell Paige, a six-year veteran and former China marine. The section chief would receive a Medal of Honor for his actions at Bloody Ridge on 26 October. His machine guns, with their timing cams modified to double the fire, were set up bordering the edge of the jungle that neared the ridge. When the enemy broke through, Paige and his machine-gun crew of thirty-six was the only force standing between a wall of Japanese and their plan to shove the marines into the sea. He directed the fire until all of his men had been killed or wounded; then he single-handedly manned the first gun until it was put out of action by a burst from a Japanese weapon that shattered the firing mechanism. When it was destroyed, he took over another gun, then continued moving from weapon to weapon. Two men were hit while they were bringing up ammunition. It had been a hectic night filled with brutal no-quarter encounters. When a new enemy force broke through at one stage, he picked up a forty-pound belt of ammunition, laced it around his shoulder, cradled the .30-caliber weapon in his arms, and headed for the oncoming Japanese, firing with fearless determination as he ran back and forth. The enemy must have thought a whole company was up there. The soldiers of Japan had run into a steel wall.

By the next morning Sergeant Paige was tired but still standing. Maj. Odell M. Conoley, the executive officer of the 2nd Battalion, 7th Marines, had collected an ad hoc force of cooks, bakers, clerks, and radiomen and joined Paige on the hill along with two platoons from Company C, 5th Marines, that were rushed to the crest.[53] In the later stages of the battle, the indomitable Paige organized and led a bayonet charge that drove off the enemy and prevented a breakthrough in the lines. The next morning approximately one thousand bodies were scattered in front of the 2/7 position. Some twenty-five hundred Japanese had attacked Paige's platoon.

Years later Mitch Paige would recall: "You know, a lot of the Japanese could speak English, and, when their assault on us began, this guy started screaming, 'Blood for the emperor! Blood for the emperor!' And [Henry] Stansberry, he was throwing hand grenades and yelling back, 'Blood for Eleanor! Blood for Eleanor!' [Eleanor Roosevelt, the wife of the president.] Bad as it was, I couldn't help but laugh."[54]

Chesty Puller had his own courageous Medal of Honor nominee, Sgt. John Basilone, a leader of two heavy machine-gun sections of Company C, 1st Battalion, 7th Marines. By 0330 on 26 October Cpl. Brandon A. Nadeau had spread the word: "They're coming!" He would be killed in the attack. The 1st Battalion, 7th Marines, reported that they were hit by six major assaults on their lines. When a pair of guns were disabled, Basilone had brought up replacements for the surviving crew members, repairing the other one, then operating it himself until help arrived. In the middle of the attacks, he had moved along the line doling out fresh belts of ammunition.[55] Much of the time he was exposed to the fury of the Japanese fire.[56]

On the 25th–26th the Sun Soldiers had carried out a bold attack against the seam between two battalions of the 164th Infantry where the trail led northward. The infantry repeatedly pushed in toward the trail, but they were driven off or killed by canister blasts from the 37-mm guns and by weapons fire from the 164th Infantry's 2nd and 3rd Battalions. An estimated 250 enemy were killed in their attempt to take the trail that dark night. The 164th reserves were on the alert, should the

Japanese manage to break through, but the lines held. The assault forces pressed ahead with reckless courage until daylight; but each was beaten back; their piecemeal attacks had no staying power.

On the 26th, the bulk of the battered Japanese forces withdrew to assess the damage. Lieutenant Miyazawa noted in his diary that Japanese losses in the attempt to take the Mukade Gata were 350 killed, 500 wounded, and 200 missing. The field hospital set up behind Mount Austen reported handling 1,600 wounded after the attack.[57] Twenty-three-year-old Pvt. Kamekichi Kusano of the 7th Company, 2nd Battalion, 29th Regiment, would write: "The 29th attacked the first day and was led into a trap and the majority of the regiment was killed. The dead were pilled three and four deep. Only two or three hundred survived the attack. The next day the 16th and the 124th Regiments attacked. The 16th led and suffered greater losses that the 124th."[58] The POW interrogation report for Pvt. Morimitsu Kikurri, 10th Company, 3rd Battalion, 16th Regiment, states: "They took their Regimental Artillery and Rapid Fire Company along with them. On 24 October they joined the remnants of the Oka Unit [124th] in the attack on the airfield from the vicinity of Mount Austen. . . . The POW [Kikurri] was sick at the time and did not go but understood the 16th bore most the blunt of the attack as they were fresh troops. They were badly defeated and only about 100 uninjured men returned."[59]

John E. Stannard, a sergeant with Company E, 3rd Battalion, 164th Infantry Regiment (Americal Division), would write: "The carnage of the battlefield was a sight that perhaps only the combat infantryman, who has fought at close quarters, could fully comprehend and look upon without a feeling of horror. One soldier of Company E, after a walk among the Japanese dead, said to his comrade: 'My God, what a sight. There's dead Japs stretched from the Corner [Coffin Corner] back along the edge of the jungle for a half a mile. There must be hundreds of them—all dead.'"[60] General Nasu, the highest-ranking officer, was mortally wounded in the battle by shell fragments and died six hours later.[61] Another diarist wrote: "26 Oct 42. Last night the night attack of the 3rd Bn [124th Infantry] did not progress as we wished. They say that [the] Oka Unit did not attack the enemy upon order, and he (Oka) left his unit and stayed at a point 2 kilometers east of the narrow [*Ippowbashi*] bridge. It seems the commander does not know what to do with him."[62]

The unsuccessful night attacks of 25–26 October marked the end of the ground phase of the October Guadalcanal counteroffensive. The headquarters of the Japanese 2nd Division was devastated, and the command center for the Seventeenth Army began pondering the sobering reality that driving the Americans off the island might be an objective whose cost the army could not afford.[63]

While the Japanese were landing troops and supplies at their end of Guadalcanal from the destroyers *Shigure* and *Ariake,* the marines were receiving reinforcements. The 1st Depot Company at Nouméa had managed to transfer a group of "greenhorn" marines, fresh from boot camp, into the form of the 2nd Replacement Battalion. They were most welcome and soon would be on the line. The old timers—the men who had been on the island since 7 August—would have to teach those "boots" how to survive.

On 29 October the Seventeenth Army's haggard and disorganized troops continued their retreat westward along the Maruyama Trail to Kokumbona, while the Shoji Butai worked its way east to *Kori Saki* (Koli Point). Meanwhile, fresh from their victory, the 1st Marine Division began to think about striking at the Japanese to the west.

13 A River Too Far

After defeating the Japanese in their last major engagement, the 1st Marine Division was determined to disintegrate the enemy forces by attacking the command center at Kokumbona, then push westward another mile and a half to the Poha River—some eleven miles west of the perimeter. What the command did not know was that more than eleven thousand determined Japanese soldiers with a handful of their guard unit troops were in that sector. In preparation for the assault, the 1st and 2nd Battalions, 2nd Marines, had been transferred from Tulagi to Guadalcanal and the 1st Engineer Battalion (less Company B) had been ordered to construct foot bridges over the Matanikau River strong enough for tanks.

The American Push

The forces were to attack westward on the morning of 1 November in columns of regiments along a 1,500-yard front starting from the Matanikau River—the "River of Death." Col. Merritt A. Edson, commanding officer of the 5th Marines and hero of Bloody Ridge, was to head the force; he was General Vandegrift's preferred combat leader, often chosen for the difficult tasks. PFC Herm Lewis (HQ/1/2) remembered Edson's blunt remarks to the troops just prior to the drive on Kokumbona. "If you don't get killed or wounded on this one," Edson told them, "I'll think you're [screwin'] off." Lewis thought it was "probably the only no-win injunction ever given to American troops."[1]

The lead formation in the drive on Kokumbona was to be the 5th Marines, backed by the 2nd Marines less the 3rd Battalion, plus Col. William J. Whaling's scout-snipers and the 3rd Battalion, 7th Marines. Additional support came from the 11th Marines (less two batteries); the weapons of Battery A of the army's 244th Coast Artillery (155-mm) and Battery B of the 5th Defense Battalion (155-mm); a small Coast Guard detachment from the Kukum naval base; and a handful of Martin Clemens's scouts. In support of the assault, SOPAC at Nouméa had ordered the cruisers *San Francisco* (CA 38) and *Helena* (CL 50) and the destroyers *Sterrett* (DD 407) and *Lansdowne* (DD 486) to shell the Japanese sector west of Point Cruz.

At 0200 on 1 November the jump-off patrol led by Lieutenant Babashanian of Company E, 2nd Battalion, 5th Marines, reinforced by the machine-gun unit, crossed the Matanikau River in rubber boats—Raider style; they reached the west side fifteen minutes later where they remained as a guard force for the area. At daybreak, heavy artillery preparation fire was concentrated on the far left bank while the remainder of 2/5 under XO Maj. Lewis W. Walt walked across the recently constructed foot bridge at 0630, engulfed in fog.[2] They were followed by the 1st and 3rd Battalions, 5th Marines.[3]

Behind Colonel Edson's 5th Marines, followed by the 2nd Marines, were Colonel Whaling's scout-snipers, who called themselves "Daniel Boone Scouts"; they moved along the grassy ridges to the south of the 5th Marines to protect the left flank. The heavy weapons companies of 3/1 and 2/5 under Lt. Col. William R. Williams remained in position amidst the thick jungle at the edge of the Matanikau River to cover the American forces as they crossed. When in place on the west side of the river, 2/5 was on the left and 1/5 on the right. At 0830, 1/5 ran into Lieutenant Mamiya's 2nd Company, 3rd Independent Trench Mortar Battalion. Mamiya's mortar men pounded the Americans and fatalities mounted; it was a bad omen of what lay ahead. The marines were in the prime area of the Japanese who fought to expel them. The Japanese 2nd Battalion, 4th Infantry, under Maj. Masuro Tamura, briefly blocked the American advance, taking casualties in doing so, but the Americans began attacking from both the river mouth and the beach. Elements of the Japanese 4th Infantry Regiment—remnants left from other encounters—were concentrated on the west bank of the Matanikau in the vicinity of the coconut-log bridges upstream, but the marines threw so much lead at the "Sun Devils" that they were able to contain them. Major Tamura's men sustained casualties caused by both ground assaults and Cactus Air Force air attacks, forcing the major to move back to the lines of Point Cruz (*Ku-ru-tsu*).[4]

Pockets of weakness had existed along the American lines, however, and the Japanese slipped through those gaps, causing havoc. The enemy assault was brutal, typical of that sustained by Cpl. Anthony Casamento of Company D, 1st Battalion, 5th Marines, a machine-gun section leader.

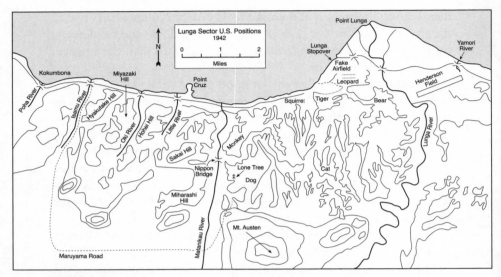

Figure 36. Based on captured Japanese map of Guadalcanal Island, November 1942.
Courtesy Mary Craddock Hoffman.

When the enemy attacked his position, his section was raked by deadly
enemy fire, though Casamento's company also exacted a toll. Nevertheless, within minutes all of Casamento's gunners either were killed or
wounded. Although the corporal was severely wounded, he had managed to knock out two enemy machine-gun emplacements, protecting
his company's flank and stalling the enemy attack.[5]

The deadly mortar fire also took a toll on the 2nd Battalion, 5th
Marines, and temporarily stymied the American advance, though it re-
sumed the next day. The Americans faced a diversified force comprising
the remnants of the Sumiyoshi Force; Lt. Tatsunosuke Takahashi's Yo-
kosuka 5th SNLF; the first three squads of WO Katsuzo Fukimoto's 2nd
Platoon, 3rd Company, Kure 3rd SNLF; members of the 84th Guard
Unit, later reinforced by the 2nd Antitank Company (2nd Infantry
Division) and the 39th Field Construction Unit; as well as the Okubo
Force, about one hundred members of the Kuma Battalion under 1st Lt.
Yoshio Okubo of the 28th Regimental Antitank Company (28th Infan-
try Regiment, 7th Infantry Division). Warrant Officer Fukimoto and
many others subsequently were killed in a skirmish on 3 November.

Col. John M. Arthur's 2nd Marine Regiment command post was set
up on the east bank of the Matanikau River; the 2nd Battalion estab-

lished a defensive position along the east bank, providing command post security. This was the Colonel's first opportunity to show leadership, as he had not seen combat before. He had spent two months in the rear area of Espiritu Santo, New Hebrides, until General Vandegrift ordered him to Guadalcanal, and thus the lesser ranks had called the colonel "Tail End Arthur"—though certainly not within earshot. Arthur later would butt heads with U.S. Army Gen. Alexander M. Patch who rebuked the colonel on his numbers that claimed an overkill of Nippon soldiers.

The 1st Battalion, 2nd Marines, moved to a defensive position on the Matanikau's west bank and in the beach area at the rear of the 5th Marines' bivouac. On 2 November, 1/2 moved again, covering a 400-yard front with the right flank on the beach. The 244th Coast Artillery Battalion opened up with their 155s on the Japanese artillery posts, the first effective counter-battery artillery available in the campaign. One cannoneer said, "If Pistol Pete can dish it out, we can serve it better." Over the course of the day, however, several men were killed by sporadic sniper fire.

Meanwhile, back at perimeter, fifty Seabees of the 6th Naval Construction Battalion had arrived on Guadalcanal—the rear echelon from the New Hebrides under Lt. (jg) Ernest K. Smith. They brought the balance of the equipment that they had been unable to ship earlier. Although ammunition, avgas, and food held a higher priority, the equipment was needed to maintain the Lunga naval operating base, which day by day was being upgraded.

The Tokyo Express—the Japanese destroyer resupply effort—continued with its mission. On the night of 2 November a convoy of five destroyers had landed troops near Tetere, east of Koli Point, members of 1st Lt. Tamotsu Shinno's 2nd Company, 230th Infantry, and 1st Lt. Yoshiaki Nagata's 6th Battery, 38th Mountain Artillery Regiment. They brought 650 bales of rice and ten bales of powdered *miso* (bean paste), which they stored in the jungle. These troops were to join Maj. Eiji Sekiya's 1st Battalion, 230th Infantry, and Maj. Ampei Onoda's 3rd Battalion, with the 9th Company commanded by Capt. Hitoshi Okada, the 10th Company led by Capt. Hikoshi Suzuki, and the 11th Company led by 1st Lt. Susumu Imai. The 9th had been ordered to the Koli Point sector to protect the debarkation and the supplies.

To the east, the 2nd Battalion, 5th Marines, had sent F and G Companies led by Capt. Harry J. Connor (now the S-3, the staff operations officer) to surround the enemy near the beach area of Point Cruz and cut the Japanese phone lines. At 0800 the next day, 3 November, E and G Companies attacked, with the marines of the weapons company as riflemen. Company F held the left flank as G advanced into the underbrush with close-in fighting; over two hundred of Tojo's soldiers were killed. 2nd Lt. Paul Moore Jr. of Company G won the Navy Cross for his assertive effort.[6]

To counter the enemy landing in the vicinity of Koli Point, General Vandegrift dispatched the 2nd Battalion, 7th Marines, under Lt. Col. Herman H. Hanneken, supported by Col. Bryant E. Moore's 164th Infantry Regiment. On the morning of 3 November, Japanese foot soldiers supported by artillery and mortar fires attacked 2/7. The battalion was forced to withdraw to the west along the coast and back across the Metapona River, then across the Nalimbiu River. A radio message requesting assistance was sent to division headquarters, which in turn asked the Cactus Air Force for help. Aircraft attacked the Koli Point sector, but unfortunately struck both American and Japanese troops, causing casualties on both sides. Because radio contact between the Koli force and headquarters failed due to the thick and damp jungle, the Koli group could not tell the command center that the aircraft were inflicting casualties on friendly troops.

The *San Francisco, Helena, Lansdowne,* and *Sterrett,* which had been supporting the drive west, were now ordered to shell Japanese pockets on Koli Point. In the bombardment of the south end of the Point, Capt. Hitoshi Okada and Capt. Fumio Dejima were killed, as well as many from Capt. Hikoshi Suzuki's 10th Company. The next morning, the 2nd and 3rd Battalions, 164th Infantry, began a march through the jungle and across the Kunai grass fields; they then proceeded to a position south of Koli Point to strengthen the marines there. Firing in support of the operation were the 1st Battalion, 10th Marines; the 1st Battalion, 11th Marines; and Battery A of the 5th Defense Battalion with their 155s left over from World War I. Meanwhile, the 1st Battalion, 7th Marines, was boated in to reinforce 2/7 at Koli Point. The plan was for the American battalions to hit the enemy force in place, while two battalions of the 164th enveloped them from the south.[7]

The Japanese 230th Infantry Regiment had placed two of its Type 97 field guns some 2,000 yards east of the Metapona River at Gavaga Creek, about one mile east of the 2nd Battalion, 7th Marines, and pounded the American positions. Meanwhile, Col. Toshinari Shoji's 230th Infantry remained in the Koli Point sector. Adding to the Americans' problems, Colonel Hanneken's 2/7 was unable to inform the division when a new enemy group had landed because the 2/7 radio had been disabled. Hanneken's marines met members of the enemy's 9th Company, 230th Infantry. By the following morning, however, elements of the 230th were anxious to exit the area and thus moved west. Hanneken's 2/7 leathernecks managed to engage the rear party, but they were hit by a blistering hail of artillery and mortar fire.

Brig. Gen. John E. Stannard, USA (Ret,), who at that time was a sergeant with Company E, 164th Infantry, later called the battle for Koli Point "the most complex land operation, other than the original landing, that the Americans had conducted on Guadalcanal up to that time." Stannard added: "Marine operations west of the Matanikau River had been as large, but they had mission bases on terrain objectives—to seize a certain location, or to clear an assigned area. At Koli Point the mission was to destroy an enemy force and this was a more complicated task. The operation was further complicated by poor communications; American forces firing on one another; and inadequate direction, control and coordination. The Americans learned once again that offensive operations against the Japanese were much more complicated and difficult than was defeating banzai charges."[8]

PhM1c Charles O. Hall of Company D, 2nd Medical Battalion, offered a corpsman's account of the push west: "The first of November, we [2nd Marines] moved up to the front crossing the Lunga River and up to the Matanikau. On November 2, we crossed the Matanikau and immediately met resistance. The battle lasted several days and we made little advance—our casualties were heavy. Early in the movement we lost three hospital corpsmen to enemy fire. In the collecting section, Bruce Bender was killed trying to rescue a wounded Marine ahead of the front line, and PhM1c Eugene Baxter was killed attempting to rescue another Marine ahead of the front lines. A sniper killed Baxter just as he was returning to the lines. Since we had no doctor, with Baxter's death, I became the senior medical NCO."[9]

Richard A. Nash, a marine with Headquarters, 1st Battalion, 2nd Marines, many years later described the events when Eugene Baxter was killed:

> Baxter, while taking over a position held by the 5th Marines[,] saw that a group of several hundred Japanese soldiers were trapped. They had the ocean at their backs and we surrounded them on the land perimeter. They had no way to escape and they would not surrender. They fought back dropping mortar fire

just yards between us and sprayed in our direction with machine gun and rifle fire. Most of us held our positions behind large logs that littered the area, but a few men were out in front with little cover. One of them was lying out there wounded and calling for a corpsman. Doc Baxter climbed over a log and ambled out to help the man, the Red Cross on his sleeve showing clearly in the morning sun. A Jap sniper shot him dead. Suddenly a jeep wheeled up towing a 37-mm anti-tank gun and Captain Andrews of D Company put a crew of men to setting the thing up to fire into the palm grove. Then I heard it—just before the gun began firing—a weird wailing and moaning, almost a religious chant . . . coming from the trapped Japanese soldiers. Then the gun fired canister shot into them, again and again, and after a while the chanting stopped and the firing stopped and for a moment it was all-quiet. Some of us went among the Lever's Brothers palm trees to look, and there, row on row, were the torn and shattered bodies of perhaps 300 young Japanese soldiers. There were no survivors.[10]

Back on 3 November the 1st Battalion, 2nd Marine, and the Whaling Scouts had continued to advance inland. Meanwhile Colonel Edson's 5th Marines successfully reduced the pocket at Point Cruz, where the Japanese paid a heavy price in casualties. The 5th Marines captured twelve 37-mm guns, one field piece, and thirty-four machine guns. In the final phase of the mop-up, they had delivered three successful attacks. After the reduction of the pocket, the 5th Marines and the Whaling Scouts were ordered back to the perimeter, and it was then that Colonel Arthur, commanding officer of the 2nd Marines, took over tactical direction of the offensive from Colonel Edson.

Cpl. James Sorensen of Company A, 1st Battalion, 2nd Marines, recalls:

Headquarters had radioed the airfield to come over and bomb and strafe . . . and break up any Jap counter concentration. The planes came all right, two of them, SBDs. They plummeted directly on us and fifty caliber slugs churned up the earth . . . while our planes strafed us. Then, as they nearly reached us, they loosened their bombs, two hundred and fifty pounds. . . . Both bombs hit dead in the center of the area where we had hurriedly dug our foxholes a few minutes before. The fighters circled out to sea and started to make another run. We feared the worst, but some guy yelled for all the skivvies, drawers, and shirts the guys had on. The idea was to get them to the ridge top to make a panel before the planes got back.... Guys all up the slopes were naked as jaybirds and the planes swooped in again and actually caught us with our pants down.... This time, all the planes did was to zoom over at tree top level. Seems the radio got hot immediately and radioed the airfield to contact the pilots to lay off the fireworks.

We later found out that we had gone beyond our objective that day and in falling back had really taken up our line on the original goal ... when we asked for plane support.... We found ourselves being bombed on our own orders.[11]

On 4 November, the American push west was officially halted, though for the men in the field the action continued. While the 2nd Marines were involved in the west, their cousin regiment, the 8th Marines, under the command of Col. Richard H. Jeschke, arrived from Apia, Samoa, with a complement of 4,010 officers and enlisted men. Although these were "fresh" troops, they soon were exhausted due to Guadalcanal's stifling heat. Within two days, on the 6th, they were in the front lines—quite a change from the dull garrison duty with the 2nd Marine Brigade on Samoa. 1st Lt. Dean Ladd of Company B, 1st Battalion, 8th Marines, wrote: "Shortly after we landed and as we observed the veterans of earlier fighting, our reaction was that they looked like men old before their time with their heavy beards with mud crusted dungarees and khakis."[12] At this juncture the 8th Marines moved south to assist the 1st Battalion, 2nd Marines, in capturing Hill 4.

The newly arrived 8th Marines began to suffer in the Guadalcanal heat, yet they continued to advance on a 600-yard front. By nightfall of 6 November 3/8 had lost touch with 2/2, but the following morning contact was renewed and the attack moved on. The 2nd Marines and the 1st Battalion, 164th Infantry Regiment, made little gains, and the 3rd Battalion, 8th Marines, was met with heavy mortar and automatic fire on its flank. By 1200, they had advanced only 400 yards. Late in the day, the 11th Marines began firing, causing confusion in the enemy lines and supporting the movement of the 2nd and 8th Marines toward Kokumbona. The attack went off as planned, with 1/164 on the right flank, 2/2 in the center, and 1/8 on the left. On the south flank 1/2 protected the sector. The troops faced mounting artillery fire and mortar fire from the 3rd Independent Trench Mortar Battalion of Lt. Col Masaji. Kitayama's 10th Independent Artillery Regiment, and from Lt. Col. Matsujiro Kaji's crack 20th Independent Mountain Artillery Battalion—all equipped with Bofors 75-mm mountain guns. The Americans progressed slowly, and each move proved costly; at 1400 orders came to halt the advance in face of the resistance. The Japanese were determined to hold the line: they wanted to protect the Maruyama Trail and the headquarters area of both the 2nd Division and the Seventeenth Army at Kokumbona. If both fell, the Japanese would be doomed.

Corporal Sorensen continues his tale: "Late on 9 November, our battalion moved up and took over the foxholes on the opposite ridge. The former occupants strung out into the jungle and hooked up with an army battalion that extended inland from the coast, and we prepared for a big drive that was to enlarge our hold of the island. A battalion of newly landed 8th Marines moved into our vacated line and was to act as a reserve unit in this push. That evening I got some mail, a post card from Al Neuman. A passage of it read, 'I wish I could be out there with you.' The next day I too wished he might have been here in my place."[13]

The leathernecks had made progress, but not without cost. The enemy had strongly defended its acreage. On 9 November orders were received from the 1st Marine Division to resume the thrust westward the following morning. On the 10th, the 3rd Battalion, 8th Marines, moved out, joining the 2nd Marines (less the 3rd Battalion) and the 1st Battalion, 164th Infantry. The 8th Marines advanced into line between 1/2 and 2/2, with 2/8 and 3/8 following, and a reconnaissance party went forward to locate a new command post. As the group passed the White River, 2½ miles west of the Matanikau, they did not see Pistol Pete's four Type 92 10-cm cannons that had been hidden after late October when he had expended all of his 798 shells. Most of the Japanese at this point were ill and low on rations. 1st Lt. Kozaburo Miyazawa of the 29th Infantry wrote in his diary:

> In these operations since landing we have been on half rations with no supplementary [portions], and with only attacking before us. The staff officers, and everyone below them[,] advanced to the attack forgetting about food. Even during the four-day lull in the battle, we only had five *shaku* [about 0.15 pint] of rice per day per man and had to escort the wounded. After that we were continuously marching and escorting the patients. Our daily ration was from seven *shaku* [0.21 pint] to one *go* [0.318 pint] of rice. Moreover, daily rains and bad roads made the officers and men extremely fatigued. On the 9th we arrived at the Matanikau

River, where the unit's supply was a little better and each man received two *go* and seven *shaku* of rice per day. However, as no salty foods were distributed, the usual sickness prevailed. The patients had chiefly intestinal trouble: beriberi, malnutrition, and dysentery problems. The cause of this illness was not seeing sunlight for days at a time, sleeping on damp ground, and the lack of proper food and medicine.[14]

At 0704 on the 10th, while moving out, assault elements of the 2nd Marines came under heavy artillery attacks, with constant mortar and machine-gun fire. Marine William J. Cannon (C/1/2) marked his eighteenth birthday while his company was in the thick of the fighting—"a hell of a way to celebrate," he recalled.[15] During the westward push, the weapons of the 11th Marines pumped 4,570 rounds of 75-mm pack howitzer, 549 rounds of 105-mm, and 212 rounds of 155-mm ammunition into the Japanese positions. The firing was so precise that not one shot fell short.[16]

Additional trouble was brewing for the Americans on the 10th when the Japanese 228th Infantry Regiment under Col. Sadashichi Doi (38th Division), fresh from Rabaul, landed at Cape Esperance then shifted to the Kokumbona sector. They shared the domain with the advanced headquarters unit, the 38th Infantry Division group, under the command of Maj. Gen. Takeo Ito. His staff of forty-eight formed the 38th Infantry group and set up offices within 200 yards of the Seventeenth Army *Ko* (command post). The sextet of destroyers that had delivered General Ito's party also embarked 206 construction workers, including Lt. Cdr. Masao Tsunomura, the engineer and architect of the Guadalcanal airstrip, and a mixed group of 142 officers and soldiers, including the rebuked General Kawaguchi.[17]

On 11 November the command post of the 8th Marines received an order by messenger: "Withdraw immediately and occupy defensive positions on the east bank of the Matanikau River extending 4000 yards inland. 2nd Marines will cover the withdrawal then move to assembly area east of the Matanikau River in Division Reserve. Brigadier General Sebree, USA the Assistant Division Commander (ADC) of the Americal Division assumed command of the Matanikau Sector."[18] The next day, 12 November, combat patrols of the 2nd Marines engaged 1st Lt. Isamiu Ito—the new commanding officer of the 9th Company, 230th Infantry—in a firefight to cover the withdrawal of the American supplies.[19] At 0730, the 1st Battalion of the 164th Infantry Regiment (Americal

Division) began to return east and back across the Matanikau River with orders to rejoin the regiment in the Lunga Point sector. Meanwhile, the 8th Marines began to leave their forward positions, and the command post of the 2nd Marines was moved to the vicinity of Point Cruz, about 1,700 yards to the rear and 300 yards inland.

The Point Cruz sector continued to be a festering sore in General Vandegrift's plans. The Japanese would jump into battle, leave, then return to fight the next day. Orders were received to shift the 1st and 2nd Battalions, 2nd Marines, into an area east of the Tenaru River effective the morning of the 13th. This move was based on a warning from the 1st Division of an expected large Japanese landing force at Koli Point, east of the Lunga perimeter. To obstruct any landing effort, the 2nd Battalion, 7th Marines, supported by the 2nd Battalion, 164th Infantry, was ordered to make a quick push to the Metapona River, about thirteen miles east of the Lunga.

At about the same time, on the Japanese side, the 228th Infantry would move to Hill 903 of Mount Austen and scatter along a line from Hill 990 (U.S. Hill 87) to Point Cruz, while the balance of Col. Akinosuka Oka's 124th Infantry was attached to the 228th Infantry forming the Ito Detachment. The 124th Infantry had received replacements in early November, recent inductees, who would make their way to the Mount Austen stronghold. From all counts the 228th Infantry had fresh troops not yet affected by the Ga Tō sickness, and they became a formidable foe that caused immense problems for the Americans. At the Mount Austen area the 124th Infantry held the center of the line, while the 2nd Battalion, 228th Infantry (Maj. Takeyoshi Inagaki), occupied the right wing lying between Hills 27 and 31. The 228th's 3rd Battalion (Maj. Haruka Nishiyama) held up the left wing of *Miharashi Dai* (Hill 54, part of Galloping Horse Ridge), situated between Hills 43 and 44 (Sea Horse Ridge). Regimental headquarters and the headquarters of the 1st Battalion, 228th Infantry, were located nearby on the west side of *Sakai Dai* (Skyline Ridge Hills 75, 78, and 80), with the 228th's 1st Battalion also covering the sector between the 3rd Battalion position on the south and elements of the 2nd Division on the north.

Admiral Turner had managed to ship much-needed supplies and reinforcements to Lunga Roads via the "Nouméa Express." The decks of the cargo ships were loaded with torpedoes and fifty-five-gallon drums of avgas. The amphibious task force in three task group echelons (TG 62.4, 67.1, and 67.4) carried 5,900 men from the 182nd Infantry Regiment (less the 3rd Battalion on Espiritu Santo); the 245th Field Artillery

Battalion, Provisional Companies B and H; the 101st Medical Regiment of the Americal Division; Battery L, 11th Marines (155-mm howitzers); plus the 1st Marine Aviation Engineer Battalion and 400 Marine replacements from the 1st Depot Company. Three heavy and light cruisers and fourteen destroyers escorted the convoy; they weighed anchor on 8 November and reached Guadalcanal four days later.

In the meantime, the U.S. Army's 147th Infantry Regiment, 1st Battalion, had just moved from Aola and was ordered to advance overland toward Koli Point to intercept any Japanese of the 230th Infantry moving eastward. While the threat to Koli Point was somewhat diminished, some spots remained unprotected. The marine command assigned the GIs of the 164th Infantry Regiment to plug the gap and move west. Col. Bryant E. Moore of the 2nd Battalion, 164th, by then a veteran of jungle warfare, assigned the task to his Company E, and the 8th Marines joined the push. But the GIs had problems with the weather and the jungle mud, as did the Sun Soldiers. The rain was relentless, causing the American offensive to move at a snail's pace. The 8th Marines, not accustomed to Guadalcanal's oppressive hot weather, advanced only 400 yards.

Meanwhile, Lt. Gen. Haruyoshi Hyakutake was determined to hold Kokumbona. The American soldiers and marines were heading his way. The 2nd Battalion, 164th Infantry, less Company E, had entered the fray and took up positions on the right of Colonel Puller's 1st Battalion, 7th Marines. At this juncture, the leathernecks and the GIs held a curved line from the beach around a horseshoe bend in Gavaga Creek. The 81-mm mortar crews of the 7th Marines would pound the enemy defenses; the Japanese mortar crews would answer them. Blocked on the east and west, the Japanese immediately attempted to break out of the web, using concentrated automatic weapons fire and grenades. One small gap in the American lines remained open—a slough in the south, because the 164th's Companies E and F, which were separated by a marsh, had failed to connect. The Japanese saw the breach and the force at Gavaga Creek made its escape, but left behind 475 bodies.

For the Americans, a pending sea threat caused a pull-back. The 8th Marines, covered by the 2nd Marines, withdrew under sporadic but effective shellfire. The 2nd was near the Maruyama Road, and the Japanese fought desperately to keep the Americans from discovering their tree-covered route, pouring a concentrated deadly fire at the marines and forcing the leathernecks to withdraw. By nightfall the 2nd Marines and the 1st Battalion, 164th Infantry, had moved back to defensive positions east of the Matanikau River. Increased artillery and mortar concentrations were fired during this maneuver and throughout the night to keep the Japanese unaware of their activity. By morning, fresh reinforced patrols were sent out to protect the troops evacuating the supplies that had been impossible to move the previous day.

The Repositioning Continues

The American withdrawal was completed within two days, leaving the sector to be reoccupied by the Japanese. By 13 November the 2nd Marines had taken up positions east of the Tenaru River, and when they added up their casualties west of the Matanikau, they had lost thirty-five killed, one hundred thirty-three wounded, and seven missing; the 8th Marines fared better, with one killed and fourteen wounded.

PFC Charles Cadwell of Battery B, 5th Defense Battalion, would write in his diary:

> November 12: At dawn our Navy started shelling Japs along the Matanikau River lines. 75 Jap landing bar craft [were] seen at Tassafaronga[.] At 1300 air raid [; at]1415 . . . 23 bomber and 8 Zeros attacked our ships. November 13: Air raid at 0200. Friday—big Jap task force reached here early this morning. Our lines near Point Cruz were withdrawn to this side of the Matanikau River to avoid being cut off. November 14: At 0300 we were awakened by heavy shell-fire around us [from the battleship *Kirishima* and heavy cruisers *Takao* and *Atago*]. Coconut trees were splintering and falling everywhere. By actual count 125 large naval shells were aimed at the airfield and shrapnel was flying like rain. When the shelling started we piled sea bags around our foxholes together in an "L" shape so we could talk during air raids. This shelling was too big for foxholes so I counted [numbers] between hearing the naval guns and when their shells hit. I took off for a covered air raid shelter as soon as I heard the guns. Unfortunately, there was a short shot and I was hit in the right knee, left chest and wrist with shell fragments and wood splinters on the way to the shelter. . . . Inside the shelter, between sheer terror and wishing the thing would stop . . . we were all entertained by Geo[rge] Noll, who had jumped into the shelter naked and the mosquitoes were finding a ready target. He looked worse than I did when it got light. This shelling lasted ¾ of an hour.[20]

Nevertheless, there was good news. While the Japanese did manage to land some troops on "the rock," of the eleven transports filled with reinforcements that coastwatcher Paul Mason had reported from his post in south Bougainville, seven had been sunk en route by the Cactus Air Force, by carrier aircraft, and by the B 17s of the Espiritu Santo-based 11th Bomb Group.[21] Eight destroyers had rescued about five thousand men from six of the sinking Japanese ships and returned them to Rabaul. From the four transports that made it to Guadalcanal's shore — the *Kinugawa Maru, Hirokawa Maru, Yamaura Maru* and *Yamatsuki Maru*—two thousand troops managed to land, including elements of the 1st Battalion, 229th Infantry, led by Maj. Sugura Orita; the 228th Infantry led by Col. Sadashichi Doi; and the rear echelon 230th Infantry, 38th Division. However, they were mostly without weapons and materiel. They reached the shore with provisions for just four days and only 260 cases of ammunition. Lost at sea were provisions for thirty thousand men for twenty days; four thousand 10-cm, three thousand 15-cm, and fifteen thousand antiaircraft shells; all varieties of ammunition for the infantry units; and seventy-six large and seven small landing craft.

The diary of an unknown Japanese soldier, dated 14 November, reads: "For the first time in my life, I have experienced a great bombing attack. First of the ships sent up one flame after another from the decks and sank. In fact, seven ships were destroyed. The remaining four ships arrived in the darkness. Oh, our fate is already decided. Since 3.30 this morning, dive-bombers have fiercely attacked our remaining ships. Finally at 5 o'clock we had to give up all hope for the ship we came on. We have landed safely on Guadalcanal. Oh, *Yamatsuki Maru!* Goodbye forever! Even if we take refuge in the jungle, there is no place without sweeping fire and bombing. This is the end! . . . I can't smoke even one cigarette or eat one grain of rice. Every one is worn out."[22]

On 14 November the Cactus Air Force had temporarily changed its name for twenty-four hours to the Allied Air Force when a Royal New Zealand Air Force (RNZAF) contingent from the No. 9 Bomb Recon Squadron, flying British-built Ventura patrol bombers (Lockheed B 34/B 37), flew up from Espiritu Santo Island to augment the Guadalcanal air units. They were followed ten days later by five Hudsons (Lockheed-Vega AT-28/AT-29) from No. 3 Bomber Reconnaissance Squadron. One of the RNZAF aircrew members, F/Sgt. David Tribe, was a radio-man who often filled in as a gunner. In an initial briefing, the airmen were advised that if lost in enemy territory, they should not expect any mercy. If their plane went down and all indications were that they would be captured, each man, rather than be taken alive, was to put a pistol to his mouth and pull the trigger. Barely on Guadalcanal's soil twenty-four hours, the New Zealanders understood the nature of the enemy.[23]

On 15 November the Americans saw that four Japanese transports were lying along the Tassafaronga area in plain sight. Battery F of the 244th Coast Artillery Battalion had brought to the beach two 155-mm guns from its field position on the west bank of the Lunga River. The battery opened fire and the transports began to burn. Meanwhile, the Cactus Air Force bombed the ships. Forty-five minutes later the 3rd Defense Battalion's 5-inch batteries—guns from 1915—opened fire. In addition, the destroyer *Meade* (DD 602) sailed from its anchorage in Tulagi Harbor to shell the four transports and the supplies on shore. The combined forces of marine, army, and navy weapons and the Cactus Air Force turned the beached Japanese ships into burning wrecks.

In his POW interrogation report, PFC Masatoshi Ikeya of the 1st Battalion machine-gun company, 229th Infantry, stated: "Four of the ships including mine [the *Yamauru Maru*] managed to reach the beach the morning of the 15th. All four of those were attacked later in the day and burned. . . . Landing operations required about 1½ hours. All the machine guns were landed but very little provisions. Of the 229th only the headquarters (120–30) men [under Col. Ryozaburou Tanka], 1st Company (140–50) [under 1st Lt. Masao Takeuchi], and one machine gun squad (20 men and 2 heavy machine guns) were landed. About 150 men of the regimental artillery also had landed but I do not know if [they had] landed any of their guns or not. On landing we went to the 38th Division Headquarters at Maruyama, a point on the Oki River [Rove Creek] about one mile from the coast."[24]

Pvt. Chino Shuji of the 52nd Independent Transport Company under Captain Watanabe had a different version. "I landed on Guadalcanal the night of 15 November 1942. My transport was bombed by U.S. aircraft, and beached ; the men had to swim ashore without their gear. They landed in the vicinity of Cape Esperance and my unit of 100 men marched to Kokumbona."[25] PFC Matsutaro Shijiri of the Lt. Col. Tsuneo Iwabuchi's engineering battalion, 38th Division, told his interrogators: "My ship was one of eleven but they were attacked by U.S. planes on the 13th and many ships destroyed. Four of the eleven managed to reach shore and were destroyed the following day. The entire Engineering Battalion landed safely. . . . They did not bring any road equipment . . . . Every thing was lost . . . . They only had chiefly picks and shovels."[26]

Private 1st Class Cadwell's diary adds: "Air raid at noon. I was temporarily treated by a corpsman because all doctors headed for the beach [following the sinking of seven Japanese ships bringing reinforcements]. Our camp was midway between the beach (between the Tenaru River and Lunga Point) and Henderson Field in the east and off Lever Brothers Coconut Plantation. The beach for hundreds of yards up and down and inland [was] covered with thousands of wounded, burned, oil blackened and exhausted sailors who were washed in debris. I counted about 20 Jap sailors [who had] washed in and were too badly wounded to resist. I remember seeing one Jap lying on a stretcher[;] he had a blanket thrown over him and there were no legs, they had packed sand over the stumps to slow the bleeding."[27]

Late in the day on 9 November the 8th Marines and the 1st Battalion of the 164th Infantry had formed the bulk of the force assigned to defend the Matanikau. They had established strong, entrenched positions on the east bank of the river and had sent out aggressive daily patrols, but this bold strategy had cost thirty-four wounded and two killed. Supported by fire from the cannoneers of the 1st and 5th Battalions, 11th Marines, the combined force executed a frontal attack on a three-battalion front, with 1/164 on the right along the coast, 2/2 in the center, and 1/2 on the left flank and rear. The Americans then dug in for the night. The next day the advance was resumed in the face of murderous rifle, machine-gun, and mortar fire. By 1200, the force had fought its way slightly beyond the point that had been reached on 4 November.

With the Americans busy east of Kokumbona, the *Iwatsuki Maru* was able to nose into that sector on 15 November and discharge Lt. Col. Tsuneo Iwabuchi's 38th Engineer Regiment. Capt. Kiyoshi Saito's 3rd Company found immediate employment on a road-building project from the upper reaches of the Mizunashi River (Dry Creek) to the entrance of the Maruyama Trail—the place where the 2nd Marines had taken heavy casualties in the November drive on Kokumbona. Capt. Kishi Akimasu's 2nd Company was attached to the 229th Infantry, mainly to move materiel; however, the project—the roadway that would help the Japanese carry supplies to the front—never fully came to fruition.

After the disastrous Japanese reinforcement run, General Vandegrift saw an opportunity to rejuvenate the drive west. On 18 November the Americans started to cross the Matanikau again. The soldiers of the 2nd Battalion, 182nd Infantry, took the lead in the renewed westward effort. On the east bank, situated on the beach, the 1st Battalion, 8th Marines, protected their crossing with the 2nd Battalion, 8th Marines, in the center and the 8th's 3rd Battalion on the left flank. The 2nd Battalion, 182nd Infantry, dug in 1,000 yards west of the river. On 19 November the 1st

Battalion, 182nd Infantry, supported by 105-mm howitzers of the newly arrived 245th Field Artillery Battalion, crossed the river with orders to seize the high ground. The Japanese resisted, pounding 2/182. The Sun Soldiers were reinforcing the sector. Maj. Suguru Orita, commander of the 1st Battalion, 229th Infantry, was wounded in the bombing and evacuated.[28]

On the morning of the 20th, a strong enemy force hit the left flank of 1/182 with every weapon at its disposal and punched a hole in the American lines. The 182nd—the Americal Division's "Minutemen from Massachusetts"—reeled back with casualties. Combat was a new experience for them. The 1st and 3rd Battalions of the 164th Infantry then were shoved across the river to support the besieged 1/182. The 2/182 stayed in position, and the 164th occupied a site adjacent to them. Bitter fighting continued, as did casualties, mostly as a result of dangerous aggressive patrolling in an attempt to make contact. The 8th Marines crossed the river, passed through the American Army lines, and engaged the enemy. The leathernecks from Samoa were becoming accustomed to Guadalcanal's blistering heat, and their combat readiness showed improvement. Meanwhile, the 2nd Marines remained east of the Tenaru until 21 November, when they returned to the perimeter west of Lunga.

Reconfiguring the Line

Company A of the 1st Battalion, 2nd Marines, which had taken a beating on the west offensive, was detailed for some better duty as guards for Fighter Strip No. 1, called "the cow pasture," east of Henderson Field. The remainder of the 1st Battalion would be in defensive positions east of the Tenaru. The 2nd Battalion was in a defensive line along the Ilu River and sent patrols to the east. Company F of 2/2 was ordered to replace one company of 2/5, which dispatched patrols to the southeast, while a segment of Company G set up an observation post 5,000 yards to the east along the coast route. Then 2/2 moved again when the 1st Battalion went into reserve along the west side of the Tenaru River; joining the 2nd Battalion in reserve adjacent to the old Japanese camp at Kukum, now the Cactus Coast Guard Station.

By 21 November, the division had issued orders for the 2nd Marines to reshape the line west of the Lunga, replacing the 2nd and 3rd Battalions, 1st Marines. The 1st Battalion, 2nd Marines, occupied an area of 1,500 yards along the beach and 1,000 yards inland, replacing the 3rd Battalion, 1st Marines. The 2nd Battalion, 2nd Marines, then manned a post on the left of the 1st Battalion's line extending southeast along the ridge; Colonel Arthur's 2nd Marines command post was now positioned in a ravine southeast of the coral-faced Fighter Strip No. 2, which would be completed by late December. On Thanksgiving Day the 1st Battalion, 147th Infantry, moved from swampy Aola to Koli Point. Three days later it was joined by its sister battalion, 3/147. The two battalions moved inland to the foot of Gold Ridge, continuing to encompass the area to offer protection to the 14th Seabees (NCB) and the new one-hundred-man medical unit of ACORN 1 (Red).[29]

Meanwhile, shortages of supplies had affected both sides. On 20 November Maj. Tadahika Hayashi, the Seventeenth Army cipher officer, reported to the Eighth Area Army at Rabaul that the Oki Army was facing an immediate food crisis. Three days later Hayashi received a message that supplies were on the way. Sea-trucks—small, slow-moving transports that traveled at six to eight knots—were plying cargo between Japan and Rabaul every day, but they were too slow to deliver materiel to Guadalcanal. The supplies thus had accumulated at the warehouses in Rabaul, and at Buin on Bougainville Island, and were not reaching the front. Thievery from the warehouses also was rampant. The rear area troops were well fed, but the foot soldiers received little or none. The Imperial Navy thus came up with a plan to use submarines for the transporting task, and on 29 November at Kamimbo Bay, a Japanese unloading point, the submarine *I-9* off-loaded 726 cases of provisions; three days later *I-31* landed 701 crates of supplies. The transport *Kyushu Maru* landed additional provisions and machine-gun ammunition. All this would be carried to the lines and would be gone in just twenty-four hours.[30]

The Americans also were in need of provisions and ammunition. Ray L. Whitaker, a crew member of the *Barnett*, remembered a November supply run:

> We made one more trip to Guadalcanal. The island needed bombs, ammunition and supplies. This was a small flotilla, the *Barnett*, the *Alchiba* (AK-6), which was a supply attack ship, and two World War I four[-]stacker destroyers. The *Barnett* was loaded with bombs and a compartment of nitroglycerine in the forward hold. In addition to supplies onboard, the *Alchiba* towed a barge alongside, also loaded with munitions. If we were attacked by a sub, and the destroyers didn't do their job, we were "toast." Fortunately, we arrived without incident. The area was becoming more secure, but subs could be a problem. The *Alchiba*

did likewise and both vessels were anchored. The destroyers were patrolling the area. It goes without saying that when anchored, the wind will keep all ships facing the same direction. A terrible explosion occurred, not from the *Barnett*, but from the *Alchiba*. She had been torpedoed by a miniature two-man sub [Type HA]. Sailors on the deck saw the torpedo coming as it barely missed the *Barnett*. It apparently had been fired in a way that it was "lopping" in the water, its power almost expended. It struck the *Alchiba* just below the bridge at the waterline. The captain got underway and beached his ship. The *Barnett*, for her own safety, got underway and left Guadalcanal for the last time. We later learned through naval reports that the Japs torpedoed the *Alchiba* two more times.[31]

On 29 November the rear echelon of the 14th NCB arrived at Koli Point from Aola via a barge shuttle service. The Seabees' first project in December was to construct a bridge span across the Nalimbiu River connecting the Koli Point area with the Lunga zone by a road to Henderson Field. The timber used was native lumber cut and sawed by the "Thick and Thin Lumber Mill," a name given to the battalion's carpentry crew. The Bees called it the "Mahogany Bridge." Mahogany was better suited for furniture than for the construction of a bridge, yet it was certainly better than coconut logs.[32] Previously, the 6th Seabees had cleared coconut trees and brush and built a road known as "Johnson Highway," which ended near the Nalimbiu River.[33] Between 5 and 17 December, the 14th NCB would start constructing an emergency airstrip (Koli No. 2) about 150 feet wide and 7,500 feet long and about two miles inland from the beach. Later the 2nd Marine Aviation Engineer Battalion would construct two taxiways on the southern side of the field.[34] Guadalcanal began sprouting airfields almost as fast as they could be built and maintained.

14 War in the Outer Islands

During the Japanese occupation lookout posts were established on Florida Island (*Fu Tō*), just north of Guadalcanal. By early July 1942 a floatplane fighter base under Lt. Cdr. Riichiro Sato had been established at Barango Bay off the village of Halavo. After the Americans conquered Tulagi, adjacent Florida became the minor theater, though it continued to occupy their attention. They believed that many Japanese troops swam to safety on Florida from Tulagi, Gavutu, or Tanambogo (actually, only a few did so). In addition, the Americans feared that the Japanese could land in force on Florida Island and use it as a jumping-off point to strike at Tulagi and Guadalcanal.

Florida Island

On 7 August 1942, D-day, at 0740 (H minus twenty minutes), Company B of the 1st Battalion, 2nd Marines, 2nd Marine Division, supported by the 4th Platoon of Company D, came ashore on Florida Island at the edge of a steaming, fetid jungle at Haleta inlet. At 0730 that day the second wave (Companies A and C, 1/2) had boarded nine LCPs, then shoved off from the *Jackson* and headed for Florida to carry out a second landing. At 0830 Lt. Col. Robert E. Hill, commanding officer of the 3rd Battalion, 2nd Marines, put Plan U in effect.[1] At H + 30 Colonel Hill was to land Company C under Capt. William S. Vasconcellos, a reinforced rifle company, to seize and hold the southeast sector. Company A under Capt. William T. Bray was to land on the eastward side of the promontory south of Halavo at H + 30 and seize Halavo village. The U.S. Navy would offer support by bombarding the Florida landing sites while the landing craft were headed for the island.[2]

The marines of this Halavo echelon (Companies A and C) had left their line of departure just as the tropical sky was beginning to break clear and they could distinguish their green objective in the distance. By this time many probably were wishing they were still in San Diego where the temperature seemed ideal. The majority were seventeen to twenty

Figure 37. Lt. Cdr. Riichiro Sato, commanding officer of the Yokohama Air Group Florida Air Unit. (Courtesy the Sato family)

years old and barely out of boot camp; one was only fifteen. Some had never shaved before. It was a mixture of high school kids, college prospects, and "old salts"—men who had been in the Argonne Forest during the Great War. All had undergone robust training, yet almost none had ever seen a jungle, much less trained in one. John H. Bowler, who was then a twenty-seven-year-old platoon sergeant, described the situation:

> I was a Plat. Sgt. 5th Platoon, Company D and while boating to Florida we were attached to Company C as a heavy weapons platoon. This platoon was to hold the ground that the rifle company had taken during the day and furnish defense at night.
>
> The 1st Battalion, 2nd Marines, had, at the time, many old time Marines, men who had served during World War I, Nicaragua and Haiti. A few names come to mind: Warren Goodwin, Walter Grant, "Doggie [Pvt. William] Wallace" and Master Gunnery Sergeant Klein. These were the "old breed Marines," China hands, men who devoted their lives to the Marine Corps and the United States of America. Warren Goodwin was a sec-

tion leader of the 5th Platoon, Company D at this time, having been up the chevron ladder numerous times; he was . . . a sergeant and was well acquainted with the water-cooled machine gun, having used the same type in the First World War. Sergeant Goodwin was respected in the Platoon and called "Pappy" because of his age and experience.

Company C, with the 5th Platoon [Company D] attached and members of Company D Medical, went ashore at Halavo Point, a short beach, to land at 0840. Their mission was to seize the village of Halavo and, if occupied, blow it away along with its defenders. The village was almost a day's march from the landing point and [there was] a very dense jungle most of the way. Midway along the march we were taken under fire by some enemy 7.7-mm machine guns that were situated on Gavutu and Tanambogo Islands in Tulagi harbor about 1,000 yards away. We all hit the deck, surprise on all our faces because everything had been so quiet up until then. Quentin Hogan of Chicago was the first to react to the revelation. When he ran over to Sergeant Goodwin and shouted "Pappy, they're shooting at us?" Goodwin very calmly said, "What did you expect? That they would come over here and kiss you?" We met no resistance in the village so we settled down for the night. . . . The first night in a combat area, even for the well disciplined troops, is the worst night any man will ever experience in his lifetime. Imaginations run wild, trigger fingers twitch, and night sounds play havoc with one's nerves. A man was fortunate to survive the first night.[3]

Florida Island had some of the most dense tangled vegetation to penetrate. With Halavo village as their target approximately a half mile away, Companies A, C, and D were to fan out, cut across the mangrove-choked beaches, and clear the area of any existing enemy force. There was none. During the landing, on a small stretch of beach, 2nd Lt. Justin G. Mills was having difficulty with his coxswain, who was afraid to get close to the beach. The sailor wanted to pilot the Higgins boat to within a short distance of the island and discharge his passengers in the foaming surf. Mills looked at the young coast guardsman sternly, slowly unlatched the flap on his pistol holster, and calmly said, "Son, take us to the shore or you will be sorry." A few seconds later the craft was beached on the shore at Halavo.[4]

Squad leader Sgt. John Zingale was assigned to the Higgins boat carrying the wave commander, Lt. Edwin Schwamer. Zingale was ordered to take position on the left side of the craft, manning the dilapidated World War I-vintage Lewis machine gun; he was instructed to open fire when they were approximately a hundred yards from the beach. The first shot went off on time; on the second, the gun jammed. Fortunately, there was no return fire.[5] As the marines were disembarking at Halavo Point, the two minesweepers went to work clearing the waters. Their orders called for them to check for floating explosive charges in the area south of Gavutu. Early that afternoon they would then head across the channel and sweep clean the Guadalcanal sector. No mines were discovered; the Japanese had not expected an attack.

Bill Cannon remembers:

> August 7 was a fairly bright, sunny morning, peaceful with a slight mist rising from the lush green jungle at Halavo. Then the destroyers opened up on various preplanned targets on Tulagi, Gavutu and Tanambogo, clobbering the target, but often hitting the Tulagi wall. We went over the side of our transport, *President Jackson,* by cargo nets to the waiting landing craft. We were ordered to stay below the gunwale, but just about everyone stood up long enough to see what was happening. I recall seeing a couple of large and several smaller splashes, including a string of machine-gun slugs hitting the water around a destroyer that was firing every now and then at Tulagi. It suddenly dawned on me that a person could get hurt doing this! Our Higgins boat grounded and we rolled over the gunwales, trying desperately to keep from being thrown under the bow every time the boat rolled from the crashing breakers and to remain on your feet with a heavy load of gear strapped to your back. Finally maintaining my footing, I landed on a small sandy beach. . . . Lieutenant Colonel Hill took off like a shot out of a gun. He was soon out of sight. There didn't seem to be much confusion and the main object seemed to be getting off the almost nonexistent beach and into the jungle by way of a fairly narrow trail. One of our objectives there was to seek out any artillery positions that might interfere with our landings on the nearby islands and destroy the hostile forces encountered. None were found.
>
> The day was beginning to get hot even early in the morning and we were beginning to feel the heat and the 70 pounds on our backs did not help this. After weeks on the *President Jackson*

I was stiff. . . . I was glad to step on land, but did not know what to expect. The company was spread out as we trudged along, but then we suddenly stopped. The word was passed back to our squad, headed by Sergeant Zingale, to move forward on the double. By the time we reached the head of the column we were hot, sticky, sweaty and very exhausted and had not yet fired one shot in anger. We were ordered to join Battalion Sergeant Major Funk and . . . Lt. Col. Hill, who were studying some nearby huts and checking for movement. (There were six native buildings, used by the Japanese airmen as quarters, and a native-built church.)

Since I was the BAR man I moved from my area into a clearing and covered the building with my gun. Hill threw three grenades at the nearest hut, . . . [the] church. One went off with a weak explosion; the other two did not. After a short period of waiting Hill carefully entered the church to check and found his grenades lying there. He picked them up and put their pins back in. The strikers were corroded to the frame. We were fighting in World War II with ammunition, rifles and machine guns produced in 1917. . . .

We were to land to the right of Haleta with Company B on the left. . . . The object was to secure the village and join forces on Florida Island, thus blocking the escape route of the Japanese from Florida Island. There was one oversight in this plan. The mangrove swamp had extended God knows how many miles in all directions and was impassable.[6]

The endeavor on Florida was described by another, an unidentified, marine:

When we hit the beach there were no Japanese. We had a Lewis Gun set up in the bow of the landing craft and fired into the foliage as we were landing. Company A came through Company C sector and moved forward, the Platoon of Company D that had accompanied our RUNABOUT (the code name for Florida Island) expedition for fire support was in the last position protecting our rear. We went along our jungle trail; it was hotter than hell! We hit a small village and sought the enemy, but found none. We did locate a cache of aviation gasoline but moved out to another village a short distance up the trail and found a second gasoline dump. That evening 1/C/2 returned to the first village and spent the night. Guards were posted and an additional guard (Pvt. Jack A. Mack) was stationed at the village well; it was thought Japanese may have poisoned it. There was rifle fire all night.[7]

Paul T. Boyd of Company A, 1st Battalion, 2nd Marines, remembered: "We landed early on the 7th and moved as quickly as possible towards the seaplane landing. I think Company C had the point. The jungle was rough and plenty of parrots making all sorts of racket. As I recall, [we moved] as quietly as possible with a lot of hand-signals and brief stops. At the village of Halavo each Company was assigned a sector and dug in for the night. [There was a] lot of shooting that night at trees and shadows. In the midst of a downpour, only like it can rain in the Solomons, we boarded a Higgins and took off for Tulagi to support the Raiders." Bill Cannon also recalled: "A machine gun was firing all night, almost like a loud chain saw, firing and firing at would-be invaders and never letting up until dawn." Maj. Wood B. Kyle remembered: "We could not get them to stop firing."[8]

The first night on hostile shores was disorganized and full of dark and moving shadows. A marine sergeant in Company D went out to relieve himself while his foxhole buddy was asleep, and on returning he was shot three times by his foxhole companion. The shooter was so distraught that he had to be evacuated. The total casualties for D-day on Florida were no enemy dead, two leathernecks wounded, and one killed. In the plan as well were two destroyer minesweepers, the *Southard* (DMS 10) and the *Zane* (DMS 14), which were to shell Bungana Island where it was reported the enemy had an outpost. At about the same time, however, the *Southard* and *Zane* were fired on by a small-caliber gun from the Japanese outpost on Bungana, but the eleven-man detachment could only hope to sidetrack the destroyers with its ineffective machine gun.

While the two minesweepers were returning the fire, the first wave of landing craft (Company C, 1/2) from the *President Jackson* passed between them on their way to the line of departure; the minesweepers offered some form of protection for the landing force. Robert Tallent of the 3rd Battalion, 2nd Marines, wrote an acerbic appreciation of the place:

Florida Island was [some of] the most inhospitable real estate I've ever patrolled.... I did considerable "snooping and pooping" on Florida. The natives existed on the shorelines. Inland, about the only fauna that could hang on were nests of purple worms, bats and a few discouraged parrots without stamina to seek better climes. . . . The Japanese who fled to Florida or were stationed there [had to] raid the native gardens to stay alive. [They] were miserably sick and war weary, as if we weren't almost in the same shape ourselves. Siota Mission . . . is the only really habitable place on the island. It was a delightful place to defend. The geography of Florida is irregular, with sharp peaks up to 1,366 feet high and rounded hills. The island is well wooded, with occasional grassy tracts bare of trees. Inland there are numerous freshwater streams, and in certain places mangroves border the sandy beaches. The water is spotted with dark coral that appears black; over the centuries, the crushed coral has become black sand.[9]

When the Americans had landed on Tulagi on 8 August, a lone Japanese, twenty-five-year-old SM Norio Ogihara of the Command Platoon, 3rd Company, Kure 3rd SNLF, escaped by swimming to Florida Island. He was captured a month later by Malaita constables (led by Corporal Eto), who located him in a native village near Halaita. He had been coexisting with the islanders, some of whom had fed him. When he encountered the police he attempted to communicate, but instead they seized him, then took him to Tulagi and turned him over to the marines. Ogihara was later sent to a New Zealand POW camp and survived the war.[10]

The Japanese had established two lookout stations when they occupied Tulagi, one at Bungana Island and the other at Cape Horn, Florida Island—a total of some twenty-two sailors plus radio operators. These stations were wiped out early in the Guadalcanal campaign by elements of the 2nd Marines; one man surrendered. The largest group of Japanese loose on Florida island was from the Halavo naval air station. The Japanese had established a floatplane base on 1 July 1942 at Halavo Bay equipped with twelve Nakajima A6M-N Type 2 (Rufe), including two spares. The planes were operated by the Hama Air Unit of the Yokohama Air Group which had Kawanishi H6K Type 97 (Mavis) flying boats headquartered nearby on the twin islands of Tanambogo and Gavutu. The sea fighter base had four commissioned officers as pilots: Lt. Cdr. Riichiro Sato, of Okegawa, Japan, commanding officer; WO Tokuchiyo Hirahashi, Sato's executive officer; and WOs Fumiro Kurozawa and Hisateru Kofuji on Sato's staff. The Halavo fighter base had seven noncommissioned officers as pilots and thirty-six others as ground crew.[11] On occasion, Commander Sato and Warrant Officer Hirahashi would take a break from

Figure 38. WO Tokuchiyo Hirahashi in front of a Type 93 trainer, Kasumigaura Naval Air Training Station, Tokako, Japan, 1935. Hirahashi was the executive officer of the Yokohama Air Group Florida Air Unit. (Courtesy the Hirahashi family)

mosquito-ridden Florida Island and travel to Gavutu where they could enjoy refreshments at the officers club, a building on the pier just south of the causeway, and the companionship of their fellow officers. The two were avid camera buffs; Hirahashi often took aerial photographs, and Sato used his Zeiss Ikon to photograph both the flying boats off Gavutu and his own squadron at Halavo.[12]

Two of Commander Sato's pilots were lost in combat in July— NAP1c Tatsuo Hori, and NAP1c Saburo Matsui—and NAP1c Shigeto Kobayashi was missing in August. All had tangled with the American B-17s. The two spare Rufes had been flown to Poporang Strait Seaplane Base #1 on Poporange Island, the Japanese air base in the Shortlands, and thus missed the 7 August American attack on Florida Island; one pilot was Warrant Officer Kofuji, the other unknown.[13] At dawn on 7 August seven Rufes at anchor off Halavo were sunk by the fighters of VF-71 from the *Wasp*. With their air station under attack, the airmen scattered inland to safer ground, but as the days passed, food there became scarce. To solve the problem, Commander Sato soon split his group of some forty men into three parties of about thirteen, each going a separate way to search for food.

Before they had been forced to split up, however, some members of Sato's group had captured a large pig for their sustenance, an action that had infuriated the natives. They wanted revenge for the loss of their own valuable food supply and boated to Tulagi to file a report, indicating that about forty Japanese had been in the area of Gumba. To pacify the islanders, the Tulagi command promised to hunt down the thieves, but it required guides to show the way. Lt. James R. Clanahan (called by the enlisted men "Fancy Clancy" or "Jungle Jim") of Company C, 1st Battalion, 2nd Marines, was selected to lead the raid patrol. His party boated to Florida Island, led by the native guides.

"Jungle Jim" Clanahan's marines hit upon a bivouac area of the Yokohama airmen. They attacked from the south and west at Gumba about noon and pressed forward when they found that no guards had been posted. They found several airmen in a clearing, under a native-style shelter, some talking, some playing games, and some sleeping—an estimated sixteen Japanese in the group, including Commander Sato, WOs Kurozawa and Hirahashi, and PO3c Mitsutaro Ito.

When the marines opened fire, the startled Japanese bolted in all directions; seven vanished into the jungle to the west. Commander Sato, who had been in the open clearing, and five others were dead. Sato's family sword would have been of little use against marines with automatic weapons. A few days after Lieutenant Clanahan's Florida Island shootout, the Malaita police constables killed a single Japanese. The papers found on his body indicated that he was one of Sato's airmen. Other members of Sato's band either starved to death or in time were killed by natives.

John R. Brakeman of Company C, 1st Battalion, 2nd Marines, part of Lieutenant Clanahan's group, relates the story in more detail:

> I do not recall whether our mission was to annihilate or to capture an isolated group of Japanese. As we knew it, this party was camped out in a grassy glade, deep in the jungles of Florida Island. A native informant, I think his name was Alex, who was a big guy and always carried a club and his leader, a little man, appeared to be in charge. They gave us a detailed description of the location and their daily living habits. The plan was to move inland as a single group and upon arriving in the general area, split up into three groups, which would surround the area, all without

detection, of course. At an assigned signal or on being detected, we were to attack the entire force.

I was the BAR man assigned to sneak up on an outpost sentry, and block any escape. The sentry was not in place; his post was a huge Banyan tree and I crawled up on the opposite side of the tree. When the signal was given to "fire," one member of the enemy group dashed out of the camp center and dived into a copse, or thicket, about 50 yards in front of me. Because a section of our patrol was directly behind him, I did not shoot and to my knowledge that one survived the raid.

The firing lasted only a few minutes, when we assembled and began the hectic and head-long "pell-mell" retreat to the location of the Higgins boats which were waiting for us. One of our Marines, a big guy, was overcome with heat exhaustion from this wild and disorganized exodus, and had to be carried out of there. This was surely indicative of Clanahan's leadership! The raid had been a big success, except for one survivor. [Actually there were three.] (Only the flying personnel were armed with pistols.)[14]

The three airmen surviving of the seven who had managed to scamper to the safety of the lush jungle were SM Shigeru Saito, PO3c Tadashi Ito, and Warrant Officer Hirahashi. Ito and Hirahashi were unhurt, but Saito had been severely wounded in the forearm. The men kept together and headed north; however, Saito's condition worsened each day. Within three days, they reached Undu Rock, Ahuha Island, off the north coast of Florida Island. At about 0800 on 23 August they approached some natives to seek food but were seized, bound, and transported by canoe to a little island where they remained tied up until the following morning. When word reached Tulagi that the Florida Islanders had seized three Japanese, Lieutenant Clanahan was ordered to pick up the "Japanese package"; with Clanahan were five members of Company C, including Pvts. B. N. "Bernie" Peipert and Charles "Rosy" Rosales. Upon their return, Saito was immediately sent to the hospital; Ito and Hirahashi were locked in the Tulagi prison.[15] Saito's badly festered arm was in critical condition, and in an attempt to save his life, the doctors used captured Japanese medical instruments to amputate the arm at the elbow. Shortly afterward, however, because of his weakened condition and the trauma of the operation, Saito died. He lies buried somewhere on Tulagi.[16]

Also escaping to Florida Island were twenty-two-year-old NAP2c Narakazo Yusura of Osaka, Japan, a pilot from the flying-boat detail on

Gavutu, and two companions. They had left the carnage on Gavutu by swimming to Florida Island on the evening of 8 August. They did not seek out any other Japanese and saw none. They ate what they could find. In September, one of Yusura's companions died from malaria, and in time, the two remaining airmen separated. On 26 December Yusura was captured by an island constable and taken to Tulagi. He eventually was sent to the POW camp in New Zealand and survived the war. The other airman was never heard from again. The marines patrolling the island, with the help of natives, occasionally would find a Japanese straggler; but most would not surrender.

Between August and December of 1942 the Marine Defense Command on Tulagi dispatched some forty-eight combat patrols to comb the jungle of Florida Island, looking for Japanese stragglers; men were drawn from the 2nd and 10th Marines and the 3rd Barrage Balloon Squadron for the task. Late in the war, one company from the 147th Infantry Regiment and one from the 132nd Infantry Regiment, U.S. Army, took over when the marines departed. The war on Florida Island is not covered in the histories of the Guadalcanal campaign, as only a few skirmishes occurred there; yet the marines trudged through and fought in that stinking jungle—and Japanese died there.

Malaita Island

Malaita Island also played a small part in the war in the Solomons, but it was a role at a grave stage of the Guadalcanal campaign. The island spans about 103 miles from northwest to southeast and twenty-three miles at its greatest width; it lies some sixty miles from Guadalcanal. A former trader, Mr. A. Brail, described it as for the most part thickly populated and called the native there "a fighter, the Gurkha of the South Seas. The interior practically unexplored. Head hunters; [along with] Malekula in the New Hebrides [one of the two] last dangerous ports of the world left. It was the most populated . . . of the major islands and its people had been the most warlike for centuries."[17] During the 1800s, it was said that a shipwrecked sailor cast up on Malaita could count his life by minutes, not by days.

Since 1909, the coastal town of Auki had been Malaita's chief port and the district officer's station. The quarters on the station were predominantly native-style leaf houses—six buildings, including the district officer's house, the ration store, a small hospital, a prison, and an armory; all had rusty, red-painted, galvanized iron roofing. For safety, most of the Solomon Island government staff had moved from Tulagi to Auki in February 1942, though Resident Commissioner William S. Marchant did not remain in Auki but instead took up quarters in the bush village of Fulisango, about four miles up the ridge and eight miles from the west coast, facing Florida Island. The Reverend Walter Hubert Baddeley, Bishop of Melanesia, and Harry W. Bullen, secretary of the Church of Melanesia diocese, also were quartered in the vicinity. With Bishop Baddeley's group were two teachers, Sister Veronica and Sister Madeline. Malaita also had its share of missionaries who had evacuated from other islands, some from Guadalcanal. Most took to the back-country and carried on their religious work.

On 4 August 1942, while the invasion force was en route to the south-ern Solomon Islands, the seaplane tender *Mackinac* (AVP-13), as an ad-vanced lookout station, arrived on Maramasike Passage, in a secluded cove on Malaita Island, which was by then code-named ECSTASY. The *Mackinac* was the mother ship to nine flying boats, all PBYs of U.S. Navy patrol squadron VP-23, which were to keep an eye peeled for any Japanese vessels. On board for a while was a U.S. Navy lieutenant who would later become one of the best-selling authors in the world, James A. Michener. Van Watts, a member of the crew, recalled:

> We would take [Michener] on what may have been, I guess, the ride of his life, picking him up and leaving him, two weeks later, at our rear base, the New Hebrides Island of Espiritu Santo. It was there, during the next eighteen months, he would write his first novel. In it, he would have his narrator say in his only partly fictionalized work, "I never saw a battleship except from a dis-tance. I never visited a carrier, or a cruiser, or a destroyer. I never saw a submarine."
>
> But . . . Michener did sail on at least one naval vessel in the first of her narrow escapes from the Solomons—the little sea-plane tender . . . called the "Mighty Mac." We . . . called her by the number on her bow—the "Lucky Thirteen"! She was lucky all right! Lucky enough to survive, with Michener aboard, "the most advanced post" in World War II's famous "First Of-fensive!"
>
> Strange—but not so strange—that modest fellow never seems to have mentioned it! But if you ever wondered where he was the day the action began—he was with us! Up front! Way up front—at an island shown on military maps behind enemy lines—refueling planes under the very noses of the enemy!

For, on 7 August 60 [miles] north of [Guadalcanal], at Malaita, the *Mackinac* would be refueling the planes that scouted the enemy. The success of one of the war's most daring exploits would depend completely on lack of detection. [The *Mackinac* had been] charged off in advance as part of the price for Guadalcanal; there was no question of her presence eventually being discovered. . . . An over-aged destroyer converted into a seaplane tender and sent into the area to refuel scouting planes in advance of our landing in the southern Solomons had been gambled and lost . . . no one could have honestly expected the *Mackinac* to return. . . .

But, on the fifth day [9 August], with still a bare chance of her own survival, the *Mackinac* would be ordered to evacuate "the most advanced post." As we upped anchor and sailed, the last of her big PBYs flew over to warn that forty Jap bombers had been sighted heading her way. . . .

Either they were after bigger game — or [they] didn't see the speck below that was us. For, tailing far behind a departing fleet . . . and, in the face of superior enemy forces, retiring as fast as it could go, the "Mighty" — and mighty lucky little — "Mac" escaped with Michener and company!

Eight days later we would head north again to set up another advance base at Ndeni [Santa Cruz Islands], leaving him at . . . Espiritu Santo. We never saw him again, but, years later, we would read in the press that he had "retreated to a jungle shack and began writing the stories that were to appear in *Tales of the South Pacific*."[18]

Back on 31 July 1942, en route in a three-masted schooner from Tulagi to their new lookout post on Malaita at the village of Afufu near Cape Astrolabe, twenty-one sea infantrymen from the 3rd and 4th Squads, 1st Platoon, 1st Company, Kure 3rd SNLF, under WO Yoshiharu Muranaka, together with two radio-men from the 85th Communication Unit, went ashore at Auki, Malaita, to investigate. The district officer, Capt. C. N. F. Bengough, having been alerted to the Japanese presence, took to the bush. Upon arrival, PO3c Kazuo Yoshida and his sailors tore down the British flag, threw it on the ground, and trampled on it. They did not replace it with their own sun-disk pennant, however, since the only flag available belonged to SME Ryutaro Minakami and that flag would later be flown over their camp on north Malaita.

Figure 39. The Muranaka platoon, led by WO Yoshiharu Muranaka, 3rd Company, Kure 3rd Special Naval Landing Force, in tropical uniforms. The photograph probably was taken at Truk Atoll, Caroline Islands, during March–April 1942. Later the 3rd and 4th Squads of the platoon served on Malaita Island. SM Shohei Fukuda, who was captured by the Americans, is sixth from right in the third row. (Courtesy Herbert R. Fuller)

The Japanese troops went from house to house in the minute Auki community, but caused no major damage, nor did they discover the important radio station located about four miles up the Kwaibla River from Auki at an elevation of 3,000 feet. The station formerly had been at Tulagi but was dismantled and shipped to Malaita in February 1942. Lt. Thomas O. Sexton of the BSIP Defense Force operated the radio station from February 1942 to January 1943 when he was replaced by Lt. Robert S. Taylor, BSIPDF, the former Tulagi government radio supervisor. Sexton was in touch with the coastwatcher network throughout the protectorate, as he maintained the link between the Australian intelligence section at Nouméa, radio CACTUS on Guadalcanal, and the resident commissioners at both Vila, Efate Island, and Port Moresby, New Guinea. In December 1942, U.S. Army Sgt. Clifford R. Kurtz arrived to assist Taylor with his work. Kurtz had logged three months on Guadalcanal as a radio operator with the 164th Infantry and was on detached service. He is the only GI known to have been assigned duty on Malaita; he remained there until March 1943.[19]

When the Japanese troops withdrew from Auki after two hours that last day of July 1942, the local islanders picked up the fallen British banner and raised it again. The Japanese continued their sail up the coast and made their camp at Cape Astrolabe. Once there and unloaded, their schooner returned to Tulagi. The Japanese began radio operations from Cape Astrolabe, contacting Tulagi as soon as the equipment was functioning. Their signal was picked up by Lieutenant Taylor, who promptly radioed both Nouméa on New Caledonia and Guadalcanal. The new enemy lookout post on Malaita was established adjacent to Rore Creek, a clear-water stream that ran into a sandy beach area; the Japanese campsite was about 200 yards inland. Seaman Minakami's flag, with his name written on it, proudly flew over the camp until 4 November 1942.[20]

Meanwhile, however, District Officer Captain Bengough had been keeping his constabulary busy observing the movements of the Japanese. As soon as his new neighbors had settled in he relayed their actions to radio KEN, the coastwatcher network station on Guadalcanal. One message reported that on 6 August four Rufes (from the Yokohama Air Group fighter unit based at Halavo, Florida Island) had dropped twenty 132-pound bombs on the Fo'ondo mission on the north coast, six miles from their spotter location, killing six islanders. The natives were stunned and frightened by the attack. Not only had death rained down on them, but they had never seen an airplane, much less four at one time.[21]

On D-day, 7 August, Admiral Fletcher's adrenaline-charged carrier pilots of Task Force 61.1.1—the air war heroes of the morning—outdid the Japanese, mistakenly bombing two "artificial" islands in Langalanga Lagoon on Malaita Island—islands that had resulted from oceanic eruptions. Possibly they mistook the very small masses for Japanese warships. Eighteen islanders were killed on one island and twenty-two on the other. One of the "Ugly Ducklings"—the PBYs, so named by crew members based in Maramasike Passage—joined in the game and planted a bomb squarely on the South Sea Evangelical mission's $15,000 launch, *Arosi*, sinking her. The plane also dropped another 250-pound calling card at the mission's bible school at One Pusu, but it failed to explode. The islanders subsequently brought the bomb to a missionary, A. J. Waite, and asked what kind of bird could have laid such a large egg. The bomb was promptly dropped into the sea. The PBYs' mission that day had not been good public relations work by the U.S. Navy.

The Japanese lookout post at Cape Astrolabe in north Malaita (the Japanese called it *Ma Tō*) received its first visitors at 1000 on 26 August, when two downed airmen walked into the station. They were dressed in full heavy flight gear, the winter heated type, which they soon shed down to their loincloths. While on a three-plane mission, a Val (Aichi

D3A Type 99) carrier bomber had lost sight of its companion planes after running into a large squall. Failing to make radio contact with the others or their base, the Val's crew eventually ran out of fuel and made a crash landing on the sandy beach at Malu Harbor. The craft overturned, but they managed to salvage a revolver, a machine gun, and four magazines of ammunition. The pilot, NAP2cYokio Hikinune, and his radio-man, PO2c Goichi Koretsune, remained at the crash site overnight. The following morning they attempted to destroy their aircraft, but it would not burn.

Naval Air Pilot Hikinune recorded his impressions: "We went ashore hungry and tired and dozed off at the foot of a large tree. Natives talking awakened us. We were on the alert, but there seemed nothing to fear for they beckoned us and did not seem to intend any harm. We were greatly relieved. By simple English and motions with our hands and body, we informed them that we were Japanese and inquired whether any white men were about. When we told them we were Japanese, they blurted out some indescribable laughs and nodded their heads. And from this we judged they were friendly."[22] The two men were invited into a house located about twenty minutes away; it did not appear to be the usual native structure. The islanders offered them cooked yams, and by all gestures were friendly. Hikinune and Koretsune rested there for the night and slept well. On the following day, one of the twenty-some islanders gathered there volunteered to lead the pair to the Japanese post at Cape Astrolabe.[23]

The Solomon protectorate had been served by missionaries since before the turn of the century; often their numbers were higher than all other Caucasians combined. Malaita had been the last major island to succumb to missionary influence, but when this occurred, in the mid-1930s, the effects became deep-rooted. When Tulagi was evacuated in February 1942 the word had gone out that the Solomons were threatened. Some missions closed down and their members returned to New Zealand, but other faiths moved their operations to Malaita, where they had established a toehold. The Reverend Canon Charles Elliott Fox was from the Melanesian mission at Siota Point, Florida Island, which later became a 2nd Marine Regiment lookout post. He later became an unofficial coastwatcher in northern Malaita. Fox had come to the protectorate when he was twenty-three; he finally returned to New Zealand at the age of ninety-eight. Archdeacon Harry Reynolds was also on Malaita, but he traveled to outer islands whenever possible to continue his work as a priest and coastwatcher.

Other mission workers at the village of Takwa, in north Malaita, included Fathers Claude Palmer and James Wall from Australia and Father Joseph Halbswach from France. The nuns came from three countries: Sisters Mary Xavier from France, Mary Duguay from the United States, and Mary Francis from New Zealand. At Buma mission in south Auki were Fathers Daniel Stuyvenberg from the Netherlands and Donatien Coicaud from France and Sisters Mary Salome and Mary Laurent from France, Mary Faustine from Italy, and Mary Immaculate from New Zealand. At Dala was Father Christopher Kamphuis from the Netherlands, and nearby at the Rohinari mission was his countryman, Father Bernard van de Walle.

In early December 1942 General Vandegrift became aware that white missionaries were still on Guadalcanal behind Japanese lines. In a daring night sortie led by Dick Horton in the *Ramada,* Bishop Aubin and the sisters were picked up and transported to Lunga. The Caucasian nuns were sent to New Caledonia, and by special permission the bishop was allowed to go to Malaita to join others in his flock. At Rokera in southern Malaita were Sisters Mary Raphael from France and Mary Methoda from Yugoslavia; Father Thomas Parsonage from New Zealand and Father E. E. Courtais from Great Britain were at the remote Wanoni Bay, San Cristobal Island.[24] The South Sea Evangelical mission at One Pusu, Malaita, headed by Dr. Norman Deck, also was very active during the conflict with the service of A. J. Waite, R. C. Vance, K. E. Griffiths, V. M. Sullivan, Clark, and J. B. Hobern.

The missionaries at the Fauabu hospital, the closest civilized locale to Malaita's Cape Astrolabe outpost, had occasional problems with the Japanese sailors there who often visited the mission hospital seeking food and medicine. Sometimes they raided, other times they came begging, depending on which NCO was in charge at the time. Cameron Buffett, originally from Norfolk Island, some 500 miles off east-central Australia, worked as a carpenter at the hospital; when the Japanese made surprise visits, he left. Nurse Nellie Stead, formerly from the Siota mission on Florida Island, worked in the bush with the islanders and returned to the hospital only when she ran out of medical supplies. Sister Talbot also worked in the bush country. Doctor Thompson remained at his station when the Japanese arrived, and they did not harm him, probably thinking that a nearby physician might be useful.

The island missionaries had an intense devotion to duty. Sister Christine Woods, a nurse at the mission hospital at remote Ugi, San Cristobal, successfully petitioned to be allowed to go to Malaita where her services might be needed more. The problem of how to get her from Ugi—actually the hospital was at tiny Pawa—to Fauabu was resolved when a church launch, the *Gwen,* well hidden in the mud flats at Fauabu, was dug out and sent to Ugi to pick up Nurse Woods. Later the *Gwen* was returned to its hiding place.

On 3 September, the Japanese at the Cape Astrolabe lookout station dispatched an urgent message to the Taivu Point Station on Guadalcanal declaring that they had two weeks of rations left. A reply three days later indicated they soon would be supplied by submarine (the *I-26*). On 20 September the men at the lookout station sent another telegram: "We are short of rations; we only have two days' rations left." A similar request followed two days later. By the 25th, the Camp Astrolabe station was out of rations and four food-seekers—Seamen Inoshita and Oneya, and the two aviators—went to a nearby village where they secured bananas, coconuts, and papaya, and the islanders put on a dance for their entertainment. No food had arrived from the outside, and thus their main subsistence was island produce and fish. On 27 September, the now-stranded garrison started eating rice gruel for breakfast, lunch, and dinner. They had expected a submarine with rations on 4 October, but none arrived. By that time the radio was useless; the batteries were dead.[25]

About then, a second Japanese aircraft crashed on Malaita; the Betty bomber apparently had been damaged by the antiaircraft gunners on Guadalcanal. This time, however, District Officer Bengough's constables managed to capture the downed Japanese aviators, NAP1c Mutsu Araki, NAP2c Masatake Kato, and NAP3c Toyo Oda. The three were sent under the guard of scouts Baethisara and Tome to coastwatcher Martin Clemens at Aola on Guadalcanal. They arrived there on 9 October and later were transferred to the POW compound at Lunga.[26]

On 27 October, the hungry Cape Astrolabe Japanese had a feast when a stray cow was rounded up and butchered. But that provided only a brief respite, for on 1 November a diarist reported: "It is exactly 20 days since we ran out of rations." On the following day, a B-17 flew a few hundred feet over the Japanese camp taking sightings. This should have been a warning that something big was brewing, as a Flying Fortress was seldom seen over their area. Emperor Meiji's birthday was on 3 November, but contrary to custom, the forlorn detachment did not celebrate. Half of the men had malaria, and the other half were too tired to pay homage. A diary entry for that date reads: "We must leave everything up to fate. I am sure there is no fear of death."[27]

Over a month earlier, on 28 September at Nouméa, Admiral Richmond Turner, in a communication to General Vandegrift, had suggested that the 2nd Marine Raider Battalion under Lt. Col. Evans F. Carlson — the renowned Carlson's Raiders — be utilized to attack the Japanese outposts at Cape Astrolabe; at Marau Sound, on the southeast end of Guadalcanal; and at Cape Hunter, on the south coast of Guadalcanal.

> Based on the foregone conjectures, now would seem to be the time to push hard as possible on the following items: (a) continue clearing out all nests of enemy troops on the north side of Guadalcanal, initial operations, continuing westward. I believe you are in a position to take some chances and go for them hard. I am glad to see Rupertus [Brig. Gen. William H.] is cleaning up Florida Island; and believe he should establish detachments on Sandfly Passage, the north coast, Matumba Bay at the eastern end of Florida, as soon as justified. Here we are working up a scheme to start out within a few days with two APDs available and two companies of Second Raiders, to attack the Jap outposts at Camp Astrolabe, Malaita; Marau Bay on Guadalcanal, and at Cape Hunter. We want to co-ordinate these operations with you, and get your approval of our plan; therefore the Commanding Officer of the Second Raider Battalion, after conference with me, will shortly fly up and see you and go over the plans with you. One question to decide is, whether or not to leave small detachments of Second Raiders at these places; at a later time, we would relieve them with other line troops.[28]

General Vandegrift, however, wanted the 2nd Raiders for other commitments.

The 2nd Marine command on Tulagi was aware of the enemy observation post overlooking Indispensable Strait on Malaita Island and had made plans to eliminate it. Maj. John Mather, the Australian liaison officer, was sent from Aola in a Vought OS2U Kingfisher amphibian to confer with District Officer Bengough. Mather remained at Auki for three days, and a plan was worked out between Maj. D. W. Fuller, executive officer of the 3rd Battalion, 2nd Marines; 1st Lt. J. Wendell Crain; and Sgt. Robert S. Suggs. A seven-team strike force was to be formed of forty men from Company I, 3rd Battalion, 2nd Marines, with Lieutenant Crain in overall command. Team #1 would be headed by Sgt. Richard E. Patch Jr.; Team #2 by Cpl. Charles F. Pyeatt; Team #3 by Sgt. Thomas I. Chapman; Team #4 by 1st Sgt. Clifford J. Robichard

Jr.; Team #5 by Cpl. Manley J. Ewait; Team #6 by Sgt. Orle S. Bergner; and Team #7 by Cpl. Arthur G. Gordon. Added to the force were a doctor and a corpsman—Lt. Robert M. Adams, MC, USNR, and PhM1c Herbert R. Fuller, Jr., USNR—and four native scouts—Alekwona, Ab Anari, Milatee, and Seleni.

The plan was set in place on 2 November. At 1400 the Malaita strike force assembled at Tulagi and boarded the slow and noisy "chug–chugs" *Nanui* and *Jones,* headed for Malaita's chief port of Auki. The force arrived at midnight after a stormy voyage and remained at Auki during that day. Lieutenant Crain made supplementary plans with Captain Bengough for the raid on the Japanese lookout post. One of the scouts reported: "The outpost had one tent covered with green coconut fronds on the main road, about 300 yards southwest of a machine gun post. Overhanging rock about 200 yards inland was used as an air raid shelter. . . . This post is well defined to our intelligence; it consists of 22 men armed with rifles and automatic weapons."[29]

The Malaita island police unit had consistently studied the Japanese schedule and movements and had obtained additional last-minute information useful to the strike force. Bengough furnished a detailed map of the enemy camp that his constable-scouts had made. When the marines were ready to shove off, the scouts led the way. Lieutenant Crain would recall the raid in detail years later:

> We stayed overnight with Bengough and heard, "This is London calling at 6:00 PM—BBC" (he had a hand cranked radio that he turned on every night for the broadcast). The next morning in an open field adjacent to his house (an old, three-room house painted white), we laid out a simulated area that the Japanese were occupying. We had seven teams of 5–7 men per team; each headed by [an] NCO. . . . The Japanese camp we were to attack was near the beach. A native road, hardly large enough for a jeep, ran along the beach area. The sandy beach was probably 20–40 yards wide, bordered by the road with the enemy camp inland from the road. The camp was in an open area, probably 150–200 yards in diameter in a clearing. A stream running into the ocean, 100 yards [farther] north from the camp[,] had been used for bathing, drinking and washing clothes.
>
> We planned to get into position, surround the camp about 4–5:00 AM, 1½ hours before daylight. We were to wait and

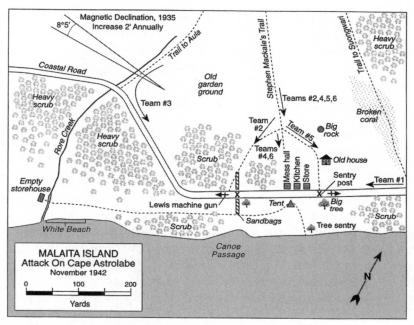

Figure 40. Map of the American plan of attack on Cape Astrolabe, Malaita Island, November 1942. (Courtesy J. Wendell Crain; map courtesy Mary Craddock Hoffman)

watch; when the Japanese got up to start their day they would usually go to an open[-]sided mess hall for their meal. That was the time we were to open fire. We had very tight timing[; we] counted them as they entered the mess hall. We were not sure of the number since it was reported 1–2 airmen had recently been shot down and swam to the camp. We estimated (the native scouts) the time it would take moving from down the beach (the British officer's house) to a point about ½ mile short of the camp. (We were moving up the native road until then.) At that point, ½ mile away, a native policeman would guide each team inland and approach the camp from there. Our goal was to spot the seven teams in an arc around the camp, move as close to the open area as each team could (yet, staying under cover in the dense jungle that surrounded the camp). We had about 40 men, moving at night, in deep jungle, led into place by natives who spoke only Pidgin English. Visibility was bad. Teams had to hold hands to keep from getting lost. We found some native roots that glowed in the dark [phosphorus] and each team member could see a faint light. Silence was imperative. We moved into position (all teams, no one lost) probably around 5:00 AM, still dark, but getting light soon. I was with a side team near the center of the camp.[30]

Another report of the events further described the situation:

It was getting light as we circled the camp. The Japs were occupying a small clearing on the coastal road built by the British. We could see four open-sided shacks, a galley, a mess hall and a storehouse. There was also a wireless shack, our main objective. We crawled on our bellies to within 15 yards of the mess hall. It was the funniest thing to lie there and watch them walking around, washing up, brushing their teeth and getting ready for chow. We waited. At a quarter to eight, 14 of them were in the mess hall. Watching them eat made us feel hungry. They were wolfing native potatoes, bananas and drinking coffee. We had waited because we hoped to get them all together, but when we saw two of them getting ready to leave, I gave the signal to fire. The plan was that no team was to open fire until our team began firing. In an emergency, a team if they had been discovered, could fire.

Support fire came in from all teams. To my knowledge, we received no return fire, although they were armed with rifles and machine guns. One or two had strolled down to the small stream for an early bath or to wash clothes. They didn't come to breakfast. They were killed or captured and one was brought back to Tulagi. The natives possibly later killed the two airmen. The firing was over in a few minutes. We picked up all gear (ammo, code books, radios and weapons) and had the natives bury the dead Japanese. We sent runners down the beach to bring the native boats back to camp.[31]

Former Pharmacist's Mate Herbert R. Fuller remembered one darkly comic moment that occurred before the teams opened fire:

Picture if you can, we [had] been lying in position for about an hour. We were waiting for the auto firing of the middle section of the team. The BARs, etc., were in very close range to the mess table area. All our senses were super alert . . . and then came the tinkling sound of someone relieving his bladder over the dump[;]

and the sound came from a stream of liquid hitting someone's helmet—not any tin can.

Some Jap was "passing yellow water" on a helmet of one of the automatic-firing group. The irate Marine was noiseless and cussing to himself half startled, but furious. Later he stated in no uncertain terms his anger and how he'd wished the order to fire [had been] given [at that instant]. . . . How he wanted to shoot that SOB then and there [even though] against orders! I suppose he never lived that down, a brief encounter that allowed the Japanese to urinate all over him while he remained motionless, then let the Jap get away with it. . . . But only briefly.

As a word of explanation, I shot that Japanese.[32]

The epilogue to the story is recounted by a member of Lieutenant Crain's force:

"When it was all over, we were treated by the natives as heroes. They had been living happily under British rule and had been severely plundered by the Japs, who had lived off their gardens and stolen their chickens. When they saw all the Japs had been killed, they made a really gala occasion and brought us all kinds of fruit and some of their native wine. The fruit was very welcome and when we had finished, they serenaded us with native songs. I felt that we ought to respond, so we all stood up and sang 'From the Halls of Montezuma' and that pleased them more than ever. When we left, they all lined up by their chief and gave three cheers in typical British fashion. We could hear them yelling as we went back to the jungle."[33]

The Japanese that had been captured was SM Shohei Fukuda, second in command of the lookout post. According to his POW report, during the skirmish he was hit in the right knee and dropped to the ground. Corpsman Fuller tended to his injury, bandaging the knee so that Fukuda could limp to the boat. After a calm ride from Malaita, Lieutenant Crain's force and the one POW arrived at Tulagi at 0605 on 5 November.[34]

On 23 July 1943, C. N. F. Bengough was killed off the New Georgia Islands while flying in a New Zealand Hudson bomber to spot targets. He had been promoted to lieutenant colonel and at the time was acting resident commissioner for the Solomon Islands. The Hudson was attacked by a Zero, and Bengough and the crew had to abandon the plane. Several members of the crew managed to get out, but the Japanese pilot machine-gunned them in the water. One man survived to tell the story.[35]

Rennell Island

Lying 160 miles south of the southern tip of Guadalcanal and nearly 100 miles south of San Cristobal, Rennell Island is one of the most isolated locales in the Solomons. At a meeting of the Royal Geographical Society in London on 6 March 1916, Charles M. Woodford, the first Resident Commissioner of the Protectorate, described Rennell and its neighbor, Bellona: "The Polynesian islands, Rennell and the adjacent Bellona, are perhaps the most interesting (in the Pacific) because they have been so seldom visited . . . and little has been recorded about their inhabitants. . . . As there is nothing that can be called a safe anchorage, and the natives have nothing to sell, the islands have been left to themselves. . . . Eastward of where I landed [on Rennell] a large lake [Lake Tengano] exists. Dr. [Norman] Deck, [of the South Sea Evangelical mission] who first discovered it, states [that] its water is brackish [and that] on the south shore of the lake, where there is considerable native settlement, . . . the natives navigate the waters of the lake in sailing canoes."[36]

In contrast to the other islands of the Solomon Protectorate, Rennell and Bellona, once low-lying atolls, rise 300 feet out of the sea like coral sentinels. Forty-five miles long and ten miles wide, Rennell Island is the world's largest raised coral atoll. It is surrounded by rugged perpendicular coral cliffs and from the air appears to be ringed by a gigantic white necklace. Rennell had been an antediluvian coral reef with an enclosed lagoon that developed around an extinct volcano; the volcano's crater forms Lake Tengano (*Te Nggano*), said to be the largest freshwater lake in the Pacific, though apparently, according to Charles M. Woodford, it was slightly salty. The island has one small open anchorage at Tuhunango.

Rennell was so remote that the inhabitants were sometimes referred to as Stone Age people. After three mission native teachers had been killed there in 1910, the government closed the island to all visitors, and it was not until 1934 that teachers and missionaries were again permitted to visit. But isolated Rennell was already blessed in one respect: its inhabitants had not contracted any of the European diseases, and it had no malaria. Although the island remained out of bounds to most Europeans, the protectorate government, through the medical officer, allowed certain missionaries periodically to make short visits there. Once every few years Doctor Deck and some of the mission staff traveled from Malaita to Rennell seeking converts; they were modestly successful, but the effort took nearly thirty years. In 1936, however, the government again closed Rennell to all visitors for fear that the islanders would contract European diseases.

Because there was no manner of communication with the remote atoll, the Allies did not know if it had been occupied by the Japanese, and thus a detachment from the rear echelon of the 2nd Marines on Espiritu Santo Island, New Hebrides, was sent to Rennell to establish a lookout station. Commanded by 1st Lt. Emmett N. Carter of Company A (motor transport), 2nd Service Battalion, the detachment comprised eight enlisted men from the 2nd Marines, three U.S. Navy petty officers, and a coastwatcher. They arrived on 12 November 1942 in a PBY flying boat, the first the islanders had seen. Lieutenant Carter kindly prepared the following account of the establishment of the lookout post at Lake Tengano and his detachment's sojourn on Rennell Island.

> My commanding officer, Capt. Robert H. Sanders, came to the tent at a meeting of the company officers; he wanted a volunteer for a unique mission. He explained what we were to do[,] saying it was unknown whether or not the Japanese had occupied the island and whether or not the natives were friendly or cannibalistic. . . . We were to establish ourselves in the native villages, without making any changes that would alert enemy aircraft. We would not engage the enemy under any circumstances except in our own defense.
>
> On the trip from the *Curtiss* I had the opportunity to spend some time with Petty Officer Andy Andresen; Andresen was on loan from the Australian Navy and had recently been shifted to Santo from Guadalcanal. An experienced coastwatcher, he discussed with me the finer points of what was ahead of us. Andresen was fluent in Pidgin English, which was a great help in communicating with many of the islanders. (Andresen had lived in the Solomons [prewar.]). Later on board the ship we found out that there were no Japanese on the island. Our radio contact would be with the *Curtiss* in code. The *Curtiss* was one of our largest aircraft support vessels and fully equipped from A to Z. It was the command post, and at this time the mother ship for Patrol Squadron 23 (VP-23).
>
> We loaded all our equipment on a PBY and were flown to Rennell Island. Our PBY landed on a very smooth lagoon, Lake Tengano, near a small village. We later learned there was one other village on the island. Before we could unload our rubber

raft the plane was surrounded by Polynesians, swimming and in their canoes. You would think the gods had sent us. They appeared to be friendly enough. Andresen, and myself were the first to step ashore and were immediately met by the Chief, Tegeta, with whom we attempted to communicate. Andresen assisted me with our first negotiations with Tegeta and then departed with the PBY to return to Espiritu Santo.

The big hit with the islanders were the trinkets we carried, as Andresen had forewarned us on how to make friends quickly in an unknown area. We had an ample supply of T-shirts [skivvies] and soon most of the women were wearing them. We also had an ample supply of black stick chewing tobacco, beads, and trinkets, but the most wanted item was machetes. Tegeta soon had vacated houses for us to move into. These houses were constructed of bamboo with leaf roofs. The one that we used for our headquarters was out over the water. If you dropped your pen, you had to dive to find it. The lake water was the principal source of fresh water for drinking, bathing, laundry, and all sanitation. We set up our own water treatment plant and latrine.

A difficult task was setting up our radio at a point where it would be well hidden and close to a good lookout for us to stand watch. The natives helped us build [something] that could protect our equipment and was close to the point we selected for observing passing vessels and aircraft. It was well hidden from the air.

After the PBY left, our team was isolated, except for wireless contact. Our first priority was to establish radio contact, and we reached the *Curtiss* before the PBY arrived back at Espiritu Santo. Our two radiomen, Bridenstine and Stone, knew their business, and with other communicators from the Marines we soon put together a system for the job.

We reported flotsam that had drifted to the island, some of which we could identify. Tegeta took us to the remains of a fighter that had crashed on the island; facts and identity were reported. We reported air flights and ship convoys that we observed.

Once a Japanese submarine sent a few Japanese sailors ashore to recon the beach at the southern tip of the island. The formation of the island made this the only feasible place for anyone to come ashore from a ship. We did not make contact. They were never aware that we were on the island.

Corpsman Carey proved to be very valuable on the mission. He had a good supply of medications and he gave our men regular physical examinations. He kept busy administering aid to the people on the island. About two weeks after we arrived, one of our watchmen, Scott, reported that a large number of islanders were headed toward us from the southern end of Lake Tengano. I alerted all hands, but it turned out to be a friendly invasion consisting of the Chief Taugongi from the other village bringing his people for medical treatment. Carey came to me shortly afterward and asked for permission to return with these islanders to their village. It seemed a girl there was dying and they wanted our "docataa" to help. This required a high[-]level conference between Tegeta, the other chief, and myself. They called me "Masatakata." As a result I sent Lovett to handle the boat and Sebby and Palmateer along with Carey to see what could be done. That mission was a success in that the pharmacist's mate was able to heal her. The treatment she was receiving from the local "healing man" was not doing enough.

After about 25 days on the island Sergeant Marsh became very ill. Marsh may have died, had Carey been less knowledgeable. I requested through our radio contact with the *Curtiss* that Marsh be evacuated from the island but got no immediate confirmation. About this time our radio began cutting out on us and we did not have spare parts to repair it. We made makeshift repairs, but they were not too successful. It was not long before a PBY arrived with radio replacement equipment and took Marsh to the hospital.

We conducted recon missions every day and encouraged the islanders to report on Japanese (or strangers) and the sighting of any vessels, so we could check it out. Nothing exciting happened and the men were busy with their particular tasks. We had our own supplies, which were supplemented with certain fruits and vegetables from the native gardens. If we had had to spend the rest of the war there on that lonely island, we would have suffered from sheer boredom.

According to Chief Tegeta, Rennell had been discovered and explored by several other countries [French and Australian traders]. Rennell is so isolated it was seldom visited by those from other islands [but] some of those visits turned out to be violent. Through the years fisherman had landed on the island and often took young women with them; they never returned. Missionaries landed several times and taught them various religions. The religion that seemed to take root was the Church of England. Young girls were often taken away to attend seminaries; only one ever returned. She taught [the islanders] Pidgin English and told [them] how the rest of the world lived. One fear that Tegeta had was of the Japanese invading the island after we left. He was also concerned that we might want to take some of his people with us when we left. . . . I was invited to give the Christmas story to the entire Lake [Tengano] population on December 25th. It was questionable whether they received very much from my story.

We closed the little station approximately on 15 January 1943; headquarters on Santo sent a PBY to pick us up. We left all our gear there, except the radio. On arrival at our base on Espiritu Santo Island, we were happy to learn that all the Santo Marines from our contingent were to be transferred to New Zealand. Our team was especially happy since New Zealand represented civilization.

On reaching Wellington we were all reassigned to our original outfits. We did our tour as coast watchers, but wished for action that would have had a positive effect on the war effort. It seemed we were on vacation, enjoying the sun while our fellow Marines were fighting the war. From my viewpoint, life would not be worth much if it had to be spent on this small bit of land. We all wanted to get back to our units and get some action; later all of us really got more than we bargained for. About six months [afterward] I received a letter from the Chief asking us to come back in the event of a Japanese attack. We did not return and the Japanese did not attack.[37]

The chief's letter to Lieutenant Carter was possibly prompted by the battle waged in late January 1943 in and about Rennell's waters, when a Zero (Model 21) of the Japanese 751st Air Group attacked the heavy cruiser *Chicago*. While the airmen clobbered her from above, a Japanese submarine fired a spread of six Long Lance torpedoes at the dying cruiser. The gallant *Chicago*, lifeless, finally rolled over and sank.

News abstracts from the *Too Daily Newspaper,* published in Aomori City, Japan, 5 February 1943, described the events:

> The latest Sea Battle Results of the Seahawks . . . Announced by the Grand Imperial Headquarters (at 16:00. the 4th) . . . Persistent counter-attacks by the enemy. Enemy damages are three times ours. Tokyo Dispatch
>
> After the great results obtained in the sea battle off Rennell Island, and the sinking of one enemy cruiser, the damaging of another enemy cruiser, and shooting down 33 enemy planes, and in the battles of Isabel Island in the New Georgia sector, . . . the number of enemy vessels sunk and damaged by the Imperial Navy in the South Pacific waters bordering the Solomons since the initial Solomon Island [assault reaches a] brilliant total of 134, and the number of enemy planes shot down to over 943. On the other hand, up to the other day we made the exalted sacrifice of a total of 41 vessels sunk or damaged in our own waters, 243 self-destroyed or missing planes, and 32 severely damaged. In comparing friendly and enemy damage, the ratio is 3.3 times greater loss for the enemy in vessels, and 3.7 times greater in planes.
>
> Comparing this recent ratio of damage to that which obtained in the initial engagement of last summer, a great decrease is evident. This fact indicates the fierceness of the battles in the South Pacific, and tells how tenacious the enemy counter attack is. Modern sea battles is truly one of the great of expendables [TN (translation), *Shomo-Sen* (a war of attrition)], and here lies the reason why it must be won by a sure victory on the production front.

While Tokyo was making these inflated claims, the Japanese Army was secretly evacuating Guadalcanal.

15 The U.S. Army Takes Over

On 28 October 1942, Maj. Tadahika Hayashi, the Seventeenth Army cipher officer, had arrived at Rabaul, New Britain Island, to confer with Maj. Gen. Akisaruro Futami, chief of staff of the Seventeenth Army rear area headquarters. The Sun Soldiers on Guadalcanal were plagued by a desperate food shortage and Major Hayashi wanted to know what immediate steps could be taken to rectify the problem. The tense meeting emphasized the difficulties being caused by the American air forces, and a consensus was reached that prompted the Imperial Navy to re-assign a number of submarines from combat patrols in the Indian Ocean to a supply mission for Guadalcanal. The 8th Base Force already had been using submarines for communications and resupply wherever possible.

By 10 November the *I-15,* the first of many Imperial Japanese Navy submarines, reached Kamimbo Bay on the far northwestern corner of Guadalcanal and unloaded supplies about one hundred yards offshore. Cdr. Nobuo Ishikawa's 354-foot-long, 2,584-ton underwater truck was one of sixteen submarines reassigned from the Indian Ocean to the RXN resupply operation. But even that effort was not enough to feed twenty thousand hungry and sick soldiers. The Imperial Navy had an impossible task. Each submarine could carry some fifty tons of supplies, yet that was just adequate for a two-day food ration. As a result, the men of the Seventeenth Army were slowly starving to death. The *I-9,* under Capt. Akiyoshi Fjii, unloaded at Kamimbo Bay on 26 November. The following day, Lt. Cdr. Inoue Endounin brought the 1,955-ton *I-31,* but she was attacked by the U.S. Navy's Tulagi-based "devil boats" (the PTs) while delivering provisions at Cape Esperance. Two torpedoes of PT-*59* had connected, sinking the *I-31.*[1]

The Seventeenth Army, determined to get food to the island, also established a chain-supply operation by sending Japanese Army daihatsu landing barges to Guadalcanal. The barges, forty-nine feet long and 6½ feet high, each could carry ten tons, but they could travel only eighty sea miles on a tank of gas at a crawling eight miles per hour, and thus a gas barge was required for a fuel resupply. If the gas barge were sunk, then they would have serious problems. The run would begin at Buin, Bougainville, the army's main supply point, and from there make a quick pass to the nearby Shortland Islands, off the tip of Bougainville, where the crews would rest during daylight hours. They then would head for Vella Lavella Island, in the New Georgia group, jump thirty-five miles to Gizo Island, and after that sneak down the 160 miles to Cape Esperance on the northwestern tip of Guadalcanal. However, the Cactus Air Force sometimes caught and sank the "ant runs," as the Americans called them, in the open sea on the long stretch between Gizo and Guadalcanal.

The Changing Forces

December 1942 saw many adjustments on Guadalcanal Island. The American troop strength had increased, while the Japanese forces dwindled. More of the U.S. Army's American Division citizen soldiers—the "weekend warriors"—were arriving from the rear areas, and the Seabees were seen walking around Guadalcanal in new gear. A post exchange opened with basic necessities plus stationery; the troops no longer had to depend on captured Japanese rice-paper on which to write their letters. One PX had a limited stock of 2.2 beer, but a small quantity of harder, bootlegged liquor could be purchased on the open market from visiting airmen at one hundred dollars-plus per bottle. Usually the Seabees, who were older, had the first pick—their average age was 33, the men the GIs and marines called "Gramps."

With the U.S. Army came tents, and for the first time in months some of the marines could sleep under cover and out of the rain. A shortage of service troops still existed—soldiers did not like being used as stevedores—but the situation began to improve on 3 December when the Solomon Islands Labor Corps was formed and islanders were put to work. Two hundred islanders in the first group were employed at the weekly rate of five shillings ($1.25); a month later, the corps would number 1,450. The natives insisted on being paid with English shilling coins, the kind they had received before the war, and thus as much as five thousand dollars in British coins had to be flown in from Nouméa. The native workers also would take American quarters, but the coins were scarce on the island.

The marines on Guadalcanal, however, were not as well situated as their brothers on Tulagi Island who could purchase a large bunch of bananas for a nickel from the Florida Island natives and a small bunch for a dime. They also could get their clothes washed each week for twenty-five cents, a luxury not available on Guadalcanal. Nevertheless, life on Guadalcanal was continuing to improve. On 3 December, in addition to the new Labor Corps, more reinforcements poured in from the rear area base on New Caledonia when the *Hunter Liggett* and the *Kenmore* (AP 62) landed elements of the 9th Defense Battalion, whose advance echelon had arrived on 21 November. The 9th was assigned as the major defense unit for the Koli Point sector, which was badly in need of antiaircraft weapons. Admiral Turner also moved additional Americal Division formations, including the 2nd and 3rd Battalions, 132nd Infantry Regiment, plus the 247th Field Artillery Battalion (less Battery A) and the 26th Signal Company. The 1st Battalion, 132nd, followed five days later.

On 9 December at Mount Mambulu, the native name for Mount Austen, twenty-eight sailor-warriors from Lt. Cdr. Akira Takizawa's Butai moved into the Gifu command post; their numbers were down from the 114 that had landed in August. Named by men of the 230th Infantry Regiment from Gifu, Japan, and the 69th Infantry Regiment, the command post was located about 400 yards northeast of Hill 27—a hill the Americans would soon come to hate. About the same time, remnants of the 228th Infantry Regiment (1st and 2nd Battalions) took up positions at the base of Mount Austen. They renamed their post Suemura Shitai for Col. Masaichi Suemura of the 228th Infantry. The position had been named Doi Shitai before the death of Col. Sadashichi Doi, the 228th commander who had been killed in a bombardment. The commanding officer of the 8th Company, 228th Infantry, 1st Lt. Iwao Fujita, established a spotter position between the first and second observation stations also the base of Mount Austen, and Capt. Yoshiyuki Sato from the 2nd Reserve Unit was in placed in charge of security. The assaulting GIs were pushing the Nippon soldiers led by Maj. Takeyoshi Inagaki (II/228i) into two valleys between Hills 27 and 31 and Hills 31 and 42 where it was said the Japanese fought like devils and the GIs took casualties.

Maj. Haruja Nishiyama, commanding officer of the 3rd Battalion, 228th Infantry (less the 9th Company under Capt. Yataro Kasugi and the 12th Company under 1st Lt. Tasuo Kobayashi), plus one machine-gun platoon, ordered his men to defend the area south of northern Miharashi Dai (Hill 54), part of the Galloping Horse Ridge mass just north of Sea Horse Ridge (Hills 43 and 44), and to extend protection to the terrain west of Hill 49 (*Inu,* Dog) and Hill 67. He also ordered the 1st Platoon, 11th Company, under Capt. Keizo Fukada, which was in the front line to "stand firm," then placed 1st Lt. Toichi Wakabayashi's twenty-seven men of the 10th Company on the left of Captain Fukada's platoon. The Japanese were determined to remain in the hills and let the American come after them.

Shuichiro Kato, a sergeant with the 2nd Battalion, 228th Infantry, machine-gun company, told his POW interrogator: "After the unit was all landed, they took the trail up the Isamu River to Hill [903; U.S. Hill 89]. Here they crossed over the Matanikau, and preceded up to the area of Miharashi Dai [Hill 54]. Then the unit split up, the 2nd Battalion going to help the Oka unit [124th Infantry], the 3rd Battalion staying at the Miharashi Dai . . . and Headquarters and the 1st Battalion assigned to Sakai Dai [Skyline Ridge—Hills 75, 78, and 80]. . . . They maintained these positions until the final push." Pvt. Isamu Kinoshita's interrogator notes: "There was plenty of ammunition for the 75-mm guns. These were covered up with green cloth. He has not heard them fire for the last ten days that he knows of; the artillery is waiting for a dark night before it really opens up. The three large guns have each about 30 rounds of badly corroded ammunition. The battalion in the front of his position has no artillery but only machine guns and mortars."[2]

The 2nd Marines (less the 3rd Battalion) had moved up between 11 and 16 December to relieve U.S. Army units at the front, the deadly Matanikau River sector where the 2nd Marines had spent part of early November. The GIs dubbed the area "the snake pit." Some deadly sparring was still occurring, with the Americans now being more aggressive as the Imperial Army still managed to hold its own. Cunning Japanese snipers infiltrated near enough to the American lines to fire off a few shots, and thus caution was the rule of the day.

The last of the American Army formations reached Guadalcanal on 13 December when the 3rd Battalion, 182nd Infantry Regiment, and part of the 57th Engineer Combat Battalion arrived from garrison duty on Espiritu Santo Island. Almost the entire Americal Division was now on the island.[3] Admiral Turner, however, was most interested in establishing Guadalcanal as a major advanced naval base; he kept sending naval construction units in bits and pieces to the island on any ships available. He transported Company B, 18th NCB, on the SS *Joseph Teal,* which reached Lunga on 3 December, followed by the bulk of Companies A and D, 18th Seabees, plus the headquarters—some fourteen officers and 552 enlisted men—that arrived at Guadalcanal on the 12th. Company C arrived the next day, and finally, on 19 December, the rear echelon of three officers and 150 men landed at Lunga. A week later the *Heywood* arrived with another load of 982 Seabees from the 26th NCB. They had been in the navy for only two months when ordered overseas, reaching Nouméa on 10 November; six weeks later they were sweating in Guadalcanal's heat.

Guadalcanal and Tulagi required an enormous amount of construction work, and the Seabees were just the right men to do it. By late December over 4,000 were at work on both islands. However, Admiral Turner was not impressed with the naval management of the Guadalcanal base. In November he had quickly replaced the first base commander, Capt. James P. Compton of Cub-1, with Capt. W. G. Greenman; a month later, he replaced Captain Greenman with Capt. Thomas M. Shook. Shook subsequently was replaced by Capt. H. L. Maples. Admiral Turner was determined that CACTUS would be the best-run advanced base in the South Pacific, even with the Japanese less than ten miles away. Progress was evident by 22 December with the opening of Fleet Post Office 145 adjacent to the airstrip; the fastest selling item was stamped six-cent airmail envelopes.

Nine months earlier, 12 March 1942, Maj. Gen. Alexander M. Patch had brought from Australia to New Caledonia a mixed bag of federalized National Guard troops that formed Army Task Force 6418 (the later Americal Division). They had been assigned as garrison troops for New Caledonia to blunt any Japanese attack. By October, however, with the enemy knocking at the door of Henderson Field, General Patch had transferred to Guadalcanal Col. Bryant E. Moore's crack 164th Infantry Regiment of the North Dakota Guard to bolster the fatigued marines. The men of the 164th would be followed later by additional elements supporting the Guadalcanal campaign, including a formation in the rear area, the 147th Infantry Regiment, which had transferred from Tonga to CACTUS via Espiritu Santo, New Hebrides Islands. The 147th pre-war had belonged to the 37th Infantry Division. No longer part of a division, it was called the "Orphan Unit," moving all across the Pacific area as an individual regiment.

On 8 December, after being on Guadalcanal for four grueling months, the 1st Marine Division moved on to Australia, relinquishing command on the island and turning control of the war to the U.S. Army's General Patch. The departing units included the 1st and 5th Marine Regiments; remaining were the 2nd, 7th, 8th, 10th, and 11th Marines, some elements of which had been in the islands since D-day, 7 August. The 1st and 5th Marines, two worn-out regiments, were eager to get away from the island of hell where they had to leave behind so many of their comrades, both in numbered cemetery graves and in unmarked and unknown places.[4]

Figure 41. The men of D-2 (Division Intelligence) Section, 1st Marine Division, in the operations bunker of the division command post, 2 December 1942. *First row, left to right*: PFC Francis Massaro, scout; Cpl. John C. Schiller Jr., senior clerk; Cpl. Joseph J. Dickhaus, observer; Pvt. Russell Esberger, lithographer; PFC Edward G. Sexton, photographer; Cpl. Robert M. Howard Jr., photographer. *Second row*: 2nd Lt. Arthur S. Claffy, assistant D-2; 2nd Lt. Karl Thayer Soule Jr., assistant D-2; 2nd Lt. James H. Whitehead Jr., assistant D-2; Capt. Sherwood F. Moran, language; Lt. Col. Edmund J. Buckley, D-2; Ensign DeLancie, USN, aerial photo interpreter; Maj. Richard Evans, assistant D-2; Ensign Sommer, USN, aerial photo interpreter. *Third row*: 2nd Lt. Levi T. Burcham, aerial photo interpreter; Cpl. Anthony Medin, draftsman; 1st Lt. Jerome J. Foley, aerial photo interpreter; Cpl. Frederic Peachy, keeper of the journal; Cpl. William F. Rogillio, lithographer; Pvt. Thomas Dudgeon, observer; Cpl. Ralph R. Wendling, lithographer; Cpl. Edward L. Hall, darkroom (back); PFC Richard K. Hance, movie photographer; PFC Earl K. Swenson, darkroom (back); SSgt. Philip A. Edmondson, chief, photolithography; Cpl. Henry Sidermann, photo interpreter (back); Sgt. Henry D. Burnham, draftsman. *Fourth row*: Cpl. Richard B. Barr, observer; Cpl. Vernon C. Stimpel, draftsman; Corporal Slaghek, section chief; Cpl. William S. Donohue, observer; Sgt. Leroy H. Wolfe, assistant section chief. (National Archives)

Those who boarded the transports included a large number with severe health problems.

In all, the 1st Marine Division had suffered 8,486 casualties; of those, 774 were killed in action or missing, with 1,962 wounded. Three men died of malaria, and the total afflicted with diseases was 5,750. They had suffered fever, chills, and dehydration, and they had been plagued with diarrhea, malaria, jungle rot, and at times almost starvation. Some of the men on stretchers directed to hospitals in Australia had been painted purple from the salve used to control jungle rot, a fungus condition they contracted from the unrelenting mud.[5] The men on Guadalcanal had endured their time in hell, undergoing 170 air raids, 64 naval bombardments, and untold hours of combat; they had survived the bombardment of 614 of Pistol Pete's 105-mm shells, which he had deposited in their midst.[6] To the Americans, the price was high, as each life was precious, yet much less costly than the "Bloody Buna" battle on New Guinea where 3,095 were killed in action and 5,451 wounded. The enemy had committed more than fifty thousand troops, and by February 1943

Figure 42. At the change of command in December 1942, Maj. Gen. A. A. Vandegrift, USMC (*right*), and Maj. Gen. A. M. Patch (*left*), USA, discuss the Guadalcanal situation just before the departure of the 1st Marine Division. Listening are Col. P. Hall Joschke, USMC (*center*), and an unidentified marine. (USMC photo)

had evacuated 10,085, leaving hundreds of sick and dying on the route to the withdrawal point.[7]

Eighteen-year-old TSgt. Joseph G. Micek, of Company G, 2nd Battalion, 132nd Infantry, American Division, debarked on Guadalcanal on 8 December, the last major element of the American to arrive. Micek recalls:

> 8 December: The first casualty I record was the death of 2nd Lt. Riley Morgan. I had known the Lieutenant back in New Caledonia, and heard he was shot through the heart while on patrol in our front lines. . . . Many patrols have often fought each other by mistake and quite a few were killed in this manner. A fellow's nerves get rather jittery and he shoots at anything. . . .
> On the 11th, three companies of my battalion occupied a defense position along the beach; others went to guard the airport. The 12th: Our mission was to send out patrols into the southern part of the island to make sure the enemy was under control. 13th: We really caught hell from "Maytag Annie" tonight as he came over about 2200 and dropped 18 bombs. Boy, did we hit our slit trenches! I could hear the shrill swishing sound of the bombs as they dropped. They do that to keep us awake.
> The 14th: new troops have been arriving almost every day. We expect to make a big push in the very near future. I also visited an American Cemetery, which was within walking distance from our encampment area. Simple, green, crude, wooden crosses on each grave marked their final resting place. One grave had a propeller stuck in it. Others had 105 shells, while still others had the lids from their meat can covers over their humble gravesite with a short epitaph inscribed: "Most of these men were killed in the October offensive."[8]

When General Patch took over on Guadalcanal, his command had been briefed by the 1st Division on aspects of the battle conditions. Patch had experience in dealing with the French in New Caledonia and had become an expert in the art of diplomatic euphemism, but he had never engaged in jungle warfare—nor had anyone in the green American Division. General Vandegrift and his 1st Division staff had witnessed the struggle since the beginning, and having seen the campaign expand day by day they had developed an eye for the unexpected. Many of Vandegrift's majors and ranks above had served in jungle detachments in the "banana countries and banana wars" of South and Central American in the late 1920s; they were familiar with tropical forest conditions and with fighting in that environment.

On 15 December, while American command adjustments were still in progress, an aggressive Japanese raiding party from the 38th Engineer Regiment, led by 1st Lieutenant Ono, broke through the lines, blew up a new P-39 Airacobra and a gasoline truck, then escaped. The engineers also had made earlier successful forays, including one on the 12th led by 2nd Lieutenant Nakazawa.[9] At this time, however, the Japanese also were in the midst of command shuffles. At the Guadalcanal naval station, the younger Lt. Cdr. Tokunaga Okamura replaced Capt. Kanae Monzen. Monzen and his staff left the island on board the destroyer *Ariake,* bound for Rabaul; both officers had been on Guadalcanal since 6 July.[10] Over the previous few months, key Japanese naval officers had departed RXN on any vessel returning to Rabaul.

On the American side of the readjustment strategy General Patch's team had not developed a coherent plan for dealing with the pressing issues. The staff, a mixed collection of Americal Division officers, inexperienced and untested, formed the initial personnel for the U.S. Army's XIV Corps.[11] Their major problem was the Japanese on Mount Austen's Hill 27. The assistant division commander, Brig. Gen. Edmund B. Sebree, believed a reinforced company supported by a battalion would be sufficient to clean up the enemy there. Sebree, a post–World War I graduate of West Point, had no combat experience and no jungle knowledge—a serious shortcoming. No one in command seriously understood the destructive pitfalls of the treacherous terrain or the Japanese military mentality, and this led to a flood of unnecessary casualties. The command therefore presented the 132nd Infantry Regiment with an almost impossible mission—to neutralize the 920-foot promontory identified as Hill 27 on the maps but called "Bullet Junction" by the GIs.

The Move on Mount Austen

The chief pursuit of the newly formed XIV Corps under the Americal Division officers was to elbow westward in two stages.[12] First they were to eliminate the Mount Austen threat, where a concentration of Japanese troops was believed to be established in and about Hill 27. Then XIV Corps would push west beyond the Kokumbona River on an extended front, with the Americans attacking on both coasts. The men of the Illinois National Guard 132nd Infantry Regiment were selected to reduce the enemy-infested Mount Austen ridge complex. On the slopes of the Mount Austen cone rising some 1,500 feet skyward, amidst ridges, valleys, rocky terrain, steep hills, and an opaque jungle that locked in the heat, the 132nd would be introduced to warfare. From atop Mount Austen, six miles from the Henderson Field perimeter, Japanese soldiers with powerful glasses would be watching all the activity at Henderson Field.

The 3rd Battalion, 132nd, was assigned to the task, commanded by Lt. Col. William C. Wright of Oak Park, Illinois. Supporting the drive was the 3rd Battalion, 10th Marines, backed by 105-mm guns of the 247th Field Artillery Battalion and Battery A of the 90th Field Artillery Battalion, with fire support coordinated by the Fire Direction Center of 3/10. The men jumped off from Bloody Ridge through some of the most challenging terrain on the island. Mount Austen was thought to be held by a weakened enemy force composed of a handful of sick troops. They indeed were sick and hungry, but they were Japanese committed to their country and they were determined to fight. Most were based in the surrounding jungle and at the steep, overgrown hills—slopes identified by peculiar names that belonged at an animal sanctuary rather than on a battlefield: Galloping Horse Ridge (Hills 50–54, 57), Dog (Hill 49), Monkey (Hill 67). Brig. Gen. John E. Stannard, USA (Ret.), wrote: "The 132nd was fresh, but without experience in combat and they were to encounter an enemy making his strongest defensive fight of the Guadalcanal Campaign, from fortified positions which were located in extremely difficult terrain."[13]

On 19 December elements of the 132nd finally hit the outer areas of Hill 27 through almost impregnable terrain and compact jungle just west of Bloody Ridge. The next day, while traversing the foothills of the Gifu stronghold they heard a terrific explosion. A U.S. Army truck loaded with land mines had exploded next to the former Japanese ice plant, sending steel shavings, and ice cubes through the air; several soldiers riding on the truck plus two others riding in a jeep nearby were killed. The 132nd found the Mount Austen fortifications to consist of more than fifty interlocking pillboxes solidly constructed with logs and piled dirt—an ingenious system of firing ports dug into the hillside and ridges. These well-built positions, each with an array of 6.5-, 7.7-, and 13-mm machine guns, were backed by a set of 50-, 70-, and 81-mm mortars. In addition, the positions were difficult to locate. Engineering officers of the Japanese Seventeenth Army—Lt. Col. Makoto Hamada, Majs. Shigemaichi Shida and Tsuneichi Shima, and Capt. Masaru Tokuda, all skilled fortifications experts—had designed this miniature stronghold. The four officers had been with the Eighth Area Army and were reassigned to temporary duty with the Seventeenth Army on Guadalcanal.[14]

The U.S. Army XIV Corps staff and their blunt plan of attacking the Japanese bastion appeared to follow the piecemeal commitment of forces and tactics that had characterized the faulty Japanese operations. The 132nd Infantry Regiment would assault the fortress in driblets, company by company, then finally a battalion. Operating in the dense jungle terrain in staggering heat, they advanced slowly, methodically. Logic would dictate that a frontal assault against a prepared defense was likely to result in catastrophic casualties for the attacking force. That is precisely what occurred.

The 132nd moved into battle with 1917-vintage C rations—the date of production clearly marked on each packet—and D rations, which were tainted white chocolate. Each man had been allotted one C and three D. The men required a tremendous amount of water; they did not have enough. Many suffered heat exhaustion before reaching the target and had to be evacuated to the rear. Hauling a sick or injured soldier out of the rugged hill country took many medics and many hours. Records of the 132nd show that on 2 January 1943 in the action at Mount Austen, 175 stretcher-bearers took five hours to transport twenty casualties.[15]

While the 132nd was in the jungle fighting weather, terrain, and the Sun Soldiers, the Cactus Air Force received two additional aircraft from Espiritu Santo. Two OS2U Kingfisher planes, #5 and #9 of VS-5-D-14, had been converted from floats to wheels back at Santo, arriving at Henderson Field on 8 December. A week later #9 would make history. On the 16th, a flight of SBD Dauntless dive-bombers returning to Henderson from a strike against Munda, New Georgia Islands, radioed that they had sighted a submarine while passing near Kulokulo Island in the Russell group and had observed propeller swirls in otherwise calm waters. The returning SBDS had no bombs left. Twenty-five-year-old pilot Lt. (jg) Roger S. C. Wolcott, USNR, and his gunner, J. B. Pattie, were on standby status. When the word came of the sighting they took off and within thirty minutes were in the vicinity of the reported submarine off Kulokulo. Pattie was the first to see the boat, on the surface, one-half or three-quarters of a mile ahead on the port side; it appeared either to be charging its batteries or in difficulty. Lieutenant Wolcott made a 360-degree turn to the right and closed in at an altitude of 750 to 1,000 feet in a sliding descent. He let go two depth charges that straddled the area of the sub's conning tower. On banking, the Americans could see the sub rise out of the water, spilling oil far and wide. What Wolcott and

Figure 43. Removing a casualty from the Mount Austen area, Guadalcanal. (Courtesy Joseph G. Micek)

Pattie sank was Cdr. Nobuo Ishikawa's *I-15* on her third resupply trip to Guadalcanal.[16]

Meanwhile, back at Mount Austen, small Japanese infantry units were spread between Hills 27 and 31 and 31 and 42; others occupied Hills 43 and 44. Hill 27 followed the Maruyama Trail and continued to Hill 43. Former PFC Robert W. Carbray, a machine gunner in Company M, describes the involvement of the 3rd Battalion, 132nd Infantry, in the attack:

> About 17 December in the morning, Company L, reinforced by our Company M, moved out from the perimeter in the direction of Mt. Austen toward the North end of Guadalcanal. To our rear was the remainder of the Third Battalion standing ready

to follow at a moment's notice. As the leading elements of the company neared the forward slopes of the hill, intensive bursts of Japanese defensive fire broke the jungle silence. Defense fire continued all day, from well concealed positions in the dense undergrowth, and came from fire of all calibers. Using rifles, light and heavy machine guns, and mortars, the Japanese had us nailed down, so we dug in to await further developments. Realizing the seriousness of this situation, Lt. Col. William C. Wright, my battalion commander, hustled the rest of the Battalion into action to endeavor to reach the crest of Mt. Austen without further delay. By late afternoon the entire Third Battalion was in position along the line of Companies L & M.

When the remainder of the Battalion was committed, it was planned that we [would] attack as soon as all troops were in position. However, the long, arduous forced march had exhausted the riflemen so that the attack could not be carried out. . . . The assault was postponed until the following morning, and so we had to set up a reconnaissance team to look over the situation. Air strikes and artillery concentrations were called upon to help soften up the Japanese resistance enough to allow the Battalion to drive through to its objective. . . . On 18 December, in the wake of intense aerial bombings and artillery fire, the Third Battalion struck forward up the slopes of Mt. Austen. Almost immediately the advance ground to a halt as the Japanese lashed forth with a tremendous hail of defensive fire. We tried to gain ground all day, but were thrown back.

On the 19th, we tried again to gain ground, but were bogged down almost as soon as [the advance] had started. [Colonel] Wright hurried forward to make a personal investigation into the cause for the delay and the lack of progress. As he was with the most forward elements of his command, fire from a well-concealed Japanese machine gun trapped and mortally wounded him with a sudden burst. We made several attempts to rescue him, but were forced to withdraw under relentless fire. . . . Finally, late in the afternoon, the Regimental S-2 formed a patrol and succeeded in reaching Colonel Wright, but he was dead. His body was brought back inside the lines.[17] . . . We were nailed down in our positions by the intense fire. . . . The 57th Engineer Battalion [A and B Companies] made supply routes to Mt.

Austen so we could bring up high explosives to knock out this
Japanese position.[18]

On Christmas Eve 1942, 2nd Lt. Albert D. Swacina of Company C,
132nd Infantry, led a patrol of eighteen soldiers to scrutinize a difficult
position 1,000 yards in front of his company. PFCs George J. Drobnack
and Orville "Elmo" Hutchison were the lead scouts, with Sgt. Nicholas
Vakola and Pvt. Russell K. Pence the point men. PFC Robert G. Hensley, a medic, was part of the team, along with PFCs Anthony A. Martinez, Charles Nolph, and John P. Kissane. The patrol checked out the
area and all went well; however, the men made the mistake of returning
over the same route. The Japanese were waiting.

Vakola and Pence were immediately struck down by machine-gun
fire; a bullet to the heart killed Hensley a moment later. Lieutenant
Swacina was hit in the neck and died within minutes. Drobnack took
a bullet in the stomach and then was hit again; he would later die of
his wounds.[19] Elmo Hutchison was hit by a grenade fragment and spent
a cold night in the brush; in the morning, on hearing the talkative enemy approaching, he managed to crawl away and eventually get back to
his own lines. In the survivors' scramble for safety, however, the dead
were left behind; they would not be recovered for some two months,
until February 1943.[20] When Sergeant Vakola's body was found, his dog
tags were missing, and Hutchison let Martinez know that they had been
taken by the enemy, as he had heard them rattle when they were being
removed.[21]

A very busy and tired GI at this time was Pvt. George F. Stanton, a
medic attached to the 132nd Infantry who handled caseloads of casualties. Stanton had retired as a lieutenant in the Chicago Fire Department
after twenty-two years of service. He was fifty-five years old but had admitted to being only forty-five so that, as he acknowledged, he could
"go overseas with the boys."[22] Like the others, Stanton got more than he
bargained for.

Arthur L. Holmes was a radio-man with Battery H, 3rd Battalion,
10th Marines; along with Battery G, Battery H supported the 132nd
Infantry. That Christmas Eve seemed quiet until the Japanese mortars
found Holmes's battery on a ridge. The enemy fire appeared to be coming from a deep ravine to the west, and the 3/10's 75-mm pack howitzers
fired back with one round every few minutes—a Christmas present, the
men decided, for Tojo's soldiers. Amidst it all, however, Holmes's bat-

tery did receive a special "gift" from the cooks of the 132nd. The "Cannibal Battalion," a name the GIs gave to the island laborers, transported rations up the long winding hill trail to Battery H's position—turkey sandwiches, plus a can of cranberry sauce for each man. For just a few moments the war almost was forgotten.

Japanese Combat Order #67 described the action that day: "The right front of the Ito Detachment is facing the enemy at 200 meters. The left front of the Ito Detachment pushed back the enemy of about 350 for five hours. About 150 made an attack in the morning at three places. The Ito Detachment sent two platoons to the northwest of Miharashi Dai [Hill 54], a Japanese observation post which was strengthened by the reserve unit of the Tamura Detachment to shore up that area. On the 24th, six men of the Tamura Detachment, after making a night attack on the enemy outpost on Sakai Dai, pushed back the enemy. Later, they found four bodies of United States soldiers and captured one light machine gun, two automatic weapons and four rifles."[23]

On Christmas Day, Companies E and F of the 132nd Infantry were guided to Hill 27 by five Fiji forces commandos led by Sgt. Frank Williams of the New Zealand Expeditionary Force (NZEF). The bush-wise Fijians were ideal as a reconnaissance team, passing information to the GIs on the disposition of Japanese troops. At 1300 on the 25th the Fijians and elements of 3/132 passed through the front lines of the Americal Division's 182nd Infantry and moved along a ridge route west of the Lunga River. Patrols of the 132nd assaulted Hills 31 and 27 from south of Edson's (Bloody) Ridge, with two rifle companies pressing the attack. Hill 31 afforded an overview of Henderson Field and Fighter Strips No.1 and 2, and the plan was to neutralize the enemy position there.[24]

What the GIs faced in those rugged foothills were elements of Maj. Kikuo Hayakawa's 1st Battalion, 228th Infantry, and Maj. Haruja Nishiyama's 3rd Battalion, 228th, plus segments of the 230th Infantry and depleted elements of Col. Akinosuka Oka's 124th Infantry, with the main strength attributed to Maj. Takeyoshi Inagaki's 2nd Battalion, 228th Infantry. The 124th had fought both battles of Bloody Ridge and lost heavily in each encounter, but Rabaul kept filtering in replacements. Although the enemy was plagued with malaria and half-starved, they were still full of fight, and the 132nd's frontal assault, involving 350 men, was stopped cold. The Japanese holding Hill 27 at Mount Austen remained potent and capable of extracting high casualties.

While the 132nd was getting battered around the slopes of Mount Austen, some major changes occurred at Henderson Field. The airstrip received a small detachment of operators from the Army Airways Communication System (AACS) who were assigned to run the control tower and navigational aids. Air strength continued to improve; the new twin-tailed and fantastic Lockeed-Vega P-38 Lightnings were assisting in commanding the Solomon air space, along with a flight of Martin B-26 Marauders from the 69th Bomb Squadron that had been transferred from New Caledonia. Meanwhile Fighter Strip No. 1 was upgraded, and No. 2 was nearing completion.

However, deep in Japanese territory, the 132nd Infantry had suffered a high number of battle casualties, and a feeling of doom began to creep through the ranks. The Illinois guardsmen began to regroup on 26 December and by the 27th had formed a defense alliance between Hills 32 and 22. While the 3rd Battalion, 132nd Infantry, was getting beaten to death attempting to assault the stronghold, the 2nd Battalion was still performing stevedore duties, unloading vessels at Lunga Roads. The 1st Battalion, 2nd Marines, then moved into position, occupying a hill to the southeast of the 132nd for flank protection.[25]

Mack Morris was on Guadalcanal at the time as a *Yank* reporter. He recorded the following on Saturday, 26 December:

> I have just come back from my first trip to the front—or as close to the front as two British and two American reporters with a Marine driver named Bill could get in a jeep. It wasn't exactly what I expected. We of course had been told that in jungle warfare you couldn't see anything at all. We could. We went over the worst roads I have ever traveled in all my life, sincerely, the worst, to a Bn CP of the 132nd Infantry—the "Men of Illinois"—sitting on the edge of the jungle on top of a hill. On the way up we were passed by, first, a casualty with blond hair leaning unconscious on the arm of a boy in a jeep, and second, by stretcher bearers carrying a dead soldier down the hill. The first boy was pale; the second's face was covered, but his pants were covered with blood. He was the first American I've seen killed in action. I don't know what I thought as they brought him by—not much, except that he was dead because his face was covered. I went on up the hill. There were men who were filthy dirty and from the look of most of them, tired. They were serious and, I think, mad. A patrol of theirs had run point blank into a machine gun. The CP is on top of a hill and men were dug in on the slope—a hell of a spot to be in. The jungle thinned a little at the edge, but deeper in it was

just a tangle of trees and vines. The advance positions were 300 or 400 yards out in that direction; they pulled back last night to let artillery shell Jap positions.

From the hill is a beautiful view of the sea, with Savo jutting up to the left and Florida lying low to the right, and Tulagi barely visible at its top. As we looked across the terrain westward we could see the Jap-held ground. We were shelling it and through an OP scope we could see shell craters on a forward slope of a hill. I traversed the scope over the ground between us and them and saw the Marines and infantry troops. I saw somebody standing on top of a ridge, stark naked, bathing. There wasn't much to see except terrain and occasional smoke shells. We apparently were shelling two different positions, one at intervals. In the distance along the rim of the island we could see beached Jap transports and some landing boats. They were all shot to hell and gone. The beaches were bare. From there we went back over the same awful road, passing artillery batteries firing over our heads at positions we'd seen. We could feel the concussion and hear the shells whistle overhead.[26]

On the 26th, while Mack Morriss was traveling to and from the front lines, the 3rd Battalion, 182nd Infantry, had set up an ambush in the Matanikau sector, but no Japanese appeared. Later in the day, after the 1st Battalion, 8th Marines, had observed a group of Japanese walking a trail, a well-armed patrol was formed, but the roving Japanese vanished. The 3/132nd made another frontal attack on Mount Austen's Hill 27; this time they moved slowly, but they were halted by massive machine-gun and sniper fire. They managed to put one machine gun out of action and killed nine, while losing five of their own with nineteen wounded. Company C lost three men missing and seven wounded when friendly artillery fire fell in the area.

Three days later, on 29 December, the Japanese reported that the Americans were observed to be very active and were increasing their strength in the Mount Austin region after having been pushed back by the small Japanese units. They noted that the Americans had shown a great interest in the Japanese area of Miharashi Dai (Hill 54) in the previous two days. The Japanese were aware that the center of the battle was gradually moving in their direction; they estimated about 400 to 500 of the enemy were opposing the Okabe Detachment and some 200 men of the Nishiyama unit.

The Mission — Regardless of Price

As the 1st and 3rd Battalions, 132nd Infantry, attempted to encircle Mount Austen, they were partially supplied with rations, water, and ammunition by what the GIs called the "Pidgin Express"—the native carriers who were part of the first contingent of the Solomon Island Labor Corps. The service company transported supplies by truck from the warehouses as far as Wright Road, the track named for Lt. Col. William C. Wright, of the American Division's 132nd Infantry Regiment, who had been killed in action. Colonel Wright was one of a family of four brothers in the 132nd. From Wright Road, the Labor Corps workers took over, carrying the materiel up the winding trail, an effort that took hours.

Meanwhile, Col. LeRoy E. Nelson, who had commanded the Illinois National Guard's 132nd Infantry Regiment since 1937, was reported to be ill and on 28 December had been replaced by forty-one-year-old Lt. Col. Alexander M. George. Colonel George was a Regular Army officer, considered to be somewhat eccentric by the men of the 132nd.[27] It was not a good exchange, but Patch was working the "old buddy" network. He eventually would replace all former National Guard officers with West Pointers. Colonel Nelson's departure had left a deep cavity that George never filled. The GIs of the 2/132 received a "pep talk" from the Colonel stressing the importance of their mission and stating that they had to accomplish it regardless of the price—small talk inasmuch as the colonel remained safe back in the command post.[28] On 30 December Field Order No. 1 from the 132nd Infantry headquarters also spelled out what was expected of the GIs. Paragraph 3 X of the order reads: "Upon capture of Hill 27 a perimeter defense will be established and will be defended at all costs."[29]

At noon on 31 December the 2nd Battalion, 132nd Infantry, arrived at the Mount Austen bivouac area; they would remain there until the following morning when they would continue the drive. The enemy positions adjacent to Hill 27 were constantly being bombarded, and some of the shells fell short, exploding on the men of 2/132. To secure themselves, they dug deep slit trenches, then bedded down for the night, knowing that the next day they would jump off for the assault on the hill.

On 1 January at Rabaul, New Britain Island, the Yano Butai (230th Infantry Replacement Unit) celebrated the start of the new year at the Tanoura district. The Yano Sun Soldiers recently had arrived from Shizuoka, Japan, where they had been part of the 34th Infantry Regiment

(3rd Division). The U.S. XIV Corps troops later would meet part of the Yano Butai, which had been sent to cover the Japanese withdrawal along the coast route to Cape Esperance. On 2 January, at the Gifu fortress, Maj. Megumi Ishido took over the command of the 1st Battalion, 124th Infantry, when Maj. Yukichi Kokusho was killed. The diary of PFC Haruguchi Mizuguchi of the 5th Company, 230th Regiment relects on the new year and the ending of the previous twelve war-torn months:

> 1942 finally comes to an end today. Looking back over this year, truly, it has been eventful and fraught with difficulties. It is more than a year since the beginning of the Greater East Asian War. I was called up to the colors again and have been in 10 months, during which time I participated in the occupation battle of Guadalcanal Island in the Solomon Islands group in October. At present, I am enduring hardships and privations in the middle of a hard battle. It is a great decisive Japanese-American War, which will never be forgotten. In the homeland it is the end of the year and a very busy period, but we, without enough food, end this year on 5 Shaku of gruel that has been our daily ration continuously for 15 days. Truly my body has become weakened. Tonight I greeted the New Year by eating 5 Shaku of gruel, imagining it to be lucky noodles of the homeland. Today I defecated for the first time since the 22nd and felt greatly relieved.[30]

At 0600 on New Year's Day the Americal Division's 2nd Battalion, 132nd Infantry, had been slowly working its way up the nearly vertical slopes of Hill 27 while the supporting artillery pounded the Japanese positions for twenty-five minutes. Companies E and F were the main attacking force, with Company G in regimental reserve. Throughout the approach to the hill the men had encountered heavy sniper fire, which took its toll. As the American guns opened up, a number of the Japanese had slipped away and retreated to the nearby jungle at the base of the knoll. When two platoons from Companies E and F finally advanced to the hilltop they met fierce automatic fire from the right flank. 1st Lt. Tasuji Tamai of the 8th Company, 230th Infantry, had taken two platoons to the position formerly held by Lieutenant Wakabayashi on the outskirts of the Gifu stronghold; Tamai was ordered to protect his position while 2nd Lt. Souichi Sawano's 3rd Platoon moved to the edge of the jungle to contain the Americans.

That night, three bold submarines crept into Cape Esperance Bay: *I–168* (Lt. Cdr. Sakae Nkajima), *I–169* (Lt. Cdr. Katsuji Watanabe), and

1–171 (Cdr. Takarō Kawasaki). The daihatsu dashed out from shore to unload the welcome cargo, but after only some fifteen tons of food provisions had been disburdened the 1,400-ton submarines were chased away by two Tulagi-based PT boats. (By February 1943 the Japanese submarines had made twenty-eight runs from Rabaul and Bougainville, delivering 1,500 tons of supplies, but it was minor compared to what actually was required.)

That afternoon of New Year's Day at Mount Austen, between 1200 and 1630—some six hours after the American artillery had been pounding Japanese troops at Hill 27—the 1st Company of the Japanese 10th Independent Mountain Artillery Regiment sent a barrage of thirty rounds of 75-mm shells back in their direction. Postwar Japanese records reveal that in contrast the Americans had sent 782 artillery rounds at the Gifu stand. Astonished that the Americans had so much firepower, the Japanese assigned an officer to count the incoming shells. That day, 1st Lieutenant Okajima of the 230th Infantry wrote in his diary: "It is really terrible to see electricity go on at the enemy airfield."[31]

In January, assorted Japanese units were occupying the hills in front of the Americans; one unit, identified as the 1st Battalion, 229th Infantry, had only 170 men. Capt. Kiyoshi Saito's 3rd Company, 38th Engineer Regiment, also had been dispatched to Mount Austen as reinforcements to strengthen the battered 124th Infantry, but the backup was only a few dozen men. On 5 January, fifty additional men from the 2nd Company, 230th Infantry, under 1st Lt. Mano Tamotsu, arrived to support the stronghold—another group of piecemeal reinforcements; nevertheless the Japanese were determined to retain the area as long as possible. An additional force—elements of the 3rd Battalion, 230th Infantry, commanded by Maj. Ampei Onada—was stationed between Hills 43 (part of Sea Horse Ridge) and 53 (part of Galloping Horse Ridge), while regimental headquarters plus the 1st Battalion were at Hills 75, 78, and 80 of Skyline Ridge (Sakai Dai).

On Hill 903 (U.S. Hill 89) was Capt. Kyohtaroh Oishi's 3rd Company, 10th Independent Mountain Artillery Regiment, but Oishi's company had only two 75-mm Model 41 mountain guns and was short of ammunition; the men had left two of their weapons on the beach. Pvt. Kosicihi Kaneko states that the "10th had observation platforms in the trees . . . only manned during daylight hours."[32] The two squads of 2nd Lt. Kazumi Yokoyama's 1st Platoon, 228th Infantry Howitzer Company, and 2nd Lt. Souhei Itani's 3rd and 4th Squads, 2nd Platoon, 228th Infantry Howitzer Company, had their Type 41 mountain guns—weapons that would duel with those of the Americans—but they also were short of ammunition. In the same sector was the 2nd Company, 228th Infantry Machine-Gun Unit, which would inflict havoc on the advancing U.S. Army's 132nd Infantry Regiment.

LCpl. (*Heichō*) Shoichi Matsushima of the 38th Engineer Regiment stated in his POW interrogation report: "There was a ration dump and small anti-aircraft trenches (but no gun emplacements) at Hill 903, and from here to the Maruyama Road, the POWs [*sic*] unit established a path for the transportation of supplies and litters."[33]

TSgt. Joe Micek recalls:

> The riflemen of Company F were forced to forsake their holes and left the LMGs to their fate. Automatic weapons aren't worth two cents without rifle support and fortunately GIs from [Company G] were placed on the right flank to reinforce the guns' support; luckily we reached there in time. . . . Private [William C.] Gately was KIA and Private Wojtke was wounded.
>
> The enemy made it so hot up here we were forced to retreat about 50 yards and in the confusion, two LMG were left behind. . . . Pvt. James M. McDonald went ahead and re-captured one of the weapons. When we attacked, we had losses; the enemy snipers accounted for many of our casualties when the other battalions failed to coordinate the strike with us. I saw men get shot in the back, head and legs and still move under their own power, and all night the enemy artillery shells dropped between us. That night we dug foxholes deep, real deep.[34]

Company K was having its own troubles assaulting Hill 31. Hugging the jungle floor was a pillbox—dubbed "The Gooseberry," because the men could neither knock it out nor contain it—with fire ports covering all directions and supported by area sector fortifications. It was the most impregnable pillbox in the complex.[35]

In his diary entry of 3 January, Micek frankly admitted, "I was never so glad to see the daylight. Our line held through the night and we were prepared to continue the attack. We did, and Pvt. George J. Riley [Company G] was killed when he walked into an enemy prepared fire lane while Private Hoelzel received two bullets in his leg and Pete Zweifler suffered from shell shock. Now the 1st Battalion is going to attack tomorrow."[36]

Meanwhile, the U.S. Army 20th Station Hospital, a well-equipped medical unit, had landed at the docks on 4 January at Kukum and moved to the Lever's plantation area along the left bank of the Tenaru River—just in time to provide medical support for the push west.[37] The 121st Medical Battalion, a component of the Americal Division, was in the grove adjacent to the hospital, which soon was packed with many serious cases of malaria. A large number of the hospital beds also were filled by the wounded, and the morgue, set in a building to the rear, was almost at capacity. The 132nd Infantry Regiment, having gained no traction, dug in for safety while rimming the Gifu post on the north, east, and south, and there the enemy would demonstrate his terrible determination. American soldiers continued to push at the Gifu strong point in order to besiege Mount Austen, and the 132nd took a large number of casualties without making appreciable progress.

On 6 January, a fresh set of faces would be seen on the "rock" when the 6th Marines arrived from LONGBOW (Wellington, New Zealand); these ex-Iceland leathernecks were getting their first sight of a jungle. Accompanying the 6th Regiment was the 2nd Battalion, 10th Marines; Companies C and F, 18th Marines; and the 2nd Platoon, Battery A, 2nd Special Weapons Company.[38] The 7th and 11th Marines, the rear echelon of the 1st Marine Division, boarded the transports that had delivered the 6th Marines; they were headed to Australia as part of TF 62 and 62.6.and were joined by 947 men of the 6th Seabees, plus 147 sailors from CUB-1. Lt. George W. Polk, USNR, one of the CUB-1 officers, ended up with a six-month stay at the 118th General Hospital in Sydney, Australia, as a result of fatigue and stress.[39]

The XIV Corps figured the Japanese were escaping west via Beaufort Bay on Guadalcanal's southwest coast. To prevent that movement they assigned a force built around Company I, 147th Infantry, led by Capt. Charles E. Beach; one platoon from Company M, led by 1st Lt. Harold L. Dubick; one platoon from the antitank company; and engineer, medical, and communication troops. The force boarded two LCTs on 7 January at Kukum to sail at night around the Japanese base at Cape Esperance on the island's northwest tip; they reached the Catholic mission at Beaufort Bay two days later. Captain Beach's troops were to guard the trails to block any movement so that the enemy did not escape southward from Kokumbona to nest in the mountains on the south coast.

At about this same time, the 11th Naval Construction Battalion arrived, on 8 January, swelling the ranks of Seabees on the island to more than five thousand men. They would help modernize the Guadalcanal base; they would extend roads, build bridges, set up telephone lines, work on airstrips, and do all sorts of tasks. In addition, a force identified as the CAM (Composite Army-Marine) Division was temporarily activated under the U.S. Army's XVI Corps, with the intent to consolidate the far-west offensive to drive the Japanese off the island. The CAM was composed of the 147th Infantry Regiment (less one battalion and one company), the 182nd Infantry Regiment (less one battalion), the 2nd Marines (less the 3rd Battalion), the 6th Marines, the 8th Marines, and the 10th Marines. The staff was that of the 2nd Marine Division.

Also on 8 January, the XIV Corps flooded the area with documents urging the Japanese to surrender; two soldiers responded. The Corps then placed a microphone to broadcast a concession message. No one in the enemy camp took up the offer, but they commented that the Americans spoke poor Japanese. The following day, the Cactus Air Force dropped 18,000 surrender leaflets on the Gifu sector; still no one surrendered.

On 9 January a formation of 170 GIs from the 147th Infantry Regiment landed at Tangarare, on the southwest coast of Guadalcanal, and moved northward to the remote village of Vurai, southwest of Kokumbona, with 125 native carriers. Their mission was to check the area, as they traveled, for the presence of the enemy. Four days later, while deep in the hinterland, the detachment had labor problems when the carriers went on strike for higher wages. The Cannibal Battalion wanted the prewar wage, which was beyond the means of the common infantryman; however, when the men of the 147th pitched in a few dollars, all was well again, and their part in the war effort continued. Also on the 9th, the "doggies" of the 132nd Infantry Regiment were instructed to police their area and pick up all discarded food cans, rifle clips, and empty cartridge cases.[40] The sector was to be taken over by the men of the U.S. Army's 25th Infantry Division, called the "Pineapple Soldiers" by the GIs of the 132nd. Maj. Gen. J. Lawton Collins, commander of the 25th, was subsequently given the sarcastic nickname of "Clean-up Collins."

By 10 January, the beat-up 132nd had lost 122 men KIA and 258 WIA, with four missing.[41] The regiment had fought hard for control of the Gifu sector for twenty-six days and endured a bloodbath. On the 14th, the 6th and 8th Marines took over Hills 66 and 76 from the 2nd Marines, and late in the day the 6th Marines and the elements of the 8th Marines began extensive patrolling. On the 15th, a patrol from the 1st Battalion, 6th Marines, located nine well-concealed log-placed pillboxes south of Hill 76 in a narrow, wooded, steep ravine. The marines knocked out two of the boxes, but deadly fire forced them to withdraw. The next day they went out again; this time the 2nd Battalion, 8th Marines, entered a hill sector they named the "Cats Ears." On the 17th, they captured a flame-thrower, clearly unused and the first they had seen. Anxious to test the "burner," the marines tried it on three occupied pillboxes with a totally devastating effect. Late that afternoon the 1st Battalion, 182nd Infantry Regiment, moved in line and prepared to hit positions in a draw between Hills 77 and 80, adjacent to the 1st Battalion, 8th Marines, in the vicinity of Hill 76 and Company G, 6th Marines.

The newly arrived Pineapple Soldiers, who would replace the battered 132nd Infantry Regiment in the Mount Austen sector, had been defending the Hawaiian Islands against a possible invasion. When that threat dissipated, plans were made to transfer the 25th Division to the Southwest Pacific area for duty in New Guinea. On 20 October the division received an alert order to move out, and on 2 November it was slated for the Southwest Pacific. With the situation on Guadalcanal still critical, new orders were issued reassigning the 25th there. The plan was to go to New Caledonia in three stages, at ten-day intervals, and then transfer to Guadalcanal. The first to leave was the 35th Regimental Combat Team, which boarded the transports on 25 November and reached Guadalcanal on 18 December. Next was the 161st Infantry, which reached Guadalcanal on 4 January; the rear echelon, the 27th Infantry Regiment, arrived three days later. Not long after the 25th Division troops had moved into a staging area near Lunga Point, they were assigned to relieve the 132nd Infantry at Mount Austen. They had orders to capture the strategically important Hill 27.

Meanwhile, on 5 January, in order to soften up the sector and help the GIs capture the territory, the SBD Dauntless aircraft of VMSB-131 began plastering the hills and valleys adjacent to Hill 27. But the Japanese were well dug in. It would take more than an occasional bombing strike of one or two flights to make a dent in the fortresses around the hill. To support the 25th Infantry Division's drive, the artillery shelled the ravines and laid a smoke line from the southwest tip of Hill 55 to the left of Galloping Horse Ridge; the smoke line was to protect the friendly troops, and no aircraft was to bomb east of it. However, events did not proceed according to plan. A short round blew up an ammunition dump on Hill 56, and with that smoke confusing the pilots, a charge was dropped on an area occupied by friendly troops. Surprisingly, no one was injured.

While the SBDs were dropping bombs in the sector, the 25th Infantry Division, with the 161st Infantry held in reserve, jumped off to strike an area to the west that had been held by the 8th Marines. While engaging the Japanese on 10 January, Company M of the 35th Infantry Regiment was hit by point-blank fire. The advance stalled around Hill 43 where it faced Maj. Tsuguto Tomoda, I/229i, who had replaced Maj. Sugura Orita, wounded in action. With units led by Capt. Kiyoshi Saito (38th Engineers), 2nd Lieutenant Ito (228i), and 1st Lieutenant Murota (228i) the troops of I/229i were ordered to repulse the attack by striking the Americans on the right flank of the Gifu strongpoint. Major Tomoda informed his company commanders that some three hundred Americans had enveloped the rear of the Gifu area.

At this same time, Company K of the 3rd Battalion, 35th Infantry Regiment, was crossing a stream en route to the Sea Horse sector (Hills 43 and 44). Part of the company was on one bank and part on the other, but the men had neglected to emplace machine guns to protect the crossing. This inattention to infantry fundamentals was a sign of the troops' inexperience, and the Japanese seized the advantage. They attacked in force; the front line was threatened and bending. Sgt. William G. Fournier, a machine-gun crew chief, stood his ground that day, when his gunner and assistant were killed. Seeing an unattended machine gun, Fournier and T/5 Lewis Hall ran to it and swung the weapon into action. Both were killed in the firefight, but the Japanese attack was halted, and Fournier and Hall received a posthumous Medal of Honor for their heroic deed.

On 13 January, the 8th Marines moved forward, supported by the 2nd Marines. Their attack, set to start at dawn, was backed up by two platoons of the 2nd Pioneer Battalion, a 75-mm platoon, and Company B of the 2nd Tank Battalion. The 2nd Marine Regiment was on the left wing, the 8th was on the right. Their task was to neutralize Hill 76 and its adjacent Hill 82 to the immediate north, as well as Hills 83 and 84, adjoining Hill 82 north-northeast. The 2nd Marines reached their objective, Hills 76 and 82, but in the effort lost six killed and sixty-one wounded. The 8th Marines managed to hit Hills 78 and 80, but also took casualties. A concentrated firefight followed, and by sheer willpower the regiment moved forward. By the 17th, the marines, pushing even harder, attacked a strongly fortified bunker just west of Hills 78 and 80. The next day the 8th Regiment managed to clean out the crevice and seize those hills.

The 35th Infantry Regiment's orders were to capture the Gifu strongpoint and then swing around and clean up the Sea Horse complex, while elements neutralized the summits of Hills 50 to 57 around Galloping Horse Ridge. (Hill 52 would be named "Sims Hill" in honor of Lt. Weldon Sims, who was killed while exploring there.) The 64th, 8th, 89th, and 90th Field Artillery Battalions would furnish fire support for the drive. The 35th's 3rd Battalion was to make an encompassing movement around the foot of Mount Austen, while its 2nd Battalion would hit key positions on Hill 27 and its 1st Battalion would be in reserve.

The 3rd Battalion, 182nd Infantry Regiment, was part of the reinforcements attached to the 25th Division; it was assigned to occupy a stretch of jungle between the 35th and 27th Infantry Regiments. During the drive, however, a leadership problem arose in the 35th Infantry when the Lt. Col. Ernest Peters, was relieved of command for not implementing an order; he was replaced by Maj. Stanley R. Larsen, who appeared to be better suited for the job.[42] By 11 January the 25th Division announced it had control of the entire Sea Horse Ridge area and its Hills 43 and 44. Other elements of the 35th Infantry struck at hills between 27 and 31.

The Changing Japanese Hold

Japanese reinforcements were fed into the Mount Austen bastion from time to time, and in January rudiments of the Seventeenth Army were still retaining the key hills. They included the 10th Company with only twenty-seven men (Wakabayashi Tai, under 1st Lt. Toichi Wakabayashi, 10/III) and the 11th Company (Fukada Tai, under Capt. Keizo Fukada, 11/III), 228th Infantry; the 3rd Machine-Gun Company (under Capt. Jitaro Murase), 228th Infantry; the 5th Company (Yamamoto Tai, under 1st Lt. Hiroshi Yamamoto, 5/II) and 8th Company (under 1st Lt. Tetsu Okaima, 8/II), 230th Infantry; and the 3rd Machine-Gun Company, 230th Infantry (under 1st Lt. Tamo Saito), as well as a few scattered remnants of the 124th Infantry. The Yamamoto Tai was quartered about 1,000 yards northwest on Hill 27. The 64th Field Artillery Battalion moved its 105-mm howitzers adjacent to Hill 34, approximately 2,000 yards northeast of the Gifu, and pounded the Japanese each day. The enemy did not budge.

By nightfall on 13 January, however, the western lines of the 25th Infantry Division extended 4,500 yards inland (south) from Point Cruz across Hill 66 to Hills 57 and 53 of Galloping Horse Ridge. The 27th Infantry Regiment, having seized all its objectives and forced the Japanese into the river gorges, was firmly seated on Hill 53, waiting for the 35th Infantry to complete its longer advance from the south.[43] The struggle was full of heroes. One was Pvt. Joseph J. Stec of the 27th Infantry who was awarded a Silver Star for his actions on the 13th. Private Stec and three other men had volunteered to destroy an enemy firing position that was blocking the 3rd Battalion's advance. The pocket was held by about twenty-five troops supported by machine guns and mortars. Stec and the other GIs threw their grenades, then rushed in and captured the position through hand-to-hand combat. In another heroic effort, Capt. Charles W. Davis, executive officer of the 2nd Battalion, 27th Infantry Regiment, with four men from Company G, ran ahead, facing enemy fire. With his clear view of the Japanese position, Davis radioed back to Company H to pour 81-mm mortar shellfire on the strongpoint, allowing his troops to advance and capture Hill 53.[44]

The Japanese Seventeenth Army meanwhile had reported the desperate situation in front of its 38th Division's position:

> American forces advancing on the southern tip of our observation point are today continuing to dig in and are rapidly bringing in supplies from the rear. Opposing them are only a few surviving troops of the Suemura Unit (228i). The front line and the headquarters as well are under American pressure around the entire perimeter. An American unit has infiltrated the jungle to the east and is advancing to the southwest. . . . In the Mount Austen sector, it is known that resistance continued until January 13, but since then the situation there [has been] unclear. . . . It has been concluded that, as of the 13th, the Headquarters Infantry Group and the unit occupying the observation post, and, as of the 12th, the men 10th Independent Howitzer Regiment, have all been killed.[45]

On 14 January at 1400 Sergeant Kachi carried an order to retreat, issued by General Hyakutake, to the headquarters of the 3rd Battalion, 228th Infantry, troops at the Gifu hold. This was a most welcome message, but some of the officers viewed it as a disgrace and vowed to stay and fight. Those that remained died.[46] On the same day, the 1st Battalion, 6th Marines, relieved the 1st and 2nd Battalions, 2nd Marines, though the 2/6 was to furnish one reinforced rifle company for the purpose of permitting Companies A and B of the 1st Battalion, 8th Marines, to shorten their lines. On the 15th, the 2nd Marine Regiment (reinforced) was withdrawn from the front lines to a rear area to await evacuation to New Zealand.[47]

The following day, 16 January, saw little progress because the 25th Division faced stiff resistance in all the hills that blocked their advance. A mix-up had occurred when an officer of the 2nd Battalion, 35th Infantry Regiment, ordered one platoon of Company G to withdraw; somehow word spread about the move, and the entire battalion departed its positions. The battalion spent the 15th regaining the ground it had captured the day before. A 75-mm self-propelled gun was brought to bear on the stronghold, but inflicted no major damage. The next day the captured flame-thrower was brought in again, and the position was reduced. The 3/35 began moving to cover the slopes overlooking the Matanikau River.

Two days later the weapons of the 2nd Battalion, 10th Marines, and the U.S. Army artillery threw 1,700 rounds of 105-mm and 155-mm howitzer ammunition at the Gifu during one ninety-minute period. On that day, Lieutenant Okajima wrote the following in his diary:

> Men are dying one after another and now the company roster has 20 men besides the CO. The enemy keeps firing from some distance so we shall have to be careful of stray bullets. I am very hungry. I wonder if this is how it is when a man is starving. Rice cakes and candy appear in my dreams. I heard the enemy talking in Japanese over a loud speaker. He is probably telling us to come out—what fools the enemy are. The Japanese Army will stick it out to the end. Position must be defended in all conditions and with our lives. There was no artillery shelling because of the broadcasts. The enemy is broadcasting something vigorously at a distance. It will have no effect at all. According to the enemy broadcasts today they are going to attack our positions. However, we have no fear. I went to Battalion Headquarters this morning and saw many propaganda sheets, which were found in First Lieutenant Kasahari's area. The writing is very poor. The enemy artillery barrage becomes fiercer and the company area was riddled with craters. The enemy artillery stopped at 15:00 and then we were [soaked] from the downpour leaking into our foxholes.[48]

At this point, the 8th Marines reported an enemy body count of 643 in their sector; they had lost five killed and thirty-three wounded. On the 18th, Company I of the 3rd Battalion, 182nd Infantry, reported little progress. The stubborn enemy was holding up the entire U.S. Army XIV Corps. Two days later the Japanese 6th Company, 2nd Battalion, 228th Infantry, now led by Maj. Haruja Nishiyama, the 3rd Battalion commander, was beating back attacks by thirty to forty aggressive GIs in the area of Mount Austen. Lieutenant Okajima reported in his diary that the commanding officers of both the 5th Company (1st Lt. Hioshi Mit-

Figure 44. Japanese bunker fire-point on Hill 27, Mount Austen, Guadalcanal, 17 January 1943. (Courtesy Joseph G. Micek)

sui) and the 8th Company (2nd Lt. Matsuro Tsurumaru) were killed on the 19th. Major Nishiyama assigned 1st Lt. Gen Fujita to replace Tsurumaru.

With all this manpower, the Japanese still had no good method to stop the Yanks' penetration. While the Americans were hitting hard at the Japanese, some of the Sun Soldiers who had heard rumors of an evacuation began to slip away and move down the coast in stages, under the cover of darkness. Some stayed, but they would not walk out alive. After days of surrounding the Gifu and taking casualties, someone in the 25th Infantry Division suggested using tanks to knock out the difficult bunkers. Three light Marine M3A1 tanks of the 2nd Tank Battalion were assigned to reduce the bastion; the GIs hoped the tanks would lessen their casualties. While en route, however, two of the iron monsters became bogged down in the mire of Wright Road, though one Stuart tank managed to crawl forward. The Stuart, commanded by Capt. Theodore Deese, was named "Mabel." Accompanied by eighteen Pineapple Soldiers as a covering guard, the steel monster blasted though the Japanese barriers on the last redoubt; its 37-mm gun knocked out nine fortifications and destroyed a 200-yard-long strongpoint, allowing a flood of doggies to enter the fortress.[49]

Back on the 18th, while the army had been slugging it out on Mount Austen, the 6th Marines had moved up the coast. Company K, 3/6, became involved in a firefight with a number of Japanese sailors from the Sasebo 5th SNLF; the engagement finally broke off about dusk. The next morning the dead were inspected; a flag found on the body of SM Makoto Kifayashida had his name and unit. The Americans continued to move forward and resupply. On the 20th, the U.S. Navy's 4th Special Construction Battalion arrived offshore at Lunga Roads. The 4th Special Seabees were trained as stevedores, with their primary duty to unload inbound cargo vessels and to transport the materiel to the storage areas. Their arrival relieved the GIs and sailors who had been doing the work for months, much to their chagrin.

On 22 January, however, a crisis developed at the Mamara River crossing when the 1st and 3rd Battalions, 6th Marines, ran into units of the Japanese 4th Infantry Regiment (eighty men) and the 16th Infantry (about one hundred soldiers) who were beginning to move west. Nevertheless, the Japanese were more intent on leaving the miserable island than stopping the Yanks' onrush. They put up resistance but continued to withdraw, leaving a few bodies for the leathernecks to bury. During the following week, the 6th Marines pushed ahead, running across a few enemy stragglers in the zone of the 2/6. Former Sgt. Rudolph E. Huisinga of Company C, 1st Battalion, 6th Marines, recalled: "We would move up the coast, then patrol inland and meet the regiment again on the beach. The following day would find us doing it again, climbing over inland hills, scouting the vanishing enemy."[50]

On 23 January, with the battle for Hill 27 almost over, forward elements of the 25th Infantry Division were now moving over rugged terrain westward toward the Kokumbona sector, an area the Americans had attacked time and time again. The 1st Battalion, 27th Infantry, advanced north and took out a small Japanese unit occupying a former native village; they then moved west again. With the Americans pounding on the doorstep, the Japanese defenders from Colonel Oka's 2nd Battalion, 124th Infantry, had managed to round up about one hundred soldiers. They knew the end of the battle was near and could have joined the evacuation, yet true to the ancient Bushido warrior code, the "Knights of Bushido" chose to attack. As they poured down the hill, most were shot and never reached the bottom standing up.[51]

Ittōhei (PFC) Takeshi Arakawa of the 2nd Battalion, 228th Infantry, an aide to Major Inagaki, stated in his interrogation report of 30 January 1943: "When the U.S. attack started, the 2nd Battalion of the Oka Unit dropped back towards the Headquarters. Major Inagaki thought that they would return to reinforce him so he held his position. [Colonel Oka and his staff left the strongpoint, and started down the coast to evacuate.

They never reached the departure site, as they were killed enroute]. After a week had passed they did not return and the U.S. forces had forged a wedge between them isolating Inagaki's Battalion They decided to make one last attack on the U.S. positions and die in the attempt. They managed to reach the American lines but the men were too weak to make the assault. Most of the unit was killed. Major Inagaki was shot down right next to me and I was wounded and then captured."[52]

Perishing in the mad dash were three first lieutenants, one warrant officer, three master sergeants, five sergeants, five corporals, nine lance corporals, twenty-nine superior privates, five candidates for NCO, seventy-one privates first class, and four medical technicians. All were part of the defending force holding a strongpoint at the Gifu complex.

The POW interrogators of *Jōtōhei* (Sup. Pvt.) Saiichi Matsueda, 2nd Company, 228th Infantry, quoted Matsueda in their report: "His company [under 1st Lt. Tomio Omasu] was reduced to about 10–12 men but a large portion was through sickness."[53]

Also on the 23rd, two Tulagi-based Royal New Zealand Navy (RNZN) minesweepers, the *Kiwi* and *Moa,* were operating off Kamimbo Bay, the most northwesterly point of the island. U.S. decoders using ULTRA were reading the enemy's "mail" at the time, and the RNZN warships and the Cactus Air Force were alerted to the possibility of the arrival of a Japanese submarine. The *I-1* under Lt. Cdr. Eiichi Sakamoto, from Submarine Division 6, subsequently became engaged in a fierce action that lasted more than an hour. The *Kiwi* rammed the sub three times and wrecked it. Of the sixty-six men aboard the sub, nineteen were able to reach the shore and scamper inland. The *I-1* also had been transporting an array of new code books; apparently the boat had been serving as the delivery agent for a number of stations. One of the sailors who reached the shore knew the value of the crypto material; he buried some of the code books and destroyed most of the others. The next morning a party from the two minesweepers boarded the submarine and captured the wounded navigation officer. According to their report, they took the sub's remaining code books, which were turned over to the commander of the Naval Operating Base, Guadalcanal.

On 25 January, large flights of Betty bombers heading for "Pot Hole Hen" (Henderson Field) were interrupted by eight F-4F and four P-38 aircraft, led by Capt. Joseph J. Foss. Although outnumbered, "Indian Joe" Foss's group shot down four of the enemy. The Americans fought with such determination that the Japanese returned to base without having dropped a single bomb, and Captain Foss received a Medal of Honor citation. The Americans on the ground slept well that night.

The Americans Regroup

While the GIs were attending to damages done and burying their dead in the Mount Austen sector, components of the newly formed CAM Division. The marines had been assigned to move west along the beach route, where they were periodically harassed by snipers. On 20 January the 147th Infantry had relieved the 182nd, which then moved into the CAM Division bivouac area. The 147th Infantry Regiment joined the 6th Marines late that day in the vicinity of the beach route. The 1st Battalion, 6th Marines, was on the right beach flank, with 2/6 positioned on the left. In the late hours of the day the CAM units ran into heavy fire and orders were issued to dig in for the night. They did not know that while they were digging foxholes, the enemy was creeping up the coast, hoping to exit with their lives.

The 6th Marines moved to higher ground in order to obtain a clearer picture of the terrain ahead, and at one juncture they encountered GIs of the 27th Infantry Regiment who had moved through the old Japanese bivouac area at Kokumbona to join the 6th Marines on the coast. Both the 27th Infantry and the 6th Marines continued to aggressively patrol the area. Other than the 22 January incident involving the 1/6 and the 3/6, who ran across the Japanese 4th Infantry Regiment, the marines met but a few scattered enemy troops, most ill or in poor health. The more hearty of the enemy were working their way up the coast a few miles ahead of the advancing CAM troops.

On 27 January, the coast force — 6th Marines and 147th Infantry — advanced to the Bonegi River. There the retreating enemy put up a stiff resistance to prevent the Americans from crossing. The CAM troops had not expected much fight as they moved along the coast route because they had met only small bands of retreating Japanese who were more interested in moving off Guadalcanal than fighting. But there, at the Bonegi, on the west bank, was Maj. Keiji Yano's Battalion, well dug in and determined to stonewall the advancing Americans. The 1st Battalion, 147th Infantry, attempted to cross the river near the coast but was stopped; the 3/147 tried to cross farther upstream, but that too was unsuccessful. Strategically placed machine guns kept the soldiers from Ohio on the east side of the river.

Meanwhile, naval gunfire liaison officers (NGLO) Lieutenants Aida and Carlin, aboard the Tulagi-based destroyers *Wilson* (DD 408) and *Anderson* (DD 411), were finally put to work. The lieutenants had been on board the two destroyers as gunfire experts when the ships had shot up the hulks of the four beached transports — the *Kinugawa Maru, Hi-*

rokawa Maru, Yamaura Maru, and *Yamatsuki Maru.* Each of the ships had two forward 75-mm antiaircraft guns, and now, in late January, the retreating Japanese passing by reboarded the grounded transports to fire the weapons in order to harass the advancing Americans. The *Wilson* and the *Anderson* silenced the Japanese guns, then moved west to some 2,000 yards off the Bonegi River basin. The 147th Infantry troopers pulled back and the destroyers fired intensely into the area with their 5-inch deck guns, clearing the way for the 147th to cross the river and continue the push west.

Sgt. Richard P. Bailey of H and S Company, 1st Battalion, 6th Marines, a BAR man, arrived on Guadalcanal on 6 January 1943. He saw more than his share of death.

> Our first night there was spent at Kukum near Lunga Point. . . .
> For several days we remained at Kukum without any apparent
> direction, although patrols were sent out at night, more for train-
> ing than to complete a mission. Shortly thereafter, about the
> second week of January, we heard scuttlebutt that we were going
> to join forces with the Army in a unit called CAM. We, the 6th
> Marines, were to form the right flank of a line that included the
> 25th Infantry Division inland.
>
> We then moved forward to the Matanikau [and] established
> an aid station and regimental headquarters on the east bank. A
> couple of days later, the 6th Regiment relieved the 2nd Marines
> who formed the left flank of the Marine's line. Our first glimpse
> of the bearded, dirty, ragged 2nd Marines, without adequate
> footwear, brought home the fact that we were enmeshed in the
> war . . . Stark combat began a few days later when we got word
> that the entire line had formed and we were all to move forward.
> Patrols were sent out and inexperience showed up immediately
> as the Japs let them go through and then closed around them.
> Fire raked the area from every direction. The Sixth had its first
> taste of battle and had been hurt, including my close friend Pfc.
> Kenneth L. Kreamer, who suffered a severe wound in the left
> knee and thigh. The dead and wounded were evacuated to the
> rear aid station across the Matanikau. The dead were eventually
> trucked back to the cemetery and the wounded to the hospital.
> On one such trip back to the aid station about the middle of
> January, I [had] overhead Doctor English complaining about
> the conditions he had to work under and wondering aloud why

the Sixth didn't have its own hearse (truck) to transport the dead to the rear so they wouldn't be lying around the aid station for hours. As luck would have it, the Protestant Chaplain, Gordon Tollefsen, was assigned a ¾-ton truck, but no driver. Before that day was over, because I was handy and no one else was, when the regimental commander decided to make an inspection of the area, and through the persuasive powers of Doc English and two chaplains, I was relieved of all other duties and assigned to Chaplains Tollefsen and Patrick J. O'Neil as their driver.

The rest of my time on Guadalcanal was heartbreaking as I often carried friends, like Dick Watson, K Company's Supply Sergeant (a very close friend)[,] and acquaintances on that long slow ride to the rear. The smell of death permeated everything. The bed of my truck was continuously full of maggots while flies and ants crawled in and out of every opening in the bodies, which were covered by ponchos.

As the CAM Division pushed even farther up the island toward Cape Esperance, about the last week of January, Regimental Headquarters, the aid station[,] and the chaplain's tent (which we shared) were moved up and established in a coconut grove adjacent to the beach. This appeared at first glance to be an ideal spot, but it proved to be otherwise because the open area between the trees and the beach was a perfect target for aircraft, surface vessels[,] and artillery. Attacks occurred [each day] during daylight hours and frequently after dark.

The proximity of the chaplain's tent to the beach gave the added advantage of being able to back the truck into the water and clean out the maggots by tossing buckets of salt water into the truck bed. Of course this left us exposed, as well as the LCMs that brought the dead and wounded to the aid station by water. On a number of occasions we had to provide whatever shelter we could for men on litters who were exposed to strafing aircraft. We never had a man hit, and we felt good about that.[54]

On 26 January portions of the CAM Division attacked the enemy from positions in and around the Poha River and moved about several hundred yards. The following day they moved further to the next river crossing, the Nueha. By the 30th, the 6th Marines and the 147th had reached the Bonegi River where they met a well-prepared enemy position on Hill 92 (*Isamm Dai*) and were temporarily halted while fighting a pitched battle. What the Yanks met were the members of the 229th Infantry at the supply and bivouac area of the Tanaka Butai who did not want to lose what foodstuffs they had cached.

As Joe Micek continued west with the American Division's 132nd Infantry Regiment (reinforced), he recorded this information about Japanese explosive devices: "January 26–27, the Japs used two types of bombs. One is a high-explosive variety generally intended for damaging the airport and the other is a personnel bomb or grass-cutters, called "Daisy Cutters." When this type of bomb explodes it sends shrapnel fragments flying in all directions, close to the ground[,] and it does not make a large hole. In the last two weeks we have spent most of our time in deep dugouts (thank God) with ... log and dirt roofing. It affords plenty of protection against shrapnel. It would practically take a direct hit to kill anyone. Of course, if you are on the surface during an air raid your chances of getting hit are excellent."[55]

During the last days of January, an ever-increasing number of Japanese transports, sea-trucks, freighters, destroyers, and battlewagons gathered in Simpson Harbor at Rabaul, New Britain, and at the Shortland Islands. Coastwatchers warned Nouméa (New Caledonia) of the buildup, causing worry at the SOPAC Command there; they passed the concern to the forces on Guadalcanal. The threat was taken seriously, as SOPAC Command suspected that the enemy was preparing to launch a new invasion. Thus it was that on 6 February the XIV Army Corps recalled elements of 25th Infantry Division (less the 161st Regiment) from the drive west. The intent was to protect the perimeter, which was now short of combat troops, and to defend the airfield against a possible new encounter from the sea. Yet despite the threat of a new attack, the 2nd Marine Division (less the rear echelon of 2/10) boarded transports at Lunga Roads and departed Guadalcanal for "milk and honey" New Zealand.

Joe Micek wrote in his diary:

> We have received an order to be prepared to move at a moment's notice. Something is in store for us, and I don't think it's good. We're off on another expedition into enemy territory. We stored our barracks bags and carried full packs to the beach at Lunga Point. Here we waited. The positions we occupied in the jungle were taken over by the 164th Infantry Regiment. Our equipment for this exercise is full field packs and battle green fatigues. Of course, we are hand carrying our heavy weapons with a normal load of ammo. We were given an address by General Sebree, Col-

onels George and Ferry [Lt. Col. George F.], who told us what a magnificent job we did on Hill 27, and how sure they were that we would also do a good job on this mission. From the information I received, our battalion will travel by Higgins boats to the enemy's rear at the northern end of the island. There, we are to establish a beachhead and place the enemy between two forces. With this stratagem by sea, we hope to clean out the island of the enemy. My company [G] was to establish the initial beachhead. Therefore, we will travel by a destroyer that we board at midnight.[56]

For the move west the force consisted of the 2nd Battalion, 132nd Infantry; Company M (antitank), 132nd Infantry (less one macnine-gun platoon); one rifle platoon of K Company, 132nd Infantry; Battery F, 10th Marines (75-mm pack howitzers); a detachment of the 65th Engineer Combat Battalion; a detachment of the Service Company, 132nd Infantry; a detachment of the Headquarters Company, 132nd Infantry; a detachment of the 26th Signal Company; and a detachment of the 101st Medical Regiment.

Micek's diary continues:

On 1 February, the 2/132 embarked on five LCTs at Kukum [Flotilla 5: LCT 58, 60, 62, 156, and 158] with supporting units, carrying a two-day supply of "C" rations and "D" bars and extra ammunition for 60-mm mortars and machine gun munitions. Standing by was the *Stringham* (APD 6), the APD that was to escort us on our journey north through the area called "Iron Bottom Bay." The sea was calm as the LCTs started their journey in single file. The island looked deceptively peaceful, the mist[-] shrouded mountain range . . . and palm trees along the beach were pictured perfect of a tropical paradise. Later that day, our convoy headed [in] to an area known as Verahue, which was to be our landing spot. At dawn, we rounded the [northwestern] tip of Guadalcanal and came in from the other side.

Our destroyer headed toward the shore area of an unknown lagoon. The DD halted and lowered its landing craft and we headed for shore. I had a strange feeling in the pit of my stomach and I wondered whether we would meet any resistance or not? We all disembarked quickly and moved inland.

As we hit the beach about noon; the sound of aircraft engines cut the air; a twin engine Japanese bomber came roaring over the hill and flew just above the beach palms. As we looked up we could see the waist gunner gazing down on us. It happened so fast that the naval gunners on the APD never fired a shot, and even with our own weapons, "loaded and locked," we didn't fire. The bomber roared down the coastline and banked to the right and attempted to gain altitude in an attempt to make second pass over our landing area, yet flew directly over our escorting destroyer. This time [the ship's fire] scored a direct hit and [the bomber] crashed as a flaming wreck. Later reports indicated that a total of three aircraft were shot down during this engagement.

We found that the landing area, the village of Nuga [Nughu, northwest Guadalcanal], had been abandoned and many of the huts were burnt. We secured the landing area and sent out patrols in the nearby hills with negative results. They found some discarded Japanese equipment, but saw no enemy. I estimated that the strength of the 2/132 and the supporting units numbered about 1,500 men. If the enemy consolidated their forces and attacked, we were informed to hold our ground until forces moving up the beach reached our position. The 65th Engineers improved the shoreline road from Verahue to Titi, enabling supplies and precious water to move forward. The main body moved southward along a beach road that ran along the shoreline without incident to a point called Titi, another Lever Brothers plantation. On the beach we found a crashed Japanese fighter plane; apparently it had made a forced landing. All the machine guns had been removed.

Each day it was the same routine. Inch-up and dig-in, then repeat the same procedure the next day. This exercise continued until 10 February. Company F was dug in and formed a defensive position from the shore on our left flank and into the grove with Company G on the right. The jungle wall we faced was approximately 300 feet to our front. Our field kitchens were set up and we enjoyed our first hot meal in days. The ocean breeze kept the heat and humidity out of the grove. The restful afternoon was shattered by the crack of Japanese rifle fire coming from the edge of the thick underbrush.

The morning of the 5th, the silence was shattered by a shell exploding when it smashed into the trunk of a palm tree and blasted near Company F's position. Everyone dove for cover. Our first impression was that the enemy had brought artillery into action, but we soon found out that our own destroyer had mistaken us for an enemy position and fired 36 rounds into our area. The firing was so close that we never heard the incoming shellfire. Was there cursing! A cease-fire was immediately ordered when a signal from shore was acknowledged. No casualties were reported. In the afternoon, a patrol from Company F was sent to probe the area along the beach road about a hundred yards into the jungle. The patrol was ambushed, with a loss of five men and a couple native scouts. The sound of gunfire was heard and an immediate alert was sounded. Members of the patrol made their way back to our lines along the beach road; our supporting field artillery, the [2nd Battalion,] 10th Marines, opened fire with their 75s.

The sound of shells passing overhead and the exploding shells covered the ambush site and gave us the impression that a new attack was looming. Suddenly, a shrill vibrating was heard and we instinctively knew that it was a "short" round falling in our midst. One killed. As night fell tensions rose, and orders were issued to remain in our foxholes regardless and that any movement would be considered as an enemy probe. Our eyes strained for anything out of the ordinary and ears were attempting to detect any sounds that differed from that of the characteristic jungle sounds.

The following morning, a patrol was organized from the 2nd Battalion and moved along the road to the ambush site. The lead scout found an enemy bayonet lying on the road and it looked "new." We saw many enemy footprints in the sand. On our patrol, we came upon the bodies of two of our GIs. The ants, maggots[,] and large blue flies had begun their aggression on their mangled remains and a sickening stench filled the air. The other missing soldiers of that patrol were listed as MIA (Missing in Action). A British . . . 303 McVickers [Vickers] machine gun was found. It had been abandoned, but no ammunition.

On the 6th we continued our advance along the coast. We passed the remains of what appeared to be a mission [the Sacred Heart mission at Visale]. The only visible object was a statue facing the ocean. I had a small camera and took a photo of it; it was untouched. Later, we passed the bodies of two enemy soldiers lying next to a heavy machine gun. In one area along the beach, we found numerous wooden landing craft. I went aboard one and found that some of the timbers had what seemed to be ax marks on some of the heavy beams. It was powered by an efficient looking diesel engine and appeared to be well maintained.

The air was filled with the stench of death as we passed many bloated and decaying bodies of enemy lying alongside the road. Clouds of flies rose and maggots filled every body opening. Due to their decomposed condition, their cause of death was unknown. We found the body of one of our ill-fated patrol MIAs along the coast route; we covered it with a half-shelter.

As night approached we dug in along high hills that overlooked a jungle valley that extended to the beach[;] two-man foxholes were the order of the day. As the darkness closed in, we could hear sounds of movements and that of muffled rumblings of motors in the distance. I wondered why our Navy or our Marine attached field artillery unit [F/2/10] didn't lay down a barrage on the area. It was later found out that our radio communication equipment was broken down and our naval escort was unable to support us at that critical juncture. Enemy movements continued all night.[57]

The 2nd Battalion, 132nd Infantry, had faced elements of 1st Lt. Michimori Ohe's 2nd Company, plus 2nd Lt. Koitsu Oichi's machine-gun company. Probation Officer Saito's 1st Platoon was active in covering the Yano Battalion's withdrawal.[58] Joe Micek's diary further describes the events: "In the morning, we advanced along the road into an area called Marovovo adjacent to Kamimbo Bay. We found all types of discarded equipment, some new and scattered about such as canteens, helmets and web equipment, plus cases of hand grenades and mortar shells. Stacks of new collapsible boats were discovered in the brush; outboard motors were wrapped in yellow rubberized sheets and had been buried in the sand at the water's edge. Some weapons were found, including an anti-tank rifle, fed by a 10 round clip that was larger in caliber than our .50 caliber machine gun. No strong enemy opposition was encountered, but our patrols inflicted casualties on the fleeing enemy."[59]

The activity on the other coast is described by W. Marshall Chaney of Company B, 1st Battalion, 147th Infantry Regiment, at that time a segment of the CAM Division:

> 19 January, the 1st and 3rd Battalions, 147th Infantry moved into the front lines, flanked by the 6th Marines on the right and the

182nd Infantry on the left. The formations were almost in contact with the enemy. Next morning, Company B's 1st Platoon was on the right of the regimental sector as the platoon went through the valley, between Hills 96 and 98. As we reached the riverbank, groups of Japanese were encountered and were full of fight. The platoon responded quickly and when the melee was over, 17 of the enemy were felled. After arriving at Kokumbona on the 24th, we remained in the reserve, for a brief period, when the XIV Army Corps ordered the regiment back into action. . . . The 6th Marines in consort with the forces of the CAM Division continued to move toward the Poha River where they made contact with scattered forces of the fleeing enemy who fought a delaying action. By the 27th, the CAM Division had reached the edges of the swollen Nueha River and crossed over.[60]

On 28 January, in a coconut grove near Tassafaronga Point, Company A, 1st Battalion, 6th Marines, encountered an ambush while acting as the point in the advance; it was a strategic Japanese delaying tactic in order to facilitate their withdrawal. Company A had many casualties, including the acting commanding officer, Lt. Blaine P. Kerr.

The XIV Army Corps added the punch of the 97th Field Artillery Battalion and Battery G of the 10th Marines to support the 147th's drive west. On 30 January, W. M. Chaney recorded: "As the regiment advanced through a grove, running parallel with the coast, [we] approached the east bank of the Bonegi River; then all hell broke loose and full-scale battle followed."[61] They had run into WO Toraji Matsumoto's 1st Platoon and the Otsuka Tai, plus members of the Yano Battalion, who were protecting the evacuation route.[62] Chaney added: "Artillery fire had been stepped up and help was sought from the Navy and the CAF. Two destroyers were dispatched from Lunga Point to shell the enemy on the west bank. Half-tracks were brought up to reinforce the 1st Battalion's sector and it became a hell-of-a-fight! Despite our aggressiveness, the 147th, however, did not cross the Bonegi River until the 5th."[63]

1st Lt. Marvin V. Ayers of the 3rd Battalion, 147th Infantry Regiment, was the supply officer. His diary covers some of the engagements of the 3rd Battalion:

> *Saturday, January 30:* 11th day in combat. The 147th took over part of the front lines supported by Company B, 57th Combat Engineers; they ran into resistance in the afternoon—quite a few casualties including Lieutenant Chadwick of Company A. The

action took place around the Bonegi River just this side of Tassafaronga. I saw a fellow from Company D blown up by a mortar hit. Snipers galore; bullets whizzing all around.

Sunday, January 31: Bonegi River, still resistance. Battalion scattered; some forward through the coconut trees, others on the ridges to the south, had a destroyer and aerial bombardment plus artillery placed on Jap positions ahead of us. What a racket! Part of the Service Company finally moved up today. Rain! Companies A and L started over ridges 118–120–121–122 and 126 to flank the Japs, tough going. Company K attacked along the coast at 1600; met strong resistance, five killed and seven wounded. Three Japanese were killed near my kitchen bivouac by [the 6th] Marines.

Monday, February 1: Still held up at this side of the Bonegi River along the coast, although Companies A and L are now across the river on the left flank up on the ridges. Couldn't get supplies to A and C Companies due to the difficult terrain. Got the engineers to start a peep [jeep] trail over Hill 117 to them, but it will take too much time. Japs bombed around while I was on Hill 117—was strafed; saw an aerial dogfight and several Japanese planes knocked down in the water. Saw a Zero outmaneuvering a Wildcat [F4F] and moved the kitchens up past Manara Point.

Tuesday, February 2: Took a platoon from Company K with a squad from Company L for guides and security and hand carried supplies to A and L Companies on Hill 124. Went through and then parallel to the front lines. The 1st Battalion pushed across the Bonegi River, so maybe I can find a peep trail now to Companies A and L with the engineers building a bridge across the Bonegi River.

Wednesday, February 3: Blazed a jeep trail to the bottom of Hill 124 and got hot grub and water to A and L.

Thursday, February 4: Took grub up at dawn and established forward ammo dumps just across the Bonegi River. Borrowed 10 mules from the 97th Field Artillery and took supplies to Company K on Hill 123, a rough grind. Battalion moved to the other side of Tassafaronga Point. Also, Condition BLACK. [Possibly an enemy invasion was on.] Contracted for mules for tomorrow.

Friday, February 5: Took supplies by mule to Company K.

The battalion held fast; to be relieved tomorrow by the 161st Infantry.

Saturday, February 6: Relieved by the 161st Infantry, 3rd Battalion by noon; back to the rest area near the Le Sage Trail where we started 18 days ago.[64]

The 161st Infantry took over the westward drive near the Umasani River, located nearly 1½ miles west of Tassafaronga, relieving the 147th. By nightfall, 3/161 had reached Doma Cove, while the 2nd Battalion moved into positions adjacent to Hill 127 and 123 as the 147th Regiment moved out. Meanwhile, 1/161 moved just west of the Bonegi River. The areas around the Segilau (Tambalolo) and Umasani Rivers were former Japanese bivouac areas. At the Sasa River Basin, a group of the enemy was seen moving west, but the Japanese scattered as the 161st Infantry pressed its advantage. The advance continued, and the Tenamba River, nearly three miles to the east of Cape Esperance, was crossed the morning of 9 February. The 161st's drive to the Cape began on the central coast of the island at the former lookout post of the 81st Guard Unit at Taivu Point, then past Koli Point, Lunga Point, Point Cruz, Kokumbona, and Doma Cove, while the GIs were moving to occupy the Japanese positions in the Cape Esperance area. At 1632 the 1st Battalion, 161st Infantry Regiment, and the advance elements (Companies E and G) of the 2nd Battalion, 132nd, met at the east bank of the Tenamba River in Tenaro village.

Back at Koli Point, the area headquarters for the 25th Infantry Division, Sgt. Charles Core (R-2 Section, 161st Infantry) wrote in his diary: "At 1835 this day—as the rain dropped down on our dark tent roof and we all sat around listing to Major [Robert Louis] Stevenson saying 'best news I've heard in a year.' Then he turned—'Can you keep it? Its unofficial still—the' (phone rings) he answers quickly 'yeah okay—okay. Well, it's official. Our forces have met near Cape Esperance and it appears all Jap forces on the island have been killed or evacuated.'"[65]

Although air, sea, and land patrols continued for months, officially the Guadalcanal campaign was over. Nevertheless, Americans continued to die from occasional snipers. It was not until 1949 that the last Japanese surrendered; he had hid in the jungle and had stolen food from the native gardens during the evening hours. He still had his rusty rifle.

16 The *Ke-go* Operation

In February 1943 the Japanese had effected an evacuation plan—the *Ke-go Sakusen*—for removing their troops from Guadalcanal. Director of the Operations Section of the First Division, Army General Staff, Col. Joichiro Sanada had visited Guadalcanal between 17 and 25 December 1942 to assess the conditions. The colonel was appalled at what he saw: the Emperor's troops were unkempt and starving. He concluded that the losses the Seventeenth Army had suffered were too great to continue the campaign; he was convinced that the army should be withdrawn as soon as possible. With this decision firmly entrenched in mind, Sanada returned to Rabaul.

On 29 December, acting on the colonel's analysis, Imperial General Headquarters formulated plans to evacuate Guadalcanal because of the drain on the Empire. The Emperor was informed of their findings: the Japanese Navy was unable to land a sufficient quantity of food to adequately feed the troops; the Seventeenth Army was facing a disaster; and the surface fleet had lost many vessels attempting to reinforce the island. The general staff had concluded it preferred to bring the losses to a halt.

The Plan in Motion

The Japanese lost no time in implementing the Ke-go Operation. Director of the 1st Division, Army General Staff, Maj. Gen. Ayabe Kitsuhu and Col. Joichiro Sanada arrived at Rabaul on 9 January with orders for the Eighth Area Army, authorizing the prompt evacuation of the Seventeenth Army from Guadalcanal. Earlier, on 3 January, Vice Adm. Shigeru Fukusdome, chief of the 1st Department, Imperial General Staff, Navy Department, had arrived at Truk Atoll, the headquarters of the Combined Fleet. The chiefs of staff for the Southeast Area Fleet and the Eighth Fleet had gathered to mull over the intricate plan and coordinate the Ke-go concept; discussion continued until late that night. The following day the Emperor issued the decree to withdraw from Guadalcanal Island, followed by Army Order Nos. 732 and 733 and Navy Order

No. 23. Order No. 733 stated that the Eighth Area Army would make the withdrawal in concert with the Imperial Navy. The essence of the Army-Navy Central Agreement was the following:

1. The troops on Guadalcanal were to be evacuated between the end of January and the beginning of February.
2. The troops were to retrench, bringing their advanced line to Munda, New Georgia Islands, in the western Solomons some 160 miles from Guadalcanal, and on the north to the Santa Isabel Islands.[1]

The New Georgia Islands had been in the overall strategy long before the plan to evacuate Guadalcanal was put in place, as some of the Imperial forces had been diverted to Munda to maintain a backup base. The New Georgia chain, a group of eleven islands, also had a barge way-station when the Gizo Island atoll was briefly occupied in March 1942. On 12 November 1942, the 2nd Battalion, 229th Infantry (Maj. Giichi Sato), 38th Infantry Division, had gone ashore on Munda from five warships as a defense unit for a naval workforce that soon followed. The landing was not unseen by the Allies; at 0900 on the morning of the 13th twelve Guadalcanal-based aircraft bombed the area.

Three days later, on the 16th, the 22nd Construction Unit landed and within days the 22nd Setsueitai began working on a secret landing strip on the southeast tip of Munda Island, well concealed beneath cleverly wired palm trees. The "Air Solomons" photographic squadron of the USAAF 4th Photo Reconnaissance and Mapping Group, recently arrived at Henderson Field, subsequently detected a hidden airstrip on 5 December and alerted air intelligence officers. The intelligence team took several days to properly identify the Japanese intention before the problem could be eradicated. Nevertheless, when their conclusions were made, the New Zealand airmen went to work. The "Kiwis" of the RNZAF in their Hudsons were a recent addition to the Cactus Air Force and usually flew their bombers without the normal fighter escort. F/Sgt. David Tribe of No. 3 Reconnaissance Bombardment Squadron, RNZAF, described what F/Sgt. Ira Page of No. 3 Squadron had written regarding that time period:

> Munda Island . . . in those days had no significance until . . . an American reconnaissance plane reported that a runway had been built on it almost overnight, apparently covered with the tops of palm trees. These treetops were to be removed . . . and there

would be an operational [airstrip]. I decided to look at Munda, which was not quite operational, so one day at midday, we flew right along the palm-covered [strip] at 200 feet and dropped a stick of bombs (depth charges, actually) . . . setting fire to several buildings at the end of the runway. This was, in fact, the first Allied attack on Munda. The result of this episode was that I got ticked off ["called down"] by the CO for "wasting" six 500-lb. depth charges since it was the whole stock for the New Zealand squadron.[2]

Also on 5 December Japanese sub-chasers had landed 1,200 troops on Ga Tō, along with a number of bags of rice. Five days later eight destroyers delivered 250 sealed drums of food by pushing them off each ship's fantail, hoping the tide would carry them to shore—an innovative manner to supply the starving Japanese, yet a drop in the proverbial rice bowl compared to what was required. During the unloading, four American PT boats disrupted the operation and tangled with the Imperial Navy. Their .50-caliber machine guns peppered holes in the floating barrels, much to the distaste of the Imperial sailors, who reacted vigorously by attacking the motor torpedo boats (MTB). PT-*43* and PT-*112* both took hits, and both were lost.

On 11 December, the Eighth Area Army issued Group Order No. 81 to the Seventeenth Army, and in compliance with this order the Yano Battalion was hurriedly organized and put together on 10 January to help support the evacuation. A fresh contingent of soldiers based at Rabaul was drawn from the Shoji Butai (Col. Toshinari Shoji), the 230th Infantry replacement unit; it was now identified as the Yano Battalion under Maj. Keiji Yano. This provisional force was a conscripted body composed of men in their thirties who formed a security detail to man the front lines of the evacuation groups. The thirty-two-year-old Yano had been a company commander of the 1st Infantry Regiment during the China incident and had participated in the capture of the "Three Wuhan Cities," Wuchang, Hankou, and Hanyang, on 27 October 1938. Before Major Yano took up his post at Rabaul he had been a company commander at the Reserve Officers School. His battalion for the Guadalcanal campaign comprised three rifle companies, one machine-gun company commanded by 2nd Lt. Koitsu Oichi (three platoons with six machine guns), and a howitzer company (75-mm weapons), led by Capt. Masanobu Doi, with about one hundred foot soldiers from the 8th Company, 38th Howitzer Regiment.

The Yano Butai was a mixture of 750 "green" troops with two or three NCOs per company, but it was led by a few officers who, like Yano, had experienced combat in China. The 1st Company was commanded by 1st Lt. Michimori Ohe, a special volunteer officer with eleven years of service; the 2nd Company was led by 1st Lt. Masashi Gomi, who had been a second lieutenant for nineteen years. The 3rd Company, however, was led by a recent call-up, 2nd Lt. Hiroshi Ohtsuka. PO2c Sankichi Kaneda wrote regarding the Yano Butai: "The Yano Battalion of [the] 38th Division, the last to be landed on Ga Tō, consisted of draftees averaging 32 years of age, poorly trained, lightly armed and in [b]rand new uniforms[. T]his was at the time when we were awaiting evacuation, so looking at this new unit, we felt uneasy. Were we still going to fight for this island? Aren't we going to be evacuated? Seeing the Yano Battalion coming ashore at *Ku-ru-tsu* [Cruz] Point, our spirits fell. We didn't know then that the Yano Butai was to be our rear guard for the evacuation operation, and it was due to their sacrifices that we escaped enemy attacks on our backs as we withdrew while the evacuation went smoothly."[3]

Adding to the overall problems just preceding the evacuation, the Seventeenth Army radio code personnel were so seriously ill with the Guadalcanal sickness that radio operations were virtually suspended. This difficulty had to be resolved for the evacuation to proceed as planned. To assist, the Eighth Area Army assigned part of the Eighth Army communication unit of about 150 men for movement to Guadalcanal. The group consisted of one army radio platoon from the 14th Signal Regiment, one army wire platoon, and one squad from the 15th Signal Regiment that was to be attached to the Yano Battalion. Accompanying the force were Lt. Col. Kumao Imoto, a staff officer with the Eighth Area Army, and Maj. Tadahiko Sato. With Colonel Imoto were two code specialists and six selected enlisted men.

On 12 January the Yano Battalion departed Simpson Harbor, Rabaul, on board the destroyers *Urakaze, Tanikaze, Arashio, Akigumo,* and *Hamakaze,* bound for Guadalcanal via the *Sho Tō* (Shortland Islands). They entered the Faisi Island anchorage at 0800 on the 13th. Major Sato and Colonel Imoto each carried identical Ke-go papers and traveled on different destroyers; should one vessel be disabled or sunk, the other would be able to deliver the instructions to Guadalcanal. At the Faisi command post, Colonel Imoto met with staff officer Maj. Einosuke Iemura and revealed the secret Ke-go Operation plan. Satisfied with the Faisi cooperation, Imoto's next step was to present the objective to the Seventeenth

Army. The team left the Shortlands for Guadalcanal, arriving that evening at Kamimbo Bay on the northwestern tip of the island.

The next day, 14 January, Colonel Imoto moved from Tenaro to the Tassafaronga area—the headquarters of the Seventeenth Army and Lt. Gen. Haruyoshi Hyakutake. Imoto explained the plan to the army staff, but most officers were hesitant. Imoto insisted: "The charge of the Eighth Area Army is to obey the Supreme Order." PO2c Kanichi Sankeda's diary noted that after two hours of heated exchange, General Hyakutake finally asserted, "Nothing shall prevent me from doing my duty." That evening, Col. Haruo Konuma of the Seventeenth Army went to the front lines to explain the evacuation order to the various commanders. At midnight, he delivered the order and the plan for its execution to Lt. Gen. Tdayoshi Sano, commander of the 38th Infantry Division, at his headquarters. Following that Konuma called upon Lt. Gen. Masao Maruyama, commander of the 2nd Division, and presented him with the plan.[4]

While Colonel Konuma had been preparing for his visit to Guadalcanal to deliver the Emperor's Order to Evacuate, PO2c Kaneda had recorded in his diary the renewed initiative to resupply the haggard troops—an effort of too much, too late. He notes: ". . . The suspended supply by destroyers was resumed on the 11th with [them] delivering provisions in sealed rubber bags. On 14 January more provisions in drums and rubber bags [were] delivered by destroyers. Apparently, they were put in the water offshore for the tide, wind and waves to float ashore." However, Kaneda's earlier entry had underscored the sense of desperation the troops had been feeling: "November and December is mostly about trying to survive, occasional small units being landed, efforts by [the] Navy to deliver supplies, and occasional sorties of no consequence. Destroyers delivered rice in metal drums overnight. Men on shore [would] light bonfires to guide [them] to areas of friendly forces." Kaneda later again wrote, listing the ironically more frequent resupply runs for the troops about to taken off the island:

> 26 January, under a half-moon, Submarine *I-26* set afloat about 15 tons of provisions in rubber bags and safely withdrew.
> 27 January, just as the night before, Submarine *I-3* set afloat rubber bags full of provisions and safely withdrew.
> 29 January, Submarine *I-3* left rubber bags of provisions afloat for us, but while taking aboard some passengers for the return

trip, was attacked by enemy torpedo boats and sunk. Our landing barges rescued crew and passengers.

30 January, at Esperance, Submarine *I-19* set afloat 25 tons of provisions and safely withdrew.

31 January, Submarine *I-20* set afloat about 25 tons of provisions and took aboard emergency passengers on its return.[5]

By 16 January the 16th Infantry had withdrawn to the area adjacent to Rove Creek, and by late afternoon on the following day it had moved to an area known as Hyakutake Hill, a line east of Isamu Gawa (White River), but still on the coast. Two days later General Maruyama issued movement directives to carry out the evacuation blueprint. Combat forces were to clear the coast route of any enemy so that the components of the 38th Division, the freshest major unit, could move to Cape Esperance with surety. However, a few days later, the 38th Infantry Division issued Order No. 304 authorizing the move of the division to Tenaro.

Although the 38th Division had issued orders to prepare to move, the commander of the 38th Transport Regiment, Lt. Col. Hideichi Yabuta, did not inform his men. Compounding the situation, on 3 February Yabuta died and the acting commanding officer, Capt. Gunji Tokunaga, likewise did not pass the evacuation order to his subordinates, but rather told them they were leaving for a final battle at the Segilau River.[6]

On 25 January elements of the 4th Infantry Regiment (eighty men) and the 16th Infantry Regiment (one hundred men) were to engage the Americans in an attempt to stall their advance. While the 4th and 16th Infantry were jabbing at the GIs, twenty officers of the Seventeenth Army rear echelon disbanded their headquarters at Tassafaronga and headed for Esperance. At sunset, elements of the 38th Division began moving forward with a detachment on the right flank as a protection screen, while elements of the Yano Battalion advanced to Kokumbona; there they engaged the Americans.

Meanwhile, elements of the 38th Division had arrived at Tenaro just after sunset on 22 January. However, the commander, seeing difficulties, ordered one unit to the front lines to remain in position, specifically to make contact with the 2nd Division, which was to maintain coastal security until the evening of the 23rd. Elements of the 2nd Division would spar with the Americans around Hills 420 and 920, and although the Americans were pushing, it was not hard enough, thus letting the Japanese flee. The 16th and 29th Regiments of the 2nd Division were to continue to be in command of the exodus while allowing the main body of the division to move west. At one juncture, the depleted 4th Infantry Regiment was also ordered to protect the withdrawal. The next day, 24 January, about 2,200 soldiers, the rear element of the 38th Division, moved from the left bank of the Segilau River, and proceeded to the Cape Esperance evacuation area to assemble there.

In support of these operations, the *Ga-shima* Guard Unit (elements of the 81st and 84th Guard Units) was to strengthen positions around Tassafaronga while the 1st Shore Patrol Unit, a provisional force, strengthened positions around the Segilau. By the 25th, portions of the 2nd and 38th Infantry Divisions were in the vicinity of the Segilau River's left bank area and formed a line to secure it; the 1st Shore Patrol Unit was responsible for receiving units moving into the area. On the 27th, the Seventeenth Army issued an order to the 38th Division to gather in the vicinity of Arrearage and Kamimbo Bay by the morning of the 29th. The Seventeenth Army issued another order at 1000 on the 28th to the navy's 1st Ship Transport Unit to embark the 38th Division, now located in the vicinity of Esperance and Kamimbo Bay, on the 31st. Meanwhile, on the morning of the 29th, the Yano Battalion retreated from the Bonegi River basin to approximately 800 yards west of the old Seventeenth Army headquarters at Tassafaronga.

What the Matsumoto company of the Yano Butai faced was the 1st and 3rd Battalions of the 147th Infantry Regiment, elements of the 6th Marines, and their half-tracks. However, after each cautious advance, sometimes only 1,000 yards, the Americans would dig in for the night, and when darkness fell, the Japanese would move out. No one in the XIV Army Corps could read the telltale signs that the Japanese were leaving, even when hundreds of decomposed bodies were found on the trails west along with scattered war materiel.

To protect the evacuation, the Eighth Fleet had carefully watched the movements of the U.S. Fleet. On 30 January the commander of the 21st Submarine Group had reported that no enemy vessels were in Lunga Harbor. However, on the following day, the 31st, the RXN Communication Base reported to the Eighth Fleet that two transports, two destroyers, and one ship resembling a light cruiser were anchored off Guadalcanal's Lunga Point. On that morning, as well, the Tokyo Express had landed the Kure 6th SNLF at Munda Island in the New Georgias, boosting the combat strength there to 2,223 troops.

The Guadalcanal evacuation plans called for all the troops to move out under the cover of darkness, with strict discipline and security to be maintained. The very sick and incapacitated were to be left behind. Any heavy vehicles and artillery pieces that the troops could not bring out with them were to be destroyed, though each man was to retain his personal weapons. The commanders were to explain to the troops that the move was in preparation for a future offensive. Important documents were to be carried safely and all others burned; materiel of no further value was to be buried. However, the physical condition of the Japanese troops had deteriorated so greatly that much of the heavy equipment was not buried as ordered but simply discarded along the route. As they advanced westward, the Japanese were pursued and nagged each day by the Americans, not far behind.

On 31 January the Eighth Area Army decided to postpone the evacuation by one day to ensure success. At 2300, on 1 February, the Seventeenth Army issued an order to the 2nd Division to carry out the evacuation operation. At that time, Col. Yutaka Matsuda, the newly appointed commander of the 28th Infantry Regiment, came under the direct control of the Seventeenth Army; he had previously commanded the 28th Regiment at Asahigawa, Japan. Colonel Matsuda's rear guard group now consisted of the Yano Butai; Maj. Kenji Ishido's battalion; the 38th Howitzer Regiment, a heavy artillery unit; and part of the 45th Field Antiaircraft Artillery Battalion.

What the U.S. Navy possessed at the Lunga roadstead in the way of warships made little difference to Rear Adm. Tomiji Koyanagi, commander of Destroyer Squadron 2. He had relieved Rear Adm. Raizo Tanaka on 31 December; Tanaka, godfather of the Tokyo Express, was returning to Japan for an assignment with the Naval General Staff.[7] The new commander was confident that his sailors would easily pluck the Seventeenth Army off RXN. In early February, two weeks after the Yano Butai had landed, the Maizura 4th SNLF, a veteran unit on Guadalcanal, moved to the Tenaro area and became the Naval Embarkation Supervision Unit, charged with the responsibility of escorting all the evacuees to the waiting destroyers. This Tokubetsu Rikusentai force had reached Guadalcanal on 15 October 1942, at which time it had a strength of 824 members. By the time it was to support the evacuation project, its roster had dropped to 361, the result of casualties and disease.

The SNLF unit was under Cdr. Namihira Sasakawa who was placed in charge of the Cape Esperance evacuees; Cdr. Tamao Shinohara was named Kamimbo Area Supervisory Chief. Commander Shinohara had been a staff officer with the both Eleventh Air Fleet and the Eighth Fleet and had come to Guadalcanal as the Japanese Navy liaison officer for the Kageyoshi Operation. A thirty-man detachment led by WO Hideo Kageyu of the 84th Guard Unit had manned dual antiaircraft guns at Esperance for the past month, and nearby were the remnants of the 11th and the 13th Construction Units, whose members had been helping unload supplies. Both formations had been on the island since July and were anxious to leave. Lt. Akira Tanabe, the ranking officer of the 84th Guard Unit, was in charge of key evacuation arrangements for the island's original naval components, assisted by WO Tetuzo Nakamura of the 81st Guard Unit mountain-gun platoon.

The Reality of Retreat

By 2 February, as the veterans prepared to leave the "Island of Death," each unit began moving out by sunset to assemble at their designated embarkation points. The evacuation was carried out in three stages during the dark of night on 2–3, 4–5, and 7–8 February. The first units to be uplifted were elements of the 38th Division, the newest complement to have arrived on the island. The next movement involved the 2nd Division, and the last took miscellaneous formations. Each destroyer had large white numbers freshly painted on the vessel's bow that would be clearly visible to the Japanese Navy men ferrying the evacuees to their respective ships. The operation plans seemed to have left nothing to chance.

The first evacuation run of twenty destroyers departed Rabaul Harbor at 0900, precisely on schedule. At 1600, however, the flotilla was attacked by Allied bombers and fighters just north of Kolombangara Island. The flagship, *Makinami,* with Rear Adm. Shintaro Hashimoto on board, was hit and suffered slight damage. The *Fumizuki* towed it back to the Shortlands, and Rear Admiral Hashimoto was forced to switch his flag to the *Shirayuki.* The first run, which had boarded 4,935 men (441 of the IJN), involved the 3rd Combination Destroyer Group; it included the 10th Squadron, of the 10th Destroyer Division, and the 17th Destroyer Division. The "lookout sector" or guard force—the *Kawakaze, Shirayuki, Maikaze, Kuroshio,* and *Fumizuki*—remained off the Tenaro waters to watch for the U.S. Navy. The *Satsuki* and the Nagasaki *Nagatsuki,* of the 16th Destroyer Division, mounted guard duty off the coast of Kamimbo Bay. The pickup destroyers assigned to pluck the remnants of the Seventeenth Army off Tenaro Point included the *Kazegumo, Yūgumo, Akigumo, Tanikaze, Hamakaze, Makikumo, Urakaze,* and *Isokaze* (replacing the *Yudachi*).[8] The *Tokitsukaze, Yukikaze, Ōshio,* and *Arashio* picked up the veterans waiting at Kamimbo Bay.

The Seventeenth Army Headquarters boarded one of the first formations to depart. They made certain they were going to leave and embarked
on the *Isokaze* with 142 remaining members of the 192 that had landed
in October; seventeen had been killed in action, one died of wounds, the
others died of sickness. The 2nd Division Headquarters was aboard the
Hamakaze, while the balance of the division—2,647 members—was
spread among the other destroyers. To combat any disruption in the
evacuation plan, the Second Fleet Battle Group, commanded by Vice
Adm. Nobutake Kondo, moved out of the Truk anchorage. It was sent
to divert the U.S. Navy's attention from the evacuation site and was well
prepared to take on the Americans. The battleships *Kongo* and *Haruna*
were backed by the heavy cruisers *Atago, Takao, Myōkō,* and *Haguro,*
and by the light cruisers *Jintsū, Agano,* and *Nagara.* The escort destroyers included the *Kagero, Asagumo, Shigure, Suzumaze, Samidare, Ōshio,
Hatsuyuki, Shikinami, Arashio,* and *Arashi.*[9] For additional safety, two
aircraft carriers were added, the *Junyō* and *Zuihō,* supported by the supply vessels *Nippon Maru* and the *Kenyo Maru.*

On 2 February, however, the destroyers *Asagumo* and *Samidare* developed engine trouble and had to return to Shortland Bay.[10] The only
thorn in the side of the Imperial Navy as they traveled to Guadalcanal
was the Tulagi-based Motor Torpedo Boat Flotilla I with its PT boats,
which attacked the evacuation armada. The PT boys believed that the
island was being reinforced again, and their task was to disrupt any Japanese warships. They, and the Cactus Air Force, harassed the evacuation
fleet, but their little stings did not counter the withdrawal. The Tenaro
evacuation group arrived off the island at 2050, and the Kamimbo Bay
destroyers arrived at 2200. The sailors from the Maizura 4th SNLF (Naval Embarkation Supervision Unit) eased the process for the soldiers by
tacking signs to trees, showing the assembly point for each unit and led
the evacuees to the barges. Each barge had a petty officer in charge and
one seaman assigned to transport the veterans to the waiting vessels. The
destroyers were not anchored, but were kept adrift in the event of attack by motor torpedo boats, and this move paid off handsomely as no
destroyers were lost. Nevertheless, while the Japanese troops were withdrawing from the nightmare that had been Ga Tō, the U.S. Army, on the
southwestern side of the island at Beaufort Bay, was watching; yet for
some unknown reason, during the eight-day evacuation, the U.S. Navy
was "dead in the water." They never appeared to halt the exodus.

1st Lt. John M. George of Company G, 2nd Battalion, 132nd Infantry, was there.

It was the most interesting and eerie night that I spent on Guadalcanal—that night on a ridge top overlooking Beaufort Bay. It was also one of the most memorable examples of lost opportunity I have ever seen. A Japanese destroyer or submarine pulled into the bay just after dusk and took on a number of evacuees. All sorts of craft—boats powered by outboard motors, rowboats, life rafts, landing barges—all were used . . . in effecting the escape of several hundreds of Japanese. One of the principal embarkation points for the operation was within spitting distance of us—less than 300 yards below and to our front.

Yet we could do nothing. We did not have the ammunition to fire blindly—we had only a few rounds of 60-mm mortar stuff. No machine gun or rifle ammunition to blaze away with at area targets. But we were sitting and watching hundreds of Japs leaving an island that rightly should have become their last resting-place!

The most tantalizing factor involved was that we had our artillery in position, in readiness to bring deadly fire to bear on a closely observed enemy. We could have engineered a wonderful slaughter with a few rounds of high explosive. But it was the ancient and honorable military problem of communication. The damned radio always weakened as night set in. Just a characteristic of that particular set—the M511. Geisel [Capt. Raymond A., HQ/2/132] struggled heroically all night in an effort to make contact with Force, but luck was not with him.[11]

Lt. Col. Yoshihatsu Onizuka, commander of the 3rd Independent Trench Mortar Battalion, had arrived on Guadalcanal on 7 October 1942; his gunners were summoned to the evacuation area to be one of the forces to help protect the withdrawal. The 6th Independent Antitank Gun Battalion and the Moritami Butai were also part of the blocking force that was to hold back the Americans, and all evacuation formations now fell under the direct command of Colonel Matsuda of the 28th Infantry Regiment.

Between 25 January and 7 February the elements of the American CAM Division had moved forward to the west at a snail's pace, averaging a daily gain of about 870 yards.[12] Matsuda's forces had succeeded in stalling the GIs while the Japanese troops continued to head for the Kamimbo evacuation site and wait their turn to withdraw. However, as the first echelon of the evacuation fleet was in full swing on the night of 2 February, they were attacked at 0540 by an assortment of aircraft from the Cactus Air Force; the proficient Japanese Navy gunners kept the planes high overhead and thus the fleet sustained no major damage. One destroyer, the *Makikumo,* ran into a mine, which momentarily slowed the fleet; but the group continued on at a speed of 30 to 33 knots, reaching Shortland Harbor at 0900. The U.S. Navy had laid mines between Doma Cove and Cape Esperance in anticipation of inhibiting any invasion efforts and disrupting the supply point; but they had caught no enemy warships in their traps until the *Makikumo* encountered their snare. The *Yūgumo* had come to the rescue, attaching a line, and it was in the process of assisting the stricken destroyer to the Shortland base when the *Makikumo* began swiftly taking on water off Savo Island and sank. Meanwhile, the evacuation fleet was attacked off Savo Island by six PTs from Motor Torpedo Boat Squadron 2, but the squadron's craft did not come away unscathed. PT-*111* took a direct hit from a destroyer's 5-inch shell, and PT-*37* and PT-*123* were smashed during the melee.[13]

The second evacuation run, on 4–5 February, was carried out in perfect weather. The night was dark and moonless, and the swells were up only slightly. Admiral Hashimoto in the *Shirayuki* considered the perfect conditions a good omen. Two platoons of the Yano Butai, plus others, managed to reach the evacuation area and quickly boarded the waiting destroyers—3,921 men (327 of the IJN). The ships headed for the Faisi Island roadstead but came under an attack by thirty aircraft from Henderson Field. The *Maikaze* was the only casualty, receiving slight damage, with one sailor killed and two wounded; it was towed back to the Shortland Base by the *Nagatsuki.*

Again, the 10th Destroyer Squadron and the 17th Destroyer Division were part of the transport group, which also included the Tenaro protection destroyers *Shirayuki, Asayuki, Kuroshio, Samidare,* and *Kawakaze.* The recovery vessels for pickup were the *Kazegumo, Akigumo, Urakaze, Isokaze, Yūgumo, Tanikaze,* and *Hamakaze.* At 1725, the *Shirayuki* developed engine trouble and Admiral Hashimoto once again was forced to transfer his flag, this time to the *Kawakaze.* The Kamimbo Bay lookout security force consisted of the *Satsuki, Nagatsuki,* and *Fumizuki,* while the pickup fleet was the *Tokitsukaze, Yukikaze, Arashio,* and *Ōshio.* Both the Tenaro and the Kamimbo Bay pickup forces reached their assigned areas at 2050.

A typical unit evacuation was that of 1st Lt. Akio Tani's 2nd Company, 7th Heavy Field Artillery Regiment. He arrived at the Kamimbo Bay evacuation point on 1 February one of eight artillerymen, the only survivors of the original 154 that had landed in October 1942 from Rabaul. When they boarded the destroyer *Ōshio* on the 4th, one of Tani's men, Pvt. Yoshihiro Miyazaki, was so weak that he had great difficulty with the Jacob's ladder and fell to the ocean, but he was rescued.[14] The evacuation of Sgt. Hisakichi Hara of the 1st Battalion, 230th Infantry, was also characteristic of the efficiency of the Japanese plan. Hara had arrived on Guadalcanal on 15 October 1942 with some one thousand others. When he reached the evacuation area that first day of February, only sixty men from his battalion remained alive. Their pickup was prompt, owing to the competence of the Naval Embarkation Group at both the Kamimbo Bay and Cape Esperance points, and as soon as the evacuees were boarded, the rescue destroyers quickly departed the area. All the ships were crowded, but no doubt many a soldier paid little heed, grateful to be leaving. Some of the unfortunate on board died only a few hours after departure and were buried at sea; the lucky ones eventually made it to Erventa, Bougainville.

The final evacuation run of 7–8 February uplifted 1,796 veterans (including seventy-five IJN). The 3rd Destroyer Squadron handled the Cape Esperance area, and the 10th Squadron took on the Kamimbo Bay sector. The ships had weighed anchors at Faisi Island at 0930 on the 7th; at 1545 they were attacked by a mass of thirty-five aircraft of the Cactus Air Force while just off the pickup site. The fleet took only minor damage, as again, the gunners kept the planes at a distance. The destroyer *Isokaze* had been part of the first two successful evacuation runs, and her captain was now part of the final effort. The destroyer received slight damage from the air attack, and ten sailors were killed and fourteen wounded, but the steadfast ship continued on its journey. The Yano Butai lost 101 men while covering the withdrawal, yet they finally arrived safely at the Shortland Naval Base at 0758 on the 8th.[15]

WO Toraji Matsumoto (commander, Masariu company) of the Yano Battalion described the evacuation role:

> On 7 February, we spent the last day in the forest [jungle] keeping guard and trying to rest up as much as possible. Soldiers had received plenty of rice and canned foods from the provision station and had their fill for the first time since landing here on Guadalcanal. They even had the luxury of warmed milk. It is regrettable that all these goods brought on land could not be carried to the front line and distributed before now. The Sekiro

areas, which we passed through the day before yesterday, and the opposite side, which is the Marovovo District, seem to be having an artillery attack that began this morning. We hear the echo of explosions but there is no sign of them bombing us. [What they heard was the U.S. Navy bombardment in error of the positions held by the GIs of the 132nd Infantry.]

That afternoon, all Japanese NCOs and soldiers were ordered to bury their weapons and equipment except knives. We were informed, "Tonight at 2100 hours our destroyers will come to carry out the last evacuation team." After sunset, before it got too dark, the barge engineer officer made the boarding arrangements. We proceeded quietly to the boarding area. At 1930, we were led aboard and jammed onto a big barge with absolutely no room for standing. If the enemy sensed what we were doing, we would have been in big trouble. The work went on secretly in the night's darkness. No one talked, of course, not even a cough. Time goes slow, when you wait. We waited and waited, but no destroyer. Is this really possible? Fear takes army soldiers as soon as they give up their weapons. They must all be thinking of the same thing as their uneasy looks are cast on the dark horizon at sea.

Suddenly over to the west of us, fierce shelling started at the shore around Marovovo. Oh no! We can't move an inch on this barge. At sea, muzzles of big guns shot out flames. [This was actually a thirty-six-plane Cactus Air Force attack on the convoy.] Sparks from the explosion look quite astonishing, to say the least. Soon, I could hear the engine sound of an American torpedo boat speeding east. Soldiers waiting to go onboard took a hard swallow. The artillery shelling stopped and the torpedo boat disappeared in the dark sea. All gave a deep sigh of relief.

Ten minutes seemed like an hour. Some time passed. Blue luminous signals offshore began flashing on and off. It's a signal from the destroyer we have been waiting for. The landing barges started engines in unison and moved rapidly toward the signal. Soon we arrived at a huge black destroyer. On deck, sailors were calling with a megaphone. "Ahoy, it's over here." The ship we approached was a destroyer, *Satsuki*. It looked big enough to be a cruiser and gave me an assured feeling. The barge was brought alongside the destroyer and a rope ladder was dropped. I let the soldiers climb on board. Some, who have exhausted their physical strength, are having difficulty climbing the rope ladder. Sailors lie on their stomachs and hold out their hands to pull up soldiers. I remained until last. I made sure the only men left on board were those who worked on the vessel and grabbed the rope ladder. I tried to climb, but oh! How heavy my body felt! Did my body weaken this badly? I put forth all energy I had left and climbed up on deck on my own. Led by a sailor I went inside and sat down. My pocket watch showed 2130. I took a communication paper and a pencil out of the pocket bag and recorded 2130: "Farewell, more than twenty thousand souls sleeping in indignation. Farewell."

After completing the last evacuation the destroyer left the coast of Guadalcanal with its engines roaring. The destroyer went west at full speed. A sailor brought out large rice balls, almost as big as an infant's head, in a basket and gave one with pickled ginger to each soldier. I got one and took a big bite. How good that rice ball tasted! I will never forget that taste as long as I live. As I ate I also tasted the true reality of being rescued.[16]

In the three evacuation efforts, the deck plates of the destroyers were crowded with soldiers. Some of the last segment to depart were 264 members of the 28th Infantry Regiment who left 1,945 of their comrades dead somewhere on Guadalcanal. The advanced echelon of the 28th Infantry—916 soldiers—had been the first of the Imperial foot soldiers to arrive, and the battered remnants of the 28th were the last to leave.[17]

1st Lt. Genjirou Inui of the 8th Independent Antitank Company was evacuated by the *Tokitsukaze* on the last run. His story is one overlaid with anticipation and apprehension. On 4 February, the second evacuation trip, he had reached the embarkation zone and was fortunate enough to board one of the landing craft. However, he was ordered off the boat by his commander, Capt. Isao Nakaoka, and directed to assist in gathering the remains of Major Kitano's battalion, including remnants of the Ichiki Shitai (Col. Kiyonao Ichiki). Lieutenant Inui finally was able to evacuate on the last run on the 7th with forty members of the 28th Infantry Regiment. Inui's company had landed on the island on 25 August 1942 with one hundred men; twenty-four survived.[18]

The remaining complement of the Maizura 4th SNLF, one of the covering and embarkation supervising units, also was able to leave on the 7th. WO Tetuzo Nakamura's howitzer gun platoon was part of the

81st Guard Unit, one of the original garrison units; the twenty-one men of the 81st that survived included Nakamura and all members of his platoon. Of the 84th Guard Unit, the organization renamed from the Kure 3rd SNLF on 1 July 1942, forty survived, with fifty-three being KIA since 25 November 1942.[19]

The ever-alert lookout destroyer covering force on the 7th, the vessels guarding against any adverse conditions, consisted of twice the number involved in the pickup. It included the *Shirayuki, Asagumo, Kazegumo, Urakaze, Kuroshio, Ōshio, Nagatsuki, Hamakaze, Samidare, Arashio, Tanikaze,* and the ever-present *Isokaze.* The *Yūgumo* and *Akigumo* had been detailed to embark the troops in the Russell Islands. A special detachment of three hundred troops from the 38th Infantry Division had landed there on 28 January, in the event the island had to be used as an alternate evacuation point. Two naval machine gun companies reinforced this unit, which then assumed the name Russell Islands Occupation Unit.[20]

Rekata Bay, Santa Isabel Island, also had been considered as an alternate staging area because Gizo was already an established barge relay base.[21] However, the Gizo plan was discarded in favor of the use of the Russell Islands, which were closer to Guadalcanal. The Imperial Navy took a major risk in going directly to Guadalcanal and won—perhaps due to their meticulous coordination. The Allies would later meet some of these same soldiers and sailors on the beaches of New Georgia Island and in the jungles of Bougainville.

The observations of Lt. Eihrchi Nakano, the assistant navigating officer on the *Satsuki,* notes the evacuees' "free ride" away from Guadalcanal with little American military interference:

> My first relation with Guadalcanal Island was the withdrawal operation of the Army forces from the island to Buin [in] the southern part of Bougainville Island on 1 February 1943 [actually 2–3 February]. We had left the Shortland anchorage at 0915 for the island with full speed adjusting the arrival time to Cape Esperance. We, of course, had expected a fierce counter attack by U.S. air sea forces before and after the operation. However, I do not know the reason why [but] we me met only a few aircraft and torpedo boats, by which we had not been damaged at all. Next morning at 1015 we returned safe back to the Shortland anchorage. After that, two more operations with the same number

of destroyers on the 5th and the 7th had been carried into effect. There were some incredible points during that operation, one of which [was] we had no serious attack by the U.S. Forces.[22]

The Repugnant Final Success

The Japanese evacuation of Guadalcanal ranks as of the most successful retreats of the war, attributable—perhaps at last—to adept planning and seamanship. When the evacuees reached the Shortlands, they were divided into two groups. The very sick soldiers were immediately transported to Rabaul for hospitalization, and the healthier individuals were transferred to Erventa, Bougainville. The Japanese Navy personnel landed at Buin, Bougainville, the headquarters of the 1st Base Force.

Japanese Personnel Evacuated—Guadalcanal

Imperial Japanese Navy

Sasebo 5th SNLF	23
Maizuru 4th SNLF	361
81st Guard Unit (incl. 5 patients)	21
84th Guard Unit	40
11th Construction Unit	228
13th Construction Unit	170
Transport crews (civilians)	27
Total IJN:	870

Imperial Japanese Army

HQ Seventeenth Army	142
2nd Infantry Division	2,647
38th Infantry Division	2.473
35th Brigade	618
28th Infantry Regiment	264
Under Seventeenth Army	1,666
Line of Communication	
Hospital	480
Army transport unit	1,500
Total IJA:	9,770
Total IJN and IJA:	10,660

After the withdrawal was completed, Vice Adm. Nobutake Kondo's battle group returned to anchor at Truk. They had maneuvered in the vicinity of Gurinitchi Island and were prepared to respond in force should the enemy interfere. The American surface fleet was deployed in an area

300 miles southeast of Guadalcanal, out of carrier aircraft range. The commander in chief of the Japanese Combined Fleet had ordered one segment to proceed 350 miles north of Guadalcanal as a diversion to lure the Americans away, if necessary. The submarine screen, after sweeping the seas southeast of Espiritu Santo Island, New Hebrides Islands, was to attack enemy vessels in the area of New Caledonia. By 8 February Kondo's advanced battle force had moved some 550 miles north of Guadalcanal when orders from the Combined Fleet directed them to return to the Truk anchorage. They reached Truk by the 9th, just as the Americans discovered that the Japanese were evacuating instead of reinforcing.

The war on Guadalcanal did not come to an abrupt halt because the Sun Soldiers had departed, for hundreds had been left behind who were too ill or too weak to make the evacuation point on time. During the next few months, individuals and small roving bands were found. Some killed themselves for fear of falling into the enemy's hands, other fought with whatever weapons they had; and some simply surrendered, too sick to fight back. They, indeed, were the wise ones. The bewildered and exhausted Japanese survivors called Guadalcanal "*Jigoku no shima*" — "hell's island." The equally war-weary marines referred to the campaign as "our time in hell." Both were right.

Epilogue

On 7 August 1942 the U.S. Marines, Navy, and Coast Guard had launched the first major Pacific Allied offensive of World War II in the British Solomon Islands Protectorate. It became a complex campaign in which the United States and its Pacific partners resolutely fought the Japanese "Sun Soldiers" and their sea infantry to a seeming standstill at Tulagi, Tanambogo, Gavutu, and Guadalcanal Islands before ultimately crushing the enemy that had not been defeated for twenty-nine hundred years.

Japanese manpower statistics on the Guadalcanal campaign indicate 31,358 troops were involved. However, the totals presented in this work, compiled from captured records, show a very different level of commitment, even if one excludes the 4,657 Imperial Japanese Navy personnel that participated in the fighting. Either Imperial General Headquarters was downplaying the extent of its losses in dissembling about Japanese victories, or it maintained unreliable records. The IGHQ had claimed that 7,646 soldiers of the 38th Infantry Division were sent to Guadalcanal, yet the total complement of the division was 18,485, and seven of the eleven transports carrying the division were sunk en route, with an estimated loss of five thousand men. The IGHQ also recorded that 10,318 men of the 2nd Division were committed, but the divisional strength was 14,300 men, and the entire division is known to have fought on Guadalcanal. Why would the high command have withheld four thousand men when clearly all of them were needed for victory?

Thousands of Japanese records were burned or destroyed in August 1945 to prevent their falling into Allied hands, but based on an examination of documents captured during and immediately after the war, I have estimated that about forty thousand Japanese participated in the Guadalcanal struggle. Apparently Japan lost more men than she cared to admit. Of the total number of Japanese on the island, some one thousand became prisoners of war, though most of those were noncombatant personnel, from construction units. It is known that 10,660 Japanese, including 870 sailors, were evacuated from the island. These figures imply that approximately 39,000 were killed or died from disease. The totals do not include unknown numbers of sailors lost at sea or aircrews on hundreds of shot-down aircraft. The U.S. Marine Corps air arm alone accounted for 427 Japanese planes.

For the Americans, Guadalcanal was a hell-hole. Many men were close to starvation. All lost body weight, and almost everyone had malaria or some sort of fever—though even with a temperature of 100° F., men were considered fit for ground combat or for flying. Most had the intestinal problems—the "trots"—at one time or another, and because there was no toilet tissue, incoming letters became a practical "gift" from home. Jungle rot was rampant; many troops had worn-out, eaten-away shoes and no socks. The men slept on the ground, and they were always wet; each new day brought another burst of rain or soaking drizzle, usually at unpredictable times. Every foxhole was a swamp, jungle-hot, with suffocating temperatures and oppressive humidity.

Under the most grueling conditions imaginable these untested American boys stood to arms and ultimately won. For six agonizing months the Americans on Guadalcanal fought the longest campaign of the Pacific war. None of the later conquests in the Pacific would have been possible without that hard-won victory. American losses were not insubstantial, but not the staggering losses sustained by the Japanese. A total of about sixty-five thousand Americans had been committed, including those of the U.S. Marine Corps, U.S. Army ground forces, and U.S. Navy construction units. The Marine Corps, which fielded two divisions, lost 1,094 killed in action, 103 dead from wounds, and 145 missing and presumed dead. The wounded totaled 3,170 and untold numbers were afflicted with malaria and tropical infections. The U.S. Navy reported 4,737 killed in action or missing at sea and 2,344 wounded. The U.S. Army's Americal Division had 334 killed and 850 wounded; the 25th Infantry Division, which arrived late in the campaign, reported 216 killed and 439 wounded. The U.S. Navy lost forty-one airmen killed and countless wounded; the Marine Corps air arm lost an undisclosed number. The USAAF's Thirteenth Air Force reported ninety-three killed and an unknown number wounded. Many Americans were captured by the enemy and never heard of again.

The Allies' first Pacific offensive halted the Japanese advance and took away the enemy's initiative; but at war's end the Japanese would feel the cost of defeat much more than just in manpower. Japan's offensive capability had been permanently affected. Her ship losses had been heavy, and the deaths of hundreds of skilled and experienced pilots would cripple future operations. With the Japanese gone, Guadalcanal became a strategically situated advance base boasting six airfields, which enabled the Allies to continue the push through the Solomon Islands toward Rabaul. Ultimately Guadalcanal became the springboard for the Pacific battles to come, for in time, hundreds of thousands of troops either would be stationed there or pass through on their way to the Philippines, Okinawa, and—eventually—the doorstep of Tokyo.

Appendix 1
Telegram to U.S. Navy Forces,
4 August 1942

U.S.S. PRESIDENT HAYES
INFORMATION TO ALL HANDS:

      Subject: Recapture of Tulagi and Guadalcanal Islands
      Reference: (a) *COMTASKFORCE* 62 Mailgram of 8/4/42
      1. Reference (a) is quoted herewith:

"PUBLISH TO ALL HANDS X ON AUGUST SEVENTH THIS
FORCE WILL RECAPTURE TULAGI AND GUADALCANAL
ISLANDS WHICH ARE NOW IN THE HANDS OF THE ENEMY X
IN THIS FORWARD STEP TOWARD CLEARING THE JAPANESE
OUT OF CONQUERED TERRITORY WE HAVE STRONG
SUPPORT FROM THE PACIFIC FLEET AND FROM THE AIR
SURFACE AND SUBMARINE FORCES IN THE SOUTH PACIFIC
AND AUSTRALIAN X IT IS SIGNIFICANT OF VICTORY THAT
WE SEE HERE SHOULDER TO SHOULDER THE US NAVY
MARINES AND THE ARMY AND THE AUSTRALIAN AND
NEW ZEALAND AIR NAVAL AND ARMY SERVICES X I HAVE
CONFIDENCE THAT ALL ELEMENTS OF THIS ARMADA WILL
IN SKILL AND COURAGE SHOW THEMSELVES FIT COMRADES
OF THOSE BRAVE MEN WHO ALREADY HAVE DEALT THE
ENEMY MIGHTY BLOWS FOR OUR GREAT CAUSE X GOD
BLESS YOU ALL X R K TURNER REAR ADMIRAL US NAVY
COMMANDING"

      /S/ H. L. PITTS
      Commander, U.S. Navy
      Executive Officer

Appendix 2
Japanese Naval Forces
in the Southern Solomons

May–15 June 1942

TULAGI ISLAND

3rd Company, Kure 3rd Special Naval Landing Force (Yano Butai, Yoshimoto
Detachment)[1]—Arrived 3 May 1942

May 1942

> Sp. Lt. (jg) Kakichi Yoshimoto
> WO Takeo Ikeda (3 men)
> Command Platoon: WO Tsurusaburo Shigeta (36 men)
> 1st Platoon: WO Tsuneto Sakado (57 men)
> 2nd Platoon: WO Sadayuki Kato [Katoh] (57 men)
> 3rd Platoon: WO Noburo Obara (56 men)
> 4th Platoon: WO Yoshiharu Muranaka (47 men)
> 5th Platoon: WO Kikuo Tanaka (38 men)
> Medical Unit: Lt. Ryoichi Chadani (6 men)
> Supply Unit: Lt. Ko Nomura (3 men)
> Communications: 3rd Section, Kure 3rd Communication Unit, PO3c Osamu
> Yamaoka (3 men)

15 June 1942

> Sp. Lt. (jg) Kakichi Yoshimoto, commanding
> Attached: WO Takeo Ikeda (3 men)
> Command Platoon: WO Tsurusaburo Shigeta (36 men)
> 1st Platoon: WO Yoshiharu Muranaka (47 men)
> 2nd Platoon: WO Sadayuki Kato [Katoh] (57 men)
> 3rd Platoon: WO Noboru Takeuchi (46 men)
> 4th Platoon : WO Katsuzo Fukimoto (46 men)
> 5th Platoon: WO Kikuo Tanka (38 men)
> Medical Unit: Lt. Ryoichi Chadani (6 men)
> Supply Unit: Lt. Ko Nomura (3 men)

Communications: 3rd Section, Kure 3rd Communication Unit, PO3c Osamu
   Yamaoka (3 men)
4th Weather Unit: Lt. Takezoh Miyagawa (Ex-8th Base Force, 6 men)

1 August 1942

GUADALCANAL ISLAND
RXI Base Commanding Officer: Capt. Kanae Monzen
   **11th Construction Unit (Under Combined Fleet, Yokosuka Construction
      Department)**—Arrived 6 July 1942
      Commanding Officer: Capt. Kanae Monzen, IJN
      Engineering Department: Lt. Cdr. Suekichi Heifuji; Engineers (civilian)
         Shiro Honma and Hyodo; Assistant Engineers (civilian)
         Naotsugu Hagiwara, Yoshizo Minami, Michiyoshi Ito, Hidesada
         Goto, Tadanari Ando, Genshiro Nakata, Shiro Yoshimura
      Medical Section: Lt. Noboru Tsuji, Lt. (jg) Hikoichi Kagata
      Paymaster: Ens. Shinzo Nagano
      Security Force: Lt. (jg) Soichi Shindo (230 men)
      Attached—Hara Construction Company (250 men) led by Inoure Hara
         (civilian)
      Attached—14th Construction Detachment (12 men), Cdr. Dairok Yokod
         (radar specialist)
      TOTAL: 1,641 men
   **13th Construction Unit (Under 8th Fleet, Sasebo Naval Construction
      Department)**—Arrived 6 July 1942
      Commanding Officer: Lt. Cdr. Tokunaga Okamura, IJNAF
      Engineering Department: Lt. Cdr. Masao Tsunomura, Lt. Yoshihide
         Miyamoto; Engineer Yoshio Kimura (civilian); Assistant
         Engineers Mitsutaro Hamada (wireless section), Kataro Aoki,
         Soichi Shinkura, Kurago Kyoguchi (civilians)
      Building Section: Engineering Petty Officer 1st Class Gisei (824 men)
      Electric Section (ex-Sasebo Arsenal): Engineering Petty Officer 1st Class
         Kohte, Engineering Petty Officer 1st Class Shokute (174 men)
      Medical Section: Lt. Toshikata Nomura
      Paymaster: Lt. (jg) Goichi Chiyo
      Security Force: Sp. Lt. (jg) Inado Yasuda (Mechanic), Ens. Seizo Fuse
         (91 seamen, plus 28 men under Engineering Petty Officer 1st
         Class Akamine). Attached—14th Construction Unit, RXI
         Detachment: Cdr. Dairoku Yokoi (21 men—2 officers, 19
         specialists)

Attached—4th Meteorological Unit: WO Takezo Miyagama (7 men, ex-8th Base Force)

85th Communication Unit: Lt. Cdr. Haruki Ito (100 men) [2]

85th Base Unit: 50 men

TOTAL: 1,395 men

81st Guard Unit, RXI Dispatched Force —1 July–2 August 1942

Commanding Officer: Lt. Yukio Endo

Headquarters: 4 men

Information Platoon: WO Kimihide Seki (21 men)

1st Platoon: WO Takezo Hasegawa (32 men)

2nd Platoon: WO Hideo Kageyoshi [ex-Rabaul, 6th Platoon, 1st Company, Kure 3rd SNLF] (45 men)

Machine-Gun Platoon: WO Kyoto Sakado (56 men)

Howitzer Gun Platoon: WO Tetuzo Nakamura (46 men)

Medical Section: Lt. (jg) Chihiro Yamaguchi (2 men)

Communications: 85th Communication Unit, Detachment (ex-8th Base Force) (WO Seiichi Sato) (21 radio operators)

Engineering Unit: 3 men from Engineering Unit, ex-8th Base Force

Pay (Intendance) Unit: 6 men (2 ex-Kure 3rd SNLF)

Meteorological Section: 9 men

Interpreters (civilians): Terushige Ishimoto, Matsutaro Ito

TOTAL: 252 men[3]

84th Guard Unit, 1st Company (Guadalcanal detachment)—Activated 1 July 1942[4]

Commanding Officer: Lt. Akira Tanabe (65 *ki*)[5]

WO Kyoto Sakado (transfer from 81st Guard Unit, machine-gun unit)

WO Hideo Kageyoshi (transfer from 81st Guard Unit, 2nd Platoon)

Warrant Officer Zenichi Maeno

WO Katsuzo Fukimoto (ex-2nd Platoon, 1st Company, Kure 3rd SNLF; Fukimoto had three squads on Guadalcanal)[6]

Medical Section: Lt. (jg) Hiroaki Imamoto

Attached—Artillery Ens. Minosuke Minamiyama

Attached—WO Kyu-chi Ishii

Attached—Engineering WO Rinjiro Yamashita

Attached—WO Noboru Takeuchi (ex-3rd Platoon, 1st Company, Kure 3d SNLF)[7]

Detached Service: WO Kikuo Tanaka (ex-5th Platoon, 3rd Company, Kure 3rd SNLF)

Attached—2 August 1942: WO Tetuzo Nakamura (5 squads, ex-81st Guard Unit)

TULAGI ISLAND

13th Construction Unit: 6 men, ex-Guadalcanal

14th Construction Unit, RXB Detachment: Technician Lt. Cdr. Kiyoshi Iida (129 men)[8]

7th Construction Unit RXB Detachment: Engineering Officers Capt. Gunji Tokunaga and Minoru Yamada. Engineering NCOs Hiroshi Furuichi and Toshimitsu Maeda

84th Guard Unit, 2nd Company (Tulagi Detachment)[9]—Formerly Yano Butai, Yoshimoto Detachment, also known as 3rd Company Kure 3rd SNLF and/or RXB Landing Force

Commanding Officer: Cdr. Masaaki Suzuki (48 *ki*) (15 July 1942)

Headquarters: WO Takeo Ikeda

Medical Section: Lt. Ryoichi Chadani

Supply Section: Lt. Ko Nomura

Paymaster: Lt. Isoa Nomura

Attached—Sp. Lt. (jg) Kakichi Yoshimoto

Attached—WO Tsurusaburo Shigeta

Attached—WO Sadayuki Kato [Katoh]

Attached—WO Yoshiharu Muranaka

Attached—WO Katsuzo Fukimoto had one squad on Tulagi [10]

Attached—23rd Meteorological Unit (ex-8th Base Force):
    SME Takeo Yaoita

Attached—85th Communication Unit

Attached—ex-*Seikawa* [seaplane tender] (20 sailors)

GAVUTU ISLAND

14th Construction Unit Detachment: communication and radar specialists

Mitsuwa Antiaircraft Unit (Miwa Unit; ex-43rd Guard Unit, Palau):
    Sp. Lt. (jg) Toshichi Mitsuwa (54 men)

Hashimoto Construction Force (civilian): Shin'ya Hashimoto (132 men)

Hara Construction Force (civilian): 50 men

7th Construction Unit Detachment: airfield construction unit

8th Communication Unit: 20 men

Maintenance Personnel: Yokohama Air Group, Halavo avgas unit (11 men)

TANAMBOGO ISLAND

Yokohama Air Group Flying-Boat Unit (303 men)

Commanding Officer: Capt. Shigetoshi Miyazaki, IJNAF

Executive Officer: Cdr. Saburo Katsuda, IJNAF

Third in Command: Lt. Cdr. Tashiro Soichi, IJNAF

Medical: Lt. Cdr. Mankichi Hoshino, IJNAF
Accountant: Lt. Tadao Shima, IJNAF
Detachment: 14th Construction Unit

FLORIDA ISLAND (at Halavo)

7th Construction Unit, Detachment (50 men)[11]
Engineering Officer: Minoru Yamada
Engineering Officer: Gunji Tokunaga
Engineering NCOs PO1c Hiroshi Furuichi and Toshimitsu Maeda
Yokohama Air Group, Floatplane Fighter Unit (Hama Air Unit) (43 men)[12]
Commanding Officer: Lt. Cdr. Riichiro Sato (66 *ki*), IJNAF
Executive Officer: WO Tokuchiyo Hirahashi, IJNAF
Third in Command: WO Fumiro Kurozawa, IJNAF

LOOKOUT POSTS—JULY–AUGUST 1942[13]

Cape Horn (East Point), Florida Island: 4th Squad, 4th Platoon, 3rd Company, Kure 3rd SNLF, under PO3c Shoichi Oishi (10 men, plus 1 radio operator). Call sign: "RO." Established 3 August 1942.[14]

Bungana Island (Florida Island): 5th Squad, 2nd Platoon, 3rd Company, Kure 3rd SNLF, under PO3c Sizuo Masuhara (10 men, plus 1 radio operator). Established 27 July 1942.

East Observation Post, Cape Taivu, Guadalcanal: 3rd Squad, 81st Guard Unit [Nakamura platoon] under Petty Officer 3rd Class Tan (6 men, plus 1 radio operator). Established 5 July 1942.[15]

West Observation Post (Nishi Post), Tsapuru (near Visale), Guadalcanal: 4th squad from 81st Guard Unit [Nakamura platoon] under PO3c Isamu Matsuda (8 men, plus 1 radio operator). Established 3 July 1942.[16]

Near Malaisu Point, Guadalcanal: under Gunner PO3c Daisaku Miyakoshi, 6 men from the 2nd Squad, 81st Guard Unit [Nakamura platoon], plus 1 radio operator. Established 10 July 1942.

Cape Hunter, Veuru, Guadalcanal: 81st Guard Unit [Nakamura platoon] (9 men, plus 1 radio operator). Call sign: "Mani." Established 15 July 1942.[17]

Marau Sound, Guadalcanal: 84th Guard Unit (38 men); plus 12 sailors from the *Kaiyo Maru No. 1* and *Kaiyo Maru No. 2* under WO Kikuo Tanaka; plus 2 radio operators, Seaman 1st Class Wusetti and SM1c Kuichi Yamada. Civilian interpreter Terushige Ishimoto. Established 5 August 1942. Closed 28 August 1942.

Cape Astrolabe, Afufu, Malaita Island: 3rd (PO3c Yojiro Tanase) and 4th Squads (PO3c Toshikazu Inoue), 1st Platoon, 3rd Company, Kure 3rd

SNLF (21 men, plus 2 radio operators). Call letter: "I." Established 31 July 1942.

Banika Island, Russell Islands: 84th Guard Unit, Guadalcanal detachment [Takeuchi platoon] (10 men, plus 1 radio operator). Established 3 August 1942.

Guard Vessels: *Kaiyo Maru No. 1, Kaiyo Maru No. 2, Daiho Maru No. 1, Daiho No. 2, Kaizu Maru, Nichiro Maru No. 3,* and the second *Taihou Maru.*

Appendix 3
Japanese 2nd Infantry Division
(Code Name, YU Division)

In October 1942 a Japanese task force on Guadalcanal, with the 2nd Infantry Division as its nucleus and a total strength of about 17,800 men, was given the mission of retaking the airfield. Listed below are November arrivals including the formations of the 38th Infantry Division that supported the drive. (Note that names and spellings presented here are taken from captured Japanese documents and may not represent current usage.) The task force was organized as follows:

Division Commander:	Lt. Gen. Masao Maruyama
Chief of Staff:	Col. Harukazu Tamaoki

Operations Section

Commanding Staff:	Lt. Col. Hiroshi Matsumoto
	Maj. Kanjiro Hirama
	Maj. Shoichi Hosokawa
Signal Officer (attached):	1st Lt. Daijiro Kose
Code Officer:	2nd Lt. Kiyosi Suzuki
Meteorology Officer:	2nd Lieutenant Takeenisu
Gas Officer:	1st Lt. Shin Nukuda
Interpreter:	1st Lt. Nagumi Tachibana
	2nd Lt. Kinso Oguro
	Tatsuo Nagata (civilian)

Adjutant Section

	Lt. Col. Shoichiro Eguchi
	Capt. Ryohei Iramura
	Capt. Miyoji Miyarkawa

Supervision Section

Section Chief:	Lt. Col. Shoichiro Eguchi (additional duty)
Personnel:	1st Lt. (jg) Ranichi Asada
Medical:	1st Lt. Taki Sakagaki

                                   1st Lt. Kiyochi Hachida

Ordnance Section
    Section Chief: Maj. Sakuzo Hosomi
    Personnel: Capt. Shinichi Yamada

Intendance Department
    Chief: Lt. Col. Tetsujiro Hirayama
    Personnel: Lt. Col. Yoshio Kima
                            Major Kachiki
                            Capt. Yatoji Endo
                            Capt. Ichiro Nakaiani
                            Capt. Konji Ouchi
                            Capt. Nasaro Shibata
                            Capt. Nobumichi Suzuki

Army Medical Department
    Chief: Lt. Col. Hideo Nishiyama
    Personnel: Capt. Akira Shirabayashi
                            1st Lt. Yataro Honda
                            1st Lt. Sadanari Uchiyama
    Apothecary: 2nd Lt. Hiroyuki Yoshida
    Veterinary Chief: Maj. Fasuusaburo Suzuki
    Personnel: 2nd Lt. Keichi Abe
                            2nd Lt. Kiyoco Akiyama

Attached Officers Forming the Seventeenth Army Artillery Group
                            Maj. Gen. Tadashi Sumiyoshi
                            Col. Senhichi Sakai
                            Lt. Col. Hojiro Takei
                            1st Lt. Ryuzo Nagashima
                            1st Lt. Yoshiharu Yamaguchi
                            2nd Lt. Toshi Aoyagi

COMPONENTS ON GUADALCANAL
        2nd Field Artillery Regiment (6th Battery, 1st Battalion, 3rd Battalion less the
            9th Battery)
            Commander: Col. Masuo Ishizaki
            Artillery: 7 Type 38-Improved 75-mm field guns

4th Heavy Field Artillery Regiment (less one battery)

    Commander: Col. Tomojiro Akamatsu

    Artillery: 12 Type 96 15-cm howitzers

7th Heavy Field Artillery Regiment (2nd Company)

    Commander: 1st Lt. Akio Tani

    Artillery: 4 Type 92 10-cm cannons

10th Independent Mountain Artillery Regiment(three batteries)

    Commander: Lt. Col. Masaji Kitayma

    Artillery: 9 Type 41 75-mm mountain guns

20th Independent Mountain Artillery Battalion

    Commander: Lt. Col. Matsujiro Kaji

    Artillery: 6 Bofors 75-mm mountain guns

21st Heavy Field Independent Mountain Artillery Regiment (two batteries)

    Commander: Capt. Junzō Tanaka

    Artillery: 4 Type 15-cm howitzers

38th Mountain Artillery Regiment (three batteries)

    Artillery: 5 Type 41 75-mm mountain guns

                       2 Type 94 75-mm mountain guns

1st Field Hospital, 2nd Infantry Division

1st Independent Artillery Mortar Regiment (three batteries)

    Artillery: 24 Type 93 155-mm mortars

1st Independent Tank Company

1st Shipping Engineer Regiment

2nd Division Communication Unit

2nd Division Medical Unit (Stretcher Company No. 2, Sanitary Company No. 2, and Ambulance Unit No. 2)

2nd Division Water Purification Unit

2nd Engineer Regiment (less 2nd Company)

2nd Field Artillery Regiment (2nd Infantry Division)(part)

2nd Field Artillery Regiment (part)

2nd Field Casualty Station

2nd Field Hospital, 2nd Infantry Division

2nd Independent Antitank Battalion

2nd Independent Rapid-Fire Gun Battalion (AT)

2nd Independent Service Regiment

2nd Infantry Group (Nasu Butai):

      4th Infantry Regiment, one battery, 10th Independent Mountain Artillery Regiment, and one battery of the 3rd Independent Infantry Mortar Battalion (less 3rd Company)

2nd Ordnance Unit

2nd Reconnaissance (Scout) Regiment

2nd Shipping Engineer Regiment

2nd Supply and Transport Regiment

2nd Transport Regiment (Headquarters and two platoons)

3rd Field Transport Headquarters

3rd Field Hospital

3rd Independent Trench Mortar Battalion

    Artillery: 36 Model 94 90-mm mortars

3rd Light Trench Mortar Battalion

4th Field Hospital, 2nd Infantry Division (one-half)

4th Infantry Regiment, Replacement Unit

6th Independent Antitank Gun Battalion

6th Independent Shipping Engineer Regiment (part)

6th Independent Trench Mortar Battalion

7th Engineer Regiment (1st Company)

7th Independent Antitank Gun Battalion

9th Independent Antitank Gun Battalion (9th Company)

10th Casualty Clearing Headquarters

15th Independent Engineer Regiment (3rd Company)

15th Telegraph Regiment (part)

16th Infantry Regiment

17th Water Purification Unit

19th Independent Engineer Regiment (part)

24th Water Purification Unit (one detachment)

29th Infantry Regiment

38th Engineer Regiment (one company)

38th Field Antiaircraft Artillery Battalion (9th and 12th Batteries)

    Artillery: 12 Model 88 75-mm AA guns

39th Independent Antiaircraft Artillery Battalion

39th Road Construction Unit (part)

41st Field Antiaircraft Artillery Battalion

    Artillery: 12 Model 88 75-mm AA guns

44th Permanent Wireless Platoon

45th Field Antiaircraft Artillery Battalion

    Artillery: 12 Model 88 75-mm AA guns

45th Independent Antiaircraft Artillery Battalion (part)

47th Field Antiaircraft Artillery Battalion (3rd Battery; less one platoon)

52nd Independent Transport Company

53rd Evacuation Platoon
53rd Independent Transport Company
54th Evacuation Platoon
61st Construction Company
67th Line of Communication Hospital (one detachment)
68th Communication Unit
75th Field Artillery Regiment (2nd Company)
76th Line of Communication Hospital
88th Independent Communication Unit
124th Infantry Regiment, Replacement Unit
230th Infantry Regiment (1st and 3rd Battalions)
3755th Independent Transport Battalion (attached to 38th Infantry Division)
5412th Independent Communication Unit
Oda engineering unit

NOVEMBER 1942 ARRIVALS
1st Field Hospital, 38th Infantry Division
1st Landing Unit
1st Shipping Artillery Regiment
2nd Field Hospital, 38th Infantry Division
2nd Landing Unit
3rd Shipping Engineers Regiment (part)
37th Field Antiaircraft Battalion (1st Company, 3rd Battery)
38th Division Hospital Unit
38th Division Infantry Group (part)
38th Division Medical Collecting Company
38th Division Ordnance Unit
38th Division Signal Unit
38th Engineer Regiment (3rd Company, less two platoons)
38th Field Antiaircraft Artillery Battalion (9th and 12th Batteries)
38th Infantry Division Communication Unit (one section)
38th Motor Transport Regiment
39th Field Antiaircraft Battalion
53rd Evacuation Platoon
106th Land Service Company
120th Land Service Company
124th Infantry Regiment, Replacement Unit
212th Independent Transport Company
228th Infantry Regiment (2nd Battalion)

229th Infantry Regiment (Regimental Headquarters, 6th Company, half of 3rd
    Company, part of 1st Machine-Gun Company, and 229th gun company)
230th Infantry Regiment (1st and 3rd Battalions)
3375th Independent Transport Battalion (attached to 38th Infantry Division)
Infantry Group Armored Car Company
Watanabe Independent Transport Company

Appendix 4
The Japanese Seventeenth Army Group
(Code Name, Oki Army)

Note that names and spellings presented here are taken from captured Japanese documents and may not represent current usage.

Commanding:	Lt. Gen. Haruyoshi Hyakutake
Chief of Staff:	Maj. Gen. Shuichi Miyazaki
Staff:	Col. Haruo Konuma
Adjutant:	Lt. Col. Yasuo Kukunaga
Attached (Imperial General Staff):	Lt. Col. Masanobu Tsuji
	Lt. Col. Taro Sugita

Staff, Branch Sections

Vessels:	Maj. Yu Shinohara
	(later Maj. Einosuke Iemura)
Rear:	Maj. Kazuo Etsuga
	(later Maj. Chikuro Yamamoto)
Communications:	Maj. Yoichiro Hiaoka
Air:	Maj. Koji Tanaka
Information:	Maj. Toyaoki Yamauchi
Operations:	Maj. Tadahiko Yamauchi
Cipher Office:	Maj. Tadahikay Hayashi

Company Officers (attached):

1st Lieutenant Toyama
1st Lieutenant Kawai
2nd Lieutenant Ito
2nd Lieutenant Nakata
Captain Niguni
Captain Takagi
Captain Kimura
1st Lieutenant Tashiro
1st Lieutenant Kawanabe

Seventeenth Army Communication Unit (38 men, arrived 9 October 1942):
   7th Independent Wireless Platoon
   80th Independent Wireless Platoon
   33rd Permanent Wireless Platoon

Attached from the Eighth Area Army:

Lt. Col. Makoto Hamada	Fortifications Engineer
Maj. Shigemichi Shima	Fortifications Engineer
Maj. Tsuneichi Yamamodo	Fortifications Engineer
Capt. Masaru Tokuda	Fortifications Engineer
Tech. 1st Lt. Genji Oba	Fortifications Officer
1st. Lt. Keishiro Nakamura	Fortifications Officer
1st Lt. Shinichi Nose	Fortifications Officer
1st Lt. Kuichi Tsuchiya	Fortifications Officer
1st Lt. Toshio Kawano	Fortifications Officer
1st Lt. Yoshi Takahashi	Fortifications Officer
1st Lt. Yoshiki Tayoshi	Chemical Intelligence Officer
2nd Lt. Hisashi Yamamura	Intelligence Information Officer
2nd Lt. Masatoshi Sato	Intelligence Information Officer
2nd Lt. Isao Yokota	Intelligence Information Officer
2nd Lt. Yozū Komata	Intelligence Information Officer
2nd Lt. Yoshiyulei Arashi	Intelligence Information Officer
Lt. Col. Tado Egusa	Military Police
Capt. Keitarō Nakayama	Military Police
Maj. Tokuji Tanaka	Photographic Reproduction Officer
Army Tech. Michio Neura	Photographic Reproduction clerk

Attached to the Seventeenth Army as required:

Col. Masaichi Suemura	(Regimental Commander)
Capt. Akira Ozaki	(Battalion Commander)
Maj. Keiji Yano	(Battalion Commander)
Capt. Yuji Nojiri	(Battalion Commander)
1st Lt. Takeyoshi Kishiguchi	(Company Commander)
Capt. Yoshiki Mori	(Company Commander)
1st Lt. Masaichi Hayata	(Company Commander)
1st Lt. Fumio Unehara	(Company Commander)
1st Lt. Fujiyoshi Yoshikawa	(Company Commander)

Notes

Chapter 1

1. Bougainville and Buka, once part of the Solomon chain, were German possessions until World War I, after which they became part of the Mandated Territory of New Guinea, administered by Australia for the League of Nations. Today they are part of Papua New Guinea.

2. Long, *Six Years War*, 15; Gillison, *Royal Australian Air Force*, 61.

3. Robson, *Pacific Islands Year Book*, 13.

4. Long, *Six Years War*, 15; Gillison, *Royal Australian Air Force*, 61.

5. Robson, *Pacific Islands Year Book*, 13.

6. W. F. Martin Clemens to author, Carlsbad, Calif., 25 Apr. 1993.

7. Nan'yo Boeki Kaisha Ltd. at one time was managed by Terushige Ishimoto.

8. The information collected by Capt. Tetsuo Toyofuku and other operatives probably was the basis for the Japanese directive "The Military Geography and Resources of the South Pacific Islands." Later promoted to major, Toyofuku was wounded in the attack on Port Moresby in August 1942. He was reassigned to Japan and at war's end was a staff officer in the Chugoku District. See Willoughby, *Reports of General MacArthur*, vol. 2, pt. 1, 24.

9. Horton, *Happy Isles*, 51.

10. In all, five Empire flying boats were taken up from civilian service and converted for general reconnaissance duties with the RAAF.

11. Creed, *PBY: The Catalina Flying Boat*, 262–63.

12. The Hudson was a light bomber, the British version of the Lockheed A-28 Electra, used for anti-submarine warfare and reconnaissance. The Wirraway fighter was a modified version of the American-designed Harvard trainer with three .303-caliber machine guns. It was often called Smokey Joe, for its tendency to smoke when hit by fire. Far from being a Zero-killing monster, as desk officers in Australia dubbed it, the plane was little more than a flying coffin. It was hopelessly outclassed by Japanese fighters.

13. See Frei, *Japan's Southward Advance and Australia*.

14. On the establishment of the Tulagi AOB and RAAF operations there, see Piper, "The Royal Australian Air Force at Guadalcanal." The official name, Tulagi Advanced Operational Base, was not strictly accurate, as the installations actually were on Gavutu and Tanambogo.

15. John Margrave Lerew, RAAF, (Ret.), conversation with author, Vancouver, Can., 19 Sept. 1994. Lerew retired as a Wing Commander in the RAAF. See also Piper,

"The Royal Australian Air Force," 27. Kennedy was then the conjoint DO of Tulagi, Savo, and Nggela. Bennett, *Wealth of the Solomons,* 400.

16. Piper, "Royal Australian Air Force," 28.

17. Ibid., 27–28. In Japanese hands, the Tanamobogo hill would be a deadly obstacle for the U.S. Marines.

18. Roberts, "Advanced Operational Base Activities Report." Hereinafter "AOB Activities Report." The report comes from an interview conducted by the No. 3 Military District Historical Team on 24 December 1944 when Roberts, who had been promoted to warrant officer, was serving at ANGAU headquarters on Bougainville. The Japanese would turn the water tank into a prepared position, which would obstruct the advancing marines of the 1st Parachute Battalion on 7 August 1942.

19. Claude T. Sinclair, RAAF, Tulagi AOB, to author, 18 Aug. 1984.

20. Piper, "Royal Australian Air Force," 28.

21. Ibid.

22. The Port Moresby facility, which included a minor repair and maintenance station, would remain the key base for the Catalinas.

23. No. 1 Independent Company, properly written as 2/1 Independent Company. The prefix 2/ indicated that this was the second time the unit had been constituted as part of the AIF.

24. John H. Mackie, CO, No. 3 Section, No. 1 Independent Company, AIF, "No. 1 Independent Company Role on Bougainville 1941–1943"; lecture to 1st Commando Regiment, Melbourne, Australia, 8 Dec. 1984.

25. In addition to the bases at Port Moresby, Rabaul, Tulagi, Vila, and Noumea, the RAAF had anchorages available at Gizo in the central Solomons; Faisi, Shortland Islands; Soraken Plantation, Bougainville; Carola Haven (Queen Carola Harbor), Buka; Kavieng, New Ireland; Samarai and Salamaua, New Guinea; Lorengau, Manus, Admiralty Islands; and Thursday Island.

26. Roberts, "AOB Activities Report."

27. Hutchinson became the first RAAF reconnaissance pilot killed as a result of enemy action in the New Guinea area (21 Jan. 1942). Gillison, *Royal Australian Air Force,* 363–64; Riddell, *RAAF Catalina Squadrons,* 7–8.

28. Theresa, "My Time on Guadalcanal."

29. McNab, *We Were the First,* 43, 63–64.

30. Roberts, "AOB Activities Report"; McNab, *We Were the First,* 44–45.

31. Ibid.; *Western Pacific High Commission Gazette,* 2 Jan. 1942.

32. Great Britain, Colonial Office, *Among Those Present,* 7–8.

33. Ibid.; see also Morison, *History of United States Naval Operations,* 11. Morison termed the BSIPDF the "Gilbert and Sullivan Army."

Chapter 2

1. Dalrymple-Hay, "Unhappy Story of Singapore"; Reg Bowley diary, 11 Dec. 1941, in McNab, *We Were the First,* 233. Cf. Piper, "Royal Australian Air Force," 29 (evacuations began on 14 Dec.).

2. Luxton, *Isles of Solomon,* 166–69; Feuer, *Coast Watching,* 1, 3; Lord, *Lonely Vigil,* 134, 139. Jack Read (quoted by Feuer) reported that the *Asakaze* departed Sohano on 19 December and arrived at Rabaul the night of the 20th.

3. The *Morinda* had sailed on 20 December 1941 via Lord Howe Island, Norfolk Island, and the New Hebrides. She departed Makambo on 14 January 1942 and arrived in Sydney on the 26th. Burns, Philp Company Ltd. to author, 14 Sept.1961, 21 Sept. 1983.

4. Burns, Philp Company Ltd. to author, 27 June 1984.

5. A. N. A. Waddell to author, 22 Dec.1993; Waddell, "Waddell to Secretary," hereinafter Waddell report. The signed three-page report, written in Suva, was based on a 16 March 1942 letter to the high commissioner from Waddell, who was then at the BSIP government offices in Sydney.

6. Mapletoft was a member of the merchandise staff at Burns Philp's Gizo branch. Burns, Philp & Company Ltd. to author, 17 Sept.1984.
    Soon after reaching Australia, Bill Klotz, with his job gone and no home, joined the army and volunteered for the commandos. Eventually he was transferred to the Far Eastern Liaison Office, part of the Allied Intelligence Bureau. William M. Klotz to author, 1 July 1993, 14 Mar. 1994.

7. A. N. A. Waddell to author, 22 Dec. 1993. Clara Scott had been divorced and Emily Cruickshank widowed in 1927. Louise Billette, a relative, had lived with Mrs. Cruickshank since the 1930s. Golden, *Early European Settlers,* 352–54, 368–71, 373–74. Because the women had no financial resources, Waddell requested that the government pay their passage. Waddell report, 1.

8. McNab, *We Were the First,* 23–26.

9. Some 133 commandos from No. 1 Independent Company, along with more than nine hundred other military and civilian personnel, would drown while being transferred from Rabaul to Japan in an unmarked, rusty old steamer, the *Montevideo Maru,* which was sunk by the submarine *Sturgeon* (SS 187) on 1 July 1942. McNab, *We Were the First,* 174–75.

10. Later a portion of the 7th CU would be transferred to Tulagi under EO Minoru Yamada and PO1c Hiroshi Furuichi.

11. John R. "Jack" Keenan would later become a coastwatcher on Vella Lavella and Bougainville. Lord, *Lonely Vigil,* passim; Feldt, *Coast Watchers,* 388.

12. Feuer, *Coast Watching,* 9; Mrs. Noelle Mason to author, Honiara, Guadalcanal, Solomon Islands, 8 Aug. 1992.

13. A. N. A. Waddell to author, 22 Dec.1993. See also "Defense Order for the R [Rabaul] Area." Kieta was not occupied until nearly six months later, 1 July 1942. The Kieta Landing Force (Asada unit) consisted of elements drawn from the 5th Base Force on Saipan and dispatched to Rabaul, plus part of the 81st Guard Unit from the 8th Base Force at Rabaul, under Lieutenant (jg) Asada. *Toyo Maru No. 9,* the vessel that transported the landing force, was sunk while returning to Rabaul.

14. Roberts, "AOB Activities Report"; McNab, *We Were the First,* 44–45.

15. Reg Bowley diary, 9 Jan.1942, in McNab, *We Were the First,* 233; Claude T. Sinclair to author, 19 Sept. 1990. In another attack, Sinclair wrote, "the enemy let a bomb drop late and [it] exploded on Florida Island[,] leaving a hole 45 feet in diameter." Eventually Sinclair fell ill with what was commonly referred to as "Gavutu syndrome," and on 25 March 1942 he was evacuated by Catalina for hospitalization. The Catalina, piloted by Flying Officer Moore, was chased by a Mavis flying boat. Moore escaped by flying low over the water until they were near Port Moresby. Sinclair confided to the author on 19 September 1990, "I was glad to get out of that hell-hole."

16. In his memoirs, Ken Hay recalled that two Japanese flying boats were involved in the raid. Dalrymple-Hay, "Behind the Japanese Lines."

17. William Murden Klotz, statutory declaration, Sydney, 17 Mar. 1942, copy in author's file; William M. Klotz to author, 14 Mar. 1994. On the Atkinsons, see Golden, *Early European Settlers,* 353, 380. The *Lofung* was named for Burns Philp's Lofung Plantation on the east side of Shortland Island adjacent to Faisi. Ibid., 352.

18. Klotz, statutory declaration; William M. Klotz to author, 14 Mar. 1994; Burns, Philp Company Ltd. to author, 17 Sept.1984. Mrs. Summerland and Val Murphy's wife, Eugenie, had left on the *Malaita* on 4 January, along with local plantation manager Carden W. Seton and his wife, Georgina. Burns, Philp & Company Ltd. to author, 27 June 1984.

19. William M. Klotz to author, 14 Mar. 1994. Father O'Sullivan, an American, evacuated from Buin to Australia; eventually he became a chaplain in the Australian army.

20. A. N. A. Waddell to author, 22 Dec.1993; Waddell report, 1–2.

21. A. N. A. Waddell to author, 22 Dec. 1993; Waddell report, 2; Klotz, statutory declaration. The laborers were still at Lofung when Klotz sailed from Faisi.
    Eric P. Monckton had a plantation and a timber mill at Kokonai, on the southern shore of Shortland Island. With his wife, Mina, and their two children, he evacuated to Sydney, probably in December 1941. The *Kamaliai* was named for Kamaliai (or Laminiai) Plantation, owned by Burns Philp, on the northern tip of Shortland Island. See Golden, *Early European Settlers,* 353, 375.

22. A. N. A. Waddell to author, 22 Dec. 1993; William M. Klotz to author, 14 Mar. 1994. Both writers state that Waddell and Murphy departed in the *Loai;* Waddell thought that the *Ramada* was not returned as promised. The accounts of the evacuation of the central Solomons, however, place the *Loai* at Gizo on 24 January and mention that Waddell and Murphy reached Kolombangara in the *Ramada* on the 27th. I have followed the latter here.

23. Miller, "Report"; Voyce, "The Cruise." The account taken from Sister Cannon's diary is titled "The Gizo Getaway." See also Rutter, "Transpacific Crossing." At the outbreak of the Pacific War the head stations of the Methodist mission were at Kokengolo and Bilua; others were at Kuboro on Choiseul and Buin on Bougainville. Rev. Aaron Bea (Helena Goldie Hospital, Munda) to author, 2 June 1994.

24. Burns Philp had taken over the *Loai* from Clara Scott for a debt she owed the company.

25. The *Alice* had belonged to Bill Binskin's father, the planter and trader Joseph K. Binskin, who died on 17 August 1941. Bill's mother, Florence, daughter of the early trader Norman Wheatley and a Solomon Islands woman, refused evacuation; when enemy troops occupied her home, she took refuge in the interior of Vella Lavella. The *Alice* was destroyed by the Japanese. See "Deaths of Islands People."

26. No one can determine who gave the Australian Broadcasting Commisssion this potentially harmful misinformation.

27. Miller reports that the two Japanese internees and their escorts also were on the *Loai,* but this is in error. Later he states that he sent them to Tulagi from Batuna on 1 February in an Seventh Day Adventist vessel.

28. En route to Tulagi, the little fleet was spooked by a Japanese seaplane, which circled but did not attack. Perhaps the pilot was out of ammunition, or perhaps he was saving it for bigger game.

29. Reverend Silvester rescued many pilots who ditched in Vella Lavella waters, and he helped save scores of survivors from ships sunk in the Battle of Kula Gulf in July 1943, among them 165 men from the light cruiser USS *Helena*. He received the U.S. Presidential Medal of Merit for assisting the landing forces during the invasion of Vella Lavella (Aug.–Sept.1943). Lord, *Lonely Vigil*, 231–54; see also "Rev. A. W. Silvester: Presentation."

30. A number apparently had been living with Florence Binskin on Bagga Island. When John Campbell came through Gizo, however, he reported that they had left and Mrs. Binskin did not know where they had gone.

31. The chief officer on the *Kurimarau* was Jack Gaskell, who had grown up in the Florida Islands. Jack Gaskell to author, 1 Jan. 1995.
    Charles Widdy left on the *Morinda*. He would return on 7 August as a guide for the 1st Marine Division. See Clemens, *Alone on Guadalcanal*, 195–96, 198–99.

32. Clemens, *Alone on Guadalcanal*, 57. Among those on board were three members of the Makambo branch of Burns Philp: John C. Mylne, manager; Robert L. Firth, accountant; and Alexander W. Glen, chief salesman. Burns, Philp & Company Ltd. to author, 17 Sept. 1984. Bob Firth would become a coastwatcher on Vella Lavella. Lord, *Lonely Vigil*, 238, 240; Feldt, *Coast Watchers*, 388.

Chapter 3

1. Miller and his wife later departed for Sydney aboard the *Morinda* on 8 February 1942. Miller retired on 13 January 1943. *Western Pacific High Commission Gazette*, 2 Mar. 1943.

2. Kennedy would use the *Marara* throughout the war. See Letter from Solomon Island Mission. On Kata Rangoso, see Golden, *Early European Settlers*, 57, 60. Kennedy later became a coastwatcher and with a small army of Solomon Islanders took the offensive against the Japanese in New Georgia. See Great Britain, *Among Those Present*, 43, 47–53; Feldt, *Coast Watchers*, 107–11, 150, 157–60; Horton, *Fire Over the Islands*, 42–45, 129–33, 148–51; Lord, *Lonely Vigil*, 155–58, 201–30.

3. Burns, Philp & Company Ltd. to author, 14 Sept. 1961.

4. Victor J. Shearwin was first clerk and boarding officer. Jack I. Blaikie was officer in charge of the armed constabulary and superintendent of prisons.

5. Clemens, *Alone on Guadalcanal*, 55–56. Most histories of the Guadalcanal campaign contain citations to Martin Clemens's unpublished "District Officer's Diary, Guadalcanal, 1942," but in fact those references are to the first draft of his book. That manuscript is organized like the diary, but it includes much explanatory material that is not in the original.

6. Attlee was the son of the later prime minister.

7. The Namatanai party consisted of Cpl. W. "Sam" Rogers; LCpls. J. Robert "Bob" MacMahon and Leo Pratt; and Pvts. Harold W. Davidson, Cecil "Snow" Evans, and John "Lofty" Moran. They took with them as a POW a German planter named Schultz, who was suspected of being an enemy alien. See McNab, *We Were the First*, 59–61.

8. Feuer, *Coast Watching*, 14.

9.   Some of the Gaskell family returned after the war.

10.   John Brett to author, 11 Dec. 1994.

11.   Pvt. Reg Bowley complained, "Our quarters not too good—very hot." Reg Bowley diary, 7 Dec. 1941, in McNab, *We Were the First,* 233.

12.   Ibid., 23.

13.   Freda Giles (daughter of Fred Jones) to author, 10 Apr. 1995.

14.   The evacuation party included Mr. D. Whitford and his wife, R. P. C. Whitford; Mr. B. A. Chapman; Mr. and Mrs. F. Batcheldor; and two New Zealand brothers who were both experienced bushmen. Ruby O. Jones to author, 18 Jan. 1985.
      Remaining at Peu were Samuel S. "Skov" Boye, the island manager for the timber company, and his wife, Ruby, the company's wireless operator. They had been in Tulagi since 1928 and had moved to Peu in 1940 when Skov was offered the manager's job. Now they were alone except for their neighbors, Mr. and Mrs. George Stokes, as well as the district officer, Colin E. J. Wilson, and Fred Jones, who had returned to Peu and kept his trading station open during the war.

15.   Rhoades was not the only coastwatcher who was guilty of inaccurate reporting. On one occasion, Macfarlan reported that twenty-five Allied aircraft had attacked Tulagi, whereas Clemens, in his "District Officer's Diary, Guadalcanal, 1942," noted only one. Clemens had to sift through the chaff to find the truth.

16.   Webster had worked at Gold Ridge earlier in the 1940s.

17.   Sandy McNab to author, 2 May 1990.

18.   See Horton, *Fire Over the Islands,* 30.

19.   Riddell, *RAAF Catalina Squadrons,* 11. Rolf Cambridge later became a coastwatcher.

20.   Father G. Lepping, statement, 26 Nov. 1945; Lt. S. Bolton, statement, 28 Nov. 1945; J. Alengi, statement, 7 Dec. 1945 (all enclosures to Lt. Col. A. N. A. Waddell, BSIPDF, Acting Resident Commissioner, BSIP, to High Commissioner for the Western Pacific, 19 Dec. 1945). See also Feldt, *Coast Watchers,* 108; Lord, *Lonely Vigil,* 156; Clemens, *Alone on Guadalcanal,* 42; Golden, *Early European Settlers,* 26, 191, 193, 228, 358.
      It is uncertain whether John Klaucke is to be identified with Johannes Klaucke (also known as Dutchy Clark), a Vella Lavella planter. Lord refers to both Klaucke and Wheatley as young half-castes; however, in the statements, the former is always called "Mr. Klaucke," whereas the latter, whose mother was a Solomon Islander, is referred to by his given name. The statements are among a series of twenty-eight taken down by Lieutenant Bolton in connection with the trial of John Henry McDonald, a lifelong resident of the Solomons and a member of one of the oldest families in the Shortlands, charged with three counts of assisting the enemy during the Japanese occupation. The case was heard by the Chief Judicial Commissioner, WPHC, on Guadalcanal in May 1946. McDonald was acquitted, but he lived the rest of his life under a cloud; he died in Honiara in 1990 at the age of eighty-seven.

21.   Golden, *Early European Settlers,* 38, 312; "Dodging Japs in Solomon Jungles."

22.   Roberts, "AOB Activities Report."

23.   The Rufes came from the seaplane tender *Kamikawa Maru,* which had been stationed in the Deboyne Islands, Louisiade Archipelago, since 21 February. Later they would be based at Halavo, Florida Island, as part of the Yokohama Air Group.

24. Searle diary, 2 May 1942, in Riddell, *RAAF Catalina Squadrons,* 17. Reprinted by permission. Cliff Searle was reassigned to the RAAF station at Port Moresby.
25. Roberts, "AOB Activities Report."
26. Kevin J. Landers, RAAF, Tulagi AOB, to author, 7 July 1993.
27. Bob Burne to Jack Riddell, 26 Apr. 1988, in Riddell, *RAAF Catalina Squadrons,* 20.
28. Roberts, "AOB Activities Report"; Ken Ryker (VS-55) to author, 14 June 1996.
29. Keith Robinson, RAAF, Tulagi AOB, to author, 25 Sept. 1995.
30. Clarence, *Yield Not to the Wind,* 166–67.
31. Clemens, "District Officer's Diary"; Duncan Ridley to Jack Riddell, 28 July 1987, in Riddell, *RAAF Catalina Squadrons,* 20.
32. Bill Binskin subsequently joined the Australian army.
33. In 1943 an enterprising Chinese borrowed five hundred pounds from the government to set up a tailor shop on Guadalcanal. Today his family is one of the wealthiest in the country, with extensive holdings in the Solomons and investments in Sydney. Sir David Trench, conversation with author, London, 9 Apr. 1985.
34. Clemens, "District Officer's Diary," 31–32.
35. W. F. Martin Clemens to author, 9 Mar. 1995.
36. Clemens "District Officer's Diary," 28.

Chapter 4

1. *Rikusentai* sometimes has been translated erroneously as "marines." The rikusentai were not specially trained amphibious assault forces but rather more akin to permanent organizations of sailors in landing parties. See Frank, *Guadalcanal,* n. 21; Smith, *Bloody Ridge,* 232. I have used the terms "naval infantry" or "sea infantry."
2. The official Japanese war history refers to the Kure 3rd Special Landing Party. Western historians conventionally use Kure 3rd Special Naval Landing Force. In 1993, Yano was living in Sasebo City; however, owing to loss of memory, he was unable to shed any light on his unit's operations in the Solomons.
3. "Defense Order for the R [Rabaul] Area."
4. "South Seas Fleet Operation Order."
5. John Winton, *Ultra in the Pacific,* 41.
6. The Miwa Butai comprised an antiaircraft gun platoon under Ensign Sanrin and light and heavy machine-gun squads. It was formerly part of the 43rd Guard Unit, 3rd Base Force, on Palau. "South Seas Fleet Operation Order No. 13" called for the unit to remain in the Tulagi area for ten days, then return to Rabaul and eventually rejoin its parent organization at Palau; but Lieutenant (jg) Mitsuwa and his men would remain on Gavutu and would be there on 7 August when the U.S. Marines invaded.
7. "Military Geography and Resources."
8. Lieutenant Maruyama returned with his 2nd Company to Rabaul, leaving his 3rd Platoon under WO Kikuo Tanaka on Tulagi to reinforce the 3rd Company.
9. "2nd Company, Kure 3rd Special Naval Landing Force."
10. Iwata, "Diary," 6 May 1942. The Kosokuka landing craft had a three-bladed propeller set at the rear; it was powered by an airplane-type gasoline engine and was

reported to be very fast. The boat was equipped with a heavy machine gun, and it could carry in excess of one hundred men.

11. Shimamoto, "Diary," 2 May 1942. Shimamoto lost his life on 14 August 1942 while on outpost duty on eastern Florida Island.

12. Warrant Officer Iwata recorded that the Yoshimoto Company brought two anti-aircraft guns and machine guns as well as supplies—perhaps extra ammunition. Iwata, "Diary," 6 May 1942.

13. Mori, "Diary," 2 May 1942.

14. Ibid., 3 May 1942.

15. Jack Riddell, *RAAF Catalina Squadrons,* 12, 24, 27. Bill Miller would earn a commission for his actions during the Battle of the Coral Sea.

16. The *Kikuzuki* was raised from the waters in October 1943 by the U.S. 34th NCB—the Seabees—and was used as a floating repair ship.

17. Those killed were SM Yaraka Sumimoto, PO3c Masazo Kasahara, and PO3c Zenichi Ikeda. Hirai, "Diary," 5 May 1942.

18. Excerpts from the diary of R. E. McCullock, USS *Astoria,* May 1942, in Wiggs, *Coral Sea Log,* 138–39. According to another source, the *Lexington* pilots reported sinking three cruisers, three destroyers, three transports, one seaplane tender, four gunboats, and eight aircraft. Shane, *Heroes of the Pacific,* 155.

19. See also Appendix 2. The redesignation was done to separate the two commands. The bulk of the Kure 3rd SNLF at Rabaul was eventually assigned as one of the invasion units for the MO operation.

20. Mori, "Diary," 27 May 1942. Mori's mention of an attack on Fiji is in reference to the FU Operation, the Japanese plan to capture Fiji, New Caledonia, and Samoa.

21. Ibid., 29 May 1942.

22. The SN Operation was the early code name for the plan to establish air facilities in the New Guinea area and the Solomon Islands.

23. Hirai, "Diary," 21 and 23 June 1942. According to Masao Tsunomura, an engineering officer at the Guadalcanal airstrip, the *Keijo Maru,* a converted gunboat, was sunk by the U.S. submarine *S-44* just south of Guadalcanal. She was transporting a cargo of aviation fuel and communications equipment. Tsunomura to author, 19 Jan. 1989.

24. The U.S. Navy did not report the sinking of the *Yomoto Maru.*

25. Temporarily assigned to the Endo Detachment from the Kure 3rd SNLF were the 4th Platoon, 1st Company, under WO Tsuneto Sakado (57 men) and the 6th Platoon, 1st Company, under WO Hideo Kageyoshi (46 men).

26. Kaneda "Memoirs."

27. Clemens, "District Officer's Diary," 4 July 1942.

28. The Japanese described the 11th and 13th Construction Units as the 11th and 13th Encampment Corps. The 124th Infantry Regiment was formally part of the 31st Division. The Horii unit comprised the following: 55th Infantry Group; 144th Infantry Regiment; 1st Battalion, 55th Mountain Artillery Regiment; 1st Company, 55th Engineer Regiment; Signal Unit, 55th Division; 2nd Company, 55th Transport Regiment; 1st Field Hospital, 55th Division; 47th Field Antiaircraft Artillery Battalion (one company).

29. U.S. records do not indicate the Japanese losses. All times given in this part of the chapter are Japanese Standard Time (JST), GMT + 9 hours.

30. "South Pacific Fleet Order No. 17." Commander of the 4th Fleet, Vice Adm. Shigeyoshi Inoue, issued the order at Truk aboard his flagship, the light cruiser *Kashima*.

31. Samuel Eliot Morison states in his *History of United States Naval Operations in World War II:* "[B]efore the end of June a convoy of 13 ships put in [at Guadalcanal], bringing a substantial force of labor troops, engineers and heavy equipment to build the landing field. It was the discovery of this by an allied reconnaissance plane on 4 July that put the heat on Operation 'Watchtower.'" (WATCHTOWER was the operational plan for the invasion of Guadalcanal-Tulagi and of Ndeni, Santa Cruz Islands.) However, Morison had the dates and details wrong. The construction units did not arrive until 6 July, and the grass was not being burned until the 8th (as reported by Martin Clemens); therefore, it was impossible for an aircraft to spot an airfield on Guadalcanal on 4 July, because one did not exist. What was spotted was the new camp of the 81st Guard Unit. See Morison, *History of United States Naval Operations,* 12.

32. Lt. Cdr. Kiyoshi Iida's construction force worked on the base at Gavutu.

33. "Intelligence Report."

34. On 6 July Clemens had relocated from Paripao to Vungana in the middle of the island. He had noted, " . . . It has a magnificent view from Savo to Rua Sura [a small island down the coast] and clear into Tulagi Harbor as far as Makambo." Clemens, "District Officer's Diary," 58–59.

35. "RXI Secret Cable No. 52." The "lucky ship" *Azumasan Maru,* which had participated in many operations, finally met her doom on 14 October 1942 off Tassafaronga, Guadalcanal.

36. The rikusentai could also purchase life insurance. For the family of a person killed in action to collect on this insurance, another person had to witness the death and confirm it.

37. "Secret Order No. 5."

38. Ibid.

39. Hirai, "Diary," 31 July, 1 Aug.1942.

40. Most of the CU workers were Korean. From a Korean design they constructed the Pagoda, the best-known building on Henderson Field (it was to become the officers club). Only a handful of the workers were killed in the bombing, but the IJN wanted the families to use the correct mailing address.

41. The 8th Base Force's order was countermanded while Endo was en route. Nothing certain is known about Ito; however, about 1935 a Japanese former naval officer named Ito had been working with local people collecting tortoise shell in the Santa Cruz Islands. Ito's ketch, *Aretgusa,* was well known and often seen in the deep waters of the group. Perhaps the Matsutaro Ito who arrived on Guadalcanal with the 81st Guard Unit was this tortoise fisherman.

42. Masao Tsunomura to author, 5 July 1991.

43. Blaknik, "Japanese Diary."

44. Kaneda, "Memoirs."

45. On 1 April 1942 the Maizuru 2nd SNLF had been split into two parts, one renamed the 81st Guard Unit, the other the 82nd Guard Unit.

46. SM Tomitaro Matsuda, 1st Platoon (Hasegawa Platoon), 81st Guard Unit, to author, 24 Jan. 1991.

47. The oil delivery was in response to a plea in a 5 August message to the 25th Air Flotilla.

48. The Mavis had red lights on the left wing, blue on the right wing, and white on the tail.

49. Lundstrom, *First Team,* 36.

50. Ibid.

51. Masaichiro Miyagawa to author, 1 Aug. 1989.

52. Herbert R. Fuller Jr., conversation with author, San Diego, Calif., 12 Nov. 1995.

53. Iwata, "POW Interrogation Report, " 21 Aug. 1942.

54. See Message, Commander Tulagi Communications Base.

55. Yoshi Sagai to author, 8 Jan.1992.

56. Boardman, "Japanese Operations at Guadalcanal," 17. Captain Boardman was Assistant R-2 of the 2nd Marines on Tulagi and an interpreter.

Chapter 5

1. Capt. M. B. Gardner, in Van der Vat, *Pacific Campaign,* 218.

2. Morison, *History of United States Naval Operations,* 12.

3. The orders reassigning the 2nd Marines were issued four days before the commanding general, 1st Marine Division, was aware of the WATCHTOWER operation.

4. Gilomen to author, 20 July 1989.

5. Ibid.

6. Robert C. Muehrcke to author, 2 Sept. 1995.

7. Arthur G. King, M.D., Col., USA (Ret.), to author, 10 Mar. 1995.

8. Horton, Josselyn, and Waddell were granted leave of absence from the BSIP for duty with naval service effective 2 August 1942. *Western Pacific High Commission Gazette,* 19 Oct. 1943, 116. They were commissioned as sub-lieutenant, RANVR.

9. William J. Cannon (C/1/2), interview by author, Carlsbad, Calif., 7 Mar. 1994.

10. Sorensen, "Memoirs."

11. Charles O. Hall to author, 12 Aug. 1991.

12. Units on board the *Hayes* did not take part in the Koro exercise. Rev. Theodore E. Franklin to author, 27 Apr. 1994. Franklin was then a second lieutenant in the Marine Corps Reserve, assigned to Company C (Motor Transport), 2nd Service Battalion.

13. Richard E. Bennink to author, 1 Jan. 2001.

14. Vandegrift, *Once a Marine,* 122.

15. Arnold, *Global Mission,* 341, 342.

16. Captain Doyle's opinion of Trevanion was transmitted to the author from Rev. Theodore E. Franklin [1st Lieutenant, 2nd Marines]. Copy of TF 62 mailgram also courtesy of Reverend. In this and the following documents the stop ("X") has been replaced with a period.

17. James Sorensen to Philip Birkitt, 31 May 1977.

18. Zimmerman, *Guadalcanal Campaign,* 13.

19. Transport Group X-Ray (62.1), the Guadalcanal landing force, consisted of four subgroups: Transport Division A—*Fuller, American Legion, Bellatrix;* Trans-

port Division B—*McCawley, Barnett, Elliot,* and *Libra;* Transport Division C—*Hunter Liggett, Fomalhaut,* and *Betelgeuse;* Transport Division D—*Crescent City, President Hayes, President Adams,* and *Alhena.*

Transport Group Yoke (62.2) carried the assault troops for the Tulagi landing: Transport E—*Neville, Zeilin, Haywood,* and *President Jackson;* Transport Division 12 (fast destroyer transports)—*Calhoun, Gregory, Little,* and *McKean;* Minesweeper Group Two—*Hopkins, Trever, Zane, Southard,* and *Hovey,* combined with the destroyers *Henley, Bagley, Helm,* and *Blue.* This force had the assignment to support the Tulagi area operation.

Report of Action at Tulagi–Guadalcanal, 6–10 Aug. 1942, courtesy Rev. Theodore E. Franklin.

20. Reverend Theodore E. Franklin to author, 27 Apr. 1994.

Chapter 6

1. Jack Riddell to author, 19 Apr. 1991.
2. Clemens, *Alone on Guadalcanal,* 135, and "District Officer's Diary," 13 June 1942.
3. Clemens, "District Officer's Diary," 16 June 1942., 136.
4. Hirai, "Diary." SME Yodoyama Mori of the 5th Platoon, 3rd Company, Kure 3rd SNLF, noted: ". . . The general feeling during the early stages of bombing of Tulagi and Guadalcanal was that the men from the cities, being accustomed to city noises, reacted much better to the bombings than the men who came from the country." Mori, "Diary," 12 July 1942.
5. Hirai, "Diary," 7 and 10 July 1942. On 17 and 23 July Hirai also reported that NAP1c Tatsuo Hori and NAP1c Saburo Matsui from the Yokohama Air Group Hama Air Unit (Floatplane Fighter Unit) on Florida Island, were killed in these confrontations. The 17 July engagement involved the B-17 that transported the Guadalcanal photographic mission of Marine Corps Lt. Col. Merrill B. Twining and Maj. William B. McKean. Japanese losses claimed on 23 July were disputed by a B-17 pilot who reported that he was compelled to take evasive maneuvers when three Rufe floatplane fighters rose up from their Halavo roost to attack his bomber. He also claimed to have shot down two of the three.
6. See Letter to Eighth Fleet. Captain Monzen's report is contradicted by the diary of CPO Yasuo Yamamiya, who recorded Shishikura's death as occurring on 31 July. This and other discrepancies in dates may be due to the diarists recording events on different days, or perhaps even to translators converting dates.
7. Jack Riddell, *RAAF Catalina Squadrons,* 28.
8. Ibid., 27–28.
9. "[There was a] woeful lack of photos, and Navy charts were badly out of date. In an effort to remedy this situation the 435th Squadron of the 19th Group during June and July had flown a number of reconnaissance missions over Guadalcanal-Tulagi area from Port Moresby." U.S. Department of the Army, *Pacific Counterblow.*
10. Carter, "All in a Day's Work."
11. Hirai, "Diary," 2 June 1942.
12. Bauer Field on Efate, with a 6,500- by 350-foot runway, was located four miles from Port Vila. It was formerly the Blandmere Plantation. The newly completed 7,000- by 200-foot dust bowl of an airfield at Plaines des Gaiacs was 371 miles southwest of Espiritu Santo.

Many of the planes sported colorful names: *The Skipper, Hellzapoppin, Typhoon McGoon II, Buzz King, Blue Goose, Galloping Gus, Madame-X,* and *Goonie.* See "98th Bombardment Squadron (H) Operational Diary," 17 July 1942; Howard and Whitley, *One Damned Island After Another,* 114.

13. Cleveland, *Grey Geese Calling,* 9–10.

14. "Long pig" is Pidgin for man. Major Sewart was killed in action on 18 November 1942 off Bougainville.

15. Joseph B. Chin to author, 15 Oct. 1993. Chin was General Rose's orderly. In May 1942 ATF 6814 would be designated the Americal Division, so named for "Americans in New Caledonia."

16. On 19 June Walcott, who had been promoted to lieutenant (jg) and was officer-in-charge of the BUTTON Detachment, had the 57th Combat Engineers construct hangars to conceal the two OS2Us. Islander bushmen covered the hangars and tent area with palm leaves to help them blend into the surroundings.

17. Arthur G. King, M.D., to Joseph B. Chin, 28 Jan. 1994. Sadie Thompson was the woman with a colorful past, in the renowned 1928 film of that name, who traveled to a South Pacific island to begin a new life; www.wikipedia.org.

18. The nine-member support unit included four enlisted men from VS-5-D-14 identified as W. Ford, George L. Cooper, Amadeo G. Schiavoni, and Merriman. Eliott would retire as a brigadier general.

19. One hectare is equivalent to 2.471 acres. Only three plantations on Espiritu Santo accepted leases: the Wrights, Chapuis, and Bencoula. The other planters' principal objection to leasing to the Americans was the automatic renewal clause without date of termination. They seemed to fear that the United States intended to retain occupancy of the island group after the war. This unwillingness to accept leases led to many disagreeable situations that were resolved only through carefully controlled dispositions and American patience in dealing with the French residents. Had the French been willing to accept leases, much bickering in regard to claim settlements could have been avoided. Kralovec, "A Naval History of Espiritu Santo," 522–23.

20. Priday, *War from Coconut Square,* 100; Joseph B. Chin to author, 15 Oct. 1993.

21. Priday, *War from Coconut Square,* 100.

22. John Gentile (57th Combat Engineers), conversation with author, 4 May 1995. The B-17s had a fuel capacity of 2,000 gallons, or forty drums of avgas.

23. U.S. Department of the Army, *Pacific Counterblow,* 8. The 11th BG sent a maximum of nine B-17s against Guadalcanal. Any antiaircraft fire had to be ineffective, as it could reach only to 4,000 meters (approximately13,123 feet). The official U.S. Army history notes that the 26th Bomb Squadron shot down three planes. Miller, *Guadalcanal,* 59. Japanese records of the Florida Island-based Hama Air Unit, however, make no mention of the loss of three aircraft at one time.

24. Yamamiya, "Diary," 31 July 1942. Kudan is a shrine of the war dead.

25. Ware, *Landing in the Solomons,* 28; Yamamiya, "Diary," 1 Aug. 1942.

26. "Note: 2 guns lack certain parts. . . . Note: There are no men in my command who are experts in firing 75mm AA guns." Lt. Yukio Endo to Comdr. Masaaki Suzuki, 16 July 1942.

27. Takahashi, "Diary," 2 Aug. 1942.

28. Ogihara, "POW Interrogation Report." Ogihara was captured on Florida Island after escaping from Tulagi on 8 August.

29. Yamamiya, "Diary," 4 Aug.1942. Yamamiya noted that the bombing on 2 August made four large holes in the airstrip, and that the airstrip and operations office were hit on the 4th.

30. Masaichiro Miyagawa to author, 3 Jan. 1990; Bernard Baeza to author, 7 Feb. 1990.

31. Jack Lee diary, 4 Aug. 1942. Lee was killed when the B-17 he was copiloting was shot down while on a raid to Buin, Bougainville, on 18 November 1942. Luie Fuller (CUB-1) to author (Lee was related to Fuller). See Lord, *Lonely Vigil,* 112.

32. National Archives, RG 165, War Department, General and Special Staffs. For information about and from prisoners, and documents captured at Attu, see Box 758, Location 390, 35/15/04.

33. Takahashi, "Diary," 5 Aug. 1942; Ogihara, "POW Interrogation Report."

34. William M. Cleveland, Historian, 11th Bombardment Group,) to author, 17 Nov. 1990. No Japanese fighter aircraft were reported in the area, and the Florida-based Rufes had been destroyed that morning. Only 512 "E" model B-17s were produced of the over 12,000 B-17s manufactured.

35. Returning from a mission, Capt. Roland Stone's B-17 was damaged and ditched two miles off Espiritu Santo when a "new" navigator got lost; another Flying Fortress crashed.

36. Craven and Cate, *Army Air Forces,* 36. SM Masakane Iwata (3rd Squad, Command Platoon, Yoshimoto Company, Kure 3rd SNLF) said that the B-17s passed up Tulagi and Gavutu and hit Florida. Iwata, "POW Interrogation Report," 14 Aug. 1942. When I questioned former MCPO Masaichiro Miyagawa (Yokohama Air Group) about the bombing of the Florida floatplane base, he reported that the B-17s did no damage at all. Masaichiro Miyagawa, interview by author, Tokyo, 15 Nov. 1990.

37. Capt. Ralph Williams, USMC, conversation with author, 27 July 1960. Captain Williams had been an enlisted postal clerk with the 1st Marine Division during the Guadalcanal campaign.

38. Frank, *Guadalcanal,* 613.

Chapter 7

1. Lundstrom, *First Team,* 39.

2. Kaneda "Memoirs."

3. In his diary entry of 8 August, Petty Officer Ueno, 3rd Base Force, listed thirteen killed and thirteen wounded from the bombardment.

4. In all, 10,819 men of the 1st Marine Division would be committed to Guadalcanal; 19,514 for the entire landing.

5. Ray L. Whitaker to author, 2 Apr. 2000.

6. The Japanese 81st Guard Unit had set up the Type 88 AA gun on 2 July. The weapon was left there when most of the Endo Detachment withdrew to Rabaul on 2 August.

7. Marion, "My First Days," 15.

8. Ingalls, "First Marine on Guadalcanal?," 11.

9. 1st Marine Division, "Operation Order No. 5." Three batteries of 5-inch guns, which the U.S. Navy had declared obsolete in 1915, arrived a month later.

10. Miller, *Guadalcanal,* 70.

11. "POW Report." The report was misfiled at the National Archives and filed with documents pertaining to the Aleutian Campaign.

12. Col. Sanford B. Hunt, USMC (Ret.), to author, 19 July 2000.

13. Alexander McNab to author, 5 July 1995.

14. Cpl. Edward S. Stelloh, USMC, Silver Star citation. Corporal Stelloh was nominated for the Navy Cross for this action, but it was never awarded.

15. Charles Hatfield to author, 14 Jan. 1993.

16. William S. Becker to author, 15 June 1996.

17. Hata and Izawa, *Japanese Naval Aces,* 136.

18. Five Vals were lost in combat, and the rest, short of fuel, ditched in the Shortlands on the way home.

19. Lamarre, "War Comes to Buka," 3.

Chapter 8

1. On the minesweepers' fire support also see the Mitsuwa antiaircraft unit, chapter 4.

2. *"San Juan* Action Report," 7 Aug. 1942.

3. Plus the 2nd Platoon, Company A, 1st Engineer Battalion; 2nd Platoon, Company A, 1st Pioneers; and 2nd Platoon, Company A, 1st Amphibian Tractor Battalion. See 5th Marine Regiment, "Record of Events."

4. Hoffman, *Once a Legend,* 176.

5. Oral statement recorded in the Office of Naval Records, Naval Historical Center, Washington, D.C. Actually the Japanese never expected Tulagi to be invaded.

6. Type 98 hemispherical anti-boat mines were large steel balls, each filled with picric acid. No barbed wire was found in the Japanese supplies.

7. Dick Horton, conversation author, London, Apr. 1993. Horton was awarded the U.S. Silver Star for his service on Tulagi.

8. Robert Caufield to author, 14 July 1998.

9. Hirai, "Diary."

10. Apparently the lessons of the Guadalcanal campaign escaped the naval commanders. Fifteen months later, in the bombardment of Tarawa, the U.S. Navy again used the wrong type of ammunition, and as at Tulagi the shelling caused few casualties among the Japanese defenders.

11. *"San Juan* Action Report," 7 Aug. 1942, 3.

12. Rosenquist, Sexton, and Buerlein, *Our Kind of War,* 40.

13. Edward G. Sexton to author, 4 Aug. 2005.

14. Hirai, "Diary."

15. Hoffman, *Once a Legend,* 180.

16. The Kato Butai was originally stationed in Chinatown but moved near headquarters and formed a defense line.

17. Captured equipment included sophisticated radar and wireless equipment with a 1942 estimated value of $750,000. Engineering Lt. Dairoku Yokoi, the detachment's radar expert, was on Guadalcanal on 7 August supervising radar network stations on Tulagi and Guadalcanal. He was evacuated to Rabaul in November.

18. Hoffman, *Once a Legend,* 180.

19. Quoted in Peatross, *Bless 'em All*, 37. "Tojo" was one of the derogatory epithets used to describe the Japanese enemy, derived from the name of Prime Minister Hideki Tojo, the tough former general who in the 1930s had led troops in the Sino-Japanese war, occupying Manchuria.

20. Frank J. Guidone to author, 20 Jan. 2001. Private Sparacino was in Frank Guidone's squad.

21. Howard Schnauber to author, 5 June 1997.

22. Cyrus J. Moore to author, 5 July 1999.

23. On the peak of Hill 281 two 3-inch guns and two 13-mm AA weapons were found.

24. McCann was awarded the Navy Cross for his heroism on Tulagi. He wanted to be a flier, and the Navy granted him his wish. Sadly, he was killed as a cadet during a flight training exercise.

25. Quoted in Ware, *Landing in the Solomons*, 65.

26. D. C. Horton to author, 23 Apr. 1995. The "Record of Events" for the 2nd Battalion, 5th Marines, dated 17 February 1943, indicates that seventeen Japanese were involved in the action.

27. Long, *Six Years War*, 130.

28. Kennedy, *Problem with Japan*, 97.

29. Nohara, "Diary." Standard tactics of the rikusentai, who trained constantly, included night assaults.

30. Alexander, *Edson's Raiders*, 99. PFC Edward Henry Ahrens, USMCR, was posthumously awarded the Navy Cross for gallantry on Tulagi. Chances are that Ahrens actually killed Sp. Lt. (jg) Kakichi Yoshimoto, a twenty-four-year combat veteran.

31. Ibid. Many of the marines received their dose of quinine powder, wrapped in toilet tissue, while in a chow line; an officer was on hand to ensure that each man took his medication.

32. Robert B. Pape to author, 4 Jan. 1989.

33. Headquarters, 2nd Battalion, 2nd Marines, was on the west side of the Tulagi hospital and near the open sea area, where a handful of LVTs (amtracs) were parked.

34. Cpl. Milton Lewis received a posthumous award of the Navy Cross. Walt recommended Red Hills for the Medal of Honor, but the award was reduced to the Navy Cross (a "spot award" given at moment). Ted Parker later was killed in action on 20 July 1943 at Bairoko, New Georgia. Ore J. Marion to author, 3 Sept. 1996. Lewis William Walt was awarded the Silver Star for conspicuous gallantry during the struggle for Tulagi. He would eventually be promoted to lieutenant general during the Vietnam War and commanded the III Marine Amphibious Force.

35. B. P. Wenver, in *New Nation Magazine* (London), May 1938, 8.

36. "*San Juan* Action Report," 8 Aug. 1942. The wounded included, 1st Lt. A. R. Gewehr, PFC V. R. Rogers, Pvt. A. L. Coffin, and Pvt. P. J. Ruane.

37. Herbert R. Fuller Jr. to author, 2 Sept. 1996. Fuller, a corpsman on the *Heywood*, landed with the paratroops on Gavutu; he received a commendation for his performance of duty from 7 to 9 August 1942.

38. Major Williams received the Navy Cross for his actions on Gavutu.

39.   Leonard Kiesel to author, 1 Apr. 1996.

40.   The paramarines' standard dress for unloading was a poncho and a jockstrap. Leonard Kiesel to author, 1 Apr. 1996.

41.   Smith, *Bloody Ridge,* 104.

42.   Masaichiro Miyagawa to author, 20 Oct. 1996.

43.   PFC Jack A. Mack (C/1/2), diary, 7 Aug.–31 Dec. 1942, in author's file. The bombardment warships had pumped a total of twelve hundred rounds into Gavutu and Tanambogo. Hoffman, *Silk Chutes and Hard Fighting,* 8.

44.   Richard E. Bennink to author, 10 Jan. 2001.

45.   Dallas Bennett (HQ, 2/22) recalled that the bombardment was so heavy and powerful that you could feel the shock waves, heat, and pressure regardless of where you were in any landing craft. Bennett, "Forty-Seven Years Late."

46   Haney, *U.S. Navy Medical Personnel,* 7–8.

47.   Vandegrift is quoted in Ware, *Landing in the Solomons,* 46.

48.   John P. Lanigan to author, 3 Sept. 1995. Lanigan eventually had twenty-one assault landings during World War II.

49.   William K. Tyler, interview by author, Guadalcanal Campaign Veterans reunion, Indianapolis, Ind., 11 Sept.1999; Col. Norman R. Nickerson, USMC (Ret.), conversation with author, Vista, Calif., 7 July 2002.

50.   Of the Reising "none-fun guns" it was said that the weapon was produced on existing machinery of Harrington and Richardson, an old gun manufacturer dating back to the Civil War, and was made out of ordinary iron rather than ordnance steel.

51.   A POW who survived the Gavutu battle reported the weapons count. Shin'ya Hashimoto was a civilian engineer assigned to the IJN. Originally stationed on Rabaul, he engineered the construction of airports and roads. On 3 May 1942 Hashimoto had arrived with the RXB Landing Force in the Tulagi area, where he assigned his men to construct defenses on Gavutu.

52.   Masaichiro Miyagawa to author, 20 Oct. 1996.

53.   See Sakurai, *Jigoku karo no Seikan [Back Alive from Hell].* Sakurai and Miyagawa, along with two others, survived; a total of 299 members of their group perished.

54.   The nickel used in the bullets may have come from the mines of New Caledonia.

55.   Meanwhile, back in Washington, D.C., at Marine Headquarters, Captain Huerth had been promoted to major on 7 August 1942.

56.   The diary entry of SM Yodoyama Mori for 24 June reads: "We constructed a strong hut for TA [antitank]." See Mori, "Diary."

57.   Givens was posthumously awarded the Navy Cross for his valiant fighting spirit.

58.   Brown said the most dangerous and exciting thing in his life was witnessing the landing of the paramarines on Gavutu on 7 August. Galen Craig Brown, telephone conversation with author, San Diego, Calif., 9 Jan. 2001.

59.   Lawrence Moran to author, 11 Apr. 1994.

60.   Leonard Kiesel to author, 1 Apr. 1996.

61.   Fordyce received the Navy Cross for action on Gavutu and was later WIA on Guadalcanal.

62.   Fuller was awarded the Navy Cross for his performance on Gavutu on D-day. Fordyce, Delia, Gagnon, and Michaud later also were presented the Navy Cross by Secretary of the Navy Frank Knox.

63.   In an article in *Guadalcanal Echoes* (date unknown), Dr. Schwartz wrote, "At Ga-
        vutu we all carried weapons and did not use the Red Cross armbands—too easy a
        target. I carried a Reising sub-machine gun." In the same article, however, Raider
        Corpsman Neil G. Kinney recalled that "he and his buddies [corpsmen] were or-
        dered by their senior medical officer to wear [the] Red Cross and carry white and
        blue blankets ashore."

64.   On 10 November 1943, Secretary of the Navy Frank Knox signed the posthumous
        Navy Cross citation for PFC George F. Grady.

65.   The following names of men from the 1st Parachute Battalion are written on the
        flag: Lt. W. W. Willard; Tom Pilant; PFC R. A. Burdok (B/1; KIA, Gavutu);
        Cpl. George F. Grady (A/1; KIA, Gavutu); Cpl. J. R. Wells (K/3). Robert L.
        Manning (B/1) was awarded the Navy Cross for his deeds on Gavutu on 7 Au-
        gust. He was later killed in action with the 28th Marines on Iwo Jima.

66.   Leonard Kiesel to author, 1 Apr. 1996.

67.   Colt M1911A1 pistols were standard issue in the Marine Corps. Some marines
        dubbed them "sauce weapons," after A-1 Steak Sauce.

68.   Robert Walter Moore to author, 9 Oct. 1992.

69.   Col. W. J. McKennan, USMC (Ret.), as quoted in *Leatherneck Magazine,* Mar.
        1986, 11.

70.   Harry Lawrence ("Torgue" or "Hal") Torgerson had served in the U.S. Army
        before transferring to the Marine Corps. He had played football for New York
        University and been an amateur hockey star.

71.   Major Enright was on Tulagi and knew little about what was happening on Ga-
        vutu; however, he was better informed than Crane about the problems there. If
        the Chutes were in deep trouble and required help, Enright should have warned
        Crane.

72.   Graham, "Observations from a Combat Hospital Corpsman," 62. Captain Crane
        was awarded the Navy Cross for his distinguished leadership at Gavutu. Later, he
        was transferred to Headquarters, 1st Marine Division, on Guadalcanal.

Chapter 9

1.   At 0600, Combat Team A withdrew from Florida Island. ADC [Assistant Divi-
        sion Commander] Reports to CG [Commanding General] 1ST MD [Marine
        Division], Subject Record of Events, 29 Sept. 1942. Guadalcanal Files, 1st Marine
        Division, U.S. Marine Corps History Division, Quantico, Va.

2.   James Sorensen to Philip Birkitt, 16 Aug. 1988.

3.   William J. Cannon to author, 15 Sept. 1991.

4.   Bennett, "Forty Seven Years Late," 17, 20.

5.   Eighteen-year-old carpenter Mamoru Hara of the Hashimoto CU fled with his
        fellow workers to a nearby cave at the foot of the eastern slope of the hill that
        dominates Gavutu. About thirty men were in the cave with him. Ten subse-
        quently left and were last seen swimming toward Florida Island, but they were
        never found. Grenades killed two of the five carpenters, then an aerial bomb
        exploded at the mouth of the cave, killing all but Hara. Further demolition by
        the attacking marines almost sealed the entrance; only a small hole remained that
        could be easily be concealed with a large stone. Hara lived in this environment
        with his dead and decaying comrades until the morning of 26 August. Appar-
        ently the stench was overpowering, even though he had covered the bodies with

dirt. During the night he crawled out to obtain a few coconuts and water from a nearby shallow well, which the marines knew about but did not use. Finally a marine from the 3rd Battalion, 2nd Marines, captured him. Whyte Papers.

6. Emory B. Ashurst to author, 24 Apr. 1996.

7. Fitch, "Securing Gavutu."

8. Ibid.

9. The Japanese encountered by Corporal Blackburn had an ID tag reading 1313.

10. Frederick W. Riggs to author, 15 Sept. 1993.

11. Baxter was later killed in action on Guadalcanal. One member of his company noted in his diary that Baxter had received two Navy Crosses.

12. Richard N. Vorwaller to author, 11 Aug. 1991.

13. Robert C. Libby to author, 10 July 1992.

14. Louis A. Carr to author, 1 Sept.1991.

15. Letter to author from "another marine," 3 Feb. 1993.

16. Louis A. Carr to author, 1 Sept. 1991.

17. Richard N. Vorwaller to author, 28 Sept. 1991.

18. Louis A. Carr to author, 1 Nov. 1991. The Japanese soldiers were, in fact, airmen.

19. E-mail, James McCoy to author, 23 Sept. 2004.

20. E-mail, Leonard E. Skinner to author, 23 Sept. 2004.

21. Later the charred remains of Cpl. Leon C. Richardt were found in the tank. Carr, "Second Week of August," 18.

22. Masaichiro Miyagawa to author, 9 July 1991.

23. Private Koon received the Bronze Star for his action on 8 August 1942.

24. Shane, *Heroes of the Pacific,* 223–24.

25. Carr, "Second Week of August," 24. Shane, *Heroes of the Pacific,* 220, reports that Koon sniped thirty Japanese.

26. Louis A. Carr to author, 19 Oct. 1991.

27. Letter to author from "another marine," 3 Feb. 1993.

28. Robert C. Libby to author, 5 Feb. 1992.

29. Jinsaku Sakurai to author, 7 July 2000. Captain Miyazaki, commander of the Yokohama Air Group, was not on the island at that time and survived the war. The author believes he left on or about 1 or 2 August, when the 11th BG started bombing.

30. Watanabe's name is not on the 3rd Company roster. Often, POWs invented names.

31. WO Noboru Takeuchi, who was on Guadalcanal, survived.

32. Survivors of the Yokohama Air Group Flying-Boat Unit included Masaichiro Miyagawa, Jinsaku Sakurai, Masaaki Nakano, Marakazu Yasuta, and Kinichiro Suzuki. From the Hama Air Unit, only Tokuchiyo Hirahashi and Makoto Ito survived.

33. Masters, *Once a Marine,* 96.

34. J. B. Hicks was the Second Clerk and Boarding Officer in the BSIP government. His house was located on the seaward slope of the ridge in the rear of the hospital area.

35. Claude R. Blanchard to author, 19 Nov. 1993.

36. John M. Braloski to author, 19 June 1994. On 24 October 1942 Braloski received a commendation from Cdr. A. W. Benson, USN, executive officer of the *Heywood,* for bravery regarding his part in the defense of Tulagi.

37. John P. Lanigan to author, 1 Mar. 1989.

Chapter 10

1. Sandy Hunt was a card-carrying cryptographer for electrical machines, one of two to have completed the course at the Brooklyn Navy Yard.

2. The war correspondents included Richard Tregaskis, Robert C. Miller, Frank McCarthy, Jack Dowling, Tomas Yarbrough, Hanson Baldwin, and Bill Kent.

3. Letter from Col. Sanford B. Hunt, USMC (Ret.), 8 Aug. 1988, to Allan R. Millett, Ph.D.; copy in author's file.

4. Kaneda, "Memoirs." Courtesy of Sachihiko Kaneda, son of Sankichi Kaneda, Toyama City, Japan.

5. Gaetano Gerace to author, 17 Mar. 1988. The Japanese octagonal tent ordinarily housed from fifteen to twenty men, although it could accommodate as many as forty. The camp comprised eighty-eight tents.

6. Kaneda, "Memoirs."

7. Raymond L. Whitaker to author, 11 Aug. 1999; Soule, *Shooting the Pacific War,* 4.

8. Harold A. Hayes to author, 7 July 1996.

9. Admiral Turner stated: " Eighty percent of my time was given to logistics during the first four months of the WATCHTOWER operation [because] we were living from one logistic crisis to another." See Dyer, *Amphibians Came to Conquer,* 68.

10. MacArthur's headquarters reportedly had the largest public relations section in the U.S. Army; its main function appears to have been the promotion of the MacArthur name. The correspondence on this subject was misfiled with the papers of the Postal Affairs Branch (Operations-20 CNO) in the records held by the National Archives. The author viewed the letters while examining the postal files in 1960.

11. Edmund L. Troccia to author, 5 June 1995. When one engine of his B-17 failed, Pease returned to his base to obtain another aircraft. Unable to find one fit for combat, he selected the most serviceable plane and rejoined the 93rd Bombardment Squadron for the attack on the Rabaul airdromes. By skillful flying he maintained his position in the formation and withstood enemy attacks until his bombs were released. After the B-17s had left the target, Pease's aircraft fell behind the formation and was lost. Captain Pease was posthumously awarded the Medal of Honor for his actions.

12. Frazer had available Company A, Company C (2nd and 3rd Platoons), Headquarters and Service Company, and the fourteen-man mapping section.

13. One of the wounded was Lt. James J. Southerland II, USNR, of VF-5 aboard the *Saratoga.* Shot down on 7 August, he landed east of Cape Esperance and worked his way back to the marine lines. Southerland, "One of the Many Personal Adventures"; Lundstrom, *The First Team,* 55.

14. WO Tsuneto Sakado was from the Yamaguchi prefecture, Japan. Unbeknown to his captors, Sakado was the leader of the deadly machine-gun platoon of the 84th Guard Unit.

15. 5th Marine Regiment, "Record of Events," Aug. 1942.

16.   In pre-war times, Ralph Cory was assigned to the Department of State and was a code breaker in the early MAGIC program that decoded Japanese messages called PURPLE.

17.   5th Marine Regiment, "Record of Events," Aug. 1942.

18.   Vernon C. Stimpel, conversation with author, Morton Grove, Ill., July 1969.

19.   Edward G. Sexton (D-2 Section, 1st Marine Division) to author, 24 Jan. 2003. The exchange was recounted by Plat. Sgt. Frank L. Few. Few spoke about the Goettge patrol in 1944 when he and Sexton were at Pavuvu in the Russell Islands; the two had been classmates at the Marine Photographic School in Philadelphia.

20.   According to Sergeant Few, when the fighting started they were so close to the Japanese that it was hand to hand. Edward G. Sexton to author, 24 Jan. 2003.

21.   Frank Few had managed to stay alive until dawn; by then, everyone else had been killed. Arndt and Spaulding must already have escaped. Few took off at top speed, dove into the surf, and swam under water as far as he could; he would come up for air, then immediately submerge again. Eventually he was able to get out of rifle range of the Japanese. When he thought it was safe, he surfaced and continued to swim to safety. Edward G. Sexton to author, 24 Jan. 2003.

       The records of the 84th Guard Unit mention the following: "Engaged in heavy fighting with the enemy, many were killed. . . . Formed a defense group by joining the 84th Guard Unit and other military forces on Guadalcanal; Captain Monzen, 11th Construction Unit, took command." Extracts from 84th Guard Unit, "Diary," 13–22 Aug. 1942.

22.   5th Marine Regiment, "Record of Events," Aug. 1942.

23.   See *War Stories,* Jan.–Mar. 1999. When I asked General Snedeker about the Goettge patrol, he said that "Vandegrift was not pleased with the prospective operation but chose not to interfere with his D-2's duties, a decision Vandegrift later regretted." Lt. Gen. Edward W. Snedeker, USMC (Ret.), conversation with author, Carlsbad, Calif. 10 Aug.1993.

24.   William J. Carroll, conversation with author, Guadalcanal Campaign Veterans reunion, Indianapolis, Ind., 12 Sept. 1999.

25.   VCNO Secret Dispatch 272049 NCR 2755, June 1942, quoting CINCPAC Secret Dispatch 260019 NCR 1811, June 1942: "Commence movement Cub Number One to FULCRUM [Auckland, NZ] from Oakland and Port Hueneme [Calif.]." The CUBs were specialists, including aviation technicians, radio-men, aviation mechanics, metalsmiths, medics, ordnance men, cooks, and even a postmaster.

       Eventually the CUB-1 camp was located on Danger Point, Guadalcanal, an ideal name for that spot. Rear Adm. Houston L. Maples, USN (Ret.), to author, 11 Aug. 1967. Captain Maples replaced Commander Compton as CO, Advanced Base, CACTUS.

26.   "Fuku/Oka Operation Order Oka #96."

27.   Later the Yokosuka 5th SNLF would relocate its camp to the Tassafaronga district. The unit remained immobile, however, and took no part in any major engagements.

28.   "A patrol [L/3/5] discovered a leg encased in a Marine legging and boondoggers [marine boots] protruding from the sand. Nearby, an oversized handless arm was sticking out of the ground. Marine Gunner Bill Rust thought it was either Goettge or Ringer, both of whom had been very large men." Hammel, *Guadalcanal,* 136.

29.   Petty Officer Sashohta and most of the other NCOs lost their lives in the encounter. A Japanese report indicates that some of the civilian construction men were also killed.

30.   Kaneda, "Memoirs."

31.   Ibid. Captain Tsunomura, who corresponded with the author for a period of eight years, died in 1994.

32.   Sugawara, *Ichiki Shitai Zenmetsu [The Annihilation of the Ichiki Detachment]*, 182A.

33.   Sugawara, *Ichiki Shitai Zenmetsu [The Annihilation of the Ichiki Detachment]*.

34.   *Guadalcanal, 50th Anniversary*, 38.

35.   Magistrate Judge Robert Hayes Scott: "Charles [Hayes] told me that his greatest contribution to the war effort was a roll of chamois [to strain the fuel] that he brought with him [to Guadalcanal] when he took command of CUB-1. Robert Hayes Scott to author, 16 Dec. 2005.

36.   Luie Fuller (CUB-1), conversation with author, Guadalcanal Campaign Veterans reunion, San Diego, Calif., 19 Sept. 1998.

37.   Graydon E. Cadwell (VMF-223) to author, 4 Oct. 1999.

38.   Wilbur F. Bewley to author, 17 Sept. 1999.

39.   Poliny, "Colonel Ichiki's Last Stand," 8.

40.   *Guadalcanal 50th Anniversary*, 39.

41.   William Whorf, phone conversation with author, 9 Aug. 2001.

42.   Sugawara, *Ichiki Shitai Zenmetsu [The Annihilation of the Ichiki Detachment]*, 178A.

43.   Merillat, *The Island*, 73.

44.   Earl J. Mowery to author, 1 June 1985. Mowery received the Navy Cross for action during the battle. Leo Case may have received the only one awarded to the tank platoon.

45.   The Collins transceiver radio (TSC) allowed for a two-way conversation.

46.   See www.pacificwrecks.com/people/verans/clark.html/.

47.   Kamei, "Island of Homesickness," Apr.–June 1991, 17; June–July 1992, 16. Other survivors included Sgt. Sadanobu Okada and Sergeant Kugagane. Smith, *Bloody Ridge*, 68–70. A few men, because of illness, had remained in the rear area.

48.   Sugawara, *Ichiki Shitai Zenmetsu [The Annihilation of the Ichiki Detachment]*, 246.

49.   1st Marine Division, "Final Report."

50.   Kamei, "Island of Homesickness," Apr.–June 1991, 17; June–July 1992, 16.

51.   Sugawara, *Ichiki Shitai Zenmetsu [The Annihilation of the Ichiki Detachment]*, 250A.

52.   Ibid.

53.   1st Marine Division, "Final Report."

54.   The RAF apparently had refused to take the Bell P-400s (P-39) it had ordered because of disappointing performance that limited aerial combat above 14,000 feet.

55.   Ferguson, *Guadalcanal*. The crews described themselves as the "Bastard Air Force."

56.   "Japanese Order—Plans for Guadalcanal."

57. Kaneda, "Memoirs."

58. Morison, *History of United States Naval Operations,* 85.

Chapter 11

1.   The Skytrains (R4D-1s, R4D-5s, R4D-6s, and R4D-7s) were used primarily in a cargo-carrying role, the Skytroopers (R4D-2s, R4D-3s, and R4D-4s) primarily in a passenger-carrying role.

2.   "Unsung Heroes of SCAT." One of the C-47s was lost on a flight from Henderson Field on 20 January 1943 carrying seventeen litter-borne and three ambulatory patients for hospitals in New Caledonia.

3.   The lookout post at Taivu Point was established by Lt. Yukio Endo's 81st Guard Unit on 5 July under PO3c Tan with five men. Later the Taivu sector was one of the major sites for Japanese troop landings and a gathering place for some older SNLF troops that remained close to the sea.

4.   Kawaguchi, "Struggles of the Kawaguchi Detachment." Yoshi Sagai to author, 22 Nov. 1994. Yoshi records that 3,545 men landed from the 35th Brigade.

5.   Smith, *Bloody Ridge,* 120.

6.   Ibid.

7.   Cpl. William D. Casey and Pvt. Seraphine "Buddy" Smith were killed. Alexander, *Edson's Raiders,* 126, 131. Their remains were found early in 1943 when a survey party returned to the area. Rosenquist, Sexton, and Buerlein, *Our Kind of War,* 86.

8.   Brig. Gen. Samuel B. Griffith II File, 6 Oct. 1945, HQ USMC, U.S. Marine Corps History Division, Quantico, Va.

9.   Kaneda, "Memoirs." *Kuma* was the Japanese code word for the 7th Infantry Division.

10. Smith, *Bloody Ridge,* 115.

11. Ibid., 116, and author's file.

12. Ibid., and author's file. According to Miller, *Guadalcanal: The First Offensive,* part of the U.S. Department of the Army's official history of World War II, the commander of the 4th Infantry Regiment was Col. Tadamasu Nakaguma. My historical contact in Japan, however, indicates it was actually Col. Naomasa Nakaguma.

13. Matsumoto, "Diary," 11 Sept. 1942.

14. Charles Farmer, Company B, 1st Battalion, 11th Marines, conversation with author, Louisville, Ky., 12 Sept. 2000. The Marine Corps later would add five times the number of grenades to a unit's allotment.

15. Matsumoto, "Diary," 11 Sept. 1942; Alexander, *Edson's Raiders,*183.

16. Sakamoto, "Diary," 13 Sept. 1942; Sonoda, "Diary," 13 Sept. 1942.

17. Sakamoto, "Diary," 13 Sept. 1942.

18. Sonoda, "Diary," 13 Sept. 1942.

19. Kashii, "Diary, 12 Sept. 1942.

20. Matsumoto, "Diary," 19 Sept. 1942.

21. Iwamoto, "Diary"; Matsumoto, "Diary"; Sakamoto, "Diary." The Bonegi River basin was a principal bivouac area for the Seventeenth Army.

22. Captured Japanese Documents, RG 127, Entry 39A, Box 14. National Archives, Washington, D.C.

23. Whyte Papers.

24. Alexander, *Edson's Raiders*, 177. Both Sweeney and Burak were awarded the Navy Cross for their actions on Bloody Ridge.

25. Smith, *Bloody Ridge*, 180.

26. 1st Marine Division, "Final Report," 12.

27. Hammel, *Guadalcanal*, 233. Fulgenzi was awarded the Silver Star.

28. Smith, *Bloody Ridge*, 178.

29. Private Dunn was awarded the Navy Cross for his heroic deed.

30. Frank, *Guadalcanal*, 225.

31. W. Ray Thomas to author, 7 Sept. 1997.

32. Lieutenant Commander (later Captain) McLarney, who was called "Butch" by the Raiders, was awarded the Navy Cross for his actions on 13–14 September 1942.

33. Martin Clemens, interview by author, Honiara, Solomon Islands, 7 Aug. 1990. On 18 September the depleted paramarine unit was shipped to New Caledonia on the vessels that had transported the 7th Marines from Samoa to Guadalcanal.
    Raider Major Bailey had already been awarded a Silver Star for his actions on Tulagi on 7 August.

34. Akio Tani to Dean Ladd, 9 Apr. 1983; copy in author's file.

35. Miller, *Guadalcanal*, 233, 235.

36. The U.S. Navy was to furnish a radio team as part of the Task Force. Lt. Gen. Edward W. Snedeker, USMC (Ret.), conversation with author, Carlsbad, Calif., 8 Aug. 1990.

37. 2nd Lieutenant Paul Moore received the Silver Star for this action.

38. Col. Joseph H. Alexander, USMC (Ret.), e-mail to author.

39. "With Second Bn. Fifth Marines," 23.

40. Cdr. Raymond J. Evans Jr., USCG (Ret.), to author, 18 June 1999. The reference is to Lt. Cdr. Dwight H. Dexter, USCG, the officer in charge of the boat pool at Lunga.

41. Michael S. Smith to author, 17 Oct. 2000.

42. W. Ray Thomas to author, 7 Sept. 1997.

43. Cdr. Raymond J. Evans Jr., USCG (Ret.), to author, 18 June 1999. Ray Evans would receive the Navy Cross for his actions during the evacuation of Lt. Colonel Puller's marines.

44. S1C Douglas Albert Munro was posthumously awarded the Medal of Honor. He is the only member of the U.S. Coast Guard ever so honored.

45. Kashii, "Diary."

46. United States Pacific Fleet, Carriers, Pacific Fleet, Scouting Squadron 3, File A16 (085), 6 Nov. 1942, Naval Historical Center, Washington, D.C. The author believes the sailors were from one squad of WO Noboru Takeuchi platoon (84th Guard Unit) that established a watcher post on Banka Island (Russell Islands) on 2 August 1942. This squad relieved a twelve-man unit of the 81st Guard Unit under PO2c Kaneda. Kaneda, "Memoirs."

47. Ted Kemper, conversation with author, Oxnard, Calif., 1 July 1989.

Chapter 12

1.   Combat Intelligence Center, Item 223.

2.   *Saiaku No Semba [The Worst Battlefield: Guadalcanal War History]*, 388–422.

3.   Charles A. Buser to author, 4 Jan. 1993. Each R4D could carry enough gasoline to keep twelve Wildcat fighters in the air for one hour.

4.   Ibid.

5.   5th Marine Regiment, "Record of Events," Unit Report No. 8, 3rd Battalion, 6–10 Oct. 1942.

6.   Akio Tani to author, 18 Apr. 1990. The Holland-manufactured guns had been captured in China.

7.   1st Marine Raider Battalion, "1st Marine Raider Battalion," 11 Oct. 1942.

8.   *Guadalcanal Echoes*, Jan. 1990, 13; "The Raider Patch," 9. Privates Thomas and Fedorak were both awarded the Navy Cross for the October action.

9.   5th Marine Regiment, "Record of Events," 19 Sept. to 9 Dec. 1942, 7.

10.   Croizat, *Across the Reef*, 55.

11.   5th Marine Regiment, "Record of Events," 19 Sept. to 9 Dec. 1942, 7.

12.   Guidone to author, 30 July 2005.

13.   Combat Intelligence Center, Item 245.

14.   *Americal Newsletter* (Feb.–Mar. 2005), 23.

15.   Dull, *Battle History*, 224.

16.   PFC Bernard Seiden of the 1st Battalion, 11th Marines, was killed in the 11th's bivouac area. He was posthumously awarded the Silver Star for his untiring efforts to rescue fellow marines. The citation reads in part: "On the morning of 14 October 1942 . . . PFC Seiden and four other Marines, with complete disregard for their own safety, rescued men from the dug-out. . . . Due to the efforts of the above man, the lives were saved."

17.   Lt. Gen. Edward W. Snedeker, USMC (Ret.), conversation with author, Carlsbad, Calif., 4 Oct. 1990. Snedeker, then a lieutenant colonel, was the 1st Marine Division signal officer.

18.   Michael J. O'Dea Jr. diary, in author's possession.

19.   Jones and Jones, *Forgotten Warriors*, 71.

20.   William W. Rogal to author, 2 Jan. 1996. Bill Rogal was awarded the U.S. Navy and Marine Corps Medal for his life-saving activities while returning to the perimeter from Aola on 13 October 1942.

21.   Louis Stark (CUB-1), conversation with author, Carlsbad, Calif., 16 Feb. 1998.

22.   "Guadalcanal Fuel," 4.

23.   Jones and Jones, *Forgotten Warriors*, 71–72.

24.   Ewan M. Stevenson to author, 8 Nov. 1999.

25.   Miyazawa, "Diary."

26.   Combat Intelligence Center, Item 203.

27.   Colonel Kaji continued to fire at the Henderson Field area until 3 November; then his unit moved to the Matanikau meeting point. On 11 November, he received a cable from headquarters at Buin that reinforcements were being shipped from RWP (Bougainville) to RXN (Guadalcanal), including three guns plus 1,200 shells. The transport carrying the reinforcements was sunk en route; sixty-five men survived. Akio Tani to author, 13 June 1990.

28. Combat Intelligence Center, Item 614, 12.

29. The Maeda Tai originally had been part of the 4th Company, 2nd Tank Regiment.

30. E-mail from Mr. Harada via Akira Takizawa, 27 July 2004.

31. Japan, Self-Defense Force, *Senshi Sōsho* files, 1968–69, 1971, 1975.

32. Banyan trees would reach a height of 75 to 100 feet and a width of several feet, with extended open roots.

33. *Saiaku No Semba [The Worst Battlefield: Guadalcanal War History]*, 392.

34. Ibid., 397.

35. Item 247, M-2 Information Bulletin 135, 28 Dec. 1942. Unknown Diarist. (Dates 1 Sept.–27 Oct. 1942), Guadalcanal File, Marine Corps Historical Center, Washington, D.C.

36. 29th Infantry, "Records."

37. Sanae Harada to author, 1 Jan. 2004.

38. The dead were from the 1st Independent Tank Company, formerly the 4th Company, 2nd Tank Regiment.

39. Shohei Haga to Akire Abuki (1st Lieutenant, Information Platoon, 1st Battalion, 4th Infantry Regiment), Itabashi, Tokyo, 9 Nov. 1991; Akio Tani, conversation with author, Tokyo, 10 Nov. 1991.

40. Merillat, *The Island,* 164.

41. Shohei Haga to Akire Abuki (1st Lieutenant, Information Platoon, 1st Battalion, 4th Infantry Regiment), Itabashi, Tokyo, 9 Nov. 1991; Akio Tani, conversation with author, Tokyo, 10 Nov. 1991.

42. Sanae Harada to author, 9 Dec. 1992.

43. History of the 1st Independent Tank Company via Akio Tani, 24 July 1990.

44. Akio Tani and Iwakichi Suzuki correspondence, 7 Feb. 1993 and 17 Mar. 1993; Akio Tani to author, 13 Apr. 1993.

45. Hoffman, "Guadalcanal," 37–38. Col. Jon Hoffman, USMCR, was the Assistant Director, History and Museums Division, U.S. Marine Corps, Washington, D.C., now with the U.S. Army Historical Office.

46. George C. MacGillivray to author, 7 Feb. 1995.

47. Juro Katsumata to author via Akio Tani, 5 June 1991. The draft narrative, edited herein, was written by James Sorensen from notes provided by Juro Katsumata. Sorensen had met Katsumata on Guadalcanal in 1978. James Sorensen to author, 1 Nov. 1978.

48. Miyazawa, "Diary."

49. Ichiji, "POW Interrogation Report." At the time of Ichiji's capture there were only sixty-five alive in his regiment.

50. Combat Intelligence Center, Item 1231.

51. Lt. Col. Herman H. Hanneken received a Medal of Honor for capturing the bandit Charlemagne in Nicaragua. The colonel reportedly cut off the outlaw's head and returned to base with it as evidence.

52. Wiens, *My Own Little Corner of the War,* 98–104.

53. 5th Marine Regiment, "Record of Events," Document #100.

54. Smith and Adams, *Beyond Glory,* 5.

55. Hoffman, "Guadalcanal," 41–42.

56.   Sgt. John Basilone received the Medal of Honor for his deeds and was later of-
       fered a commission, which he refused.

57.   Miyazawa, "Diary," 30 Oct. 1942, via Akio Tani to author, 18 Apr. 1990.

58.   Kusano, "Diary."

59.   Kikurri, "POW Interrogation Report."

60.   Stannard, *The Battle of Coffin Corner,* 99.

61.   Letter to author from Akio Tani, 18 Apr. 1990.

62.   Combat Intelligence Center, Item 223.

63.   Boardman, "Japanese Operations at Guadalcanal."

Chapter 13

1.   Herm Louis, conversation with the author, Victorville, Calif., 7 Jan.1997.

2.   *Military Affairs,* Winter 1947, 211.

3.   "With Second Bn. Fifth Marines," 26.

4.   Tamura, "A Japanese Commander Tells His Story."

5.   Anthony Casamento of Brooklyn, New York, received the Navy Cross for the
       action on 1 November. Thirty-eight years after the battle, on 22 August 1980, the
       award was upgraded to the Medal of Honor. Ibid.

6.   "With Second Bn. Fifth Marines," 26.

7.   Stannard, *Battle of Coffin Corner,* 182–83.

8.   Ibid., 185.

9.   Charles O. Hall to author, 9 Sept. 1996.

10.   Richard A. Nash to author, 1 Nov. 1994.

11.   Sorensen, "Memoirs."

12.   Ladd, *Faithful Warriors,* 45.

13.   Sorensen, "Memoirs."

14.   Miyazawa, "Diary," 9 Nov. 1942. One *shaku* is approximately 0.030 pint.

15.   William J. Cannon made it home alive. In 1992, during the fiftieth anniversary
       of the Guadalcanal Campaign, he and the author toured some of the areas where
       Cannon had spent that eighteenth birthday.

16.   William W. Rogal to author, 18 Mar. 1998.

17.   Frank, *Guadalcanal,* 421.

18.   2nd Marine Regiment, Reinforced, "Record of Events."

19.   1st Lt. Isamiu Ito took over the company when Captain Okada was killed on 4
       November.

20.   Charles Cadwell to author, 7 July 1995; copy in author's file.

21.   The *Arizona Maru, Brisbane Maru, Canberra Maru, Nagara Maru, Nako Maru,
       Sado Maru,* and *Shinanogawa Maru*—the seven transports sunk—represented
       44,855 tons and twenty antiaircraft guns.

22.   "Diary, 14 Nov. 1942."

23.   David Tribe to author, 18 Aug. 1998.

24.   Ikeya, "POW Interrogation Report," 28 Jan. 1943; copy in author's file.

25.   Shuji, "POW Interrogation Report," 27 Jan. 1943; copy in author's file.

26.   Shijiri, "POW Interrogation Report," 30 Jan. 1943; copy in author's file.

27. Charles Cadwell to author, 7 July 1995; copy in author's file. About one thousand Japanese sailors died, including two admirals, and hundreds were wounded.

28. Akio Tani to author, 18 Mar. 1990.

29. ACORN—Aviation, Construction, Ordnance, Repair, Navy—was an airfield assembly unit designed to construct, operate, and maintain an advanced landing field and/or seaplane base to provide facilities for operation. A Naval Construction Battalion and an ACORN unit usually made up a team. However, the only segment of ACORN 1 sent to Guadalcanal was the medical section; the balance of the unit remained on Espiritu Santo Island.

30. According to extracts from a captured diary, two large landing vessels and one small barge arrived at Tassafaronga on 10 December. The diary states that a small submarine arrived at Kamimbo Bay and that the other submarines also were the small type. The diarist further notes that on 16 December a large landing barge was camouflaged. "It seems the enemy planes are off guard and they have not been able to detect the barge when moored. Our pilots are laughing at the enemy pilots' failure to detect it." Guadalcanal File, SOPAC 0440: M-2 015889, Naval Historical Center, Washington, D.C.

31. Ray L. Whitaker to author, 2 Apr. 1999. Eight midget submarines were reported lost in and around Guadalcanal waters.

32. Rothermel, "The 14th NCB History of Guadalcanal."

33. Named for Roy H. Johnson, Machinist's Mate 1c, USN, of Minneapolis, Minn.

34. Subsequently the 26th, 46th, and 63rd Naval Construction Battalions, plus the 810th Army Engineer Battalion and the 873rd Aviation Engineer Battalion, would work on Bomber Strip No. 2, or Carney Field. By 22 April 1943 Bomber Strip No. 2 was operational for B-17s and B-24s of the 13th Air Force.

Chapter 14

1. CG1st MarDiv Operations Order No. 5 (revised), 4 Aug. 1942.

2. 2nd Marine Regiment, "Report Record of Events."

3. John A. Bowler to author, 11 Dec.1991.

4. Lieutenant Mills was known to his friends as "No Guts, No Glory." He was killed on Tarawa.

5. John Zingale to author, 4 July 1996.

6. William J. Cannon interview with author, Carlsbad, Calif., 3 Mar. 1994.

7. 2nd Marine Regiment, "Report Record of Events."

8. Paul T. Boyd to author, 23 Mar. 1992; William J. Cannon interview with author, Carlsbad, Calif., 3 Mar. 1994; Maj. Gen. Wood B. Kyle to author, Carlsbad, Calif.

9. Robert Tallent to author, 13 June 1992.

10. Ogihara, "POW Interrogation Report"; POW list, Fetherston Camp near Wellington, NZ, copy in author's file.

11. Lt. Commander Sato kept a notebook with the names of the men in his unit. The Hama Air Unit on Florida Island consisted of the following (asterisk indicates flying personnel): Lt. Cdr. Riichiro Sato*, WO Tokuchiyo Hirahashi* (XO), WO Fumiro Kurozawa,* WO Hisaterau Kofuji,* NAP1c Tatsuo Mori*, NAP1c Shigeto Kobayashi*. NAP1c Saburo Matsui*, PO1c Anado (Senior NCO), NAP2c Noboru Nomura *, NAP2c Shojiro Tsuji*, NAP2c Tadash Yusa*, NAP3c Kawamura *, NAP3c Yoshio Omishi *, PO1c Tamotsu Ito, PO3c Masahiko Ito,

PO3c Yonesaku Kaneyama, PO3c Sumisei, PO3c Eihi Suzuli, PO3c Fukujiro Tamura, PO3c Najkagawa Tsuchida, PO3c Hideo (or Toshio) Yanazaki, SM Murakami, SM Shigenaru Nakagawa, SM Onuma, SM Masakaazu Ota, SM Mitsuaro Saito, SM Shigeru Saito, SM Tsuyoshi Yamazaki, SA Tomomi Abe, SA Hiroshi Fukuda, SA Risuke Hasegawa, SA Masayoshi Katyo, SA Mitsuaki Sakurai, SA Toshio Sasaki, SA Tadashi, SA Yoshio Takahashi, SA Minoru Takeshita. Boardman, "Japanese Operations at Guadalcanal."

12.   Both of Sato's photos still exist. Boardman, "Japanese Operations on Guadalcanal," 11.

13.   Ibid.

14.   John R. Brakeman to author, 27 Sept. 1942.

15.   Ibid.

16.   2nd Marine Regiment, "Report Record of Events." The Japanese medical instruments apparently were of better quality than those the marines were using.

17.   From AWM 54, Written Records Section, World War II, Australian War Memorial, Canberra.

18.   Van Watts to author, 2 Sept. 1993. Used by permission from Van Watts, as printed in the *Tin Can Sailor,* Jan. 1993.

19.   Clifford R. Kurtz to author, 26 Mar. 1987.

20.   The flag is in the possession of Herbert R. Fuller Jr.

21.   Rev. Harry Voyce Auckland, NZ, to author, 2 Sept. 1991.

22.   Hikinune, "Diary."

23.   Ibid.

24.   Dick Horton to author, 15 Dec. 1994.

25.   "Diary [Unknown Writer]."

26.   Boardman, "Japanese Operations at Guadalcanal," 14.

27.   "Diary [Unknown Writer]."

28.   Vandegrift, *Once a Marine,* 168.

29.   "Coastwatcher Report [Bengough]," 2 Nov. 42.

30.   J. Wendell Crain to author, 21 Jan. 1991.

31.   Ayling, *Semper Fidelis,* 62.

32.   Herbert R. Fuller Jr. to author.

33.   Ayling, *Semper Fidelis,* 62.

34.   Fukuda, "POW Interrogation Report."

35.   *Western Pacific High Commission Gazette,* 7 Sept. 1943, copy in author's file.

36.   *The British Solomon Islands Gazette,* 6 Mar. 1916.

37.   Emmett N. Carter to author, 3 Aug. 1993.

Chapter 15

1.   Breuer, *Devil Boats,* 84.

2.   Kato, "POW Interrogation Report"; Kinoshita, "POW Interrogation Report."

3.   The last element of the Massachsetts National Guard's 182nd Infantry Regiment had been on garrison duty on Espiritu Santo, New Hebrides, and was transferred to Guadalcanal when the 129th Infantry Regiment (37th Division) replaced them.

4. No American prisoner of war was ever found on Guadalcanal, nor any graves of the men captured by the Japanese.

5. The scaly jungle rot, usually contracted from the soil, was cured only in colder climates.

6. Miller, *Guadalcanal: The First Offensive,* 350.

7. The figure of fifty thousand-plus is taken from eighteen pages of records of Japanese formations in the author's files. Most Japanese records were destroyed at Rabaul just before the surrender,

8. Joseph G. Micek diary, in author's file.

9. Frank, *Guadalcanal,* 528, 748.

10. Captain Monzen was evacuated to Japan, but on 9 June 1944, while aboard the destroyer *Matsukaze* in command of a transport convoy escort group, he was lost when his ship was torpedoed off Chichi Island (Tokyo Prefecture). Kaneda, "Memoirs."

11. The fully staffed permanent U.S. Army XIV Corps arrived on Guadalcanal on 12 March 1943.

12. When the complete U.S. Army XIV Corps arrived in March 1943 the Americal officers were replaced. Elements of the Americal Division began leaving Guadalcanal beginning on 1 March (125th Quartermaster Company, 245th Field Artillery Battalion, and 246th Field Artillery Battalion); they were followed by units leaving on 24 March and 1, 6, and 7 April.

13. Stannard, *Battle of Coffin Corner,* 203.

14. Eighth Army Staff Radiogram #122.

15. Miller, *Guadalcanal,* 249.

16. Ryker, *The VS-55 Newsletter;* U.S. Department of the Navy, *United States Naval Chronology,* 42. VS-5-D-14 became Scouting Squadron VS-55 on 1 February 1943.

17. Muehrcke, *Orchids in the Mud,* 114.

18. Carbray, "Wright's Road."

19. Muehrcke, *Orchids in the Mud,* 125–27.

20. Ibid., 127–28.

21. Ibid., 127; Anthony A. Martinez to author, 16 Apr. 1990; NUMA [code name for 38th Division] Ito Intelligence Report No. 8, covering 20–27 Dec. 1942 (abandoned identification tags [dog tags] and personal notes, letters, diaries, picked up from positions occupied by the 124th Infantry and Major Nishiyama, 3rd Battalion, 228th Infantry), National Archives, Washington, D.C.

22. Muehrcke, *Orchids in the Mud,* 18.

23. "Combat Order #67."

24. Fighter Strip No. 2, also known as Kukum Field, three-fifths of a mile southeast of Kukum Beach, was completed on 1 January 1943.

25. Joseph G. Micek diary, in author's file.

26. Morriss, *South Pacific Diary,* 53.

27. Dr. Robert C. Muehrcke, conversation with author, Guadalcanal, 8 Aug. 1992. According to Muehrcke, the men of the 132nd called Colonel George "Crazy George" because of his unusual behavior before and in combat. The *Chicago Tribune* correspondent Robert Cromie labeled the diminutive Colonel George a "Tiny Pepperpot." Harold Ashe (Service Company, 132nd Infantry Regiment)

told the author that the men called Colonel George "Wet Pants." Harold Ashe, interview by author, Chicago, Ill., 2 July 1993.

28. Joseph G. Micek diary, in author's file.
29. "Field Order No. 1."
30. Mizuguchi, "Diary."
31. Okajima, "Diary," 1 Jan. 1943.
32. Kaneko, "POW Interrogation Report."
33. Matsushima, "POW Interrogation Report."
34. Joseph G. Micek diary, Jan. 1943, in author's file.
35. The Japanese pillbox was analogous to a thorny gooseberry bush, whose fruit is very difficult to pick.
36. Joseph G. Micek diary, 3 Jan. 1943, in author's file.
37. Steve Sokal, ex-medic, conversation with author, Chicago, Ill., 10 June 1981.
38. A redesignated unit, formerly the 2nd Pioneer Battalion.
39. George Polk was murdered in Athens in 1948 while covering the Greek civil war as a CBS news correspondent.
40. Muehrcke, *Orchids in the Mud,* 155. It is believed this was the only time during World War II that such an order was given on a battlefield.
41. The short drive by the 132nd against this Japanese position would cost the men of the Illinois National Guard about ten percent of the marines killed in action in the four months of fighting. The American Division would lose 533 killed and 902 wounded on Guadalcanal, about half the marine casualties.
42. Stanley R. Larsen later would be promoted to major general.
43. Miller, *Guadalcanal,* 278.
44. Captain Davis received the Medal of Honor and retired as a colonel.
45. Seventeenth Army Report No. 46, Akio Tani to author, 4 Jan. 1995.
46. Akio Tani, conversation with author, Tokyo, Japan, Nov. 1991.
47. Zimmerman, *Guadalcanal Campaign,* 160.
48. Okajima, "Diary." Lieutenant Okajima died on 22 January 1943. At times there may be a confusion or disagreement with other records regarding dates of events; the only sustainable explanation is that in the field, combatants forget the date details. In many POW reports the individuals even get the months confused.
49. Captain Deese received the Silver Star for this engagement.
50. Rudolph E. Huisinga, conversation with author, Chicago, Ill., 23 May 1998.
51. Frank, *Guadalcanal,* 567, lists 888 Japanese KIA, 29 POWs, and 188 KIA by artillery.
52. Arakawa, "POW Interrogation Report."
53. Matsueda, "POW Interrogation Report."
54. Richard P. Bailey to author, 18 Jan. 1998.
55. Joseph G. Micek diary, 26–27 Jan. 1943, in author's file.
56. Ibid., 31 Jan. 1943.
57. Ibid., 1–6 Feb. 1943; see also Muehrcke, *Orchids in the Mud,* 174.
58. Lieutenant Oshi was to assist in the withdrawal and remained behind; however, he was too tardy and was captured.
59. Joseph G. Micek diary, 7 Feb. 1943, in author's file.

60. Chaney, *Good Old Days*, 11. Company B earned more Purple Heart medals on 30 January 1943 than any other time on Guadalcanal.

61. Ibid. The Bonegi River basin was the last Japanese Naval Headquarters station and also the location of the 67th Line of Communication Hospital and the Katteril Medical Unit.

62. McLeod, *Always Ready*, 108.

63. Chaney, "Ah! Yes We Remembered!," 27.

64. Lt. Col. Marvin V. Ayers, USA (Ret.), to author, 7 Jan. 1992.

65. Charles Core diary, 9 Feb. 1943; Charles Core, conversation with author, Carlsbad, Calif., 15 Jan. 1999.

Chapter 16

1. The plan was to retain rudiments in key sectors, such as the 958th Air Group at Rekata, Santa Isabel Island, plus elements of the Kure 7th SNLF, the Sasebo 6th SNLF, and the 6th and 17th Air Defense Units. (Later, they would move to the Bougainville area and the New Georgia Islands.) The 12th Air Defense Unit was stationed on Rekata after 28 April 1943. The Japanese Navy moved a small segment of the Kure 7th SNLF and the 20th Air Defense Unit to Choiseul Island. Information on Army Order No. 733 courtesy of Capt. Kawaro Teruaki (Ret.), JMDF, from Defense Research Office, War History Division, Tokyo, Hara correspondence.

2. David Tribe, Hamilton, NZ, to the author, 12 Aug. 1998.

3. Kaneda, "Memoirs."

4. Statements by Colonel Imoto and General Hyakutake, from Capt. Teruaki Kawano (Ret.), former head of the History Division, Japanese Maritime Defense Force, Tokyo, to author.

 Although the general Order to Evacuate was issued by the 38th Infantry Division on 5 February 1943, the acting commanding officer of the 38th Transport Regiment, Capt. Gunji Tokunaga, did not pass the evacuation order to his subordinates, but told them they were leaving for the final battle at the Bonegi River.

5. Kaneda, "Memoirs."

6. Yokoyama, "POW Interrogation Report."

7. On 1 October 1943 Rear Admiral Tanaka became commander of the 13th Base Force at Rangoon, Burma.

8. Eighth Fleet, Outer South Seas Force Signal, Radio Operations Order No. 80, dated January 1943.

9. The *Kagero* was part of Destroyer Division 15, which in company with five other destroyer divisions had transported the first army troops to Guadalcanal. Ldg. SM Ichiro Kunisada of the *Kagero* reported that the last phase of the evacuation "went like clockwork."

10. Japan, *Senshi Sōsho*, Vol. 28, Pt. 2, *Guadalcanal–Buna Operations*, 565.

11. George, *Shots Fired in Anger*, 148.

12. Muehrcke, *Orchids in the Mud*, 180.

13. Conversation with K. R. H. Davidson (former lieutenant with MTB Squadron 9), Chicago, Ill., 20 Nov. 1987. All PT-boat records were lost in June 1943 when a 500-pound bomb destroyed the MTB squadron office.

14. The other known survivors of Lieutenant Tani's company were Sgt. Royuichi Murano, Cpls. Ichirou Nemoto and Horju Okabe, and Pvts. Motomi Nakazaki, Kaju Takahashi, Kioshi Tanaka, and Takeo Watanabe.

15. Details on the Ke-Go Operation were drawn from Japan, *Senshi Sōsho,* Vol. 28, Pt. 2, *Guadalcanal–Buna Operations,* 454–91. Akio Tani, letter # 212 to author, 19 Jan. 1990.

16. McLeod, *Always Ready,* 120.

17. Ohtomo Gentaro, Kai, Hokkaido, Japan, to the author, 7 July 1996.

18. The Kitano Battalion was more like a platoon or small company, formed in October 1942 from various remnants of the Ichiki Detachment; it performed services of engineering and unloading.

19. Survivors from the 84th Guard Unit included Lt. Akira Tanabe (commander), Lt. (jg) Hiroaki Imamoto (MC), Ens. Mitsuzo Kaneko, WO Hideo Kageta, WO Noboru Takeuchi, WO Zenichi Maeno, and WO Rinjiro Yamashita.

20. Sub/Lt. A. M. "Andy" Andresen, RANVR, made a trip from Guadalcanal to the Russell Islands with Lieutenant Campbell and F/Lt. R. A. Robinson, RAAF, on 29 January. En route the party was chased back from Savo by enemy aircraft. When Andresen, the group's radio specialist (station CAM), finally reached Eaua, across the bay from the former Japanese outpost at Lingatu, he looked around. Natives had reported that three thousand Japanese were on the island and that one thousand more had joined them at Bayce. The number of evacuees could range from two thousand to four thousand, depending how the natives calculated. Their figures were always unreliable; three hundred could be three thousand. Andresen files, U.S. Navy Historical Center, Washington Navy Yard, Washington, D.C.

21. Rekata Bay was occupied 8 September 1942.

22. Nakano, "Poignant Remembrance."

Appendix 2

1. Also identified as the RXB Landing Force. Note that names and spellings presented in Appendix 2 are taken from captured Japanese documents and may not represent current usage.

2. One hundred men of the 85th Communication Unit were on the *Matsumoto Maru,* along with five hundred laborers; fifty men of the 85th Base Unit were on the *Kinai Maru* with five hundred IJN laborers. All arrived on 6 July 1942.

3. The remnants of the 81st Guard Unit departed RXN (Guadalcanal) for Rabaul, New Britain Island, on 2 August 1942 leaving the Nakumara platoon on Guadalcanal under the administrative control of the 84th Guard Unit.

4. Formed from elements of the Kure 3rd SNLF and one platoon of the 81st Guard Unit. Lt. Akira Tanabe was transferred from Rabaul to command the unit.

5. The number "65 *ki*" indicates the officer graduating class of the Japanese Naval Academy (see also "48 *ki*" and "66 *ki*").

6. WO Katsuzo Fukimoto's 1st, 2nd, and 3rd Squads were on Guadalcanal. He remained on Tulagi while his 4th and 5th Squads were on guard duty on East Cape, Florida Island.

7. WO Noboru Takeuchi took command of WO Katsuzo Fukimoto's three squads on Guadalcanal. Fukimoto was on Tulagi on 7 August 1942.

8. Organized 21 June 1942; the bulk of the 14th Construction Unit was at Rabaul, New Britain Island, staging for the Buna campaign.

9. Activated 1 July 1942 from elements of the 3rd Company, Kure 3rd SNLF.

10. WO Katsuzo Fukimoto remained on Tulagi with the 4th Squad.

11. On 1 May 1942 the 7th Construction Unit was transferred to the jurisdiction of the 4th Naval Civil Engineering Department (Fourth Fleet). The 7th CU arrived on RXB (Tulagi Island) on 3 May with the invasion forces. The unit had constructed the air base at Rabaul, New Britain Island, and at Florida and Gavutu Islands. The unit is believed to have returned to Rabaul before 1 August 1942.

12. Eleven men from the Hama Air Unit (gas crew) were on Gavutu on 7 August 1942.

13. All posts were equipped with short-wave portable transceiver apparatus and transmitters. See 81st Guard Unit, "War Diary," 28 June–30 July 1942; Endo, "81st Garrison War Diary," copy in author's file.

14. The Cape Horn lookout post was located at the height of a 693-foot hill.

15. The East Observation Post was one mile west of Cape Taivu at the eastern part of Tasimboko Bay.

16. The West Observation Post was on a 1,177-foot hill at the northern foot of Cape Esperance.

17. The Cape Hunter lookout post was halfway up the mountain at a 1,577-foot elevation.

Glossary

Definitions are followed by country of origin when necessary for clarity.

A/1/2; 3/132	System for identifying U.S. Marine Corps and U.S. Army units: here, Company A, 1st Battalion, 2nd Marine Regiment; 3rd Battalion, 132nd Infantry Regiment
1st Marine Division	As organized for the Guadalcanal campaign, the 1st Marine Division was composed of three infantry regiments (1st Marines, 5th Marines, and 7th Marines), each with three battalions, and one artillery regiment (11th Marines) with five battalions
2nd Marine Division	Attached to the 1st Marine Division for the Guadalcanal campaign, the 2nd Marine Division was composed of three infantry regiments (2nd Marines, 6th Marines, and 8th Marines) and one artillery regiment (10th Marines), each with three battalions
II/29i	Abbreviated numbering system for Imperial Japanese Army battalions and regiments: here, 2nd Battalion, 29th Infantry Regiment
AA	Antiaircraft
AACS	Army Airways Communication System
AAF	Army Air Forces (USAAF). Before May 1941, Army Air Corps
ACM	Air Chief Marshal
ACIDITY	U.S. code name for Gavutu Island
ACORN	U.S. Navy airfield assembly unit designed to construct and operate a land and seaplane base and facilities for operations: Aviation, Construction, Ordnance, Repair, Navy
AD	Destroyer tender (U.S.)
ADC	Assistant Division Commander (U.S.)
Adm.	Admiral
AEA	Air Efficiency Award (GB)
AF	Store ship (U.S.)
AH	Hospital ship (U.S.)
AIF	Australian Imperial Forces

Airacobra	Bell P-39 single-engine fighter plane; see also P-39, P-400 (U.S.)
AK	Cargo ship (U.S.)
AKA	Attack cargo ship (U.S.)
AM1c	Aviation Metalsmith 1st Class (U.S.)
Americal Division	New U.S. Army division formed in May 1942 in response to the Pearl Harbor attack; composed of the 132nd Infantry Regiment of the Illinois National Guard, the 164th Infantry Regiment of the North Dakota National Guard, and the 182nd Infantry Regiment of the Massachusetts National Guard; named for a combination of "America" and "New Caledonia"
Amtrac	Amphibian tractor (U.S.)
ANGAU	Australian–New Guinea Administrative Unit
AO	Oiler; fuel-oil tanker (U.S.)
AOB	Advanced operational base (Aus.)
Aoba	Name of detachment commanded by Col. Naomasa Nakaguma, 4th Infantry Regiment; *Aoba Butai*
AP	Transport (U.S.)
APA	Attack transport; configured for carrying LCVPs and LCMs (U.S.)
APD	High-speed transport.; flush-deck destroyers ("four-stackers") modified for carrying troops. (U.S.)
APHE	Antipersonnel high-explosive; armor-piercing high-explosive
APRICOT	U.S. code name for Ndeni Island, Santa Cruz Islands
ARM2c	Aviation Radio-Man 2nd Class
ARS	Salvage ship (Jap.)
AT	Antitank
ATF	Army task force (U.S.)
AUS	Australia
AV	Large seaplane tender (U.S.)
AVD	Seaplane tender; AVDs were converted flush-deck destroyers ("four-stackers") (U.S.)
AVP	Small seaplane tender (U.S.)
Avenger	Grumman TBF single-engine torpedo bomber; see also TBF (U.S.)
Avgas	Aviation gasoline
AVP	Small seaplane tender (U.S.)
B-17	Boeing four-engine heavy bomber; the Flying Fortress (U.S.)
B-26	Martin two-engine medium bomber; see also Marauder (U.S.)

Banzai	Japanese war cry
BAR	Browning automatic rifle (U.S.)
Battalion	In U.S. Marine Corps, a unit comprising 750 men under the command of a major or lieutenant colonel
BB	Battleship (U.S.)
BBC	British Broadcasting Corporation
BEACH BLUE	Landing site on western side of Tulagi
BEACH RED	Shoreline site of the Allied Guadalcanal landings; some 6,000 yards east of Lunga Point
Bees	See Seabees
BELMONT	Special U.S. code name for 1st Marine Raider Battalion
Betty	Allied code name for Mitsubishi G4M1, Navy Type 1 two-engine attack bomber
BG	Bomb group; bombardment group (U.S.)
BLEACHER	Code name for Tonga Island (U.S.)
Bluejackets	Navy enlisted men (U.S.)
BM2c	Boatswain Mate 2nd Class
Bn.	Battalion
Boondoggers	U.S. Marine boots
Brig. Gen.	Brigadier General
BSIP	British Solomon Islands Protectorate
BSIPDF	British Solomon Islands Protectorate Defense Force
Bug out	Slang: to leave
Butai	Unit or group; e.g., Tanaka Butai (Jap.)
BUTTON	U.S. code name for Espiritu Santo Island, New Hebrides Islands
C-47	Army Air Forces version of Douglas DC-3 two-engine transport plane; called the Flying Boxcar; see also R4D; Skytrain (U.S.)
C rations	Canned foods for consumption while in the field (U.S.)
CA	Heavy cruiser (U.S.)
CACTUS	U.S. code name for Guadalcanal Island
Cactus Air Force	Hodgepodge of U.S. Army, Navy, and Marine Corps aviation units that defended U.S. forces in the Guadalcanal campaign
CAM Division	Composite U.S. Army–Marine Division
Capt.	Captain
CarDiv	Carrier division (U.S., Jap.)
Cat	See Catalina

Catalina	Consolidated-Vultee twin-engine flying boat; also called Cat or Catboat; see also PBY (U.S., Aus.)
Catboat	See Catalina
CB	Construction battalion; see also Bees; NCB; Seabees (U.S.)
CBE	Commander of the Order of the British Empire (GB)
Cdr.	Commander
CG	Commanding General
Chutes	Nickname for personnel of the 1st Parachute Battalion
CINCPAC	Commander in Chief, United States Pacific Fleet
CINCPOA	Commander in Chief, Pacific Ocean Area
CINCSWPA	Supreme Commander [Commander in Chief], Southwest Pacific Area (Allied Forces)
CL	Light cruiser (U.S.)
CM	Minelayer (U.S.)
CMG	Commander of the Order of St. Michael and St. George (GB)
CMM	Chief Machinist Mate (U.S.)
CNO	Chief of Naval Operations (U.S.)
CO	Commanding Officer
Coastwatchers	Civilian observation network established in 1922 by the Royal Australian Navy throughout New Guinea and the Solomon Islands; activated after the onset of World War II, in 1941 it numbered about 1,000 men, with some 100 stations linked by radio
Col.	Colonel
COMAIRSOLS	Commander Air Solomons (U.S.)
COMAIRSOPAC	Commander, Aircraft, South Pacific Force (U.S.)
COMAMPHIBFORSOPAC	Commander, Amphibious Force, South Pacific Force (U.S.)
COMINCH	Commander in Chief, United States Fleet
Company	In U.S. Marine Corps, a unit of approximately 250 men under the command of a captain; companies were composed of varying numbers of platoons and squads
COMSOPAC	Commander, South Pacific Area and South Pacific Force (U.S.)
COMTASKFORCE	Commander, Task Force (U.S.)
CP	Command post
CPA	Central Pacific Area (U.S.)
CPhM	Chief Pharmacist Mate (U.S.)

Cpl.	Corporal
CPO	Chief Petty Officer
Crash boat	Generally a small craft (some up to 100 feet) used to rescue aircraft personnel
CruDiv	Cruiser division (U.S., Jap.)
CU	Construction unit; also called Encampment Corps, *Setsueitai* (Jap.)
CUB	Combined use base: a U.S. Navy advanced base unit consisting of all the personnel and materiel necessary for the establishment of a medium-sized advanced fuel and supply base
CV	Aircraft carrier (U.S.)
CW	Continuous wave: radio code transmission (U.S.)
CWO	Chief Warrant Officer (U.S.)
CYANIDE	U.S. code name for Santa Cruz Islands
D – 1	D minus 1: in U.S. military terminology, the day before D-day (the beginning of an attack); the Japanese called this "X-day"
D + 1	D plus 1: in U.S. military terminology, the day after D-day
D-2	The intelligence officer or section of a U.S. Marine Corps division: "D" was a generic label for staff sections of a division; similarly, "R" was used in regiments, "S" in staff offices, "Bn" in battalions
Dai	Hill (Jap.)
Daihatsu	Landing barge; 49 feet long, 6½ feet high (Jap.)
DAN	Code letters for 10th Independent Mountain Artillery Regiment (Jap.)
Dauntless	Douglas SBD single-engine scout-bomber; see also SBD (U.S.)
DD	Destroyer (U.S.)
D-day	In U.S. military terminology, the day set for the beginning of a planned attack; the Japanese called this Y-Day. In *Hell's Islands*, D-day refers to 7 August 1942, the date of the Allied invasion of Guadalcanal and its environs; also called Dog-day. See also Y-day
DesRon	Destroyer squadron (U.S., Jap.)
Devastator	Douglas TBD single-engine torpedo bomber; see also TBD (U.S.)
Devil boat	Nickname for motor torpedo boat; see MTB; PT; also called Mike Tare, Peter Tare
DFC	Distinguished Flying Cross (GB, U.S.)
DFM	Distinguished Flying Medal (GB)

Digger	Australian slang for a soldier in the AIF
Division	In U.S. Marine Corps, a field-size unit of 15,000 men under the command of a major general or brigadier general
DL	Deputy Lieutenant (GB)
DM	Destroyer-minelayer
DMS	Destroyer-minesweeper
DO	District Officer, an administrative position in British and Australian overseas territories
Doggies	Nickname for U.S. Army troops; see also GI
DSC	Distinguished Service Cross (GB)
DSIO	Deputy Supervising Intelligence Officer (Aus.)
ECSTASY	U.S. code name for Malaita Island
Emily	Allied code name for Kawanishi H8K, Navy Type 2 four-engine flying boat; see also Kawanishi
Empire	Short S23 C-class four-engine flying boat (GB, Aus.)
Eng.	Engineer (U.S.)
Ens.	Ensign (U.S., Jap.)
EO	Engineering Officer (U.S.)
F4F	Grumman Wildcat single-engine fighter plane; see also Wildcat (U.S.)
FEAF	Far East Air Force (USAAF)
1st Lt.	First Lieutenant
1st Sgt.	First Sergeant
F/Lt.	Flying Lieutenant (RAAF)
Flying Boxcar	Nickname for Douglas C-47 two-engine transport plane; see C-47, R4D, and Skytrain (U.S.)
Flying Fortress	Boeing B-17 four-engine heavy bomber (U.S.)
F/O	Flying Officer (Aus., GB)
Foot loggers	Slang for U.S. Marine Corps infantrymen; also called "loggers"
FS	The Japanese plan for the occupation of New Caledonia and other territories in order to isolate Australia from the United States and pressure it to surrender; initials are thought to be taken from "F" of Fiji and "S" of Samoan Islands
F/Sgt.	Flying Sergeant (RNZAF)
FU Operation	Japanese plan to capture Fiji, New Caledonia, and Samoa
FULCRUM	U.S. code name for Auckland, NZ
Fu Tō	Abbreviation for Florida Island (Jap.)

G-2	Intelligence Officer, Headquarters
Gadarukanaru	Guadalcanal Island; abbreviated as *Ga-Tō* (Jap.)
Gateway	U.S. Marine nickname for Henderson Field
Ga Tō	Abbreviation for Guadalcanal Island (Jap.)
Ga Tō sickness	Illness commonplace on Guadalcanal: fatal malnutrition and malaria (Jap.); see also Guadalcanal sickness
GB	Great Britain
G/Capt.	Group Captain (Aus., GB)
GCMG	Knight Grand Cross of St. Michael and St. George (GB)
Gen.	General
GI	Nickname for U.S. Army enlisted soldier (a sarcastic abbreviation for "government issue"); see also Doggies
Gifu	Japanese strongpoint adjacent to Mount Austen on Guadalcanal, occupied and defended by troops that came from Gifu, a region in Japan
Go	Unit of measurement; one *go* is equivalent to 0.318 pint (Jap.)
GO	Code name for Japanese Eighth Area Army
GMT	Greenwich Mean Time
GU	Guard Unit (Jap.); see Guard Unit, see *Keibitai*
Guadalcanal sickness	Illness commonplace on Guadalcanal: Malaria (U.S.); fatal malnutrition and malaria (Japan); see also *Ga Tō* sickness
Guard Unit	Japanese security unit; see also GU, *Keibita*
Gunji-Gokuhi	Top Secret (Jap.)
Gyrene	Nickname for a U.S. Marine
H	The hour proscribed for the beginning of a mission (H + 4 = designated time plus four hours) (U.S.)
HA1c	Hospital Apprentice 1st Class (U.S.)
Half-shelter	Small two-sided, V-shaped tent; similar to Pup tent (U.S.)
Heichō	Japanese for Leading Private or Lance Corporal
Higgins boat	Landing craft, vehicle and personnel, manufactured by Higgins Industries (U.S.); also called H-boat, Papa boat, Peter boat; see LCVP
HMAS	His Majesty's Australian Ship (Aus.)
HMSO	His Majesty's Stationery Office (Aus.)
Hudson	A-28/A-29 Lockheed-Vega attack cargo transport, twin-engine medium bomber, or reconnaissance aircraft
HYO	Japanese 124th Infantry Regiment outpost; means "leopard"

HYPO	U.S. code name for Navy Combat Intelligence Center, Pearl Harbor, Hawaii
IGHQ	Imperial General Headquarters, Tokyo
I-	Japanese submarine designation; e.g., *I-15, I-31*
ID	Identification
IGHQ	Imperial General Headquarters
IJA	Imperial Japanese Army
IJN	Imperial Japanese Navy
IJNAF	Imperial Japanese Naval Air Force
IMAR	Independent Mountain Artillery Regiment
ITMB	Independent Trench Mortar Battalion
Ittōhei	Japanese for Private 1st Class (PFC)
Jacob's ladder	A rope ladder used on ships and boats
JCS	Joint Chiefs of Staff (U.S.)
JLMG	Johnson light machine gun—the "Johnny Gun"
JMDF	Japanese Maritime Defense Force
Jōtōhei	Superior Private (Sup. Pvt.) (Jap.)
JST	Japan Standard Time (JST = GMT + 9 hours)
Kawanishi	H8K, Japanese Navy Type 2 four-engine flying boat, Allied code name Emily; H6K4, Navy Type 97 four-engine flying boat, Allied code name Mavis; see also Emily, Mavis
KCMG	Knight Commander of St. Michael and St. George (GB)
Ke-Go	Shortened form of *Ke-Go Sakusen* (*Ke-Go* Operation), the plan for evacuating the Japanese troops from Guadalcanal
Keibitai	Guard unit (Jap.)
KIA	Killed in action
Kingfisher	Vought-Sikorsky OS2U, single-engine U.S. Navy scout-observation seaplane; see also OS2U
Ko	Japanese command post
Kori Mura	Japanese name for Koli Village
Kori Saki	Japanese name for Koli Point
Kosokuka	Japanese landing craft with a gasoline-powered airplane-type engine
Kuma	Japanese code word for 7th Infantry Division; means "bear"
Kure 3rd SNLF	The Kure 3rd Special Naval Landing Force (*Kure Dai 3 Kaigun Tokubetsu Rikusentai*); see Special Naval Landing Force; see also SNLF and *Tokubetsu Rikusentai*

LAC	Leading Aircraftman (Aus.)
LCM	Landing craft, mechanized (U.S.); also called Mike boat.
LCP	Landing craft, personnel (U.S.)
LCpl.	Lance Corporal (U.S.); see also *Heichō* (Jap.)
LCT	Landing craft, tank (U.S.)
Ldg. Pvt.	Leading Private; see also *Heichō* (Jap.)
Ldg. SM	Leading Seaman (Jap.)
Leatherneck	Slang for a U.S. Marine
LION	U.S. Navy specialized, large, advanced base unit
LMG	Light machine gun (U.S.)
LONGBOW	U.S. code name for Wellington, NZ
Lt.	Lieutenant
Lt. Col.	Lieutenant Colonel
Lt. Cdr.	Lieutenant Commander
Lt. Gen.	Lieutenant General
Lt. (jg)	Lieutenant (junior grade)
LVT	Landing vehicle, tracked (amtrac) (U.S.)
M3	The Stuart light tank with three .30-caliber (7.62-mm) Browning machine guns; traveled at approximately 36 mph
MAG	Marine Air Group (U.S.)
MAGIC	U.S. code name for intelligence obtained from breaking Japanese coded messages called PURPLE
Maj.	Major
Maj. Gen.	Major General
Marauder	Martin B-26 two-engine medium bomber; see also B-26 (U.S.)
Ma Tō	Abbreviation for Malaita Island (Japan)
Mavis	Allied code name for Kawanishi H6K4, Navy Type 97 four-engine flying boat; see also Kawanishi (Jap.)
MAW	Marine Air Wing (U.S.)
MBE	Member of the Order of the British Empire (GB)
MC	Military Cross (GB); medical corps
MCPO	Master Chief Petty Officer (Jap.)
MDB	Marine Defense Battalion (U.S.)
MG	Machine gun; machine gunner (U.S.)
MIA	Missing in action

MLR	Main line of resistance
MM	Military Medal (Aus.)
MO	The Japanese plan for the attack on and occupation of Port Moresby
MP	Military Police (U.S.)
MSgt.	Master Sergeant (U.S.)
MTB	Motor torpedo boat; see also Devil boat, PT; also called Mike Tare, Peter Tare (U.S.)
Mukade Gata	Japanese for "Centipede Hill," site of the Battle of the Ridge—Bloody Ridge; also called "Edson's Ridge"
MV	Motor vessel
NAPıc	Naval Air Pilot 1st Class (Jap.)
NCB	Naval Construction Battalion; see also Bees, CB, Seabees (U.S.).
NCO	Noncommissioned officer
NGK	U.S. Navy radio station land-base call signal for Guadalcanal
NGLO	Naval Gunfire Liaison Officer (Aus.)
NLF	Northern Landing Force (U.S.)
NLO	Naval Liaison Officer (Aus.)
NOB	Naval Operating Base (U.S.)
NPA	North Pacific Area (U.S.)
NUMA	Code name for Japanese 38th Infantry Division
NZEF	New Zealand Expeditionary Force
OIC	Officer in charge
Oki	Code name of Japanese Seventeenth Army
OP	Observation post
ORANGE airfield	U.S. code name for the Guadalcanal airstrip before it was renamed Henderson Field (ORANGE was the name for the prewar plan of operations for war with Japan)
OS2U	Vought-Sikorsky single-engine Navy scout-observation seaplane; see Kingfisher (U.S.)
P-39	Bell Airacobra single-engine fighter plane; see also Airacobra, P-400 (U.S.)
P-400	Export version of P-39; see P-39; see also Airacobra (U.S.)
Paramarine	Member of specialized Marine Corps units skilled in parachute-drop invasion that saw service from 1940 to 1944
PBY	Consolidated-Vultee twin-engine Navy patrol bomber; see Catalina (U.S.)

P.E.	Professional Engineer
PESTILENCE	The general operational plan for the seizure and occupation of the New Britain–New Ireland–New Guinea area, including the capture of Rabaul (U.S.)
PFC	Private 1st Class (U.S., Jap.); see *Ittōhei* (Jap.)
PhM	Pharmacist Mate (U.S.)
Plan Q	The landing on Guadalcanal's BEACH RED (U.S.)
Plan S	The landing on BEACH RED and the subsequent move inland (U.S.)
Plan T	The operational concept for the invasion of Tulagi (code name RINGBOLT) (U.S.)
Plat. Sgt.	Platoon Sergeant (U.S.)
PO	Petty Officer
P/O	Pilot Officer (Aus., GB)
PO1c	Petty Officer 1st Class; PO2c, PO3c (U.S., Jap.)
POA	Pacific Ocean area (U.S.)
POW	Prisoner of war
PT	U.S. Navy hull nomenclature, with numbering, for motor torpedo boat (e.g., PT-*59*); see also MTB, Devil boat; also called Mike Tare, Peter Tare
Pvt.	Private
PX	Post Exchange
QSM	Queen's Service Medal
R-2	Regimental intelligence section; intelligence officer (U.S.)
R-3	Regiment operations section; operations officer (U.S.)
R-4	Regiment supply section; supply officer (U.S.)
R4D	U.S. Navy version of Douglas DC-3 two-engine transport plane, fitted with oversized cargo doors and reinforced landing gear. The R4D-1s, R4D-5s, R4D-6s, and R4D-7s (Skytrains) were primarily cargo carriers; the R4D-2s, R4D-3s, and R4D-4s (Skytroopers) were primarily passenger aircraft. See Skytrain; see also C-47
RAAF	Royal Australian Air Force
RAF	Royal Air Force
Raiders	Four elite U.S. Marine Corps World War II commando-type battalions: 1st Raider Battalion, 2nd, 3rd, 4th; existed only two years as a special USMC organization
RAN	Royal Australian Navy
RANVR	Royal Australian Naval Volunteer Reserve

Rear Adm.	Rear Admiral
Recon	Reconnaissance
Rev.	Reverend
Rikusentai	Infantry of the Imperial Japanese Navy
RINGBOLT	Code name for the invasion of Tulagi (U.S.)
RM	Radio-man
RN	Royal Navy (GB)
RNZAF	Royal New Zealand Air Force
RNZN	Royal New Zealand Navy
RT1c	Radio Technician 1st Class (U.S.)
Rufe	Allied code name for Nakajima A6M2-N, Navy Type 2 floatplane fighter (Jap.)
RUNABOUT	U.S. code name for Florida Island
RWH	Japanese code for Shortland Bay, Faisi, Shortland Islands
RWP	Japanese code for Bougainville Island
RX	Japanese code for Solomon Islands
RXB	Japanese code for Tulagi Island
RXC	Japanese code for Buka
RXI	Japanese code for the Guadalcanal airfield (later Henderson Field)
RXL	Japanese code for Salamaua
RXM	Japanese code for Lae
RXN	Japanese code for Guadalcanal Island
S, S1c, S2c	Seaman, Seaman 1st Class, 2nd Class (U.S.)
S-2	Staff intelligence officer (U.S.)
S-3	Staff operations officer (U.S.)
S	Submarine (U.S.): note also: *Amberjack* (SS 219) submarine
SA	Seaman apprentice (Jap..)
Sake	Rice-fermented alcoholic beverage (Jap.)
Sapper	Military engineer (GB)
SB2C	Curtiss Helldiver dive-bomber (U.S.)
SBD	Douglas Dauntless single-engine scout bomber (U.S.). See also Dauntless
SCAT	South Pacific Combat Air Transport Command, USMC
Seabees	Personnel of U.S. Navy construction battalions (Cbs); see also Bees, CB, NCB

Seagull	Supermarine single-engine amphibian (Aus., GB); Curtiss SOC-4 single-engine U.S. Navy scout-observation biplane; see also SOC-4
2nd Lt.	Second Lieutenant
SEPA	Southeast Pacific Area (U.S.)
Setsueitai	Construction unit; see also *CU* (Jap.)
Sgt.	Sergeant
Shaku	Unit of measurement; one *shaku* is equivalent to approximately 0.030 pint (Jap.)
Shiba	Lion. Japanese code name for a mountain on Guadalcanal
Shitai	Detachment; e.g., Kawaguchi Shitai (Jap.)
Skytrain	U.S. Navy R4D-1, R4D-5, R4D-6, or R4D-7 two-engine transport plane; see also R4D, C-47, Flying Boxcar
Slot, The	Allied name for the body of deep water running northwest to southeast through the main islands of the Solomons group, bordered on the north by Choiseul, Santa Isabel, and Malaita and on the south by Vella Lavella, New Georgia, Guadalcanal, and San Cristobal
SM	Seaman (Jap.); also Society of Mary
SME	Seaman Engineer (Jap.)
SM1c	Seaman 1st Class (Jap.)
SN	Early Japanese code for the operational plan to establish air facilities in the New Guinea area and the Solomon Islands
SNLF	Special Naval Landing Force; a regimental-sized unit of Japanese naval infantry comprising both deck and engineering personnel; see also *Tokubetsu Rikusentai*
SOC-4	Curtiss single-engine Navy scout-observation biplane; see Seagull (U.S.)
SOPAC	South Pacific Area, South Pacific Force (U.S.)
SPA	South Pacific Area (U.S.)
SPD	Douglass Dauntless dive-bomber (U.S.)
Sp. Lt. (jg)	Special Lieutenant (junior grade). Officers of this rank had completed a special course, as opposed to graduating from the Naval Academy; they had joined the Imperial Japanese Navy when young and needed a long year of service to qualify for a commission. (Jap.)
SR	Seaman recruit (also called Seaman third class (S3c) (Jap.)
SS	Merchant steamship; Silver Star; submarine, as in *Amberjack* (SS 219) (U.S.)
SSgt.	Staff Sergeant (U.S.)

Sub/Lt.	Sub-Lieutenant (RAN)
Sunderland	Short four-engine flying boat (GB)
Sup. Pvt.	Superior Private; *Jōtōhei* (Jap.)
SWPA	Southwest Pacific Area (U.S.)
T/5	Technician 5th Grade (U.S.)
Tai	Company (Jap.)
TBD	Douglas Devastator single-engine torpedo bomber; see also Devastator (U.S.)
TBF	Grumman Avenger single-engine torpedo bomber; see also Avenger (U.S.)
TBX	A type of radio used by the U.S. forces contained in four canvas cases with pack straps; it included a transceiver set, a battery box, a generator, and an antenna.
TF	Task Force (U.S.)
Tokubetsu Rikusentai	Special Naval Landing Force; see also SNLF (Jap.)
Tokyo Express	U.S. nickname for the massive, largely unopposed deliveries of troops to Guadalcanal by Japanese ships
TORO	Code name for Japanese outpost near Henderson Field, Guadalcanal; means "tiger"
TSC	Collins transceiver radio (U.S.)
TSgt.	Technician Sergeant (U.S.)
Tsuragi	Japanese name for Tulagi
ULTRA	U.S. cryptographic system first developed to intercept and decode highest level German codes and ciphers; later used for high-level Japanese codes
USA	United States Army
USAAF	U.S. Army Air Forces; before May 1941, Army Air Corps
USCG	U.S. Coast Guard; during World War II, the USCG was a component of the U.S. Navy
USFISPA	U.S. Army Forces in the South Pacific Area
USMC	U.S. Marine Corps; during World War II, the USMC was a component of the U.S. Navy
USMCR	U.S. Marine Corps Reserve
USN	U.S. Navy
USNR	U.S. Naval Reserve
Val	Allied code name for the Japanese Aichi D3A, Navy Type 99 carrier bomber
VCNO	Vice Chief of Naval Operations (U.S.)

VF	U.S. Navy fighting squadron
Vice Adm.	Vice Admiral (U.S.)
Vice AM	Vice Air Marshal (NZ)
VMF	U.S. Marine fighting squadron
VMJ	U.S. Marine utility squadron
VMO	U.S. Marine observation squadron
VP	U.S. Navy patrol squadron
VMSB	U.S. Marine scout bombing or dive-bombing squadron
VS	U.S. Navy scouting squadron
VT	U.S. Navy torpedo squadron
WATCHTOWER	The operational plan for the invasion of Guadalcanal–Tulagi
W/Cdr.	Wing Commander (Aus., GB)
WHITE POPPY	U.S. code name for Nouméa, New Caledonia; POPPY was code name for New Caledonia
WIA	Wounded in action
Wildcat	Grumman F4F single-engine fighter plane; see also F4F (U.S.)
Wirraway	Single-engine fighter plane (Aus.)
WO	Warrant officer
WP	White phosphorus
WPHC	Western Pacific High Commission (GB)
X-day	Japanese military equivalent of D – 1 (D minus 1); see D – 1, Y-day
XO	Executive Officer (U.S.)
Y-day	In Japanese military usage, the equivalent of D-day; see also D-day, X-day
YP	Yard craft, patrol; district patrol vessels, former California tuna fishing boats converted for naval service; also called Yippies (U.S.)
YU	Code letters for Japanese 2nd Infantry Division

Bibliography

PUBLISHED WORKS (ENGLISH)

Alexander, Joseph H. *Edson's Raiders: The 1st Marine Raider Battalion in World War II*. Annapolis: Naval Institute Press, 1999.

Americal Newsletter (Feb.–Mar. 2005): 23ff.

Arnold, Henry H. *Global Mission*. New York: Harper & Bros., 1949.

Ayling, Keith. *Semper Fidelis: The U.S. Marines in Action*. Boston: Houghton Mifflin, 1943.

Bennett, Judith A. *Wealth of the Solomons: A History of a Pacific Archipelago, 1800–1978*. Honolulu: University of Hawaii Press, 1987.

Blakeney, Jane. *Heroes, U.S. Marine Corps, 1861–1955*. Washington, D.C.: Guthrie Lithographic Co., 1957.

Blaknik, Ted. "Japanese Diary [of William Burke]," *Guadalcanal Echoes* (Mar. 1990): 19ff.

Blundon, J. Paul, ed. *Saga of the Sixth: A History of the Sixth U.S. Naval Construction Battalion, 1942–1945*. N.d., n.p., 1946.

Breuer, William. *Devil Boats: The PT War against Japan*. Novato, Calif.: Presidio Press, 1995.

British Solomon Islands Protectorate. Lands and Surveys Department. *The Solomon Islands Gazetteer: A List of Place Names in the British Solomon Islands Protectorate*. Honiara, Guadalcanal, Solomon Islands: Government Printing Office, 1969.

Buckley, K., and K. Klugman. *The History of Burns Philp: The Australian Company in the South Pacific*. N.p. [Sydney]: Burns, Philp & Co. Ltd., 1981.

———. *The Australian Presence in the Pacific: Burns Philp 1914–1946*. Sydney: George Allen & Unwin, 1983.

Bueschel, Richard M. *Japanese Code Names*. Vol. 1, no. 4, *World War II*. West Roxbury, Mass.: Aero Publishers, 1966.

Carbray, Col. Robert W. (Ret.). "Wright's Road & 'M' Co. 132nd Inf.," *Guadalcanal Echoes* (July 1987): 7ff.

Carr, Louis A. "Second Week of August 1942," *Guadalcanal Echoes* (May–June 1999): 18, 24.

Carter, Lloyd B. "All in a Day's Work," *Guadalcanal Echoes* (May–June 1987).

Chaney, W. M. *Good Old Days. Purple Hearts of B Company, 147th Infantry*. Indianapolis, Ind.: Veterans of the 147th Regiment, July 1991.

———. "Ah! Yes We Remembered!" *Indianapolis News*, 14 Aug. 1985, 27.

Chant, Christopher. *The Encyclopedia of Codenames of World War II*. London: Routledge & Kegan Paul, 1986.

Clarence, Margaret. *Yield Not to the Wind*. Sydney: Management Development Publishers Pty. Ltd., 1982.

Clemens, Martin. *Alone on Guadalcanal: A Coastwatcher's Story*. Annapolis: Naval Institute Press, 1998.

Cleveland, W. M., ed. *Grey Geese Calling: A History of the 11th Bombardment Group Heavy (H) in the Pacific, 1940–1945*. Askov, Minn.: American Publishing, 1981; Portsmouth, N.H.: W. M. Cleveland, 1992.

Craven, W. F., and J. L. Cate, eds. *The Army Air Forces in World War II*. Vol. 4, *The Pacific: Guadalcanal to Saipan, August 1942 to July 1944*. Chicago: University of Chicago Press, 1950; Washington, D.C.: Office of Air Force History, 1983.

Creed, Roscoe. *PBY: The Catalina Flying Boat*. Annapolis: Naval Institute Press, 1985.

Croizat, Victor J. *Across the Reef*. Quantico, Va.: Marine Corps Association, 1992.

Dalrymple-Hay, Ken. "Unhappy Story of Singapore in the Solomons," *Pacific Islands Monthly* 42(7) (May 1971): 53–55.

———. "Behind the Japanese Lines on Wartime Guadalcanal," *Pacific Islands Monthly* 42(8) (Aug. 1971): 71–73, 75, 77.

"Deaths of Islands People: Mrs. Florence Binskin," *Pacific Islands Monthly* 43(3) (Mar. 1972): 107.

"Dodging Japs in Solomon Jungles," *Pacific Islands Monthly* 13(8) (Mar. 1943): 28.

Dull, Paul S. *A Battle History of the Imperial Japanese Navy (1941–1945)*. Annapolis, Md.: Naval Institute Press, 1978.

Dyer, George C. Vice Adm. *The Amphibians Came to Conquer: The Story of Admiral Richard Kelly Turner*. Washington, D.C.: Government Printing Office, 1969.

Feldt, Eric A. *The Coast Watchers*. Melbourne: Geoffrey Cumberlege; Oxford University Press, 1946.

Ferguson, Robert L. *Guadalcanal—The Island of Fire: Reflections of the 347th Fighter Group*. Blue Ridge Summit, Pa.: TAB Books Inc., 1987.

Feuer, A. B., ed. *Coast Watching in the Solomon Islands: The Bougainville Reports, December 1941–July 1943*. New York: Praeger, 1992.

Fitch, Warren. "Securing Gavutu," *Guadalcanal Echoes* (May-June 1993): 11–12.

Frank, Richard B. *Guadalcanal*. New York: Random House, 1990.

Frei, Henry P. *Japan's Southward Advance and Australia: From the Sixteenth Century to World War II*. Melbourne: Melbourne University Press, 1991. See www.users.bigpond.com/

battleforaustralia/battaust/AustInvasion/Throttle_Australia.html.

George, John M. *Shots Fired in Anger.* 2nd ed. Washington, D.C.: National Rifle Association, 1981.

Gillison, Douglas, *Royal Australian Air Force 1939–1942. Australia in the War of 1939–45,* Series 3, *Air,* vol. 1. Canberra: Australian War Memorial, 1962.

Golden, Graeme A. *The Early European Settlers of the Solomon Islands.* Melbourne: Medlow Bath Books, 1993.

Graham, William F., CPhM, USNR. "Observations from a Combat Hospital Corpsman, World War II," in *Second Marine Division Association 1988 Reunion Annual Directory.* Grand Prairie, Tex.: Second Marine Division Association, 1988.

Great Britain. Colonial Office. *Among Those Present: The Official Story of the Pacific Islands at War.* Prepared by the Central Office of Information. London: His Majesty's Stationery Office (HMSO), 1946.

Guadalcanal Echoes (Jan. 1990): 13ff.

Guadalcanal, 50th Anniversary. Paducah, Ky.: Turner Publishing Company, 1992.

"Guadalcanal Fuel," *Guadalcanal Echoes* (Nov.–Dec. 1997): 4ff.

Hammel, Eric. *Guadalcanal: Starvation Island.* New York: Crown Publishers, Inc., 1987.

Handbook of the British Solomon Islands Protectorate. Suva: Government Printer, 1923.

Handbook of the British Solomon Islands Protectorate, with Returns up to 31st March, 1911. Tulagi: Published by Authority, 1911.

Haney, Ken. U.S. *Navy Medical Personnel in Marine and Raider Battalions in WWII.* Jackson, Tenn.: Privately published, 1990.

Hata, Ikuhiko, and Yasuho Izawa. *Japanese Naval Aces and Fighter Units in World War II.* Translated by Don Cyril Gorham. Annapolis: Naval Institute Press, 1989. [Originally published as *Nihon Kaigun Sentoki-tai.* Rev. ed., Tokyo: Kantosha Publishers, 1975.]

Hoffman, Jon T. "Guadalcanal, Chesty Puller's Defense of Henderson Field," *World War II* (Nov. 2002): 37–42.

———. *Once a Legend: "Red Mike" Edson of the Marine Raiders.* Novato, Calif.: Presidio Press, 1994.

———. *Silk Chutes and Hard Fighting: U.S. Marine Corps Parachute Units in World War II.* Washington, D.C.: History and Museums Division, Headquarters, U.S. Marine Corps, 1999.

Horton, D.C. *Fire Over the Islands: The Coast Watchers of the Solomons.* Sydney: Reed, 1970.

———. *The Happy Isles: A Diary of the Solomons.* London: Heinemann, 1965.

Howard, Clive, and Joe Whitley. *One Damned Island After Another.* Chapel Hill, N.C.: University of North Carolina Press, 1946.

Ingalls, Philip G. "First Marine on Guadalcanal?" *Guadalcanal Echoes* (Mar.–Apr. 1994): 11ff.

Jones, Arvil, and Lulu Jones. *Forgotten Warriors: Challenge at Guadalcanal.* Paducah, Ky.: Turner Publishing, 1997.

Kamei, Hiroshi. "Island of Homesickness," *Guadalcanal Echoes* (Apr.–June 1991): 17ff.

———. "Island of Homesickness," *Guadalcanal Echoes* (June–July 1992): 16ff.

Kennedy, Malcolm D. *The Problem with Japan.* London: Nisbet, 1935.

Ladd, Dean, *Faithful Warriors: Memories of World War II in the Pacific.* Spokane, Wash: Teen-Aid Inc., 1993.

Long, Gavin. *The Six Years War: A Concise History of Australia in the 1939–1945 War.* Canberra: Australian War Memorial and the Australian Government Publishing Service, 1973.

Lord, Walter. *Lonely Vigil: Coastwatchers of the Solomons.* New York: The Viking Press, 1977.

Lundstrom, John B. *The First Team and the Guadalcanal Campaign: Naval Fighter Combat from August to November 1942.* Annapolis: Naval Institute Press, 1994.

Luxton, C. T. J. *Isles of Solomon: A Tale of Missionary Adventure.* Auckland: Methodist Foreign Missionary Society of New Zealand, 1955.

MacCleary, Lt.(jg) E. E., USNR, Base Historian. *History of U.S. Naval Advanced Base Guadalcanal, 1942–1945.* Pts. 1 and 2. Lunga, Guadalcanal. British Solomon Islands: Base Printing Office, FPO 145, 1945.

Marion, Ore J. "My First Days," *Guadalcanal Echoes* (Aug.–Sept. 1996): 15ff.

Masters, Mike. *Once a Marine, Always a Marine.* Winston, Ore.: Privately published, 1988.

McLeod, Tom. *Always Ready: The Story of the United States 147th Infantry Regiment.* Texarkana, Tex.: Privately published, 1996.

McNab, Alexander. *We Were the First: The Unit History of No. 1 Independent Company.* Loftus, Aus.: Australian Military History Publications, 1998.

Merillat, Herbert C. *Guadalcanal Remembered.* New York: Dodd, Mead & Co., 1982.

———. *The Island: A History of the First Marine Division on Guadalcanal, August 7–December 9, 1942.* New York: Houghton Mifflin Co., 1944; Washington, D.C.: Zenger Publishing Co., Inc., 1979.

Military Affairs (Winter 1947): 211ff.

Miller, John Jr. *Guadalcanal: The First Offensive. The United States Army in World War II: The War in the Pacific.* Washington, D.C.: Government Printing Office, 1949; Washington, D.C.: Center for Military History, United States Army, 1989.

Morison, Samuel Eliot. *History of United States Naval Operations in World War II.* Vol. 5, *The Struggle for Guadalcanal, August 1942–February 1943.* Boston: Little, Brown & Co., 1948.

Morriss, Mack. *South Pacific Diary, 1942–1943*. Edited by Ronnie Day. Lexington, Ky.: University Press of Kentucky, 1996.

Muehrcke, Robert C., ed. *Orchids in the Mud: World War II in the Pacific—Pain, Boredom, Adventure*. Chicago: R. C. Muehrcke, 1985.

Nakano, Eihrchi. "Poignant Remembrance." *Guadalcanal Echoes* (Jan.–Feb. 1988): 18.1ff.

Peatross, Oscar F. *Bless 'em All: The Raider Marines of World War II*. Irvine, Calif.: Review Publications, 1995.

Piper, Robert K. "The Royal Australian Air Force at Guadalcanal," *Australian Defense Force Journal* 87 (Mar.-Apr. 1991): 27–34.

Poliny, Andy. "Colonel Ichiki's Last Stand," *Guadalcanal Echoes* (Apr. 1995): 8ff.

Priday, Lewis H. E. *The War from Coconut Square: The Story of the Defence of the Island Bases of the South Pacific*. Wellington, New Zealand: Reed, 1945.

"Rev. A. W. Silvester: Presentation of Medal of Merit," *Open Door* 29(4) (1950): 5.

Riddell, Jack. *RAAF Catalina Squadrons, First and Furthest*. Murwillumbah, NSW: Privately published, 1992.

Robson, R. W., ed. *Pacific Islands Yearbook*. 4th ed. Sydney: Pacific Publications, 1942.

Rosenquist, R. G., Col. Martin J. (Stormy) Sexton, USMC (Ret.), and Robert A. Buerlein. *Our Kind of War: Illustrated Saga of the U.S. Marine Raiders of World War II*. Richmond, Va.: American Historical Foundation, [1990].

Rothermel, James D. Jr. "The 14th NCB History of Guadalcanal," *Guadalcanal Echoes* (Feb.–Mar. 1999): 6, 27.

Rutter, Allen G. "Transpacific Crossing in the *Fauro Chief*," *Open Door* 20(4) (1942): 6–7.

Ryker, Ken. *The VS-55 Newsletter* [Benbrook, Tex.] (Jan. 2000): 1ff.

Shane, Ted. *Heroes of the Pacific*. New York: Julian Messner, 1944.

Smith, Larry, and Eddie Adams. *Beyond Glory: Medal of Honor Heroes in Their Own Words*. New York: W. W. Norton & Co., 2003.

Smith, Michael S. *Bloody Ridge: The Battle That Saved Guadalcanal*. Novato, Calif.: Presidio Press, 2000.

Soule, Karl Thayer. *Shooting the Pacific War*. Lexington: University Press of Kentucky, 2000.

Southerland, Lt. J. J. "One of the Many Personal Adventures in the Solomons," *U.S. Naval Institute Proceedings* (Apr. 1943): 539–47.

Stannard, Brig. Gen. John E., USA (Ret.). *The Battle of Coffin Corner and Other Comments Concerning the Guadalcanal Campaign*. Gallatine, Tenn.: Privately published, 1992.

Stanton, Shelby L. *World War II Order of Battle*. New York: Galahad Books, 1991.

Tamura, Maj. Masuro. "A Japanese Commander Tells His Story," *Guadalcanal Echoes* (Mar. 1992): 7, 13.

"The Raider Patch," *Guadalcanal Echoes* (Mar. 1983): 9ff.

Theresa, Sister Mary SM. "My Time on Guadalcanal," *Guadalcanal Echoes* (Oct. 1989).

"The Unsung Heroes of SCAT," *The Yellow Sheet*, 25 (Fall 1996): 1–3.

U.S. Department of the Army. Army Air Forces. *Pacific Counterblow: The 11th Bombardment Group and 67th Fighter Squadron in the Battle for Guadalcanal: An Interim Report.* Wings at War Series, no. 3. Washington, D.C.: Headquarters, Army Air Forces, 1945. Reprinted. Washington, D.C.: U.S. Government Printing Office, 1992.

U.S. Department of the Navy. *United States Naval Chronology: World War II.* Washington, D.C.: Naval Historical Center, March 1955.

Van Dam, Theo. *A Century of War Dates.* Anaheim, Calif.: Theo Van Dam, 1996.

Vandegrift, A. A. *Once a Marine: The Memoirs of General A. A. Vandegrift, United States Marine Corps.* As Told to Robert B. Asprey. New York: W. W. Norton & Co., 1964.

Van der Vat, Dan. *The Pacific Campaign: World War II, the U.S.–Japanese Naval War, 1941–1945.* New York: Simon & Schuster, 1991.

War Stories (Jan.–Mar. 1999).

Ware, Leonard. *The Landing in the Solomons, 7–8 August 1942.* Washington, D.C.: Naval Historical Center, 1994.

Western Pacific High Commission Gazette. 2 Jan. 1942; 2 Mar., 7 Sept., 19 Oct. 1943.

Wiens, Harry. *My Own Little Corner of the War, A Look Back . . . After 50 years to Guadalcanal.* Fargo, N.Dak.: Privately printed, 1993.

Wiggs, Audrey F., compiler. *Coral Sea Log.* Townsville, Aus.: Coral Sea Battle Association of Australia, 1992.

Willard, Warren Wyeth. *The Leathernecks Come Through.* 5th ed. New York: Fleming H. Revell, 1944.

Willoughby, Charles A., ed. *Reports of General MacArthur. Japanese Operations in the South Pacific Area.* Vol. 2, pt. 1; vol. 2, pt. 2. Prepared by His General Staff. Washington, D.C.: Government Printing Office, 1966.

Winton, John. *Ultra in the Pacific: How Breaking Japanese Codes and Cyphers Affected Naval Operations Against Japan.* Annapolis: Naval Institute Press, 1993.

"With Second Bn. Fifth Marines," *Guadalcanal Echoes* (Apr.-May 1995): 23–26.

Zimmerman, Maj. John L., USMCR. *The Guadalcanal Campaign.* Marine Corps Monographs. Washington, D.C.: Historical Division, Headquarters, U.S. Marine Corps, 1949.

PUBLISHED WORKS (JAPANESE)

Japan. Self-Defense Force. Defense Research Institute. Office of War History. *Senshi Sōsho. Minami Taiheiyo Rikugun Sakusen, 1, Poto Moresbi–Gatō Shoki Sakusen [War History Series.* Vol. 14, *South Pacific Army Operations.* Pt. 1, *Port Moresby–Guadalcanal, Early Operations].* Tokyo: Asagumo Shinbunsha, 1968.

———. Self-Defense Force. Defense Research Institute. Office of War History. *Senshi Sōsho. Minami Taiheiyo Rikugun Sakusen, 2, Gadarukanaru–Buna Sakusen [War History Series.* Vol. 28, *South Pacific Army Operations.* Pt. 2, *Guadalcanal–Buna Operations].* Tokyo: Asagumo Shinbunsha, 1969.

———. Self-Defense Force. Defense Research Institute. Office of War History. *Senshi Sōsho. Nantōhōmen Kaigun Sakusen, 1, Gatō Dakkai Sakusen Kaishimade [War History Series.* Vol. 49, *Southeast Area Naval Operations.* Pt. 1, *To the Beginning of Operations to Recapture Guadalcanal].* Tokyo: Asagumo Shinbunsha, 1971.

———. Self-Defense Force. Defense Research Institute. Office of War History. *Senshi Sōsho. Nantōhōmen Kaigun Sakusen, 2, Gatō Tesshumade [War History Series.* Vol. 83, *Southeast Area Naval Operations.* Pt. 2, *To the Withdrawal from Guadalcanal].* Tokyo: Asagumo Shinbunsha, 1975.

Kamei, Hiroshi. *Beigun ga Kirokushita Guadalcanal no Takakai [The War on Guadalcanal as Recorded by the U.S.].* Tokyo: Kojinsha, 1995.

Saiaku No Semba [The Worst Battlefield: Guadalcanal War History]. Pacific War Eye-Witness Series, Maru. Vol. 5, 54–71 (Yasuo Yamamiya); 72–100 (Hajime Yamamoto); 388–422 (Hisakichi Hara). Tokyo: Takagi Hajime, Shio Bookstore, 1987.

Sakurai, Jinsaku. *Jigoku karo no Seikan [Back Alive from Hell].* Tokyo: Mamenoki Kobo Co., 1995.

Sugawara, Susumu. *Ichiki Shitai Zenmetsu [The Annihilation of the Ichiki Detachment].* Minamu-ku, Saporo, Japan: Privately published, 1969; Tokyo: Privately Published, 1979.

Tsunomura, Masao. *Kaigun Shisetsukei Gijutsukan No Kiroku [Navy Engineer Facility Record].* Tokyo: Privately published, 1969.

UNPUBLISHED WORKS AND DOCUMENTS

Arakawa, PFC Takeshi. "POW Interrogation Report." 30 Jan. 1943. HQ XIV Corps, Cactuōs G-2 Section. Marine Corps Historical Center, Washington, D.C.

Bennett, Dallas R. "Forty-Seven Years Late." History of Headquarters Company, 2d Marines, at Tulagi and Guadalcanal. Manuscript, n.d. [Copy in author's file.]

Boardman, Capt. Eugene, USMC. "Japanese Operations at Guadalcanal." Undated handwritten manuscript, written at Guadalcanal. Boardman Papers. Marine Corps Historical Center, Washington, D.C.

Clemens, W. F. M. "District Officer's Diary, Guadalcanal, 1942." Original manuscript. Central Archives of Fiji, Suva, Fiji [1967].

"Coastwatcher Report [Bengough]." Post at Camp Astrolabe, 29 Aug. to 2 November 1942. Guadalcanal Files. Marine Corps Historical Center, Washington, D.C.

Combat Intelligence Center, South Pacific Force. Translations of Captured Japanese Documents. Items 203, 223, 245, 614, and 1231. Naval Historical Center, Washington, D.C.

"Combat Order #67." RG 127, Entry 39A, Box 41. Captured Japanese Documents. National Archives, Washington, D.C.

"Defense Order for the R [Rabaul] Area, 8th Base Force." RG 127, Entry 39A, Box 21, 370/23/22/4. Captured Japanese Documents. Guadalcanal Files. National Archives, Washington, D.C. [Translated copy in author's file.]

"Diary, 14 Nov. 1942." RG 127, Entry 39A, Box 15. Captured Japanese Documents. National Archives, Washington, D.C.

"Diary [Unknown writer]." RG 127, Entry 39A, Box 15. Captured Japanese Documents, National Archives, Washington, D.C.

Eighth Army Staff Radiogram #122, 29 Nov. 1942, Item #706. Naval Historical Center, Washington, D.C.

81st Guard Unit. "War Diary." RXI Defense Unit. Japan Defense Agency, Office of War History, Tokyo, Japan.

84th Guard Unit. "Diary." RG 127, Entry 39A, Box 17. Captured Japanese Documents, National Archives, Washington, D.C.

Endo, Lt. Yukio, IJN. "81st Garrison War Diary." Endo File. Military History Department, National Institute for Defense Studies, Tokyo, Japan.

"Field Order No. 1." 30 Dec. 1942. 132nd Infantry Regiment. History Department, U.S. Army War College, Carlisle Barracks, Pa.

5th Marine Regiment. "Record of Events." 26 June–9 Dec.1942. Document #10C, 19 Sept–9 Dec. 1942; Document #100, 25 Oct. 1942; 17 Feb. 1943. Marine Corps Historical Center, Washington, D.C.

1st Marine Division. "Final Report, Guadalcanal." Phase 4, Annex G. Marine Corps Historical Center, Washington, D.C.

1st Marine Division. "Operation Order No. 5 (revised)." CG1MarDiv, Annex G (Artillery), 4 Aug. 1942. Guadalcanal File. Marine Corps Historical Center, Washington, D.C.

1st Marine Raider Battalion. "1st Marine Raider Battalion in the Field." Report of Operations. 11 Oct. 1942. Marine Corps Historical Center, Washington, D.C.

"Fuku/Oka Operation Order Oka #96." Military Secret (Gongokuhi), 14 Aug. 1942. RG 127, Entry 39A, Box 17. Captured Japanese Documents. National Archives, Washington, D.C.

Fukuda, SM Shohei. "POW Interrogation Report." 3 Dec. 1942. POW Files. Marine Corps Historical Center, Washington, D.C.

Hikinune, Yokio. "Diary." RG 127, Entry 39A, Box 15. Captured Japanese Documents. National Archives, Washington, D.C.

Hirai, Tomisaburo. "Diary." RG 127, Entry 39A, Box 16. Captured Japanese Documents. National Archives, Washington, D.C.

Ichiji, Sup. Pvt. Yabuchi. "POW Interrogation Report." 26 Jan. 1943. HQ XIV Corps. POW Files. Marine Corps Historical Center, Washington, D.C.

Ikeya, PFC Masatoshi. "POW Interrogation Report." 28 Jan. 1943. 1st Battalion, 229th Infantry. POW Files. Marine Corps Historical Center, Washington, D.C.

"Intelligence Report." RG 127, Entry 39A, Box 15. Captured Japanese Documents. National Archives, Washington, D.C.

Iwamoto, Hiroshi. "Diary." RG 127, Entry 39A, Box 21. Captured Japanese Documents. National Archives, Washington, D.C.

Iwata, SM Masakane (serial no. K 3595). "POW Interrogation Report." Command Platoon, Yoshimoto Detachment, Kure 3rd SNLF. 14 and 21 Aug. 1942. POW File. Marine Corps Historical Center, Washington, D.C.

Iwata, Takeo. "Diary." RG 127, Entry 39A, Box 14. Captured Japanese Documents. National Archives, Washington, D.C.

"Japanese Order—Plans for Guadalcanal." August 1942. Translation by Akio Tani. Captured Japanese Documents, RG 127, Entry 39A, Box 39. National Archives, Washington, D.C.

Kaneda, Sankichi. "Memoirs." Toyama City, Japan. [Translated copy in author's file.]

Kaneko, Pvt. Kosicichi. "POW Interrogation Report," 25 Jan. 1943. G-2 Cactus, POW Files. Marine Corps Historical Center, Washington, D.C.

Kashii, 2nd Lieutenant. "Diary." RG 127, Entry 39A, Box 21. Captured Japanese Documents. National Archives, Washington, D.C.

Kato, Sgt. Shuichiro. "POW Interrogation Report," 8 Feb.1943. HQ XIV Corps. Marine Corps Historical Center, Washington, D.C.

Kawaguchi, Kiyotake. "Struggles of the Kawaguchi Detachment." Partial translation. Samuel B. Griffith Personal Papers. Marine Corps Historical Center, Washington, D.C.

Kikurri, Pvt. Morimitsu. "POW Interrogation Report." William H. Whyte Collection, POW Report. History Division, U.S. Marine Corps, Quantico, Va.

Kinoshita, Pvt. Isamu. "POW Interrogation Report," 8 Feb.1943. HQ XIV Corps. Marine Corps Historical Center, Washington, D.C.

Kralovec, Lt. D. W., USNR, Base Historian. "A Naval History of Espiritu Santo, New Hebrides." Command File, World War II, No. 231, BUTTON. Naval Historical Center, Washington, D.C. [1945].

Kusano, Kamekichi. "Diary." Item 867, RG 127, Entry 39A, Box 17. Captured Japanese Documents. National Archives, Washington, D.C.

Lamarre, Father Joseph. "War Comes to Buka." Typewritten manuscript, n.d. Files, Archdiocese of Honiara, POB 237, Honiara, Guadalcanal, Solomon Islands.

Letter from Solomon Island Mission of Seventh Day Adventist, Honiara, 6 July 1948. Subject: Statement on MV *Marara*. Archives, Seventh Day Adventist Mission Kukum, POB 63, Honiara, Guadalcanal, Solomon Islands.

Letter to Eighth Fleet, 5 Aug. 1942. RG 127, Entry 39A, Box 16. Captured Japanese Documents. National Archives, Washington, D.C.

Matsueda, Sup. Pvt. Saiichi. "POW Interrogation Report." 30 Jan. 1943. HQ XIV Corps, Cactus G-2 Section. Marine Corps Historical Center, Washington, D.C.

Matsumoto, Kenji. "Diary." RG 127, Entry 39A, Box 14. Captured Japanese Documents. National Archives, Washington, D.C. [Copy in author's file.]

Matsushima, LCpl. Shoichi. "POW Interrogation Report." Jan. 1943. 132nd Infantry Regiment. POW Files. Marine Corps Historical Center, Washington, D.C.

Message, Commander Tulagi Communications Base to Commander 8th Base Force, 7 Aug. 1942. AWM 54, Written Records Section, World War II. Australian War Memorial, Canberra.

"The Military Geography and Resources of the South Pacific Islands." RG 127, Entry 39A, Box 16, 370/23/22/4-. Captured Japanese Documents. National Archives, Washington, D.C.

Miller, H. C. C. "Report to the Resident Commissioner," undated. File BSIP/6-F.11/42. Solomon Islands National Archives, Honiara, Guadalcanal, Solomon Islands.

Miyazawa, Kozaburo. "Diary," SOPAC 0500 N-1: 016467. Guadalcanal File. Marine Corps Historical Center, Washington, D.C.

Mizuguchi, Haruguchi. "Diary." RG 127, Entry 39A, Box 15. Captured Japanese Documents. National Archives, Washington, D.C.

Mori, Yodoyama. "Diary." RG 127, Entry 39A, Box 14. Captured Japanese Documents. National Archives, Washington, D.C.

"98th Bombardment Squadron (H) Operational Diary." 17 July 1942. USAF Historical Research Agency, Maxwell Air Force Base, Montgomery, Ala.

Nohara, Giichi. "Diary." RG 127, Entry 39A, Box 14. Captured Japanese Documents. National Archives, Washington, D.C.

Ogihara, SM Norio. "POW Interrogation Report." 7 Nov. 1942. William H. Whyte Collection, POW Report. Marine Corps Historical Center, Washington, D.C.

Okajima, 1st Lieutenant. "Diary." RG 127, Entry 39A, Box 40. Captured Japanese Documents National Archives, Washington, D.C.

"POW Report." HQ, U.S. Army Forces in the South Pacific Area (USFISPA), APO 502 (1 Jan. 1943) unnumbered. National Archives, Washington, D.C.

Roberts, Howard J. "Advanced Operational Base Activities Report." No. 1 Section, A-Platoon, No. 1 Independent Company, AIF, Tulagi. Interview conducted by No. 3 Military District Historical Team, 24 Dec. 1944. [Copy in author's file.]

"RXI Secret Cable No. 52." RG 127, Entry 39A, Box 17. Captured Japanese Documents. Guadalcanal. National Archives, Washington, D.C.

Sakamoto, Haste. "Diary." RG 127, Entry 39A, Box 14. Captured Japanese Documents. National Archives, Washington, D.C. [Copy in author's file.]

"San Juan Action Report." 7 Aug., 8 Aug. 1942. Naval Historical Center, Washington, D.C.

"2nd Company, Kure 3rd Special Naval Landing Force, Order No. 1, 30 Apr. 1942." RG 127, Entry 39A, Box 14. Captured Japanese Documents. National Archives, Washington, D.C.

2nd Marine Regiment. Reinforced. "Report Record of Events." 7 Aug.–1 Nov. 1942. Marine Corps Historical Center, Washington, D.C.

2nd Marine Regiment. Reinforced. "Record of Events." 27 Oct.–30 Nov. 1942. Marine Corps Historical Center, Washington, D.C.

"Secret Order No. 5, 16 July 1942." RG 127, Entry 39A, Box 17. Captured Japanese Documents. Guadalcanal. National Archives, Washington, D.C.

Shijiri, PFC Matsutaro. "POW Interrogation Report." 30 Jan. 1943. HQ XIV Corps Cactus. POW Files. Marine Corps Historical Center, Washington, D.C.

Shimamoto, Tameichi. "Diary." RG 127, Entry 39A, Box 14. Captured Japanese Documents. National Archives, Washington, D.C.

Shuji, Pvt. Chino. "POW Interrogation Report." 27 Jan. 1943. 52nd Independent Transport Unit. POW Files. Marine Corps Historical Center, Washington, D.C.

Sonoda, Kiyoshi. "Diary." RG 127, Entry 39A, Box 14. Captured Japanese Documents. National Archives, Washington, D.C. [Copy in author's file.]

Sorensen, James. "Memoirs." Manuscript. Based on his diary of service with the 2nd Marine Regiment on Florida, Tulagi and Guadalcanal Islands. [Copy in author's file.]

"South Pacific Fleet Order No. 17, 24 June 1942." RG 127, Entry 39A, Box 17. Captured Japanese Documents. Guadalcanal. National Archives, Washington, D.C.

"South Seas Fleet Operation Order No. 13, 23 Apr. 1942." AWM 54, Written Records Section, World War II. (Information taken from Japanese records dated 29 Apr. 1942.) Australian War Memorial, Canberra.

Takahashi, Shizuko. "Diary." RG 127, Entry 39A, Box 15. Captured Japanese Documents. National Archives, Washington, D.C.

29th Infantry. "Records." RG 127, Entry 39A, Box 21. Captured Japanese Documents, National Archives, Washington, D.C.

Voyce, Rev. Arthur H. "The Cruise of the Fauro Chief." Mimeographed compilation from the journals of Dr. Allen G. Rutter and the diaries of Sisters Vera Cannon, Lina Jones, and Effie Harkness. Methodist Church of New Zealand, Solomon Islands District, Auckland [1949].

Waddell, A. N. A., "Waddell to Secretary," Western Pacific High Commission, Suva, 14 Sept. 1942. Subject: Evacuation of the Western Districts of the British Solomon Islands Protectorate in January and February 1942. Typewritten report. Central Archives of Fiji, Western Pacific High Commission Government Building, Suva, Fiji.

Whyte Papers, POW Files. Marine Corps Historical Center, Washington, D.C.

Yamamiya, Yasuo. "Diary." RG 127, Entry 39A, Box 15. Captured Japanese Documents. National Archives, Washington, D.C.

Yokoyama, Sup. Pvt. Motozo. "POW Interrogation Report." 38th Transport Regiment. POW Files. Marine Corps Historical Center, Washington, D.C.

Special Acknowledgments

Akira Abuki Information Company (Japan), 4th Infantry Regiment, Seventeenth Army, Guadalcanal Island

Dr. Dean C. Allard, Director (1989–95), Naval History, Naval Historical Center, Washington, D.C.

Harold J. Ash, 132nd Infantry Regiment, Guadalcanal Island

Emory B. Ashurst, Company D, 2nd Pioneer Battalion, Gavutu Island

Lt. Col. Marvin V. Ayers, AUS (Ret.), 147th Infantry, Guadalcanal and Florida Islands

Bernard Baeza,(France), Guadalcanal Island

Richard P. Bailey, 6th Marine Regiment, Guadalcanal Island

Capt. Leonard J. Baird, USN (Ret.), USS *Helena,* Guadalcanal waters

John Bakeman, Company C, 1st Battalion, 2nd Marine Regiment, Florida Island

Jimmy A. Bayers, 2nd Marine Regiment, Tulagi Island

Rev. Arron Bea, Methodist missionary, Munda Island, New Georgia Islands

William Bethard, photo credit, Gavutu Island cemetery

Wilbur F. Bewley, 1st Marine Regiment, Guadalcanal Island

Maj. Theodore L. Billen, DFC, USAF (Ret.), 19th Bombardment Group, Tulagi and Guadalcanal Islands

Rev. Canon David H. V. Bindon, QSM., JE, Guadalcanal Island

Ted Blahnik, Editor, *Guadalcanal Echoes*

Claude R. Blanchard, Company L, 3rd Battalion, 2nd Marine Regiment, Makambo Island

Rear Adm. Joseph P. Blundon, USNR (Ret.), 6th Naval Construction Battalion, Guadalcanal Island

Reginald A. Bowley, No. 1 Independent Company, Australian Independent Forces, Tulagi Island Advanced Operational Base

Paul T. Boyd, Company A, 1st Battalion, 2nd Marine Regiment, Aola raid, Guadalcanal Island

John M. Braloski, USS *President Hayes,* Tulagi and Guadalcanal Islands

James S. Bratton, Company C, 1st Battalion, 2nd Marine Regiment, Florida and Guadalcanal Islands

Jack Britt, RAAF, Tulagi Island Advanced Operational Base

Chester Brown, Headquarters Company, 2nd Battalion, 2nd Marine Regiment, Siota mission, Florida Island

Buzz Brown, 3rd Battalion, 10th Marine Regiment, Florida Island

C. W. Brown, CEO, Guadalcanal Plains Limited, Honiara, Guadalcanal Island

Alvin E. Brunson, Company D, 1st Battalion, 2nd Marine Regiment, Florida Island

Edgar L. Bryant, Company C, 1st Battalion, 2nd Marine Regiment, Aola, Guadalcanal Island

Harold L. Buell, Ph.D, Scouting Squadron 5, Guadalcanal Island

Graydon Cadwell, VMF-223, Guadalcanal Island

William J. Cannon, Company C, 1st Battalion, 2nd Marine Regiment, Florida, Tulagi, and Guadalcanal Islands, and Aola raid

Frank Capos, 132nd Infantry, Guadalcanal

Louis Carr, Company M, 3rd Battalion, 2nd Marine Regiment, Gavutu and Tanambogo Islands

Rear Adm. H. Robert Carson Jr., USN (Ret.), CUB-1, Espiritu Santo and Guadalcanal Islands

Emmett N. Carter, 2nd Marine Regiment, Lake Tengano, Rennell Island

L. H. Carter, VP-71, Tulagi Island

Sister Mary Teresa Cartier, SM, missionary, Guadalcanal Island

Robert Caufield, Company F, 2nd Battalion, 5th Marine Regiment, Tulagi Island

W. Marshall Chaney, 147th Infantry Regiment, Guadalcanal Island

Joseph Chin, 182nd Infantry Regiment, Americal Division, Espiritu Santo and Guadalcanal Islands

Margaret I. Clarence (Australia; daughter, Charles Bignell, Fulakora, Santa Isabel Island)

William F. Cleveland, 11th Bombardment Group, Guadalcanal Island

Edward M. Coffman, Ph.D., Sato papers, Florida Island

Charles Cole, 161st Infantry Regiment, Guadalcanal Island

S. B. Coleman, No. 1 Independent Company, Australian Independent Forces, Tulagi and Bougainville Islands

Allan C. Colin (New Zealand), Peu, Vanikoro Island, Santa Cruz Islands

Brig. Gen. Manley L. Curry, USMC (Ret.), 3rd Battalion, 10th Marine Regiment, Gavutu, Tulagi, and Guadalcanal Islands

Harold W. Davidson, No. 1 Independent Company, Australian Independent Forces, Tulagi Island Advanced Operational Base

A. R. Evans, Royal Australian Naval Reserve, Kolombangara Island

Cdr. Raymond J. Evans Jr. (Ret.), USCG, Point Cruz, Guadalcanal Island

Warren H. Fitch, Company L, 3rd Battalion, 2nd Marine Regiment, Florida Island

Rev. Theodore E. Franklin, 2nd Marine Regiment POW Camp, Espiritu Santo Island, New Hebrides Islands

H. E. Frost, Company I, 3rd Battalion, 2nd Marine Regiment, Tulagi Island

Herbert R. Fuller, USNR, Gavutu and Malaita Islands

Lt. Col. Ritchie Garrison, USA (Ret.), Efate Island, New Hebrides Islands

J. R. Garrett, Company I, 2nd Battalion, 11th Marine Regiment, Guadalcanal Island

Father Frederic B. Gehring, CUB-1, Guadalcanal Island

Gaetano Gerace, 5th Marine Regiment, Guadalcanal Island

Freda Giles (Frederick Jones's daughter; Nendi Island, Santa Cruz Islands), Port Vila, Vanuatu Island

William J. Gilomen Sr., Company G, 3rd Battalion, 10th Marine Regiment, Tulagi and Gavutu Islands

James L. Given, Company E, 3rd Battalion, 2nd Marine Regiment, Florida Island

Graham Golden (Australia)

William F. Graham, USNR, Company B, 1st Battalion, 2nd Marine Regiment, Florida, Gavutu, and Tanambogo Islands

Brig. Gen. Samuel B. Griffith II, USMC (Ret.), Tulagi Island

Francis J. "Frank" Guidone, 1st Raider Battalion, Tulagi and Guadalcanal Islands

Charles O. Hall, Company D, 2nd Medical Battalion, Fiji, Tulagi, and Guadalcanal Islands

Noburo Hara (Japan), 3rd Company, 1st Battalion, 4th Infantry Regiment, Seventeenth Army, Guadalcanal Island

Charles E. Hatfield, 2nd Weapons Company, Tulagi Island

Col. Harold A. Hayes, USMC (Ret.), Company A, 2nd Pioneer Battalion, Florida, Gavutu, and Guadalcanal Islands

SME Tomisaburo Hirai family (Imperial Japanese Navy, Kure 3rd SNLF)

Arthur L. Holmes, 3rd Battalion, 10th Marine Regiment, Tulagi and Florida Islands

MSgt. Harry R. Horsman, USMC (Ret.), 1st Battalion, 1st Marines, Guadalcanal Island

Joan Humphreys, Archivist, Burns Philp & Company Ltd., Sydney, Australia

Col. Robert D. Jacobs, USMC (Ret.), 3rd Battalion, 10th Marine Regiment, Makombo and Guadalcanal Islands

Robert W. Johnsmiller, 3rd Battalion, 2nd Marine Regiment, Gavutu, Tanambogo, and Tulagi Islands

Arthur S. Johnson Jr., Company M, 182nd Infantry Regiment, Americal Division, Santa Cruz Islands

Randall E. Johnson, 2nd Marine Regiment, Florida and Islands

Frederick J. Jones, Santa Cruz, South Espiritu Santo, and New Hebrides Islands

Ruby Olive Boye Jones (Penshurst, NSW, Australia), Vanikoro Island, Santa Cruz Islands

Mark H. Jordan, P.E., 6th Naval Construction Battalion, Guadalcanal Island

Pat Josselyn (Mrs. Henry E. Josselyn, England)

Sankichi Kaneda (Toyama City, Japan), Imperial Japanese Navy, 81st Guard Unit, Guadalcanal Island

Franklin J. Karal, 3rd Battalion, 2nd Marine Regiment, Tulagi Island

Capt. Juro Katsumata, Imperial Japanese Army, 29th Infantry Regiment, 2nd Infantry Division, Seventeenth Army, Guadalcanal Island

Kisaburo Kawakami, Imperial Japanese Navy, 81st Guard Unit, Guadalcanal Island

B. G. Kenner, 2nd Marine Regiment, Gavutu and Florida Islands

Benjamin Kevu, Western Solomons Islands evacuation (Gizo, Solomon Islands)

Donald Klotz, VP-23, eastern Solomons

William M. Klotz (Australia), Shortland Islands evacuation, 1942

T. Kosuge (Japan), South Sea Trading Company, 1941 Rabaul

Mahlon R. Kruse, R-2, Santa Cruz and Espiritu Santo Islands

Clifford R. Kurtz, 164th Infantry Regiment, Americal Division (detached service), Malaita Island radio operator

H. Y. Kwan (Sydney, Australia, and Honiara, Guadalcanal Island), O.B.E., Chinese on Malaita and Guadalcanal Islands

Maj. Gen. Wood B. Kyle, USMC (Ret.), 2nd Marine Regiment, Florida Island

Lt. Col. Dean Ladd, USMC (Ret.), 1st Battalion, 8th Marine Regiment, Guadalcanal

Kevin Landers, Royal Australian Air Force, Tulagi Island Advanced Operational Base John P. Lanigan, USS *Heywood,* landings on Gavutu and Makombo Islands

Jack E. Lee, Headquarters Company, 3rd Battalion, 2nd Marine Regiment, Florida Island

Jack T. Lent, R-2, Santa Cruz and Espiritu Santo Islands

Group Capt. John M. Lerew (Vancover, BC, Canada), Royal Australian Air Force (Ret.), Tulagi Island Advanced Operational Base

Herm Lewis, 2nd Marines, Florida and Mandoliana Island

Robert C. Libby (New Zealand), Company M, 3rd Battalion, 2nd Marine Regiment, Gavutu Island

Timothy Longoba, Malaita Island, north Malaita Island, Solomon Islands

Capt. F. Kent Loomis, USN, (Ret.), Naval Historical Center, Washington, D.C.

Howard Lorsch, Company L, 3rd Battalion, 2nd Marine Regiment, Makombo Island

Huey M. Love, USNR, Company A, 1st Battalion, 2nd Marine Regiment, Tulagi Island

Jack A. Mack, Company C, 1st Battalion, 2nd Marine Regiment, Guadalcanal Island

Rear Adm. Houston L. Maples, USN (Ret.), Guadalcanal Island

Ore J. Marion, 5th Marine Regiment, Tulagi and Guadalcanal Islands

Michael A. Masters, Company A, 1st Pioneer Battalion, Tulagi Island

Tomitaro Matsuda (Yamagata, Japan), Imperial Japanese Navy, 81st Guard Unit, Guadalcanal Island

Thomas McCarthy, 7th Battalion, Australian Independent Forces, Munda Island, New Georgia Islands

Brother Peter McDonaugh (Australia), SM, Catholic mission, Marau Sound, Guadalcanal Island

Alexander "Sandy" McNab, No. 1 Independent Company, Australian Independent Forces, Bougainville Island, historian

Ronald Melicher, Company M, 3rd Battalion, 2nd Marine Regiment, Gavutu Island

Henry C. Michalak, Headquarters Company, 3rd Battalion, 2nd Marine Regiment, Florida Island

Joseph G. Micek, 132nd Infantry Regiment, Americal Division, Guadalcanal Island

V. F. Miller, Head, Military Records Branch, Marine Corps Historical Center, Washington, D.C.

Masaichiro Miyagawa (Japan), Yokohama Air Group, Gavutu and Tanambogo Islands

Cyrus J. "Jim" Moore, Company E, 2nd Battalion, 11th Marine Regiment, Tulagi Island

Robert W. Moore, 1st Parachute Battalion, Gavutu, Island

Jack R. Moran, No. 1 Independent Company, Australian Independent Forces, Tulagi Island Advanced Operational Base

Lawrence E. "Roy" Moran, Company B, 1st Parachute Battalion, Gavutu Island

Vice AM Ian G. Morrison, Royal New Zealand Air Force (Ret.), Guadalcanal, Island

Col. Joseph N. Muller, USMCR (Ret.), Guadalcanal Island, Goettge patrol

Mrs. Eugenie Murphy (Australia), Faisi, Shortland Islands

Maj. Gen. Raymond Murray, USMC (Ret.), 6th Marine Regiment, Guadalcanal Island

William E. Neff, Jr., M.D., 7th Marine Regiment, Samoa and Guadalcanal Islands

C. M. Nelson, Squadron 1, Guadalcanal Island

Col. Norman R. Nickerson, USMC (Ret.), Company A, 1st Parachute Battalion, Gavutu Island

Frank B. Niehaus, 147th Infantry Regiment, Aola, Guadalcanal Island, and Florida Island

John Gen Nishino (Japan), war correspondent, Mainichi newspapers, 35th Brigade, Guadalcanal Island

Col. Susumu Nishiura , Imperial Japanese Army (Ret.), Chief, War History Office, Japan Self-Defense Force (1960–65)

Michael J. O'Dea Jr., 6th Naval Construction Battalion, Guadalcanal Island

Mrs. Yuko Okazaki (Japan; daughter, Mr. T. Ishimoto)

Larry Padrons, Company B, 1st Battalion, 2nd Marine Regiment, Florida, Gavutu, and Tanambogo Islands landings

Felix J. Perko, Company C, 1st Battalion, 2nd Marine Regiment, Florida Island

Robert K. Piper, Royal Australian Air Force, Historical Section, Canberra, Australia

Larry L. Pressley, Company F, 2nd Battalion, 2nd Marine Regiment, Tulagi Island

Jack Ranken (Australia), 1st Commando Company, Australian Independent Forces, Port Vila section, New Hebrides Islands

David R. Rapley, Company B, 1st Battalion, 2nd Marine Regiment, Aola raid, Guadalcanal Island

John A. Remar, Company M, 2nd Battalion, 2nd Marine Regiment, Florida Island

Frederick W. Riggs Jr., Company K, 3rd Battalion, 2nd Marine Regiment, Florida Gavutu, and Guadalcanal Islands

Howard J. Roberts (Australia), No. 1 Section, 1st Independent Company, Australian Independent Forces, Gavutu Island

Keith Robinson, Royal Australian Air Force, Tulagi Island Advanced Operational Base

David A. Rolla, Company B, 7th Naval Construction Battalion, Espiritu Santo Island, New Hebrides Islands

Pat Rollins, M.D., Company D, 2nd Medical Battalion, Tulagi and Guadalcanal Islands

Jinsaku Sakurai, Imperial Japanese Naval Air Force, Yokohama Air Group, Gavutu Island

W. D. Sandquist, Company I, 3rd Battalion, 2nd Marine Regiment, Gavutu Island

Hiroako Sato and Takuya Sato (Japan) (family of Cdr. Riichiro Sato, Imperial Japanese Naval Air Force, Yokohama Air Group)

Howard Schnauber, 2nd Battalion, 11th Marine Regiment, Tulagi Island

Raymond Schneider, Headquarters Company, 2nd Battalion, 2nd Marine Regiment, Tulagi and Guadalcanal Islands

Clifford Searle, Royal Australian Air Force, Tulagi Island Advanced Operational Base

Edward G. Sexton, D-2 Section, Headquarters, 1st Marine Division, Tulagi and Guadalcanal Island

Clyde Sinclair, Royal Australian Air Force, Tulagi Island Advanced Operational Base

Gershon Smith, CUB-1, Guadalcanal Island

Ian Smith, Head, Research Section, Australian War Memorial, Canberra, Australia

WO2 Michael S. Smith USN, Bloody Ridge, Guadalcanal Island

Richard J. Sommers, Ph.D., archivist-historian, U.S. Army Military Institute, Carlisle Barracks, Pa.

Karl Thayer Soule Jr., D-2 Section, Headquarters, 1st Marine Division, Guadalcanal Island

Col. Wayne F. Staford, USMC (Ret.), 2nd Battalion, 2nd Marine Regiment, Florida Island

Louis Stark, CUB-1, Guadalcanal Island

Capt. Michael A. Stefanowicz, USMC (Ret.), 5th and 14th Marine Defense Battalions, Tulagi Island

Vernon C. Stempel, D-2 Section, Headquarters, 1st Marine Division, Guadalcanal Island

Bert Townsand, Royal Australian Air Force, Port Moresby, New Guinea

Margaret Thompson, Assistant Curator, Australian War Memorial, Canberra, Australia

Sir David Trench (England), GCMG, MC, DL, Tulagi and Guadalcanal Islands

Edmond L. Troccia, 93rd Squadron, 19th Bombardment Group, raid on Vunakanau airfield, Rabaul, New Britain Island

John C. VanDyke, Company G, 3rd Battalion, 2nd Marine Regiment, Tulagi Island

Ray Van Winkle, 1st Battery, 3rd Battalion, 10th Marine Regiment, Gavutu and Florida Islands

Richard N. Vorwaller, Company M, 3rd Battalion, 2nd Marine Regiment, Gavutu Island

Col. Hawley C. Waterman, USMC (Ret.), 1st Service Battalion, Guadalcanal Island

Van Watts, USS *Makinac,* Vanikoro Island, Santa Cruz Islands

Stanley Wedlock, Headquarters, 2nd Battalion, 2nd Marines, Florida Island

Elmer R. Wetsel, Company D, 1st Battalion, 2nd Marine Regiment, Gavutu and Tanambogo

Jester P. Whigham, South Pacific Combat Air Transport Command, mail officer

Raymond L. Whitaker, USS *Barnett,* Guadalcanal Island landing

Sir Colin E. J. Wilson (New Zealand), Vanikoro Island, Santa Cruz Islands

Yasuo Yamamiya, Imperial Japanese Navy, 11th Construction Unit, Guadalcanal Island

Capt. Minoru Yano, Imperial Japanese Navy (Ret.), Kure 3rd SNLF, Rabaul, New Britain Island–New Guinea

R. W. Young, 64th TC Squadron, 410th Signal Company, Fourteenth Air Force, USAAF

Ward A. Zimmerman, USNR, USS *Heywood,* Tulagi and Gavutu Islands

John P. Zingdale, Company C, 1st Battalion, 2nd Marine Regiment, Florida Island and Aola, Guadalcanal

Index

506 Index